THE LAND WAS FOREVER: 15,000 YEARS IN NORTH-EAST SCOTLAND

THE LAND WAS FOREVER: 15,000 YEARS IN NORTH-EAST SCOTLAND

Excavations on the Aberdeen Western Peripheral Route/ Balmedie-Tipperty

Kirsty Dingwall, Matt Ginnever, Richard Tipping, Jürgen van Wessel, and Don Wilson

OXBOW | books

Oxford & Philadelphia

Published in the United Kingdom in 2019 by
OXBOW BOOKS
The Old Music Hall, 106–108 Cowley Road, Oxford, OX4 1JE

and in the United States by
OXBOW BOOKS
1950 Lawrence Road, Havertown, PA 19083

Hardback Edition: ISBN 978-1-78570-988-3
Digital Edition: ISBN 978-1-78570-989-0 (epub)

A CIP record for this book is available from the British Library

Library of Congress Control Number: 2018963072

Printed in the United Kingdom by Short Run Press, Exeter

Typeset in India by Versatile PreMedia Services. www.versatilepremedia.com

For a complete list of Oxbow titles, please contact:

UNITED KINGDOM
Oxbow Books
Telephone (01865) 241249
Email: oxbow@oxbowbooks.com
www.oxbowbooks.com

UNITED STATES OF AMERICA
Oxbow Books
Telephone (800) 791-9354, Fax (610) 853-9146
Email: queries@casemateacademic.com
www.casemateacademic.com/oxbow

Oxbow Books is part of the Casemate Group

Front cover: Top right – Milltimber in the Mesolithic. Top left – Standingstones in the Mesolithic. Bottom left – Gairnhill through the Bronze Age. Bottom right – Roman Milltimber. All images by Mano Kapazoglou and copyright Headland Archaeology (UK) Ltd.
Back cover: Left – Milltimber from the air. Right – The coastal plain at Charlestown from the air. All images copyright Transport Scotland.

'...the land was forever, it moved and changed below you, but was forever, you were close to it and it to you...'
Title quote taken from from Lewis Grassic Gibbon's 1932 novel Sunset Song, set in the north-east of Scotland.

Contents

Acknowledgements

The Aberdeen Western Periphery Route/Balmedie-Tipperty (AWPR/B-T) project was funded by Transport Scotland, Aberdeen City Council and Aberdeenshire Council and was managed on their behalf by the Managing Agent. The archaeological works, both in the field and during the extensive post-excavation programme was supervised by Jacobs UK, with involvement from Rob McNaught, Ed Danagher, Al Curtis, Jonathan Dempsey and Pete Fasham at various stages of the works.

The authors are indebted to several friends and colleagues who have provided advice and comment on our interpretations over the duration of the project. It would be impossible to name them all, but particular thanks must go to Stephen Carter (Headland Archaeology) for visiting the site and providing advice on formation processes, to Caroline Wickham-Jones (University of Aberdeen) and Graeme Warren (University College Dublin) for providing feedback on early versions of the Mesolithic period material, to Beccy Jones (Historic Environment Scotland) for the same on the Roman material and to David Mason (Principal Archaeologist with Durham County Council) for commenting on the potential of the Roman Navy in Aberdeenshire. Bruce Mann of the Archaeology Service for Moray, Angus and Aberdeen City Councils provided invaluable guidance and support throughout the project.

Thanks must be given not only to the many specialists who have contributed to the volume but to the field team who worked tirelessly throughout 2012–2015, sometimes in rising groundwater, to ensure successful completion of the archaeological programme. With apologies for any omissions, in the field over the course of three phases of work, the teams comprised Abby Cooper, Ali Cameron, Anne Marot, Antony Clifton-Jones, Aris Palyvos, Callum Allsop, Calum Henderson, Carmen Dahlke, Claire Christie, Dave Harding, Fraser McFarlane, Fraser Stewart, Helen Rickwood, Jason Murphy, Joe Turner, Josh Gaunt, Juan Ferrando-Ortiz, Juliette Mitchell, Jürgen van Wessel, Kieran Boyle, Laura Bailey, Linn Glancy, Magda Benysek, Magnar Dalland, Mairead McLaughlin, Matt Ginnever, Meaghan Dyer, Nuala Woodley, Paul Masser, Phil Karsgaard, Rafael Maya-Torcelly, Richard Tuffin, Robert Williams, Rowena Thomson, Sandra Mulligan, Sarah Munro, Sheryl McKimm, Simon Mayes, Steve Cox, Steve Roe, Steve Thomson, Stuart Farrell, Sue McGalliard, Tony Taylor and Val Dufeu. Other than myself, Alistair Robertson, Don Wilson and Ross Murray were the Senior Archaeologists in the field. They were supported in this by our two Ecological Clerks of Work; Doug Blease and Alice Murphy.

Specialist processing and analysis beyond the named authors was completed by Aisling Fitzpatrick, Amy Koonce, Catherine Longford, Georgina Barrett, Heather Smith, James Lowe, Sarah-Jane Haston, Scott Timpany and Val Dufeu. Additional editing was undertaken by Julie Franklin and Luke Craddock-Bennett.

The creative team of Julia Bastek-Michalska, Rafael Maya-Torcelly and Mano Kapazoglou led by Caroline Norrman have succeeded in converting the relatively dry site plans into attractive and informative illustrations, with Mano's artist's impressions being particularly effective in evoking the character of each period. Leanne Whitelaw produced the lithics illustrations for all chapters, which have greatly enhanced the monograph.

Although I have been responsible for managing the publication in its latter stages, Sorina Spanou was the Project Manager for most of the project's duration, from 2012 through to 2017. She inspired the teams in the field and through the post-excavation and publication design, maintaining the enthusiasm of the team throughout the challenging post-excavation programme. Sorina's support as I took up the reins of project management has proved invaluable, as has her insight into the discoveries made in the field.

Many thanks must also go to Professor Richard Bradley, who very kindly agreed to provide comments on the text, a considerable task. His input has ensured the manuscript is more robust than it would otherwise have been; naturally all opinions expressed (and any errors remaining) are the authors' own. Val Kinsler undertook copy-editing and offered editorial guidance for which I am most grateful.

Finally, the fieldwork would quite simply not have been possible without the tireless efforts of Iain Miskelly. From an original phone call requesting a cost for a single tracked machine, he (along with his brother Stuart, and all his plant operators) quickly became an essential part of the delivery team. Despite an extremely challenging programme he remained good-humoured throughout and became a true friend to many on site. Iain sadly passed away unexpectedly in late 2016, and this volume is dedicated to him.

Kirsty Dingwall
Edinburgh
June 2018

List of illustrations

List of tables

Abbreviations

ADS	Archaeology Data Service	NL	Northern Leg
AMA	Archaeological Monitoring Areas	NRHE	National Record of the Historic Environment
AMS	Accelerator Mass Spectrometry	OIL	Oblique Incident Light
AOD	Above Ordnance Datum	OS	Ordnance Survey
AWPR/B-T	Aberdeen Western Peripheral Route/ Balmedie to Tipperty	OSL	Optically stimulated luminescence
		PCSC	Plano-convex slag cake
BGS	The British Geological Survey	pOSL	Pulsed Optically Stimulated Luminescence
BP	Before Present	PPL	Plane Polarised Light
CB	Carinated Bowl	RCAHMS	Royal Commission on the Ancient and Historical Monuments of Scotland
CBNE	North-Eastern style Carinated Bowl		
CJV	Construction Joint Venture	RF	Refit complex
EDINA	Centre for digital expertise and online service delivery at the University of Edinburgh	RS	Runned slag
		SAIR	Scottish Archaeology Internet Reports
		ScARF	Scottish Archaeological Research Framework
EDS	Energy dispersive X-ray spectrometer		
ES	Environmental Statement	SEM	Scanning Electron Microscope
FAO	Food and Agriculture Organisation of the United Nations	SEPA	Scottish Environment Protection Agency
		SF	Small find
FAS	Low-density fuel ash slag/vitrified ceramic	SL	Southern Leg
GD	Greatest Dimension	SMR	Sites and Monuments Records
GIS	Geographic information system	SUERC	Scottish Universities Environmental Research Centre
Ha	Hectares		
HES	Historic Environment Scotland	TLP	Total land pollen
HLA	Historic Land-use Assessment	U/S	unstratified
HS	Hammerscale	UIS	Unclassified Iron Slag
LiDAR	Light Detection And Ranging	VC	Vitrified Ceramic
LMA	Land Made Available	XPS	cross polarised light
MVR	Magnetic vitrified residues		

Lithics glossary

Term	Definition
Abraded	When an edge has been flattened and smoothed through motion
Arris	The ridge formed at the intersection of two negative scars on the dorsal side of a flake
Bipolar	A technique where the core is seated on an anvil and struck from above
Blade	A flake twice as long as it is wide
Blank	A piece from which an object is retouched
Broad blade	This could refer to a particularly broad blade, where the width is still less than half the length but at the wider end of the scale. It may also refer to an early Mesolithic industry favouring broader blades
Burin	A flake or blade that has been modified by the removal of a narrow splinter (spall) from a break
Chip	A small piece less than 10 mm in maximum dimensions
Chunk	Large indeterminate piece
Core	Nodule or pebble that has been used to detach pieces, will only show dorsal surfaces
Core trimming flake	Removals carried out in order to get rid of irregularities in the core. These can be along the platform or down the body of the core
Cortex	The outer skin of the rock
Crescents	A microlith of crescent shape
Crested pieces	The use of alternate flaking to create a ridge that can act as a removal guide
Debitage	All flaked waste material, including blades, flakes and chips
Distal	The end directly opposite the proximal
Dorsal	The side opposite the ventral
Drop zone	The place where pieces fall while knapping
Edge retouch	Any tool with a retouched edge that cannot be placed in a more specific category
En eperon	Platform preparation that results in a spur on the edge of the platform. Used for guiding and precision removals
Facetted platform	The removal of small flakes to the platform surface to prepare it for removals
Flake	Any detached piece with a ventral surface
Fragment	The term fragment is used to indicate a broken piece
Indeterminate piece	A piece that cannot be identified as a flake or core
Knapping	A general term for the use of percussion to break apart stone with the purpose of creating tools
Krukowski 'microburin'	What appears to be a long microburin, often from the distal end. This could be an uncompleted microlith, a failed microlith or a microburin
Lateral	The edges of the flake or blade; there is a left and right lateral.
Levallois-ism	It is characterised by overlapping flake removal scars struck from edges on a horizontal rather than vertical plane. This technique prepares the nodules for removal or certain shaped blanks

Term	Definition	Term	Definition
Microblade	A small blade	Retouch	Removal of small flakes from a piece in order to shape it further
Microburin	A waste product from microlith production. This is a small piece snapped off from one end to create the desired microlith shape	Secondary flake	Some of the dorsal is covered in cortex
Microlith	A range of small tools made during the Mesolithic. They are composite	Scale-flaked	Retouch that overlaps in a pattern reminiscent of 'scales'
Platform technique	A reduction technique where percussion is applied to a platform to detach pieces	Scalene triangle	A microlith of scalene triangle shape
Piquant triédre	The traces visible on the extremity of a blade or bladelet when part of it has been removed by the microburin blow technique	Scraper	A type of tool with abruptly angled blunt edge of retouch
		Sur enclume technique	'on anvil' retouch
		Tang	A projection created to assist the hafting of the tool
Polished-edge	Abrasion that causes smoothing and shining of the edge	Tool	Any secondary modification (retouch)
Primary flake	The dorsal is entirely covered in cortex	Tertiary flake	No cortex is present
Proximal	The end of the flake that received the blow or pressure	Toss zone	The areas within a knapping surface where pieces are thrown to keep the working location clear
Raw material	The different types of stone that were used to knap	Truncated	A line of regular continuous retouch truncating either the proximal, distal or lateral part of a piece
Refit	When pieces can be joined to another	Ventral	The surface of the flake or blade that originally faced into the core

Chapter 1

Introduction

Kirsty Dingwall and Don Wilson

1.1 The route

Plans for a bypass route for Aberdeen were first mooted in the 1950s, with several possible routes proposed, including an eastern route with a bridge over the harbour. After going quiet for decades, in the early years of the new millennium Scottish Ministers announced new plans for a bypass, which was subsequently approved in late 2009. The new road was opened in 2018.

The aim was to improve travel in the region by constructing an entirely new road around the western periphery of the city; the Aberdeen Western Peripheral Route/Balmedie to Tipperty (AWPR/B-T). The works would include improvements to twelve junctions along the route, two new river crossings, the need to cross five major pipelines, construction of three wildlife bridges and over 100 other ancillary structures. Two sections of the A90 were also widened to ease the flow of traffic.

Prior to construction, the 58 km long Aberdeen Western Peripheral Route/Balmedie to Tipperty project (AWPR/B-T) comprised four sections:

AWPR Northern Leg: 16.1 km – from North Kingswells to Blackdog

AWPR Southern Leg: 18.7 km – from Charleston to North Kingswells

AWPR Fastlink: 11.5 km – from Stonehaven to Cleanhill

A90 Balmedie to Tipperty: 12 km – from Blackdog to Tipperty. This included the construction of 9 km of new dual carriageway, alongside the improvement of 3 km of existing dual carriageway.

This cut across an area nearly 35 km north to south and 10 km from the coast inland (Illus 1.01). It joined the A90 in the south close to Stonehaven, ran across the moors to the south of the Dee, skimmed the outer suburbs of Aberdeen such as Peterculter and Kingswells, and joined the A90 again to the north of Aberdeen. Across the total 58 km of the new route a variety of different types of landscape and communities were encountered (Illus 1.02).

In conjunction with the main road project, additional archaeological investigations were carried out at the Third Don Crossing and the A96 Park and Ride Scheme. This comprised several phases of work including geophysical survey (Bartlett & Boucher 2012a), topographic survey (Murray 2012a), historic building recording (Murray 2012b; Holden 2012), trial trench investigations (Dalland 2013a; 2013b) and excavation (Thomson 2015; Taylor 2016). This work has been reported separately and does not form part of this volume.

The AWPR/B-T road scheme naturally required a variety of investigations and activities to understand and safeguard the cultural heritage present, both previously known and newly discovered. This volume presents the results of five years of investigation and analysis.

1.2 Project background

An Environmental Statement for the AWPR (Northern Leg, Southern Leg and Fastlink) was prepared by Jacobs in 2007 for the AWPR Managing Agent (on behalf of Transport Scotland, Aberdeen City Council and Aberdeenshire Council who funded the AWPR) while a separate Environmental Statement for Balmedie to Tipperty was prepared by Grontmij (now Sweco) and Natural Capital on behalf of Transport Scotland in 2007.

The Environmental Statements identified known cultural heritage assets along the routes, and areas of potential for the presence of unknown sites (Jacobs 2007; Grontmij and Natural Capital 2007). Clearly, given the length of the routes and the areas passed through, a large number of sites within the route might be expected; in total, 409 sites were recorded within the study area across the four sections of the route. These comprised Scheduled Monuments, Listed Buildings, Conservation Areas and undesignated sites. The Environmental Statements also assessed potential impacts on these cultural heritage assets and identified measures to mitigate these impacts. The

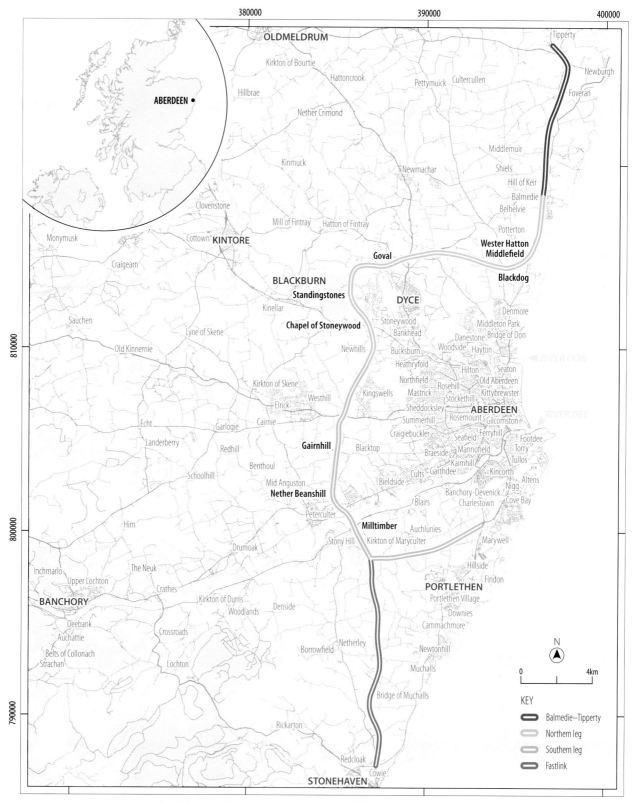

Illus 1.01 The Aberdeen Western Peripheral Route/Balmedie-Tipperty

Illus 1.02 The AWPR/B-T route intersected with coastal plain (Charlestown), river valley (Milltimber) and rougher uplands (Gairnhill)

range of known sites and their distribution is discussed further in 1.3 below.

As the first stage of a programme of archaeological investigations to implement the mitigation measures identified in the Environmental Statements, Headland Archaeology (UK) Ltd was appointed to undertake non-invasive archaeological investigations comprising geophysical survey, topographic survey, palaeoenvironmental assessment and a metal-detector survey, along with historic building recording and photographic surveys. These took place between July and November 2012.

Nearly 460 ha were subject to geophysical survey resulting in the detection of 118 anomalies, only 36 of which were thought to be of potential archaeological significance.

Topographic surveys were carried out on a total of 34 sites, comprising 16 sections of dyke, two cairns, two stones, four sheepfolds or pens, a pumping station, the remains of a croft and a field system, two farmsteads, a stone-lined well, two sections of railway, an area of rig cultivation and an enclosure wall (van Wessel 2012a; 2012b; 2012c). The majority of the sites subject to topographic survey were post-medieval in date and largely concentrated around Charleston in the south-east of the route and Kingswells near the crossover between the Northern and Southern Legs. Not all sites would be directly impacted by construction, but they lay in sufficiently close proximity that detailed recording of them was deemed necessary.

Historic Building Recording was undertaken on three sites across the scheme. English Heritage level 3 surveys were undertaken for Dyce Airfield Radio Station and Kingcausie Bridge (van Wessel 2012d; 2012e) with a basic photographic record made of Silverburn Bridge (van Wessel 2012e). Further topographic and photographic surveys were undertaken at Snarleshow (Dambrae) Possible Lade, Kirkhill Upright Stone, Overhill Cattle Rubbing Stones and Mill of Foveran Lade (all van Wessel 2012f) and Walton Farmhouse (van Wessel & Bailey 2012). A Level 2 HBR survey of Silverburn Bridge was undertaken as part of the CJV works (Wilson 2017; Appendix 1.4).

Palaeoenvironmental survey in the form of manual auger survey was undertaken at four locations across the scheme (Timpany 2012a; 2012b; 2012c); two along the Fastlink section (Red Moss and Blackburn Moss), one on the Southern Leg (Hare Moss) and one from the Northern Leg (a second site called Red Moss).

A metal-detector survey was carried out at the Hill of Muchalls, the supposed location of a battle between Royalist and Covenanting forces in 1639. The location of the battle is shown on Roy's Military Map of the following century. The survey identified a small number of finds that could date to the 17th century, two of which could have military associations (Franklin 2012).

Following completion of the non-invasive phases of work, trial trenching and a series of sample excavations were carried out in 2013. Sample excavations were undertaken at 16 sites across the Northern and Southern Legs (Table 1.01), largely concentrating on known sites

Table 1.01 Sample excavation on Northern and Southern Legs

Site	Name
NL-EX02	Overton stone wall
NL-EX01	Cranfield farm
SL-EX01	West Charlestown dyke
SL-EX02	West Charlestown dyke
SL-EX03	Lochview Croft dyke
SL-EX04	Charlestown consumption dyke
SL-EX05	Hillhead, Charlestown consumption dyke
SL-EX06	Hillside dyke
SL-EX07	West Charlestown dyke
SL-EX08	Newpark ruined farmstead
SL-EX09	Newpark ruined farmstead
SL-EX10	Auchintoul Croft
SL-EX11	Burnhead cairns
SL-EX12	West Hatton dyke
SL-EX13	Denhead of Cloghill dyke
SL-EX14	Denhead of Cloghill dyke

of post-medieval date that would be removed during the construction of the road (Dingwall 2013; Robertson 2014). Fourteen sections were cut across consumption dykes, and targeted excavation of a farmstead took place at Auchintoul Croft (SL-EX10; ES Site 121). The site of Burnhead (SL-EX11; ES Site 443) was also targeted for excavation to establish whether mounds recorded here were cairns or natural features. These sites are not presented in any detail here, although they provide context on the more recent past along the road line (see Illus 1.03). A single clearance cairn on the Fastlink section was subject to sample excavation; it does not form part of this report and the associated records have been archived separately from the material relating to the Northern and Southern legs. The various geophysical, topographic, metal-detecting and photographic surveys, along with the palaeoenvironmental assessment and historic building recording were reported in stand-alone reports that have been submitted to NHRE as part of the archive from the project. The sample excavations were reported as part of the trial-trenching report and are available digitally through the Archaeology Data Service (see 1.7 below; Appendices 1.1 and 1.2).

For the purposes of trial trenching, the route was split into the four sections outlined above. CFA Archaeology Ltd carried out works on the Fastlink (Kirby 2014) and Balmedie to Tipperty (Moore 2014) sections, while Headland Archaeology (UK) Ltd carried out those on the Northern Leg (Robertson 2014) and Southern Leg (Dingwall 2013). Nearly 3000 trenches totalling 148,017 m² were excavated. From these, 225 features were identified, and 20 areas of archaeological potential were flagged up for further investigation.

Having identified sites of interest, mitigation excavations were carried out between March and November 2014. The

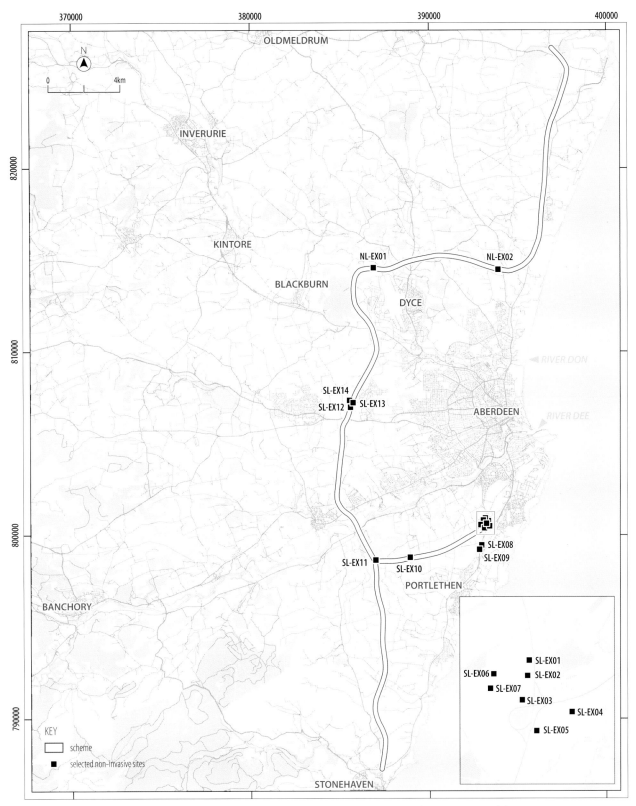

Illus 1.03 Sites subject to sample excavation; these were largely consumption dykes

mitigation excavations for the Fastlink and Balmedie to Tipperty sections were undertaken by CFA Archaeology Ltd (Kirby 2015a; 2015b; 2015c; Savory 2015; Suddaby 2014; 2015a; 2015b). In general, the results from these two sections were limited. The majority of features identified

were found to be non-archaeological in origin and are not included in this publication.

Headland Archaeology undertook mitigation excavations on the Northern and Southern Legs (Illus 1.04). On the Northern Leg, six areas of potential

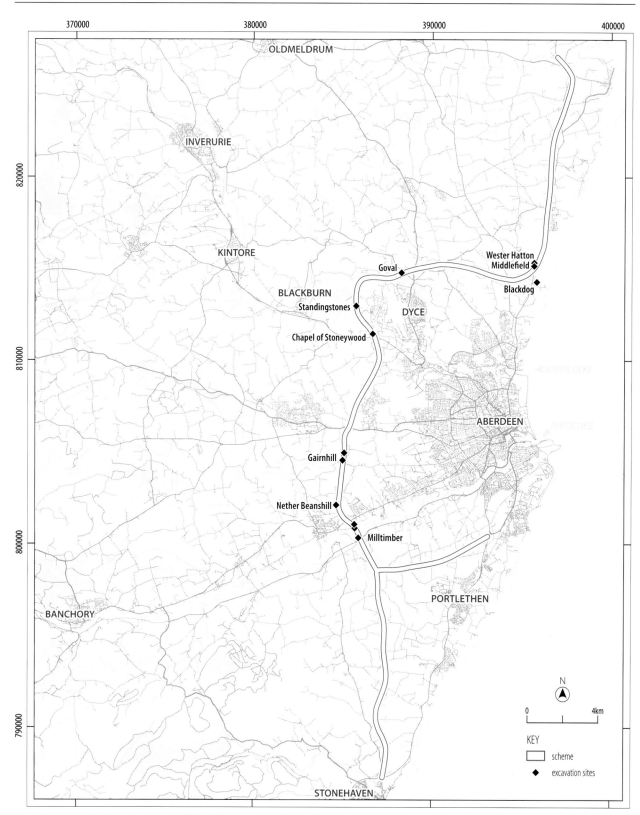

Illus 1.04 Sites excavated along the route of the AWPR/B-T

interest were identified. In addition to these areas, isolated features were also found during the trial trenching that merited further investigation, resulting in topsoil stripping at 13 different locations (Robertson 2014; Appendix 1.1). On the Southern Leg, five areas of potential were

identified (Dingwall 2013; Appendices 1.2 and 1.3). In total, 243,638 m² were stripped of topsoil and investigated.

All areas identified as potential sites were given area numbers indicating which leg the site was on. Multiple but separate areas at one location were given alphanumeric combinations, eg SL/002A, SL/002B etc. During the construction phase, areas to be monitored were given a new sequence of numbers as 'Archaeological Monitoring Areas' (AMA).

Context numbers for each site or area had prefixes representing the site. During the construction phase, the AMA number was used as the prefix eg AMA09 for Milltimber. Plans and sections in this publication use both prefixes throughout. All context numbers are four digits long.

Areas SL/003A, C and D, SL/005, NL/001A and B, all of NL/002, NL/003A, NL/004, NL/005, NL/006C and D, NL/007, NL/008, NL/010, NL/011 and NL/014 either proved to contain no archaeological features, or features were limited to those already investigated during the trial trenching phase. No further work was undertaken and these do not form part of the works presented here.

By the completion of the mitigation excavations, sites of varying date and scale had been discovered at: Milltimber on the River Dee; Nether Beanshill, a short distance to the north of Peterculter; Gairnhill close to Gairnhill Woods; Chapel of Stoneywood, immediately overlooking the modern A96; Standingstones on the east-facing slopes of Kirkhill Forest; Goval on the northern banks of the River Don; and at Middlefield and Blackdog, near the coast around three miles to the north of the city of Aberdeen (see Illus 1.04). All these sites were subsequently subject to post-excavation assessment and the production of an updated publication design providing guidance for the post-excavation analysis.

Owing to lack of access, a number of sites could not be mitigated before the construction phase of the road scheme commenced in 2015. These sites were completed during construction under the aegis of the Construction Joint Venture (CJV). During this phase, the route was divided into three (South, Central and North); however, as the majority of discoveries were made during the enabling works, this publication continues to use the original four sections described above.

Under the management of the CJV a total of 28 archaeological mitigation areas were identified. These were largely areas where archaeology was known or suspected to exist but had not been accessible previously, either due to access issues or because of the presence of services. The full results of the construction phase mitigation are presented in an assessment report (Wilson 2017; Appendix 1.4); however, the main findings were the presence of further extensive archaeological remains at Milltimber (CJV site AMA09), one of the stand-out sites from the enabling works, and the excavation of a known cropmark site (ES Site 362) at Wester Hatton (CJV site AMA22). The results of these two sites are incorporated into this volume.

1.3 Archaeological background

The Aberdeenshire landscape is one rich in cultural heritage, from the early prehistoric right through to the modern day. The road line cuts across river valleys, hillsides, bogs, through the suburbs of the city and runs close to the airport at Dyce. This encompassed a variety of 'landscapes', all of which have been altered to some degree or another.

The relatively low number of known sites across the extent of the road scheme was likely to be a reflection of the limited intrusive investigation along much of the higher ground between the Dee and the Don, and from the Don to the coast (Illus 1.05). That said, there are sites that clearly indicate human activity from the Mesolithic through to the recent past. The central part of the route (primarily along the Southern Leg) has a greater density of archaeological sites, and certainly has the most extensive evidence of early prehistoric material. All along the Dee from Milltimber up as far as Banchory, flint scatters have been identified on both sides of the river. A large proportion of these sites were identified in the 1970s by Dr John Grieve, who carried out fieldwalking of ploughed fields mostly on the northern banks of the River Dee. One of the sites identified at Nethermills Farm near Crathes was excavated under JB Kenworthy of St Andrews University between 1978 and 1981. Flints were also identified by Dr Grieve from the field immediately to the west of the road line at Milltimber.

Other flint scatters have been recorded along the Aberdeenshire coast, both immediately north of Balmedie (HER NJ91NE0094) and some distance to the north of the AWPR/B-T route, at Sands of Forvie (NK02NW 29) and Menie Links (NJ92SE 13), but in general the northern portion of the route has limited sites of Mesolithic date.

The Neolithic in Aberdeenshire is largely represented by large-scale monuments dedicated to funerary or ceremonial activities. The long cairn at Cloghill to the west of Kingswells is a typical example of how the evidence presents itself, surviving as an upstanding mound of stones some 55 m long, which reportedly contained a cist burial and is presumed to represent a communal burial site. Equally, findspots of artefacts dating to this period, such as polished stone axes, give an indication of the spread of activity across the region.

In comparison, structural evidence for this period in Aberdeenshire is limited, particularly that relating to settlement activity. A handful of sites provide evidence. The timber hall excavated at Balbridie (Fairweather & Ralston 1993) on the southern bank of the Dee at Crathes in the late 1970s was one of the first examples of this type of site seen in Britain. A second timber hall of similar layout was excavated nearly 30 years later at Warren Field (Murray *et al.* 2009) on the northern banks of the Dee, slightly further back from the river and a few hundred metres downstream.

Recumbent stone circles form one of the most characteristic field monuments of north-east Scotland. The most prominent in relation to the road line is that at Tyrebagger (NJ81SE 11), on a hill to the west of Dyce. These are stone circles that include a large stone lying on its side between two uprights. They date to the late third

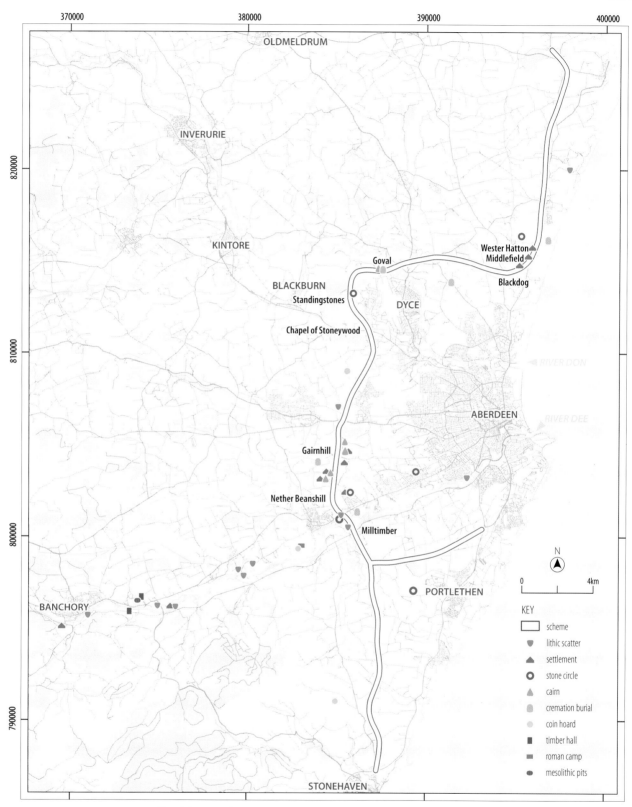

Illus 1.05 Distribution of known sites in the vicinity of the AWPR/B-T

millennium and relate to funerary practices, although this may not be their exclusive use.

Other evidence of burial practices is known from cremation burials. Many of the discoveries are historic, such as the Beaker burial found in a cist approximately 500 m to the east of the road line at Milltimber in 1899, or the urn found at Upper Kirkton to the north-west of Dyce in the early 19th century, which it is presumed would have related to a cremation burial; no further details are known.

By the later prehistoric period (Bronze and Iron Age), more of the known sites represent settlement. Upstanding settlement remains in the form of low stone walls covered in vegetation are present at Beans Hill to the north of Milltimber. A number of hut circles of probable Bronze Age date are recorded, along with evidence of cultivation in the form of cairnfields from stone clearance. From the number of structures recorded in a relatively small space, this seems to be a particular focus of settlement activity. Settlement sites may also include features such as souterrains, but again, most examples from the area are known from cropmarks rather than excavations.

The Roman period is represented by a series of temporary camps that run from near Stonehaven to at least as far as Keith in Moray (Jones 2011). Camps in proximity to the road line include Raedykes and Normandykes, with Kintore lying some distance to the north-west of the route, but which has been extensively excavated. It seems certain now that at least some of these camps belong to the Agricolan campaigns of the late 1st century AD. The presence of Romans or contact with Romans is further attested by a number of findspots of Roman date, including a coin hoard at Silverburn to the north-west of Beans Hill.

Features or sites of confirmed medieval date are few and far between, and the extent and character of medieval activities is often extrapolated back from the post-medieval period. From this it is assumed that settlement took the form of fermtouns (a collection of cottages for farm workers).

In summary, although sites of all periods are known from the wider area, the majority are unexcavated upstanding early prehistoric monuments or cropmarks whose dates have not been confirmed through excavation.

1.4 Geological and topographic background

Richard Tipping

1.4.1 A landscape approach to the presentation of the archaeological excavations in this volume

The geography of the AWPR/B-T forms the basis for the organisation of this volume. This, rather than chronology, is the organising principle, with the assumption that there are different landscapes to be found along the road line. However, the word 'landscape' has become a slippery and ambiguous term. Shorn of its apparent objectivity by post-processualist thinkers (eg David & Thomas 2012), landscape seemingly exists only in the eye of the beholder. That landscape is experienced (Tilley 1994) is a significant and liberating observation (when done well), but this approach also condemns landscape to be largely inaccessible to us. Reading the landscape becomes intuitive, with no frame of reference and little accountability (Fleming 2005).

This way of thinking tends to marginalise the role of the environment in landscape (Thomas 1999), whether because 'determinism' seems always to be bracketed with 'environment' (and determinism has become a dirty word) or because the skills needed in its understanding are not those of anthropologically-minded archaeologists. Recently there has been a return to older, more solid ways of understanding landscape and people; a move away from speculation, particularly from writers at the interface between archaeology and history. Williamson (2003; 2015) observed that 'boundaries of human, and of natural, landscapes often corresponded', that people – farmers, after all – responded to 'patterns of soils, the urgings of topography' (2003, 23). Rippon has also argued this for early historic landscapes (Rippon *et al.* 2012). Soils, and the character of superficial, Quaternary deposits in particular, are argued in later chapters to underlie prehistoric settlement patterns in lowland Aberdeenshire; this will not have seemed novel to earlier historical geographers of these landscapes.

The best example of this in lowland Aberdeenshire, though away from the road line, is the Garioch, in the interior of Donside, west and north of Hatton of Fintray and across to Insch. The marked contrast in settlement patterns in any period, from nearly all monument types and other sources (RCAHMS 2007) in this area has to be explained in a deterministic way, with the disposition of soil types (Illus 1.06). Neolithic stone axes (Gannon *et al.* 2007, fig 5.43) are used as a way in to the data (cf Chapter 3.4 and above) because they are abundant, albeit often with imprecise locations (*ibid.*, 75), are distinctive, likely to be reported when found and noted by antiquarians but are less affected by destruction than monuments. They are a good measure of the reflection of Neolithic human activity. The great majority of stone axes in the Garioch are found on one soil type only; Insch Series brown forest soils. These have formed from till, but one rich in local basic igneous rocks; gabbro and norite. These soften the acidity of Tarves Association soils to the east. Walton (1950) recognised the significance of Insch Series soil in sustaining the population of the Garioch before 1696, though he clouded its importance by focusing on small patches of deep, dry Insch series soils which we might today consider anthropogenic, plaggen soils. Nevertheless, Walton could demonstrate the long-term sustainability of a soil that reaches to the Neolithic, equally recognised as important by the earliest farmers.

Clearly, geography can have cultural significance. The road line, for example, crosses the River Don at Overton just north of Dyce Airport. It would probably have been easier to bridge the river at the Mill of Dyce, where surfaces of glaciofluvial sand and gravel project out into the valley, narrowing its width to less than 100 m, but the rich assemblage of early historic symbol stones surrounding St. Fergus Chapel are protected, which influenced the design. The new road crosses the Don a kilometre downstream at an old crossing, the Forked Ford, the crossing-point until erection of the Bridge of Dyce in 1803. St. Fergus is seen as originally a pre-Christian cult centre (Fraser & Halliday 2007, 128), and lying at the extremity of the

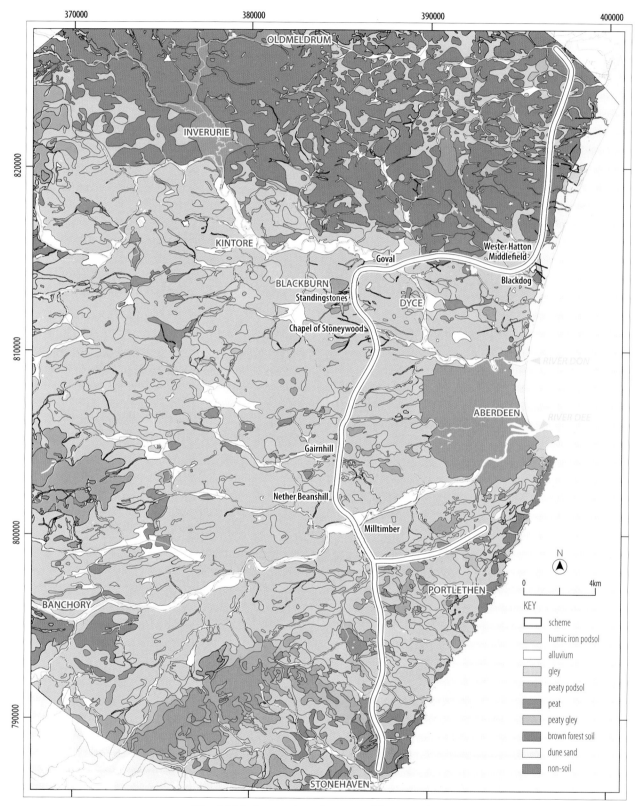

Illus 1.06 Soil types along the route of the AWPR/B-T

medieval parish, it defined the edge of a territory. Pictish symbol stones line the River Don from St. Fergus upriver to Inverurie (*ibid.*, fig 7.3) and later medieval parish boundaries follow the line of the Don from St. Fergus to Kintore. The northern side of the river has long been seen as separate from the Dee–Don upland. Only below Dyce was there medieval ecclesiastical unity between land north and south of the river in St. Machar Parish.

1.4.2 Topography and bedrock geology along the road line

Topographically, the deep valley floors of the Rivers Dee and Don form alluvial corridors; ways for people to penetrate the interior. The Dee in particular, with its west–east alignment, provides contrasts between the south-facing (and therefore sunny), densely populated north side and the colder south side from at least the late 17th century AD (Walton 1950). The old Deeside road, now the A93, separates the alluvial corridor discussed in Chapter 2 from the upland between the Rivers Dee and Don, the subject of Chapters 3 and 4. The upland between these rivers is not terribly high. The summit of Brimmond Hill, some 8.5 km north of the bridge at Milltimber, is only 266 m AOD. Tyrebagger Hill, 3.7 km further north, is lower at 250 m AOD, but the road line doesn't breast either Brimmond or Tyrebagger Hills. It passes to the east of both and rises higher than 200 m AOD only on the Hill of Marcus, north-east of Tyrebagger. The Don provides fewer topographic controls on settlement, partly because it is less deeply incised and partly because of its north-west/south-east orientation in the lower part of its course. East of the Don the plateau surface rarely exceeds 100 m AOD (Chapter 5) and falls gently to the North Sea coast at Blackdog, considered in Chapter 6.

The bedrock geology of the central and northern parts of the road line is simple. The A93 at Milltimber also marks the line of a geological fault, a linear dislocation traced from near Banchory into Aberdeen itself (Munro 1986) that controls the alignment of the valley of the Dee in its lower course. There is no significant change in rock-types either side of the fault. South of the fault are rocks called meta-sediments, originally sandy and clay-rich sediments that have been altered by being subject to low-grade metamorphism. These belong to the Aberdeen Formation. North of the fault are very similar meta-sediments, also of the Aberdeen Formation. The Banchory-Aberdeen fault that guided the Dee in pre-glacial times and therefore guided the glaciers descending from the Cairngorm deepened the Dee valley floor. In doing this, the valley sides became steeper.

The road line follows the outcrop of meta-sediments across Brimmond Hill. The hill itself is made of metamorphosed sediments. Just to the north-west of the summit, at Tulloch, meta-sediment is replaced by the Clinterty granite, a coarse-grained igneous rock. In plan this is a roughly circular body of granite and granodiorite, a granite-like rock, some 4 km across, forming the low ground between Westhill and Blackburn. It was intruded as magma, rising into the meta-sediments, which are older. It is the granite that metamorphosed the meta-sediments by baking them. The Clinterty granite is a pink colour with large (up to 15 mm across) crystals of pink feldspar. Chemically it is a granodiorite, with c50% quartz and c50% feldspar (Munro 1986, 81). The rock was quarried on Elrick Hill in the early 20th century (NJ81SW 92). To the east of the road line across Brimmond Hill, a second, larger granite pluton outcrops; the Aberdeen granite. Its flattened southern edge between Cults and Aberdeen has come about because the Banchory–Aberdeen fault has sliced off its southernmost part. The granite pluton underlies much of Aberdeen and supplied the city with a great deal of its building stone. The 150 m deep quarry at Rubislaw, now in Aberdeen's suburbs, is just one of many quarries. The granite lies under Dyce Airport and the Don catchment east of Cothal, the outcrop being around 17 km at its longest and some 6 km wide. As with the Clinterty pluton, it forms the low ground east of Brimmond and Tyrebagger and has little impact on the topography of the upland. The granite is typically grey, more fine-grained than the Clinterty mass, with more uniform crystals some 2–3 mm across. Aberdeen Formation meta-sediment forms the bedrock between Goval and the coast at Blackdog. Reflecting the uniformity of this geology, Glentworth & Muir's (1963) characterisation of landform elements in north-east Scotland subsume the entire length of the road line to a single element, the Skene Lowlands, the lowest of a series of plateau surfaces in the eastern Grampians between 100 m and 150 m AOD. A lower surface still is locally etched along lower Donside at 45–90 m AOD, possibly a pre-glacial marine embayment (Walton 1963; Merrit *et al.* 2003). Despite the emergence of the granite at the surface, areas of pre-glacial deep chemical weathering, so important as foci of prehistoric and historic settlement and agriculture to the west, are rare in the Garioch (Walton 1950; Hall 1986) owing to the intensity of glacial and glaciofluvial scouring and burial beneath thick masses of glacial till. Munro (1986, 104) reported some 12 m of glacial tills in a continuous section across Dyce Airport.

1.4.3 Glacial landforms and deposits

Bedrock is rarely at the surface anywhere along the road line, usually concealed by superficial deposits. The detail of these differs markedly along the road line, although a map appears disarmingly simple (Illus 1.07). Late Devensian glaciofluvial and Holocene fluvial sediments fill the valleys of the Dee and the Don. At Milltimber where the road line crosses the River Dee (Chapter 2), there is an intimate relationship between these deposits and the archaeology present, such that new work on understanding their chronology was needed and is presented in Chapter 2.

Very extensive surfaces of glaciofluvial sand and gravel (the Lochton Formation) are found above, rather than confined within, the valley of the Don from near Parkhill House (NJ 896 140) in the west to Hillhead of Mundurno in the east (NJ 940 135). They may mark a course that meltwater took along the Don valley after the last glaciation some 20,000 years ago (Murdoch 1975; Munro 1986). Deposits around Loch Hills Farm (NJ 910 145) have an area of 96 ha. Well-drained substrates that are argued to have been very important for founding farming communities next

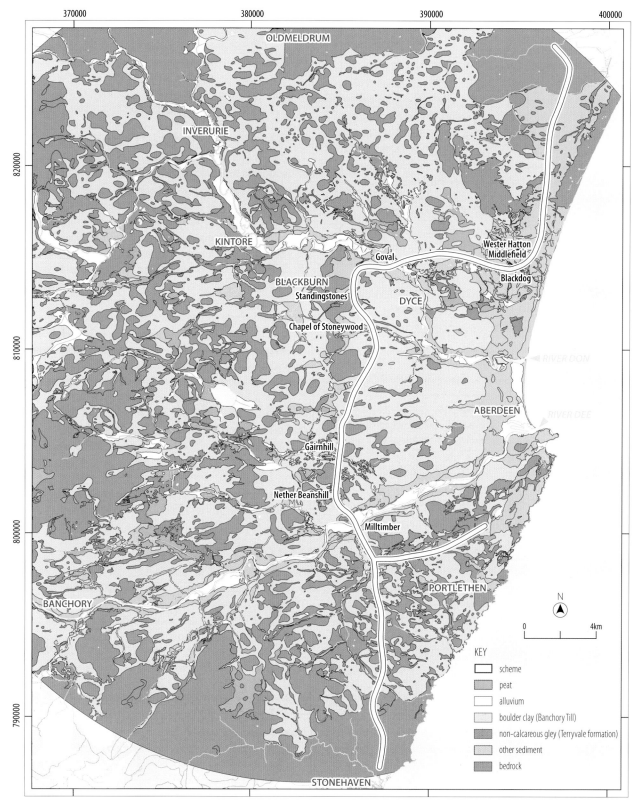

KEY

▢ scheme

▨ peat

▢ alluvium

▨ boulder clay (Banchory Till)

▨ non-calcareous gley (Terryvale formation)

▨ other sediment

▨ bedrock

Illus 1.07 Geological deposits along the route of the AWPR/B-T (Superficial deposits)

to the River Dee (Chapter 2.7.2) are here away from the river. This mostly occurs as discrete rounded mounds of sand elongated west to east, with a few more sharp-crested (Munro 1986, fig 36). The former are kames, the latter

eskers, both indicative of flowing water inside (englacial) or at the base (subglacial) of a glacier or ice-sheet.

The present course of the Don below Dyce is younger. During deglaciation, the river fell into what was probably an old course, glacially deepened to –20 m AOD at the coast, and filled with glacial debris. Radiocarbon dating of two samples of organic matter in lacustrine or fluvial sediment beneath a surface at around 50–55 m AOD at the Mill of Dyce gravel pits, ascribed to an early part of the Windermere Interstadial (Harkness and Wilson 1979; Aitken 1995), suggests excavation of the gorge downstream by the River Don after the youngest date, c13,000 BP, in the latter part of the Windermere Interstadial and into the Younger Dryas Stadial. Wide glaciofluvial terraces line the lower course of the Don on both sides of the channel below Stoneyhill (Illus 5.02). Bremner (1921) recorded suites of up to five terrace surfaces created during deglaciation within the gorge of the lower Don. Before this a large lake filled the floor of the Don at least as far west as Kintore.

The upland plateau surfaces are covered in boulder clay or, more correctly, glacial till (Illus 1.07). Two types are recognised, which differ in their source and origin and therefore in their attributes. Across the Dee–Don upland, and east of the Don, the ground surfaces of the uplands are of the Banchory Till Formation, formed beneath the ice sheet that emanated from the granite of the Cairngorm Mountains and flowed across the outcrop of the Clinterty granite. It is in many places between the Dee and the Don extraordinarily sand-rich, with frequent very large granite boulders but negligible clay content. In Chapter 3.7 a case is built up that this distinctive geology, very well drained because of its high permeability, had major implications for where Bronze Age farmers settled and, more particularly, where they chose not to, which in turn leads to a consideration about the density of later prehistoric settlement (Chapter 7.1.5). On the North Sea coast above Bridge of Don is a second clay-rich till; the Hatton Till Formation, originating off-shore from ice pushing westward.

There are also marked differences between the Dee–Don upland (Chapter 3) and above the Don (Chapter 5) in glacial landforms. The ice that deepened the Dee and the Don valleys streamed eastward over the high ground between Dee and Don, striating and stream-lining rock knolls. The cols that separate Brimmond Hill and Tyrebagger, and smaller gaps such as between Tyrebagger and the Hill of Marcus, were eroded by subglacial meltwater channels. These can have strange long-profiles that are raised in the middle (arched or up-and-down channels) because water beneath ice can be forced uphill. The most prominent meltwater channel flows east from a low col between Brimmond and Kingshill Wood, originating in the col itself and flowing east for 8 km into Aberdeen where it is called the Den Burn. As meltwater waned, the channel was filled with glaciofluvial sand and gravel. Between Brimmond and Tyrebagger, several tributary channels flow up from the west, crossing the watershed and isolating Elrick Hill before coalescing into two parallel curving channels south of Dyce Airport and to the Don at Bankhead.

South of Kingshill the meltwater channels fall into the Dee valley (Chapter 2.4.1). Rather than falling perpendicular to the slope, they form graceful incised arcs aligned with the flow-lines of the glacier. West and north-west of Peterculter are the Gormack and Leuchars Burns, which are parallel with the Dee below them for a long distance. The Ord Burn is also an arched channel with a col at Gairnlea before falling into the Den of Murtle. These channels give a more complex, corrugated structure to the climb from Milltimber to the uplands. There are many slopes that carry smaller, delicate, nested meltwater channels, their courses parallel but often only tens of metres apart, and these too lie across the slope, cutting into it by only a few metres before falling gracefully to the nearest large channel. Some of these channels were – like the River Dee itself – infilled after their incision by well-drained glaciofluvial sands and gravels, such as the Ord Burn north of North Westfield, which has two terraces, both equated with the Lochton Formation (Chapter 2.4.1), or in particular the Leuchars Burn between Garlogie and Inverord. The Ord Burn created a one-kilometre wide alluvial fan as it fell to the Dee, which merged with the glaciofluvial terrace along the Dee. Deposits of Camphill Terrace age seem to be absent in the upland or are undifferentiated. Glaciofluvial gravel can also occur as isolated fragments on the slopes themselves, as at South Lasts above Peterculter.

1.4.4 Holocene landforms and deposits

North and east of the Don the plateau above c60m AOD is studded by large kettle-holes formed by 'dead' stagnating ice. Corby Loch, 1 km to the east of Goval Farm (Illus 5.02), may have been one originally conjoined to Lily Loch; Bishop's Loch is another. Fen peat in the early Holocene has in-filled and isolated them. These extensive peat accumulations are totally absent across the road line over the Dee-Don upland. They occupy enormous areas, even today after millennia of cutting and nibbling at their edges. Illus 1.06 plots their extents from mapping by the Soil Survey of Scotland (Sheet 77) because soil surveyors would have described these more carefully than would the British Geological Survey: to be mapped as peat, the surface organic horizon had to be more than 30 cm thick and have organic contents >60% (Glentworth & Muir 1963, 190). On Hawkhill, north of Cothal, two parallel mosses on either side of a granite ridge occupy some 80 ha of the plateau. To the east, the Red Moss of Parkhill covers some 220 ha despite peat cutting affecting an estimated three-quarters of it. To its north, the Red Moss of Whitecairns covers 70 ha. South of the road line and the fen at Corby Loch, which covers some 40 ha, Grandholme Moss also extends around 40 ha, but this has been very heavily reduced to perhaps one-third of its original size. Diameters of smaller mosses of more than a kilometre are common. At their largest, raised mosses probably occupied more than 20% of the area depicted in Illus 5.02. In addition, the spreads of

Terryvale Series gley soils in Illus 5.02 may also indicate the former existence of peat.

Some of these mosses began to form as fens, gradually in-filling areas of open water (Durno 1957). Some such as Corby, Lily and Bishop's Lochs have remained fens, and are Sites of Special Scientific Interest for their freshwater habitats. Stratigos & Noble (2014) report a crannog in Corby Loch. Other mosses are thought to have originated in bedrock and till depressions rather than in open water (Munro 1986, 117). Glentworth & Muir (1963) recorded peat depths (and so the profiles of underlying substrates across several mosses north and south of the River Don) and argued that some large mosses are mixtures of peats initially confined to basins and peats forming on shallow slopes (blanket peat). However, the need is to understand where peat began to accumulate first, and this is most likely in basins. There are probably several basins beneath each of these mosses, and peat inception may have been triggered at several foci. The ponding of water is critical and yet the glacial till is often sandy. This paradox is hard to resolve because Glentworth & Muir (1963) did not describe the mineral substrate at the base of their profiles and very few civil engineering boreholes have been sunk through them. Where these have been sunk along the road line east of Corsehill (NJ 906 152), both clay-rich and sandy substrates are noted.

Fens initially supported open vegetation, with grass and sedge communities on dryer ground, with *Calluna* (ling heather) and other heathers. Trees like birch and willow would have colonised when the water table was low. Several basin peats in Aberdeenshire probably began to form very early in the Holocene epoch, certainly within the first 1000 years. None have been radiocarbon dated, but correlation of their pollen records with other radiocarbon-dated pollen records using regionally synchronous features (Tipping 2007, 33), suggests this for Strichen Moss (Fraser & Godwin 1955) and at nearby St. Fergus (Durno 1956) in the Buchan Lowland near Peterhead, at Skene Moss (Glentworth & Muir 1963: Chapter 3.2) and south of the River Dee at Netherley Moss (Durno 1956).

Fen peat will grow vertically as long as the water table will allow. To continue to grow, vertically and laterally, fen peat has to be transformed to a raised moss by changes in water chemistry or changes in climate to increasing wetness (Hughes & Barber 2004). Then sphagnum species spread across the peat surface, a moss that is 95% water, floating without roots on the peat surface, pulling the water table up as it grows. Sphagnum on a peat surface accumulates on dead sphagnum and the peat surface grows higher and spreads laterally. Raised mosses can be more than 10 m thick in the centre of the low dome. Water in the peat becomes increasingly acid, causing trees to decline. No detailed work has been done east of the Cairngorms on when this transition occurred, but at St. Fergus Moss near Peterhead, and Skene Moss on Deeside, the increases in sphagnum occurred just prior to the rise in alder (*Alnus*),

perhaps around 5750 BC (estimated from Glentworth & Muir 1963, figs 20–22).

The Dee–Don upland was until quite recently also characterised by very large lakes (Brown 1995), also of glacial origin, which lie to the west of the road line. Some are mapped by the British Geological Survey, where their distinctive sedimentology results in them being named the Glen Dye Silts Formation. They are delicately laminated (eg beds <2 mm thick) olive-grey silts and clays, probably the product of deposition into lakes fed by meltwater streams during deglaciation. The flat surface at Woodend, just up the hill from Peterculter, was formerly one small lake, and directly east of Westhill, under Kingsgrove House, was a lake whose mapped extent has a diameter of around 1.2 km. The Neolithic long cairn at Longcairn (NJ 8512 0705; NJ80NE 13) stands almost at the edge of the mapped Glen Dye Silts and may have looked to the south-west across open water. Set within the Glen Dye Silts are extensive spreads of peat and gravel (Munro 1986, 114), formed some time in the Holocene. They indicate that shrinkage of the lake was a staggered rather than gradual process. The lake is drained by the now canalised Brodiach Burn. This burn formed part of the western boundary to the 'freedom lands' (Chapter 3.5) and Boundary Marker 28, at Borrowstone Farm (NJ80NW 17) seems to skirt the present burn, so maybe there was open water in the early modern period. Roy's mid-18th century survey depicts only a spread of moorland (Roy 1747–55). Just west of the gap punched through the granite of Elrick Hill by meltwater channels, perhaps ponded as the ice-front fell westward away down-slope of the col, a third large spread of Glen Dye Silts some 2 km long drains along the Black Burn through Blackburn. The name suggests peat, and Auton & Crofts (1986, 18) found a humic sand in boreholes, though none is mapped by the British Geological Survey. The area of the silts was drained in association with 19th-century enclosure fields but whether the lake was drained then is not clear. Ponds still remain on the floor of the former lake.

Bremner (1935) traced the old shorelines and histories of larger lakes. He considered the Loch of Skene, still 249 acres (100 ha) in extent, to be a kettle-hole lake formed when 'dead' ice, isolated from an ice-front retreating westward, slowly melted *in situ* leaving a hollow. Bremner saw the Loch of Skene originally connected to a lake in the former meltwater channel of the Leuchars Burn. Geological mapping by the British Geological Survey shows the latter filled with gravel, but though civil engineering boreholes record glaciolacustrine clays (Glen Dye Silts Formation), they are beneath the gravel and the lake must have quickly infilled with gravel. A small spread of alluvium east of Broadwater may have survived to be drained artificially in the last few centuries. The Loch of Skene remains, although shrunken in size. Durno (in Glentworth & Muir 1963) analysed around 5.7 m of peat at Skene Moss for its pollen content at a location sadly not recorded, and demonstrated that peat began to form between c8000 BC and c6500 BC.

To the south-west, the Loch of Park has almost vanished today. It is now a marsh, only 0.5 km long, between Crathes and Drum Castle but Bremner reckoned it was once the largest lake on Deeside, at 719 acres (290 ha), extending westward some eight kilometres along the Bo Burn to Raemoir beneath the Meikle Tap. The loch was dammed by till, morainic material left at a phase in deglaciation. The Bo Burn flows along a meltwater channel and the early Loch of Park was a series of beaded stretches of open water separated by narrow channels. East of Hirn the lake swelled and covered over 400 ha. Bremner thought the water surface fell around 4 m in two stages, the first before Keith's survey of the agriculture of Aberdeenshire in 1811, when Drum Loch, the Loch of Park, was only some 300 acres (120 ha). Gordon's 17th-century map (Adv. MS.70.2.10: Gordon 25) shows a small lake, his more detailed map (Adv. MS.70.2.10: Gordon 28) depicting a lake extending west some four kilometres to Hirn but Gordon (31: Adv. MS.70.2.10) shows the lake barely larger than the present marsh. Roy's Military Survey does not show the lake. The second and final stage was between 1811 and 1845 during agricultural 'improvements', and finally in 1943 (Vasari & Vasari 1968).

Just outside Banchory and less than a kilometre south of Raemoir was the Loch of Leys, extant to some extent when a crannog was constructed (NO79NW 3), its later stages of medieval date. Gordon's detailed map (Adv. MS.70.2.10: Gordon 28) shows both the lochs of Leys and Park. The Loch of Leys was drained first in 1755 (Bremner 1935, 32) and almost completely in 1850. If both Park and Leys Lochs were extensive open water in the Neolithic, they might have made passage along the glaciofluvial gravels of the Dee almost necessary.

1.4.5 Landscape character along the road line

Landscape character (Usher 1999) is one way of defining individual elements of landscape. From analysis of landforms, visibility, plant communities and anthropogenic influences over time. Nicol *et al.* (1996) identified five landscape character types outwith the urban areas. When applied to the road scheme these comprised: (1) the valleys of the Dee and Don, (2) the hills of Westhill, Brimmond and Elrick and Kirkhill Forest, (3) wooded farmland, (4) open farmland and (5) the coast. We recognise the alluvial corridor of the River Dee (Chapter 2) to be different from the Dee-Don interfluve (Chapter 3). The hills have little significance for us, although the Mesolithic site of Standingstones (Chapter 4) is on their eastern flank. The road line east of the crossing of the Don is not considered in detail by Nicol *et al.* (1996) but accords with the Dee–Don upland in being open farmland: we see the late Quaternary peat-land along the road line as distinct from the soils between the Dee and Don (Chapter 5). The coast is considered in Chapter 6.

An interesting character type in this context is the wooded farmland, a linear strip barely 2 km wide rising

from the Dee valley urban strip from Cults to Peterculter, west of Craigiebuckler, to the treeless landscape north of the Aberdeen-Alford road, the A944. To Nicol *et al.* (1996) this is largely an enclosure landscape, the woodland of 18th-century origin in the large amalgamated estates that came after the 'freedom lands' colonisation, but in Chapter 3 we try to define a more fundamental pedological divide between this and the open Dee–Don upland that can be traced to the Bronze Age.

The historical dimension is more explicit in Historic Environment Scotland's HLA mapping (Macinnes 2004; 2010; http://hlamap.org.uk/). Little survives along the road line, even of the medieval period. This is a predominantly modern, 17th–18th century farmed landscape (see also Dixon & Gannon 2007) of rectilinear fields, farms, designed landscapes and managed woodland.

1.5 Project aims and objectives

The overarching aim of the project was to reduce the effect of the scheme on the archaeological resource through the acquisition of a full archaeological record and an evidence-based interpretation of that record. For each site, following topsoil stripping the remains present were categorised and quantified and a strategy for excavation devised. The intention was to place each site in a wider context in terms of type, date and the archaeology of the wider area.

Potential research objectives were identified following the trial-trenching phases of work and then further refined during the mitigation excavations, coming to full expression in the Post-Excavation Assessments (Appendices 1.1–1.4; Dingwall 2015; Murray 2015; van Wessel 2015; Wilson 2017). These research objectives were tied into period-specific research agendas as laid out in the Scottish Archaeological Research Framework (ScARF). A summary of these objectives is presented below:

Landscape and Sites – Each of the sites had a specific landscape setting. Understanding how that landscape impacted on and was impacted by the site was key to placing them in their context. What was the character of the landscape of north-east Scotland over time? What impact did the Rivers Dee and Don have on these landscapes?

Mesolithic Period – What activities do the sites of Mesolithic date represent? Are these consistent across the sites or are we seeing different activities at different locations and how does this relate to a 'mobile Mesolithic'? Do the lithic spreads represent single visits or multiple periods of activity over a longer duration? What can be gleaned from refits within the assemblages? What function do the large pits serve, and are they a type of feature that has been missed or poorly recognised in the past?

Neolithic Period – The Neolithic period is represented by a range of features, some of which would typically be represented as 'ritual' activities, others more directly related to settlement. What is the relationship between these types of features and activities and can any distinction really be identified? To what extent can pits be used as a proxy for evidence of settlement in this period? How does the structure at Milltimber compare to other settlement evidence?

Neolithic Transition/Chalcolithic Period – Do the timber settings represent an entire site or do they extend beyond the limits of excavation? What was the function of the features and are they strictly speaking structural? Are they focused on a particular alignment and, if so, what is the significance of this? How does the site fit into known patterns of distribution of sites of this nature?

Bronze Age and Iron Age Periods – How are settlement and related activities represented as a whole along the entire route of the AWPR/B-T? Are there differences in settlement patterns dependent on date, location or environment? Where multiple structures are present, can phasing be distinguished, or evidence of the development and alteration of a settlement? What does the presence of apparent settlement structures in close proximity to burial activities say about the relationship between these two aspects of Bronze Age life? With the resource of burnt timbers and material from the structures at Gairnhill, is it possible to be any clearer on the specifics of roundhouse construction and layout from this evidence? Can the site economies be reconstructed from the environmental remains? How does metalworking and the presence of furnaces near the River Don relate to the broader settlement activity in the area?

Roman Period – What is the chronology of the site during the early first millennium and does a refined dating chronology allow an understanding of the duration of activity? What can the environmental evidence tell us about the use of the ovens and the materials used to construct and cook in them? How did the landscape at the time of their construction influence and affect their distribution and appearance? What do the ovens represent in terms of the advance of the Roman military in north-east Scotland?

Early Historic and Medieval – What does the presence of a number of relatively isolated features of these dates tell us about activity in the later first millennium AD and into the early centuries of the second millennium AD? Why are these sites rarely identified and does this reflect a genuine distribution pattern or a lack of excavation in such locations? How do such features relate to known sites of Pictish date and could they be classified as such?

1.6 Technical methodologies

Standard methodologies were followed for stripping topsoil, initial identification and quantification of features, and methods of excavation and recording. Where sites had been identified through trial trenching, a generous buffer was stripped beyond known features to ensure that, as far as possible, the full limits of sites within the road corridor were revealed (Illus 1.08). Exceptions to the standard methodology had to be proposed in two situations, both at the multi-period site at Milltimber on the River Dee. The presence of an apparently *in situ* lithic spread of likely

Mesolithic date required a more targeted approach, and the discovery of 90 ovens of possible Roman date also necessitated an alternative proposal.

1.6.1 Lithics spread

The discovery of a potential *in situ* spread of lithics at Milltimber was highly significant. However, it was initially unclear whether the material genuinely was *in situ* or was the result of hill wash or other movement down the hill. Should it be *in situ*, much of the value of the information was linked to specific material's location within the spread, so the excavation process needed to record this. An evaluation excavation on a grid system (explained below) was carried out, along with a site visit conducted by Dr Stephen Carter to understand the formation processes occurring at the site (Illus 1.09).

A 1 m × 1 m grid was laid out over the spread and each grid box assigned a unique number. A selection of these grids were 50% excavated in 50 mm spits and 10 l samples taken for flotation assessment and the remaining material wet sieved for artefact retrieval. This evaluation phase confirmed the Mesolithic date of the lithic material, and also established that although there had been some degree of vertical movement of lithics within the spread, horizontally their location was still unchanged and the deposit could indeed be considered *in situ*. Recording the remains spatially would be worthwhile and an appropriate methodology for excavation. As a result, 159 grid squares were excavated in a systematic manner, with around half distributed evenly across the preserved deposits and another 60 excavated in areas of higher density. A further 20 were held in reserve and excavated where the density proved to be greater or where additional finds retrieval was recommended.

For finds retrieval purposes, dry-sieving was carried out on site using a 5 mm mesh, and 25% of the dry sieved material was then wet sieved through a 3 mm mesh using a frame and hose. A lithics specialist based on site was able to examine all the material extracted and provide recommendations for further sampling and excavation of grids.

1.6.2 Roman ovens

Initially only 13 ovens were revealed following the primary stripping at Milltimber. Subsequently a larger area was stripped revealing in total 90 suspected ovens (Illus 2.33). Although this was a substantial resource, initial excavation indicated that there was very limited variety in the stratigraphic sequences and structural form of the features. The overall objective of mitigating their loss by obtaining as much information as possible needed to be balanced with the time constraints of the project as a whole. The interest in the ovens lay more in their groupings and potential date rather than the details of their structure.

Discussions between Headland Archaeology (UK) Ltd, Jacobs and Historic Scotland (now HES) took place and it was agreed that 50% of the ovens would be

Illus 1.08 Excavation of the road corridor at Gairnhill (Chapter 3)

Illus 1.09 Grid excavation of lithic spreads at Milltimber (Chapter 2)

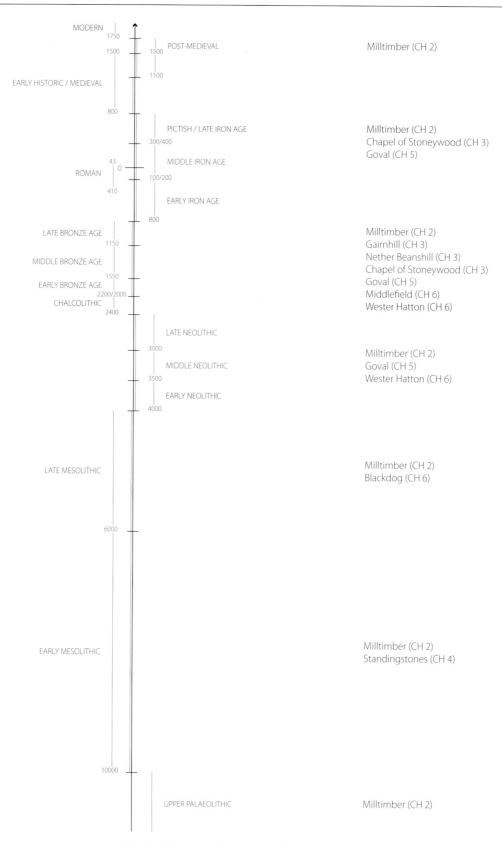

MODERN		
1750		
1500	POST-MEDIEVAL	Milltimber (CH 2)
	1500	
	1100	
EARLY HISTORIC / MEDIEVAL		
800		
	PICTISH / LATE IRON AGE	Milltimber (CH 2)
	300/400	Chapel of Stoneywood (CH 3)
43	MIDDLE IRON AGE	Goval (CH 5)
0		
ROMAN	100/200	
410		
	EARLY IRON AGE	
	800	
LATE BRONZE AGE		Milltimber (CH 2)
1150		Gairnhill (CH 3)
MIDDLE BRONZE AGE		Nether Beanshill (CH 3)
1550		Chapel of Stoneywood (CH 3)
EARLY BRONZE AGE		Goval (CH 5)
2200/2000		Middlefield (CH 6)
CHALCOLITHIC		Wester Hatton (CH 6)
2400		
	LATE NEOLITHIC	
	3000	Milltimber (CH 2)
	MIDDLE NEOLITHIC	Goval (CH 5)
	3500	Wester Hatton (CH 6)
	EARLY NEOLITHIC	
	4000	
LATE MESOLITHIC		Milltimber (CH 2)
		Blackdog (CH 6)
6000		
EARLY MESOLITHIC		Milltimber (CH 2)
		Standingstones (CH 4)
10000		
	UPPER PALAEOLITHIC	Milltimber (CH 2)

Illus 1.10 Timeline showing periods, sites and chapters

excavated, provided the ovens were uniform in terms of types, morphology and sequence of deposits. The 50% would be spread across the spatial groups that could be identified prior to excavation. If any of the excavated ovens were unusual or did not conform to examples previously excavated, additional ovens from that group would be chosen for investigation.

All the ovens investigated would be half-sectioned, and 10 l samples taken from any firing layers identified. In addition to those half-sectioned, a single oven would be picked from each group for full excavation and 40 l samples of all deposits relating to the oven would be taken, including underlying material the ovens were cut into and overlying deposits representing collapse or abandonment. Again, should atypical elements be recognised during the full excavation of an oven, consideration would be given to full excavation of further examples from the group.

All ovens were metal detected prior to excavation to assist in deciding which to excavate; in the event no positive signals were present. Dr Richard Tipping also visited the site during the excavation to advise and inform on further analysis, and OSL dating was undertaken on selected samples.

1.7 Organisation of the report

This publication is organised by site, starting with the southernmost discoveries and moving north. Some sites were relatively short-lived and only represent a single period of activity while others are extensive multi-phase palimpsests with a wide variety of types of evidence;

this is reflected in the text. There was a strong similarity in evidence from Nether Beanshill, Gairnhill, Chapel of Stoneywood and Wester Hatton. All four revealed evidence of settlement and related activities in the later prehistoric period. Owing to their proximity to each other the sites at Nether Beanshill, Gairnhill and Chapel of Stoneywood have been grouped together in a single chapter (Chapter 3). Similarly, the discoveries at Middlefield, Blackdog and Wester Hatton were sufficiently relatable to merit discussion together and are contained within Chapter 6.

A timeline has been produced (Illus 1.10) to aid the reader and provide a guide to the dates and periods presented within the various chapters of this monograph. These are based on current models produced by ScARF and the latest available research in Scottish Archaeology.

A large number of specialist assessments and analysis has been undertaken in relation to the variety of sites investigated as part of this project, and what is presented here is a synthesis of that information, intended to be suitable for an informed general reader. All the technical specialist reports, along with the assessment reports from each phase of the project are publicly available online through the ADS website (https://doi.org/10.5284/1050093).

Appendices 1 and 2 list the individual reports and their location within the digital report. Appendix 4 provides a concordance table of analysis undertaken at each site.

The archive from the site has been lodged in the National Record for the Historic Environment, held by Historic Environment Scotland.

Chapter 2

A landscape through time: Milltimber and the River Dee

Kirsty Dingwall, Richard Tipping and Don Wilson

2.1 Introduction to the circumstances of discovery at Milltimber

2.1.1 Background to the archaeological works at Milltimber

This chapter presents the results of excavations at Milltimber on the north and south banks of the River Dee. The Environmental Statement (Jacobs UK 2007) did not identify any sites within the road corridor at Milltimber, although it was clear that the valley of the Dee had higher potential owing to the number of known sites in the surrounding area (see 2.2 below). Geophysical survey identified a handful of anomalies within the road corridor and trial trenching confirmed the presence of a small number of features; however, many were shown to relate to geological or natural features. The trial trenching also revealed concentrations of features in three or four locations across the valley floor. Based on this, five mitigation areas were identified for stripping.

This process revealed a far more extensive and complex archaeological landscape than the trial trenching had predicted. As additional features were identified, topsoil stripping was extended to find the limits of activity. A slope of relatively shallow gradient on the valley floor north of the River Dee had been partially masked by the presence of extensive colluvial deposits. Removal of the topsoil revealed a relatively steep bank forming the northern edge of a palaeochannel (the location of which is shown on Illus 2.33 and is clearly visible in Illus 2.49). The edge of the slope was lined with pit-like features containing extensive burnt deposits, and other similar features could be seen lining the edge of other slightly shallower banks bordering the palaeochannel.

To the north of the palaeochannel, the topsoil was much shallower, and the geological substrata formed a broad terrace of sands and gravels, extending for nearly 350 m north at which point the ground rose relatively

steeply, forming the northern limit of the valley floor (a contour map showing the slope of the valley sides is displayed on Illus 2.26). Below the topsoil here deposits were encountered containing extensive Mesolithic flint assemblages. Whilst the deposits did not form a prehistoric ground surface, the spatial distribution of the flint reflected the pattern of deposition on the original land surface. This is explained further in Chapter 2.14.2. Initial stripping revealed a number of small, often charcoal-rich, pits with very diffuse edges and with no clear cuts. While a methodology for investigating the lithics spread was being agreed the site was left to weather. A dry summer combined with periodic heavy rain resulted in numerous additional features weathering out of the ground, usually surrounding the poorly defined features initially identified.

By the end of nearly six months of excavation at Milltimber, an extensive, complex and rich archaeological landscape had been revealed, comprising approximately 500 features and (following analysis) proving to represent at least eleven individual phases of activity and potentially as much as 15,000 years of human interaction at this one location. The role the river played in shaping the valley was key, influencing the resources available and both restricting and enhancing the land available for people to live in and exploit.

2.1.2 Site location and extent of mitigation

As indicated above, the original five areas identified for investigation were expanded during the excavation and eventually the stripped area covered 48,760 m² linking three of the five original areas (Illus 2.01). Further targeted evaluation trenches were also excavated to confirm blank areas of the site. During the construction phase of the road building programme further monitoring extended the known limits of the site by an additional 23,410 m². This was predominantly towards the northern extent of

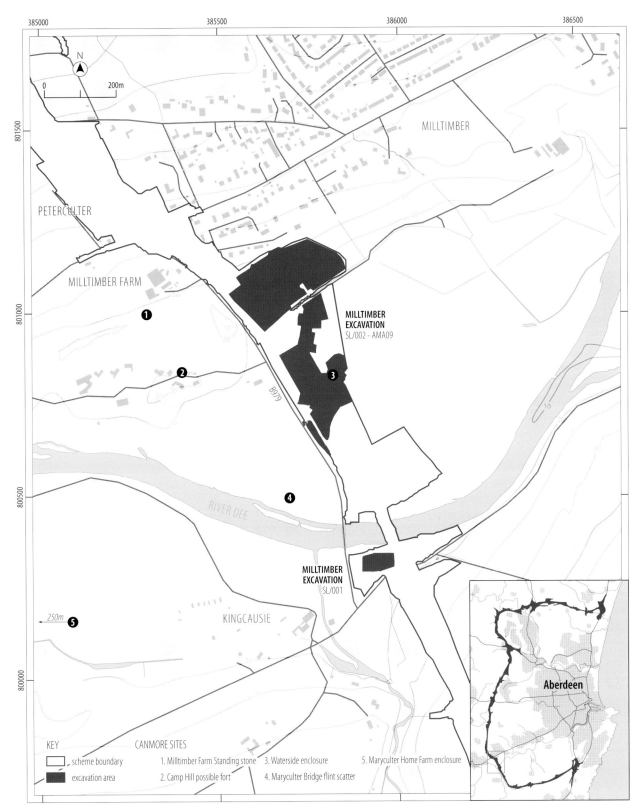

Illus 2.01 Location of sites at Milltimber

the site and features relating to this phase of works carry the prefix AMA09.

The site at Milltimber comprises the northern part of the flat valley floor to the north side of the River Dee, along with the south-facing slope defining the northern side of the valley. It also includes a small area on the south side of the river. At the time of excavation, all the fields in question were in use for rough pasture, with one field containing horse jumps.

During excavation, specific methodologies were developed to excavate the lithic spread, the large pits and the features lining the bank of the palaeochannel, which had been shown to be of early first millennium AD date through early targeted radiocarbon dating (see 1.6).

2.2 Background to the archaeology of the River Dee valley

Although no sites had been identified within the road corridor at this location, and no previous archaeological investigations had taken place, it was still broadly recognised to be an area of some potential. To the south-west of the site, within the field immediately to the west along the northern bank of the River Dee, an assemblage of over 8000 flint pieces (NJ80SE 36) was collected by a local individual. The exact location of the findspots are not known, and the assemblage has not been examined in detail. It is unclear what period the lithics date to, beyond prehistoric; however, extensive work on lithics distributions along the River Dee point to a Mesolithic origin.

A record from the 19th-century antiquarian Jervise mentions a standing stone at Milltimber Farm to the west side of the B979, apparently the single surviving upright from a full stone circle (NJ80SE 10). Also to the west side of the B979 the historic record of a 'camp' is recorded on the Ordnance Survey first edition map. Jervise (1875, 19) suggested that the earthworks are 'British', Meldrum interpreted the very slight upstanding remains as a possible motte (1957, 20), while the Ordnance Survey notes from the 1960s refer to it as an alleged fort (NJ80SE 17). Some 550 m east of the mitigation areas a cist containing a Late Neolithic/Early Bronze Age Beaker (NJ80SE 11, Eeles 1899) was unearthed during sand and gravel extraction.

Two cropmark enclosures identified from aerial photographs are also listed in the NHRE. The first of these (NJ80SE 42) is located immediately east of the road corridor with the second (NJ80SW 27) 500 m to the west. Both were undated but provided further evidence of previous activity in the area.

2.3 Radiocarbon results and dating

In total, 82 radiocarbon dates were obtained from a range of features (Table 2.01; Illus 2.02a–f). Where possible, short-lived species or small branch wood were used in order to achieve as tight a date-range as possible. Given the extent of features, the presence of earlier spreads of deposit with later features cut through and the general lack of artefactual material (other than lithics, which are of limited use in dating individual features), a great many features identified remain effectively unphased. Unless these features can be specifically related to a known phase of activity, they have not been included in illustrations. The issue of undated features is discussed below (see 2.12).

A considerable number of features were cut into the edge of a palaeochannel. These, along with a number of

other similar features considered to be contemporary, were broadly dated to between the 2nd century BC and the 4th century AD, with most of the dates clustered in the first two centuries AD. Given the potential Roman origin of the features, it was considered that Bayesian analysis might further clarify the date range of the activity and assist in understanding its origins (see 2.10.3 below).

Proxy dating for the prehistoric periods was also provided by pottery and lithic material (see 2.14 below). In addition, detailed analysis of the lithic material produced evidence for a previously unrecognised Late Upper Palaeolithic phase of activity, although no specific features can be assigned to this phase.

2.4 Introduction to the landscape of the Dee at Milltimber

Richard Tipping

The topography of the site could be described as a typical wide river plain, with the current River Dee located close to the southern limit of the valley floor, a broad flat plain that appeared susceptible to flooding to the north of this, and then the northern edge of the valley rising up and defining its limit as shown in Illus 2.03.

2.4.1 The alluvial corridor of the Dee

The alluvial corridor of the River Dee, a prehistoric route into the interior (Murray *et al.* 2009; Wickham-Jones *et al.* 2017) with its free-draining soils formed on fluvial gravel and sand, can be traced up the valley sides around 50 m above the river. They date to the last glaciation. The British Geological Survey (BGS Geoindex; accessed 2016) defines three separate spreads of sand-and-gravel above the valley floor at Milltimber (Illus 2.03) that originally formed continuous valley-wide flattish surfaces of gravel, sloping downstream. The highest is called the Lochton Formation, found up to 40–42 m AOD at Milltimber (Illus 2.04). East of Milltimber a second terrace is mapped set below this, also described as the Lochton Formation, at around 26 m AOD on the south side of the valley. The Lochton Formation is not dated. On the northern side of the valley these terraces are not seen, probably because the south-facing slope has been more prone to erosion as a result of the unequal warming of the two valley sides. The sunny side also attracted more urban development from at least the late 17th century (Walton 1950; Coull 1963). The alluvial corridor is connected to the upland slopes to the north by a series of glacial meltwater channels: the valleys of the major channels, the Leuchar Burn above Peterculter, immediately west of Milltimber, and the Ord Burn at Milton of Murtle, 1 km east of Milltimber, all contain Lochton Formation gravel in them.

Below Lochton Formation gravels are discontinuous fragments of younger gravels. One forms a surface at Milltimber around 16–17 m AOD (Illus 2.03) on the north

Table 2.01 Radiocarbon determinations from Milltimber

Context	Lab no	Material	Radio-carbon age BP	Calibrated age 95.4% probability
(2D-1777) fill of small Mesolithic pit [2D-1776]	SUERC-68101	Nutshell: *Corylus avellana*	8897±29	8220–7970 cal BC
(2D-1119) fill of Mesolithic pit [2D-1089]	SUERC-68106	Charcoal: *Salix sp*	8848±29	8210–7820 cal BC
(2C-0147) fill of Mesolithic pit [2D-0143]	SUERC-54050	Charcoal: *Salix sp*	8657±29	7730–7590 cal BC
(2D-1028) fill of Mesolithic pit [2D-1009]	SUERC-68096	Charcoal: *Corylus avellana*	8620±29	7710–7580 cal BC
(2D-1015) fill of Mesolithic pit [2D-1014]	SUERC-68100	Charcoal: *Pomoideae Sp.*	8313±30	7490–7200 cal BC
(AMA09-2217) fill of small Mesolithic pit [AMA09-2216]	SUERC-73594	Nutshell: *Corylus avellana*	8176±31	7310–7070 cal BC
(2D-1489) fill of Mesolithic pit [2D-1485]	SUERC-68095	Charcoal: *Corylus avellana*	8142±30	7290–7060 cal BC
(2D-1035) fill of Mesolithic pit [2D-1008]	SUERC-58021	Charcoal: *Betula sp*	8054±30	7080–6830 cal BC
(2D-0008) fill of Mesolithic pit [2D-1003]	SUERC-54051	Charcoal: *Ilex aquifolium*	7963±27	7040–6710 cal BC
(2D-1716) fill of Mesolithic hearth [2D-1715]	SUERC-58189	Charcoal: *Corylus avellana*	6843±31	5790–5660 cal BC
(2D-1144) fill of tree bowl [2D-1102]	SUERC-68113	Charcoal: *Corylus avellana*	6251±30	5310–5080 cal BC
(2D-1274) fill of Mesolithic fenceline pit [2D-1273]	SUERC-68115	Charcoal: *Corylus avellana*	5962±29	4940–4770 cal BC
(2D-1226) fill of Mesolithic fenceline pit [2D-1225]	SUERC-68116	Charcoal: *Corylus avellana*	5780±30	4710–4550 cal BC
(2D-1128) fill of Mesolithic pit [2D-1127]	SUERC-68110	Nutshell: *Corylus avellana*	5737±30	4690–4500 cal BC
(AMA09-2244) fill of Mesolithic pit [AMA09-2241]	SUERC-73592	Charcoal: *Corylus avellana*	5280±31	4230–4000 cal BC
(2D-1898) fill of Neolithic pit [2D-1895]	SUERC-58617	Charcoal: *Salix sp*	5097±28	3970–3800 cal BC
(2D-1435) fill of Neolithic post-hole [2D-1433]	SUERC-58188	Nutshell: *Corylus avellana*	5092±29	3960–3800 cal BC
(2D-1467) upper fill of Mesolithic pit [2D-1193]	SUERC-58023	Charcoal: *Corylus avellana*	5091±30	3960–3800 cal BC
(2D-1636) fill of structure hearth [2D-1638]	SUERC-58194	Charcoal: *Corylus avellana*	5081±30	3960–3800 cal BC
(2D-1259) fill of Neolithic hearth [2D-1258]	SUERC-68112	Charcoal: *Corylus avellana*	5076±30	3960–3800 cal BC
(2D-1824) floor deposit of Neolithic structure	SUERC-68114	Charcoal: *Corylus avellana*	5050±29	3950–3710 cal BC
(2D-1266) fill of Neolithic post-hole [2D-1267]	SUERC-68104	Charcoal: *Ilex aquifolium*	5036±29	3950–3720 cal BC
(2D-1881) fill of Neolithic hearth [2D-1879]	SUERC-68102	Charcoal: *Corylus avellana*	5026±29	3940–3710 cal BC
(2D-1786) upper fill of Mesolithic pit [2D-1714]	SUERC-68105	Charcoal: *Ilex aquifolium*	5024±29	3940–3710 cal BC
(2D-1509) fill of Neolithic post-hole [2D-1495]	SUERC-58193	Charcoal: *Corylus avellana*	5017±29	3940–3710 cal BC
(2D-1408) fill of Neolithic hearth [2D-1400]	SUERC-68120	Charcoal: *Corylus avellana*	5014±29	3940–3710 cal BC

Mesolithic Features (rows: (2D-1777) through (AMA09-2244))

Early Neolithic Features (rows: (2D-1898) through (2D-1408))

Table 2.01 Radiocarbon determinations from Milltimber (Continued)

	Context	Lab no	Material	Radio-carbon age BP	Calibrated age 95.4% probability
Middle and Late Neolithic Features	(2D-1214) fill of Neolithic hearth [2D-1210]	SUERC-58604	Charcoal: *Corylus avellana*	4633±28	3510–3360 cal BC
	(2D-1149) fill of Neolithic pit [2D-1137]	SUERC-58022	Charcoal: *Corylus avellana*	4534±30	3360-3100 cal BC
	(2D-1235) fill of Neolithic hearth [2D-1234]	SUERC-58605	Charcoal: *Corylus avellana*	4494±29	3350-3090 cal BC
Chalcolithic Features	(2C-0160) fill of chalcolithic post-hole [2C-0157]	SUERC-58517	Charcoal: *Quercus sp*	3909±28	2470–2300 cal BC
	(2C-0017) fill of chalcolithic post-hole [2C-0016]	SUERC-58516	Charcoal: *Corylus avellana*	3886±29	2470–2290 cal BC
	(2C-0019) fill of chalcolithic post-hole [2C-0018]	SUERC-54055	Charcoal: *Corylus avellana*	3851±26	2460–2210 cal BC
	(AMA09-2014) fill of pit [AMA09-2011]	SUERC-73593	Charcoal	3664±31	2140–1950 cal BC
Middle Bronze Age Features	(2D-1613) MBA burnt spread	SUERC-68103	Charcoal: *Corylus avellana*	3154±29	1500–1320 cal BC
	(2B-2429) fill of MBA pit [2B-2428]	SUERC-59044	Charcoal: *Alnus glutinosa*	3080±29	1420–1270 cal BC
	(2C-0128) fill of MBA hearth [2C-0127]	SUERC-54056	Charcoal: *Corylus avellana*	3041±29	1400–1220 cal BC
	(2C-0070) fill of MBA pit [2C-0068]	SUERC-68094	Charcoal: *Corylus avellana*	2990±29	1370–1120 cal BC
	(2B-0044) upper fill of Ditch [2B-2075]	SUERC-68091	Charcoal: *Corylus avellana*	2951±29	1260–1050 cal BC
	(2D-1576) fill of MBA pit [2D-1575]	SUERC-68111	Charcoal: *Betula sp*	2948±29	1260–1050 cal BC
Iron Age Features	(AMA09-2090) fill of Iron Age pit [AMA09-2089]	SUERC-74402	Charcoal	2158±29	360–110 cal BC
Roman Ovens	(2A-0108) fill of oven B21	SUERC-68064	Charcoal: *Betula sp*	2067±29	170 cal BC–cal AD 1
	(2B-2111) fill of oven E03	SUERC-58505	Charcoal: *Quercus sp*	2067±28	170–1 cal BC
	(2B-2180) fill of oven F19	SUERC-58498	Charcoal: *Calluna vulgaris*	2003±29	90 cal BC–cal AD 70
	(2A-0062) fill of oven B20	SUERC-54188	Charcoal: *Alnus glutinosa*	1995±30	50 cal BC–cal AD 70
	(2B-2629) fill of oven C04	SUERC-68066	Charcoal: *Betula sp*	1984±29	50 cal BC–cal AD 70
	(2C-0108) fill of 2C-0108	SUERC-56395	Charcoal: *Calluna vulgaris*	1975±38	50 cal BC–cal AD 120
	(2B-2277) fill of oven A10	SUERC-58500	Charcoal: *Calluna vulgaris*	1970±29	40 cal BC–cal AD 80
	(2A-0116) fill of oven B13	SUERC-54187	Charcoal: *Ulnus sp*	1960±30	40 cal BC–cal AD 120
	(2B-2019) fill of oven A05	SUERC-68060	Charcoal: *Calluna vulgaris*	1960±29	40 cal BC–cal AD 120
	(2A-0018) fill of oven B13	SUERC-54189	Charcoal: *Alnus glutinosa*	1957±30	40 cal BC–cal AD 120
	(2B-2294) fill of oven D04	SUERC-68071	Charcoal: *Alnus glutinosa*	1947±29	20 cal BC–cal AD 130
	(2B-2272) fill of oven A08	SUERC-68062	Charcoal: *Calluna vulgaris*	1942±29	20 cal BC–cal AD 130

Table 2.01

	Context	Lab no	Material	Radio-carbon age BP	Calibrated age 95.4% probability
Roman Ovens	(2B-2028) fill of oven E09	SUERC-68074	Charcoal: *Salix sp*	1938±29	cal AD 1–130
	(2A-0090) fill of oven C08	SUERC-68070	Charcoal: *Alnus glutinosa*	1937±29	cal AD 1–130
	(2B-2261) fill of oven G01	SUERC-58497	Charcoal: *Calluna vulgaris*	1931±29	cal AD 10–130
	(2A-0122) fill of oven B16	SUERC-68083	Charcoal: *Betula sp*	1928±29	cal AD 10–130
	(2B-2113) fill of oven E03	SUERC-59043	Charcoal: *Ilex aquifolium*	1926±29	cal AD 1–130
	(2B-2119) fill of oven F13	SUERC-68075	Charcoal: *Corylus avellana*	1917±29	cal AD 10–210
	(2B-2038) fill of oven D06	SUERC-58504	Charcoal: *Alnus glutinosa*	1911±28	cal AD 20–210
	(2B-2083) fill of oven E01	SUERC-68072	Charcoal: *Alnus glutinosa*	1903±29	cal AD 30–210
	(2A-0083) fill of oven B09	SUERC-68063	Charcoal: *Calluna vulgaris*	1902±29	cal AD 30–210
	(2A-0073) fill of oven C01	SUERC-68065	Charcoal: *Alnus glutinosa*	1901±29	cal AD 30–210
	(2B-2191) fill of oven G07	SUERC-68076	Charcoal: *Calluna vulgaris*	1900±29	cal AD 30–210
	(2A-0049) fill of oven C09	SUERC-58509	Charcoal: *Ilex aquifolium*	1897±28	cal AD 30–210
	(2B-2094) fill of oven F08	SUERC-68085	Charcoal: *Alnus glutinosa*	1894±29	cal AD 50–210
	(2B-2433) fill of oven G08	SUERC-68080	Charcoal: *Ilex aquifolium*	1885±29	cal AD 60–220
	(2B-2003) fill of oven A02	SUERC-58499	Charcoal: *Calluna vulgaris*	1883±28	cal AD 70–220
	(2B-2200) fill of oven D02	SUERC-68090	Charcoal: *Calluna vulgaris*	1877±29	cal AD 70–220
	(2B-2242) fill of oven F06	SUERC-68084	Charcoal: *Calluna vulgaris*	1875±29	cal AD 70–220
	(2B-2180) fill of oven F19	SUERC-68086	Charcoal: *Calluna vulgaris*	1873±29	cal AD 70–230
	(2B-2078) fill of oven E04	SUERC-68073	Charcoal: *Alnus glutinosa*	1870±29	cal AD 70–230
	(2A-0141) fill of oven B15	SUERC-68082	Charcoal: *Calluna vulgaris*	1842±29	cal AD 90–240
	(2B-2227) fill of oven A07	SUERC-68061	Charcoal: *Calluna vulgaris*	1838±29	cal AD 90–240
	(2B-2049) fill of oven A11	SUERC-68081	Charcoal: *Corylus avellana*	1818±29	cal AD 90–320
Early Historic Features	(01-0014) fill of early historic kiln [01-0015]	SUERC-58187	Cereal: *Hordeum vulgare*	1613±29	cal AD 390–540
	(2C-0010) fill of early historic pit [2C-0009]	SUERC-59291	Charcoal: *Alnus glutinosa*	1532±29	cal AD 430–600
	(2B-2448) fill of enclosure ditch [2B-0063]	SUERC-58507	Cereal: *Hordeum vulgare*	1334±29	cal AD 650–770
	(2B-0110) fill of pit/post-hole [2B-0109]	SUERC-68093	Charcoal: *Corylus avellana*	1112±29	cal AD 780–1010
	(2B-0081) fill of pit/post-hole [2B-0080]	SUERC-68092	Charcoal: *Alnus glutinosa*	1066±29	cal AD 900–1020
Medieval Features	(2B-0090) fill of pit/post-hole [2B-2089]	SUERC-58506	Nutshell: *Corylus avellana*	1051±28	cal AD 900–1030
	(2B-2331) fill of small pit [2B-2330]	SUERC-58508	Nutshell: *Corylus avellana*	314±29	cal AD 1490–1650
	(2B-0059) fill of pit [2B-0057]	SUERC-59296	Charcoal: *Pinus sp*	104±26	cal AD 1680–1930

Kirsty Dingwall, Richard Tipping and Don Wilson

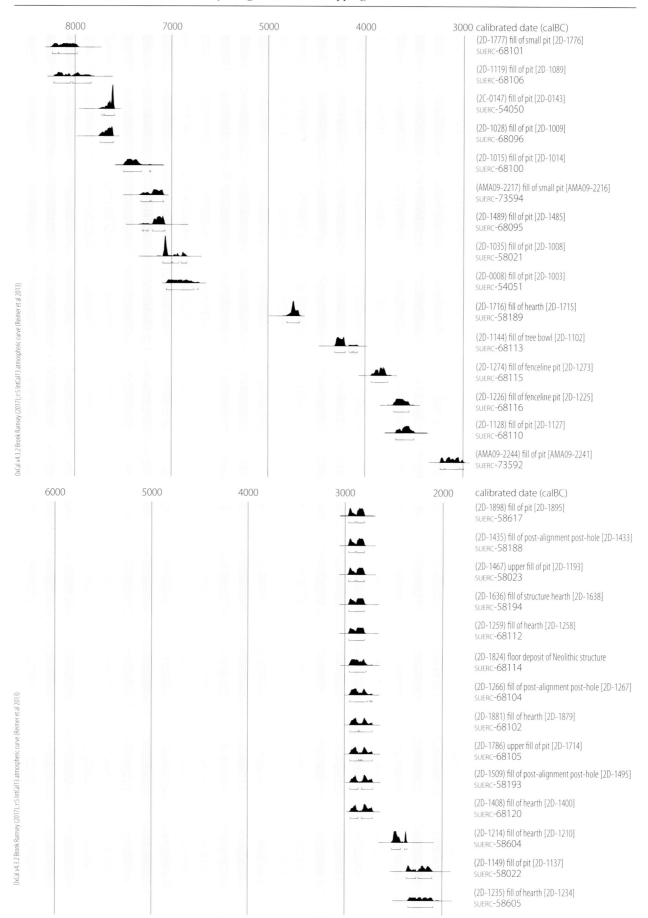

Illus 2.02A-F ^{14}C graphs from Milltimber

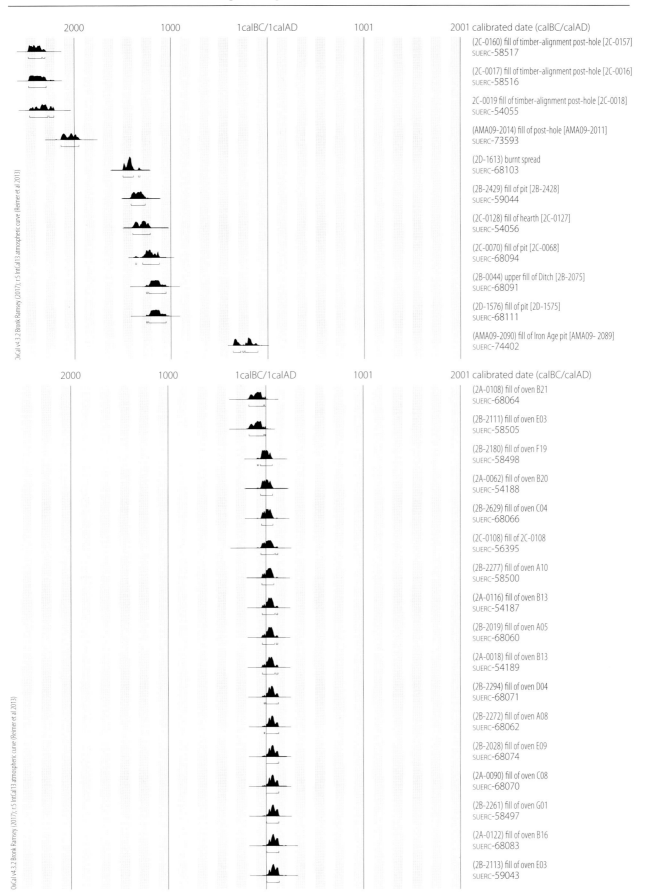

Illus 2.02A-F ^{14}C graphs from Milltimber

28

Kirsty Dingwall, Richard Tipping and Don Wilson

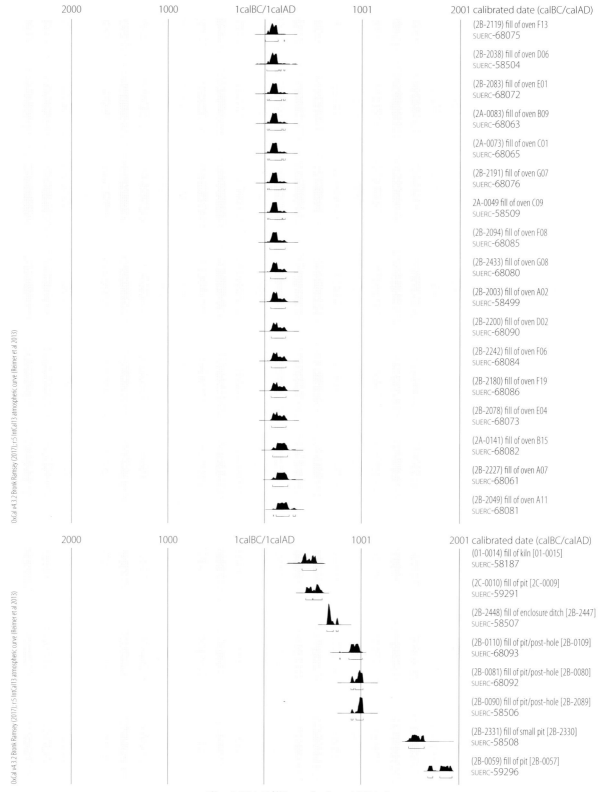

Illus 2.02A-F ¹⁴C graphs from Milltimber

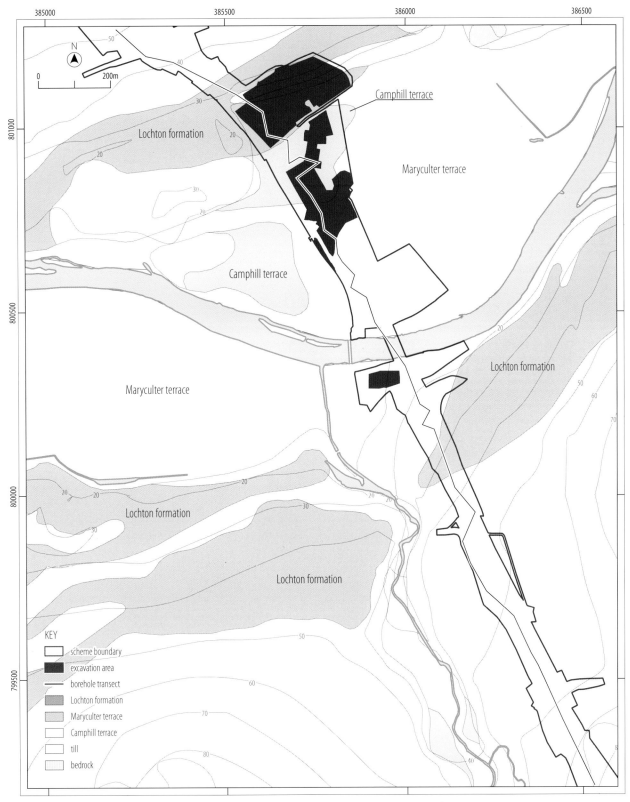

385000 385500 386000 386500

801000

800500

800000

799500

N

0 200m

50

40

30

20

20

30

20

Lochton formation

Camphill terrace

Maryculter terrace

Camphill terrace

Maryculter terrace

Lochton formation

Lochton formation

Lochton formation

20

30

50

60

70

20

20

20

30

50

60

70

80

40

KEY

scheme boundary
excavation area
borehole transect
Lochton formation
Maryculter terrace
Camphill terrace
till
bedrock

Illus 2.03 Plan of the geological formations at Milltimber

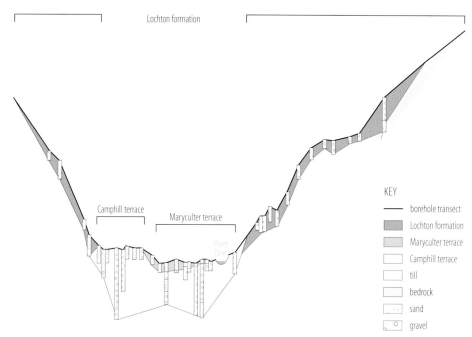

Illus 2.04 Section across the alluvial corridor of the River Dee at Milltimber, showing the disposition of outcropping gravels (Lochton Formation) and terrace surfaces (Camphill Terrace; Maryculter Terrace) from civil engineering boreholes along the road-line

side of the valley where it is around 200 m wide, some 5 m above the valley floor. This and other fragments are mapped by the British Geological Survey but not named, called 'undifferentiated gravel, sand and silt'. The terrace is named the Camphill Terrace. Illustration 2.05 (a height–distance diagram of altitudes on the surfaces of these fragments) shows clearly that the terrace surface at Nethermills of Crathes (Wickham-Jones *et al.* 2017), approximately 10 km to the west, is correlated with fragments of the same age at Milltimber and Garthdee Road (Murray and Murray 2014), 8 km to the east and Duthie Park in Aberdeen. The two surviving fragments within urban Aberdeen are at the same altitude, suggesting that the river graded to a mean sea level at that time of around 9 m AOD.

The valley floor at Milltimber is around 12–13 m AOD and some 400 m wide (Illus 2.04). It is underlain by glaciofluvial gravels that have been truncated by later fluvial erosion. Over this gravel, unconformably, is an almost stoneless sand or silty sand called the Maryculter Terrace, deposited when the river did not have the power to transport gravel.

2.4.2 The chronology of deglaciation in the Dee Valley

Ballin's identification of Late Upper Palaeolithic elements in the flint assemblage (see 2.14.2 below) necessitates discussion of the timing of deglaciation of lower Deeside, to define the earliest that occupation was possible. If the Camphill Terrace did grade to a sea level around 9 m AOD, an understanding of Later Devensian relative sea-level change helps constrain its age. On the Moray coast, the St. Fergus Silt Formation represents glacio-marine

deposition. The surface of the formation is generally between 7 m and 10 m AOD but locally up to 16 m AOD. Two calibrated radiocarbon assays on samples of marine shells (Hall & Jarvis 1989) date to around 18,000 BP (Merritt *et al.* 2003). The Camphill Terrace might relate to this time. Full deglaciation of lower Deeside at c15,000 BP is suggested by Clark *et al.* (2012). Although the timing of deglaciation along the Dee valley is poorly dated (Brown 1993), Ballantyne (2010) has suggested deglaciation within the Cairngorm Mountains by c15,000 BP. Several localities record full sediment sequences dating to the Devensian Lateglacial, probably from around 14,000 BP (Tipping 2007, 29), throughout the Dee valley, at Loch Builg (Clapperton *et al.* 1975) 50 km north west of Milltimber, above Braemar at Morrone (Huntley 1994) 55 km to the west and in lowland landscapes at Loch Kinord in the Muir of Dinnet (35 km to the west) and the infilled Loch of Park, west of Peterculter (Vasari & Vasari 1968; Vasari 1977). The lithic assemblage is seen as Hamburgian/Ahrensburgian in affinity, which is of Windermere or Lateglacial Interstadial age, correlated (Lowe *et al.* 2008) with Greenland Interstadial 1 (GI-1d: 14,692 to 12,986 years BP; Rasmussen *et al.* 2008).

2.4.3 Climate and environment in the Devensian Lateglacial

Detailed quantitative mean July temperature estimates from the Devensian Lateglacial to the early Holocene have recently been made for a site at Abernethy Forest in the western Cairngorms, around 60 km from Aberdeen (Brooks *et al.* 2012). As a guide, mean July temperature at Aberdeen between 1921–1950 was c14.5°C (Glentworth

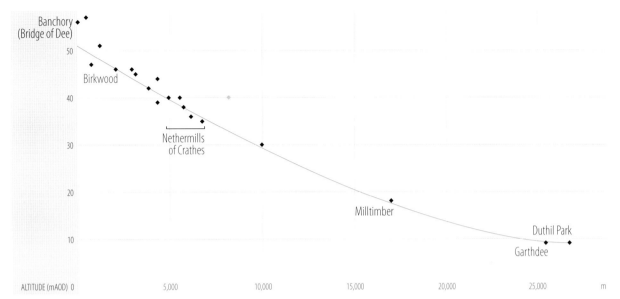

Illus 2.05 Height-distance diagram of fragments of post-Lochton Formation (undifferentiated sand and gravel) mapped by the British Geological Survey, showing their altitudinal correlation

& Muir 1963, 27). The Abernethy Forest record begins before 14,000 BP when mean July temperatures were around 11°C. Mean July temperatures fell to around 8°C at roughly 14,100 to 13,950 BP, rising to around 13°C after this for a short period before returning to a mean of 8°C. Fluctuations of around 1°C led to falls of around 7°C in the early Younger Dryas c13,000 BP, in agreement with other north-west European estimates (Denton *et al.* 2005). These authors stress that mean winter temperatures may have fallen far more dramatically, by 20–22°C in the earlier part of the Younger Dryas. Mean July temperatures at Abernethy Forest rose during the later Younger Dryas, after c12,100 BP to around 10°C (Brooks *et al.* 2012).

We have few measures of precipitation from the British Isles for the Lateglacial. The Aberdeen region must have been relatively dry, lying east and in the rain-shadow of the Cairngorms, which in turn is in the rain-shadow of the western Grampians: the very small size of Younger Dryas glaciers in the Cairngorm is because of the relative aridity downwind of prevailing westerlies. What the River Dee was like is unclear; there is no dated evidence. It certainly would not have been tidal at Milltimber after c14,500 BP. On the continent, most rivers were single-channel meandering systems in the Windermere Interstadial. Some became gravel-rich and braided in the Younger Dryas. Bohncke *et al.* (1988) described the early part of the Younger Dryas as very dry.

The Loch of Park pollen record (Vasari & Vasari 1968; Vasari 1977) serves to describe lower Deeside in the Windermere Interstadial and the Younger Dryas. It is radiocarbon dated at two horizons, the lower calibrated by Tipping (2007, 29) to 14,570–13,286 BP, the second 85 cm higher to 12,554–11,072 BP. Trees may have been absent around Loch of Park in the Windermere Interstadial,

contra Tipping (2007, 28). Birch (*Betula*) is the only tree in the British Isles in the interstadial (Walker *et al.* 1994) but birch pollen at Loch of Park is recorded at quite low values. A sedge-rich grassy heath is probable, with juniper (*Juniperus*) and willows (*Salix*) the only tall shrubs, with herbs that thrive in bare ground and heath plants like crowberry (*Empetrum*), suited to dry and nutrient-poor soils (Bell & Tallis 1973). The Younger Dryas saw the destruction of organic-rich soils and many of the interstadial plant communities.

2.4.4 The Early Holocene River Dee and the Camphill Terrace

Glaciofluvial gravels of the Lochton Formation and the Camphill Terrace extend up- and downstream of Milltimber (Illus 2.04). Palaeoenvironmental data from Nethermillls of Crathes (Ewan 1981; Boyd & Kenworthy 1982) have considerable relevance for Milltimber in the Mesolithic period.

Ewan (1981) defined a series of former stream-courses (palaeochannels) across the surface of the 75 m wide Camphill Terrace surface. Such abandoned channels usually represent criss-crossing meltwater-fed, sediment-charged braided rivers and their channels are usually filled with sand from the last floods (eg Maizels & Aitken 1991). However, on the Camphill Terrace surface there are several very different palaeochannels. They run broadly parallel to the present river, with low sinuosity, bifurcating around sand 'islands'. At least one is filled with peat. The channels are barely two-thirds the width of the present river at their widest. The channels may have formed at different times, but they may also have been contemporary, and may represent a floodplain characterised by anastomosing stream-courses, with multiple channels, a type of floodplain rare nowadays. How this may have looked at Milltimber is depicted in Illus 2.90. Such river forms have long been suggested as preceding single-channel rivers in the Holocene (eg Brown 1995). The channel examined by Ewan (1981) was around 20 m wide but only 70 cm deep. The channel then filled with peat. Pollen analyses show that peat inception occurred c9300 BC, some 400 years after the beginning of the Holocene epoch, when mean July temperatures at Abernethy Forest rose to around 14°C (Brooks *et al.* 2012).

The surface of the Camphill Terrace at Nethermills may have been the floodplain of the Dee in the early Holocene, and Mesolithic sites there may represent human activity on the active floodplain of the Dee. Up-valley at Birkwood (NO 717 962), near Banchory, Paterson & Lacaille (1936) excavated *in situ* later Mesolithic flint assemblages on the Camphill Terrace in sand that continued to accumulate (Kenney 1993, 227–28; Tipping 2007, 36).

The Camphill Terrace was also the active floodplain of the River Dee at Milltimber in the Mesolithic, although the course/s of the river cannot be defined. The surface appears to have retained little sediment from this time except for an 80 m long, 15 m wide palaeochannel filled with sand. The sediments in this channel were not directly dated but Kinnaird, Tipping & Sanderson (Appendix 2.8.18) sampled eight depths in a c70 cm thick vertical profile (Profile 4) and seven depths in a c50 cm thick accumulation of sand lying on top of the gravel (Profile 6) and assessed their luminescence properties using a portable optically stimulated luminescence (pOSL) reader, which rapidly allows the identification of trends with depth as indicators of the uniformity of sediment accumulation (Sanderson & Murphy 2010). The study identified that the basal sand is relatively much older than overlying sediments and may pre-date the Holocene epoch. It also indicated that the sediments in Profiles 4 and 6 on the Camphill Terrace are generally much older than the Late Iron Age, except for the uppermost sediments of Profile 4 (P4/1 to 3; Table 2.2 in Appendix 2.1.18). Though pOSL measurements do not always indicate age, these three samples might suggest that the Camphill Terrace may have been over-topped by flood waters from the River Dee long after it had been abandoned by the river.

There are a small number of Mesolithic features cut into the sand and gravel of the Camphill Terrace including four large pits (see 2.6.2 below). One of these, pit [2C-0143], is radiocarbon dated to 7730–7590 cal BC (SUERC-54050). Pit digging per se need not indicate that the surface of the terrace was permanently dry, only that water did not impede digging, probably over a very short period, perhaps even a day. It is entirely possible that the sediments filling pit [2C-0143] were deposited in a water-lain environment such as the active floodplain, although this was not clearly identified in the deposits of this pit. The marked difference in the abundance of pits between the base of the slope cut in eroded Lochton Formation gravel and the surface of the

Camphill Terrace might also suggest that the surface of the latter was usually avoided. This may also have implications for the use of the pits in this area. Would water ingress be a problem when digging the pits? This seems unlikely as it makes no sense expending energy digging a pit that would rapidly silt up.

Existing anastomosing river systems are often described from environments different from the temperate woodland zone of north-west Europe, but Gradziński *et al.* (2003) described such a system from the Narew River in Poland that is close in many aspects to what is visualised for Milltimber in the Mesolithic. The valley floor of the Narew is mostly peat, a wetland only 30–40 cm higher than the mean water level, the valley floor gradient is low, and channels carry negligible amounts of mineral sediment. Channels are of varying dimensions and discharges, usually 5–35 m wide and 3–4 m deep, steep-sided, bifurcating by avulsion (eg by cutting new channels) round bars ('islands') in a maze-like pattern at all angles, some >90°, but channels generally flow parallel to the valley sides, with low sinuosity, as at Nethermills (Ewan 1981). The vast majority of channels carry water, even at low flow. Abandoned channels quickly fill with aquatic plants. Inter-channel areas are flat, waterlogged quagmires and densely vegetated, predominantly with tall wetland grasses and sedges with willows rather than trees, because of the high water table.

2.5 Evidence for the Late Upper Palaeolithic on the River Dee

The very earliest evidence for human activity at Milltimber is solely in the form of a lithics scatter (2D-1939) towards the northern limits of the valley floor. The date of the activity was proposed on the basis of the typology of sub-assemblages within the overall assemblage and does not relate to any features on the ground. The artefactual evidence is not presented in any detail here as it relates to specific comparisons between lithics of various periods and in-depth analysis of material, typology and technological schemata. A full presentation of the evidence is provided below (see 2.14.2).

In summary, there are at least two zones within the overall scatter where there is a small but notable assemblage of lithic material that is thought to be of Late Upper Palaeolithic date. This cannot be dated using radiocarbon techniques but is thought to come from the time span between 13,000–10,000 BC.

2.6 Mesolithic activity

2.6.1 Mesolithic valley floor environments, plant communities and resources

Richard Tipping with contributions from Tim Holden

Ewan's (1981) pollen analyses at Nethermills are the only data along the lower Dee on early Holocene floodplain or riparian plant communities (Tipping 2007). This was a habitat that clearly attracted Mesolithic people, though Ewan's analyses were few and skeletal, the percentage-based diagram was calculated on a sum that makes comparisons difficult, and the peat was not radiocarbon dated. The pollen site has a small diameter, implying that most pollen at the site came from close by but the source area will have included the northern valley side as well as the valley floor.

Birch (*Betula*) is one taxa on the valley floor. The tree colonised north-east Scotland around 9600 BC (Tipping 2007, 33) on every substrate and habitat; very little deflects birch growth except other trees. Birch was abundant at Braeroddach Loch, near Loch Kinord (30 km west of Milltimber) by c8140 BC (Edwards 1979a) but was more poorly represented at Nethermills (Ewan 1981). Willow (*Salix*) will already have grown along Deeside by the time that birch colonised, growing on most substrates. Birch establishment may have forced willow on to the valley floor where it is competitively superior. Willow is the dominant plant on the Narew River inter-channel areas (Gradziński *et al.* 2003) and willow scrub probably dominated the Dee valley floor until the establishment of alder at c5750 BC (Tipping 2007, 38). Willow was burnt in pit [2C-0143] at Milltimber, radiocarbon dated to 7730–7590 cal BC (see 2.6.2 below).

Grasses and sedges are not abundant in the pollen record at Nethermills and the valley floor of the Dee may have differed from the Narew today in having less open vegetation. Grassy habitats persisted at Nethermills, however, rich in meadowsweet (*Filipendula*), tormentil (*Potentilla*) and other members of the Rosaceae, and ferns. Spores of horsetails (*Equisetum*) were common before the establishment of hazel type (Coryloid) pollen c8000 BC, possibly *E. palustre* or *E. fluviatile* in wet-meadows.

Coryloid pollen includes both hazel (*Corylus avellana*) and bog myrtle (*Myrica gale*). On mineral sediment away from the palaeochannels, the pollen is probably of hazel. Values start to increase at Braeroddach Loch between around 8140 and 7700 BC. A date between 8500 and 8000 BC for lower Deeside would be in accord with other estimates (Boyd & Dickson 1986; Birks 1989; Tipping 2007, 33). Hazel will also have grown on dry valley sides.

Open-ground habitats declined at Nethermills after c7500 BC. More shade may have been cast on dryer inter-channel areas in time by the colonisation of oak (*Quercus*). The establishment of oak is radiocarbon dated at Braeroddach Loch (Edwards 1979a) to 5613–4913 cal BC, but one piece of oak charcoal was found in pit [2C-0143] at Milltimber, the pit radiocarbon dated to 7730–7590 cal BC. Oak will also have colonised valley-side slopes above the valley floor. Boyd & Kenworthy (1982) and Wickham-Jones *et al.* 2017) record oak charcoal in abundance at Nethermills, and it can be assumed that these

trees were nearby. The growth of more trees on the valley floor will have stabilised stream-banks and inter-channel areas, slowing channel change (avulsion). The higher accumulation of woody debris will also have reduced water-flow, but would lead to temporary flooding along some reaches, encouraging channel instability and the forcing of new channels around blockages (Harwood & Brown 1993; Gurnell 2014). Vegetation change may also have been provoked by reductions in discharge, leading to fewer floods, and less sediment being supplied by floods, increasing soil stability in the areas between channels.

Valley-floor woods were again disturbed by the colonisation of alder (*Alnus*), estimated to have been around 5750 BC in the Dee lowlands (Tipping 2007, 38). Alder competes poorly with already-established trees (Bennett & Birks 1990), and disturbance to a stable wetland habitat is one way alder gets a foot-hold. At Nethermills, however, the proportion of alder was never high.

The last major vegetation change recorded at Nethermills saw a total transformation of the valley-floor woodland, with the total loss of willow and the collapse of the local oak population, shown most clearly from the near-absence of spores of *Polypodium*, which is commonly an epiphyte growing on oak. The valley-floor woodland was apparently rapidly replaced by birch and by grassy habitats. Alder was unaffected, but equally it did not gain from this disturbance, which is unusual. Willow may also have lost to birch with changing hydrology. It may be that what is recorded at Nethermills was a shift from riparian woodland on marshy soils to a valley floor woodland that grew on a mineral substrate, with the introduction of floodplain sands and silts. This event almost certainly affected the valley side woodland also, because the dry ground grazing indicator, ribwort plantain (*Plantago lanceolata*) became more common. The event may well have been anthropogenic in origin, although the woodland at Nethermills was not cleared, only altered substantively. The age of the rapid shift from alder–willow to birch woodland at Nethermills cannot be defined; it was after c5750 BC. At Braeroddach Loch, the first ribwort plantain pollen grains are radiocarbon dated to 4551–3782 cal BC (Edwards 1979a).

The edge of the marshy valley floor at Milltimber, the base of the slope where the vast majority of Mesolithic finds are, would have been a sharply defined ecotone between two different woodland habitats (see Illus 2.06). Birch will have grown on the valley floor and valley sides from around 9600 BC, and hazel will have been confined to dry valley sides after its establishment around 8000 BC (Tipping 2007, 33). Because the assemblage of Mesolithic pits at Milltimber are from these lower valley-side slopes, environmental reconstruction has been detailed, but also a little beyond the available evidence.

Calibrated radiocarbon age-estimates for the pits mostly span the period between c8200 BC to c6700 BC. For most, if not all, of this time the dry woodland on the valley side

Kirsty Dingwall, Richard Tipping and Don Wilson

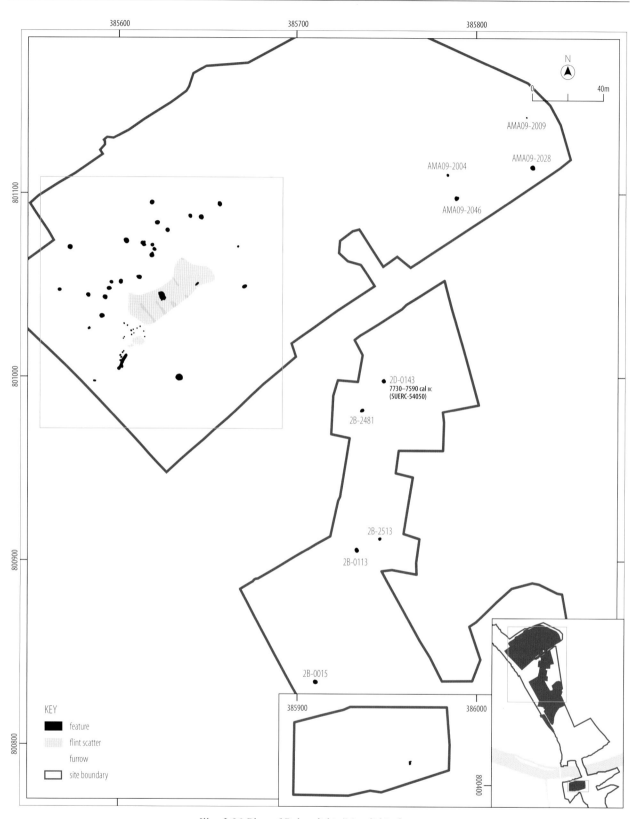

Illus 2.06 Plan of Palaeolithic/Mesolithic features

was entirely of birch and hazel. Elm (*Ulmus*) appears not to have colonised the ground around Braeroddach Loch before 7021–6051 cal BC.

Davies *et al.* (2007) analysed five pollen samples from near the base of a Mesolithic pit at Warren Field (Murray *et al.* 2009; Context 5/14) on Lochton Formation gravel. Charcoal identified as alder from this pit was radiocarbon dated to 7040–6690 BC and 7260–6840 BC: the charcoal is thought to have been wrongly identified (contra Murray *et al.* 2009, 19; cf Timpany 2014a, 16). The very small diameter of the pit at Warren Field means that most pollen will have come from the surface of a soil within a few tens of metres around the pit, so these analyses relate more to surrounding plant communities than either the lake sites of Braeroddach Loch or Loch Davan. The five pollen samples in this pit contained pollen of birch (30–40% total land pollen – TLP) and hazel type (*Corylus avellana*-type: 15–20% TLP), which here can be assigned to *Corylus avellana* (hazel).

Hazel can be assumed to have been a tree, not a tall shrub (Rackham 1980, 203) and, with birch, formed the canopy of the woodland. The proportions of birch and hazel pollen from Pit 5 (above) are probably equivalent to their percentages in the vegetation (Andersen 1970). It seems most likely that the two trees were growing mixed together because the proportions are constant in all five samples (cf Birks 1973, 175). The pollen of trees other than birch and hazel were not recorded at Warren Field at values signifying their presence. Palynologically rare tree taxa such as rowan (*Sorbus aucuparia*), aspen (*Populus tremula*) and bird cherry (*Prunus padus*) are recorded from this period, though what role they played in the woodland is unclear. Scrub elements like hawthorn (*Crataegus*) have been found as macro-plant remains on archaeological sites in the period 8000–6000 BC (Bishop *et al.* 2013).

The woodland at Warren Field is thought not to have had a closed canopy; light penetration is important for both birch and hazel to flower and set seed (Cameron & Ives 1997). There was an under-storey of heathers. For example, ling (*Calluna* pollen); cf bell heather (*Erica* pollen) and perhaps bilberry (*Vaccinium/Erica* pollen) with a small amount of grasses and grassland herbs of the daisy/dandelion family (*Asteraceae*), campions (*Caryophyllaceae*), buttercups (*Ranunculus*) devil's bit scabious (*Succisa*), and ferns, close to McVean's (1964, 151) bilberry-rich birchwood association today. Birch–hazel woodland like this covered Deeside and the Dee–Don upland in the early Mesolithic period (Chapter 4). Nowhere in lower Deeside is high enough to have been above the tree-line (Birks 1988). This woodland type is seen at every pollen site in eastern Deeside (Durno 1957; 1970; Vasari & Vasari 1968), further west (Edwards 1979b; Edwards & Ralston 1984; Edwards & Rowntree 1980) and throughout the country (Bennett 1989; Tipping 1994). Birch and hazel had co-existed for around 1000

years before Mesolithic people dug pits at Warren Field (Murray *et al.* 2009), Milltimber (this chapter) and made camp at Standingstones (Chapter 4). In many parts of the country, birch populations seem to have lost out rapidly to hazel, but this was not so in north-east Scotland, where birch remained important. Such woods today grow on acidic but not markedly podsolised brown forest soils (McVean 1964, 152; Birks 1973, 175). The presence of bilberry at Warren Field suggests the soil there was acidic by c7000 BC. Soils like these occurred almost everywhere across the Dee–Don upland, the Counteswells, Charr and Dess Series (Glentworth & Muir 1963). The climate enveloping these types of wood today is cool, wet, windy and cloudy (Rodwell 1991), though our data are skewed by their present distribution in Scotland on the wet and wind-pruned Atlantic coast (Coppins & Coppins 2010). Huntley (1993) argued that early Holocene climate prior to c6250 BC encouraged the abundance of hazel through its greater tolerance to heightened seasonality (cf Davis *et al.* 2003), to seasonal drought and to cold winters and cool summers, than oak or elm (see also Tallantire 2002 and Finsinger *et al.* 2006).

What was it like to walk through this wood? Here we have no modern parallels. Hazel scrub on the west coast today forms dense, compact stands, shaded and dark in summer (Coppins & Coppins 2010), but this was probably not the habit it assumed in the early Holocene. Birch trees will commonly grow today to 25 m in height, hazel much less. Fyfe *et al.* (2013) estimated the openness of the woodland around Loch Davan to have been around 30% throughout the first half of the Holocene. If we assume that early Holocene birch–hazel woodland was uniform over long distances, and we have no evidence it was not, then this woodland was to a greater extent more open than woods became after c6000 BC (Whitehouse & Smith 2010). Birch is a single-stemmed tree while hazel coppices naturally, new stems replacing dying ones from a stool. This might not imply that naturally-growing trees will be multi-stemmed, but Coppins & Coppins (2010) argue that it does, with different-aged stems on one stool, which is pretty much self-perpetuating. The spacing of trunks is very hard to reconstruct because many variables affect this but perhaps trees were a few metres apart; Coppins & Coppins (2010, 46) report the creation of gaps (hazel 'rings') around stools up to 2.3 m. Sansum (2004, 248) recorded an average density of all trees of around 400 per ha in a wood, Glen Nant, Argyll, dominated by hazel and birch. It would probably have been easy to see a long way under the canopy. From the Warren Field data, under-storey shrubs were few. The ground cover would have been complete under undisturbed conditions, an acidic heath or grass-heath, easy to step over, but the amounts of dead wood, suggested from coleopteran reconstructions (Whitehouse 2006) or from possible modern analogues (Sansum 2004, 251) will have inhibited movement if not taken to use or burnt (Simmons 1996, 178–81). Burning as 'housekeeping', maintaining through fire a woodland floor relatively free of straggling undergrowth, is attested (Pyne 2013, 92).

The woodland was dynamic, disturbed at different temporal and spatial scales from individual trees dying, creating small gaps, to stand-scale impacts (Pickett & White 1985). There would have been short-lived edges because birch finds it hard to regenerate beneath its own canopy. Dying trees would have been replaced after a gap phase with fast-growing saplings. This phase of open canopy around individual trees may have persisted for more than decades, however, if browsing animals were drawn to saplings (Simmons 1996). Stand-scale disturbance might be from fires, drought, frost or storms (Peterken 1996; Tallantire 2002). Because Aberdeen is among the least windy regions of Scotland, gap-phase replacement may have been most common. Ecotones will have allowed shade-intolerant shrubs to establish, many of which are fruit- or berry-bearing, and spiky, like *Ilex* (holly), recovered from Mesolithic pit [2D-1018] at Milltimber.

The birch–hazel woodland was joined by elm and oak after c7500 BC. Oak and hazel were both resources used by people at Nethermills (Boyd & Kenworthy 1982). Whitehouse & Smith (2010) suggested that southern English woodlands became more closed in canopy after c6000 BC, though Fyfe *et al.* (2013) did not report this at Loch Davan. If the cessation or at least reduction of Mesolithic pit-digging at Milltimber is assumed to have been after c6700 BC, then this might, broadly, relate to denser valley-side woodland. Whether this vegetation change meant that the pits no longer served the function they once did is unclear.

Hazel nuts were abundant at Nethermills (Boyd & Kenworthy 1982) where the south-facing valley-edge ecotone might have promoted abundant growth of hazel trees (cf Holst 2010). Hazel nuts were common too at Milltimber, though there is no evidence for the extensive or repeated processing of hazel nuts that has been seen elsewhere in Scotland (eg Mithen *et al.* 2001, 225). It was clearly a significant resource. Seeds of goosegrass (*Galium aparine*) were recovered from a fill in pit [2D-1714], a rambling, clingy tall herb of stream-banks and the dryer parts of wetlands, and grasses, implying an open environment nearby. Both would have been very common away from the alluvial corridor. There is some evidence for the processing of hazel nuts at the Mesolithic site of Standingstones (Chapter 4), and the possible effects of people in enhancing hazel trees in the Mesolithic is discussed there.

No sources of economic information were recovered at Milltimber. A wide diversity of plant foods would have been utilised. These foods tend to leave very little evidence in the archaeological record (Bishop *et al.* 2013, 53). With this in mind the site was comprehensively sampled for charred remains with over 271 samples

taken, of which 152 were processed by flotation and wet sieving (Appendix 2.1). Sorting the remains was done with particular attention paid to fragments that could represent traces of starchy plant tissues (parenchyma) that on occasion survive in early archaeological assemblages (Holden *et al.* 1995) but nothing was recovered. Like the extremely sparse and fragmentary bone remains, it is important to note that this absence was not for want of looking. Clarke (1978, 20) recognised the very high primary and edible productivities of wetland systems. Inter-channel areas in the Narew River, as would the Dee, sustain abundant stands of common reed (*Phragmites australis*), floating sweet grass (*Glyceria fluitans*), reed mace and greater reed mace (*Typha angustifolia* and *T. latifolia*), water plantain (*Alisma plantago-aquatica*), yellow-cress (*Rorippa amphibia*) and mint (*Mentha* sp), and the slow-flowing channels support water lily (*Nuphar lutea*; Gradziński *et al.* 2003), all listed as of economic value to Mesolithic people by Clarke (1976) or Price (1986). Colonisation of the Dee valley floor by alder at c5750 BC will have reduced aquatic resources through shading, suppressing the abundance of the ground-flora, but biodiversity will have increased within riparian woodland because there are many more niches than in open ground, from short-lived dams formed by woody debris to overhanging vegetation falling in to supply invertebrates and leaf-litter to aquatic fauna. Woody debris will have included tree trunks, much slower to decompose than on dry ground. Driftwood may have formed this tangle (Boyd & Kenworthy 1982).

In the Narew River, Penczak (2009) identified an assemblage of fish associated with low shade, of which species thought to be native to Scotland include stone loach (*Barbatula barbatula*), and another on reaches with high shade, including pike (*Esox lucius*), perch (*Perca fluviatilis*) and roach (*Rutilus rutilus*). Salmon (*Salmo salar*) would have passed seasonally. Kenney (1993, 225) found that Mesolithic activity was invariably within 1 km of the River Dee, and that the concentration of Mesolithic lithic scatters east of Banchory might be related to the 19th-century observation that salmon fishing was profitable only east of the town. Kenney argued that 'the suitability [of the lower Dee] for catching salmon would seem to be an adequate explanation for the concentration of Mesolithic activity here' (1993, 230), conceivably sufficient to encourage sedentism (*ibid.*, 261).

Wildfowl (waders, swans, geese and ducks) should be added to the list of aquatic resources, both residential birds and seasonal migrants (Grigson 1986). Otter and beaver and other aquatic animals will have been common: some of the changes in wetland plant communities at Nethermills might have been beaver-induced (Coles 2001; Tipping 2010a, 61–62). The relative abundance of birch, willow and aquatic plants would also have attracted elk (*Alces alces*; Yalden 1999). Elk was a critical resource at camps focused on wetland resources, killed mainly from summer

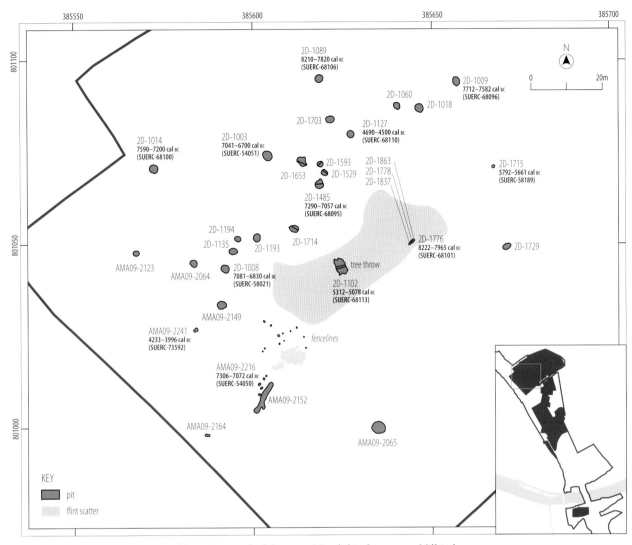

Illus 2.07 Detail of the main Mesolithic features at Milltimber

into winter for its meat, marrow, grease and antlers, which are best shaped in these months (Chaix 2009). The marshy valley-side locale has been suggested as the habitat of aurochs (Lynch *et al.* 2008), perhaps when faced with increasing maturation and closure of the dryland tree canopy (Noe-Nygaard *et al.* 2005).

2.6.2 Milltimber during the Mesolithic – 8200–4500 BC

Mesolithic human activity was primarily located at the northern end of the site along the base of the slope that forms the boundary between the Lochton Formation sands and gravels and the Camphill Terrace glaciofluvial gravels. The focus of this activity was the digging of 30 large deep pits and the production of tools, represented by a large flint scatter (Illus 2.06). The pits, distinguished by their substantial size and relative invisibility, were mainly clustered along the break of slope, but five outlying examples were seen further to the south on the Camphill Terrace itself. The flint scatter was concentrated in one area although could be divided into five zones of

activity related to tool preparation and production (see 2.14.2.3 below).

The pits were concentrated around the 16 m–17 m AOD contour, generally located immediately north of the lithic scatter (Illus 2.07; Table 2.02). Although broadly similar, they ranged in diameter between 1.4 m and 2.9 m and can be divided into two groups; those with steeper sides, which tend to be deeper (frequently over 2 m in depth), and those with moderately steep sides, slightly flatter bases and depths of under 1 m with the shallowest pits only 0.6 m deep. The process of discovery and excavation of these features involved a degree of 'weathering' of the feature before excavation commenced. Before this the edges were often near invisible and it is likely that some of the excavated edges are relatively poorly defined (see 7.3.4). This factor was also apparent at Blackdog where three similar pits were recorded (see 6.6.1).

The sequence of deposits within the pits was similar among all those excavated. A series of basal deposits comprised sands and silty sands, generally the result of wind-blown deposition or slumping of surrounding

Table 2.02 Summary of large Mesolithic pits

	Feature no	Length (m)	Width (m)	Depth (m)	Recut	Radiocarbon date
Larger, deeper pits	[2B-0113]	2.35	1.85	0.85		
	[2D-1194]	1.76	1.31	0.94	-	
	[2D-1018]	2.4	2.3	0.95	-	
	[2D-1060]	1.64	1.38	0.97	-	
	[2D-1593]	1.8	1.65	1.1	[2D-1595]	
	[2B-0015]	2.3	1.9	1.1		
	[2D-1008]	2.26	1.95	1.36	-	7080–6830 cal BC SUERC-58021
	[2D-1089]	2.26	2.2	1.45	[2D-1117]	8210–7820 cal BC SUERC-68106
	[2D-1127]	2	1.86	1.54	[2D-1092]	4690–4500 cal BC SUERC-68110
	[2D-1529]	2.08	1.6	1.56	[2D-1580]	
	[2C-0143]	1.8	1.8	1.8		7730–7590 cal BC SUERC-54050
	[2D-1135]	2.19	1.75	1.9	[2D-1173]	
	[2D-1193]	2.2	2.18	2.02	[2D-1632]	
Shallower, flatter pits	[2B-2513]	1.5	1.5	0.65		
	[2D-1703]	2.45	2	0.75	[2D-1706]	
	[2D-1014]	2.3	2.3	0.8	-	7590–7200 cal BC SUERC-68100
	[2D-1009]	2.55	2	0.86	-	7710–7580 cal BC SUERC-68096
	[2B-2481]	2.05	1.41	0.98		
	[2D-1003]	2.63	2.25	1	-	7040–6710 cal BC SUERC-54051
	[2D-1485]	2.4	1.7	1	-	7290–7060 cal BC SUERC-68095
	[2D-1729]	2.5	1.8	1.05	-	
	[2D-1714]	2.68	1.75	1.1	[2D-1941]	
	[2D-1653]	2.9	2.9	1.19	-	
	[AMA09-2028]	2.35	2.1	1.69		
	[AMA09-2004]	1.25	1.0	0.59		
	[AMA09-2046]	2.4	2	0.6		
	[AMA09-2064]	1.8	1.4	0.86	[AMA09-2077]	
	[AMA09-2065]	3.3	3.3	1.6	[AMA09-2230]	
	[AMA09-2123]	1.5	1.2	0.7		
	[AMA09-2149]	2.65	1.9	1.38	[AMA09-2268]	

material. Some pits then had patches of siltier deposits with inclusions of small fragments of probably wind-blown charcoal. This was sometimes found to occur alongside deposits that may represent stable phases of infilling or even soil formation. Over this were layers of gravelly silt. Finally, some pits had upper deposits of silt with frequent charcoal fleck inclusions. Some pits contained evidence to suggest they may have held a timber post. At least six of the pits feature insertions of secondary deposits into the centre of the original pit. In three cases traditional Carinated Bowl (CB) pottery dated to the Early Neolithic was recovered. Evidence for recutting was also proposed, representing reuse of the original pits.

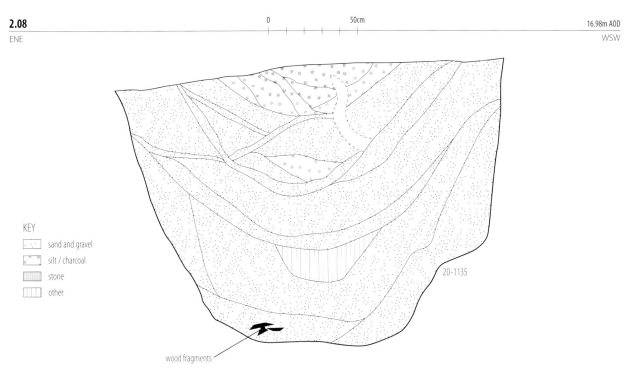

2.08   ENE   0   50cm   16.98m AOD   WSW

KEY
- sand and gravel
- silt / charcoal
- stone
- other

2D-1135

wood fragments

Illus 2.08 Section of Mesolithic pit [2D-1135]

2.6.2.1 Larger, deeper pits

The pits defined as 'deeper' were generally 1.1 m or more in depth and had either near-vertical or close to vertical sides. The bases tend to be narrow and curved. In general, they were filled with thick layered deposits of redeposited sands and gravels, overlain by layers of more silt-rich material, which occasionally contained fine-grained ash and charcoal. In many examples, there were several layers of the sequence of redeposited material and silt-rich material, with varying amounts of charcoal contained within. The smallness of the charcoal fragments, along with their abraded appearance, seemed to suggest they had washed or blown into the features, usually once they had been infilled at least a third of the way up with eroded sands and gravels.

Despite the narrow/vertical form of the pits, there was generally no evidence to suggest they had held posts. The exceptions to this were two pits lying around 8 m apart; [2D-1135] and [2D-1193]. One of the basal fills of pit [2D-1135] contained 'rare wood fragments' (Illus 2.08) and there is some evidence to suggest some sort of disturbance or removal above the basal fills. Deposit (2D-1178) (marked 'other' on the illustration) was a gravelly sand containing rare amounts of charcoal, which appeared to sit in a hollow or possible cut. This could suggest there had once been a post within the pit, although the evidence was far from conclusive. The upper deposits had been subject to burrowing and biological activity and were mixed.

Pit [2D-1193] (Illus 2.09) in comparison was one of the very few pits to have a silty deposit at the base, dark in colour and similar to soil, which may have washed in immediately after digging. Once filled to just under half of its excavated depth, the boundaries between deposits became much more vertical, potentially indicative of a post or vertical element having been removed. Immediately above these was a deposit containing large amounts of nutshell and some charcoal, in turn covered by a greyish loamy material possibly representing a stabilisation layer or soil formation. This pit is one of the few which has strong evidence for reuse, with a relatively clear recut present, the later fill containing layers of redeposited material along with a layer of charcoal-rich sandy loam. Hazel charcoal from this deposit was submitted for radiocarbon dating and returned a date range of 3960–3800 cal BC (SUERC-58023). This period of activity is discussed in more detail below (see 2.7.3.3).

Pit [2D-1127] also showed evidence of a recut, although the upper edges of this pit were very indistinct because of the slumping of natural gravels. A 'ledge' was also apparent around halfway up. A possible stabilisation layer, potentially where a turf line had started to form, was present over the basal deposits of this pit. A later recut contained three deposits, the upper one of which contained a small amount of charcoal and pottery fragments. Radiocarbon dating of hazel charcoal from the middle deposit returned a date range of 4690–4500 cal BC (SUERC-68110), towards the end of the Mesolithic. The secure context immediately above contained sherds of Early Neolithic Carinated Bowl ware.

Located slightly further up slope on the 19 m contour, above which the ground becomes rapidly steeper, pit

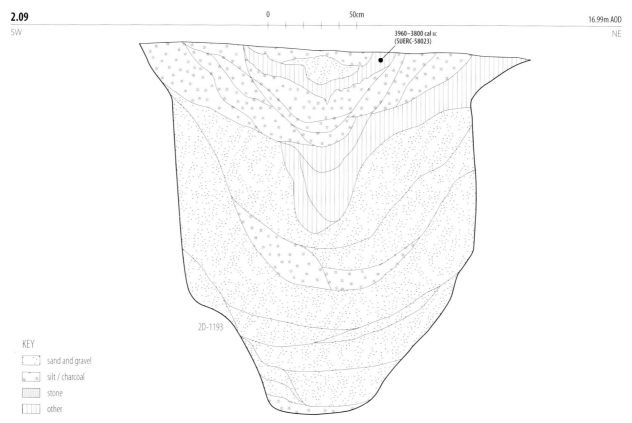

Illus 2.09 Section of Mesolithic pit [2D-1193]

[2D-1089] not only contained occasional silty layers, potentially representing periods of stabilisation close to the base, but also appeared to have a much higher sand content in the upper deposits. A central hollow at the top of the pit contained a deposit of charcoal-rich loamy sand that also contained angular and possibly heat-affected stones. Willow charcoal from this deposit returned a date range of 8210–7820 cal BC (SUERC-68106), the earliest date obtained from any of the large pits, and notably from a similar type and sequence of deposit as those that produced Early Neolithic dates elsewhere.

Pit [2D-1018] provides an example of a simpler sequence (Illus 2.10), with a basal fill of silty sand, layers of gravelly sand and then of charcoal across the pit, which appeared to have been washed in rather than dumped.

A number of large pits were recorded away from the main cluster. Pit [AMA9–2028] was located at the eastern extent of the excavated area (Illus 2.06). The upper fills were a complex sequence of alternate lighter and darker bands (Illus 2.11), predominantly undiagnostic of age except the final fill. This included a small lithic assemblage comprising mostly flint-knapping debitage, but also a later Mesolithic/Early Neolithic crested narrow blade. Three of these pieces had been affected by fire.

Three pits were found to the south, on the Camphill Terrace. Pit [2C-0143] was unusual in that it contained basal sand and gravel deposits (Illus 2.12) that included,

at well over 1 m depth, a large fragment of carbonised timber (willow) radiocarbon dated to 7730–7590 cal BC (SUERC-54050) and flints diagnostic of a Mesolithic narrow blade industry.

2.6.2.2 Shallower, flatter pits

The shallower, flatter-based pits ranged in diameter from 1.5 m to nearly 3 m and ranged in depth from 0.6 m to 1.2 m. Their sides were less steep, and they frequently had a broader flatter base. They tended to be found further up slope, although some examples were present much further to the south and east on the Camphill Terrace. Fills were predominantly layers of gravel and sand deposited by slumping.

The dates obtained from the shallower pits were broadly similar to those from the deeper ones. Charcoal from one of the upper layers of pit [2D-1014] returned a radiocarbon date range of 7590–7200 cal BC (SUERC-68100). A deposit of ash and then charcoal lay in the upper deposits of pit [2D-1003] (Illus 2.13) though there was no evidence of *in situ* burning. Holly charcoal from this layer was dated to 7040–6710 cal BC (SUERC-54051), providing further evidence of the Mesolithic date of the upper deposits in the majority of the pits.

At the base of pit [2D-1009] was an unusual deposit of loamy sand containing heavily abraded charcoal, hazel nutshell and a barley grain. Above this were redeposited

2.10

0   50cm   17.21m AOD

NW   SE

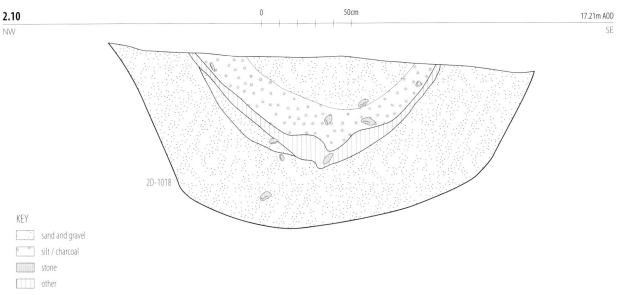

2D-1018

KEY

- sand and gravel
- silt / charcoal
- stone
- other

Illus 2.10 Section of Mesolithic pit [2D-1018]

Illus 2.11 View of pit [AMA09–2028] during excavation

natural sands and gravels, more extensive on the uphill side of the pit, and then extensive deposits of mottled loamy sand. A date range of 7710–7580 cal BC (SUERC-68096) was returned from hazel charcoal recovered from one of the basal fills. The inclusion of a barley grain is problematic given the early date of the feature, and it is probable this grain is intrusive.

Above the basal deposits in pit [2D-1714] (Illus 2.14) were two large stones in an upright position on the north-western side. Towards the centre, two charcoal and nutshell-rich deposits collected in a hollow that might have been created by removal of a post (marked 'other' in the illustration). The sequence of deposits above this follows a familiar pattern, with dished layers of loamy sand with occasional charcoal fleck inclusions. The upper deposit contained Carinated Bowl pottery, but the relationship between this deposit and those below is not clear.

Two further shallow pits provided potential evidence of having held a post. Above the slumped basal layers

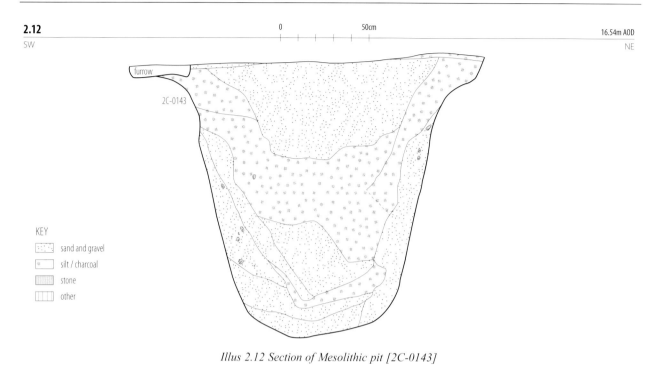

Illus 2.12 Section of Mesolithic pit [2C-0143]

2.13

KEY

sand and gravel

silt / charcoal

stone

other

Illus 2.13 Section of Mesolithic pit [2D-1003]

of pit [2D-1485] was a dark organic-rich loam, which could represent the remains of a decomposed post. Above this was redeposited geological material that probably slumped in from the surrounds once the post had been snapped/cut off and begun to rot. Hazel nutshell recovered from this pit returned a date range of 7290–7060 cal BC (SUERC-68095). Pit [AMA09–2123] included a dark grey central deposit that had been interpreted as the remains of a post-pipe although the diffuse interface of the deposits made this difficult to clarify.

Pit [AMA09–2064] had a sequence of at least four slightly mixed deposits with very diffuse interfaces (Illus 2.15) including a darker deposit characteristic of stabilisation processes. These had been truncated by a conical recut, filled with lighter and darker deposits with clear banding visible in the upper darker sands. The shape of the recut could be interpreted as being formed during the removal of a timber post. Upper layers contained frequent hazel nutshell fragments and flint debitage and tools. Among the debitage were ten rock crystal flakes, unique

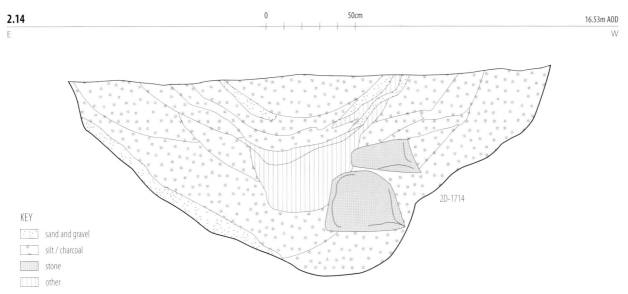

2.14 0 50cm 16.53m AOD
E W

KEY
sand and gravel
silt / charcoal
stone
other

Illus 2.14 Section of Mesolithic pit [2D-1714]

on this site and more widely in the Scottish Mesolithic. Further conical recuts may be present in pit [AMA09–2149] and [AMA09–2065].

Pit [AMA09–2004] did not fully conform to typical profiles (Illus 2.16): at 0.59 m it was not particularly deep, though fills were representative of what was recorded elsewhere with occasional stabilisation layers present over redeposited sands and gravels. Another smaller example was seen in pit [AMA09–2046], which included a poorly defined stepped cut on one side (Illus 2.17). As was noted above, the edges of all the large pits were very indistinct and therefore some were potentially under-excavated.

As with the steeper pits, a number of shallower pits were also identified scattered across the Camphill Terrace. Pits [2B-2481] and [2B-2513] lay on the terrace, some distance from any other features (Illus 2.06). Approximately 80% of the finds were recovered from pit [AMA09–2028], one of the large deep pits discussed above. The large number of pieces found here may represent evidence of a knapping floor or disposal of knapping debris (see 2.14.2 below).

2.6.2.3 Mesolithic lithic scatter, fencelines and other activity

A truncated and sporadic silty spread was present to the south of the main concentration of pits, covering an area c65m × 24 m (Illus 2.18). Within the spread, 10,057 pieces of (mostly) flint were recovered from a site total of 11,565 pieces. Analysis showed that the majority dated to the Mesolithic, with a small but notable sub-assemblage of Late Upper Palaeolithic material (detailed below, 2.14.2.4). Early and Middle Neolithic material was also present.

The lithics spread was excavated using a 1 m grid (Illus 2.19; see 1.6.1 for methodology). By analysing the grids, it was possible to divide the scatter into five discrete 'zones' of activity (Zones 1–5), with four further zones defined from the CJV phase of works (north, east, south and west; Illus 2.18) that represent the four areas adjacent to each side of the main flint scatter, where flint was recovered from various pits and post-holes. Lithic pieces were also recovered from features cut into both the soil spread itself and the geological substrate below. These features are discussed below, as are the specifics of the results of the zoned analysis which are presented in detail below (see 2.14).

A dogleg arrangement of post-holes was recorded, effectively separating Zone 1 from Zone 2 (see Illus 2.07). The majority of the post-holes were between 0.25 m and 0.4 m in diameter and under 0.15 m deep. All but two had single fills and none showed any evidence of post-pipes surviving. The alignments formed likely two fencelines, either sheltering an area of activity, or separating one area from another. A small number of lithics derived from the fills of five of these pits. Dating of the fencelines was provided by hazel charcoal taken from post-holes [2D-1273] and [2D-1225], which gave a combined date of 4940–4550 cal BC (SUERC-68115 and SUERC-68116) and place the features in the Late Mesolithic.

The area west of the flint scatter (Illus 2.07) included a series of five small pits and an unusual shaped linear cut [AMA09–2152] immediately west of Zone 1. The cluster of five small circular pits ranged in size from 0.4 m to 0.7 m diameter, each no more than 0.15 m deep. They all contained a single homogeneous sandy fill along with a variety of lithic pieces. Pit [AMA09–2179] yielded a relatively large short end-scraper (CAT11779; Illus 2.85) and a worn serrated blade (CAT11780; Illus 2.85). Both are forms that would better fit a Neolithic rather than a Mesolithic date. Two of the other pits in this cluster – [AMA09–2216] and [AMA09–2218] – contained, among other things, a microburin (CAT11781; Illus 2.85) and a

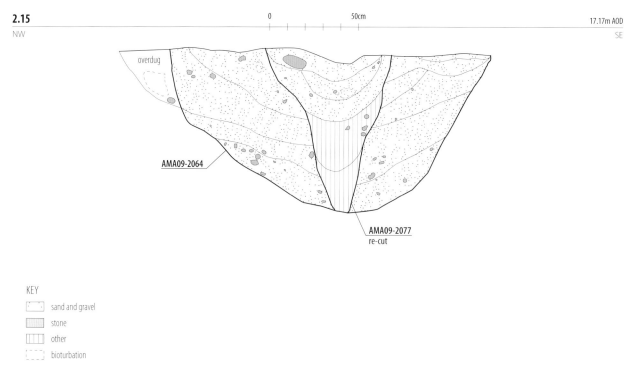

KEY

	sand and gravel
	stone
	other
	bioturbation

Illus 2.15 Section of Mesolithic pit [AMA09–2064] showing the recut. Photo shows the upper part of the pit during excavation

Levallois-like flake (CAT11713), datable to the Mesolithic and the later Neolithic respectively. Pit [AMA09–2218] contained a crested Mesolithic narrow blade and crescent (CAT11782; Illus 2.85, CAT11783), as well as a jasper flake and blade. These could point to non-functional deposition given their uniqueness on the site, though within abundant functional material. Hazel charcoal from pit [AMA09–2216] dated to 7310–7070 cal BC

(SUERC-73594). Despite the presence of some Neolithic material in this cluster of features, they are all thought to be Mesolithic in date, and relate to the shallow linear cut [AMA09–2152] immediately south of the five pits. The linear feature was very shallow and poorly defined in plan and its function is unclear.

Pit [AMA09–2164] lay to the south-west of the cluster and, although not radiocarbon dated, contained 44 lithic

Illus 2.16 Section through Mesolithic pit [AMA09–2004]   *Illus 2.17 Section through Mesolithic pit [AMA09–2046]*

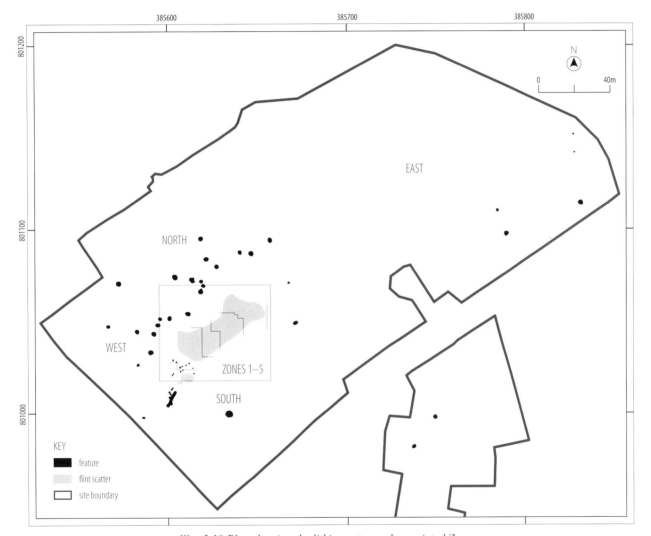

Illus 2.18 Plan showing the lithic scatter and associated Zones

artefacts including a fragment of a microlith or backed bladelet (CAT11777) likely to be Mesolithic or Early Neolithic. At least 11 of the flint pieces (a quarter of the total) were heat affected. All the charcoal from this pit was oak, potentially from large branches or a trunk. It also produced a small quantity of hazel nutshell.

Hazel nutshell from the fill of pit [AMA09–2241] returned a radiocarbon date range of 4230–4000 cal BC (SUERC-73592), providing evidence of a transitional

Mesolithic/Neolithic period of activity. The upper two fills included frequent charcoal and hazel nutshell plus a small lithic assemblage of knapping debitage.

Four inter-cutting pits (see Illus 2.07) were identified in Zone 5, towards the south-eastern limits of the lithics scatter. They all contained charcoal-rich silty sand with a small quantity of burnt bone and nutshell, although no evidence of *in situ* burning was recorded. Nearly 200 lithic pieces were recovered from these pits, although they are

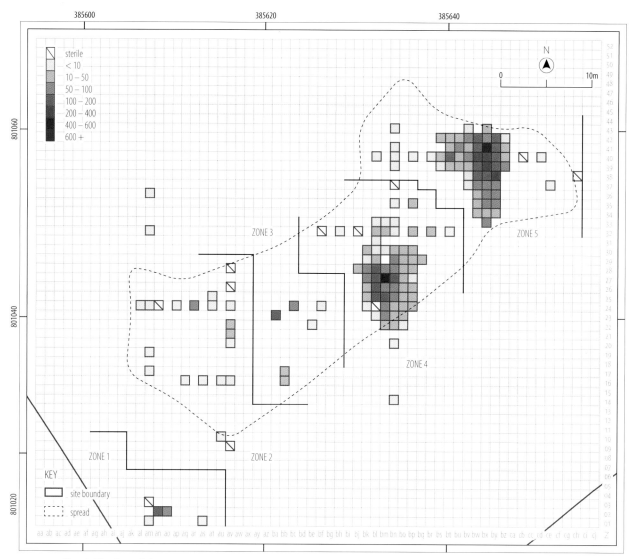

Illus 2.19 Plan of the gridded excavation of the lithic scatter, showing Zones identified during lithics analysis

likely to be residual given that the assemblage primarily comprises chips and flakes. The pits also contained a small number of microliths with scalene triangles and two crescents. This mixing of microlith types not usually found together seems to confirm the residual nature of this assemblage. Hazel charcoal from the fill of pit [2D-1776] returned a date range of 8220–7970 cal BC (SUERC-68101); the earliest dated feature on site. It was unclear what these pits represented as the spatial arrangement was not indicative of a structure.

More broadly, the features east of the flint scatter are limited in number and in general fairly isolated from each other (see Illus 2.07). An isolated hearth feature [2D-1715] was dated to 5790–5660 cal BC (SUERC-58189) from hazel charcoal recovered from the fill, although the lithic assemblage from this pit was undiagnostic regarding chronology.

In summary, the Mesolithic at Milltimber is represented by three strands of evidence; the large pits, which mostly date to the period between 8000–7000 BC, the lithics

scatter, which dates to any time between c8500 and 4100 BC, and a handful of pits, hearths and fencelines that likely both pre- and post-date the scatter. All of this suggests repeated visits to the site, which is further supported by the artefactual evidence (see 2.14 below).

2.6.3 Optically stimulated luminescence (OSL) dating of the earliest sediments of the Maryculter Terrace

Richard Tipping and Tim Kinnaird

Following incision from the Camphill Terrace, the Dee then began to deposit sand and sometimes sandy silt across the eroded part of the valley floor. These accumulated vertically to form the Maryculter Terrace (Illus 2.03 & 2.04). These largely uniform sediments are characteristic of lowland river systems (Lewin & Macklin 2003; Lewin *et al.* 2005) and called overbank sediments (deposited by floodwater). Overbank sediments are most commonly thought to be derived from rivers that flowed as single channels and

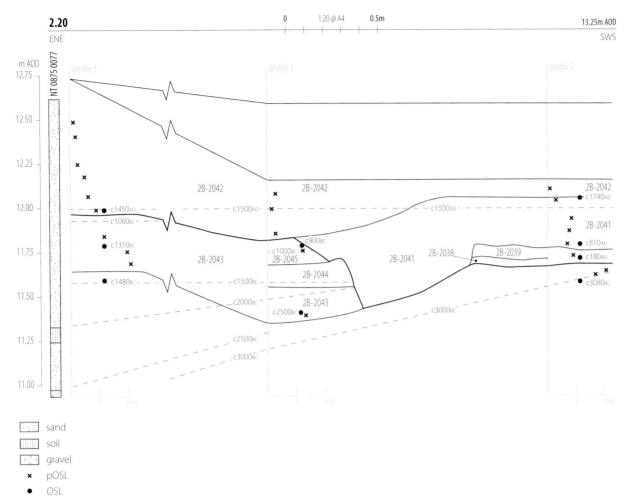

Illus 2.20 The sediment stratigraphy of the fluvial sediments and anthropogenic material in and around oven D06, and of the sediment stratigraphy at NJ 8575 0077 plotted against altitude (m AOD), with the relative position of OSL Profile 1 to 3

not the several anastomosing threads that might have characterised the Mesolithic Camphill Terrace (Brown 1995). They may also represent a substantial increase of fine-grained sediment carried by the river.

Age estimates from OSL analyses for the formation of the Maryculter Terrace (Appendix 2.1.18) focused on three closely spaced vertical sediment stratigraphies (profiles) around one of the ovens cut into the north bank of a palaeochannel (oven D06, see 2.10.2 below; Illus 2.45). A Google Earth image (1/1/2001) shows the palaeochannel as a dark scar appearing to depart from the present northern bank of the Dee close to NJ 853 006, now around 4–5 m higher than the present Dee. The channel at its western end lies between bedrock surfaces where the surface is around 16 m AOD. As the palaeochannel approaches the western site boundary, it lies between fragments of the Camphill Terrace, making it either contemporary with or later than the Camphill Terrace in origin. Nothing is known of the sediment filling the channel at this point. The surface of the channel then falls eastward to around 13 m AOD in the excavated area, where it grades to the Maryculter Terrace. For the channel to grade in this way, it may have remained an active channel for a long time; sediment accumulating

in the channel near its lowest point is of later Neolithic age (below). Excavation exposed the full c20m width of the channel in places, much less than the 60–70 m width of the present river channel. The ground surface at the time of recording is likely to have been around 12.5 m AOD.

The sediment stratigraphy and contexts were recorded during excavation of oven DO6 (Illus 2.20). Samples for pOSL and OSL on Profiles 1 and 2 were obtained from this standing archaeological section. Although records of the oven indicate a sharp edge between the fill of the palaeochannel and the fill of the Maryculter Terrace, the youngest unit (2B-2042) is laterally continuous between the channel and the terrace.

Profile 2 is located at the head of oven DO6, 0.56 m deep below a ground surface at 12.18 m AOD at the time of excavation. The poorly seen substrate beneath the basal oven deposit (2B-2037), below c11.65 m AOD, is a coarse gritty sand. The basal anthropogenic deposit (2B-2037) is a thin layer of heat-affected reddish-brown silty sand spread across the neck and head of the oven. Above this and spread over the whole of the head is a 6 cm-thick layer of charcoal-rich black loamy sand (2B-2038), and a further layer of heat-affected orange sandy silt (2B-2039) spread over the head of the oven and into the neck. Overlying the oven deposits in Profile 2 is unit (2B-2041), a mid-brown clay-rich silt loam extending to the south-west. This represents infilling of the oven with fluvial sediment, probably after it had gone out of use. This is overlain by unit (2B-2042), a light brown clay-rich silt representing a later phase of flooding. Not drawn on Illus 2.20 is c0.45 m of mid-brownish-grey sandy silt (2A-0001), which was stripped before excavation. The original ground surface across the section, not shown here, would have been around 12.6 m AOD.

Profiles 1 and 3 are considered together because several sediment units are shared and are laterally continuous. Profile 1 is c2m south-west of oven DO6, 0.85 m deep below the ground surface at the time of recording at 12.17 m AOD. Profile 3 is tens of metres south-east of oven DO6, within a baulk left *in situ* across the palaeochannel deposits. The profile was not surveyed to OD: it is likely that at the time of recording it was around 12.75 m AOD. Profile 3 is a little over 1.12 m deep. The basal sediment in both profiles is gritty sand, called the substrate. Above this is a dark brown, humic, structureless sandy clay-rich silt (2B-2043). The overlying units in Profile 1 (2B-2044) to (2B-2045) were not traced to Profile 3. Unit (2B-2043) is a 0.135 m thick orange-brown silty clay: unit (2B-2044) is very similar and the boundary between these units is very diffuse. Unit (2B-2045) overlies (2B-2044) in Profile 1 with a sharp boundary, a dark brown clay-rich silt loam c0.11 m thick. This is overlain in Profile 1 by 0.27 m of unit (2B-2042), seen in Profile 2 and in Profile 3 where it is 0.40 m thick.

The three profiles displayed interpretable luminescence behaviours and are therefore amenable to OSL dating. More detailed luminescence characterisation was accordingly obtained using calibrated screening measurements. Nine samples were prepared for OSL dating, comprising both fluvial sediment and anthropogenic materials associated with Profiles 1, 2 and 3. Methods and data are presented in Appendix 2.1.18. The positions of these samples are shown in Illus 2.20. As a test of the OSL chronology, assay SUTL-2733, the age range materials within oven DO6 (AD 180 ± 90) can be seen to agree very well with a calibrated radiocarbon date on charcoal of *Alnus glutinosa* from this oven, of cal AD 20–210 (SUERC-58504). What follows in this section is a consideration of the ages and rates of accumulation of sediments older than oven DO6.

The substrate of gritty sand at 11.63 m AOD in Profile 2 is dated to 3080 ± 380 BC (SUTL-2731). Fluvial sediment above this is truncated by the oven (2B-2037; Illus 2.20). Sediment at Profile 1 in the basal part of unit (2B-2043) is dated to 2500 ± 500 BC (SUTL-2728). Sediment at the top of the substrate (an assumed 11.63 m AOD) in Profile 3 has an age of 1480 ± 460 BC (SUTL-2736), while unit (2B-2043) is dated to 1310 ± 360 BC (SUTL-2735), showing that there is no hiatus or unconformity between the substrate and unit (2B-2043). Rates of sediment accumulation at Profile 3 between these assays were around 16yrs/cm. At Profile 2, sediment accumulation was lower at around 41yrs/cm. The isochrones in the model of sediment accumulation

show that Profile 3 was probably within the palaeochannel at c2500 BC. The effect of these differences in sediment accumulation rate was probably to allow the deeper parts of the palaeochannel to fill with sediment faster, so that by and after c1500 BC, all parts of the sediment system lay at roughly the same altitude. Reworked sediment with only partially re-zeroed luminescence characteristics, suggestive of large floods depositing eroding sand at too high a rate to be fully bleached, are identified once in Profiles 1 and 3 in later prehistory, both dating to between 1500 and 1000 BC. Sediment units (2B-2044) and (2B-2045) in Profile 1 are part of this aggrading sequence.

Taken together, the archaeological evidence for human occupation of the Camphill Terrace from, perhaps, the Early Neolithic, and probably by the Middle Neolithic is in good agreement with a date prior to 3460–2700 BC on fluvial sediment near the base of the Maryculter Terrace in this section. It is very probable that the later Chalcolithic clusters of post-holes and associated features on the Camphill Terrace were constructed when it was unaffected by floods because the River Dee had incised to a level some six metres below this surface (see 2.8.1 below). It is possible at a local scale that down-cutting caused, through the drying of formerly waterlogged soils, the rapid though undated change at Nethermills from willow-alder woodland to birch woodland (Ewan 1981).

Abandonment of the Camphill Terrace by down-cutting is the largest Holocene fluvial change on the lower Dee. During abandonment through incision of the Camphill Terrace, the River Dee cut into and truncated glaciofluvial gravel to around 10–11 m AOD. To a large degree the channel is locked in place, confined during incision at points where it touches the valley sides (Lewin & Brindle 1977). A change in the river system of this magnitude, in the Neolithic, when the palynological evidence for woodland clearance suggests only small and local impacts, will have been driven by a large-scale phenomenon such as climate change (Macklin & Lewin 2003; Macklin *et al.* 2005; Jones *et al.* 2010). The period c4400–3800 BC represents one such period of climatic deterioration in north-west Europe (Tipping 2010b). A possible second, but less likely, period is centred on c3200 BC (Roland *et al.* 2015). Nevertheless, after incision, OSL dating suggests that initial fluvial sedimentation on the Maryculter Terrace was slow and intermittent, with fine-grained sediment supply limited, possibly reflecting a largely natural woodland cover upstream into later prehistory, considered further in Chapter 3.

2.7 Settlement activity at Milltimber in the Neolithic

2.7.1 Earliest Neolithic woodland clearance along the alluvial corridor

Richard Tipping

Murray *et al.* (2009) have recently suggested that the alluvial corridor of the Dee drew people along it from the coast in the earliest Neolithic, possibly migrants from across the North Sea (see also Sheridan 2010; Murray & Murray 2014). The pairing of earliest Neolithic timber halls at Balbridie (Fairweather & Ralston 1993) and Warren Field, Crathes (Murray *et al.* 2009), on the south and north side of the valley respectively, generates ideas about control of and ease of passage along this route; these halls are some way inland. One advantage both have over coastal locations is that in our present climate, they experience a mean maximum temperature some 2°C warmer than the coast, with concomitant increases in the growing season of crops.

Bayesian analyses of the radiocarbon assays at Warren Field (Marshall 2009) suggest that the use of the hall here was for a very short time, something in the range of 1–90 years. Similarly detailed analyses are awaited from Balbridie. Marshall & Cook (2014) argued that the smaller house at Garthdee Road was occupied for longer, perhaps a century or so, between 3850–3700 cal BC and 3765–3610 cal BC. The available evidence suggests that these structures appear in the archaeological record over a fairly short timeframe, between c3900 BC and 3700 BC (ScARF 2012b).

Though travel by water is probably implied by this connectivity, land still had to be cleared for farming. Ideas that Neolithic cereal cultivation could be undertaken with limited removal of the tree canopy (Goransson 1982; 1986: see Edwards 1993) have been replaced with interpretations that suggest sedentism and a commitment to maintain fields in areas cleared of trees (Bogaard & Jones 2007; McClatchie *et al.* 2014). Our understanding of the scale of earliest Neolithic woodland clearance along the lower Dee is very limited. Ewan's (1981) pollen analyses at Nethermills may cease before the Neolithic period. Those at Loch of Park, 5 km east of Crathes, reflect plant communities growing on till soils, and best describe the landscape considered in Chapter 3, but around the Loch of Park, birch, oak, perhaps a little elm, alder and hazel grew barely disturbed by woodland loss (Vasari & Vasari 1968): the pollen diagram ceases soon after c4000 BC. On the Lochton Formation gravel at Warren Field, Crathes around 3800 BC, only hazel survived of the mid-Holocene woodland cover around the timber hall (Lancaster 2009, 47). The pollen source area at Warren Field will have been very small. Tipping *et al.* (2009) tried to model the size of the pollen source area and suggested that the nearest hazel trees may have been up to 2.5 km around the hall. Nevertheless, the spatial impact of this clearance was argued to have been very limited, such that a woodland clearance of this extent would not have registered in pollen records from more conventional peat bogs or lochs (see also Edwards and Ralston 1984, 29).

2.7.2 Fluvial change and Early Neolithic arable agriculture along the lower River Dee

There is a strong association between earliest Neolithic timber halls and free-draining soils on glaciofluvial gravel river terrace surfaces (Brophy 2007). A similar association can be suggested for smaller, probably domestic, sites (Brophy 2016). The availability of and access to good-quality soils were fundamental to the first farmers. The Warren Field hall (Murray *et al.* 2009) is 17 m above the present Dee, at around 55 m AOD, on a still extensive surface of Lochton Formation gravel. Pollen analyses show that crop-growing was one activity immediately around the hall (Davies *et al.* 2009; Tipping *et al.* 2009), with plant macrofossil evidence of bread/club wheat and naked barley. Arable agriculture here was practiced on soil formed from Lochton Formation sand and gravel, which had been leached of nutrients for the best part of 6000 years. The Wardend of Durris site (Russell-White 1995), though a long distance from and a considerable altitude above the Dee, is nevertheless situated on a terrace of Lochton Formation gravel lining the Burn of Sheeoch. The as yet undated lithic scatter at Park Quarry, Drumoak, and the isolated Neolithic-age pit at Park Quarry, Durris (Noble *et al.* 2016a), above the Dee are both on mounded Lochton Formation gravel (Brown 1993). The later Neolithic structure reported by Noble *et al.* (2012) at Green Bogs, Monymusk, is on undifferentiated glaciofluvial gravel.

These old gravel terraces may have been foci for nascent agriculture. However, the creation through river incision of extensive, newly drained, fresh and comparatively nutrient-rich soil on the Camphill Terrace by the Early Neolithic may have been particularly attractive to Early Neolithic colonists. The hall at Balbridie (Fairweather & Ralston 1993) lay very close to narrow but laterally extensive surfaces of Camphill Terrace gravel. In the 1790s, the minister for Durris parish noted Balbridie as one of the few places in his parish with deep soil (Withrington & Grant 1982). The Neolithic structures at Durris Bridge (Brophy 2016) are on Camphill Terrace gravels, as is the series of Early Neolithic pits interpreted as a house at Garthdee Road, Aberdeen (Timpany 2014a). The pollen record for cereal cultivation at Warren Field implies local cultivation, though it is not known whether the ground cleared for crops around the hall (Davies *et al.* 2009; Tipping *et al.* 2009) had a duration beyond the burning down of the hall, or whether the farmland that existed around Balbridie was abandoned with the hall.

The Neolithic–Chalcolithic charred plant assemblages at Milltimber were characterised by hazel and oak with low occurrences of gorse/broom. Cereal grain was recovered from a range of features including hearths and pits. Naked barley was present in hearth [2D-1137] and pits [AMA09–2080] and [AMA09–2058]. Barley has been recorded from other Neolithic sites in Scotland (Greig 1991, 300) and was an important crop (McLaren 2000, 91), with emmer (Fairweather & Ralston 1993; Murray *et al.* 2009; Murray & Murray 2014). Occasional 'weed' seeds, primarily from Neolithic deposits, included cleavers (*Galium aparine*), corn spurrey (*Spergula arvensis*), chickweed (*Stellaria media*), fat hen sp (*Chenopodium* sp) and knotgrass (*Polygonum aviculare*), species characteristic of open ground and nitrogen-rich soils typical of agricultural fields or human settlement of any permanence.

2.7.3 Early Neolithic settlement activity at Milltimber – 4200–3700 BC

Early Neolithic human activity at Milltimber is represented by the partial remains of a structure at the north-east of the site, three alignments of post-holes towards the north valley-side slope, a number of hearths/hearth-like deposits occupying the lower slopes below the post-hole alignments and a number of more isolated pits (Illus 2.21). A large curvilinear ditch recorded on the Camphill Terrace had the potential to represent further Early Neolithic activity although the dating of this feature was problematic; it is presented in detail below (see 2.9). A pottery assemblage amounting to 30 vessels (65% of the site total) was recovered from a number of these features. Scientific dating along with diagnostic pottery and lithic assemblages provided a consistent date range across the features, placing the activity in the first three hundred years of the fourth millennium BC.

2.7.3.1 The structure

The remains of a structure were positioned in a small hollow towards the eastern end of the foot of the northern valley edge. A shallow cut [2D-1917] defined the western and southern edges, with post-holes presumably forming the wall-line (Illus 2.22). Material was banked up around the location of the roof supports. The presumed dimensions were around 4.5 m wide and at least 5 m long, although the northern limit of the structure was poorly defined. To the east, a metalled surface (2D-1950) may represent the entrance, which was also cut through by further post-holes. Within the structure a series of patches of compacted gravel surfaces were found, the best surviving of which was (2D-1824). Holly charcoal from this was dated to 3950–3710 cal BC (SUERC-68114). Towards the northern end of the structure was presumably the main hearth [2D-1638]. Hazel charcoal from this was submitted for radiocarbon dating and returned a date range of 3960–3800 cal BC (SUERC-58194).

Immediately to the south of the structure was a spread of silty sand (2D-1916) roughly 10 m by 5 m in plan, thought to represent the remnants of an old ground surface. A pit lay to the west of the surviving surface and may have acted as an external hearth, containing considerable amounts of charcoal and having a burnt basal fill. A leaf-shaped flint arrowhead was recovered from the charcoal-rich material and an overlying deposit contained sherds of Carinated Bowl pottery, both of which would be consistent with the date range for the structure of 3960–3710 cal BC.

2.7.3.2 Post alignments

Around 75 m to the south-west of the structure lay three lines of post-holes, very roughly parallel and aligned north-west/south-east (Illus 2.23). The westernmost line

was formed of three post-holes in close proximity and a fourth continuing the line 5 m further to the south-east. They were between 0.3 m and 0.4 m in diameter and contained single homogenised deposits. The fill of the northernmost example [2D-1267] contained holly charcoal that was dated to 3950–3720 cal BC (SUERC-68104).

The middle and eastern lines were constructed of more substantial post-holes. In the middle line [2D-1436], [2D-1433] and [2D-1670] all had vertical sides and slightly curved bases. At the northern end of the line [2D-1673] was much smaller. It seems likely that pits [2D-1371], [2D-1675] and [2D-1693] are all associated with this line. Post-hole [2D-1433] was the only feature to show indication of a post-pipe, and nutshell from that deposit was dated to 3960–3800 cal BC (SUERC-58188). This deposit also contained Carinated Bowl pottery (02-V30; see 2.14.1 below).

The eastern alignment comprised five post-holes in a line, with a small stake-hole between the two northernmost examples. Pits [2D-1629], [2D-1495] and [2D-1518] are also thought to relate to the alignment. Hazel charcoal from pit [2D-1495] was dated to 3940–3710 cal BC (SUERC-58193), confirming at least some of the pits surrounding the alignment as contemporary.

2.7.3.3 Hearths and hearth-deposits

Across the site, eleven features were identified either as *in situ* hearths dating to the Early Neolithic period or that contained quantities of artefactual material corresponding to this period. Hazel charcoal from hearth [2D-1258] was dated to 3960–3800 cal BC (SUERC-68112). Pit [2D-1399], a short distance down the slope, was a wide shallow hollow that contained silty sand layers below a layer of charcoal-rich material showing evidence of *in situ* burning. Sherds of Carinated Bowl pottery (02-V31) were recovered from this layer. The deposits above this were consistent with an abandoned feature gradually silting up.

The most complex of the hearth features was pit [2D-1895]. It was roughly oval in plan, with a deeper 'bowl' to the north-western end of the pit, the remainder forming a hollow 0.65 m deep. The feature had basal layers of gravelly sand, overlain by a series of mixed layers containing charcoal that were mostly contained within the 'bowl' end of the feature but had spread across shallower parts. Radiocarbon dating of willow charcoal from this returned a date range of 3970–3800 cal BC (SUERC-58617). Above this was a light grey ashy deposit that contained large parts of a Carinated Bowl (02-V40; see 2.14.1 below), which may have been deposited intact. The deposition of a complete pot may point to non-domestic activities taking place here.

In general, these features were characterised by layers of charcoal-rich silty material, either the result of *in situ* burning, or dumped/infilled material from burning nearby. This kind of deposit was also encountered in the upper

Illus 2.21 Plan of the Neolithic features at Milltimber

parts of three of the large pits dated to the Mesolithic. The recutting or reuse of these pits was thought to have occurred in the Early Neolithic, identified by either radiocarbon dating or by the presence of artefacts of Neolithic date. Pits [2D-1193], [2D-1714], [2D-1127] contained this material.

In pit [2D-1193], 0.2 m from the top of the pit, a thin but distinct layer of charcoal was recorded, which

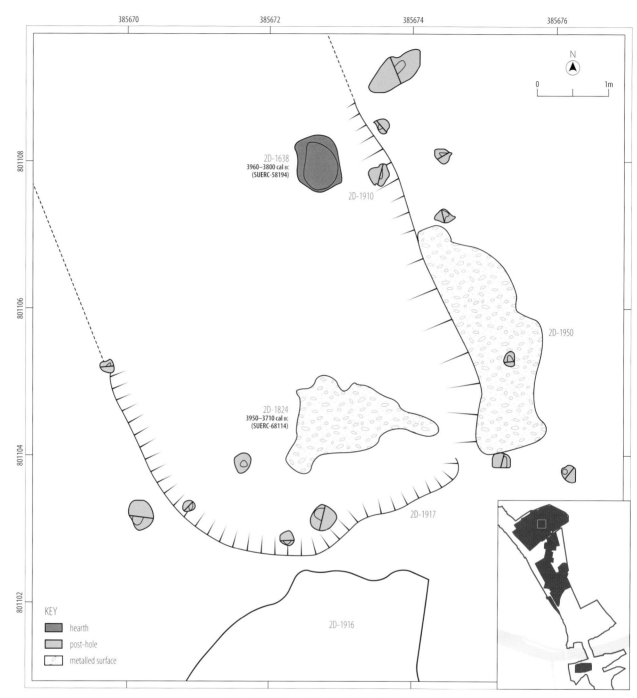

Illus 2.22 Plan of the Neolithic Structure

was dated to 3960–3800 cal BC (SUERC-58023). This pit is one of those where there was reasonably strong evidence for a post having been present at some stage. Pit [2D-1714] also had evidence of a post being present (see Illus 2.14). Here, the uppermost deposit of the pit not only contained Early Neolithic pottery but holly charcoal from the same deposit was dated to 3940–3710 cal BC (SUERC-68105). The recut in pit [2D-1127] contained a lower deposit that was dated to the mid-fifth millennium BC, but the uppermost deposit contained pottery of Early Neolithic date.

Further dated features assigned to this phase of activity include hearth [2D-1879] and pit [2D-1400]. The hearth contained hazel charcoal dating to 3940–3710 cal BC (SUERC-68102). Pit [2D-1400] was heavily truncated but probably originally formed a figure-of-eight shape and appeared to be a short-lived hearth. Hazel charcoal from the main bowl was dated to 3940–3710 cal BC (SUERC-68120). Hearths [2D-1755] and [2D-1076] have also been included in this group due to their proximity to the post alignments described above, although were not radiocarbon dated. Pit [AMA09–2222] lay close

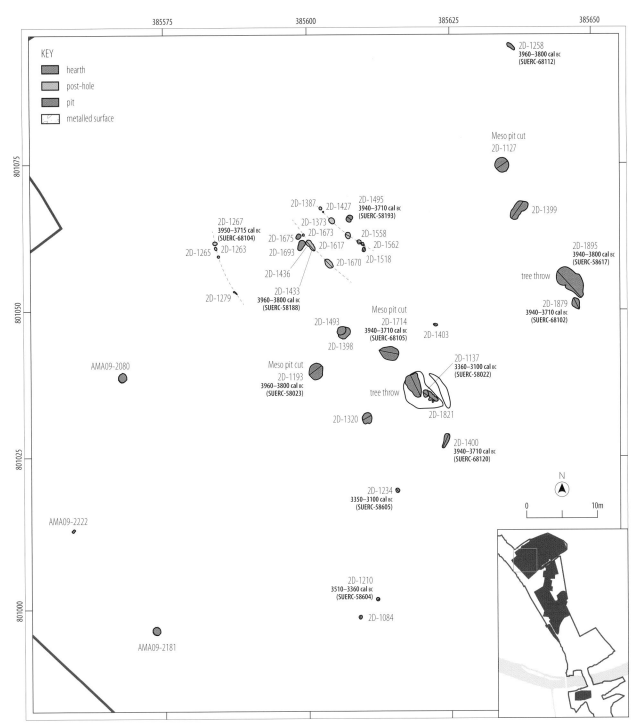

Illus 2.23 Detail of Neolithic features at Milltimber

to the western limit of excavation and contained lithic knapping debitage, half of which was heat-affected. It also contained a bipolar core representative of post-Mesolithic activity, pointing to a Neolithic date. The environmental evidence comprised a small quantity of hazel nutshell.

A complex pit recorded as two inter-cutting features [2D-1398] and [2D-1493] was undated but contained a crested flake (CAT10156), probably an informal sickle used to cut vegetable matter. It may indicate a further example

of deliberate deposition based on the fact that it contained only this solitary and heavily used tool.

The concentration of activity in the Early Neolithic was concentrated around the northern part of the site. However, two pits were recorded nearly 350 m to the south (Illus 2.21), on the Maryculter Terrace. The pits were both small (around 1 m in diameter) and had fills of dark greyish sandy silts. The larger of the two [2B-2550] contained sherds of Carinated Bowl North East style (CBNE; 02-V01), which was broadly in use in the Early Neolithic.

2.7.4 Middle and Late Neolithic activity at Milltimber – 3500–3100 BC

The northern part of the site also included a spread of later Neolithic features, although these formed a more disparate group. A cluster of three small pits (Illus 2.21) at the base of the slope represented one aspect of this limited activity. Pit [AMA09–2058] contained 75 sherds of pottery from two Impressed Ware vessels (02-V43 and 02-V45, Illus 2.24), a pottery type synonymous with this period (see 2.14.1 below). Owing to the near completeness of one of the pots it is suggested that this represents deliberate, possibly ritualised, deposition. The pit also included a modest quantity of charred barley and oat. The other two pits [AMA09–2054] and [AMA09–2056] proved undiagnostic although their similarity and alignment suggests they were contemporary.

Further prehistoric pottery sherds (02-V44), along with lithic debitage, burnt bone, charred hazel nutshell and cereal grain were recovered from pit [AMA09–2080] (Illus 2.23). The cereal grain comprised charred barley and emmer wheat and charcoal from this pit predominantly derived from oak, with lesser quantities of alder and elm present. This mix of material may suggest some form of midden material.

Three further features dated to this period were similar to the Early Neolithic hearths. Possible hearth [2D-1210] (Illus 2.23) appeared to represent short-lived activity and, along with charcoal, also contained lithics and pottery. Hazel charcoal from the hearth was dated to 3510–3360 cal BC (SUERC-58604). A few metres to the south-west an undated pit [2D-1084] included a bipolar core of Middle Neolithic date, suggesting it may be contemporary with the hearth. Another hearth [2D-1234] to the north-east was of similar proportions to [2D-1210] and was dated from hazel charcoal to 3350–3090 cal BC (SUERC-58605).

A further hearth complex was in many ways similar to [2D-1895], comprising at least three and potentially four individual hearths. These had been cut into or utilised the hollow created by a fallen tree (labelled as [2D-1821] on Illus 2.23). Hearths [2D-1152], [2D-1137], [2D-1823] and [2D-1822] were all cut into the western half of the tree throw, along with a number of potentially associated

features such as pit [2D-1086] that included a quantity of coarseware sherds, and several possible post-holes or stake-holes. Hearth [2D-1137] was the best preserved and may be the latest in the sequence. Sherds of coarseware pottery were recovered from the burnt deposits, along with charred naked barley. Hazel charcoal from the hearth was dated to 3360–3100 cal BC (SUERC-58022).

Hearth [AMA09–2181] measured 1.15 m diameter with steep sides 0.2 m deep and a flat base included a charcoal-rich loam basal fill over which was a thin layer of dark grey brown loam; the upper deposit contained frequent fire-cracked stones (Illus 2.25) and was typical of all the hearth deposits described above. No diagnostic material was recovered from the pit; its similarity to pit [AMA09–2080] and its location, close to the main Mesolithic and Neolithic activity, are the signifier of a likely prehistoric date. An edge-retouched broadblade (CAT10278; Illus 2.64) was recovered from pit [2D-1320] (Illus 2.23) that potentially dated to the Middle Neolithic. No other dating material was recovered from the feature, but it is assigned to this phase.

Sherds of Neolithic pottery and a moderate assemblage of Neolithic lithic industries were also recorded within the material that made up the large flint scatter. Notable quantities of pottery were also recovered over the area to the south-east of pit [2D-1895] and a further concentration of Early Neolithic pottery was found within Zone 2; however, no directly relatable feature could be identified as the source of the material.

2.7.5 The preservation of Mesolithic and Neolithic features at the base of the slope above the Camphill Terrace
Richard Tipping

The majority of the features considered above are located just above the surface of the Camphill Terrace, at the base of the gravel-rich slope eroded in Lochton Formation gravel. Mesolithic pits in particular are predominantly found in a line bordering the Camphill Terrace between 16 and 18 m AOD. A number of Early Neolithic features and

Illus 2.24 View of the pottery under excavation in pit [AMA09–2058]

Illus 2.25 View of hearth [AMA09–2181]

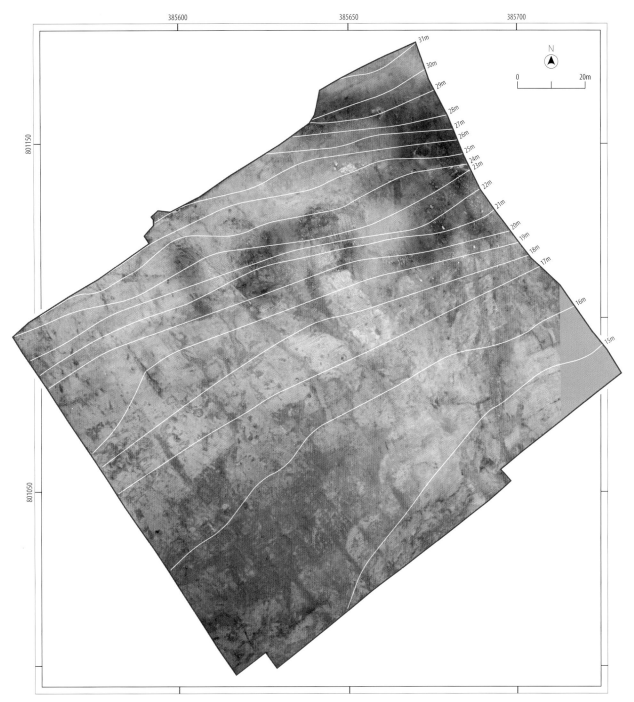

Illus 2.26 Contour data and aerial photograph showing evidence for soil erosion at some time in the Holocene, which probably protected Mesolithic and Neolithic archaeological features on the northern valley side of the River Dee alluvial corridor formed in Lochton formation gravels. The routes of soil erosion are highlighted in purple

the few dated Middle Neolithic features also occupy the same position. Their preservation is remarkable and begs the question as to the completeness of their distribution.

It is possible that these features were sealed beneath aggrading fluvial sediment. None was recognised in excavation save for a scattered few tens of centimetres of sand, but a largely organic substrate would have oxidised and left nearly nothing. There is evidence, however, for the formation of a former colluvial spread of eroded soil,

or small alluvial fans that redeposited sediment from the hillside above, but which went unrecorded in topsoil-stripping. Illus 2.26 combines contour data showing two areas of comparatively steep slope (gradients around 18%) in the north-east corner and generally from 23 m to 19 m AOD, a Google Earth image prior to excavation (22/03/12) showing areas of light-coloured soils made shallow by erosion, and an aerial photo taken during the excavation, showing a series of parallel gullies descending perpendicular to the slope (shown in purple) that would have transferred eroding soil downslope. These were cut at some time in the Holocene and may have eroded archaeological features higher up the side of the valley, with the concentration of surviving features from selective preservation where eroded soil accumulated.

2.8 Enclosing and defining spaces: the Chalcolithic at Milltimber – 2500–2200 BC

2.8.1 Late Neolithic reduction in flood frequency and incipient pedogenesis on the Maryculter Terrace

Clare Wilson and Richard Tipping

To comprehend the development and changes in the landscape and topography at Milltimber, it is necessary to understand the changes occurring within the palaeochannels across the valley floor. As part of the OSL work undertaken to date the incision of the channels, investigation of the stratigraphy associated with Profile 3 was undertaken. This revealed sediment with field characteristics suggestive of pedogenesis between 1.21 m and 1.32 m depth. This was explored through soil micromorphology on an 8.0 cm × 6.0 cm thin section impregnated and prepared from a Kubiena tin spanning this unit, examined using a lightbox and an Olympus BX51 polarising microscope under oblique incident light (OIL), plane polarised light (PPL), and cross polarised light (XPL) at magnification of between ×20 and ×100 (see Appendix 2.1.18).

The thin section showed no differentiation within it indicative of either sediment deposition or soil horizonation because the sediment had been disturbed post-depositionally and bioturbated. There are clear indications that this material has been affected by pedogenesis. These include:

(a) the frequent channel voids that had predominantly been formed by plant roots from surface vegetation, evidenced by their distinctive interlaced, vertical and horizontal orientation and the absence of excremental pedofeatures within the channels, and

(b) the intimately mixed fine organic and mineral material, together with the presence of heavily coalesced, mammilate excremental pedofeatures (Stoops 2003), clearly indicating the activity in the past of earthworms and other soil macrofauna within the A horizon of a soil.

No evidence of recent biological activity was identified. The only indicators of current/recent pedogenesis are impregnative orthic (*in situ*) iron nodules, found throughout the thin section, including within the excremental pedofeatures, indicating that they formed after the phase of past biological activity. The absence of impregnations of root material also suggests they formed after traces of the roots that formed the channel microstructure had decomposed (Wilson *et al.* 2013). Iron nodules develop in conditions of alternating oxic and anoxic conditions

in moist soil and are typical of sub-surface horizons in groundwater and stagno-gley soils that are influenced by a fluctuating water table (FAO 2006).

Pedogenesis thus occurred within the accumulating fluvial sediment. Correlation with the model of sediment accumulation generated for adjacent Profile 3 in Illus 2.20 indicates that this phase occurred slightly before 2000 BC. For a time long enough to establish a vegetated surface and promote biological activity, alluviation was interrupted and flood frequency probably halted. One implication of this is that in later prehistory, sediment was discontinuously supplied, and that fluvial sediment represents a series of discrete pulses. This sets the scene for activity at Milltimber in the later prehistoric period and through into the early centuries of the first millennium BC.

2.8.2 Free-standing timber settings

The Chalcolithic at Milltimber is primarily represented by five alignments, groups or single post-holes that together may form a timber monument (Illus 2.27). The overall alignment of the timber settings is south-west/north-east, although there are individual lines of posts running north-west/south-east. These occupy part of the exposed north-eastern section of the Camphill Terrace and extend over an area around 65 m long by 20 m wide. The post alignments were divided into four (Clusters A–D) based on their locations (Illus 2.28). A further post-hole was identified during the construction phase further to the north, which is of Early Bronze Age date, slightly later than the other groups of features.

Cluster A comprised a double line of post-holes around 1.5 m apart. The north-east row consisted of five post-holes and the south-west, three, with one of the post-holes in the north-east row partially disturbed by a modern cut. All were roughly circular, between 0.5 m and 0.75 m in diameter and up to 0.6 m in depth. On average, the post-holes of the south-west row were slightly larger and deeper than those in the north-east row.

In the north-east row, evidence showed the majority of the posts had been removed after the monument had gone out of use, on the basis of central deposits with sloping lines on their edges and the relatively loose compaction of this material. One post-hole in each row contained what appeared to be an *in situ* post-pipe, suggesting posts of between 0.25 m and 0.4 m diameter. Where evidence of packing material was present, it comprised mottled sandy silt, likely originating from the surrounding natural sediment. Post-hole [2C-0001] also had a single surviving packing stone. Dating of the group comes from radiocarbon determinations of hazel charcoal from the fills of [2C-0016] in the northern row and [2C-0018] in the southern row (Illus 2.29), with dates of 2470–2290 cal BC and 2460–2210 cal BC respectively (SUERC-58516 and SUERC-54055).

Cluster B lay 25 m to the south-west and was another double row of post-holes. The two rows were 3.95 m apart

Illus 2.27 Aerial shot of timber settings

and were generally larger and more widely spaced than Cluster A. They followed the same alignment, with four post-holes in the northern row and two in the southern. They had average diameters between about 1 m and 1.2 m and were up to 1.2 m in depth. Of particular note in this arrangement was that below the base of the rotted remains of the post in [2C-0050] a complete Beaker pot (02-V05; see 2.14.1 below) was found, apparently *in situ* (Illus 2.30). The Beaker can be dated to between 2400 and 1800 BC.

The post-holes of the northern row all showed evidence of the posts having been removed or at least partially removed. This must have taken place long enough after their erection for them to have begun to rot, as in both post-hole [2C-0050] and [2C-0094] the bottom part of the post survived as a post-pipe that had subsequently rotted, but the upper part had clearly been deliberately removed. The two post-holes forming the southern row contained much more homogenised fills, with no post-pipe apparent, indicative of the posts rotting *in situ* but experiencing extensive biological alteration over time. Near the base of post-hole [2C-0092] was a half-ring of large stones, presumed to be packing stones from around the post.

Clusters C and D were situated 15 m and 25 m further to the south-west, each comprising two sets of two post-holes, all of which were generally smaller and shallower than those to the north-east. In the case of both post-holes in Cluster C, the fills were fairly mixed and contained

both silts and sandy gravels. Due to the mixed nature, it is thought that the posts had been removed from the ground. Oak charcoal from the fill of [2C-0157] was submitted for radiocarbon dating and returned a date range of 2470–2300 cal BC (SUERC-58517) although it is unclear if this date range has been subject to the 'old oak' effect or not. The two post-holes in Cluster D were around 0.6 m to 0.7 m in diameter and 0.4 m deep. The evidence for the presence or otherwise of *in situ* posts is unclear; however, the size of the post-holes would suggest that the posts were smaller than the ones further to the north.

The final element of the settings was a single pit [2C-0075] located between the two double rows of post-holes. It was around 1.75 m in diameter and relatively shallow at 0.2 m deep. The fill of the pit comprised a single deposit of black sandy loam containing frequent charcoal inclusions, weed seeds, fragments of burnt bone and three fragments of pottery, identified as Beaker (02-V04). It should be noted that the pit is very similar in form to pit [2C-0068], which lies a few metres to the south-east and dates to around 1000 years later than the timber setting is likely to be, or when Beaker pottery would be in vogue. Another pit, which is not dissimilar, lies around 10 m to the north and dates to the mid-first millennium AD; therefore, we should be cautious about directly relating the pit to the timber settings.

Post-hole [AMA09–2011] was located approximately 50 m to the north of the post alignments (Illus 2.28),

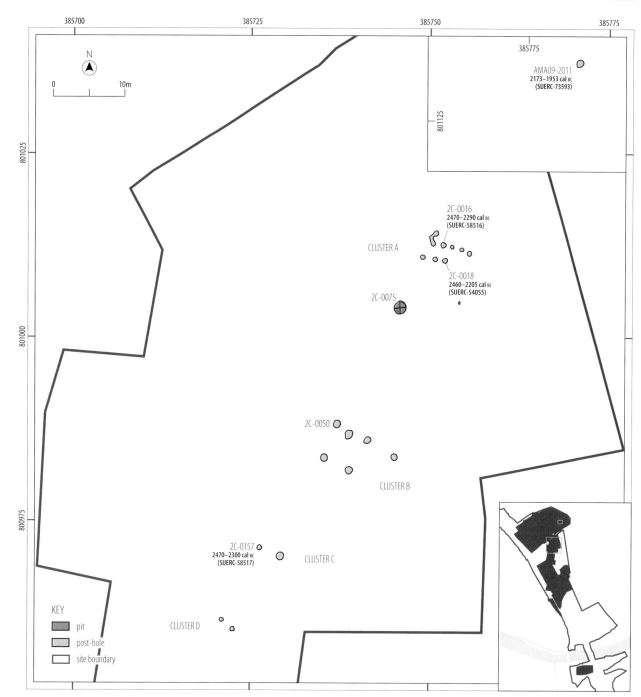

Illus 2.28 Plan of Chalcolithic features

and charcoal from its fill dated to 2140–1950 cal BC (SUERC-73593). This was a substantial post-hole, 0.95 m in diameter and 1 m deep, with a 0.2 m post-pipe visible. A small assemblage of lithic debitage was also recovered from the fill along with oak and hazel charcoal. Although slightly later in date than the radiocarbon determinations from the clusters, it could be broadly contemporary.

2.9 Milltimber in later prehistory – 1550–100 BC

Although limited, there is evidence that Milltimber in the later prehistoric period was still a location to which people

returned. The most prominent of these features was a large curvilinear ditch [2B-2075] lying towards the south-east of the Camphill Terrace (Illus 2.31). This was 94 m in length, up to 3.5 m wide and 1.15 m deep. It covers an arc c77m long and 25 m wide defining an area above the slope leading down to the Maryculter Terrace. Deposits within the ditch comprised a series of sandy slumping layers (largely confined to and thicker towards the outer edge of the curve), compacted silty layers from infilling of the feature, and upper deposits similar to topsoil representing the final infilling of the hollow of the ditch. The slumping

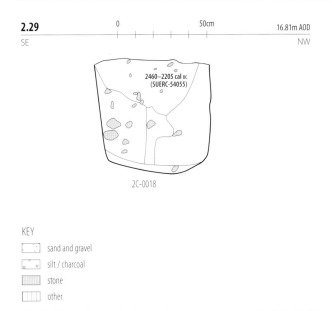

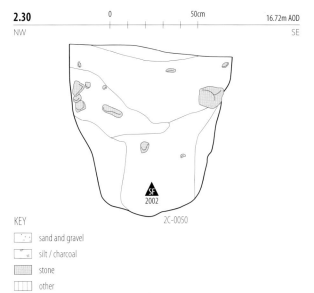

KEY

sand and gravel

silt / charcoal

stone

other

KEY

sand and gravel

silt / charcoal

stone

other

Illus 2.29 North-east-facing section through post-hole [2C-0018]

layers to the outer edge imply there may have been an outer bank. The profile of the ditch was also steeper on the outer edge than the inner, with a relatively narrow curved base.

The fills of the ditch were uniformly lacking in significant environmental or artefactual material, with many of the samples taken being deemed 'archaeologically sterile'. By the very nature of their formation, much of the slumped material relates to periods after the feature had gone out of use. Hazel charcoal from one of the upper layers of slumping returned a date range of 1260–1050 cal BC (SUERC-68091). The outer edge of the ditch had subsequently been cut into by a series of Roman ovens, recorded exclusively on the outer edge, showing it had certainly gone out of use and had silted up by the late 1st century AD (see 2.10.2 below).

At its north-eastern extent, both the edges and fills of the ditch had been heavily disturbed by probable quarrying for sand and gravel, related most probably to the post-medieval period. The southern limit of the ditch, lying on the slope separating the Camphill Terrace from the Maryculter Terrace, is argued to have been eroded, probably by fluvial activity because the depth of the ditch shallows to only a few tens of centimetres. If erosion of the southern side of the Camphill Terrace and the ditch occurred during incision of the River Dee below the Camphill Terrace, the ditch must have been created before c3300 BC (see 2.6.3 above). Lateral erosion by the River Dee after this date is problematic because an undisturbed fluvial stratigraphy is recorded at oven DO6. This date is significant as the ditch had initially been interpreted as a henge monument, based primarily on its plan and the potential existence of an outer bank: a pre-c3300 BC date would preclude it being a henge. It is possible the ditch represents the remains of an Early Neolithic enclosure of unknown form. Two other substantial linear ditches were identified further to the

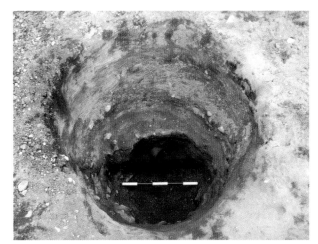

Illus 2.30 South-west-facing section through post-hole [2C-0050] showing location of Beaker (02-V05) at the base of the removed post. B. Beaker under excavation C. Beaker following cleaning

north and may belong to this period of activity, but both of these were undated (see 2.12 below). Their location is shown on Illus 2.31.

Of the remaining six features dated to the late prehistoric period, three were unprepossessing hearths, very similar to

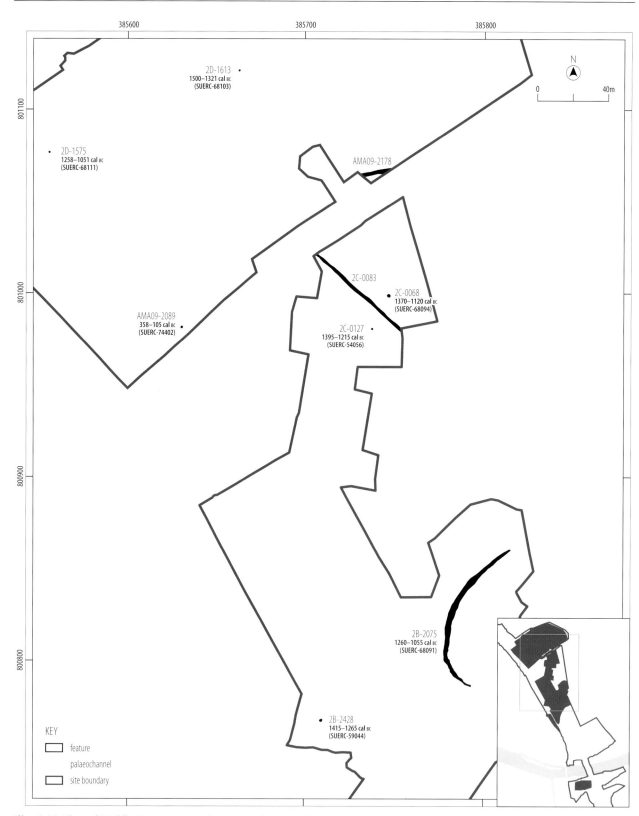

Illus 2.31 Plan of Middle Bronze Age and Iron Age features (ditches [2C-0083] and [AMA09–2178] are presumed of this phase of activity)

the hearths seen in the earlier prehistoric period. Two of these – [2D-1575] and [2D-1613] – were located slightly further upslope than Neolithic examples, with one – [2C-0127] – found near the Chalcolithic timber setting. The hearths all appear to be single or short-lived use. They date to 1500–1320 cal BC, 1400–1220 cal BC, and 1260–1050 cal BC respectively (SUERC-68103, SUERC-54056 and SUERC-68111), indicating no specific period of focus.

Illus 2.32 Pit [AMA09–2089]. The pit contained part of a saddle quern and undiagnostic pottery and was dated to the Early Iron Age

Also in the vicinity of the Chalcolithic timber setting was pit [2C-0068], 1.5 m in diameter and 0.65 m deep, filled with successive layers of sandy silts and redeposited sand and gravel. This was conclusively not a hearth feature, despite the presence of charcoal in the middle deposit. This material was dated to 1370–1120 cal BC (SUERC-68094), effectively contemporary with hearth [2C-0127] described above, lying 18 m to the south-east.

A single isolated pit [2B-2428] was also identified at the very southern extent of the Camphill Terrace. This shallow feature contained fragments of alder charcoal dated to 1420–1270 cal BC (SUERC-59044). However, the fill of the features was entirely from in-washed material; the features near it were of Early Historic date and it may be more sensible to view this pit as contemporary with the Early Historic enclosure (see 2.11 below).

Through dating of selected features across the Milltimber site, it was also established that there was at least one visit during the first millennium BC. Pit [AMA09–2089] contained fragments of saddle quern, 13 sherds of undiagnostic pottery (02-V46) and lithic debitage (Illus 2.32). Charcoal from this pit was dated to 360–110 cal BC (SUERC-74402), which was unexpected. However, the wide range of dates obtained from features across the site, along with the presence of a great many undated and undatable features means that this feature likely represents a small and short-lived period of activity at the site, of which this is the only evidence.

2.10 A military presence: the Romans at Milltimber – AD 83/84

In total, 90 Roman ovens were identified across the site. These comprise the largest body of data after lithic material. It seems highly likely that more are present in the unexcavated strip in the far south-west of the site between Groups 12 and 13, and that at least a handful more may be present following the line of ovens beyond the eastern limit. The ovens were located on the slope of the (for Roman purposes, interestingly named) Camphill Terrace and cut into sediments of the younger Maryculter Terrace on the

north side of the River Dee at 11–13 m AOD (Illus 2.33). The majority of the ovens utilised the banks of two large palaeochannels that had dried up or were vegetated by the later prehistoric age.

The presence of extensive secure, datable material within the ovens allowed a wide-ranging programme of dating to take place with two-thirds of the excavated ovens scientifically dated. Bayesian analysis was undertaken that allowed a refined chronology of the date and duration of the activity to be proposed (see 2.10.3 below). The ovens were arranged in 13 groups, with two additional ovens found to the north in association with an undated prehistoric ditch. Apart from Group 7, all the ovens were cut into sloping ground of some description or another. Where their full extent is known (ie the group had clearly defined limits with obvious gaps between one group and the next) they ranged in size between five and eight ovens, although one of the groups with no defined southern end (Group 12) was made up of at least 15 ovens.

Ovens were given feature numbers with a letter suffix during the excavation phase, based on their location. The process of discovery and excavation of these ovens occurred over several phases of work; Ovens B17 and F05 were first identified during trial trenching. Subsequent topsoil stripping over larger areas revealed the remainder; pits containing larger amounts of charcoal, almost universally set back into the slopes on the side of palaeochannels. In particular at the northern extent of the main palaeochannel route, soft sands on the side of the channel had slumped over the features, making defining their extents and plans challenging. At this stage many of the ovens (most of Group 4 and some of Groups 3 and 6) were investigated through the medium of arbitrarily placed slots. This process confirmed the existence of the overlying sandy deposits, that the charcoal material did in fact belong to cut features of roughly keyhole shape and resulted in further topsoil stripping to remove the overburden.

No artefacts of Roman or Iron Age date were recovered from this part of the site. A residual amount of metalworking slag was recovered from the palaeochannels that may relate to the Roman phase of activity; however, this cannot be confirmed.

2.10.1 The fluvial context of the Roman ovens
Richard Tipping

As most of the ovens were cut into the outer banks of two prominent palaeochannels within the Maryculter Terrace (Illus 2.33), it follows the palaeochannels must have existed prior to construction of the ovens. The Maryculter Terrace began to form before c3100–3300 BC (see 2.6.3 above). Both channels are much smaller than the present course of the Dee but neither need have been the only channel when they were cut: sandy islands called inches abounded in the past and still exist.

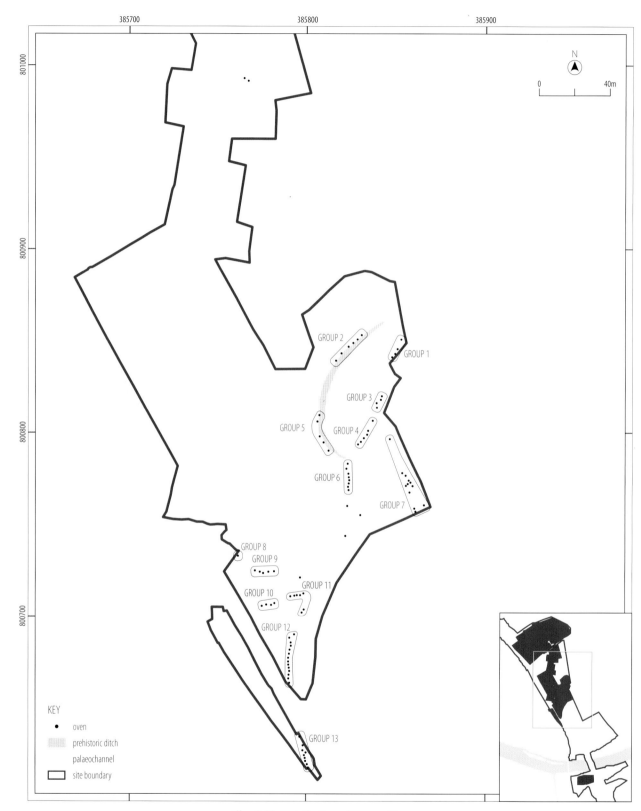

Illus 2.33 Distribution of Roman Ovens

This positioning of ovens in relation to a pre-existing floodplain morphology is not seen with the Roman ovens at Kintore (Cook & Dunbar 2008). At Milltimber, the builders seem likely to have sought pre-existing steep banks in the sides of the palaeochannels and the partly filled ditch [2B-2075], so that ovens could be constructed at closer to waist to shoulder height. However, several ovens were dug into both ditch/channel fills as well as adjacent terrace sediment, implying that these were filled with sediment when these ovens were constructed. At oven DO6, the modelling of sediment accumulation (see 2.6.3 above; Illus 2.20) suggests that the palaeochannel was filled to the level of the surrounding terrace surface long before the ovens were dug, indicating it was completely filled before the 1st century AD. There are open questions, then, as to how the builders knew where the channel banks were, and why they positioned the ovens where they did. Given the majority of the ovens were cut into the outer bank of the palaeochannels the conclusion must be that the raised banks of the channels were visible at this time.

The ovens imply access to part of the contemporary floodplain. Group 7 ovens are the farthest distance across the floodplain, around 30 m from the slope down from the Camphill Terrace (Illus 2.33). The existence of the ovens implies that the floodplain surface was dry when the ovens were used, but this period may have been short. Overbank sediment accumulation may have continued. pOSL analyses of sediment infilling a section of palaeochannel on the Camphill Terrace, maybe 4 m higher than the Maryculter Terrace in the Late Iron Age, showed that the youngest sediments in that palaeochannel have mean IRSL and OSL net signal intensities equivalent to those in Profiles 1–3 that formed on the Maryculter Terrace in the later Iron Age (see 2.6.3 above). These suggest, but cannot conclusively demonstrate, that very large floods, with water depths of around 4 m, deposited sand on the Camphill Terrace in this period.

Alluviation took place in a freshwater environment. Relative sea-level curves in the region indicate that the tide would not have reached Milltimber (Smith *et al.* 1999). The river was probably a single channel supplying overbank sediment, but this has not been located. The dimensions of the river are not known, nor whether it or its estuary at New Aberdeen was navigable. Jackson (2002) suggested that until the early modern period and the advent of large-scale engineering the estuary was more of a barrier to the Dee than a passage. Having said that, it is clear that the river formed an access route in the early prehistoric period, and there is no reason why this should not continue into later millennia.

2.10.2 The ovens

The following describes the locations of the individual groups and gives an analysis of the excavated ovens. A full list of the ovens is given in Table 2.03.

2.10.2.1 Group 1

The four ovens of Group 1 (A07–A10) had been cut into the western bank of the later palaeochannel (Illus 2.34). They were keyhole-shaped in plan, with their tails relatively undefined as they dropped down into the palaeochannel. They were located right next to the limit of excavation, so the full extent of the tails and the relationship between the tail deposits and the palaeochannel deposit was generally not visible. Three had stone linings at the head end of the oven (some better constructed than others), and one was unfired (Illus 2.35). It is entirely possible that oven A09 was not only unfired but was actually incomplete, with an intended stone lining never finished. A07 (Illus 2.36) was the northernmost example and survived the best. In addition to burnt material, the fills also included a patch of heat-affected silty clay found overlying the latest layer of charcoal, and a further deposit of clay found beyond the neck of the oven. These deposits are the remnants of clay seals that were used in the firings of the ovens. Overlying this in the tail end of the oven was another silty clay deposit, which extended well into the limits of the palaeochannel. This could be the decayed collapse of a clay superstructure of the oven, starting to erode down the slope.

Within the heads of the ovens, layers of burnt sand and charcoal were present. Of the fired ovens, the charcoal was identified as a mix of heather or gorse and some birch, suggesting that the fuel used was being collected locally and was made up of what was readily available, rather than what might burn most efficiently. A07 showed evidence of two firings, while A08 and A10 both only had a single firing. Dates of cal AD 90–240 (SUERC-68061), 20 cal BC–cal AD 130 (SUERC-68062) and 40 cal BC–cal AD 80 (SUERC-58500) were obtained from ovens A07, A08 and A10 respectively.

2.10.2.2 Group 2

The six ovens of Group 2 (A01–A06) were dug into the outer edge of ditch 2B-2075. It is presumed that, along with Group 5, they were located here owing to the contemporary presence of a bank on the outer edge (Illus 2.37). Two of the six ovens were excavated (A02 and A05), although two of the group had been so heavily truncated that they did not merit intrusive investigation (A01 and A03).

Both A02 and A05 were keyhole-shaped, although the tails were relatively indistinct against the backfill of the ditch. What was clear from the two examples was that the ditch was at least partially infilled at the time of the construction of the ovens. Oven A02 had evidence of a single firing (but may have been truncated), A05 had two firings, with a layer of heat-affected sand between the two layers of charcoal (Illus 2.38). The sand may have been used to douse the fire once cooking was completed. Of interest in relation to A05 was a deposit found in a section excavated across the ditch immediately to the south-west of the oven. A mounded spread of sand was present at the same level as the oven tail deposits, similar to the geological subsoil through which the oven was cut. When the head of the oven was constructed, the excavated material must have been thrown to the side (left-hand side) by the person digging it (Illus 2.39). This was not the only example where this type of material was identified, and it would seem likely that this process would apply to each oven.

The charcoal used in both ovens was largely heather, with some oak, hazel and birch. Where oak was used, it tended to be larger branches with a mix of small, medium

Table 2.03 Roman ovens

Group	Oven no	Length (m)	Width (m)	Diameter (m)	Height OD at base (m)	In situ firings	C14 date	Wood	Notes
–	2C-0106	–	–	1.1	16.4	0	–	–	
Group 2	A01	1.2	0.8	-	15	-	-	-	Unexcavated
	A02	–	–	1.1	–	1	cal AD 65–218	–	
	A03	0.4	0.2	–	–	–	–	–	Unexcavated
	A04	–	–	0.9	–	–	–	–	Unexcavated
	A05	–	–	1.5	14.8	2	40 cal BC–cal AD 120	*Calluna*	
	A06	1.4	1.3	–	–	–	–	–	Unexcavated
Group 1	A07	–	–	1.5	12.3	1	cal AD 86–244	–	
	A08	–	–	1	12.8	1	19 cal BC–cal AD 129	–	
	A09	–	–	1.7	12.4	0	–	–	
	A10	1.4	1	–	12.8	1	43 cal BC–cal AD 82	–	
Group 5	A11	–	–	1	15.3	2	cal AD 94–321	*Betula, Corylus*	
	A12	–	–	1.4	15	0	–	–	
	A13	1.2	–	–	–	–	–	–	Unexcavated
	A14	–	–	1.3	14.2	1	–	–	Unexcavated
	A15	1.4	1.2	–	15.1	0	–	–	
Group 6	B01	1.8	1	–	–	–	–	–	Unexcavated
	B02	–	–	1.2	–	–	–	–	Unexcavated
	B03	–	–	1.5	–	–	–	–	Unexcavated
	B04			1.4	–	–	–	–	Unexcavated
–	B05	–	–	0.7	11.9	1	–	–	
–	B06	–	–	0.8	11.5	0	–	–	
–	B07	–	–	1.6	–	–	–	–	Unexcavated
–	B08	2.1	1.3	–	11.6	0	–	–	
Group 6	B09	–	–	1	11.5	3	cal AD 27–212	*Calluna, Betula*	
	B10	–	–	1.2	11.6	2	–	*Prunus, Corylus, Calluna, Quercus*	
	B11	–	–	0.9	12.5	1	–	–	
	B12	–	–	1.2	12.5	1	–	–	
Group 4	B13	–	–	1.4	11.7	2	39 cal BC–cal AD 123; 40 cal BC–cal AD 121	–	
	B14	–	–	1.3	11.6	2	–	*Ulex/Cytisus, Calluna*	
	B15	–	–	1.4	11.5	2	cal AD 86–240	*Calluna*	
	B16	–	–	1.6	11.5	1	cal AD 7–131	–	
	B17	–	–	1.4	11.6	3	–	*Calluna*	

Table 2.03

Group	Oven no	Length (m)	Width (m)	Diameter (m)	Height OD at base (m)	In situ firings	C14 date	Wood	Notes
Group 3	B18	1.9	1.5	–	11.4	1	–	–	
	B19	–	–	1.1	–	1	–	–	Unexcavated
	B20	–	–	1.3	11.2	2	52 cal BC–cal AD 71	Betula, Prunus, Corylus, Quercus	
	B21	–	–	1.4	11.6	3	171 cal BC–cal AD 1	Quercus	
Group 7	C01	–	–	1	11.2	1	cal AD 28–212	–	
	C02	2.2	–	–	–	–	–	–	Unexcavated
	C03	–	–	0.9	–	–	–	–	Unexcavated
	C04	–	–	1.5	11.2	1	46 cal BC–cal AD 74	–	Underwater; base data from section
	C05	–	–	1.4	11.3	–	–	–	Underwater; base data from section
	C06	2.7	1.8	–	–	–	–	–	Unexcavated;
	C07	2.6	1.5	–	11	–	–	–	Full length and width of feature provided; base measurement from section
	C08	–	–	1.23	11.2	1	cal AD 3–129	–	
	C09	–	–	1.3	11.2	1	cal AD 33–214	–	
	C10	2	1.2	–	11	0	–	–	
Group 9	D01	–	–	1.1	–	–	–	–	Unexcavated
	D02	–	–	1.5	11.5	0	cal AD 69–221	–	
	D03	–	–	1.1	–	–	–	–	Unexcavated
	D04	–	–	2	11.3	0	21 cal BC–cal AD 127	–	
	D05	–	–	1.3	–	–	–	–	Unexcavated
Group 8	D06	–	–	1.5	11.8	1	cal AD 21–208	–	
Group 10	E01	1.2	1.2	–	1.7	1	cal AD 27–211	–	
	E02	–	–	0.9	–	–	–	–	Unexcavated
	E03	1.7	1.1	–	1.8	0	cal AD 3–129; 171–1 cal BC	–	
	E04	1.4	1.2	–	1.3	2	cal AD 74-225	Betula, Quercus, Calluna	

Table 2.03 Roman ovens (Continued)

Group	Oven no	Length (m)	Width (m)	Diameter (m)	Height OD at base (m)	In situ firings	C14 date	Wood	Notes
Group 11	E05	–	–	–	–	–	–	–	Unexcavated
	E06	–	–	1.2	11.4	1	–	–	
	E07	–	–	1.3	–	–	–	–	Unexcavated
	E08	–	–	1.3	–	–	–	–	Unexcavated
	E09	–	–	1	11.6	1	cal AD 2–129	–	
	E10	–	–	–	–	–	–	–	Unexcavated
	F01	–	–	1.3	12	0	–	–	
	F02	–	–	1.1	–	–	–	–	Unexcavated
Group 12	F05	0.6	0.5	–	12.3	0	–	–	Base measurement from section
	F06	–	–	1.5	11.9	2	cal AD 70–224	*Quercus, Calluna*	
	F07	–	–	1.6	–	–	–	–	Unexcavated
	F08	–	–	1.6	12.2	1	cal AD 54–214	–	
	F09	–	–	1.2	–	–	–	–	Unexcavated
	F10	–	–	1.1	12.4	0	–	–	Base measurement from section
	F11	–	–	1	–	–	–	–	Unexcavated
	F12	–	–	1.5	12.5	0	–	–	
	F13	–	–	1.5	12.4	1	cal AD 5–205	–	
	F14	–	–	1.5	–	–	–	–	Unexcavated
	F15	–	–	0.9	12.4	0	–	–	
	F16	–	–	1.1	–	–	–	–	Unexcavated
	F17	–	–	1.5	12.2	3	–	*Alnus, Betula, Ulex/Cytisus*	
	F18	–	–	1.5	–	–	–	–	Unexcavated
	F19	–	–	1.7	12	2	87 cal BC–cal AD 68	*Ulex/Cytisus, Calluna, Corylus*	
Group 13	G01	–	–	1	12.4	1	cal AD 5–130	–	
	G02	2.5	–	–	–	–	–	–	Unexcavated
	G03	–	–	1.4	12.5	0	–	–	
	G04	–	–	1.3	12.5	0	–	–	
	G05	–	–	1.3	–	–	–	–	Unexcavated
	G06	–	–	1.3	–	–	–	–	Unexcavated
	G07	–	–	1.8	12.4	2	cal AD 29–213	*Ulex/Cytisus, Calluna*	
	G08	–	–	1.2	12.4	1	cal AD 61–218	–	
	G09	1.5	–	–	–	–	–	–	Unexcavated

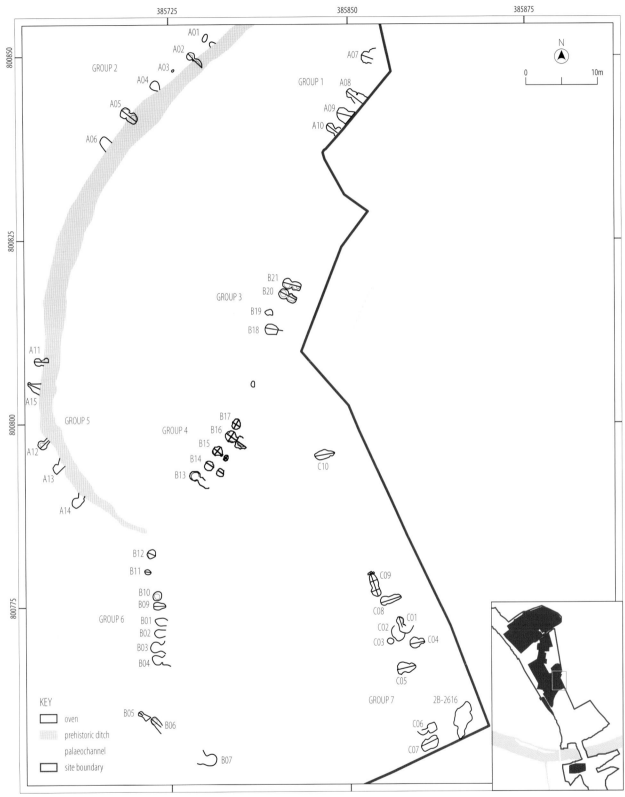

Illus 2.34 Detail of Groups 1–7

Illus 2.35 Group 1 ovens cut into edge of palaeochannel. The very edge of the palaeochannel can be seen as a dark line to the right of the heads of the ovens

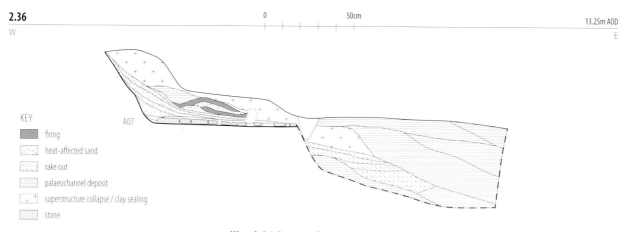

Illus 2.36 Section through oven A07

and large branches of hazel and heather. Oven A02 was dated to cal AD 70–220 (SUERC-58499) and oven A05 to 40 cal BC–cal AD 120 (SUERC-68060).

2.10.2.3 Group 3

Group 3 comprised four ovens (B18–B21) dug into the north-western bank of the palaeochannel (Illus 2.34). Compared to Group 1, the ovens were dug at a lower elevation into the slope; roughly 11.5 m AOD, with Group 1 closer to 12.75 m AOD.

Unusually, ovens B20 and B21 both had well-defined tails contained by a pit. Also relatively unusually, B18 may have had up to four firings partially *in situ*, and it could be argued that there is evidence of three firings within B21 (two *in situ* and one in the form of rake-out pre-dating the two firings; Illus 2.40). The only other ovens to have strong evidence of more than two firings were ovens B09 and B17, which both lay a short distance to the south.

Excavation of oven B19 provided evidence that surviving charcoal in the ovens was not deliberately

Illus 2.37 Group 2 and 5 from above, cut into the earlier ditch

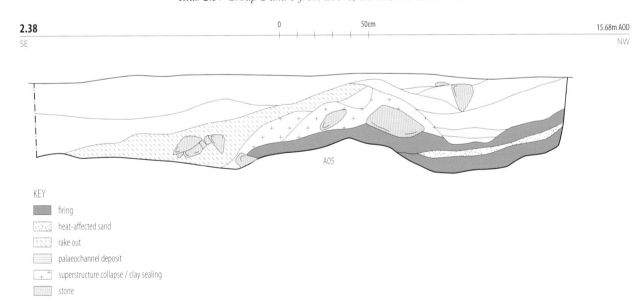

2.38 0   50cm   15.68m AOD

SE   NW

A05

KEY

■ firing

▨ heat-affected sand

▧ rake out

▤ palaeochannel deposit

⊞ superstructure collapse / clay sealing

▦ stone

Illus 2.38 Section through oven A05

arranged, but rather was roughly scattered across the bowls. It is also notable that all of the ovens of this group except B19 were extensively using oak as fuel, in comparison to other groups where a range of scrubby wood was commonly used. Oven B20 was dated to 50 cal BC–cal AD 70 (SUERC-54188) and oven B21 to 170 cal BC–cal AD 1 (SUERC-68064).

2.10.2.4 Group 4

Group 4 comprised five ovens (B13–B17; Illus 2.34) dug into the north-western bank of the later palaeochannel and located around the 11.6 m AOD mark. All the ovens apart from B16 had multiple firings, with most showing evidence of two firings and B17 showing three layers of charcoal *in situ*. In comparison to Group 3 to the north, the charcoal used for the fuel was generally a mix of heather

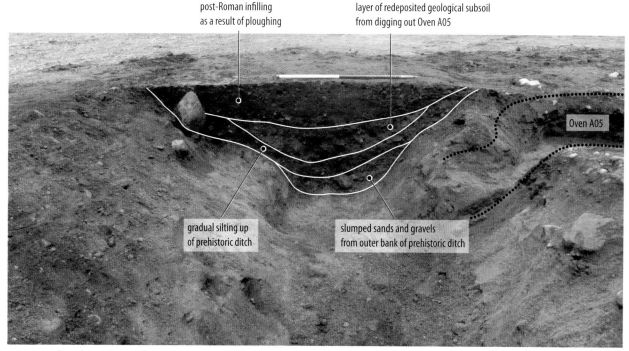

post-Roman infilling
as a result of ploughing

layer of redeposited geological subsoil
from digging out Oven A05

Oven A05

gradual silting up
of prehistoric ditch

slumped sands and gravels
from outer bank of prehistoric ditch

Illus 2.39 Photo of prehistoric ditch and oven A05 showing mound of redeposited subsoil from digging out oven

and gorse, with smaller amounts of hazel and birch present. These seem to display a deliberate trend towards more scrubby resources as opposed to large timbers or stores of firewood (Illus 2.41).

Also of interest in this group is B15, which appears to have a deliberately cut/eroded pit tail rather than the deposits petering out into the palaeochannel. The pit measured 0.8 m by 0.6 m. Two dates were obtained from B13, 40 cal BC–cal AD 120 and 40 cal BC–cal AD 120 (SUERC-54187 and SUERC-54189). Oven B15 was dated to cal AD 90–240 (SUERC-68082) and oven B16 to cal AD 10–130 (SUERC-68083).

2.10.2.5 Group 5

The five ovens of Group 5 (A11–A15) were dug into the western (outer) edge of ditch [2B-2075] (Illus 2.34). Again, the presumption is that a bank must have been present to provide an attractive location for siting the ovens. All five of the ovens were excavated, and two were found to be unfired.

None of the ovens survived particularly well, and the group seems 'unfinished'. The best example is A11, which had two firings present, mostly using hazel and birch as the fuel. A14 had a large stone present in the neck of the oven, similar to the sealing material seen in other ovens. Dating of material from A11 returned a range of cal AD 90–320 (SUERC-68081).

2.10.2.6 Group 6

Group 6 comprised eight ovens (B01–B04 and B09–B12) dug into the outer bank of the later palaeochannel (Illus 2.34). Four out of the eight ovens were excavated, and as a group their survival was poor with several tails

lost. B12 was also excavated early in the sequence, and the features were not fully understood at this point. Two ovens had single firings (B11 and B12), while B10 had two firings and B09 had three surviving (Illus 2.42). The fuel used was a mix of heather, birch, gorse, hazel and oak. It is important to note that the samples identified as mostly oak came from the earlier firing of B10 and from the very poorly preserved oven B11, which only survived as a circular hollow with a single deposit of charcoal.

The presence of oak in the lower deposits could be an indication of the intentional use of more woody material (or planks/spare wood?) during the first phase of use of this group of ovens, with a more opportunistic approach once this material had run out or there was an awareness that the brushy material would burn well. Oven B09 was dated to cal AD 30–210 (SUERC-68063).

2.10.2.7 Group 7

Group 7 is unusual in that there were no clear topographic features that explain the specific location of the ovens. This group had ten ovens, C01–C10, that were spread out over a relatively large area in comparison to the other groups (Illus 2.34), with no consistent alignment of direction. Excavation of this group of ovens was challenging as they lay at the level of or under the water table (causing problems during heavy rain). Of the ten ovens, seven were investigated.

The ovens were a variety of shapes in plan; C05 and C07–C10 are oval, with no real distinction between the head and the tail prior to excavation. Ovens C01, C04 and C06 were more keyhole-shaped. The remainder were not investigated, and their form was not particularly clear as the area rapidly filled with water.

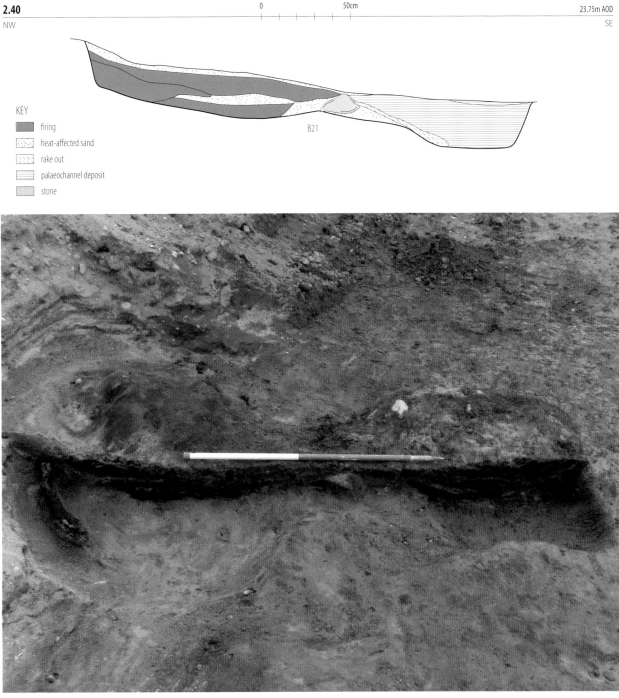

2.40

NW

0   50cm   23.75m AOD

SE

KEY
- firing
- heat-affected sand
- rake out
- palaeochannel deposit
- stone

B21

Illus 2.40 Section through oven B21. B. Photo shows the layers of charcoal and the pit-defined tail

The topographic location of Group 7 was fundamentally different from all other ovens recorded. The action of the River Dee over at least 6000 years had scoured away the Camphill Terrace, which previously occupied a height of c15.5 m OD, leaving most of the area between the palaeochannel and the current location of the river at a height of c11.3 m and forming the Maryculter Terrace (see 2.4.4 above). The whole area within the Maryculter Terrace that was stripped as part of this scheme seemed broadly flat and uniform in terms of topographic features; however, some very slightly elevated sandy 'islands' seem

to have been present and, for whatever reason, proved comparatively attractive as a location for some of the ovens.

In general, and where it could be identified, the head of the ovens were towards the western end. The exceptions to this were C01, which had the head at the north, and C09 which, conversely, had the head at the south. In some, for example, C01, C05 and C09, the head was slightly higher, or there was a rise between the head and tail. C10 was also unusual in being a relatively deep pit, with no apparent difference between head and tail. From

Illus 2.41 Group 4 ovens from above. The palaeochannel has partially filled with water during a period of rain

Illus 2.42 Group 6 ovens cut into the bank of the palaeochannel

the direction of rake-out, it is assumed that the head was towards the west.

The majority of the ovens showed evidence of being fired only once, although the conditions during excavation made it difficult to be certain. Oven C08 had only one firing deposit *in situ* (Illus 2.43), but it appeared to have two or three episodes of rake-out in the tail, suggesting more extensive use. Where secure samples could be recovered, the fuel used was a mix of oak, birch, hazel and gorse, with oak present in three out of four samples analysed. As the ovens generally only had a single firing, there was no way to assess this relatively high presence of oak against the proposition that it tended to be more abundant in the earlier ovens or firings.

Four of the ovens from this group were dated; C01 was cal AD 30–210 (SUERC-68065), C04 was 50 cal BC–cal AD 70 (SUERC-68066), C08 was cal AD 1–130 (SUERC-68070) and C09 was cal AD 30–210 (SUERC-58509).

There is a gap between Groups 1–7 and Groups 8–13 (Illus 2.44). This does appear to be real (as opposed to an artifice of the limits of excavation) and may be due in some part to the shallowness of slope of the north-western bank of the palaeochannel, or the allocation of this area to other activities not involving ovens and leaving no trace.

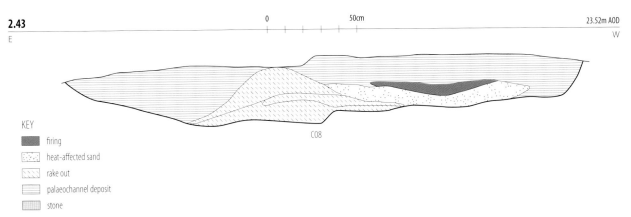

2.43

0   50cm   23.52m AOD

E   W

KEY

▬ firing

▨ heat-affected sand

▨ rake out

▤ palaeochannel deposit

▦ stone

C08

Illus 2.43 Section through oven C08

2.10.2.8 Group 8

Only one oven lay within the excavation area belonging to Group 8; D06. While it could be considered a stray individual oven, the location adjacent to the limit of excavation makes it likely the oven is the southernmost of a group continuing to the north-west.

Oven D06 was keyhole-shaped, with a single firing (Illus 2.45). Analysis of the charcoal showed the fuel used was a mix of oak and heather. The oven was dated to cal AD 20–210 (SUERC-58504). OSL dating was also undertaken of deposits above, below and around this feature (see 2.6.3 above).

2.10.2.9 Group 9

Group 9 comprised five ovens (D01–D05; Illus 2.44), two of which were investigated. Oven D01 appears to represent the furthest point east at which it was felt the slope of the palaeochannel was worth using and this relatively gentle slope is apparent in the two excavated ovens (Illus 2.46). They were dug at a relatively low level into the slope and, similar to Group 7, this made excavation of the features with rising water levels a challenge, and it was not possible to retrieve secure material for sampling. Therefore, the types of fuel used are not known. Dating of this group was obtained from rake-out from both ovens, rather than *in situ* material. Oven D02 was dated to cal AD 70–220 (SUERC-68090) and D04 to 20 cal BC–cal AD 130 (SUERC-68071).

2.10.2.10 Group 10

The four ovens of Group 10 (E01–E04; Illus 2.44) lay on the opposite side of the earlier palaeochannel from Group 9, occupying the southern bank where the ground rose up to a small sandy plateau. Three of the ovens were investigated and were keyhole-shaped in plan, although the tail of E04 was relatively indistinct. The tails of the ovens seemed to be more intentionally cut into the slope of the channel, creating a stepped profile to the features (Illus 2.47), in comparison to the sloped appearance of other ovens. This stepped characteristic was seen in all three excavated examples.

The number of firings present was more difficult to assess with Group 10 as they had been more efficiently or intentionally cleaned out, both during their use, and following the final use. However, of the two ovens that had firings *in situ* the fuel used was a mix of birch and oak, with a small amount of heather present in E01. Dating of the ovens included one sample of oak, which illustrated the issue of the 'oak effect' where two dates from the same oven differed substantially (one from oak charcoal and one from holly). The original date obtained from oven E03 was 170–1 cal BC (SUERC-58505), whereas the second sample of holly returned a date of cal AD 1–130 (SUERC-59043). Dates of cal AD 30–210 (SUERC-68072) and cal AD 70–230 (SUERC-68073) were obtained from ovens E01 and E04 respectively.

2.10.2.11 Group 11

The ovens comprising Group 11 were probably the most artificial collection (E05–E10 and F01–F02; Illus 2.44). They are located on the north and south-eastern banks of the palaeochannel at the confluence of the two different branches. The surface of the palaeochannel was particularly low at this point and the shallow nature of the banks meant the heads of the ovens were sometimes cut into earlier palaeochannel deposits. It was also the location of the most concentrated coverage of later field systems, obscuring and truncating many of the ovens. It is entirely possible that the ovens with the prefix E and those with the prefix F belonged to different groups, but as limited material was recovered from F01, they have been grouped together. Of the eight ovens present, a full plan could only be discerned for six of them, and three ovens were investigated.

As far as could be seen, these were keyhole-shaped in plan. All three of the excavated ovens showed evidence of at least one firing. Where material was still *in situ* and could be analysed it was shown to be a mix of birch, hazel and heather, with a small amount of gorse in oven E06 (Illus 2.48) and extensive use of oak in E09, although at least some willow was present from which the oven was dated to cal AD 1–130 (SUERC-68074).

74   *Kirsty Dingwall, Richard Tipping and Don Wilson*

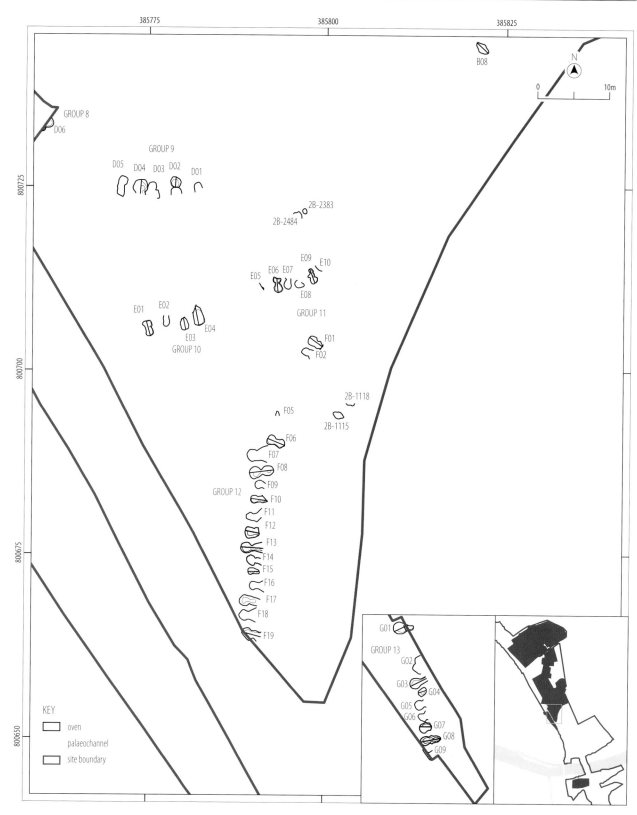

Illus 2.44 Detail of Groups 8–13

2.10.2.12 Group 12

Group 12 comprised 15 ovens (F05–F19) cut into the south-western (outer) bank of the later palaeochannels (Illus 2.44 & 2.49). The southern limit of the group was not defined, so it is possible that further members of Group 12 are present in the unexcavated area to the south of F19. Generally, the ovens were cut in from around 12.3 m to 12.5 m AOD through the geological subsoil; however, the

Illus 2.45 Oven D06 during excavation

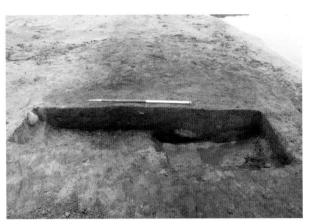

Illus 2.47 Section through oven E01

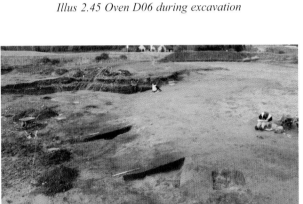

Illus 2.46 View of Group 9 ovens from south-east

depth to which they had been excavated varied, ranging from 11.9 m AOD at the base of the head of oven F06, to 12.45 m AOD at the base of F10. The ovens are also much closer together than the majority of the other groups. This could be an indication that this suite of ovens was either not all constructed at the same time or perhaps by a small group of individuals who preferred to cook in a different manner.

The ovens are still keyhole-shaped but the tails of at least two of the ovens (F06 and F08) are closer to the pits seen in B20 and B21, although circular and indistinct. Several of the ovens (F08, F10, F12, F15 and to a lesser extent, F13) were very truncated, only surviving to a depth of around 0.1 m. Most of the shallow ovens only contained a single firing, and it is not thought that evidence of further firings has been lost due to truncation. Ovens F06, F17 and F19 all showed evidence of at least two firings, with potentially more present through evidence of rake-out. All three ovens also had the remnants of clay and stone sealing material from either the final use of the ovens or, in the case of F17, potentially even earlier firings, mixed up with rake-out. In addition, ovens F06 and F17 also contained patches of mottled heat-affected material in the heads of the ovens, lying above the final burnt deposits (Illus 2.50). It is thought that these deposits represent collapse (or deliberate slighting?) of probable turf superstructures.

Charcoal was recovered from F06, F08, F13, F17 and F19, which could be identified to species and indicated that the fuel was largely a mix of heather and gorse, with some birch present in F13 and F17, and small amounts of oak also present in F06.

2.48

0   50cm   12.08m AOD

S   N

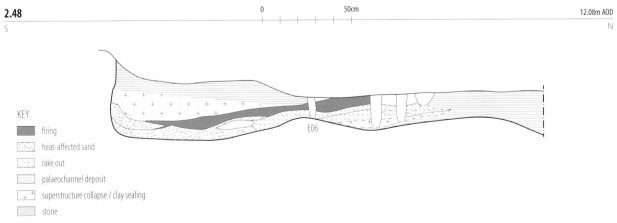

KEY

▨ firing

▨ heat-affected sand

▨ rake out

▨ palaeochannel deposit

▨ superstructure collapse / clay sealing

▨ stone

Illus 2.48 Section through oven E06

Illus 2.49 Group 12 ovens from south

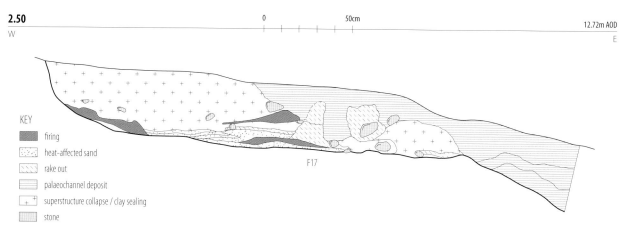

2.50   0   50cm   12.72m AOD

W   E

KEY
- firing
- heat-affected sand
- rake out
- palaeochannel deposit
- superstructure collapse / clay sealing
- stone

F17

Illus 2.50 Section through oven F17

Dates were obtained from F06 of cal AD 70–220 (SUERC-68084), F08 of cal AD 50–210 (SUERC-68085) and F13 of cal AD 10–210 (SUERC-68075). Two samples were dated from F19, from the same material. This returned two significantly different date ranges – 90 cal BC–cal AD 70 (SUERC-58498) and cal AD 70–230 (SUERC-68086). This would seem to provide evidence that material was being collected that had been lying around or items were burnt that were no longer needed but had been carried there by those building the ovens. This also suggests that there was no wide-scale programme of tree felling to fuel the ovens.

2.10.2.13 Group 13

The nine ovens of Group 13 were cut into the south-western bank of the later palaeochannel, of which five were investigated (Illus 2.44). Neither the northern or southern extent of the group could be defined within the limits of the excavation. There is a small 3.5 m gap between oven G01 and G02, which could suggest that G01 does not belong to the group but rather to Group 12, or to another unrecorded group lying between Groups 12 and 13. For the purposes of current analysis, G01 has been placed in Group 13.

All the ovens were roughly keyhole-shaped in plan. The ground sloped off relatively steeply into the palaeochannel,

Illus 2.51 Section through oven G07

so the tails of the ovens were not well defined. One of the excavated examples (G04) appeared to be unfired with no evidence of burning. Of the remaining four, most had evidence of a single firing, with G07 (Illus 2.51) showing two successive episodes. Where charcoal was analysed, there was a clear preference for gorse as fuel, with only small amounts of heather present, and no other species. Three ovens from the group were dated, with G01 dating to cal AD 10–130 (SUERC-58497), G7 to cal AD 30–210 (SUERC-68076) and G08 to cal AD 60–220 (SUERC-68080).

2.10.2.14 Ovens elsewhere at Milltimber

There were a handful of ovens identified that could not be assigned to any group. Ovens B05–B08 were located on either bank of the palaeochannel to the south of Groups 6 and 7 (see Illus 2.34). They were so distant from the groups that they could not reasonably be connected to either one. Each one also appeared to be sitting in isolation, rather than in a group. Oven B08 seemed similar in form to the flat oval ovens of Group 7, but it lay centrally to the palaeochannel.

In the vicinity of the Chalcolithic monument to the north of the concentrations of ovens, there was a ditch [2C-0083] running across the area from south-east to north-west (Illus 2.31). The function or date of the ditch is unknown, although it is presumed to post-date the monument. It certainly must have been in existence prior to the 1st century AD, as it had two ovens [2C-0106] and [2C-0111] cut into the south-western side of it, sitting adjacent to each other. Both were excavated but [2C-0111] was heavily truncated by a post-medieval furrow. Oven [2C-0106] contained a single firing, dated to 50 cal BC–cal AD 120 (SUERC-56395), contemporary with the other groups of ovens.

2.10.3 Bayesian analysis and dating the ovens
Derek Hamilton (SUERC)

Thirty-four of the radiocarbon dates from Milltimber were single-entity charcoal samples on either short-lived species or from twiggy roundwood. The samples were processed at the Scottish Universities Environmental Research Centre (SUERC), with the full methods provided in Dunbar *et al.* (2016). A Bayesian approach was taken

to interpreting the chronology of the Roman ovens. This enabled a move away from the specific individual calibrated radiocarbon dates and allowed exploration more generally of the date of activity across the site, as well as the duration of the use of the features. The Bayesian approach allowed the chronology of this activity to be estimated by using the absolute dating derived from the radiocarbon measurements and the relative dating information provided by the archaeological analysis. Bayliss (2009; 2015) and Hamilton & Krus (2017) provide informative backgrounds to the Bayesian chronology building methodology, while an in-depth report on the chronological modelling is provided in the digital appendices (Appendix 2.1.19).

The dating strategy was two-fold and aimed to provide dating evidence that allowed the investigation of the timing of the Roman camp presumed to be associated with the ovens as well as the longevity of that activity. While it was not necessary to date every single oven, the aim was to provide at least one date from each group, while ensuring a few groups spread across the site had three or more dates so that the internal consistency could be investigated. Furthermore, the spread of the ovens over more than 200 m and the fact that they formed clearly discrete spatial groups provided the opportunity – if the Roman presence did in fact extend over a protracted period – to investigate the temporality of the activity from a spatial point-of-view.

Three different chronological models were produced. The first model followed two basic assumptions: (1) the activity associated with the Roman ovens at Milltimber was relatively continuous, and so without any significant breaks, and (2) the samples selected from across the site are uniformly distributed from throughout the period of Roman activity. This primary model also allowed for the production of a single date estimate, assuming that the activity all occurred over a very short period of time (ie a single year). The alternative models investigated the possibility of spatio-temporal ordering of the dates, which might be expected if the area was visited periodically over time, which would result in temporal differentiation between the individual groups.

If the activity associated with the construction and use of the ovens at Milltimber did occur over a number of years, the model estimates that this activity began in 10 cal BC–cal AD 140 (95% probability; see Appendix 2.1.18, Fig 1), and probably in cal AD 60–130 (68% probability). The activity is estimated to have ended in cal AD 100–185 (95% probability), and probably in cal AD 115–165 (68% probability). The overall span of the activity modelled is 1–165 years (95% probability; see Appendix 2.1.18, Fig 2), and probably 1–85 years (68% probability).

If the activity associated with the ovens occurred over a very short period of time, then the single best date for the Roman camp at Milltimber is cal AD 40–170 (95% probability), and probably in the range cal AD 90–145 (68% probability).

In addition, the second model proposed looked at the apparent north-to-south progressive trend in terms of the dates of each group of ovens as a whole. This split the groups into independently modelled Northern (Groups 1–7) and Southern (Groups 8–13) groups. The model provides an 89% probability that the start of the Northern groups began before the start of the Southern groups, therefore confirming the overall apparent trend from north to south.

2.10.4 Local–Roman interaction in Deeside: a palynological debate

Whittington and Edwards (1993) advanced the hypothesis that the Roman advance into eastern Scotland was far from peaceful, and instead led to a significant agricultural collapse. Two pollen records used in that re-assessment were from Deeside in the Howe of Cromar, some 40 km west of Milltimber. One is Loch Davan (Edwards 1978), a large 36 ha lake with a large, regional pollen source area where 'dramatic regeneration of *Betula* and perhaps hazel woodland, and substantial declines in open land taxa and the levels of charcoal' ... indicate ... 'An apparently massive abandonment of farmed land' (Whittington & Edwards 1993, 18). This change occurs equidistant between two radiocarbon dates, bulk radiometric assays of 0.10 m thick sediment samples calibrated in 2016 to 352 BC–AD 315 and 95 BC–AD 399 respectively. Clearly a Roman age is possible but is not demonstrated. These vegetation changes cannot be dated to the Roman interlude: that much is clear. Their interpretation has been criticised (Tipping & Tisdall 2006) as has the seemingly catastrophic impact of a modest military intrusion (Hanson 2003, 214). The suggestion that increases in birch and hazel pollen represent the suppression of farming activities must be set against the evidence from radiocarbon dating for considerable soil in-washing (Edwards & Rowntree 1980; Edwards & Whittington 2001), which belies intensive agricultural activity in the catchments: with old, in-washed soil might come old, in-washed pollen and a distorted pollen record (Tipping 2010a, 58). A second issue is that the birch–hazel woodlands around these lochs show no evolution through time, no succession to trees like oak, which would have occurred on abandoned land. It may be that these two pollen records describe woodland held at an early successional stage by management, not abandonment.

2.11 Agricultural expansion at Milltimber: Early Historic enclosures and a kiln – 400–1000 AD

The Roman activity at Milltimber was tied to the late 1st century AD. Following this, there is no evidence that Romans returned to this camp during the campaigns in Scotland of the mid-2nd century or the 3rd century AD. The hiatus in activity lasts until the late 5th or more likely 6th century AD when low-level activity began to occur, mostly concentrated around the southern end of the Camphill Terrace, above the floodplain, and on the southern bank of the River Dee (Illus 2.52). The archaeological features indicate a landscape geared for agricultural production, which then largely continues through to the present day.

On the southern bank of the River Dee, a single isolated grain-drying kiln was excavated. This lay around 50 m to the south of the current line of the river. The kiln was an elongated oval in plan, aligned roughly east–west and measuring 0.9 m by 0.75 m. The eastern end of the kiln was lined with roughly shaped river cobbles (Illus 2.53). A later (probably 19th century) pit cut through the centre of the kiln, removing part of the stone lining. Across the base of the kiln was a charcoal-rich deposit that also contained abundant charred barley. No *in situ* burning was identified at either end of the kiln and it was not clear which would have functioned as the fire pit owing to the later disturbance. The barley was dated to cal AD 390–540 (SUERC-58187), placing the kiln in the Early Historic period, which in this region could be described as Pictish.

Of similar date, a pit was found in proximity to the earlier Chalcolithic monument. Pit [2C-0009] was broad and shallow pit, with a charcoal-rich basal fill that was dated to cal AD 430–600 (SUERC-59291). No other material was recovered from the feature to point to function.

On the southern edge of the Camphill Terrace, the partial remains of a sub-rectangular enclosure ([2B-0063]; Illus 2.52) were found. This measured roughly 60 m × 35 m, although the south-western edge of the enclosure had been removed by a modern sewer pipe and a field boundary of post-medieval date. The enclosure had an entrance around 4 m wide on its north-western side, slightly set back from the south-western corner of the enclosure. The enclosure ditch was shallow – it survived only to a maximum of 0.3 m and had very gently sloping sides – and would not have functioned as a useful enclosure for animals (Illus 2.54). A barley grain recovered from the fill of [2B-0063] was submitted for radiocarbon dating and returned a date in the range of cal AD 650–770 (SUERC-58507). Inside the enclosure in the north-western corner were eight post-holes defining a rectangular structure measuring 11 m × 3.3 m. Outside the enclosure to the south-west of the entrance were four further post-holes, which form a structure 3.3 m square. The two structures are relatively small, and no other evidence was recovered to indicate their function. Given the location in relation to the enclosure it is proposed the three are related.

Around 50 m to the north-east of the enclosure was an L-shaped arrangement of pits and post-holes (Illus 2.52). The features at the southern end of this arrangement were recorded as small post-holes, while the northern features were mostly formed of pits. The function of this arrangement of features was poorly understood, not helped by the lack of material found in either the pits or post-holes. Dates of cal AD 780–1010, cal AD 900–1020 and cal AD 900–1030 were recovered from charcoal from [2B-0109], [2B-0080] and [2B-0089] respectively (SUERC-68093, SUERC-68092 and SUERC-58506), indicating that they were contemporary at least. The overall size of the features

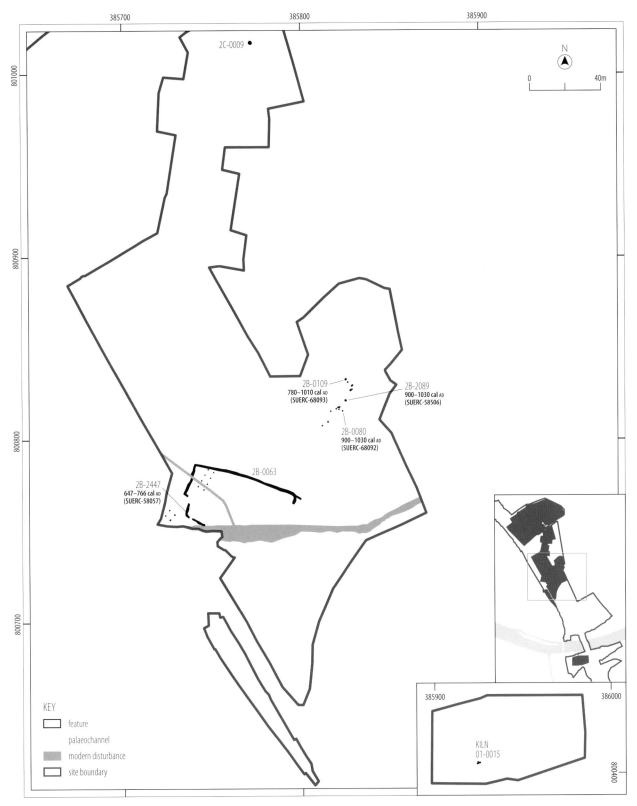

Illus 2.52 Plan of Early Historic Features

in plan (covering an area approximately 30 m × 15 m) seemed to imply it did not represent the remains of a building. The arrangement could represent a wind-break or part of a small enclosure, the pits marking out an area where a specific activity occurred, possibly relating to medieval agricultural practices.

A number of barley grains were recovered from the fills of three pits [2B-0105], [2B-0112] and [2B-0133], the

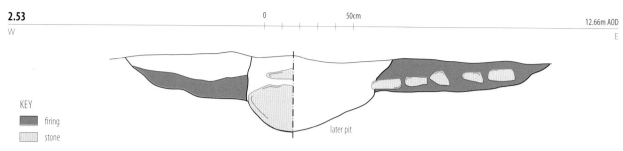

Illus 2.53 Section through kiln [01–0015] on the south side of the River Dee

Illus 2.54 View of Early Historic enclosure from north during topsoil stripping

majority of identified grain being hulled barley (*Hordeum vulgare*), providing further evidence of farming in this area. It seems these agricultural activities continued into the post-medieval period as evidenced by the frequent rig and furrow cultivation that truncated the Palaeolithic and Mesolithic lithic spread at the north of the site, and by the field systems that criss-cross the southern extent of the Maryculter Terrace and the palaeochannels.

Further formalisation of this landscape as one of enclosure is indicated by the construction of a metalled road cutting across the excavation area from north-west to south-east, which was certainly in place by the mid-18th century but may have been built in the 15th or 16th centuries. Cartographic representations from the 18th century onward shows how the landscape along this part

of the Dee has been enclosed and 'improved' to form neat fields, roads and associated farms.

2.12 Undated features

The sheer quantity of features recorded across Milltimber meant it would not be possible to date all the features present, even with a robust radiocarbon dating programme. Phasing many of the features was either reliant on the recovery of datable artefactual material or on establishing that features were identifiably part of a larger group or cluster, one of which could be dated. Where possible, groups were dated using radiocarbon determinations; however, in some cases the sterile fills meant even this was not possible.

Two linear ditches, neither of which provided any datable material, represent the most notable consequence of this problem (although undated they are shown on Illus 2.31). A 15 m long section of east to west aligned ditch [AMA09–2178] was recorded at the base of the Lochton Formation gravels (not shown in plan). The lower fills of this ditch were gravel rich and slumped to the steeper south side, indicating the potential for a bank on this side. Unfortunately, not enough of the ditch survived to enable it to be properly defined. A second undated section of ditch [2C-0083], not dissimilar to ditch [AMA09–2178] in width and depth, ran across the middle of the Chalcolithic timber settling, aligned roughly north-west to south-east. It was 1.3 m wide and up to 0.6 m deep, with variable steep to gradual sloping sides. The fills were quite variable with less evidence of slumped material, although the lower fills on the whole included frequent poorly sorted stone inclusions. As with ditch [2B-2075] the upper fill had been partially truncated by two Roman ovens, indicating the ditch must pre-date the 1st century AD. In places the profile of the ditch was like that of [AMA09–2178] and potentially both could have formed two sides of a large enclosure based on their alignments, although this was tenuous. A number of trial trenches were excavated to the south of the mitigation area in order to identify the extent of this ditch, but no further evidence of the feature was identified.

2.13 Environmental synthesis

Tim Holden and Angela Walker

2.13.1 Mesolithic and Neolithic

The Mesolithic features were of interest because sites of this period are often short-lived, and linear infrastructure projects such as this offer a rare opportunity to identify and investigate them. Archaeological remains encountered comprised pits, including those with associated lithic assemblages, hearths and spreads of charred material.

We know from other Mesolithic sites (eg Bishop *et al.* 2013, 9; Zvelebil 1994, 35) hazel nutshell and wood charcoal are commonly recovered and Milltimber was no exception. Hazel nuts were clearly an important resource in this and later periods but many researchers (eg Mason in prep; Appendix 2.1.11) also recognise that the survival properties of hazel, particularly as a result of charring, significantly exceeds that of other plant foods that are likely to have made an important contribution to the Mesolithic diet. On the Scottish coast Mesolithic middens containing bone and shell occasionally survive (eg Mithen *et al.* 2001), but elsewhere the archaeological evidence provides little evidence for Mesolithic subsistence. With this absence of evidence one of the few sources left to us is the ethnographic record and a study of more recent hunter-gather groups, particularly those using similar resources and in broadly analogous environments should provide

subsistence models that can be tested. These suggest that a wide diversity of plant foods including tubers/roots/nuts/leaves would have been utilised and there is no reason to believe that hunter-gatherers in these isles would be any different. Unfortunately, these foods tend to leave very little evidence in the archaeological record (eg Bishop *et al.* 2013, 53), and with this in mind sorting of the remains from sample processing was done with particular attention paid to fragments that could represent traces of starchy plant tissues (parenchyma) that on occasion survive in early archaeological assemblages (eg Holden *et al.* 1995). In this instance, nothing along these lines was recovered and, like the extremely sparse and fragmentary bone remains, it is important to note that this absence was not for want of looking.

Hazel nutshell was recovered from both the Neolithic and Mesolithic contexts, illustrating both hazel's continuing importance in the environment and its importance as a collected food resource. There is no evidence for the extensive or repeated processing of hazel nuts that has been seen elsewhere in Scotland (eg Mithen *et al.* 2001, 225) but it was clearly a significant resource. The use of hazel has also been identified at Standingstones and a more detailed discussion of this has been undertaken there (see 4.6).

Cereal grain was recovered from a range of Neolithic features, including hearths and pits. Naked barley was present in hearth [2D-1137] and pits [AMA09–2080] and [AMA09–2058]. Barley has been recorded from other Neolithic sites in Scotland (Greig 1991, 300) and appears to have been an important crop in that period (McLaren 2000, 91), having previously been found at a number of sites in Aberdeenshire including Crathes, Warren Field (Lancaster 2009), where it was the main cereal along with emmer. Both naked barley and emmer were also found in Neolithic deposits from excavations at Garthdee Road and Balbridie (Fairweather & Ralston 1993).

Occasional 'weed' seeds, primarily from the Neolithic deposits, were also identified and included cleavers (*Galium aparine*), corn spurrey (*Spergula arvensis*), chickweed (*Stellaria media*), fat hen sp (*Chenopodium* sp), and knotgrass (*Polygonum aviculare*). These species are characteristic of open ground and nitrogen-rich soils that would be typical of agricultural fields or human settlement of any permanence.

The number of prehistoric features containing organic remains is low and therefore any analysis of the charcoal may not be representative of the environment as a whole. A number of observations, however, may add to the bigger picture. In general, the species present are in keeping with the vegetation suggested in pollen analyses undertaken at Nethermills (Ewan 1981). The Mesolithic charcoal assemblage was principally hazel and birch with rarer occurrences of willow, gorse/broom and hazel. Although the sample size was small only one fragment of oak was recovered. Whether this was a function of ease of collection (because of the size of the trees or lack of dead wood) or local availability of oak trees is uncertain. By contrast the Neolithic–Chalcolithic charcoal assemblages was characterised by hazel and oak and the Neolithic/Chalcolithic pollen by oak with low occurrences of gorse/broom.

2.13.2 Roman ovens

The environmental evidence in the Roman period derives primarily from a number of ovens containing layers of spent fuel. These are very similar in character to those excavated at the Roman Camp at Kintore, Aberdeenshire (Cook & Dunbar 2008) and one of the key questions about this site was the way that the ovens were used. The archaeobotanical evidence adds some detail to this discussion.

Very few grains were recovered from the ovens, with the largest concentrations from oven B05. The majority of grain recovered was hulled barley, with occasional oat grains (*Avena* sp) and very rare bread wheat (*Triticum aestivum*). It seems very likely that the bread wheat had been imported from further south, ie brought with the Romans in the form of grain. The barley and oats could either represent local crops 'acquired' by the Romans or intrusive material from later periods. This paucity of cereal grain noted here was also seen at nearby Kintore Roman Camp (Cook & Dunbar 2008) and both sites support suggestions that the ovens were to make bread, with grains occasionally becoming charred incidentally. The presence of even small amounts of whole grain does at least suggest that some of the cereal was brought to site as whole grain rather than meal.

The wood charcoal assemblage indicates the utilisation of a wide range of species and wood types ranging from small twigs to more substantial branch and trunk wood and generally supports the character of local environment suggested from other sources (Timpany 2012c; Tipping 1994). The charcoal shows trees such as birch, hazel and oak as present with heather, and broom/gorse more representative of open ground. Fifty-seven samples were analysed in some detail in the hope that the species utilised could help identify duration of occupation as, for example, soldiers were forced to forage wider for fire wood or utilise larger trees over time (Illus 2.55 and 2.56). However, interpretation of archaeological wood charcoal is notoriously difficult because it is not possible to know whether collection was made on a minimum effort basis or through deliberate selection and therefore whether the species composition is a direct reflection of the local environment. At a crude level however, the ovens in Groups 1–4, 6 and 11–13 appear to contain more twiggy material (typically heather, gorse, and small diameter birch and hazel) while those in Groups 7, 8 and 10 contained more oak and larger diameter branches of birch and alder. Potentially the twiggy material would have been easier to collect as long as it was growing locally so these ovens could represent the earliest on site, ie those made by the first soldiers to arrive or during the first days of settlement.

This fits with the evidence indicated by the Bayesian analysis (see 2.10.3 above).

2.13.3 Medieval

A number of barley grains was recovered from the fills of three pits [2B-0105], [2B-0112] and [2B-0133] (Illus 2.52, pits to north-east of enclosure [2B-0063]). Although originally thought to be Neolithic they have since been reassigned to the medieval period on the basis of radiocarbon dating of associated features. The majority of identified grain was hulled barley (*Hordeum vulgare*) and while this cereal is known from the Neolithic period it is not common (Fairweather & Ralston 1993, 318; Boyd 1988, 104) and is far more typical of later periods. In this case the archaeobotanical evidence supports the archaeological phasing of the features.

2.14 Material synthesis

Julie Lochrie

2.14.1 The pottery

The assemblage comprises 415 sherds and 289 fragments belonging to an estimated 46 vessels, albeit a very small percentage of each actually remains. It is likely that some of the Early Neolithic sherds found in close proximity may belong to the same vessels, but they do not conjoin. As the Early Neolithic fabrics and surface treatment are so homogeneous it has proved difficult to directly attribute them to each other unless they refit.

The pottery clusters into three broad periods: Early Neolithic, Middle Neolithic and Chalcolithic. The vast majority of these, at least 30 of the 46 vessels, are Early Neolithic in date. Nine are Middle Neolithic, two are Chalcolithic and five cannot be assigned a date. A substantial suite of radiocarbon dates provides a chronological backdrop to the pottery assemblage. There are 11 Early Neolithic dates from features that cluster within a tight date bracket of c3970–3700 BC (see Table 2.01). Three Middle Neolithic dates spanning c3500 to 3090 BC indicate two or three intermittent periods of activity, but this chronological detail cannot be seen in the pottery assemblage. Finally, the Chalcolithic pottery is associated with three overlapping dates bracketed to 2470–2200 BC.

2.14.1.1 Context, condition and deposition

The Milltimber site covers a large area between the river and valley sides and a summary of the locations of pottery retrieval is given in Table 2.04. The circumstances of discovery can be broadly summarised by three main scenarios. The first of these is where a substantial quantity from a single vessel was found in a single feature eg [2C-0050] and [AMA09–2058]. The second is where few sherds from a small number of vessels were found within cut features and the third is where few sherds of

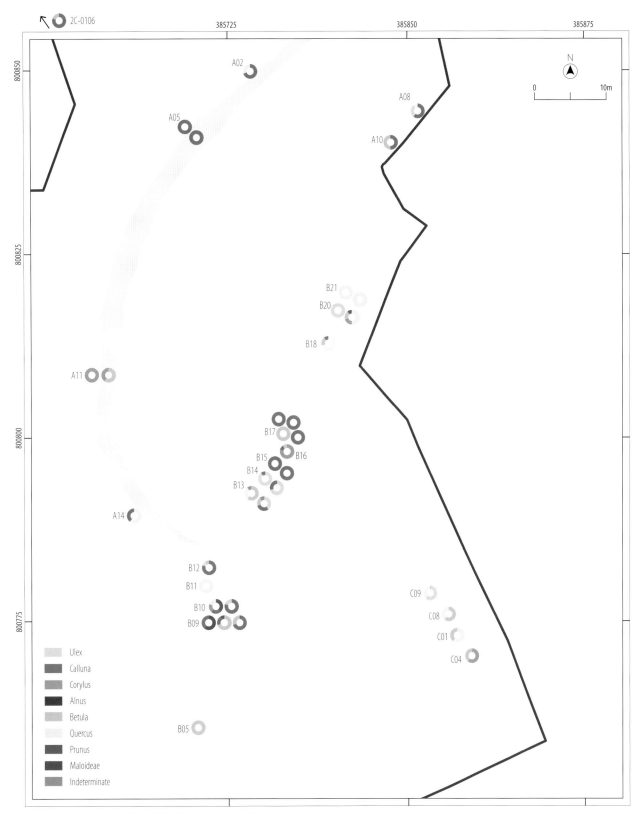

Illus 2.55 Plan of the wood charcoal assemblage utilisation in the Group 1–7 ovens

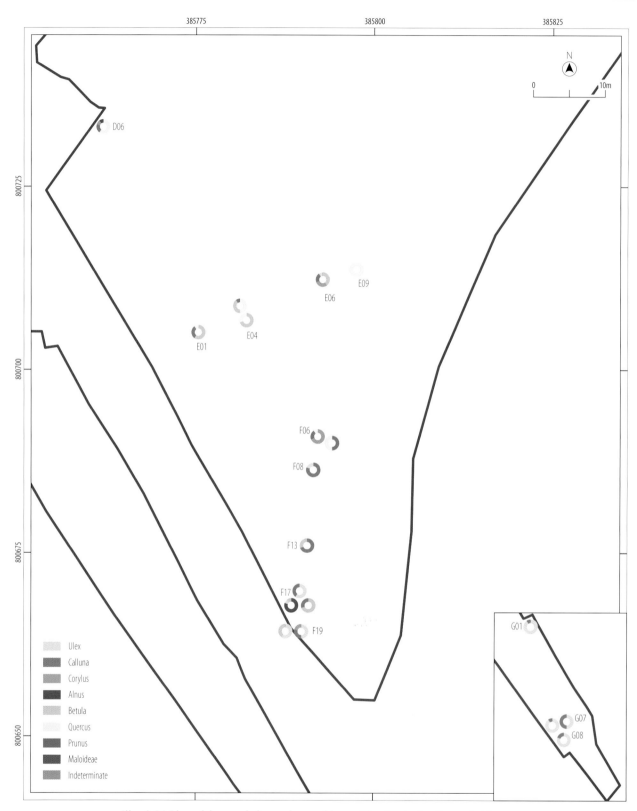

Illus 2.56 Plan of the wood charcoal assemblage utilisation in the Group 8–13 ovens

Table 2.04 Milltimber vessel summary

Date of pottery	Area	Feature	Context	Vessel no	Vessel qty	Sherd count
Early Neolithic		Pit [2B-2550]	2B-2551, 2B-2552	02-V01	1	4
	North	[2D-1012]	2D-1013	02-V23	1	1
	North	Upper deposit of Mesolithic pit [2D-1127]	2D-1093	02-V25 to 02-V26	2	9
	North	[2D-1399]	2D-1439	02-V31	1	2
	North	[2D-1403]	2D-1404	02-V29	1	2
	Post alignment	Post-hole [2D-1433]	2D-1435	02-V30	1	1 + 2 fragments
	North	Upper deposit in Mesolithic pit [2D-1714]	2D-1786	02-V37 to 02-V39	3	5
	North	Hearth [2D-1895]	2D-1901	02-V40	1	100
	Neolithic structure	Pit [2D-1927]	2D-1928	02-V41 to 02-V42	2	4
	Zones 1–5	Spread (2D-1939)	2D-1939	02-V06 to 02-V22	17	45 + 45 fragments
Middle Neolithic	North	Hearth [2D-1822]	2D-1751	02-V34 to 02-V36S	3	56 + 111 fragments
	North	Pit [AMA09-2058]	AMA09-2059	02-V43 and 02-V45	2	75 + 119 fragments
Chalcolithic	Timber setting	Post-hole [2C-0050]	2C-0134	02-V05	1	Complete vessel
	Timber setting	Pit [2C-0075]	2C-0076	02-V04	1	3
Undated	–	Pit [2B-0109]	2B-0110	02-V02	1	1
	Palaeochannel	[2B-2650]	2B-2656	02-V03	1	5
	North	Pit [2D-1086]	2D-1087	02-V24	1	68
	North	Hearth [2D-1210]	2D-1214	02-V28	1	14
	North	Hearth [2D-1137]	2D-1149, 2D-1150	02-V27	1	6
	Post alignment	Post-hole [2D-1495]	2D-1509	02-V32	1	5 fragments
	North	Pit 2D-1529	2D-1590	02-V33	1	1 fragment
	North	Pit AMA09-2080	AMA09-2081	02-V44	1	1 + 1 fragment
	North	Pit [AMA09-2089]	AMA09-2090	02-V46	1	13 + 6 fragments

up to 17 vessels was retrieved from across a large spread of surface material.

All pottery from the site, excepting 02-V05 and 02-V45, is abraded to some degree. The sherds are all very small; most are less than 40 cm and indicate highly fragmented vessels. They are mostly body sherds, which is unsurprising given the level of fragmentation. There are also examples of laminar breaks where the sherds have either split down the middle or lost their surface. Other notable breakage is present on 02-V40 where the vessel has broken along its coil joins. Clearly burnt examples

were infrequent, only present on the vessels from 02-V03, 02-V04 and 02-V46 which were soft, delicate and completely oxidised.

The vessels are summarised in Table 2.04, based on the dating characteristics of the material. It should be noted that some of the 'undated' material comes from features that have been radiocarbon dated to a specific period.

As a strong contrast to the rest of the assemblage, a complete and unbroken pot, 02-V05, was retrieved from post-hole [2C-0050]. It dates to the Chalcolithic and is one of two vessels of this date found on site. The pot was lying on its side and the weight of the soil has flattened it slightly to be more oval-shaped in plan; other than this it is in near perfect condition. It was found in the base of a deep post-hole and as difficult as it is to believe that this fine-walled pot would have survived under such pressure, the stratigraphic sequence indicates the post rotted *in situ*, meaning the pot was deposited before the post. The scenario implies that someone carefully reached in and laid it into the base of the feature; had it been tossed in it would certainly have smashed. The survival of the pot must relate to exactly how the post was lying, as thin-walled beakers found in cists are typically crushed (eg at Beechwood Park the beaker was crushed with only 0.3 m on top, Sheridan & Hammersmith 2006; the beaker from West Torbreck was crushed within a cist of 0.51 m depth, Ballin Smith 2014).

No other unbroken vessels were found but at least 25% of an Early Neolithic bowl, 02-V40, was recovered from the top of pit [2D-1895] and 80% of a Middle Neolithic bowl, 02-V45, was found in pit [AMA09–2058]. The sherds from 02-V40 are larger than most of those found on site and large sections of profile conjoin. The breaks on this vessel are mostly along the coil joins rather than an irregular breakage pattern through impact. The combination of these characteristics indicates it fragmented *in situ* and a large section of the vessel, if not all of it, was originally deposited. Unlike 02-V05, this vessel was in the uppermost deposits of the feature and therefore not as protected.

The sherds from 02-V45 are a little different as they have clearly been broken through impact. Of the 20% of the vessel that is missing, 10% is likely to be a recent loss, indicated by fresh breaks. The other broken edges are unabraded and appear to have occurred in antiquity, within the pit or shortly before deposition. It is certain this vessel was largely intact and complete upon deposition, with perhaps a small break to the rim.

The small quantities of pottery spread across a mixture of features appear to be typical of domestic activity. They are low in quantity, abraded and usually small body sherds. Their likeliest functional explanation is that they derive from domestic refuse and were either deliberately dumped into open features or incidentally accumulated within open or partially open features over time. The pottery found in the spread could derive from the same domestic activity, being the result of either general discard on the ground or having been displaced from nearby Neolithic features ploughed out by more recent agricultural practices.

2.14.1.2 Form, fabric, manufacture and function

EARLY NEOLITHIC – 4200–3700 BC

Almost all the Early Neolithic pottery belongs to the Carinated Bowl tradition, which spans c3950 BC–3650 BC. These are finely burnished, thin-walled vessels, bipartite in form with an everted neck and carination leading to a round base. The small portions of the vessels that survive at Milltimber make it impossible to reconstruct

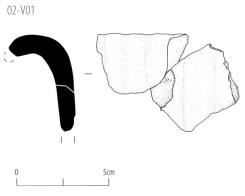

02-V01

Illus 2.57 Vessel 02-V01

and discuss their precise form. Nine rim sherds survive; all are simple, rounded and everted. Vessel 01-V040 has a rim that is slightly rolled over to create a small lip, but this varies around the circumference, sometimes appearing rolled and other times not. All the Carinated Bowl pottery has been given some form of surface treatment, almost exclusively in the form of burnishing and usually carried out on both the interior and exterior surfaces. The fabric of all the Neolithic pottery is sandy with a fine micaceous shimmer. They mostly contain sub-rounded to sub-angular quartz inclusions, small to large in size and are always well distributed through the vessel and never more than moderate in frequency. They have been well fired and are of an even thickness; usually the fabric looks mid-brown and is reduced throughout.

While all the other pottery is very traditional in form, two rim sherds of Vessel 02-V01 from pit [2B-2550] are from a fluted Carinated Bowl of Henshall's north-eastern style (CBNE; Illus 2.57). These have been found in the north-east at many sites, including Blackdog and Wester Hatton (Chapter 6), Garthdee Road (Murray & Murray 2014), Port Elphinstone (Lochrie 2013), Westgate, Inverurie (Lochrie 2010a), Warren Field (Sheridan 2009) and Deer's Den (Alexander 2000). The example at Port Elphinstone was associated with dates of 3707–3636 cal BC (SUERC-42979), which is much later than some other dates for fluted CBNE, showing it was a long-lived type (Murray & Murray 2013).

Another example is more substantial in size (Vessel 02-V40; Illus 2.58) and allows closer analysis of both overall form and how it was made. It is a traditional Carinated Bowl, meaning it is open, everted and bipartite with a rounded base and no decoration. It has a rolled rim which begins at 4.5 mm thickness, increasing to 6 mm before thinning dramatically to 3.5 mm before a sharply angled carination. The base is hemispherical but a little flattened right at the very base. The burnishing has left a black leathery effect on the exterior, which has worn variably across the vessel. Clay joins on the vessel run along a slight diagonal rather than horizontal, which may suggest the use of a coil rather than slabs or rings but without the remainder of the vessel it is not certain.

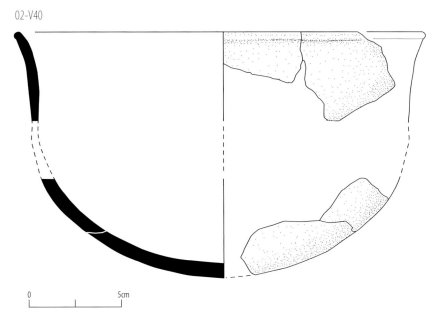

Illus 2.58 Vessel 02-V40

Overall, the Early Neolithic vessels impress with the talent and skill used to create them. The fabrics are hard, smooth and thin with a change in angle. The defining characteristic when identifying Carinated Bowl pottery at Milltimber is undoubtedly the surface treatment and thin walls. Evidence from two vessels on site may give further clues to the manufacture of these vessels. Vessels 02-V39 and 02-V40 both show coil joins that are practically flat but with almost undiscernible short sharp lips along the edge. The horizontal flat join means the clay has not bonded together well and left a point of weakness, along which the coils have later become detached. This is not an uncommon feature on this pottery; it has also been noted at Kirkton of Fetteresso (Lochrie 2016) and Westgate, Inverurie (Lochrie 2010a). This seemingly points towards little manipulation of the clay at the joins, perhaps to maintain the uniform wall thickness. If the walls were heavily manipulated, stretching the clay at these points would more likely result in concave/convex or oblique joins. Another method that may have been used to maintain the thin and even walls would be by cutting or slicing away parts of the surface, which would also account for the weak joins. Slicing the walls for uniform thickness would have left cut marks on the surface, perhaps explaining why much care was subsequently taken to perfect the surface by smoothing and burnishing; unfortunately, this treatment removes any evidence of slicing. On 02-V39 the lip at the very edge of the sherd could have been created by slicing off part of the surface where at one time a larger lip was holding together the clay.

MIDDLE NEOLITHIC – 3500–3100 BC

The Middle Neolithic pottery includes six vessels, 02-V34 to 02-V36, 02-V43, 02-V45 and 02-V46. They all belong to the Impressed Ware tradition, a long-lived type of pottery

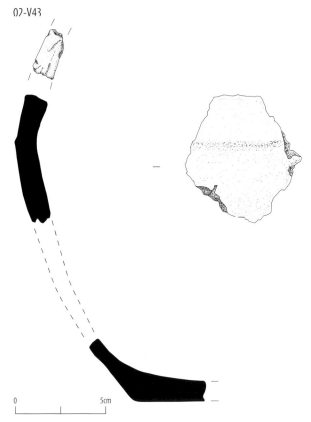

Illus 2.59 Vessel 02-V45

in use between c3500 BC and 2900 BC (Kinbeachie, 3500–2920 BC, MacSween 2001, table 1, 63; Kintore, 3530–3340 BC, MacSween 2008, 181; Meadowend Farm, 3350–3000/2900 BC, Jones *et al.* 2018).

Vessel 02-V45 from pit [AMA09–2058] comprises an almost complete vessel (Illus 2.59) with a rim diameter

02-V45

02-V034

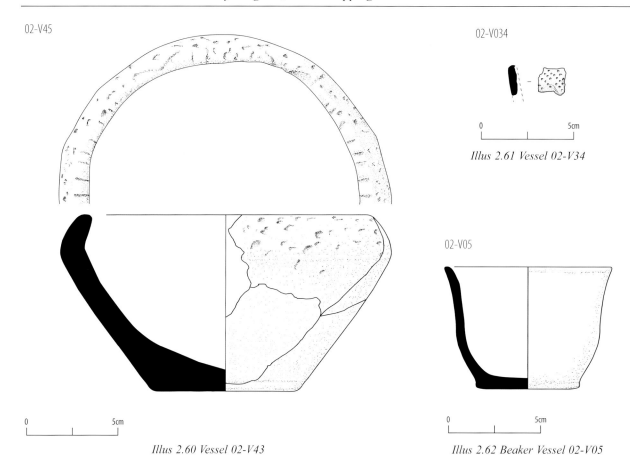

0   5cm

Illus 2.61 Vessel 02-V34

02-V05

0   5cm

Illus 2.60 Vessel 02-V43

Illus 2.62 Beaker Vessel 02-V05

of 135 mm, a carination diameter of 150 mm and a base diameter of 50 mm. The form is bipartite with a closed collar-like rim decorated with rows of impressions. The very edge of the rim has vertical impressions or incisions, likely done with a small stick or dry grass, which has left vertical striations in the impressions. The point of the same tool could have created the impressions on the collar, and its length could have created the vertical lines around the lip of the rim. The shape of the vessel, especially the collar, is very proto-Unstan in form. Proto-Unstan vessels from Oldmeldrum are dated to 3370–3090 cal BC but it is assumed these had round bases (Johnson 2010, 20) and not the flat base seen on the Milltimber vessel. Pots with decorated collars and trunconic forms with flat bases are also part of the wider Impressed Ware repertoire. They were present at Meadowend Farm, Clackmannanshire, where they were radiocarbon dated to c3350–3000/2900 cal BC (Jones *et al.* 2018) and Deer's Den where they dated between c3300 and 3000 (3130–2910 cal BC, OxA-8177 and 3360–3030 cal BC, OxA-8176, Alexander 2000, 64). The Meadowend Farm vessels are slightly more trunconic in shape and the collars slightly more pronounced than the Milltimber vessel but the basic stylistic features are the same. Both proto-Unstan and Impressed Ware vessels date to the latter few hundred years of the fourth millennium BC and this certainly fits the Milltimber vessel. The closest specific comparatives for this vessel include those from Culduthel, Inverness (P35, Sheridan forthcoming) and from Deer's Den, Aberdeenshire (P49, P51 and P62, Alexander 2000, 45).

A second vessel (02-V43) from the same pit [AMA09–2058] includes sherds from a flat-based, bipartite pot (Illus 2.60) with an upright, gently inturned, internally bevelled rim. The rim of this vessel also has linear incised decoration positioned directly upon the bevel. Too small a portion survives to discern the true pattern, but they appear to be located as pairs running parallel to the interior and exterior edges.

Hearth [2D-1137] included small quantities of three vessels, 02-V34 to 02-V36. Among these are a simple gently curving squared rim (02-V035), a single rounded upright rim (02-V36) and five sherds decorated with diagonal lines of small, sub-rectangular dot-impressions, which could be from a comb (02-V034; Illus 2.61). At Wester Hatton similar comb impressions were present on Vessel 06-V12 (see 6.10.1.2). Vessel 02-V035 and 02-V034 belong to the Middle Neolithic but the single rounded sherd 02-V36 is burnished and may be residual from an Early to Middle Neolithic uncarinated cup.

CHALCOLITHIC – 2500–2200 BC

The pottery found in association with the timber setting includes two vessels, 02-V04 and 02-V05, both Beaker pottery. Vessel 02-V05 is complete and unbroken, comprising a small, squat, well-finished, low-bellied Beaker (Illus 2.62) with an everted, gently rounded rim. It stands at 75 mm tall and has an estimated diameter of 100–110 mm. This vessel is well made with thin, even walls and well finished, with evidence for smoothing/burnishing. There are long facets located around the belly that may indicate where the clay was joined together or where tools were used to aid shaping and smoothing. Charcoal from features that make up the timber monument have been radiocarbon dated to between 2470 and 2200 cal BC (SUERC-54055, SUERC-58516, SUERC-58517), which matches the date range expected for this vessel form. Other sites within the Aberdeenshire area with similar early Chalcolithic dates include the cremation complex at Midmill (with four dates ranging between 2470–2060 cal BC, Lochrie 2010b) and the cist at Slap (3803 ± 35 uncal bp; Sheridan 2007).

Undecorated Beakers are not very common in Scotland but have been found in the north-east at Slap, Aberdeenshire (Ledingham 1874), Boghead, Moray (Burl 1984), West Torbreck, Invernesshire (Ballin Smith 2014) and Beechwood Park, Invernesshire (Sheridan & Hammersmith 2006), all in burial contexts. Of these, the Slap Beaker would appear to be closest in profile and dimensions to the Milltimber Beaker, although at 150 mm it is twice as tall. However, at Ascoilemore (Davidson 1939–40) a small vessel identified at the time as a food vessel urn looks almost identical to the Milltimber Beaker. Its dimensions (120 mm height, 150 mm rim diameter and 70 mm base diameter) are also closer than any other examples available. As an antiquarian discovery it has not been subject to modern analysis so little information is currently available on either the pottery or the site.

The Beaker sherds comprising 02-V04 from pit [2C-0075] are much burnt and extremely delicate. The sherds join to form part of the everted neck and rim and there are clear horizontal lines covering the exterior. Unfortunately, it has not been possible to discern how the decoration was created, but based on the radiocarbon dates retrieved from site and the early form of the other Beaker they are most probably 'all over cord' impressions (Needham 2005).

UNDATED

A group of 108 sherds and 13 fragments belonging to up to nine vessels could not be identified by type; these are summarised in Table 2.04. Five fragments, representing vessel 02-V32, from [2D-1495] are associated with an Early Neolithic date, 3940–3710 cal BC (SUERC-58193). Two vessels are associated with Middle Neolithic dates and may belong in this category. Vessel 02-V27 is represented by six undiagnostic, greatly abraded, small body sherds and two fragments and associated with a radiocarbon date of 3360–3100 cal BC (SUERC-58022). Vessel 02-V33 is represented by a single fragment that is associated with charcoal radiocarbon dated to 3510–3360 cal BC (SUERC-58604)

Two further vessels were associated with radiocarbon dated material. The burnt sherds comprising 02-V46 from [AMA09-2089] are associated with an Early to Middle Iron Age date of 360–110 cal BC (SUERC-74402). This date is thought to relate to intrusive material as the pit also contained fragments of a saddle quern, although the quern fragments could quite easily be of Iron Age date.

The pottery from [2B-0110] is associated with a date of cal AD 780–1010 (SUERC-68093).

2.14.2 The lithic assemblage
Torben Bjarke Ballin, with microwear analysis contributions from Karen Hardy and synthesis by Julie Lochrie

To the south of the large pits and at the northern extent of the Camphill Terrace, a truncated and sporadic spread of soil material was present (see Illus 2.18) within which a large lithic assemblage was identified. Due to the differential survival of the undisturbed sediments it is unclear if the lithic distribution in this spread reflects activity limits or simply survival. The sediments were deposited too early for the presence of the lithics to be explained simply by burial under accumulating sediment deposits. It is equally implausible that they were transported from elsewhere in the Late Glacial Period to be deposited as part of the sediment. Therefore, it must be assumed that the lithics were incorporated into the soil profile at a later date, long after the deposition of the sediment.

Lithics, when deposited on the surface of a biologically active nutrient-rich soil (as would have existed on the site in the early to mid-Holocene) will become buried by the action of surface-casting earthworms and other invertebrates. This will lead to progressively deeper burial until the fragments reach the base of the biologically active layer. This is essentially a matter of vertical movement with some potential for a little localised horizontal movement. The prehistoric ground surface would have been close to the present-day ground surface and this suggests burial to a depth of 0.4–0.5 m. While the spatial distribution of the flint may be essentially intact, it must be recognised that vertical integration could have led to temporal mixing of material.

The biological mixing would have ended with acidification of the soil, which would also have led to the formation of a podzol soil horizon. The evolution of nutrient-rich 'brown' soil profiles to nutrient-poor podzols is widely recognised in freely draining soils of eastern Scotland and is sometimes explained as a consequence of the loss of tree cover from the Neolithic period onwards. As the lithics have been detected in the remains of the lower podzolic horizon, not the base of a biologically active topsoil, it indicates a relatively early date for the assemblage.

It is concluded that the lithic assemblage was originally deposited on the surface of the soil profile, more or less directly above the locations where it occurs today. If this interpretation is correct, it follows that no actual prehistoric ground surface survives, nor do any features directly associated with the human activity that led to deposition of the lithics. However, the spatial distribution of the flint will still reflect the pattern of deposition on that original land surface.

The *in situ* character of the assemblage is supported by refits from several grids (see 2.14.2.3 below). Rig and furrow cultivation identified when the site was stripped also appears to have had some level of impact on the archaeology held within the podzol sediment and the artefacts within (see Illus 2.06). The furrows seem to correlate to areas where fewer lithics were retrieved.

In total, 11,565 lithic artefacts were recovered and analysed (Appendix 2.2.8; Table 2.05); these are listed in Table 2.06. The analysis focused on the lithics from the scatter as the quantity and presence of *in situ* spreads of material provided the highest potential to understand activities taking place. This revealed that the majority of the lithics date to the Mesolithic, with a small but notable sub-assemblage of Late Upper Palaeolithic date, and handfuls of Early and Middle Neolithic material. Debitage forms 94% of the assemblage, with 1% cores and 5% tools.

The Late Upper Palaeolithic presence at Milltimber was recognised exclusively from the lithic assemblage and located primarily from the flint scatter but with individual artefacts also present elsewhere on site. A date range of 13,000–10,000 BC is suggested as defining this period. The Scottish Late Upper Palaeolithic can be aligned with contemporary industries on the north-west European mainland (listed earliest to latest: the Hamburgian, Federmesser-gruppen, and the Ahrensburgian techno-complexes; Ballin 2016a; Ballin & Bjerck 2016; Brooks *et al.* 2012; Sturt *et al.* 2013).

Late Upper Palaeolithic pieces found at Milltimber include large blades from opposed-platform cores, crested blades, platform rejuvenated flakes and a small number of blades and scrapers. It is not possible on the basis of the recovered fragments to narrow the date down to a specific industry or material culture. During the Mesolithic there is a transition in Britain from broad to narrow microliths. On the basis of analysis of microliths from Cramond, Edinburgh, and the radiocarbon dates relating to transition, it is suggested that the switch took place at approximately 8500 BC (Saville 2008).

Use-wear analysis has been carried out on a selection of artefacts from Milltimber and Standingstones; the results have been referenced here and a comparison of all the results is presented in Chapter 4. The following is a synthesis of the full lithics analysis report, which is available online (Appendix 2.2.25). It presents a basic outline of the methodology used for analysis, the raw materials used, the zones identified and the overall strategies for future research that could be learnt from analysing all material from each period.

2.14.2.1 Methodology

The lithics derive from both the fills of features and from the 1 m² gridded scatter (Illus 2.19). Based on the spread and quantity of lithic pieces within these grid squares it was possible to divide this scatter into five discrete 'zones' of activity (Zones 1–5). It was thought that the individual zones might represent individual visits to the site. To allow this hypothesis to be tested each zone was investigated separately. Four further zones were identified (north, east,

south and west) that represent the four areas adjacent to each side of the main flint scatter. These further zones are defined by concentrations of flint within various features. An additional Zone (Structure east) dealt with the only evidence of prehistoric occupation.

Owing to the high artefact numbers and the complexities of the sites the following recording principles were followed:

SPATIAL ANALYSIS

The internal chronology of the two numerically richest and most complex scatters, Zones 4 and 5, was tested by the application of intra-site spatial analysis, and spatial analysis was also applied to gauge prehistoric site activities. There are numerous different forms of spatial analysis available (Cziesla *et al.* 1990), but as far as analysis of small hunter-gatherer sites is concerned, the present writer favours:

1. the use of contour maps for the presentation of distributions of artefact types present in large numbers;
2. dot-mapping for the presentation of distributions of artefact types present in smaller numbers; and
3. the application of a Binfordian approach and terminology in terms of the interpretation of the distribution patterns (Binford 1983).

The most important elements of the Binfordian approach are:

1. the distinction between drop-zones (small pieces of waste 'dropped' and left where they were produced) and toss-zones (larger pieces 'tossed' into the site periphery immediately after production to avoid future problems to traffic across the site);
2. the distinction between two different site maintenance strategies, preventive maintenance (tossing) and post hoc maintenance (the collection and removal of larger pieces of waste to middens some time after production).

Table 2.05 Lithics recording principles

Type	Recording
Blades/Microblade	Measured length, width and thickness
Blade/Microblade fragments	Measured width
Flakes	Not measured
Chips	Not measured
Indeterminate piece	Not measured
Cores	Measured length, width and thickness
Core fragments	Greatest dimension only
Tools and core preparation pieces	Measured length, width and thickness
Microliths	Measured length, width and thickness, to a decimal point
Microlith fragments	Measured width, to a decimal point

Table 2.06 Full assemblage list by artefact type and zone location

Artefact	Zone 1	Zone 2	Zone 3	Zone 4	Zone 4/5	Zone 5	Neolithic Structure	North	East	West	South	Unstratified	Total
Debitage													
Chips	82	100	427	1,263	12	2,285	94	83	30	79		262	4608
Flakes	100	63	191	1,048	126	1,779	46	68	11	44	2	198	3619
Blades	43	12	45	428	50	653	11	28	1	9		64	1334
Microblades	14	8	35	227	11	513	9	10	1	11		20	847
Indeterminate pieces	19	14	11	138	22	199	3	11		8		19	436
Crested pieces		4	8	37	6	21	1	1	1	1		4	82
Platform rejuvenation flakes		1	4	8	1	4						1	19
Total debitage	258	202	721	3,149	228	5,454	164	201	49	152	2	568	10,945
Cores													
Split pebbles						1							1
Core rough-outs												1	1
Single-platform cores: conical	1	1	1	6	2	12						4	27
Single-platform cores: plain	1		1	2	1	2				1		1	8
Opposed-platform cores				1					1				1
Cores with 2 platfs at angle												1	1
Discoidal cores, plain		1		1								1	3
Irregular cores		1	2										3
Bipolar cores	1					4			2	1		1	6
Core fragments						3						1	4
Total cores	3	3	4	10	3	22	0	0	3	2	0	10	55
Tools													
Microlith preforms						1							1
Obliquely blunted points			1			5		1					7
Scalene triangles	1			1	2	38		1					43
Crescents	1			7		12				1		1	21
Edge-blunted pieces						3						1	4
Idiosyncratic microlith forms						1							1
Frags of microliths			1	6		7						1	15
Frags of microliths or backed bladelets	1			7		27		1		1		3	39
Backed bladelets				2		3							5
Truncated bladelet						2							2
Microburins	7	2	6	25	2	117			2	18		5	166
Krukowski 'microburins'				1		5							6

Table 2.06 Full assemblage list by artefact type and zone location (Continued)

Artefact	Zone 1	Zone 2	Zone 3	Zone 4	Zone 4/5	Zone 5	Neolithic Structure	North	East	West	South	Unstratified	Total
Frags of tanged or angle-backed points?				1									1
Idiosyncratic points				1									1
Backed blades (points?)				2									2
Db truncations (points?)				1									1
Leaf-shaped arrowheads						1							1
Discoidal scrapers						1							1
Short end-scrapers	2		1	3	2	6		1		1		1	16
Blade-scrapers			1			1							2
Double-scrapers						1							1
Side-scrapers	2			1									3
End-/side-scraper												1	1
Scraper-edge fragments	1					1				1			2
Piercers	3		1										4
Backed knives												1	1
Curved truncations				1									1
Straight truncations				1		3							4
Oblique truncations				1		4							5
Serrated pieces						1				1			1
Heavily abraded implements	1				1	157							159
Combined tools (scraper-piercers)												1	1
Scale-flaked knife										1			1
Pieces w edge-retouch	6	1	2	11	3	19			1	1		4	46
Burins										1			
Gunflints					1								1
Total tools	25	3	12	73	11	415	1	6	1	10	0	19	565
TOTAL	286	208	737	3,232	242	5,891	165	207	53	164	2	597	11,565

The combination of the mapping strategy indicated above, and a Binfordian approach, allows a number of general spatial zones to be identified, such as the central hearth, the knapping floor(s), other activity areas, and disposal areas.

BLADE WIDTH AS A CHRONOLOGICAL TOOL

As blades frequently break (either in prehistory or later), the most reliable way to measure blade size is by measuring blade width, as this dimension is usually unaffected by the fragmentation process. It is possible to characterise individual blade assemblages in different ways, such as by calculation of the average blade width of that assemblage, as well as by the production of a curve that shows the distribution of the site's blades, from narrow to broad. If a site is undisturbed, and the assemblage represents one visit to the site, the curve should show a statistical 'normal' distribution with one peak and a distinct bell-shape.

This approach allows an assemblage to be dated in relative terms through its average blade width, but it is also an easy and practical way to test whether an assemblage is undisturbed or not (is the curve single-peaked and bell-shaped or is it multi-peaked?).

2.14.2.2 Raw materials

Apart from 22 quartz flakes/chips and one retouched jasper flake (CAT10264 from Zone 4/5), the Milltimber assemblage consists entirely of flint (99.8%). The Palaeolithic finds and the Mesolithic finds are associated with two different sizes of flint, representing two different procurement patterns. Artefacts belonging to the former category are generally fairly large and those belonging to the latter category small. This suggests that most of the flint reduced by the site's Palaeolithic knappers was procured in the form of up to 150 mm long flint pebbles, whereas that reduced by the Mesolithic knappers took the form of 40–70 mm long pebbles. Flint of the former size would not generally have been available along the present or Mesolithic coasts of eastern Scotland, but they could probably have been procured from sources on Doggerland; those parts of the North Sea that were dry land during the early post-glacial period (Ballin 2016a; Ballin & Bjerck 2016; Brooks *et al.* 2011; Sturt *et al.* 2013). Relatively large pebbles are only available from the Buchan Ridge Gravels near Peterhead in Scotland (Bridgland *et al.* 1997) but the Palaeolithic flints from Zone 4 are generally based on a type of flint considerably better in quality (ie, fewer faults and impurities) than the ones available from there. The colours also differ, with the Buchan Ridge flint varying between different hues of brown and grey, with other colours also being present (*ibid.*, 46), whereas most of the Palaeolithic flint is in mottled grey forms akin to so-called Yorkshire flint (Ballin 2011b). In the discussion of the finds from Howburn in South Lanarkshire (Ballin *et al.* 2010), it was suggested that the highly mobile settlers from this Late Upper Palaeolithic, Hamburgian site may have procured their stocks of large flint pebbles when they passed through Yorkshire or parts of Doggerland on their treks, possibly following herds of migrating reindeer.

2.14.2.3 Lithic zones

Some small quantities of lithics were found spread through other areas, including a few pieces of debitage from the timber avenue and from pit [2B-2550]. Table 2.06 outlines the full assemblage, including a breakdown of material found in each zone.

In Ballin (1999), the author demonstrated that the chip ratio of sieved assemblages usually varies between c30% and 55%, and the present chip ratio (Table 2.07) is within this framework. A relatively high chip ratio at a specific location usually indicates that primary production took place there.

ZONE 1 ASSEMBLAGE

The Zone 1 assemblage of 286 lithic artefacts was recovered predominantly from gridded squares, with a small number of artefacts deriving from the fills of five pits and post-holes distributed evenly across the zone (Illus 2.18 and 2.19).

The widths of the recovered blades and microblades form a bell-shaped curve with a small peak to either side. This suggests that the finds may generally date to one prehistoric period, although a small number of pieces may have been left by earlier or later visitors to the area. With the curve's peak at 9 mm, the zone's main visit is likely to have taken place within the Mesolithic-to-Early Neolithic period, and the recovered microliths narrow the probable date down to between 8500 and 4100 BC.

Mesolithic artefactual dating elements in Zone 1 include the presence of a small number of microliths and microburins, regular conical microblade cores, a group of regular narrow blades with a width centred around 9 mm, and small expedient scrapers. Two radiocarbon dates from fenceline post-holes [2D-1225] and [2D-1273] date the Zone 1 Mesolithic lithics between 4940 cal BC and 4550 cal BC (SUERC-68115 and SUERC-68116).

Approximately one-quarter of the finds were recovered from five pits or were scattered among a cluster of pits distributed across the zone. A radiocarbon date from pit [2D-1210] suggests that this group of pits dates mainly to the Middle Neolithic period (3510–3360 cal BC; SUERC-58604). CAT10153, a bipolar core (Illus 2.63), was recovered from pit [2D-1084] and this piece may be contemporary with the zone's Middle Neolithic pits, in contrast to the pits' probable residual knapping waste. Apart from the core, it is suggested the other lithic finds are residual pieces that formed part of a Mesolithic knapping floor and became incorporated into the later activity.

A total of 128 pieces in this zone are affected by fire although no cores had been visibly exposed. As many as 91 of these were recovered from grid AN02 (Illus 2.19),

Table 2.07 Percentage of lithics in each zone

	Zone 1	Zone 2	Zone 3	Zone 4	Zone 5	Zone 4/5	Structure	North Zone	East Zone	West Zone
Debitage (%)	90	97	98	97.5	92.6	94	99.4	97.1	92	93
Cores (%)	1	1.5	0.5	0.3	0.4	1	0.6	0	6	1
Tools (%)	9	1.5	1.5	2.2	7	5	0	2.9	2	6
Total number	286	208	737	3,232	5,891	242	165	207	53	160

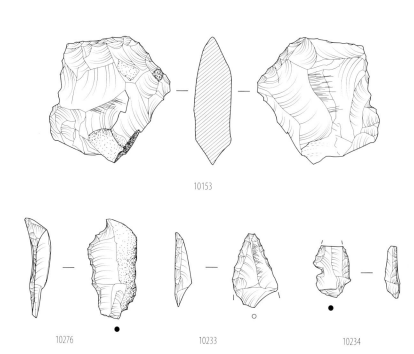

Illus 2.63 Zone 1 bipolar core and 3 piercers

with smaller numbers from the surrounding squares. This suggests that AN02 lay exactly over the central hearth relating to the period of the main visit. Ten burnt pieces were recovered from the five flint-bearing pits; they are generally thought to be residual pieces pre-dating the pits. Eighteen of the nineteen indeterminate pieces are burnt, supporting the suggestion put forward for Standingstones that, at the Aberdeen sites, many indeterminate pieces were formed when flakes and blades were exposed to fire and subsequently lost their ventral faces (see 4.7.1). Twelve of the tools, or approximately half of the implements, are burnt. This corresponds to the burnt ratio of the debitage.

Three of Milltimber's four piercers were retrieved from Zone 1 (CAT10276, CAT10233, CAT10234; Illus 2.63). They form a more homogeneous category than the Zone 1 scrapers, and they are all based on short blades or elongated flakes, which have been provided with a distal tip. Zone 1's non-microlithic pieces dominate the tools (microlithic pieces:other tools provide a ratio of 88:12).

ZONE 2 ASSEMBLAGE

The distribution of the finds across Zone 2 does not seem to have an obvious centre and the number of visits it may represent is uncertain (Illus 2.19). The zone is best described as a palimpsest and its assemblage has little research potential. Apart from the edge-retouched broadblade CAT10278 from pit [2D-1320] (Illus 2.64), which may be either a Palaeolithic or a Middle Neolithic object, the

typo-technological attributes of this sub-assemblage is consistent with a general date in the Mesolithic period. Diagnostic elements include microblades and narrow-blades, a conical microblade core, and two microburins. The width of the blades suggests either one or two visits to the site during this period. The diagnostic elements of this sub-assemblage are predominantly datable to the Mesolithic period, although a radiocarbon date from hearth [2D-1234] is evidence that the area may have been visited during the Middle Neolithic without leaving any lithic evidence. Although dominated by Mesolithic material, this sub-assemblage is likely to include later pieces as well, and the zone was almost certainly visited on a number of different occasions and periods.

ZONE 3 ASSEMBLAGE

Approximately two-thirds of the finds from Zone 3 were retrieved from gridded squares, with roughly one-third deriving from tree-throws (Illus 2.19). The assemblage from BB16/17 and neighbouring features includes a high proportion of microblades and narrow-blades, one typical conical core, as well as some microliths and microburins, whereas the assemblage from BA23/BC24 and neighbouring features includes broader blades, considerably higher numbers of preparation flakes and flakes with finely faceted platform remnants. This suggests the southern group is dominated by early finds and the northern by later ones. The finely faceted platforms could technologically date to the Late Upper Palaeolithic

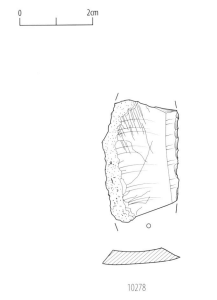

Illus 2.64 Zone 2 retouched blade fragment

period as well as the later Neolithic; cf Ballin 2011b; Ballin *et al.* 2010. Although it is generally impossible to divide the full assemblage into chronologically unmixed sub-assemblages, three radiocarbon-dates from the northern concentration suggest that the area may have been visited at least three times during prehistory: Mesolithic – 5310–5080 cal BC (SUERC-68113); Early Neolithic – 3940–3710 cal BC (SUERC-68120); and Middle Neolithic – 3360–3100 cal BC (SUERC-58022). The southern concentration is not covered by any of these radiocarbon dates.

Like the sub-assemblage from Zone 2, this sub-assemblage is best described as chronologically mixed, and the zone as a palimpsest with little research potential. An end-scraper and a piercer are items of note within the assemblage (CAT10227 and CAT10241; Illus 2.65)

ZONE 4 ASSEMBLAGE

Almost all the lithic artefacts from Zone 4 were retrieved from the gridded lithic scatter (Illus 2.19). Given the volume of the sub-assemblage, all lithic artefacts were fully analysed to establish as full an understanding as possible of the zone's internal chronology and on-site activities. The spatial analysis revealed six concentrations or possible hearths (Illus 2.66), although no physical evidence (ie cut features) is present for the individual hearth locations. .

The sub-assemblage from this area includes objects from both the Late Upper Palaeolithic and the Mesolithic periods. The relative distribution of microblades and macroblades suggests that Concentration 2 may have been the centre of the Late Upper Palaeolithic activity, which is supported by the absence of microliths in and around this concentration. However, it is likely that the scatter of large flint objects left by the pre-Mesolithic activity

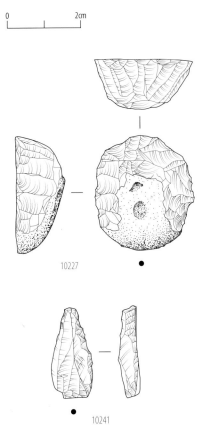

Illus 2.65 Zone 3 end scraper and piercer

was 'mined' by later Mesolithic people because of the easily accessible raw material source it represented. This explains the presence of large blades, crests and core tablets dispersed throughout Zone 4, and in neighbouring Zones 3 and 5. No radiocarbon-dated features lay within this zone and all dating is based on the lithic assemblage.

Owing to the importance of the Late Upper Palaeolithic finds to research into the first post-glacial settlers in Scotland, an effort was made to characterise them in detail, gathering evidence from across the site to include the operational schema responsible for their production. This forms a separate section, combining evidence from across Milltimber and beyond (see 2.14.2.4 below).

Quantities of burnt flint in Concentrations 1, 2 and 5 support the theory that the areas were possibly hearths. In Concentrations 3, 4 and 6 the presence of a hearth can only be theorised from the surface map (Illus 2.66). The distribution of the chips represent what Binford (1983, 153) referred to as the drop zone – finds too small to be a problem to the general traffic across the site, and which were therefore generally left where they fell. They show the position of a number of knapping floors. It has been noted that knapping floors tend to be near hearths (cf Ballin 1998).

The distribution of the blades is interesting, as the broad blades and the microblades appear to have slightly different distribution patterns. It is possible that

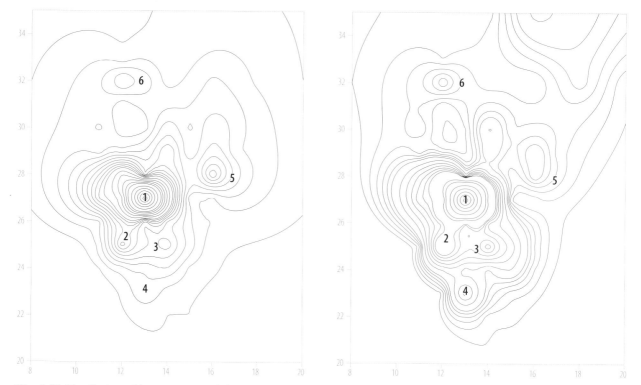

Illus 2.66 Distribution of burnt pieces and distribution of chips in Zone 4 – the numbers indicate where hearths may have been located. The position of some hearths is more clearly indicated by the distribution of the chips, which are thought to represent the knapping floors immediately next to the hearths

Concentration 2, with its broad blades, was the centre of the Late Upper Palaeolithic settlement in the area, and that the presence of many broad blades and other Palaeolithic pieces in Concentration 1 is the result of Mesolithic settlers there mining Concentration 2 for all larger pieces, whereas Concentration 5, with its microblades, seems to be entirely Mesolithic. The preparation flakes (crested pieces and platform rejuvenation flakes) are mainly found around Concentrations 1 and 2.

Most of the Zone 4 cores are burnt; however, only two pieces were recovered at the centre of a perceived hearth (BM27, Illus 2.19), whereas most of the burnt cores were found scattered across the area. This suggests that either one or more hearths were deliberately manipulated (either cleared out or reconstructed), or later visitors to the area have kicked these objects around. Most of these are large, and it is thought that many of them are pre-Mesolithic. It is possible that some of the pieces around Concentration 2 represent Palaeolithic 'tossing' (Binford 1983, 153), whereas the mostly large crests and core tablets found around the Concentration 1 fireplace may be scavenged pieces used by the Late Mesolithic settlers responsible for this concentration.

The microliths of this zone are found within the hearth areas of Concentrations 1 (eight pieces) and 5 (two pieces), as well as scattered around those two concentrations. The microliths from the possible hearth locations may indicate microlith production, as light and warmth would likely be sought for these activities. The microliths further away from

the fire may relate to various other activities, including hafting, caching, etc. The microburins, which are simply waste products from microlith production, have a tighter distribution, with these pieces either having been found within the fireplaces of Concentrations 1 (six pieces) and 5 (one piece), or within a circle surrounding the hearth of Concentration 1, probably all representing 'dropping' in the Binfordian sense. This tighter distribution supports the suggested link between microlith production and fireplaces around which the knapper(s) would have been seated (eg Ballin 2013b). The area around the hearth is also where hafting and 're-tooling' would have taken place (*ibid.*; Keeley 1982).

The probable Late Upper Palaeolithic objects are included in Table 2.12. Some pieces were recovered from the centre of the hearth grid of Concentration 1 (BM27), but most were found around this concentration and towards Concentration 2. The distribution of these pieces probably reveals little, as most of them are likely to have been affected by the activities of later settlers in the area.

The sub-assemblage from Zone 4 includes a number of pieces that have been characterised as likely Late Upper Palaeolithic. One opposed-platform core (CAT10059; Illus 2.67) is smaller than one would have expected on the basis of the size of the broad blades from opposed-platform cores recovered from the area (CAT899, CAT11371, CAT3090, CAT3186; Illus 2.67), but in morphological and technological terms it corresponds

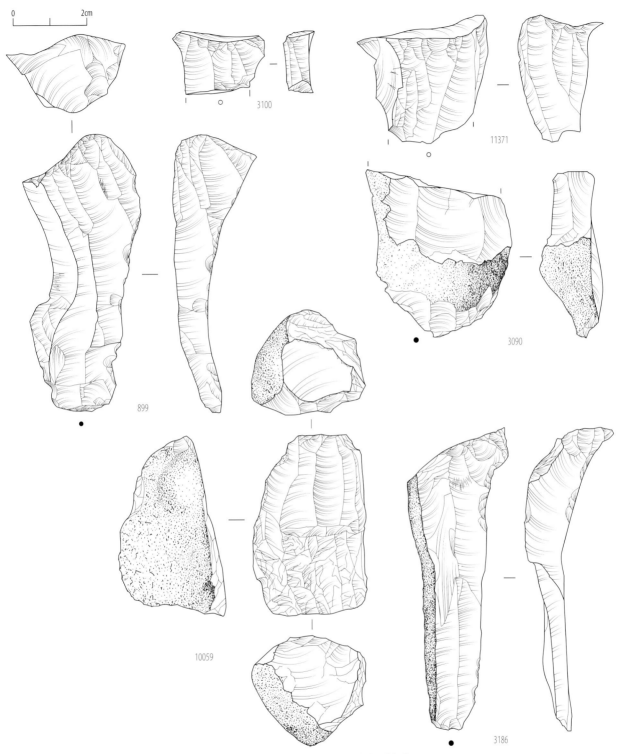

Illus 2.67 Waste from Upper Palaeolithic blade cores

precisely to the cores described by Bo Madsen in his analysis of later Hamburgian flintwork (1992, fig 81; also see Weber 2012, fig 32). However, related cores have been found in other Late Upper Palaeolithic contexts (eg, Vermeersch 2015), and at the present time this core should only be perceived as indicating an unspecified Late Upper Palaeolithic presence in Zone 4, ie pre-dating c10,000 BC. A selection of conical cores is presented in Illus 2.68.

The dating of the lithic points from Zone 4 shows that they include a number likely to be of Late Upper Palaeolithic date, including a fragment from a tanged or angle-backed point (CAT10265), one idiosyncratic point (CAT10456), two backed blades (CAT10289, CAT10567),

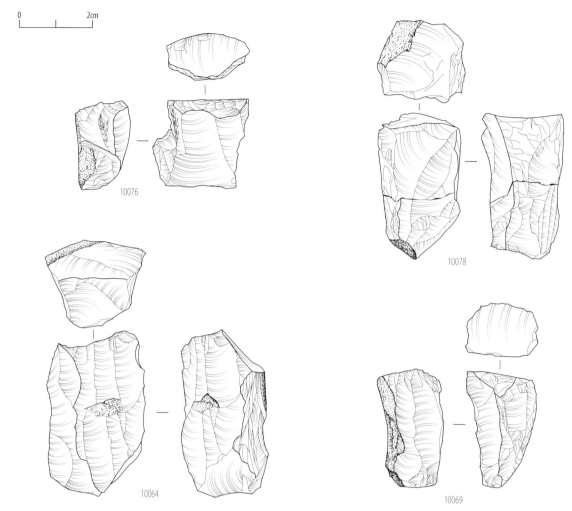

Illus 2.68 Zone 4 conical cores

and one double-truncated piece (CAT10236), all shown in Illus 2.69. CAT10265 is similar to tip fragments from Howburn; broken off late Hamburgian Havelte points (Ballin *et al.* 2010, fig 6). Although the piece from Zone 4 is smaller than the tip fragment on the Howburn point, it has the same general angle against the opposed lateral side, the same thickness, and both pieces were produced by the use of *sur enclume* technique. CAT10456 corresponds to another piece recovered from Howburn. It is a roughly triangular point with a straight base and, like the Howburn piece, may be a reused/remodified tip fragment from a broken tanged point. The two backed blades from Zone 4, CAT10289 and CAT10567, find their best parallels in the assemblage from the Federmesser site Kilmelfort Cave, near Oban (Saville & Ballin 2009), although some backed pieces were also recovered from Howburn (Ballin *et al.* forthcoming). The double-truncated piece is unusual, and it has preliminarily been interpreted as a potential Upper Palaeolithic point (see for example Jacobi 2004), although it cannot be ruled out that the piece is post Mesolithic. The general absence

of diagnostic Neolithic pieces within Zone 4 speaks against this.

Two large scrapers (CAT10214 and CAT10507; Illus 2.70) are also likely to date to the Late Upper Palaeolithic period. The former is an oval flake scraper (L 45 mm), and the latter a blade-scraper (L 70 mm), and the dorsal scars indicate that both blanks were struck off a large blade core (see 2.14.2.4 below). In addition, the working edge of the blade-scraper, which is based on a crested piece, is distinctly acute, a feature associated with pre-Mesolithic scrapers (Ballin *et al.* 2010, figs 8–9). Further examples of end-scrapers that cannot be conclusively dated to the Mesolithic are CAT10215 and CAT10217 (Illus 2.71).

A solitary obliquely blunted point (CAT10466; not illustrated) is relatively broad with a width of 10.8 mm and could be Early Mesolithic (Butler 2005, 96). However, owing to this being the only piece of its kind in Zone 4 it is difficult to determine whether it represents a brief visit to the site or whether it could be later, like the narrow obliquely blunted pieces from Zone 5.

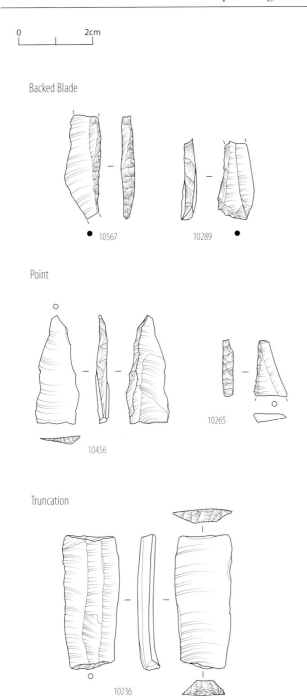

0   2cm

Backed Blade

10567   10289

Point

10265

10456

Truncation

10236

Illus 2.69 Zone 4 lithic points likely to be of Late Upper Palaeolithic date

first and foremost aimed to produce blanks for microliths by the application of soft percussion. Illus 2.73 plots the width of all Zone 4's intact blades and shows the curve is almost perfectly bell-shaped, with a peak at W 8–9 mm, suggesting that the area's Mesolithic blades may have been produced and/or deposited within a very narrow chronological horizon. Some of the minor peaks or 'dimples' at the right side of the curve may represent larger specimens that, as mentioned above, are almost certainly Late Upper Palaeolithic pieces.

In summary the distribution of the lithic artefacts across the area suggests that it may have been visited six or more times.

The identification of part of the sub-assemblage as dating to the Late Upper Palaeolithic period adds to the small group of pre-Mesolithic sites in Scotland known to date, including Howburn (Hamburgian; Ballin *et al*. 2010), Kilmelfort Cave (Federmesser Culture; Saville & Ballin 2009) and Rubha-Port an t-Seilich on Skye (Ahrensburgian; Mithen *et al*. 2015). At the present time it is not possible to determine to which part of the Late Upper Palaeolithic the pre-Mesolithic finds from Zone 4 date, but these finds clearly relate to a time prior to 10,000 BC (cf Saville 2004). The Late Upper Palaeolithic settlers appear to have focused on the production of large blades from opposed-platform cores using raw material collected elsewhere on their travels, possibly in Doggerland. Some tools and tool fragments suggest that these blanks may have been intended for points, which would have formed tips and/or edges in composite hunting gear.

Most of the non-microlithic implements are likely to be Palaeolithic. Zone 4 was visited at least once during an unspecified part of the Late Upper Palaeolithic period, as well as several times during the Mesolithic. It is thought that during at least one of these visits the original Palaeolithic remains may have been scavenged by the later knappers.

Most of these scatters are the remains of short-term visits during the Mesolithic, probably to replace lost and damaged microlith inserts in composite hunting tools and weaponry, supplemented by small numbers of other implements (mainly scrapers and truncated pieces/knives). The distribution patterns, as well as the almost complete absence of structural evidence, suggest that these concentrations may represent individual hunter-gatherer open-air sites, rather than visits involving sophisticated structures (eg, Howburn and Echline Fields; Waddington 2007; Robertson *et al*. 2013) or light shelters (eg, Standingstones, this volume; Fife Ness, Wickham-Jones & Dalland 1998). It is possible that the difference between the numbers of artefacts recovered from each concentration, as well as the density of the burnt flint, indicates visits to the zone of varying duration, or that the concentrations may represent the remains left by different sets of activities.

Most of the lithic material retrieved from the zone clearly represents a microblade industry (Illus 2.72). It is not possible on the basis of the technological attributes, or the operational schema associated with the microblade production, to date this industry more precisely than to the Mesolithic into Early Neolithic (Table 2.13; Ballin 2014a), although other available evidence (such as the microliths/microburins) narrows this down to the Late Mesolithic period. This Mesolithic microblade industry

0   2cm

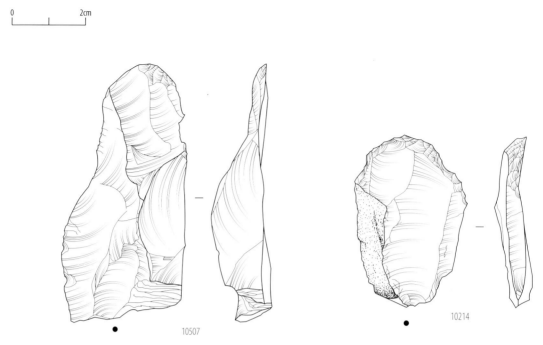

Illus 2.70 Zone 4 scrapers likely to be of Late Upper Palaeolithic date

0   2cm

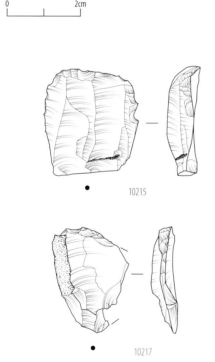

Illus 2.71 Zone 4 Mesolithic end scrapers

ZONE 5 ASSEMBLAGE

Approximately 5700 lithic finds from Zone 5 were recovered from gridded squares, with less than 200 deriving from a line of four pits in the southern half of the zone. The lithic artefacts make up six concentrations (Concentrations 7–12; Illus 2.74), each of which may have had its own central hearth and therefore probably represents an individual visit to the area. Approximately two-thirds of the finds were retrieved from Concentration 7. Again it must be noted that no physical remains of a hearth were identified in any of the concentrations of Zone 5.

The typo-technological composition of the lithic sub-assemblage here suggests that the finds may almost exclusively date to the Mesolithic, supported by a radiocarbon date from a feature in the zone's southern half which dates to 8220–7970 cal BC (SUERC-68101). There is also a small Late Upper Palaeolithic element and one clearly identifiable Early Neolithic object (serrated knife CAT10237; Illus 2.75). In Concentration 7 heavily abraded implements were present in high numbers. These have been subject to more detailed technological characterisation (see 2.14.2.4 below).

Similar to Zone 4, all lithic artefacts from Zone 5 were fully analysed with the aim of increasing understanding of the zone's internal chronology and on-site behaviour.

The Milltimber distribution patterns are generally quite neat, and from this evidence there is no indication of major plough-induced disturbance. However, there is evidence some individual pieces were moved by ploughing. A core (CAT10162) and refitting overshot blade (CAT10163; neither illustrated) connects grids BS41 and BW35, which lie c7m apart. The linear alignment of the two find spots is almost exactly parallel with the Milltimber furrows and it is likely they were dragged during ploughing.

The general distribution patterns of small open-air hunter-gatherer sites were touched upon by the author in his analysis of the middle Mesolithic site Lundevågen 31, Vest-Agder County, Norway (Ballin 2013b). Lacking a built fireplace, the central hearth is defined by the distribution of

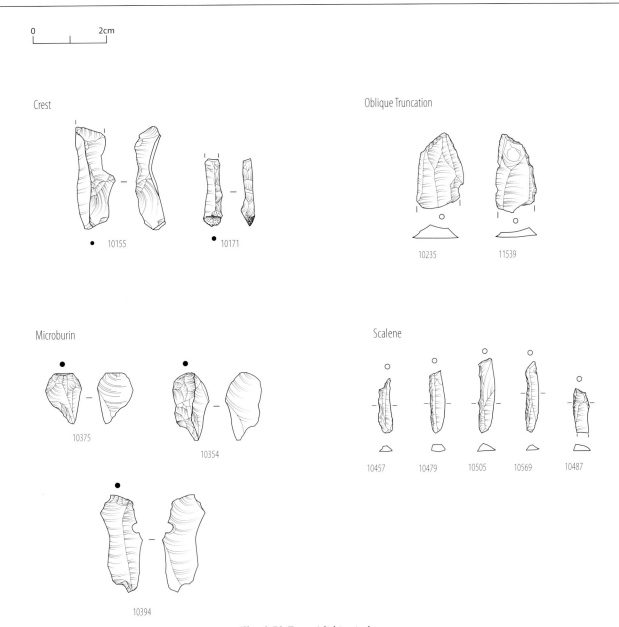

Illus 2.72 Zone 4 lithics industry

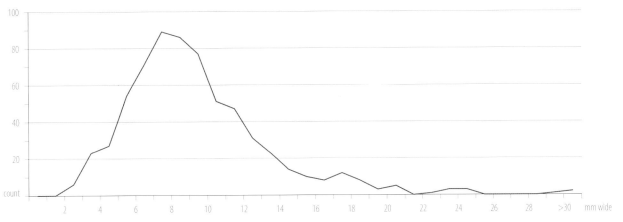

Illus 2.73 The width of all unmodified blades and microblades from Zone 4 (655 pieces)

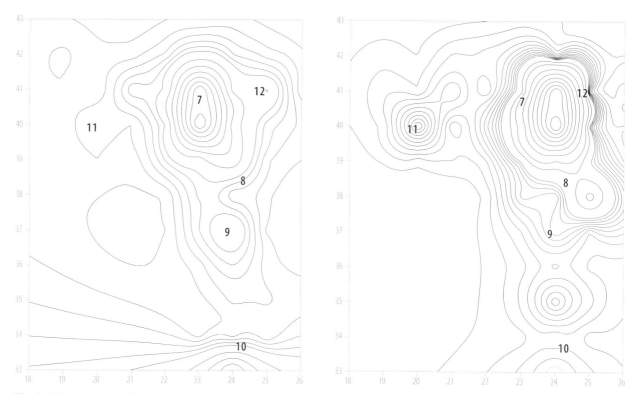

Illus 2.74 Distribution of burnt pieces and distribution of chips in Zone 5 - the numbers indicate where hearths may have been located. The position of some hearths is more clearly indicated by the distribution of the chips, which are thought to represent the knapping floors immediately next to the hearths

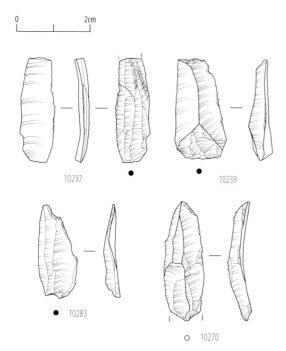

Illus 2.75 Zone 5 Early Neolithic serrated knife and oblique truncation lithics

burnt flint; the chips (Binford's drop zone) then define the main knapping floor, which is usually located immediately next to the hearth; slightly further away from the hearth are specific activity areas where individual tool types were used, and furthest from the site's centre is the heavy lithic waste, defining the site's toss zone.

Zone 5 has six centres or focal points. Each was likely associated with a hearth, although only the hearths of Concentrations 7, 9 and 10 stand out. The probable presence of a hearth in Concentration 8 is indicated more clearly in the surface map (Illus 2.74), which even indicates a possible sixth concentration at Grid BY41 that has been almost entirely obscured by the neighbouring main concentration.

The position of Concentrations 7–11 is most clearly shown by the distribution of the chips. These pieces represent the waste material from tool production and show the likely position of a number of knapping floors, which in general tend to be located immediately next to hearths (cf. Ballin 1998). This is also where most of the blades were found.

The cores and preparation flakes, in contrast, are relatively large and thus tend to be found further away from the hearth in a 'toss' zone. Only Concentrations 7 and 9 contain enough cores and preparation flakes to show a pattern, and both indicate a toss zone around the concentrations' fireplaces. At Mesolithic sites microblades, microliths and microburins generally tend to be found together, overlapping the concentration of burnt flint (Cziesla *et al.* 1990, 81). The microliths of Zone 5 were apparently manufactured next to the hearths, where the knappers would have been seated.

The most notable scatter of microliths is around the hearth in Concentration 7, with a general scattering of

Table 2.08 Sub-assemblages from the four intercutting pits in Zone 5

	Chips	Flakes	Blades	Micro-blades	Indet pieces	Crested pieces	Core frags	Scalene triangles	Crescents	Microlith frags	Scrapers	Total
Pit [2D-1211]	6	4		1				1				12
Pit [2D-1776]	91	20	6	2	11		1	1		4	1	137
Pit [2D-1837]	1	2				1						4
Pit [2D-1863]	2	19	6	3	3				2			35
Total	100	45	12	6	14	1	1	2	2	4	1	188

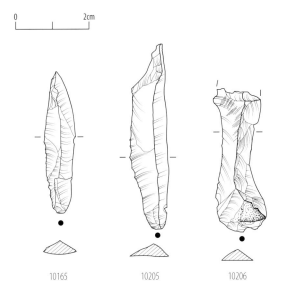

Illus 2.76 Zone 5 crested pieces

microliths across the zone indicating that they were also produced and used around the other hearths. The microburins define Concentrations 7 and 9 in particular, but, like the microliths, they also indicate that microliths were produced throughout the zone. Interestingly, the area appears to be divided into a northern (Concentrations 7–8 and 11–12) and southern part (Concentrations 9–10), separated by an area with relatively few microliths. The northern part includes almost exclusively scalene triangles and the southern part almost exclusively crescents. Unfortunately, the northern part is not associated with any radiocarbon dates. A string of radiocarbon-dates from Fife Ness (Wickham-Jones & Dalland 1998, 6) suggested a date for a crescent-dominated assemblage there of c7600–7400 cal BC.

As the tight concentration of these pieces coincides quite precisely with the other artefacts in Concentration 7, including many scalene triangles, this is likely to have been created in a single visit to the area during the Mesolithic. The distribution of the zone's unusual heavily abraded implements supports this interpretation of a single event, associated with the processing of presently unknown materials.

Four inter-cutting pits in Zone 5 (Illus 2.07; see 2.6.2.3 above) contained nearly 200 lithics (Table 2.08); however, this assemblage is primarily chips and flakes and likely to be residual. This is further supported by the presence of scalene triangles recovered from two of the pits and two crescents in a third pit. It is rare to find two microlith types together and they must have become mixed post-deposition.

The four intercutting pits in Zone 5 are unlikely to be related to anything structural and the absence of other features in the area suggests that the fireplaces defined by burnt flint may relate to open-air sites. In terms of the intra-site spatial patterns, there is little directly relevant material from Scotland that can be compared to Zone 5, as Scottish early prehistoric sites have traditionally been excavated in contexts rather than grids or, when excavated by grid units, many turned out to be palimpsests that could not be disentangled (eg, Nethermills Farm; Ballin 2013a).

It is tempting to compare the patterns above with those of recently discovered Mesolithic huts from Scotland (eg, Echline Fields on the Forth; Robertson *et al.* 2013) or northern England (eg, Howick, Northumberland; Waddington 2007), but the organisation of space on open-air sites and inside structures may have followed quite different principles. On open-air sites, the spatial patterns are very much governed by 'drop and toss' (Binford 1983, 153), whereas order within the confined space of dwellings would have been more structured and include features like door dumps, actual middens, wall-defining debris, tongues of micro-waste in the entrance area, etc (*ibid.*, 176; also see the distribution patterns associated with the Early Bronze Age house at Dalmore on Lewis; Ballin 2002a; 2008c). However, some universal trends are present at sites of both types, such as the focus on the central hearth, around which most activities took place.

Dating of the pieces suggests a number of broad blades, large crested pieces (CAT10165, CAT10205, CAT10206; Illus 2.76) and core tablets from Zone 5 probably relate to the Late Upper Palaeolithic presence at Milltimber. These pieces were generally produced by the reduction of large opposed-platform cores, and they may either represent activities in Zone 5 by the Palaeolithic visitors of Zone 4 or represent 'mining' of the Zone 4 Palaeolithic scatter by Zone 5 Mesolithic knappers.

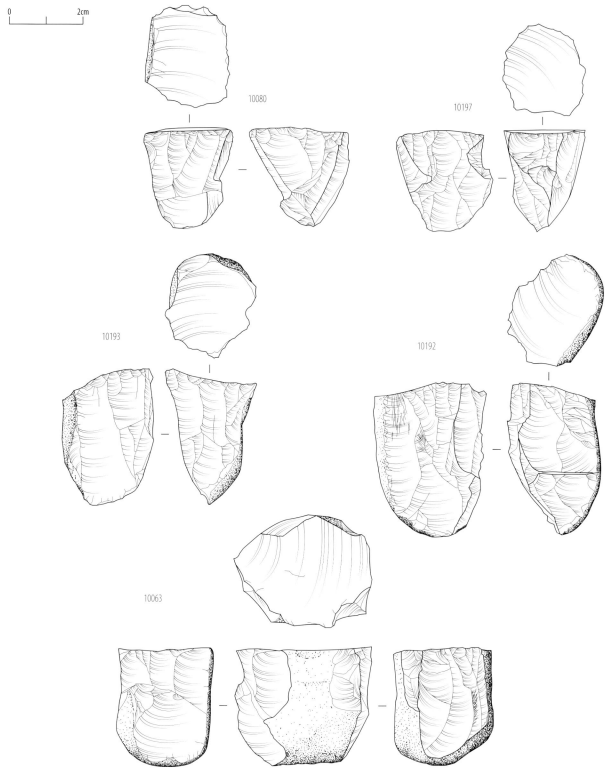

Illus 2.77 Zone 5 conical cores

The bulk of the lithic material recovered from the various concentrations in Zone 5 clearly represents a microblade industry. This industry first and foremost aimed to produce blanks for microliths by the application of soft percussion. More robust tools like scrapers were manufactured mainly on waste flakes from the preparation of the blade cores, although truncated pieces (knives) were predominantly made on the sturdy blades. The size and character of the zone's blades and conical cores (CAT10080, CAT10197, CAT10193, CAT10192, CAT10063; Illus 2.77) are consistent with a date in the Late Mesolithic period. Illus 2.78A and 2.78B shows the

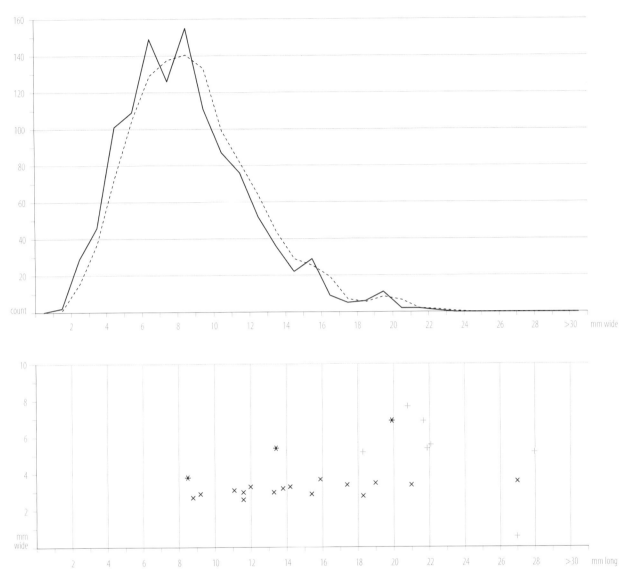

Illus 2.78 (A) The width of all unmodified blades and microblades from Zone 5 (red). A dashed trendline (moving trendline) has been inserted (1,166 pieces); (B) The main dimensions of the scalene triangles, crescents and edge-blunted pieces from Zone 5; scalene triangles (exes); crescents (crosses); and edge-blunted pieces (stars)

width of all intact blades and microblades in Zone 5. The diagram's curve has two peaks immediately next to each other, almost forming a statistically 'normal' distribution. The curve's adjusting trendline forms a perfectly bell-shaped figure. This suggests that, even if the area was visited more than once, most of the blades are likely to have been produced and/or deposited during one relatively narrow chronological horizon, such as a segment of the later Mesolithic. The fact that the cores, microliths and microburins also form two size groups supports the indication of more than one visit to the zone. The radiocarbon date from pit [2D-1776] (8220–7970 cal BC, SUERC-68101) may give a terminus ante quem date for most of the Mesolithic material of Zone 5. The microliths are almost exclusively micro-blade scalene triangles and crescents, with the northern part of the zone being

dominated by the former and the southern part by the latter. It is uncertain whether the preference for a particular type of microlith is diagnostic, relates to function, or simply is a matter of personal 'taste'. Bipolar cores are shown in Illus 2.79, scrapers in Illus 2.80.

Obliquely blunted points are traditionally associated with the Early Mesolithic (Butler 2005, 96), but some do occur in later contexts (see the characterisation of the more than 500 microliths from Nethermills Farm; Ballin 2013a). The five pieces from Zone 5 are all microblade versions (av width 5 mm), and clearly date to the Mesolithic. The fact that the crescents from this zone are generally substantially broader than the area's scalene triangles (Illus 2.81) may therefore also signify a chronological difference.

The 157 heavily abraded implements form a highly unusual group of tools that display coarse abrasion and

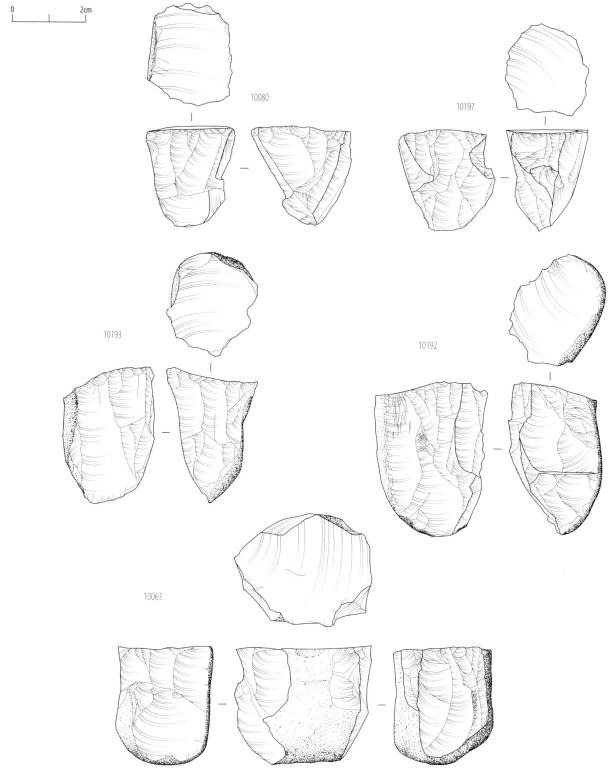

Illus 2.79 Zone 5 bipolar cores

macroscopically visible striations. Their recovery from the area's main concentration, which is also defined by the presence of numerous scalene triangles and microburins, suggests that these pieces probably date between 8500–4000 BC. Only the solitary serrated piece (CAT10237)

is an obvious later form, probably dating to the Early Neolithic period (Saville 2006). Serrated pieces, scything microdenticulates, have been associated with either sawing (eg, wood, bone, antler) or cutting/sickling vegetable matter (Juel Jensen 1994, 59). This piece may relate to

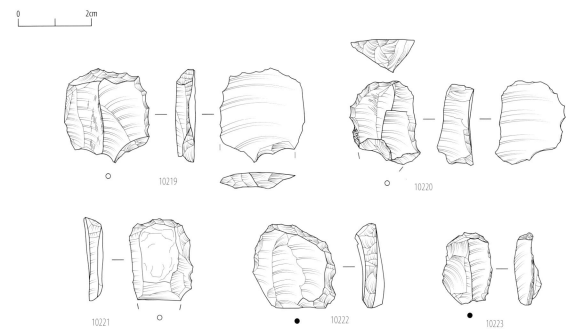

Illus 2.80 Zone 5 scrapers

the Early Neolithic radiocarbon date from pit [2D-1879] (3940–3710 cal BC, SUERC-68102) and it may be linked to the Early Neolithic activities over the rest of the site.

In summary the lithic distributions in Zone 5 point towards a number of visits during the Mesolithic. It is uncertain whether pieces relating to an earlier broadblade industry represent Late Upper Palaeolithic activity here, or whether they are objects 'mined' from Zone 4 (the focal point of Milltimber's Palaeolithic activity) as raw material or ready-made blanks.

The lithic debris forms six concentrations, and the distribution patterns suggest that these concentrations represent individual Mesolithic open-air sites. It is possible that the difference between the numbers of artefacts recovered from each concentration, as well as the density of the burnt flint, indicates visits to the zone of varying duration. It is also possible that the concentrations may represent the remains left by different sets of activities, although only Concentration 7 stands out as such. In general, the concentrations are dominated by waste from the production of microblades and microliths/microburins, but Concentration 7 yielded a sub-assemblage of unusually heavily abraded implements.

The distribution of scalene triangles and crescents across Zone 5, in conjunction with the fact that the crescents are generally approximately twice as broad as the scalene triangles, suggest a potential chronological relationship between the two groups of microliths, with crescents possibly being earlier and scalene triangles later. This scenario is supported by the fact that the microblades from the two main parts of the zone (north and south) also form two size-groups, with microblades from the north (and associated with the narrow scalene triangles) being

narrower (average width 8.8 mm), and those from the south (and associated with the broad crescents) being broader (average width 9.5 mm). At Fife Ness, the microliths (as defined here) are almost all crescents, and in this case the authors suggested a functional explanation (Wickham-Jones & Dalland 1998, 15). Mostly, crescents and scalene triangles appear together (as at Gleann Mor on Islay; Finlayson & Mithen 1997), but in many cases the available sites are either obvious palimpsests (eg, Nethermills Farm; Ballin 2013a), or it is not entirely certain whether sites have single- or multi-occupation status. It is also quite possible that some pieces defined as crescents in old reports may be poorly produced triangular microliths or edge-blunted pieces with a somewhat convex retouch.

The heavily abraded implements presently form a unique collection of tools, partly defined by modification and partly by use-wear. They are probably functionally similar to the later Neolithic polished-edge implements discussed in Ballin (2011b), where a specific function could not be identified. The use-wear analysis of a number of these pieces suggested a probable function for processing vegetable matter.

ZONE 4/5 ASSEMBLAGE

The finds referred to 'Zone 4/5' are predominantly finds from the initial identification of the lithics scatter prior to grid excavation. The dominance of quite large blades suggests a Late Upper Palaeolithic element to the assemblage. The crested pieces, as well as the solitary platform rejuvenation flake, are all fairly large and their size, as well as their general appearance, suggests a Late Upper Palaeolithic date. The zone's very small microblades are most likely datable to the Mesolithic. The solitary

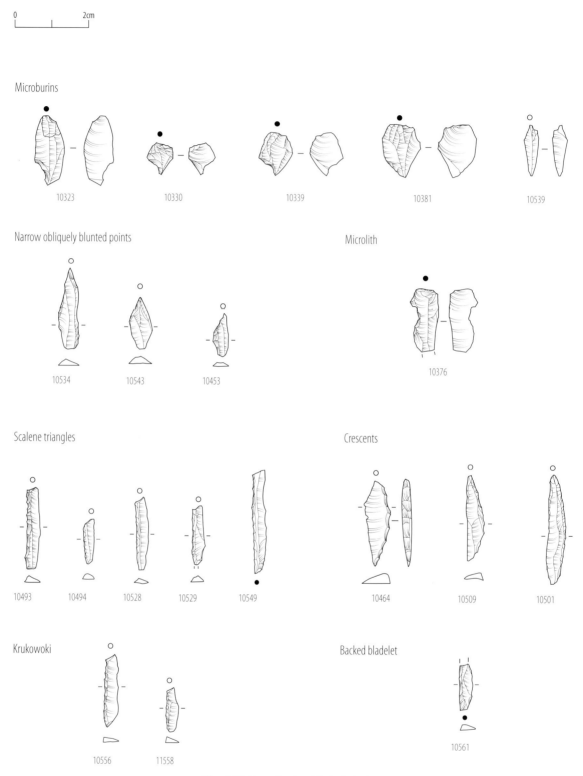

Microburins

10323   10330   10339   10381   10539

Narrow obliquely blunted points

10534   10543   10453

Microlith

10376

Scalene triangles

10493   10494   10528   10529   10549

Crescents

10464   10509   10501

Krukowoki

10556   11558

Backed bladelet

10561

Illus 2.81 Zone 5 microblade industry

heavily abraded implement (CAT10753) links this sub-assemblage to that of Zone 5.

NEOLITHIC STRUCTURE ZONE ASSEMBLAGE

This group of lithics were predominantly recovered from within the Neolithic Structure or its immediate surroundings (Table 2.09). A single tool was retrieved from pit [2D-1927] immediately to the south of the structure. It was a very small drop-shaped arrowhead (CAT10060; Illus 2.82) belonging to Green's type 4A (1980, 72) and dating to the Early Neolithic. Thirty-four pieces of debitage were found in an upper layer of the same pit. The arrowhead

Table 2.09 The distribution of lithic artefacts across Neolithic Structure Zone

Features	Chips	Flakes	Blades	Micro-blades	Indet pieces	Crested pieces	Leaf arrowhead	Total
Structure and interior								
Floor (2D-1766)	27	12	2	3				44
Trample (2D-1824)	13	4	4	1	1	1		24
Tumble (2D-1775)	12	2	1		1			16
Pit [2D-1648]	2		1					3
Post-hole [2D-1783]		1						1
Post-hole [2D-1865]	10	7						17
Features surrounding structure								
Spread (2D-1916)	8	7	1					16
Pit [2D-1927]	18	10	2	4			1	1
Pit [2D-1754]				1				1
Post-hole [2D-1827]		1						1
Outlying features								
Pit [2D-1747]		1						1
Pit [2D-0015]	4	1			1			6
Total	94	46	11	9	3	1	1	165

0   2cm

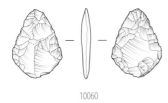

10060

Illus 2.82 Neolithic Structure, leaf-shaped point

is compatible with the radiocarbon dates obtained for the structure, which place it in the first 300 years of the fourth millennium BC.

NORTH ZONE ASSEMBLAGE

This sub-assemblage was recovered from features to the north of the lithics scatter (Illus 2.18 and Table 2.10). Diagnostic artefact types and technological attributes, as well as a number of radiocarbon dates, define the bulk of the activities in this area as dating to either the later Mesolithic or the Early Neolithic. A radiocarbon-date of 1260–1050 cal BC (SUERC-68111) from a hearth indicated later activity but no artefacts are identifiable as being from the later period.

One crested flake (CAT10156; Illus 2.83) is probably an informal sickle with both edges displaying macroscopically visible gloss, indicating that the piece may have been use for cutting or scything vegetable matter (Juel Jensen 1994). It was recovered from pit [2D-1398], and was the only artefact in the pit, in contrast to the spread of debitage found in most lithic-bearing features. This could suggest deliberate deposition, although it was from the uppermost deposit and is likely residual.

Other than the sickle, most of the flint is in the form of plain knapping debris and it is suggested that this material may relate to one or more small domestic scatters in the area.

Four of the microliths and microburins of this sub-assemblage were recovered from features in the area's north-western corner, including the lithic-rich pit [2D-1014]. Microburins, as a by-product of lithic production, are likely to be located near where microliths are produced; this kind of work would most likely have involved sitting down for some time. A radiocarbon-sample from this pit suggests a date of 7490–7200 cal BC (SUERC-68100).

The radiocarbon-dated Early Neolithic hearths, pits and post-holes are all contemporary with the Neolithic structure. It cannot be said with certainty whether the knapping debris found in the features with Early Neolithic dates could be also of Mesolithic date.

EAST ZONE ASSEMBLAGE

The sub-assemblage from the East Zone was recovered entirely from cut features (Illus 2.18 & 2.21). Approximately

Table 2.10 The distribution of lithic artefacts in the North Zone

Feature	Chips	Flakes	Blades	Microblades	Indet pieces	Crested pieces	Microliths	Microburins	Scrapers	Total	Date of feature from 14C determination
[2D-1258]	2		1							3	Early Neolithic
[2D-1575]	1									1	
[2D-1691]			1							1	
Pits											
[2D-1003]		1	2							3	
[2D-1009]	1									1	Mesolithic
[2D-1014]	13	7	12	3	2		1	2		40	Mesolithic
[2D-1052]		12	3	4	1					20	
[2D-1127/1092]	13	10	1	1	2					27	Mesolithic
[2D-1117/1089]							1			1	Mesolithic
[2D-1393]	1									1	
[2D-1399]	2									2	
[2D-1485]		1								1	Mesolithic
[2D-1493]	1									1	
[2D-1522]	1	1								2	
[2D-1529/1580]		1								1	
[2D-1658]		1								1	
[2D-1714/1941]	4	1	1		2					8	Early Neolithic
[2D-1717]		1								1	
[2D-1904/1895]	16	11			3				1	31	Early Neolithic
[2D-1942]	4	2	1							7	
Post-hole											
[2D-1265]	1									1	
[2D-1279]		1								1	
[2D-1398]						1				1	
[2D-1427]		1			1					2	
[2D-1433]	9	6	1	1						17	Early Neolithic
[2D-1495]	2	2	1							5	Early Neolithic
[2D-1617]	1	1								2	
[2D-1670]			1							1	
Tree-throw											
[2D-1759]	7	3	2	1			1			14	
[2D-1761]	4	5	1							10	
TOTAL	83	68	28	10	11	1	3	2	1	207	

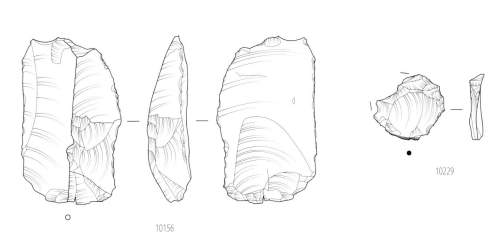

Illus 2.83 North Zone, informal sickle

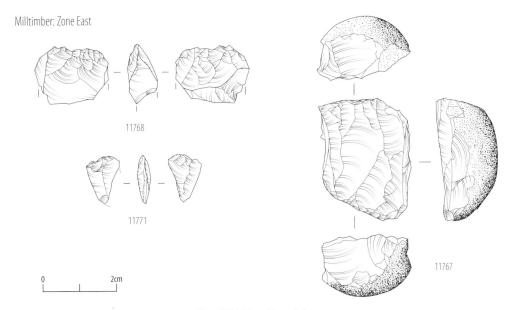

Illus 2.84 East Zone lithics

80% of the finds were recovered from pit [AMA09–2028]. Although many of the cut features were first interpreted as probably dating to the Mesolithic period, due to their content of some small cores and microblades, they only provide a terminus post quem for digging the features.

Like most of the flint from the features in the North Zone, the sub-assemblage from pit [AMA09–2028] is in the form of plain knapping debris. The size of the six microblades suggests that most of the lithic material may date from c8500 BC to the Early Neolithic, whereas the size of blade fragment CAT11763 (W 16 mm) indicates that this piece may relate to before or after this timeframe. A selection of lithics from the East Zone is presented in Illus 2.84.

WEST ZONE ASSEMBLAGE

Apart from ten rock crystal chips, one flake and a blade in jasper, and one chip in quartz, all pieces in this zone are flint. This sub-assemblage was recovered entirely from cut features (Table 2.11 and Illus 2.18 and 2.21). It is thought that most of the lithic debris in the features may be residual material from scatters, which entered the later features with the backfill. Although many of the cut features were initially interpreted as potentially dating to the Mesolithic period, because of their content of mainly Mesolithic style blanks, cores and tools, these finds only provide a terminus post quem for digging the features. This suggestion is supported by the fact that some of the cuts also included Neolithic blanks, tools and pottery.

Table 2.11 The distribution of lithic artefacts in the West Zone

Feature	Feature type	Total finds	Including
[AMA09-2077]	Pit	12	Ten rock crystal chips
[AMA09-2078]	Hearth	1	
[AMA09-2080]	Pit	2	Indeterminate pottery sherd
[AMA09-2152]	Ditch	40	Single-platform core, burin, scale-flaked knife
[AMA09-2164]	Pit	44	Frag of micro or backed bladelet
[AMA09-2170]	Pit	4	
[AMA09-2179]	Pit	2	End-scraper, serrated blade
[AMA09-2209]	Pit	2	
[AMA09-2214]	Pit	1	
[AMA09-2216]	Pit	7	Levallois-like flake, microburin
[AMA09-2218]	Pit	21	Crested microblade, crescent, two pieces in jasper
[AMA09-2220]	Pit	7	
[AMA09-2222]	Pit	18	Bipolar core
[AMA09-2241]	Pit	2	
[AMA09-2268]	Pit	1	
Total		160	

Although the bulk of the finds are undiagnostic, some are chronologically informative or interesting in other ways. The ten small chips of rock crystal were recovered from a likely Early Neolithic recut in Mesolithic pit [AMA09–2064]; however, the date of these pieces is uncertain. As the vast majority of finds from Milltimber are flint, these rock crystal chips are notable and may indicate unspecified non-functional deposition. Linear features [AMA09–2152] contained 40 pieces of worked flint (Illus 2.85), including a pre-Neolithic burin (CAT11773), a single-platform core which may be Mesolithic or Neolithic (CAT11776), and a probably later Neolithic scale-flaked blade-knife (CAT11774). Three microblades, measuring 4–8 mm wide, are thought to date between 8500 and 4000 BC.

Pit [AMA09–2179] associated with feature [AMA09–2152] yielded a relatively large short end-scraper (CAT11779; Illus 2.85) with extended retouch along both lateral sides and a worn serrated blade (CAT11780; Illus 2.85). Both are forms that would fit a Neolithic date better than a Mesolithic date. Two of the other pits in this cluster, pits [AMA09–2216] and [AMA09–2218], contained, among other things, a microburin (CAT11781) and a Levallois-like flake (CAT11713; not illustrated), datable to the later Mesolithic and the later Neolithic respectively. Pit [2D-2218] contained a crested microblade (CAT11783; not illustrated), a crescent (CAT11782; Illus 2.85), as well as a flake and a blade in

jasper. The former two pieces are of a later Mesolithic date, and this date is supported by the presence in the pit of four delicate microblades (W 5–7 mm). It is uncertain whether the jasper pieces could represent non-functional deposition. Pit [AMA09–2220] contained some debitage, but three of these pieces are broad blades with widths up to 14 mm, suggesting potential activity in the Neolithic period.

Pit [AMA09–2164] in the south-western corner of the area included 44 lithic artefacts, one of which is the fragment of a microlith or backed bladelet (CAT11777; not illustrated). All other pieces from this feature are chips and flakes. CAT11777 is most likely to date to the later Mesolithic or the Early Neolithic. Pit [AMA09–2222] in the northern half of the area yielded one bipolar core (CAT11784; Illus 2.85). Two broad blades (W 9–13 mm) from this feature may suggest a post-Mesolithic date.

In summary the lithic evidence suggests that the West Zone was the focus of activity during the later Mesolithic, as well as during the Neolithic period, as is confirmed by radiocarbon dating of the features. Some of the Neolithic finds are not datable within this period, but a Levallois-like flake from pit [AMA09–2216] and a scale-flaked blade knife from cut [AMA09–2152] may be later Neolithic. Both features also contained Mesolithic objects. As mentioned in connection with the discussion of the sub-assemblage from, among other areas, the North, minuscule debris like chips may indicate that pits were dug through existing knapping floors and entered the features with the backfill. The fact that several closely situated features in the south-eastern corner of the area contain diagnostic Mesolithic material as well as mainly later Neolithic objects supports this interpretation. Pit [AM09–2241] included two small pieces of worked flint, and a radiocarbon date indicates that this feature may date to the very end of the Mesolithic (4230–4000 cal BC; SUERC-73592); however, it is not certain that the Mesolithic material from the area's other pits dates to the same segment of the later Mesolithic. Pit [AMA09–2080] only contained two undiagnostic pieces of flint and one indeterminate pottery sherd.

The nature of the various lithic-bearing features is uncertain, but some finds may represent non-functional deposition, such as unusual raw materials (eg, rock crystal chips and jasper flakes and blades) and well-executed tools (eg, the scale-flaked blade-knife and the short end-scraper). Three features [AMA09–2152], [AMA09–2164], and [AMA09–2222], contained higher than expected proportions of burnt lithics (between two-thirds and one-quarter). It was possible to refit several burnt pieces from cut [AMA09–2152], and it is thought that probably many more bits from this feature may conjoin with the established refit complexes. A vitrified flake from pit [AMA09–2164] suggests activities that involved more intense use of fire than that associated with ordinary domestic fireplaces, such as cremation or industrial activities (cf. the finds from Skilmafilly cremation cemetery; Ballin 2012a).

Milltimber: Zone West

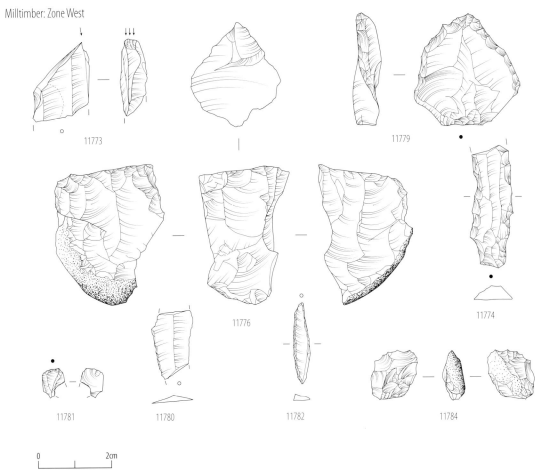

11773

11779

11776

11774

11781   11780   11782   11784

0   2cm

Illus 2.85 West Zone lithics

SOUTH ZONE ASSEMBLAGE

Two flakes were recovered from pit [AMA09–2089]. They may or may not be residual in relation to the feature; an Early to Middle Iron Age radiocarbon date was retrieved from charcoal from the pit (360–110 cal BC, SUERC-74402) although the pit itself was potentially Neolithic, based on the pottery retrieved from the fill.

2.14.2.4 Technological approaches

LATE UPPER PALAEOLITHIC TECHNIQUES

A Late Upper Palaeolithic (LUP) presence at Milltimber was recognised primarily in Zone 4 but individual artefacts were also recovered from other parts of the site. The identification is made on the basis of technology, incorporating an operational schema that differs fundamentally from the knapping styles of the Mesolithic of eastern Scotland. Table 2.12 details some probable Late Upper Palaeolithic pieces found at Milltimber. It is not possible on the basis of the recovered fragments of tanged and backed points to narrow the date down to a specific industry or material culture. On the Continent all are associated with blade production from large opposed-platform cores. However, the broadblade industry discovered at Milltimber must date to the period c13,000–10,000 BC.

This operational schema includes meticulous core preparation, in contrast with that associated with Mesolithic to Early Neolithic microblade/narrow-blade production from small conical cores. The LUP knappers produced large crested blades and core rejuvenation flakes as a by-product of their artefact manufacture. In fact, the opposed-platform blades and crested blades from Zone 4 are so big that the German term Riesenklingen ['giant blades'] seems appropriate, although it is not possible to assign the material from Milltimber to any specific Late Upper Palaeolithic sub-division.

The knapping technique for Late Upper Palaeolithic visitors to Milltimber comprises:

1. Procurement: Several of the raw flint nodules procured would have been up to, and possibly larger than, 150 mm. Flint pebbles presently available along the North Sea coast would mostly have been between 40–70 mm. It is therefore likely that the flint procured by Palaeolithic settlers in Zone 4 was from sources no longer available, such as outcrops on Doggerland (Ballin 2016a; Ballin & Bjerck 2016; Brooks *et al.* 2011; Sturt *et al.* 2013). It is known that, today, flint corresponding in type and quality to the first-class

Table 2.12 Selected likely Late Upper Palaeolithic pieces

Type	Zone	CAT	Fragment	L (mm)	W (mm)	Th (mm)	Estimated original length	Cortex	Other observations
Large blades from opposing-platform cores	–	8391	Medial-distal	25	13	5	c45 mm		Reg trimmed platform-edge at distal end
	3	8395	Intact	79	38	15			
	4	899	Intact	74	30	18			Reg trimmed, rejuvenation platform-edge at distal end
	4	2775	Medial	37	18	7	c60 mm	Soft	
	4	3090	Proximal	42	36	15	Poss 150 mm or more		
	4	3100	Distal	16	24	7	c100 mm or more		Reg trimmed platform-edge at distal end
	4	3186	Intact	81	24	15		Soft-ish	Reg trimmed platform-edge at distal end; probably used
	4	6592	Medial-distal	56	21	13	c75 mm		Reg trimmed platform-edge at distal end
	4	11371	Distal	31	34	20	Poss 100 mm or more		Reg trimmed platform-edge at distal end
	4/5	9953	Intact	118	68	25			Reg trimmed platform-edge at distal end
	4/5	10020	Intact	60	28	11			Reg trimmed platform-edge at distal end
	5	3945	Intact	43	18	7			Reg trimmed platform-edge at distal end
Crested blades	3	10117	Intact	71	22	9			10117–18 refits dorsal-ventrally
	4	3187	Intact	65	23	8			
	4	10102	Proximal-medial	56	24	12	c68 mm		From opposing-platform core
	4	10103	Med-distal	59	21	9	c68 mm		
	4	10110	Med-distal	93	33	19	At least 105 mm		
	4	10183	Med	52	28	15	Poss 120 mm or more		From opposing-platform core
	4/5	9929	Med	59	31	11	c110 mm		From opposing-platform core
	4/5	10118	Intact	63	25	12			
	4/5	10121	Intact	66	24	14			From opposing-platform core; use-wear from cutting
Platform rejuvenation flakes	–	10120	Intact	83	32	16			Platform length at least 83mm; use-wear from cutting
	3	10104	Intact	34	17	7			10104, 10182, 10184 refit, one on top of the other
	3	10182	Intact	37	33	6			10104, 10182, 10184 refit, one on top of the other
	3	10184	Intact	26	26	4			10104, 10182, 10184 refit, one on top of the other
	4/5	10138	Intact	43	33	12			

Table 2.12 Selected likely Late Upper Palaeolithic pieces (Continued)

Type	Zone	CAT	Fragment	L (mm)	W (mm)	Th (mm)	Estimated original length	Cortex	Other observations
	5	10129	Intact	47	26	11			10129/10157 almost refit (same core)
	5	10157	Intact	52	29	13			10129/10157 almost refit (same core)
Opposing-platform cores	4	10059	Intact	48	28	27			Typical UP opposing-platform core, but very small
Idiosyncratic point	4	10456	Intact	29	11	3			Sur enclume retouch; straight base
Tip of tanged or other point	4	10265	Distal	15	8	2	Original size uncertain		Similar frags are known from Howburn, S Lanark
Backed blade (point?)	4	10567	Proximal-medial	27	9	4			Sur enclume retouch
Backed blade (point?)	4	10289	Proximal-medial	20	9	3	c28 mm		
Piece with double truncation (point?)	4	10236	Intact	36	16	4			Truncations are straight and oblique, and 10236 angle-backed
Large oval end-scraper (non-Mesolithic)	4	10214	Intact	45	31	8			
Blade-scraper with acute scraper-angle	4	10507	Intact	70	34	15			On crested blade from opposing-platform core
Large blade with abraded retouch	4	10291	Intact	91	24	10			With abraded retouch (pol-edge imp); use-wear from cutting

flint mined or collected in prehistoric Yorkshire or East Anglia is available from sources in the North Sea (Harker 2002).

2. Opening: As the target blanks of this industry were long broad blades, rather than microblades, core rough-outs were not created by splitting small pebbles into two, but by removing a primary opening flake from large nodules (for example rejuvenation flake CAT10120). This allowed sizeable opposed-platform core rough-outs to be formed, and subsequently very long and broad blades to be produced.

3. Core preparation: The recovery of several partially cortical crests (eg, CAT10102; Illus 2.86) suggests that cresting was used in connection with the initial formation of the core rough-outs, with some cortex-free crests (eg, CAT10103) being detached as part of the adjustment to the shape of the cores during the actual blank production. Although this is unlikely to be an absolute rule, first-generation crests (from the formation of the core rough-outs) are in many cases bilateral (that is, with small flakes having been detached to either side of the crest), whereas second-generation crests

(from the adjustment of core-shape during blank production) tend to be unilateral (that is, with small flakes having been detached to one side of an existing dorsal arris left by previous blade detachments). There is also a trend towards many of the Late Upper Palaeolithic crests being located very close to one lateral side of the blade, rather than at the centre of the dorsal face (eg, CAT10118). Crests were frequently detached serially: if the detachment of one crest resulted in the production of an irregular blade, or if the resulting core shape was not satisfactory, other crests would be formed below the first one, and then detached (eg, dorsal-ventrally conjoining crests CAT10117 and CAT10118; although they refit, there is space between them for a third crest).

During blade production the cores were carefully curated. Both opposed platforms were regularly adjusted (eg, CAT10059 where both platforms of the opposed-platform core have been rejuvenated, Illus 2.67), and several refit complexes testify to the serial detachment of core tablets. CAT10129 and CAT10157 do not fit exactly (Illus 2.87), but the

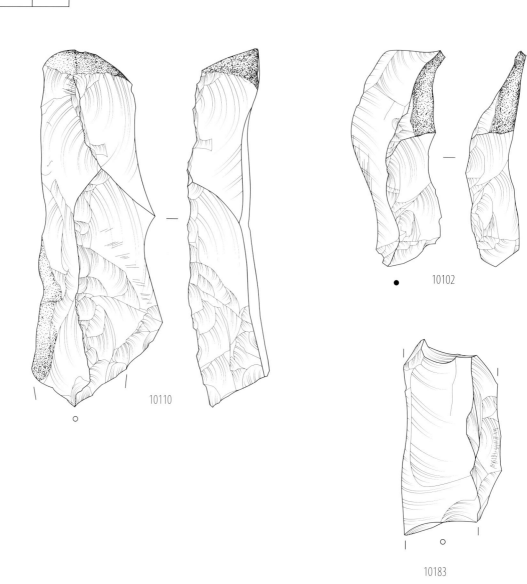

Illus 2.86 Zone 4 Late Upper Palaeolithic large crested pieces

patterns of the cortex of one core-side are so distinct that these two pieces must have been detached from the same parent core. The missing flake between the two would almost certainly have been a third core tablet. In this case, three core tablets were detached, one after the other, without any blades having been detached; presumably, the knapper perceived each consecutive platform as unsatisfactory. CAT10104, CAT10182 and CAT10184 from Zone 3 form another complex of refitting core tablets. In this case, a first core tablet was detached, then a few blades were produced, a second core tablet was then detached, with the later platform-edge having moved a few millimetres back, and then this process was repeated a third time.

The platform-edges are generally well-trimmed and occasionally also abraded (CAT5757, CAT754,

CAT8317 and CAT3554; Illus 2.88). Some of the crested pieces also display dorsal blade-scars detached from opposed directions (eg, CAT10102, CAT10110, CAT10183; Illus 2.86, and CAT10121; not illustrated). The relative dimensions of the frequently elongated core tablets suggest that the Late Upper Palaeolithic opposed-platform cores may have looked very much like the cores described by Madsen (1992, fig 81B) as typical Hamburgian cores, with a main flaking-front, and two opposed, sloping, elongated platforms (also see Weber 2012, fig 32).

4. Blank production: The Late Upper Palaeolithic visitors to the site focused on the production of long, wide and sturdy blades (length up to 150 mm; width in many cases between 20–40 mm) by the application of mainly soft percussion. As might be expected, some of the

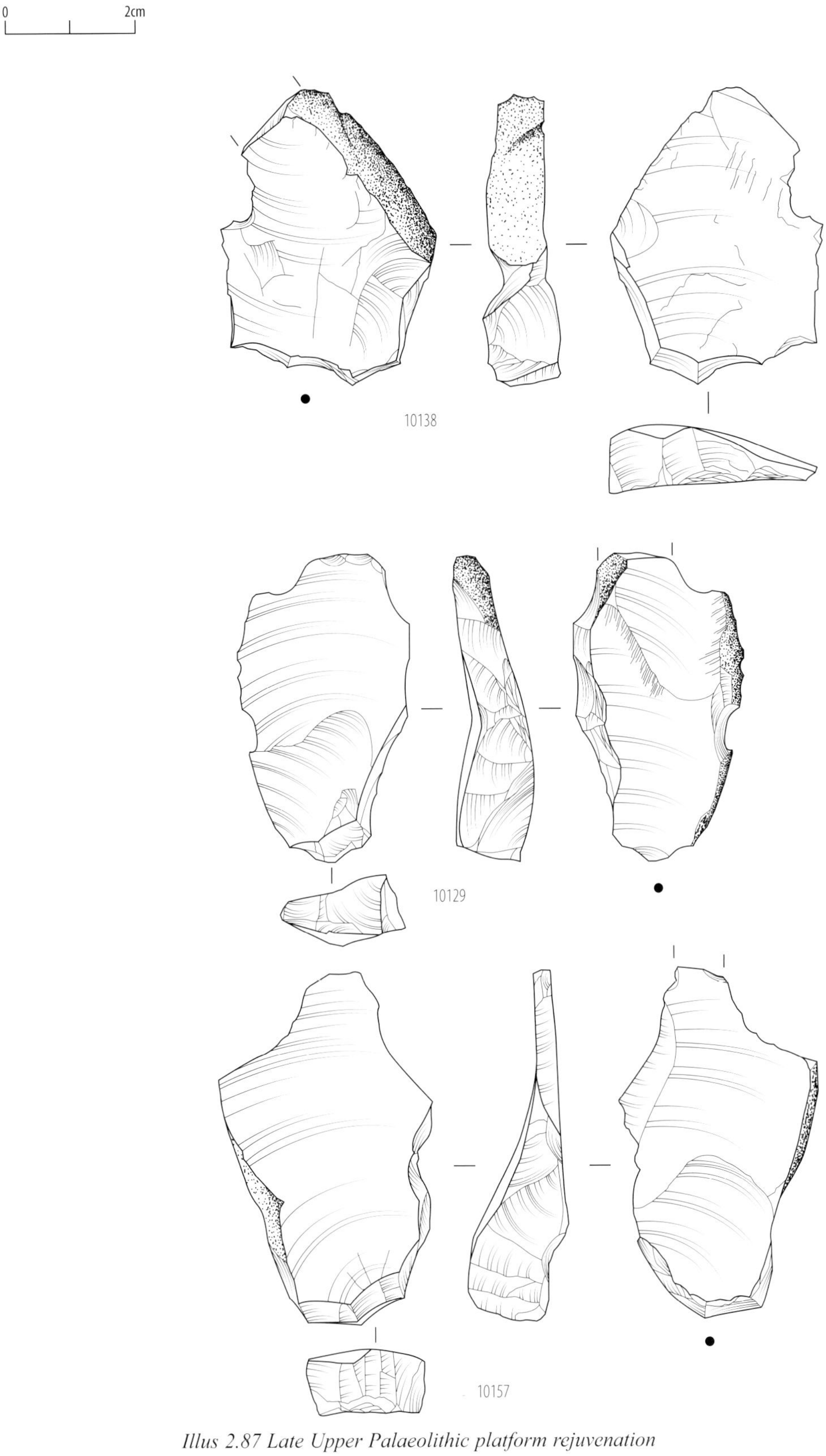

0   2cm

10138

10129

10157

Illus 2.87 Late Upper Palaeolithic platform rejuvenation

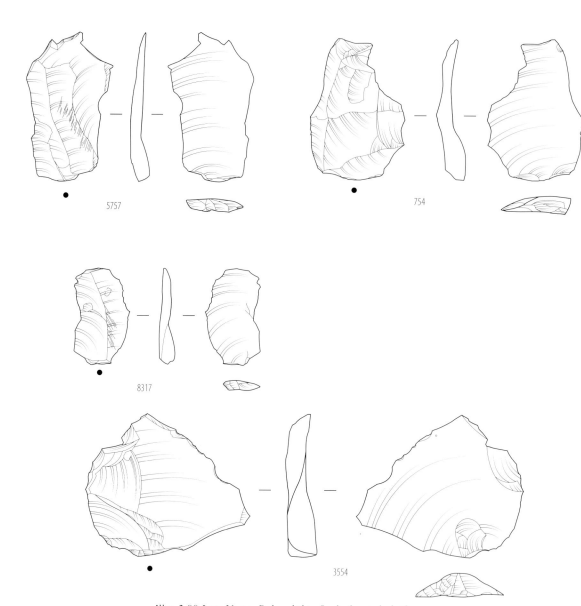

Illus 2.88 Late Upper Palaeolithic finely faceted platforms

largest (particularly crested) blades were detached by hard percussion (eg, crested blade-scraper CAT10507 (Illus 2.70). Some flakes would also have been produced as part of the preparation process (decortication, and cresting), but it is impossible to distinguish these from Mesolithic flakes.

5. Tool production: A number of implements and implement fragments from Milltimber are likely Palaeolithic. These include five points, three scrapers and two truncated pieces or knives. It is difficult to say whether other large Palaeolithic tools were absent, as these

pieces could have been recycled by later Mesolithic visitors to the site.

MESOLITHIC TECHNIQUES

Mesolithic reduction techniques were compiled from the evidence of Zone 4, Zone 5, and through comparison to the Standingstones (Chapter 4) pieces. Mesolithic production in Zone 4 appears to have focused almost entirely on the manufacture of microliths. Table 2.13 provides a comparison of the Upper Palaeolithic and Mesolithic schemata.

Table 2.13 Comparison of the Late Upper Palaeolithic and Late Mesolithic operational schemas responsible for the lithic sub-assemblage from Zone 4

		Late Upper Palaeolithic	Late Mesolithic
Procurement	Material	Procurement of flint nodules with GDs of up to, and possibly beyond, 150 mm.	Procurement of flint pebbles with GDs of c40–70 mm
	Provenance	Most likely outcrops on Doggerland.	Most likely North Sea beaches
Preferred core type		Large opposed-platform macroblade cores.	Small conical microblade cores
Opening		The character of the core tablets (only one opposing-platform core has been recovered) suggests that nodules were opened by detaching a primary opening flake.	Platform-to-platform refitting of cores (Standingstones) suggests that pebbles were generally split into two rough-outs with immediately available plain striking platforms
Heat treatment			Only clearly indicated at Standingstones
Core preparation	Prior to production	Extensive cresting (eg CAT10110) and trimming.	No cresting, but extensive platform-edge trimming
	During production	Serial cresting (eg refit CAT10117-8) and platform rejuvenation (eg refit CAT10129, CAT10157, and refit CAT10104, CAT10182 and CAT10184).	Little or no platform rejuvenation, but adjustment of core shape by cresting
Blank production	Target blanks	Large macroblades with lengths of up to 120 mm, and widths of 20-40 mm.	Microblades and narrow-blades with intended widths of c5–11mm
	Percussion technique	Soft percussion.	Soft percussion, probably generally pressure-flaking
Tool production	Main tool forms	Large blade-scrapers and oval scrapers and fragments of points have been recovered from Site 2D. Crested blades and large blades were used as knives without modification.	Predominantly microliths, but some small piercers, scrapers, and truncated pieces (knives) have also been recovered. A large assemblage of heavily abraded implements was retrieved from Zone 5
Core abandonment		Uncertain, as only one small opposing-platform core was recovered. The large UP cores may either have been 'tossed' out of the site (Binford 1983), exported out of the site when the settlers left, or scavenged by LM settlers 'strip-mining' the UP site. Bipolar technique not applied.	The conical cores were generally abandoned when they were deemed useless due to the development of deep hinge- or step fractures, or overshot

1. Procurement: The dimensions of the recovered microblades/narrow-blades and cores, in conjunction with the presence of abraded cortex, suggest that pebbles were collected from North Sea beaches approximately 12 km away. The site at Milltimber was located close to the River Dee, which would have made transport of raw flint easy. The size of the artefacts and the curvature of the outer surfaces of the cores suggest a general size of these nodules of c40–70 mm.

2. Opening: Sometimes cores are refitted platform-to-platform, indicating that rather than opening pebbles by detaching a primary so-called 'opening flake', pebbles are opened by simply splitting them across, thus forming two core rough-outs with ready-made plain striking platforms. This may have been the approach followed by the Mesolithic visitors to Zone 4.

3. Heat-treatment: Sometimes the raw flint pebbles are heat-treated. The indicators (burnt pebbles, blades and

cores with shiny surfaces) are not present in the Zone 4 Mesolithic sub-assemblage, but the possibility that heat-treatment of flint took place cannot be excluded.

4. Core preparation: Prior to initiation of blank production, the Mesolithic cores received little core preparation other than platform-edge trimming. Some narrow crests are sometimes created during the reduction process to adjust core shape between blade series. The character of the mostly plain platforms of the conical cores supports the view that, during this period, platforms were in most cases not rejuvenated. The surviving cores are predominantly neat conical single-platform cores from the focused production of narrow blades (widths c5–13 mm), most likely for the manufacture of microliths.

5. Blank production: The Mesolithic visitors to the Milltimber area produced two forms of blanks, namely squat, mainly hard-hammer flakes (most of the 1051

pieces from Zone 4), and elongated microblades/narrow-blades (most of Zone 4's 652 pieces).

6. Tool production: The tools from the area include four main groups, namely microliths and microlith-related implements (24 pieces, supplemented by 34 microburins), points (five pieces), scrapers (five pieces), and truncated pieces or knives (three pieces). The microliths are all based on regular soft-hammer microblades or narrow-blades. As indicated by the approximate numerical parity between microliths and microburins (24:34), most microliths were manufactured by the application of microburin technique, although some may have been produced either by simply snapping off the proximal end or by retouching obliquely through the bulbar area (approaches demonstrated at Standing-stones and at Milltimber's Zone 5). In this zone, the microliths are dominated notably by scalene forms, supplemented by a small number of obliquely blunted pieces, Krukowski pieces, and backed bladelets. Owing to the mixture of Late Mesolithic and Late Upper Palaeolithic material, it is not possible to determine whether different types of blanks were preferred for different types of non-microlithic tools during the Late Mesolithic visits to the area.

HEAVILY ABRADED IMPLEMENTS

This technological summary is based on an approach linked specifically to heavily abraded implements primarily found in Zone 5. In terms of form and use, the assemblage of heavily abraded implements come across as a homogeneous category, and the fact that the vast majority of them were recovered from one well-defined cluster centred on grids BX/BY41 (84% of all heavily abraded implements), indicates that they were made, used and deposited by the same person or group of persons within a very narrow time span, and that this well-defined scatter represents one event focusing on the execution of one specific task.

Table 2.14 shows the location of the use, edge preparation, whether an edge or a pointed part was abraded, and the degree of abrasion of this assemblage. In total, 306 used 'parts' were identified on the 157 heavily abraded implements.

The left and right lateral edges were used to an equal extent, as would be expected. The distal end was also commonly used. If the distal end was broad, its edges would be used, and if it was pointed or had protruding corners, these parts were used. The proximal end was used less commonly, but the edges and protruding parts of this end were also occasionally employed.

More than half of the used tool parts were modified by steep edge-retouch prior to use, with approximately one-third being unmodified pieces. In 8% of the cases, platform remnant edges were used, and in 9% of the cases, the used edges are break facets. The employment of break facets suggests that some of these pieces are

Table 2.14 Characterisation of the heavily abraded implements from Zone 5

Location	Number	Edge prep	Tip/edge	Degree
Proximal	44			
Left lateral	91			
Right lateral	81			
Distal	89			
Dorsal	1			
Unmodified		99		
Modified		156		
Edge of platform remnant		24		
Break facet		27		
Tip			44	
Edge			260	
Platform surface			1	
Uncertain			1	
Barely notable				120
Light				159
Heavy				27
Total	306	306	306	306

recycled blanks or tools (eg CAT10639, CAT10645, both on Illus 2.89; CAT10695–6, CAT10743). Most used parts have a retouched base indicating the edges or points were modified to make them usable for a specialised task. Although the used parts are mostly edges (85%), a notable proportion of these are tips, or pointed/protruding parts.

The assessment of the degree of use is based on the analyst's subjective impression. A total of 39% of the pieces have barely notable but macroscopically visible use-wear; as many as 52% have light use-wear; and 9% of the implements are characterised by heavy use-wear. If all edges and pointed parts of all lithic artefacts from Zone 5 were inspected by the consistent use of a microscope, this tool category would almost certainly expand exponentially.

In addition, four pieces have lateral use-wear from cutting (CAT10605, CAT10643, CAT10704, CAT10721; not illustrated), and CAT10650 seems to have a degree of gloss, possibly indicating the processing of vegetable matter.

General technological analysis of the implements shows that they:

1. are mostly based on dense, opaque, monochrome or marbled grey flint;
2. include five crested pieces (CAT10618, CAT10633, CAT10721, CAT10745; not illustrated and CAT10754; Illus 2.89);
3. are partly based on thick flakes/flake fragments and whole or broken blades/microblades (flake:blade ratio 63:37);

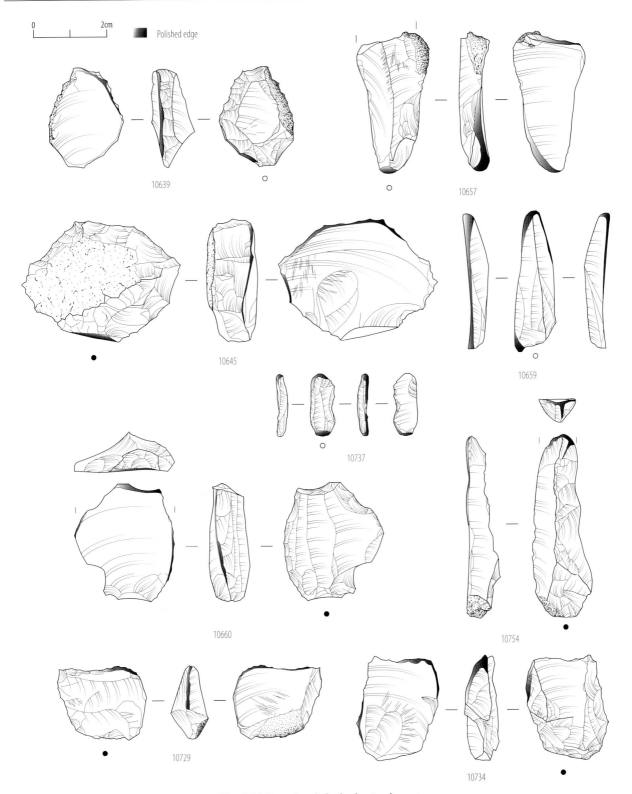

0   2cm

Polished edge

10639

10657

10645

10659

10737

10660

10754

10729

10734

Illus 2.89 Zone 5 polished-edge implements

4. include mostly broad-blades (blade:microblade ratio 93:7; average width 13 mm); and
5. most of the blades are hard percussion specimens (hard: soft percussion ratio of definable pieces 59:41). The curvature of some of the blades indicates that these pieces were struck off conical single-platform cores,

rather than representing scavenged material from the Late Upper Palaeolithic Zone 4 concentration, which is based on opposed-platform technique.

Ten of the polished edge pieces were submitted for use-wear analysis (CAT10639, CAT10645, CAT10657,

CAT10659, CAT10605, CAT10660, CAT10729, CAT10734, CAT10737 and CAT10754). The pieces submitted are all 'blade-like flakes' and are a similar size and shape (mean length 31 mm, mean width 20 mm, mean thickness 8.5 mm), with wide, rounded, distal ends and relatively short, straight, lateral edges. They are all heavily rounded around these edges and have the same polish pattern. This extends along the edges and round into the dorsal. The polish pattern on the ventral side begins at the edge and does not extend into the ventral surface of the artefact. This suggests they were held with the ventral face upwards, and used in a pulling fashion, on soft material.

This roundness of edges was so pronounced that they must have been heavily used in this way. The nature of the polish distribution and the rounding, suggests they were used as a smoother of some sort on a soft material. For example, they could have been used on hide, to remove the fat or smooth and soften the material. In terms of size and shape, there appears to be little correlation with their use. Artefact lengths range from 31–48 mm, shape (width/length) ranges from 0.3 mm (long and thin) to 0.87 mm (short and squat); however, edge angles are almost universally low (average 18.40).

In summary, the area's heavily abraded implements were used to rub, scrape, or smooth some as yet unknown soft materials in a number of different ways (the use of edges as well as tips).

In terms of dating this event, the use of relatively large, predominantly hard percussion blades indicates a date in the later Neolithic, suggesting that this group of objects may indeed be contemporary with the later Neolithic polished-edge implements from, for example, sites near Overhowden Henge in the Borders (Ballin 2011b), but the general distribution of artefacts across Zone 5 suggests a different scenario. The distribution of chips, blades and burnt pieces indicates the presence of at least six concentrations and hearths, with the most notable one being centred on grids BX/BY41. This concentration also includes many narrow blades, microliths (almost exclusively scalene triangles) and microburins, and it is highly likely that the heavily abraded implements are contemporary with these pieces, and therefore Mesolithic.

2.14.3 The coarse stone
Julie Lochrie

A broken edge from a large saddle quern, in two conjoining parts, was retrieved from pit [AMA09–2089]. The original dimensions and shape are not known but it would have been heavy and not an easily portable object (the fragments measure 29.5 mm × 14.5 mm × 97 mm). This was the only example from Milltimber.

Dating the saddle quern is not an easy task; they are used from the Neolithic to the Iron Age with no fixed

date when they become obsolete. This example is likely to be Early to Middle Iron Age given a radiocarbon date of 360–110 cal BC (SUERC-74402) from the pit where it was discovered.

The grinding surface shows the quern is well used and would have performed an essential domestic function that indicates likely occupation in the vicinity. The deposition of querns is often discussed in terms beyond discard, relating to how quernstones have a wider meaning to the household and community. It is often theorised that they embody the life cycle and of seasonal change, especially since they are such an essential component of food production (Culduthel, Inverness, McLaren in prep; North Kessock, Inverness, Lochrie in prep; and Kintore, Aberdeenshire, Engl 2008). However, strong evidence for the Milltimber deposit being deliberately structured is scant. Pit [AMA09–2089] is isolated and cannot be phased alongside any other features. There were also several other large but natural stones in the deposit that could just as likely point towards small-scale area clearance. If Iron Age in date, comparative examples of structured deposition from this period can be found at Birnie (ScARF 2012d) and Kintore (Engl 2008, 223–24).

2.14.4 Industrial waste
Dawn McLaren

An assemblage comprising a limited quantity (782.3 g) and range of vitrified material was recovered during excavations at Milltimber. With the exception of two small fragments of low-density fuel ash slag, the assemblage is dominated by waste indicative of ferrous metalworking activities, specifically blacksmithing. All of the waste identified is residual material that was recovered from secondary contexts, including from an abandonment deposit in a probable Roman oven, an isolated probably medieval post-hole and soils within a palaeochannel. None of the ironworking slags recovered are chronologically distinctive but they could be Iron Age or later in date.

2.14.4.1 Classification
The material was subject to macroscopic examination to enable classification based on morphology, density and colour. Overall, this is a small quantity of vitrified debris that provides limited evidence for ironworking, probably smithing. A summary of the vitrified material is presented in Table 2.15 and a full catalogue of the material is given in the archive report (see Appendix 2.2.21).

2.14.4.2 Diagnostic ferrous metalworking waste
Only two types of diagnostic ferrous slag types were present; these consisted of two plano-convex slag cakes (PCSC) and a limited quantity of hammerscale (HS). Plano-convex slag cakes are typically sub-circular or oval accumulations of slag formed during ironworking. These can survive in a range of sizes and can vary considerably

Table 2.15 Summary of vitrified material by type

Type	Mass (g)
Plano-convex slag cake (PCSC)	656
Hammerscale (HS)	1.1
Unclassified iron slag (UIS)	111.3
Low-density fuel ash slag/vitrified ceramic (FAS)	13.9
Total	782.3

in weight and density, making it difficult to be sure whether they were produced during smelting or smithing based on visual examination alone (McDonnell 1994, 229; Bayley *et al.* 2001, 14).

Two plano-convex slag cakes (SF 1 & 2) were recovered from the fill of palaeochannel [2B-2650]. Their dimensions, texture, weight and form is consistent with smithing hearth bottoms from Iron Age and later sites in Scotland (eg McDonnell 1994, 230; McDonnell 2000, 219). These smithing hearth bottoms are recognisable by their characteristic plano-convex form, having a rough convex base with frequent small charcoal impressions and a smoother, vitrified, upper surface; they are formed as the result of high-temperature reactions between iron, hammerscale and silica from the hearth lining or flux, which accumulate at the base of the smith's hearth (McDonnell 1994, 230; Starley 2000, 338). Both examples from Milltimber are substantially complete compact cakes of small dimensions. They are 85.5 mm and 88.5 mm in diameter, 38 mm to 76 mm in thickness and are 229.8 g and 426.2 g in weight respectively. One cake, SF 1, is a particularly thick and heavy example and appears to comprise a series of small cakes superimposed on one another, suggested by the traces of at least two layers observed on the external curving edges of the cake. A similar amalgam was recovered from an Iron Age hearth at Seafield West, Inverness, where chemical and microstructural analysis confirmed that the cake consisted of two superimposed hearth bottoms indicative of distinct but sequential phases of smithing within the same hearth (Heald *et al.* 2011, 21–22). Layered smithing hearth bottoms, such as the example from Milltimber and from further afield at Seafield West, are thought to occur when sequential episodes of smithing take place prior to the hearth being cleaned out, allowing a hearth bottom to form and fuse to an existing cake at the base of the forge hearth (*ibid.*, 22). The second slag cake from Milltimber, SF 2, appears to represent only a single phase of metalworking activity. As the methods of blacksmithing within a simple forge saw little change from the Iron Age onwards, it is impossible to date hearth bottoms closely simply on the basis of their form alone.

Further evidence of smithing activities was recovered in the form of a limited amount of magnetic hammerscale flakes (1.1 g) from post-hole [2B-0080]. Micro-debris of this form

is usually found in the immediate vicinity of the smithing hearth and anvil and, where found in significant quantities, can indicate precisely the focus of the blacksmithing activity (Starley 1995; Heald 2002, 71). No *in situ* metalworking features or hearths were noted in the vicinity of post-hole [2B-0080] but the presence of diagnostic micro-debris implies that blacksmithing took place in the area.

In addition to these classifiable, diagnostic, ironworking slags are small quantities (111.3 g) of unclassified iron slag (UIS). These are amorphous, small and fractured pieces of iron-rich vitrified material which, although likely to be debris from ironworking, are not possible to assign to a particular stage in the process (Crew & Rehren 2002, 84). These are likely to represent rake-out from an iron-smelting furnace or smithing hearth. The pieces from Milltimber came from upper soils within oven F17 [2B-2123] and post-hole [2B-0080] and are likely residual.

2.14.4.3 Other vitrified materials

A small amount of material from Milltimber (13.9 g) is a low-density slag characterised by its vitreous and vesicular nature, low density and friability. This type of slag is typically called fuel ash slag and is formed when material such as earth, clay, stones or ceramics are subjected to high temperatures, for example in a hearth (Bayley 1985, 41–43; Bayley *et al.* 2001, 21). These can be formed during any high temperature pyrotechnic process and do not necessarily indicate deliberate industrial activity. This material was recovered from the fill of post-hole [2B-0080] and is likely to be domestic hearth waste. Similar material was recovered with fuel debris and hearth sweepings associated with later prehistoric roundhouses at Oldmeldrum, Aberdeenshire (McLaren 2010, 19).

2.14.5 Finds discussion

Milltimber has played host to communities over millennia. The wealth of material culture found at the site only scratches the surface of helping us understand how useful and important the site has been for people through the centuries. To describe the occupation in popular terms, the finds from Milltimber may be associated with Late Upper Palaeolithic 'reindeer hunters', Late Mesolithic 'hunter-gatherers of the forest', Early and Middle Neolithic 'farming communities', Chalcolithic 'ceremonial landscapers' and possibly, Iron Age metalworkers.

2.14.5.1 Late Upper Palaeolithic

The first stage in the search for a Scottish Late Upper Palaeolithic has been the recovery of diagnostic implement forms dating to this period, in particular the well-known and highly diagnostic pre-Mesolithic tanged and backed points (eg, Livens 1956; Ballin & Saville 2003; Ballin & Bjerck 2016). The inclusion of a technologically based approach now allows us to identify Late Upper Palaeolithic activity where typological evidence may be absent or sparse, such as at Milltimber. The importance of this discovery goes beyond simply being able to state the presence of a Late Upper Palaeolithic site in eastern Scotland – only the fourth such site to have been discovered in Scotland (in addition to Howburn, Kilmelfort Cave and Rubha Port an t-Seilich; Ballin *et al.* 2010; Saville & Ballin 2009; Mithen *et al.* 2015). It also introduces a new approach for the identification of Late Upper Palaeolithic settlement sites in Scotland.

Another aspect when considering the Scottish Palaeolithic in the future is the possibility that Upper Palaeolithic lithic scatters may have been used by later visitors, who found in the large cores, blanks and implements a ready-made source of raw material

In terms of the interpretation of the Late Upper Palaeolithic activity discovered at Milltimber it is important to note the composition of this assemblage and how it differs from other assemblages from this period. Where Scottish Mesolithic sites may yield a relatively low number of burins (eg, Glentaggart in South Lanarkshire and Donich Park in Argyll – four and two pieces, respectively; Ballin & Johnson 2005; Ballin 2012b), Scottish Upper Palaeolithic sites occasionally yield notably higher numbers (eg Howburn Farm in South Lanarkshire – 34 pieces; Ballin *et al.* 2010; forthcoming). The Late Upper Palaeolithic sub-assemblage from Milltimber includes no burins at all, adding to the impression that activities at this location and at this time were 'narrow-spectred' and corresponded to activities taking place at the site in Mesolithic times, namely the production of blanks for making points and microliths to replace lost and damaged ones – in Keeley's (1982) terms, 're-tooling'.

2.14.5.2 Mesolithic – 8200–4500 BC

The Mesolithic scatters generally seem to be the remains of short-term visits to the site by small groups of people, probably hunting parties. The lithic finds are heavily dominated by primary waste from the production of blades and microblades, supplemented by some fragments of points and numerous microliths. The latter are associated with roughly equal numbers of microburins, which were discarded during the production of the microliths. Most likely, the reason for these groups to make a stop at Milltimber was to produce blanks, which were then transformed into points and microliths to be inserted into composite hunting equipment, to replace broken or lost pieces. Other flint implements are rare at the site, such as scrapers and knives, adding to the impression that the site's scatters are most certainly not the remains of base camps, or parts of such camps, but ad hoc pieces produced for subsistence-related tasks during the short-term visits to this location. Certainly no settlement structures were identified here and the interpretation of the large pits as hunting traps could imply the area was primarily a known hunting site that was returned to seasonally.

The evidence from the zones within the scatter points to short-term visits to Milltimber. Most likely, the visiting groups were small bands of hunter-gatherers who stopped at a location for a short period of time – possibly as little

as hours or days – with the main purpose of manufacturing large numbers of microblades and microliths to replenish their depleted hunting equipment. Small numbers of scrapers and knives may represent subsistence-related activities, such as preparing food, although some may also have been used to process killed prey.

Generally, the lithic industry can be defined by the production of microblades from conical cores, followed by the modification of these blanks into a number of microlith forms. At Milltimber, these microlith forms are predominantly scalene triangles and crescents, supplemented by small numbers of edge-blunted and obliquely blunted pieces. Non-microlithic implement forms are relatively rare. As at Nethermills Farm (Ballin 2013a), the microliths seem to have been manufactured almost exclusively by the application of microburin technique, with microliths and microburins being almost equally numerous. The microlith:microburin ratio is 47:53 in favour of microburins. Comparing this scenario with assemblages from the west coast of Scotland, a clear east–west split becomes apparent, as the microburin technique seems to have been used considerably less frequently in the west than in the east.

The lithic assemblage from Shieldaig, Loch Torridon, for example, includes roughly the same number of microliths and microburins, with each sub-assemblage containing c25 microliths and one microburin; that is, microburins made up c4% of the two microlithic sub-assemblages (Ballin 2001). These results are supported by the assemblages recovered by Mercer from Mesolithic sites on Jura, such as Lealt Bay (Mercer 1968), which had a microburin ratio of only 16%. West coast assemblages recovered more recently also have relatively few microburins, and at Camas Daraich on Skye (Wickham-Jones & Hardy 2004) microburins make up only 3% of pieces and fragments with microlithic retouch.

It is possible that this difference reflects the use of different raw materials in the two regions, with the Mesolithic of Aberdeenshire being defined by the almost exclusive use of high-grade flint, whereas quartz and other raw materials with relatively poor flaking properties (eg bloodstone, baked mudstone, flint-like chert) were used extensively in the west (Ballin 2014b). It is also possible that the fewer microburins in the west reflect more widespread use of bipolar technique (for example adapting to the region's small flint pebbles and quartz), and the use of naturally pointed bipolar spalls as blanks, rather than true microblades. Although this difference is likely to be real, it is also possible that the microburin ratio of older assemblages from the west represents less meticulous examination. Examination of the lithics from the present project involved every single chip examined in magnification (8×) to allow microburins with GDs of as little as 2 mm to be identified. To test this hypothesis, it would be helpful if older west-coast assemblages could be re-examined.

During the investigation of the lithics from Zone 5, it was noticed that scalene triangles and crescents were recovered from different parts of the zone, that crescents were approximately twice as wide as scalene triangles, and that the two microlith forms were based on microblades of different width. This scenario led to a discussion of the reasons for this variation, where one interpretation is that the different width of the diverse microlith types may indicate different ages. However, it is presently not possible to rule out that the variation may indicate functional differences, or simply idiosyncratic preferences among the Late Mesolithic knappers. The Late Mesolithic microlith assemblage from Fife Ness (Wickham-Jones & Dalland 1998) is also based predominantly on crescents, with other Late Mesolithic microlith assemblages from Scotland – not least from the West Coast and Hebridean regions – being dominated by scalene triangles or being mixed.

It has been suggested that the presently unique group of polished-edge implements – which in terms of appearance differ somewhat from related Neolithic pieces (Ballin 2011b) – may date to the Late Mesolithic period. They were clearly used to process soft materials, causing the development of rounding, facets, and striations, but at the present moment their specific use is somewhat enigmatic. In terms of future research, it would be possible to carry out analysis of wear-patterns on the later Neolithic polished-edge implements, defined by more shining and mirror-like surfaces, with the intention of defining the differences between these two related groups of heavily abraded implements.

2.14.5.3 Early Neolithic – 4000–3700 BC

The finds dating to the Early Neolithic period include a few scattered lithics and the remains of up to 30 Carinated Bowls. The activity is mainly clustered at the north of the site.

Overall, only a handful of lithics were interpreted as Neolithic. The technology of the Mesolithic through to Early Neolithic relied on the production of small blades, making it difficult to tease them apart. When these small blades are found within a mass of Mesolithic tools it must be assumed that most are Mesolithic. Therefore, identifying Early Neolithic debitage is not simple and likely underestimated. Tools, on the other hand, are easier to identify to period. A leaf-shaped point recovered from a pit close to the dated Early Neolithic structure was one such Neolithic implement. A serrated blade from Zone 5 was also defined as Neolithic (cf Saville 2006; Suddaby & Ballin 2010), and the delicate nature of this piece defines it as more likely to be Early Neolithic than later Neolithic. An informal sickle from pit [2D-1398] is also likely to be Early Neolithic.

Traditional Carinated Bowl pottery is known at other sites in Aberdeenshire with similar date brackets to those obtained from the radiocarbon dating at Milltimber (Deer's Den, Alexander 2000; Pitdrichie, Lochrie 2010c; Westgate, Lochrie 2010a). The date of the CBNE is also likely to fall within this period. CBNE is part of the Carinated Bowl tradition at a time when the traditional styles began to include modifications. This 'style drift' in the north-east

saw the addition of fluting as an early modification, such as in vessel 02-V1, and began from as early as c3800 BC (eg OxA-8132, OxA-8131, Oxa-8133, Deer's Den, Alexander 2000, 17; GU-9155, Dubton Farm, MacSween 2002, 41; Warren Field, Sheridan 2009, 92).

The period between c3970–3700 BC is a time of great change in the British Isles, with the introduction of ceramics, agricultural practices and new construction techniques. These new elements are certainly borne out by the evidence from Milltimber. Here for the first time we have domestic refuse in pits, evidence of a roofed structure and some small evidence for spreads of refuse, left where it was dropped. Even at later Mesolithic sites with solid evidence for roofed structures there is a proliferation of knapping debris across living surfaces (Howick, Howburn, Waddington 2007; Echline Fields, Robertson *et al.* 2013). This would suggest that by the Neolithic there are different patterns of behaviour relating to the organisation of space, particularly in relation to rubbish and removal of items from general circulation.

Consideration of how conscious Neolithic people would have been of the traces of Mesolithic activity left visible on the ground (see also Chapter 6.10) is relevant at Milltimber. In two instances Early Neolithic pottery was found in the top of Mesolithic features. The quantities of pottery are small and they are abraded, suggesting they form part of general refuse accumulating or dumped in the hollow left by the Mesolithic hunting pits. This occurrence of Neolithic material appearing in the top of Mesolithic features is recognised at other sites (eg Blackdog, Chapter 6; Warren Field, Murray *et al.* 2009; Chapelfield, Atkinson 2002; Port Elphinstone, Lochrie 2013; Garthdee Road, Murray & Murray 2014). The deposition of the pottery in a hollow seems to be intentional; whether they recognised the hollows as being man-made, and whether the placement was acknowledging previous activity on the site, is another question.

The circumstance of deposition of 02-V40 needs to be considered in a little more detail as a much higher quantity of this vessel was found compared to the rest of the Early Neolithic pottery assemblage. It was found in the top of a pit [2D-1895], a complex hearth feature that may have enlarged or enhanced an earlier tree throw or natural hollow. The deposition of a near-complete vessel could signify a ritual purpose for this feature, beyond a simple hearth.

The lithic assemblage also shows two Early Neolithic artefacts of note. Pit [2D-1927], associated with the Neolithic structure, contained a leaf-shaped point which, being a so-called 'special' object, could be interpreted as a deliberate, ritual deposition. However, it is also accompanied by small abraded fragments from several Carinated Bowls. The pottery sherds, in contrast to the leaf-shaped arrowhead, are nothing remarkable. Also of note is a sickle recovered from pit [2D-1398] within the flint scatter. This solitary and heavily used sickle was all that was found within this feature and it seems unusual as a chance or accidental loss. Despite these two possible examples of something more ritualistic, the Early Neolithic assemblage is overall typical of domestic activity.

2.14.5.4 Middle and Late Neolithic – 3500–3100 BC

The artefactual evidence for Middle Neolithic activity is small and primarily comes from six Impressed Ware vessels and a couple of lithics. The evidence comprises too small a group to support any level of continuous occupation, which is supported by the radiocarbon dates from features in this period, suggesting more spasmodic activity.

Despite being a long-lived pottery typologically, the Impressed Ware vessel found in [AMA09–2058], could be narrowed to a probable date of between around 3300 and 3000 BC. The completeness of the vessel is remarkable, and unrepresentative of the pottery found elsewhere at Milltimber. Parallels can be drawn with the complete Beaker placed in a post-hole from the Chalcolithic timber setting further to the south. Even if a small portion had broken off, necessitating discard, it has clearly been placed consciously in the pit with care and the pit filled in not long after its deposition, thus preventing further damage.

Very little definitive evidence for lithic use or manufacture can be identified across the main areas of activity during this period although there are some indications they may be present. Bipolar technology becomes more prevalent through the later Neolithic, becoming notable in the Early Bronze Age, and it may be that a large bipolar core from pit [2D-1084] might represent Middle Neolithic deposition. The recovery of a scale-flaked blade-knife from cut [AMA09–2152] and a Levallois-like flake from [AMA09–2216] may also represent evidence of this period.

2.14.5.5 Chalcolithic – 2500–2200 BC

Two Beakers found in relation to the timber setting are the only datable artefacts from the Chalcolithic. The complete Beaker is interpreted as a foundation deposit relating to the construction of the setting. It is unclear whether the burnt beaker sherds from pit [2C-0075] represent activity from construction, use or abandonment/destruction of the features, or is merely residual material. No *in situ* burning was present in the pit, and the pottery must have been incorporated from elsewhere.

Most strikingly the complete Beaker from post-hole [2C-0050] has survived intact, to some extent against all odds. Complete fine-walled, non-'domestic' Beakers are rarely found in this state of preservation outside funerary contexts. Direct comparison of this discovery is not possible, given the unique circumstances. No published examples of Beaker pottery used as a construction deposit are known. However, Beaker use in closing deposition is quite well documented. This is typically seen as a closing ritual at Neolithic sites (Lelong & MacGregor 2007; Mercer 1981; Barclay 1983).

2.14.5.6 Iron Age or later – 360 BC–1000 AD

The small assemblage of vitrified material from Milltimber is dominated by ferrous metalworking waste indicative of blacksmithing activities. All of the debris was recovered from secondary contexts within prehistoric, Roman or Early Historic features, is residual and cannot be closely dated. Despite this, the ironworking waste from Milltimber provides a glimpse of craft activities taking place in the area.

Slags produced from ferrous metalworking are rarely intrinsically datable and as a result any chronological information about the craft activities that this material represents must derive necessarily from any associated stratigraphic evidence, datable artefacts or directly datable organic material, such as charcoal, which is not present here.

Small quantities of unclassified iron slag came from upper deposits within oven F17 [2B-2123]. The soils containing the unclassified iron slag fragments post-date the use and abandonment of this structure, indicating that the metalworking activities that the slag represents are likely to be Roman or later in date. Vitrified material, resulting from both metalworking and other, non-metalwork related pyrotechnic activities, were recovered from the fill of Roman ovens at Forest Road, Kintore, Aberdeenshire (Heald 2008, 209). Like that seen at Milltimber, much of this waste was secondary and intrusive within the ovens and did not relate directly to the use of the features themselves.

The recovery of hammerscale, indicative of blacksmithing, alongside fragments of unclassified iron slag and fuel ash slag from post-hole [2B-0080] suggests that ironworking was taking place in the vicinity but the date or location of this activity cannot be determined from the available evidence. Similarly, the residual smithing hearth bottoms that came from the palaeochannel [2B-2650] attest to blacksmithing activities but the associated features or datable material makes it difficult to draw any useful comparisons.

2.15 Discussion

Our understanding of the archaeological remains at Milltimber is heavily dependent on understanding the environmental change and development of the landscape of the river valley and edges over the past 15,000 years. Prior to excavation, the site could have been described as a fairly typical wide river plain, with the current River Dee route sitting close to the southern limit of the valley floor, a broad flat plain that appeared susceptible to flooding to the north of this, and then the northern edge of the valley rising up and defining its limit.

Both through excavation and extensive geoarchaeological investigation it is clear that the story complex and the landscape of the Dee has been both influenced by and impacts on the location and type of archaeological remains that have been found. Only by understanding these changes have we been able to place the features against the appropriate backdrop. Illus 2.90 summarises this understanding to show the major changes to the

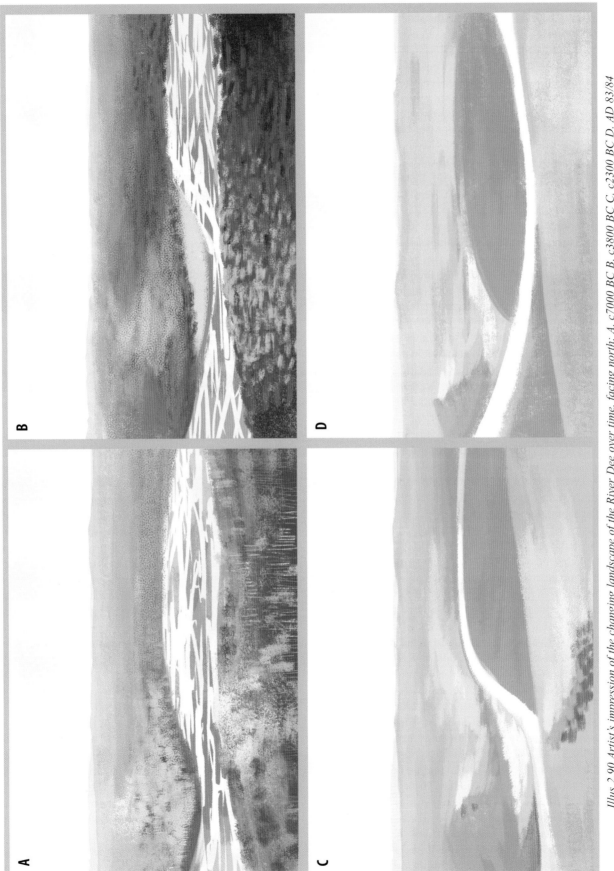

Illus 2.90 Artist's impression of the changing landscape of the River Dee over time, facing north: A. c7000 BC B. c3800 BC C. c2300 BC D. AD 83/84

river and its surroundings from the Mesolithic through to the Roman period. In the Mesolithic, the River Dee is a characteristic anastomosing river system, formed of many shallow braided streams with dry islands between them. The river itself and river edges would have been one of the main methods of accessing the interior of the region, with the ground beyond the river valleys having extensive, although not impenetrable tree cover.

Over time, the extent of the river channel changes, cutting down through the terrace that previously formed the river floor, increasingly moving towards a single channel system. During the Early Neolithic, the river would still have been relatively braided, but covering a narrower area and gradually becoming a deeper, faster single channel. This allowed some of the terraces previously occupied by the river to dry out and become suitable areas for settlement and associated activity.

By the Chalcolithic, in the late third millennium BC, the appearance of the valley had changed dramatically. The river was now a single channel formation that had cut down through the Camphill Terrace. Either side of the river would be occupied by lush meadow, against which the timber settings of the Chalcolithic would stand out.

The history of environmental change was key to understanding the activities of the Romans in particular. The attraction provided by the banks of the dried up palaeochannel for construction of the ovens directed their presence to this location. By undertaking detailed investigation into the deposits above and below the ovens, it was possible to create a timeline for the cutting of the river, the change into a dried-up channel and the subsequent flooding events across the valley floor, through into the medieval and post-medieval.

2.15.1 Upper Palaeolithic activity

One of the most significant aspects of the discoveries at Milltimber, owing to the scarcity of similar material elsewhere in Scotland, is the evidence for a Late Upper Palaeolithic phase at the site. In Scotland these sites are still uncommon and generally consist of lithic material such as at Howburn, South Lanarkshire (Ballin *et al.* 2010). The assemblages are dominated by European typologies rather than those of southern England, implying the spread of shared ideas across vast distances. The potential use of material sourced from Doggerland points to a high degree of mobility. The technological industry discovered at Milltimber must date to the period c13,000–10,000 BC. At this time, the north-east region must have been dry, lying east of and in the rain-shadow of the Cairngorm mountain range. These dry conditions would have depleted the nutrients within the soils and, as with the pollen records at Loch Park (Walker *et al.* 1994), the nutrient-poor soils would have suited the spread of grassy heath with juniper and willows predominating. The scant remains found at Milltimber relating to the Late Upper Palaeolithic are indicative of a brief visit to the site, seemingly to prepare tools used for hunting and food preparation.

To some extent, the importance of the discovery of this phase of activity is in the methodology used to identify it; it was entirely based on post-excavation analysis of the lithics assemblage that had been excavated in such a way as to allow the material to be examined against the background of detailed spatial information. Not only could the existence of the activity be confirmed, but the location of that activity identified within the lithics scatter as a whole.

2.15.2 Mesolithic activity
2.15.2.1 Mesolithic pit digging

The 30 pits grouped in this category all show strong similarities in terms of size, location (for the most part), sequence and process of use, infill and abandonment, and – broadly speaking – date. However, within this block of similar characteristics, there are a multitude of variances that make interpretation challenging.

At the outset it is important to note that although nine pits have been scientifically dated to the early part of the Mesolithic, only one of these dates has been obtained from material collected from the bottom half of a pit. That example – pit [2C-0143] – is not from the main concentration at the north of the site but from one of the isolated features further south. While it is morphologically very similar to the main group, location wise, it is unusual. The dated material from the remainder of the pits, reflecting a presence mostly in the early part of the Mesolithic, tends to be from the upper half and overlies nearly half a metre of eroded sand and gravel in some cases. It is likely that the lower deposits entered the pits fairly rapidly after the initial cutting, although this cannot be conclusively established.

The dates for the pits span nearly 4000 years, c8200–4500 BC, from the Mesolithic almost through to the transition into the Early Neolithic. While it might seem simplistic to present over four millennia of activity as a single phase or suggest that activity has been identical over such a long time span, the morphological evidence from the pits does seem to point to repetition of the same action. The material dated is also generally not primary deposition: broadly speaking the majority of fills above come from natural infilling. This dated material is highly likely to originate from immediately adjacent to the pit and allows us to broadly date the period of activity, but it does not date the act of creation.

In general the dates recovered (see Table 2.01) represent activity as early as c8200 BC, with continuous (if sporadic) presence over the course of the following 1200 years to 7000 BC. Further activity then occurs at around 4500 BC, on the cusp of the Neolithic transition period, although this seems limited in comparison with the suite of earlier dates. The bulk of the dates do seem to confine the core of the activity to the 8000–7000 BC period.

The most striking factor about the pits (and one that sets them apart from many comparative pits of similar date) is their size. Allowing for some degree of truncation of the upper part of the pits over the intervening years, these features might have been nearly 2.5 m deep at their largest and often over 2 m in diameter.

It has been stated two different types of pits are present; steep-sided and very deep, and shallower with more gentle gradients. Despite the difference in shape, there is still consistency in deposits and the processes by which they were formed, indicating essentially a similar function for all. There was no real evidence to suggest deliberate (or ritual) dumping or placing of material within the features had taken place. The degree of gravel-rich material of any single deposit can usually be directly tied to the localised make-up of geological subsoil, even to the extent that if bands of gravel or larger pebbles are present in the geology on one side of the pit, the material originating from erosion on that side of the feature will likewise contain more of this type of material. This potentially indicates a fairly rapid initial infilling of the pits. In some pits (such as pits [2D-1529] and [2D-1593]) the gravel layers appear somewhat disturbed and mixed up.

The upper portions of the pits are also filled with further material resulting from erosion, but there is also an increase in material washing in, with deposits generally becoming more silty or loamy in nature. These fills are evidence of a more gradual infilling process than before, incorporating elements of the surrounding topsoil or other degraded organic material, likely to relate to processes occurring after the abandonment of the pits. This could have provided an opportunity to identify contemporary activities; unfortunately, the almost complete lack of environmental evidence within these upper fills limited this prospect. It may be that the material washing in originates from further up-slope whereas the main focus of activity was located down-slope (as indicated by the extent of the lithic scatter).

Even in upper layers containing charcoal that could be dated to the Mesolithic, the material is generally small, abraded and reflective of gradual natural infilling processes (washing in, blowing in etc). The implication is that although there is no direct evidence of burning, some form of wood-burning must have been occurring in the immediate locale. This is evidenced by the presence of other features such as fencelines, hearths and the extensive lithics spread, although whether they were contemporary with the large pits is unclear.

In a small number of the large pits there is some suggestion that stabilisation processes had taken place, with possible soils forming, usually when the pits are around two-thirds full and the slope of the interface with the material below is relatively shallow. Could this be taken as an indication that activity within the pits, and potentially in the wider vicinity of the pits, had largely stopped? Is vegetation beginning to form on the surface of the infilled hollows?

There is little in the taphonomy of the pits to provide conclusive evidence of their original function. The rapid

and extensive infill of sand and gravels from the edges of the features would seem to suggest that in use they were intended to be open – these deposits only built up once they were abandoned or the intended activity had ceased. Given the loose nature of the superficial geology these pits are cut into, it might be expected that they would have been lined, particularly if they were intended to be open for any extended period of time. In all cases no such lining was identified. Although this may imply to the contrary that the pits were only required to be open for a short period, either way survival of unburnt organic material from this period is extremely unlikely.

An excellent summary of the current knowledge (or lack of it) of Mesolithic pits is provided in a recent publication largely concentrating on the Neolithic of mainland Scotland (Noble *et al.* 2016a). Within the north-east, they summarise a total of seven sites where there are pits that can be conclusively dated to the Mesolithic. Of these, only three can be said to have any close comparisons with the Milltimber pits in any real sense; Warren Field (Murray *et al.* 2009), Spurryhillock (Alexander 1997) and Skilmafilly (Johnson & Cameron 2012). Further to this we now have additional comparable pits at Blackdog (Chapter 6).

Both Spurryhillock and Skilmafilly are sites with single pits and Blackdog had three. The pits from all three sites have been dated to the Mesolithic, and are all of a comparable size to those at Milltimber. At Spurryhillock near Stonehaven, the 1.35 m deep pit contained a sequence of layers of alternating sand and charcoal, with the upper deposits in particular being relatively abraded and likely to be the result of in-washing (Alexander 1997, 20). It is of note that the excavator originally considered that the feature might be natural in origin, a similar process of investigation and understanding initially applied to the Milltimber pits. A small handful of diagnostically Mesolithic flint was recovered from the pit and its surrounds. The lowest present charcoal deposit was radiocarbon dated, providing dates of 4720–4370 cal BC and 4910–4540 cal BC (*ibid.*, 22; note that the dated charcoal is oak), placing it in the Late Mesolithic. In form, the pit is closest to the shallower examples from Milltimber, being more oval in plan and having a less steep profile (at least along its short axis).

The single pit from Skilmafilly some 40 miles to the north of Milltimber shows a sequence of deposits near identical to the large pits under discussion. In particular, a series of relatively steep tip lines of sterile material (Johnson & Cameron 2012, 17) mirrors that recorded in the majority of the deposits at Milltimber. No conclusive interpretation for function is provided for either Skilmafilly or Spurryhillock. It was also difficult to conclusively determine a purpose for the pits at Blackdog, although evidence for recuts was strong. This is one of the major difficulties in understanding this class of feature – they are only recently beginning to be recognised in any numbers, they contain almost no material from which to imply a function and they generally tend to be found in isolated circumstances.

The most closely comparable site to Milltimber, in both form and proximity, is that of Warren Field, Crathes, 13 km upstream on the River Dee. The site lies in an area of extensive Mesolithic activity, with a stretch of around 2 km of the northern bank of the river a likely focus during this period. Around 600 m to the north of the current location of the river an alignment of at least 12 (from excavation) and potentially 17 (from cropmarks) large pits was identified on a gravel ridge running south-west to north-east. Of the 12 confirmed pits, seven were excavated over the course of two seasons' work. It is of note that the pits excavated during the first season had to be re-excavated in the second season to establish their full size (Murray *et al.* 2009, 5), and that the excavator notes that four of the pits may be larger than their recorded size (*ibid.*, 5). This chimes sharply with the experience of excavating at Milltimber, where the large pits were initially only recognised owing to upper charcoal or silt deposits. The edges of the features were incredibly hard to define, and in some cases, the true original edge has probably been lost.

This issue of a lack of clarity over the edges of features cut into this geology at both Warren Field and Milltimber is of relevance, as there is considerable difference in the size of the pits at Warren Field, ranging from 1–2.6 m diameter and 0.55–1.3 m deep. This is used to argue that there is no pattern in the difference in sizes (*ibid.*, 12), when in fact, it could be because some features are actually larger than their recorded size. This could imply that there is actually more consistency in size than previously thought. This also applies to the depth of the features – the deepest recorded is 1.3 m, considerably less than the 2 m of pit [2D-1193]. The implications of the shallower depths are discussed below.

The sequence of deposits present at Warren Field was broadly similar to Milltimber; fills in the bottom half of the pits were sandy or gravelly in nature and the result of erosion. Six out of the seven pits were identified as having recuts or later features cut into the top of them, a similar pattern as interpreted at Blackdog. Although the sequences at Milltimber largely did not conclude that the upper material represented recuts, the deposits were very similar in nature. Two of the excavated pits at Warren Field were also thought to have held posts (*ibid.*, 13), or more likely small stakes; comparable to six of the pits at Milltimber.

Where the Milltimber and Warren Field pits differed is in the presence of apparently deliberately placed deposits of charcoal-rich material in the base. Three or possibly four of the pits at Warren Field were found to contain such material (*ibid.*, 13); there was no conclusive evidence for this at Milltimber. The deposits found at Warren Field were found at a depth of between 0.45 m and 0.7 m, the shallower examples of the features investigated. At Milltimber and Blackdog there was a general tendency for the pits to be deeper. Given that the excavator indicates

there the possibility that some of the pits at Warren Field may be larger than originally thought, it seems likely that these deposits are not in fact, basal deposits, but layers within a larger sequence. Raising this possibility is of significance in understanding the Milltimber features and their function; certainly, any charcoal-rich deposits recorded in the Milltimber pits were within the upper portions of the features.

Unlike the linear alignment identified at Warren Field the arrangement at Milltimber seems to have been much more random. They are not found in only one location or one type of location, although the majority are found at the boundary between the Lochton Formation and the Camphill Terrace. Although there are patterns and similarities within their make-up, these do not appear to be rigidly adhered to. All of this would seem to point to a more practical reason for their creation. The very few that have evidence of posts or stakes may assist in understanding their function. The size of the pits is considerable – a tall human would struggle to get out of one unaided. Their vertical or near-vertical sides also make access and egress a challenge. Could these have acted as trapping pits, possibly with an array of stakes or sharpened posts in the base to spear any animal that might fall in? The location, in proximity to the edge of the River Dee, could support this. The presence of the flint scatter to the south of the pits, representing the remains of knapping floors associated with the repair of composite tools, provides further potential evidence of hunting activities here.

The large mammal fauna that might typically have been hunted in the Mesolithic in a north-eastern Scottish context would include aurochs, deer (both red and roe), elk and wild boar (Maroo & Yalden 2000, 245). No features have been found previously in Scotland that have been confidently interpreted as prehistoric trapping pits; however, it is almost certain that trapping occurred.

Hunting traps for large animals of early prehistoric date are known from Scandinavia, and in particular there is evidence of them being used in groups to channel or funnel animals in to the traps. In a review of five hunting traps from Almemoen to the north-west of Oslo, dates spanning 6500–5500 BC were recovered from charcoal deposits near the base of the pits (Bergstøl 2015). These pits were of a similar dimension to those at Milltimber, and showed a similar sequence of deposits, other than the presence of wood charcoal near their bases. The interpretation of the sequence of excavation, construction and collapse provided by the author of the paper could equally apply to the examples at Milltimber. Where there is some divergence of the evidence it is in the lower deposits of charcoal; in Norway the presence of this was used to argue for timber lining of the pits, presumably to reinforce the sides, which were excavated into loose unstable sands. In Scotland, no such evidence was present, and it seems highly unlikely that the pits were lined with charred timbers (bases charred to improve their durability). It is

Illus 2.91 Artist's impression of Milltimber during the Mesolithic period, around 7500 BC. The forests would have had hunting traps scattered through them, strategically placed across game trails leading down to the edges of the River Dee. In the distance, a hearth is the focus for lithics repair

not impossible that uncharred timber linings were present, and the similarity of the sequence of deposits, particularly those with a V-shaped profile, could point in this direction, although this was not satisfactorily established. With or without a lining, the potential for these pits to represent some form of hunting trap is thought to be the best reasonable interpretation for the features on the basis of current knowledge (Illus 2.91).

There was no direct stratigraphic relationship between the lithics scatter and pits; however it is feasible they were both being created within the same broad timeframe. The proximity of pits to spread is not problematic, and

in fact supports the multiple visits interpretation for the accumulation of the spread. Assuming trapping was successful, the river bank would provide an attractive spot to process the carcasses, repair tools and generally take advantage of the resource over a short period of time. However, this location would be avoided for any kind of settlement activity of longer duration, lest it impacted on the behaviours of the animals being trapped.

2.15.2.2 Other activity at Milltimber

The other scattered features identified in the northern limit of the Milltimber site are best interpreted against the background of activity represented by the lithics scatter and the large pits. The evidence from the scatter suggests that there were several short-term visits to the site, likely over an extended period. Much of the material fits well with the interpretation of these groups being hunting parties, but it is important to remember that lithic tools would also be used expediently, not just as projectiles. The focus certainly seemed to be on the production of blades and microblades, along with points and microliths.

In general, there is limited evidence that any of this lithic production was associated with any kind of structures, even of the temporary kind seen at Standingstones (Chapter 4). The lithics work occurs in an open-air context, around a series of hearths that would be entirely temporary in nature. Features such at the fencelines at the west of the scatter could act either as wind breaks around these open-air camps, or potentially provide some form of definition to the extent of the area used for camps. In the absence of conclusively identifying any of the specific hearth locations and having datable material, features such as the fencelines and pits within the scatter may provide the most relatable dates for the activity, and highlight the extended duration. Dates from one of the pits within the scatter lie in the centuries before 8000 BC, while those from the fencelines are focused in the early fifth millennium BC. There is little question that although the individual visits were brief, the activity as a whole continued for many thousands of years.

2.15.3 Early Neolithic settlement

The Early Neolithic period brings with it the first appearance of an identifiable structure at the site. The issue of recognising the truly 'domestic' in Neolithic Scotland is one which has been much discussed (ScARF 2012b). Having said that, there are now a small number of reasonably comparative structures that mirror some of the elements seen in the Milltimber structure.

A short distance downstream from Milltimber, at Garthdee Road on the northern bank of the River Dee, an irregular, roughly oval structure was recorded in 2005 (Murray 2005; Murray & Murray 2014), defined by shallow post-pits and containing a notable amount of artefacts and environmental data. It had a date range of 3800–3650 BC, a couple of hundred years beyond that of the Milltimber structure. Both were similar in their 'roughness' – these do not appear to be long-standing buildings. Interpretations of the structure at Garthdee have revolved around its temporal relationship with the much larger timber halls at Crathes, Balbridie and Claish, with suggestions that upon the arrival of the Neolithic incomers from the Continent, they initially may have lived communally in the large halls, and then rapidly separated off to smaller, more typically 'domestic' situations (ScARF 2012b; Sheridan 2010). The Milltimber structure seems to be at odds with this theory, pre-dating the range of the early halls.

Other possible comparators are found in the structures at Drumoig in Fife (pits defining an area c4.5 m by 2.6 m) and Kingarth Quarry, Bute (7 m by 3.5 m, dated to the Early–Middle Neolithic) but there are still differences in date, size and establishment of function. It is recognised that there is a large degree of ambiguity when considering the limited collection of known structures of this type in Scotland, and they certainly do not form a homogeneous group, as seen with similar structures in Ireland (Brophy 2016, 212–15).

The presence of several hearths or hearth-like deposits spread across the north of the Milltimber site could be taken as evidence of further structures, the remains of which have simply not survived. The hearths and hearth material can be broadly dated to between 3900 and 3700 BC, with a later phase of similar activity in the latter half of the third millennium BC. The material from the hearths seems to be typical of general domestic waste, and for many of the features there is clear evidence of *in situ* burning. However, when the deposits are found in the tops of pits dating to the Mesolithic, the activity 'type' becomes more complex. This sequence was seen at Warren Field, Crathes and at Blackdog (Chapter 6). At Warren Field, the interpretation for the original pits and for the periods of reuse were thought most likely to be ritual activity (Murray *et al.* 2009, 26–27), with the concept that although the specific meanings of the activities might change, the power of the place remains the same over millennia. The evidence suggested that the upper parts of the pits had been deliberately recut and dug out during the Early Neolithic, and material then intentionally placed in. This was also implied for the recut pits at Blackdog. Unlike the Blackdog pits, however, this proposal for Warren Field seems at odds with the assertion that the Neolithic fills largely comprised in-washed material; small charcoal fragments with minor amounts of other material such as burnt bone and grain. This is certainly what is generally seen at Milltimber; in the handful of Mesolithic pits that contain later material, it is washed in rather than *in situ* and comprises heavily degraded material. The evidence that this has been deliberately 'placed' is simply not there. The similarity between the hearth features and the hearth material would suggest they have a similar origin. The distinction between this interpretation and that for the pits at Blackdog is another indication of how pits of near identical type may have different functions and have been treated differently once they were abandoned.

The post alignments are located on a slight but noticeable slope to the west of the structure. The alignments and spacing of these seem to imply they all represent a similar function. The linear arrangement is more typical of fencelines or enclosures, but the short lengths of line makes this unlikely. The fact that the alignments are roughly parallel, but not exact, may suggest that the north-west

2. A landscape through time: Milltimber and the River Dee

to south-east arrangement was of importance. Could the alignments be drying racks, taking advantage of breezes funnelling up and down the river valley?

Several isolated pits and a small pit cluster provide further evidence of activity during this period. The purpose of these pits is poorly understood. The pit cluster in particular seems to be a fairly common feature of the Neolithic, although their purpose has never been clearly defined. This practice was more prevalent at Wester Hatton and to lesser extent at Blackdog (both Chapter 6, where the practice is discussed in more detail; see 6.11.2), although in the case of Wester Hatton the pits were predominantly Middle to Late Neolithic.

One type of feature present across Milltimber, but not extensively studied or understood in archaeological literature, were the tree throws. These were uneven and poorly defined pits that seem to consistently contain lithic debitage and occasionally pottery (see Illus 2.07 & 2.23). These features could represent evidence of clearance of the site although no clear proof of this was identified. These enigmatic features are noteworthy and their presence should not be completely ignored when investigating sites of this period.

In summary, to some extent the evidence for the Early Neolithic is broadly similar to the Mesolithic at Milltimber, indicating the northern part of the site remained a location of interest, continuing the traditions from earlier. Groups of people were visiting the site in small numbers, still processing flint and repairing tools, setting campfires of some description, but potentially also clearing larger areas of forest, undertaking more work that involved shaping their immediate environment, while still not treating the location as a place of permanent settlement.

2.15.4 Middle–Late Neolithic activity

The later Neolithic activity at Milltimber was sparse and disparate in comparison to the earlier occupation. The features comprise a number of hearths, two potential pit clusters plus the occasional larger pits. The dated features ranged between 3510 and 3100 cal BC, which is comparable to the Neolithic pit clusters at Wester Hatton and to a lesser extent those at Blackdog (both Chapter 6).

The function of the features at these two coastal sites was not really understood and seemingly represented a combination of both ritual and mundane depositional practices. The features recorded at Milltimber did not convincingly mirror those at Wester Hatton, although it seems similar patterns of deposition occurred. Certainly pits [AMA09–2058] and [2D-1895], both containing numerous pottery sherds from a variety of predominantly Impressed Ware vessels, could imply evidence of ritualised deposition. In general though, the remaining assemblages at Milltimber seem to be a result of more mundane depositional practices. Little more can be added to the story at Milltimber beyond the fact it illustrates that not only were people still returning to this site, albeit intermittently and probably over short

periods of time, but they seemed to be carrying out similar practices.

2.15.5 Chalcolithic timber settings

Matt Ginnever

Timber- and pit-defined settings dating to the transitional period between the Neolithic and the Bronze Age have been identified at a number of sites across Scotland, primarily from cropmark evidence. Excavated examples are still comparatively rare, with only two timber settings currently published, and direct comparisons with undated cropmarks can be problematic. Both of the excavated examples, from Forteviot and Leadketty in Perth and Kinross (Noble & Brophy 2011; 2014), are entrance avenues leading up to large (c250m in diameter) palisaded enclosures. The avenues themselves are also considerably larger than those at Milltimber, with the Forteviot avenue extending over 50 m in length. Unexcavated entrance avenues seen from cropmarks at sites such as Dunragit (Thomas 2004) and Meldon Bridge (Speak & Burgess 1999) are of a similar large scale in comparison with Milltimber.

Free-standing avenues consisting of pits rather than post-holes have been excavated at Holm Farm in Dumfries and Galloway (Thomas 2007) and Upper Largie in Argyle (Cook *et al.* 2010). Both of these avenues are again considerably larger than those seen at Milltimber, although in form the alignments do appear similar with uneven (in number of posts) rows that curve slightly over their length. An unexcavated avenue at Sprouston (see Millican 2016, 152) is especially similar in form to the northernmost avenue at Milltimber.

The Milltimber settings date to between 2470 and 2205 cal BC. The Beaker placed in post-hole [2C-0050] is also considered to be a foundation deposit and is of a style dating to between 2400 and 1800 BC and fits well with the narrower range provided by the radiocarbon dates. Although the Upper Largie avenue was dated to the Early Neolithic (AMS date of 4230–2960 cal BC), this was thought to be residual and likely to come from timber related to the nearby timber-defined cursus. The avenue also appeared to respect the Early Bronze Age timber circle, or vice versa, suggesting that the avenue was likely to be closer to the circle in date. Similarly, dating of the avenue at Holm Farm, Dumfries and Galloway (Thomas 2007) is unclear as the two dates taken from the pits produced widely discrepant dates of 2210–2020 cal BC and 1380–1040 cal BC. A recent summary of Neolithic timber structures in Scotland (Millican 2016) suggests that most avenues or timber settings date from the Late Neolithic into the Early Bronze Age. The Milltimber timber settings broadly support this observation.

Another possible comparison with the Milltimber alignments can be made with cropmark evidence for open-ended trapezoidal or rectangular structures often referred to as 'Timber settings' (Millican 2016, 148–49). Although these monuments have traditionally been assigned to the Early Neolithic, none of the thirteen known examples from Scotland have ever been excavated or dated. Their attribution to the earlier period of the Neolithic comes from morphological similarities to post-built structures leading up to long barrows seen from sites in England. No evidence for mortuary monuments associated with the timber settings at Milltimber was found.

The timber settings at Milltimber do not lead into or out of any apparent structures or enclosures, a feature also noted at Holm Farm and Upper Largie, despite their association with cursus features. Likewise, many of the settings seen from the cropmark data are free standing. The timber settings at Milltimber were seemingly also set too far apart to suggest that they supported a roof or platform. They most likely functioned to control or lead movement through a defined space or spaces in the landscape, as processional ways. An archaeoastronomical assessment of the avenue at Upper Largie (Cook *et al.* 2010, 196) suggested an alignment with the midwinter solstice sunset. It is possible that the two potential alignments of the structures at Milltimber were also linked to astronomical features or to nearby landmarks that are no longer visible owing to modern development. A single surviving upright from a full stone circle (NJ80SE 10) at Milltimber Farm near the site implies the area was part of a ceremonial landscape during this period.

2.15.6 Late prehistoric period activity

Those remains that date largely to the Middle Bronze Age at Milltimber are consistently isolated features, generally relating to single-use hearth type features that do not add much to the story of activity on the riverside. They do further support the concept of periodic, occasional visits to the site, which seems to mirror the activity in the earlier periods here. This intermittent use of the site also contrasts with the almost nucleated settlement activity occurring at Gairnhill in particular and to a lesser extent at Wester Hatton, both sites located away from the river valleys.

The only potential anomaly to the minimal activity at this time was the presence of a large curvilinear ditch immediately north of the palaeochannel. The difficulty in interpreting this feature was twofold. Firstly, although it was dated to the Bronze Age, the material from which the date derived was an upper deposit of slumping material, therefore does not date the construction. Secondly, the stratigraphic sequence relating to both the erosion of the southern end of the ditch and the cutting of the palaeochannel was complex and inconclusive. The OSL dating of the palaeochannel indicated that it had initially cut the Camphill Terrace c3300 BC. Therefore, if the ditch had been eroded by the palaeochannel it would imply the ditch was older than this event, placing its construction firmly in the Neolithic. It is also entirely possible that the southern end was eroded away by later

flood events that did not extend beyond the outer edge of the palaeochannels, this also being the slightly raised edge of the Camphill Terrace.

The ditch was substantial and would have required a significant amount of work to construct. This implies it was not built by people who were just 'passing by' but by people investing time and energy in the place. Could the ditch represent remains of an Early Neolithic enclosure? There is certainly a contemporary period of settlement. Evidence of an outer bank for the ditch had drawn comparisons with henge monuments and this cannot be dismissed. Canmore lists at least four such features within a 30 km radius of Milltimber, although only two of these (Broomend of Crichie; NJ71NE 248 and Hill of Tuach NJ71NE 27; Bradley 2011) have been excavated. In both cases no comparable evidence could be identified. The Chalcolithic timber settings immediately north of the ditch and evidence of a stone circle at Milltimber Farm imply a rich ceremonial landscape through to the Bronze Age. Given the potential loss of the southern end of this ditch to flood events it may even represent early Iron Age activity, although given the paucity of evidence of this date at Milltimber this seems unlikely and would also require rapid infilling and settling of deposits to allow the later Romans to use it for oven construction. At present the only secure evidence available is that it pre-dated the cutting of the ovens during Roman occupation of the site. It seems that, as with two other ditches recorded to the north of the curvilinear ditch, the absence of suitable dating material from the basal deposits has reduced our ability to interpret these features satisfactorily.

More broadly, the identification of these later prehistoric features also highlights the importance of a wide-ranging radiocarbon dating programme. Assumptions could be (and indeed to some extent with these features, were) made about the presumed date of these features on the basis of their proximity or similarity to other features. Had an extensive programme of dating not been undertaken of some of the more mundane and easily interpretable features, eg hearths, then the presence of people in the Bronze Age at Milltimber would largely have been missed.

2.15.7 Roman occupation

2.15.7.1 Dating

Following the discovery of the ovens at Milltimber, the most immediate and key questions to be answered was to establish their date and origin. Were these, as they initially appeared, one of the largest groups of Roman ovens excavated, or were they the result of Iron Age construction (possibly copying Roman examples) and therefore later in date than the known periods of Roman activity in the area? The two questions are closely interlinked; a series of dates in the 4th century AD would attest to a Late Iron Age origin; however, dates from any of the three main phases of Roman presence in Scotland (the Flavian campaigns in the 1st century, during the Antonine occupation of

Scotland in the mid-2nd century when the Antonine Wall was constructed, and during the northern campaigns of Septimius Severus in the early 3rd century) would not automatically imply they were Roman.

The layout of the ovens was explicitly tied to the natural and archaeological features that the builders encountered when they arrived at the site; the relatively steep slopes provided by the partially infilled and grassed over palaeochannels and the bank of the earlier prehistoric ditch higher up on the terrace above the contemporary floodplain. However, the ovens were not set out equally along the slopes – some areas that appeared to provide an attractive location (eg between A10 and B21) were ignored. Other locations requiring a higher input of effort (eg all of the Group 7 ovens) hosted multiple examples. The 13 groups identified above are based on the locational data – where clear gaps exist between ovens, and in particular in areas where ovens would be expected, is an indication that the ovens formed discrete groups. The discrete nature of the groups could imply that the ovens were being used at different times, although this would be difficult to establish with any confidence. The Bayesian analysis undertaken suggested that in general the trend of oven creation was from north to south, which is further supported by the progression from the use of local scrubby material to larger timbers as time went on. It is important to remember that the full limit of ovens to the north (continuation of Group 1), west (continuation of Group 8) and south (continuation of Group 13) cannot be defined from the current works.

The presence of these distinct groups, although not conclusive, does point to the ovens being of Roman military origin rather than Iron Age. This is further supported by the dates obtained for the ovens. Of the 90 ovens identified, dates were obtained for firings (or, for a handful of examples, rake-out) from 31 ovens, with multiple dates taken from three ovens (B13, E03 and F19). The dates returned gave a broadest range for the ovens between 155 cal BC and cal AD 321. The Bayesian analysis undertaken established that the activity had to have taken place sometime between the Flavian and Nerva-Antonine Dynasties (AD 69–192).

2.15.7.2 The question of a camp

From the evidence presented above, it seems clear that the ovens are indeed Roman in origin, and that they most likely date to the period of the Flavian campaigns of the late 70s and 80s AD. This interpretation immediately raises the question of whether or not the ovens lay within some sort of temporary camp and can they be taken to infer the presence of such a camp, the absence of any other evidence notwithstanding?

Recent work categorising and quantifying the resource of Roman camps in Britain (Jones 2011; 2012) has established that over 500 examples are recorded across the country, a higher quantity than is currently known from any other Roman province. This spread may be real; however, it is likely to be in part due to the efforts of aerial survey and antiquarian tradition in Britain. It is notable that the vast majority of recorded camps in Scotland are known through aerial survey (Jones 2011, 1) and only a very small number have been tested through excavation. At the same time, we are lucky enough to have a temporary camp in the same region as the Milltimber discovery that has been subject to extensive excavation and provides a variety of parallels and comparisons (Kintore near Inverurie; Cook & Dunbar 2008).

Ovens of this style and broad date (ie Roman, rather than specifically Flavian) are known in Scotland from camps at Inchtuthil II and III, Lochlands III, Inveresk I, Kintore, Lochlands Three Bridges, Normandykes and possibly also from Glenlochar, Drumlanrig II, Dalginross and Carronbridge (Jones 2011, 82). There are also some ovens of Roman date that appear to lie outwith any known camp defences and some distance from the known camp eg 500 m west of Elginhaugh at Melville Nurseries (Raisen & Rees 1996). Other possible Roman field ovens have been identified outwith Roman military structures (see Jones 2011, 83), and it is possible that some of these relate to camps for which no defensive perimeter has been identified. But these are usually small in number, in single figures, although in some instances this will be the result of the scale of the excavations (for example, see Dundee High Technology Park – Gibson & Taverner 1989). However, there are no records anywhere within the Roman provinces of large numbers of ovens where they are not either specifically enclosed by the defences of a camp, or at least clearly tied to an annexe of a camp.

Camps can to some extent be grouped by analogy in terms of size and morphology, and individual camps of these groups can then be tentatively dated. This is the case with one of the recorded groups (those enclosing 44 ha/110acres), dated to the later 1st and early 2nd centuries AD through radiocarbon dating ovens found at Kintore (Cook & Dunbar 2008, 145). By inference, the ovens at Milltimber could be taken to represent evidence of a previously unrecognised camp at a crossing point on the River Dee, although it lies a short distance (not a proposed day's march) from Normandykes, which is in the same series as Kintore. It is possible that a smaller camp was located here. If the river was used as the southern boundary of the camp (although this is more likely in the case of fort annexes than camps), the northern edge could be beyond the limit of excavation to the north of the site, but only if a very large camp was sited here. Equally, the maximum width of excavation at the site was around 175 m, so further defences could lie to the east and west of the stripped area. However, either by means of evaluation trenches or from open-area stripping, a near-continuous section through all deposits and of the underlying geological subsoil was seen from c20m from the edge of the river, right up to the current cycle path, which bordered the northern extent of stripping. The only east–west running strip that was not excavated (or the ground seen) was the current track leading from the A979 to the quarry in the east – around 16 m wide.

Of almost 250 temporary camps in Scotland and Northumberland (Jones 2011, 29), only a couple of dozen have been investigated to any degree in their interior (rather than the focus being on the survival of the defensive ditches and ramparts, often undertaken to prove whether a site was Roman or not). This focus makes it difficult to find comparanda for Milltimber – some of these examples have some form of upstanding remains, still visible in the landscape today, or have remnants of their defensive perimeter ditches visible through differential crop-markings on aerial photos. There is only one other example of a camp proposed purely on the evidence of ovens with no ditches recorded – this was as a result of recent excavations in Ayr (Hunter 2017, 327).

The suggestion of a camp with this many ovens but no defensive perimeter is largely unprecedented, but the Roman author Tacitus referred to the general Germanicus pitching camp with earthworks to front and rear but only palisades on his flanks (Annals I.49; Bryant 1942). Detailed topographic survey of camps in England concluded that the rampart was the most important feature of the camp, with the ditch serving as additional defence (Welfare and Swan 1995, 17). It has been argued that the potential non-construction of a ditch around a camp would explain some of the significant gaps in the archaeological record, particularly in areas where arable activity would have ploughed away any traces of ramparts (Jones 2012, 80). However, it also appears that the construction of a perimeter ditch was standard practice by the Flavian period (Jones 2012, 106). Although limited, there are certainly specific locations at Milltimber where defensive ditches or structures could have run and not been picked up during the AWPR/B-T works (either to the northern limit of excavation, or to the east, or potentially even along the line of the track cutting east–west linking the B979 to the quarry). This could point to a very large camp, which would fit with the 44 ha grouping that includes Normandykes to the west and Kintore, Ythan Wells I and Muiryfold to the north.

Further to this, the higher outcrop to the west of the current B979 is named Camphill in current mapping and Ordnance Survey maps back to the mid-19th century. First edition OS maps note that the higher ground is the 'Site of Camp', although this changes to 'Site of Fort' by the second edition produced at the end of the 19th century. This seems to confirm the presence of a fortified earthwork of some description that survived into the modern era.

However, the map evidence is not as straightforward as it seems. Although the camp is noted in Ordnance Survey maps, no record is made of it in other reliable maps of the early 19th century (eg Robertson 1822; Thomson 1826),

nor does any mention of it appear on Roy's Military map of the mid-18th century which does include camps such as Raedykes to the south. Where substantial ditched defences were present in the Roman period, the evidence suggests they do survive to some small degree. The site at 'Camphill' has also been interpreted as a medieval motte (Yeoman 1988). Despite this, what is certain is that no evidence of any ditched defence was identified during the excavation, and therefore until further research is conducted into the ground surrounding the site, the assumption must be that ditches were not present, and therefore that the collection of ovens is unusual.

2.15.7.3 Form and function of the ovens

In all other aspects, the ovens are fairly typical of those excavated elsewhere. They comprise a bowl end where the firings took place, and a less formally constructed 'tail' end. Due to the slope of the palaeochannel and ditch, the tail was largely defined only by the spread of raked out material from the bowl; only two examples (B20 & B21) showed evidence of cut pits forming the tails. The bowls were usually circular in plan and, based on excavated examples, up to 1.9 m in diameter, although most were between about 1.2 m and 1.4 m. The recorded depth of the bowls was very much dependent on a combination of truncation (through recent agriculture) and the extent to which they were overlain by later alluvial deposits. The best-preserved examples were up to 0.8 m deep (oven A10) at the bowl end.

Little evidence of any superstructures could be gleaned from the excavated material; a handful of ovens contained patchy heat-affected deposits overlying the final firings that could be interpreted as partially burnt turf superstructures. None of the ovens had evidence of stakes or wooden supports for any superstructures, and it is presumed that branches may have been roughly placed over the top, with turf from digging out the oven placed over that. A handful of ovens (in Group 12 in particular) had stones and clay in the necks of the ovens that had clearly been used to seal the ovens during the cooking process.

The differing heights of the base of the bowls in individual groups (eg B20 and B21 are 0.4 m different) gives us a hint of the hand of the individual in digging the ovens, and potentially reflects the preferences of those who constructed them, perhaps as a result of different backgrounds, diet and ethnicity (Jones 2009). It must be assumed the ground surface within the channel was roughly the same for its length, and it would be expected the soldiers would dig the ovens so that they were around chest to shoulder height for ease of access (Illus 2.92). This would suggest that each group of ovens was constructed by more than one individual.

In terms of how the ovens were being used, the environmental evidence is limited. Only a very small amount of grain was recovered, mostly from oven B05 and

Illus 2.92 Artist's impression of Milltimber in AD 83/84. Roman soldiers take advantage of all available slopes of the infilled river channel. The camp at Normandykes would occupy the higher ground in the distance

in the main hulled barley, although some oat and bread wheat was also present (see 2.13.2 above). This supports the (traditionally ascribed) notion that these structures were built for cooking, rather than to dry or process grain. However, the presence of even small amounts of grain does suggest it was brought to the site in that form, rather than as meal. This is consistent with records of the Roman army on campaign generally, where it is thought the grain would have been threshed before issue to the troops; however, it would then have been ground and bread produced per contubernia (group of 8 men; Roth 1999, 49).

2.15.7.4 Evidence for presence of Romans

Milltimber is notable in lacking any other features of Roman date. This is not because features of possible Roman date went undated. Extensive areas around the ovens were stripped of topsoil and none were found in close proximity or relation to the ovens. The handful of features found towards the south of the excavation areas were radiocarbon dated to other periods of activity. The absence of associated pits appears real. This is in stark contrast to the range of features seen at Kintore. There, along with the ovens, 40 rubbish pits were identified, generally found in pairs and often with metal objects (Cook & Dunbar 2008, 131). They were thought not to be related directly to the ovens.

What does the site represent? The evidence seems fairly conclusive that the ovens represent a previously unknown site of Roman date and origin, almost certainly relating to the Flavian campaigns of the 80s AD. What this means for our understanding of this period is more complex. As noted above, it is far from clear that this is a new marching camp. Even if it is, it is most unusual that no trace of perimeter defence has been found, given that this practice appears to have been the norm in northern Britain. The evidence for defences of any sort is not strong, nor is the evidence for any level of sustained occupation in the form of rubbish pits or any other internal features that would suggest soldiers occupying the ground. The location of the ovens is overlooked by higher ground on several sides and is far from the ideal with regard to establishing such a camp (Gilliver 1999, 70), although it is clear that numerous factors were in play in site selection. There are plenty of camps across Britain that are overlooked by higher ground, but in most instances the important feature seems to have been proximity to a watercourse.

The 44 ha camp at Normandykes (NO89NW 1), which lies just 3 km further upstream, also on the northern bank of the Dee, but in a far more defensible position, is thought to belong to the sequence of camps constructed to support the Flavian campaigns through Angus and Aberdeenshire (Jones 2011, 110). A secondary camp a short distance away would not be unheard of. The smaller more northern camps of Auchinhove and Ythan Wells II lie near to 44 ha (110 acre) camps at Muiryfold and Ythan Wells II respectively; excavations at the latter have demonstrated that the smaller camp was earlier than the larger (St Joseph 1970).

The proximity of the site at Milltimber to the River Dee is notable and may in some part explain the presence of the ovens. It is generally acknowledged that the Roman Navy in Britain (the Classis Britannica) would have played its part in the campaigns, and this is directly noted by Tacitus in his account (Tacitus' *Agricola*, Chapter 25). Studies on the role of the Roman Navy in Britain highlight the fact that these combined operations are poorly represented in the archaeological record (Mason 2003, 102); however, it is difficult to see how a naval camp or interaction would be identified, considering no sites are known anywhere, despite some speculation (Jones forthcoming). The Dee is likely to have been navigable for at least some of its length, and it is not impossible that boats could have reached as far as Milltimber. If the two arms of the Roman military machine were meeting up intermittently, as is noted in Tacitus (*Agricola* 25), might it be possible that the navy would arrive at the rough location (eg the next major river crossing) ahead of the army and have to arrange

provisions for themselves without the normal defences that the army were specifically set up to construct quickly and with the minimum of fuss? In which case, some form of defensive perimeter would have been expected to have been constructed, even if it was a rampart only and such remains have long been ploughed out. Would the sailors have made the best of a bad situation by staying on their boats, protected, but briefly going on land to undertake food preparation?

The connection with the Roman Navy at Milltimber is purely speculative. However, the fact remains that this site is extremely unusual. In order to be able to confirm or disprove any of these theories, more excavation within known camps needs to be undertaken, with focus beyond the defences and entranceways; and a reappraisal of possible Roman ovens found elsewhere with no apparent perimeter enabling their interpretation as a camp.

2.15.8 Historical agricultural activity

Evidence for Early Historical activity within the excavation area at Milltimber is extremely limited, comprising a 5th/6th century cereal-drying kiln and a 9th/10th century enclosure. This seems to be reflected in the wider region, where very few sites associated with this period are known. Locally, a single potential comparable kiln is known at Foggieton, north of Bieldside (Shepherd 2009), unfortunately undated. Further to the west at Kintore three kilns were identified, with the earliest dated to cal AD 770–980 (Cook & Dunbar 2008). As with the Milltimber kiln these contained hulled barley, although some emmer wheat was also present at Kintore. At present little is known about these types of feature and little can be said beyond the fact that they provide clear evidence of simple farming and crop processing. This must have been a relatively common practice across the fertile river valleys of the area throughout the Early Historic and medieval periods.

This agricultural activity did not take place in isolation and coincides with the emergence and consolidation of regional powers and elites in the wider area. This can be seen in the proliferation of hillforts in the Strathdon area dated to between the 4th and 8th century (Cook 2011, 211). At this time, we also begin to see the appearance of the Class 1 Pictish carved stones (RCAHMS 2007, 118). These are considered to date between AD 400 and 700 (Carver 1999). Two of these symbol stones (NJ90SW 6 & NO79NE 44.10) are known locally, although in both cases it seems their original location has been lost. A further five have been recorded in the area around Kintore (Cook & Dunbar 2008).

Evidence for settlement activity in the surrounding area during the Early Historic to medieval period is negligible. Excavations at Portmahomack on the Tarbat Peninsular, Easter Ross (Carver *et al.* 2016), has provided us with a few clues as to the practices being undertaken at this time. Metalworking was still important, and rye, wheat and barley were staple crops of the period. Plough pebbles were identified, and scratch-plough marks were evident. However, very few secular sites with dwellings or enclosures dating to the early medieval period have been identified across Scotland. Those that have are generally close to ecclesiastical structures (eg Portmahomack, Carver *et al.* 2016; Coleman & Photos-Jones 2008). In both these cases the enclosures were rounded or curvilinear. The purpose of the rectilinear enclosure at Milltimber is not known and no real comparators could be found. It is assumed that the enclosure represents a change in farming practices from crop production to the management and corralling of livestock. The pits and post-holes to the east of the enclosure represent further 9th/10th century activity here, although again no clues regarding its purpose or function could be found. Certainly, these features can be added to the growing corpus of Early Historic and medieval secular sites in north-east Scotland.

It is not known what the transport routes through the Dee valley would have been like in the medieval period although they are likely to have been poor. Thus, the rural economy at the time would likely have revolved around small self-sufficient farmsteads. People would have been producing crops and rearing livestock as well as foraging for wild foods. Even the river would have been an invaluable source of food. One potential reason no farmsteads or settlements were identified during the archaeological investigations is that they may have been situated on the slightly higher ground, away from potential flood events, the area now occupied by the string of towns and villages lining the main road through to Aberdeen. There is also the potential that the dwellings at this time were constructed of stone and turf, the evidence of which has since washed away by one or more of the frequent flood events. Settlement evidence for this period in general is limited, with the occasional rectilinear post-built structure identified, such as at Kintore (Cook & Dunbar 2008, 160) and the 14th/15th century farm building at Kintore Substation (HER NJ71SE0107).

Agricultural activity continued to be one of the primary activities in the area as the villages and towns started to emerge along the higher ground from the post-medieval period onwards. The more fertile lands were enclosed and, in many cases, cleared of stones. Embankments were constructed in an attempt to limit the damage by flooding events, and drainage systems were installed. Since these agricultural improvements, mostly undertaken in the 18th and early 19th century, little in the area has changed. At Milltimber, quarrying to the east of the site and the gradual expansion of the town seems to represent the only real change to have taken place in this area over the last 200 years, the new road presenting a further chapter in this area's expansive history.

Chapter 3

Between the Dee and the Don: Settlement, life and death in the Bronze Age

Matt Ginnever and Jürgen van Wessel

3.1 Introduction to the circumstances of discovery at Nether Beanshill, Gairnhill and Chapel of Stoneywood

3.1.1 Background to the archaeological works between the Dee and the Don

This chapter covers the archaeological discoveries north of the River Dee crossing at Milltimber (Chapter 2), on the higher ground between there and the river valley of the Don at Goval (Chapter 5). It excludes the Mesolithic site found at Standingstones, described in Chapter 4. Four archaeological sites, identified during the preliminary works, were investigated along this c10km stretch (Illus 3.01); Nether Beanshill and Gairnhill in the south, an area to the south-west of Brimmond Hill (SL/005) and Chapel of Stoneywood in the north. These areas were selected for further mitigation through topsoil stripping and excavation. Prehistoric remains were discovered at three of these sites and included a single pit dated to the Neolithic, an Early Bronze Age burnt mound, a Middle Bronze Age cremation cemetery and nine Middle to Late Bronze Age roundhouses.

3.1.2 Site locations and extents of mitigation

At Nether Beanshill four areas were stripped, only one of which contained any significant archaeological remains. At Gairnhill all four stripped areas contained archaeological remains. A site to the south-west of Brimmond Hill (SL/005) was stripped and consisted of seven mitigation areas covering 31,444 m², but revealed no archaeological remains of any note. The features identified as of possible archaeological origin were reinterpreted as recent agricultural clearance of field stones. Chapel of Stoneywood at the northern extent of this landscape consisted of four mitigation areas, only one of which contained significant archaeological remains.

3.1.2.1 Nether Beanshill

Nether Beanshill is approximately 1.6 km north-east of Milltimber (Chapter 2), to the east of Nether Beanshill Farm, between Culter House Road and Contlaw Road. The archaeological remains of a roundhouse and a cremation cemetery were situated on a plateau of a south-facing hill, away from an area of outcropping bedrock at a height of 110 m AOD. A tributary of the River Dee was located approximately 500 m to the south-west. At the time of excavation, the land was used for pasture.

3.1.2.2 Gairnhill

Gairnhill lies to the west and north of Gairnhill Wood, Blacktop, Aberdeenshire, approximately 2.3 km north of Nether Beanshill. A Neolithic pit, an Early Bronze Age burnt mound and seven Middle to Late Bronze Age roundhouses were identified across four separate stripped areas. The site occupies the south-western slope of a hill overlooking the Silver Burn, a tributary of the River Dee. The site sloped down from 140 m AOD in the north-east to 110 m AOD in the south-west and the slopes were relatively steep in places. At the time of the excavation the land was a mix of pasture in the north and rough ground towards the south.

3.1.2.3 Chapel of Stoneywood

The site at Chapel of Stoneywood was located to the south-east of Dyce, north of the A96 trunk road. The site lay approximately 6.8 km north of the excavations at Gairnhill. Only one of the four stripped areas contained archaeology, in the form of a Middle Bronze Age roundhouse that lay on a south-east facing grassy slope which ran from 109 m AOD in the north to 104 m AOD in the south. The site was under arable crop.

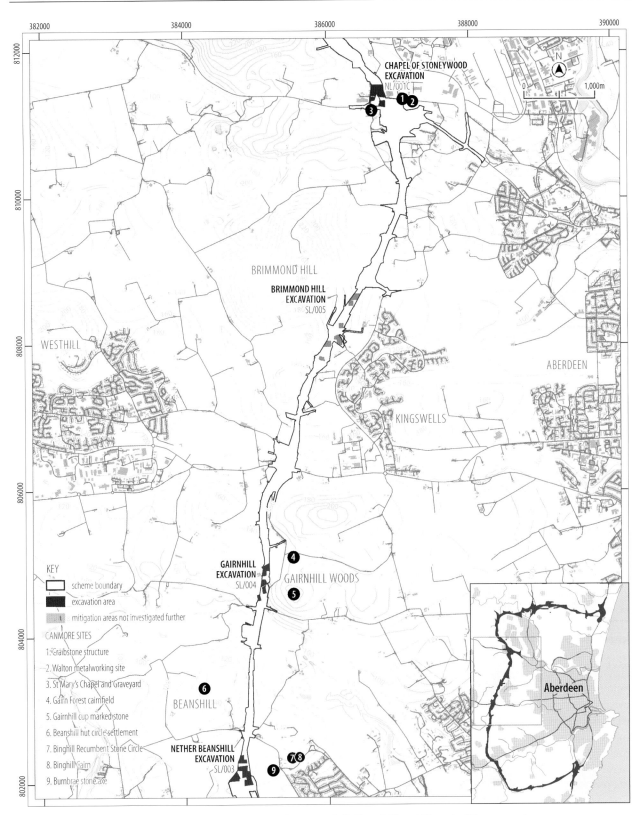

Illus 3.01 Location of sites at Nether Beanshill, Gairnhill and Chapel of Stoneywood

3.2 Background to the archaeology of the Dee to Don landscape

Prior to the works associated with the AWPR/B-T no archaeological investigations had taken place within any of the sites. Previously known sites in the area were compiled as part of the Environmental Assessment (Jacobs UK 2007) and are summarised below.

3.2.1 Nether Beanshill

At Nether Beanshill, activity in the prehistoric period is represented by the find spot of a stone axe at Burnbrae, Milltimber (NJ80SE 59), 500 m to the east of the excavation area, and by the presence of Binghill Recumbent Stone Circle (NJ80SE 16), and cairn (NJ80SE 12) also to the east. A number of hut circles, cairns and a cup-marked stone are recorded at Beanshill (NJ80SW 50) around 1.3 km to the north. Fragments of lazy bed cultivation also survive. The only other sites of archaeological interest from the area date to the medieval and post-medieval periods and are primarily related to agriculture.

3.2.2 Gairnhill

To the east of the mitigation areas at Gairnhill, within Gairnhill Wood, a cup-marked stone (NJ80SE 5), cultivation remains and possible cairnfields (NJ80SE 6 and NJ80NE 64) are recorded. Similar to Nether Beanshill there is an apparent gap in recorded sites until the medieval and post-medieval period when a number of farmsteads are known, generally to the south and west of the mitigation areas.

3.2.3 Chapel of Stoneywood

The 14th-century St. Mary's Chapel (NJ81SE 10.01) is located to the south of the A96, is one of the few known medieval sites in the area of Chapel of Stoneywood and gives the area its name. A post-built structure comprising an arc of post-holes was encountered during a watching brief for the installation of a gas pipe to the east at Craibstone (NJ81SE 209). These were preserved *in situ* rather than excavated so no further information is available. Significant excavation was undertaken some 500 m to the east in advance of the construction of a park and ride facility at Walton (NJ81SE 196 and Woodley forthcoming), which revealed a complex palimpsest of post-holes and pits, few of which formed recognisable structures. Radiocarbon dating from the site revealed two main periods of activity, in the Iron Age and the early medieval period. Abundant evidence for metalworking in the form of iron smelting and smithing was recovered related to both periods of the site's use.

3.2.4 The wider context

The wider landscape prior to the AWPR/B-T works shows sparse prehistoric activity in the form of hut circles, a recumbent stone circle and cairnfields, mostly clustered around Binghill, Gairnhill Wood and Beanshill

in the southern part of the Dee–Don higher ground. Other prehistoric remains are known from near Brimmond Hill in the form of the find spot of a stone axe (NJ80NE 70) and a possible stone circle (NJ80NE 33). West Hatton Croft Long Cairn (NJ80NE 13) is also situated between Kingswells and Westhill and is the only evidence of Neolithic activity within this landscape unit beyond a single pit found to the west of Westhill at Broadshade, which was dated to between 3940 and 3660 BC (SMR NJ80NW0308). Further to the north a recumbent stone circle is present on the eastern slope of Tyrebagger Hill (NJ81SE 11). Prehistoric remains are few and far between, with most settlement sites situated on south-facing hill slopes such as at Beanshill and Brimmond Hill.

Early medieval and medieval sites are also largely unknown beyond the Chapel of St Marys at Chapel of Stoneywood and sporadic remains of undated rig and furrow agriculture. Most other recorded sites relate to later medieval and post-medieval agricultural practices and include the large 19th century consumption dykes to the south of Brimmond Hill (Dingwall 2013).

3.3 Radiocarbon results and dating

Twenty-six samples were submitted for AMS dating (Illus 3.02 and Table 3.01). The dates show that excavated activity within the Dee–Don landscape was mostly from the Bronze Age with a single Iron Age date from Chapel of Stoneywood (see 3.6 below). Proxy dating for the Neolithic period and Bronze Age was also provided by pottery and lithic material (see 3.8 below).

Where possible, short-lived species or small branch wood were used to date features, to achieve as precise a date-range as possible. Multiple features were chosen for sampling from each set of structural remains in order to minimise the chance of anomalous dates.

3.4 Nether Beanshill

Matt Ginnever

The excavation area at Nether Beanshill contained two clusters of features on the south-western slope of a gentle hill (Illus 3.03). In the south-western corner of the site was a post-built roundhouse dated via radiocarbon assays to the Middle Bronze Age. Approximately 50 m to the north-east a second cluster of features formed a small cremation cemetery, with radiocarbon dates that place it roughly contemporary with the roundhouse.

A topsoil of mid-greyish brown sandy silt varied in thickness between 0.2 m and 0.4 m. It was shallowest in the north-east at the top of the slope and deepest towards the south-west. The superficial geological subsoil deposits were a mix of yellow-brown silty sands and gravels across the whole excavation area and contained frequent small, medium and large angular boulders.

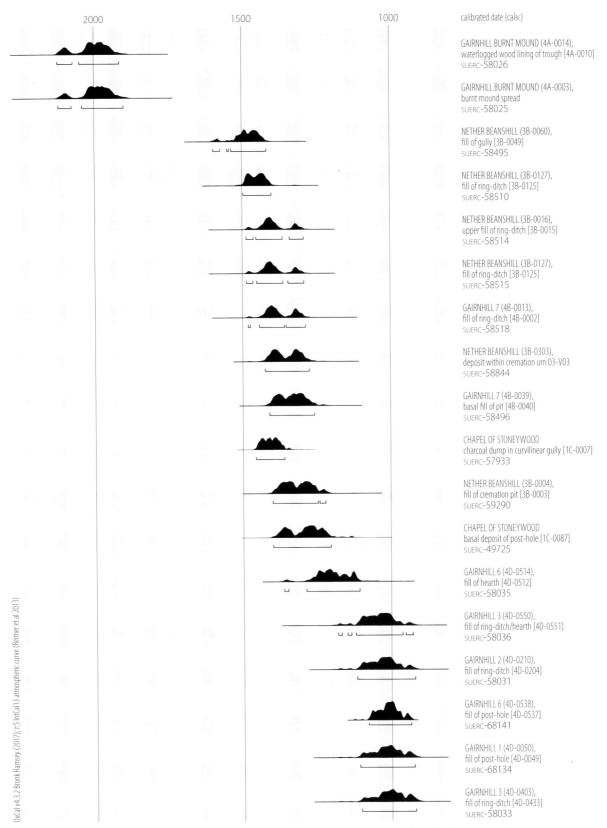

Illus 3.02A-B ^{14}C graphs from Gairnhill, Nether Beanshill and Chapel of Stoneywood

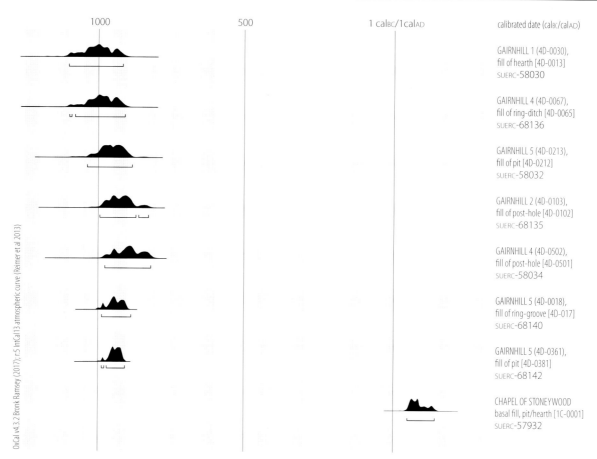

Illus 3.02A-B ¹⁴C graphs from Gairnhill, Nether Beanshill and Chapel of Stoneywood

3.4.1 Nether Beanshill roundhouse: Middle Bronze Age: 1550–1150 BC

3.4.1.1 The structural elements

The roundhouse was formed of two rings of post-holes and a south-east facing entrance (Illus 3.04). Two sections of ring-ditch were present within the interior of the building. The inner post-ring (Illus 3.04A) consisted of larger load-bearing post-holes that would have supported the roof via a ring-beam construction. The outer post-ring (Illus 3.04B) consisted of more numerous but smaller post-holes that probably formed the supports for an outer wall made either of wattle panels or from timber planks.

The eight post-holes of the inner post-ring were symmetrically placed. Post-holes [3B-0287] and [3B-0289] stood on either side of the entranceway with post-hole [3B-0039] placed equidistant between the two, at the back of the building. Three post-holes were equally spaced along the north-eastern arc between the back post and entrance post, and although only a single post-hole of the south-western arc was recovered, it is assumed that this is due to being obscured by the ring-ditch. It is noticeable that features along the western edge of the building were in general more shallow than on the eastern side and this is most likely the result of greater truncation downslope.

The post-holes of the inner ring were larger than others within the building (compare the sizes of post-hole in Illus 3.05A and B), being on average at least 0.4 m in diameter. They likely formed the main support for the roof of the building, holding up a ring-beam construction to which the rafters of the roof were attached.

Twenty-one post-holes formed an outer ring with a gap between post-holes [3B-0293] and [3B-0273] respecting the south-eastern entrance. This post-ring provided support for an outer timber or wattle panel wall, making the likely overall diameter of the building approximately 8.3 m.

On the interior of the two post-rings, a further nine post-holes were arranged in a penannular arrangement, with a gap on the south-east. Most of these post-holes were less than 0.15 m in depth, suggesting they did not contribute to the structural integrity of the building. These post-holes likely held up an internal partition wall or fence separating the central area from the surrounding periphery of the building.

Pottery was recovered in small amounts from a number of the post-holes. These fragments provide little information other than confirming a broad prehistoric date for the structure. More substantial amounts were found in post-hole [3B-0039] but the condition and type (flat-rimmed ware) means it adds little to our understanding of the structure.

Table 3.01 Radiocarbon determinations from Nether Beanshill, Gairnhill and Chapel of Stoneywood

Site	Context	Lab No	Material	Radiocarbon Age BP	Calibrated age 98.4% probability
Gairnhill Burnt Mound	(4A-0014), waterlogged wood lining of trough [4A-0010]	SUERC-58026	Wood: Alder	3642±30	2130–1930 cal BC
	(4A-0003), burnt mound spread	SUERC-58025	Charcoal: Alder	3634±30	2130–1910 cal BC
Nether Beanshill	(3B-0060) fill of gully [3B-0049]	SUERC-58495	Charcoal: Alder	3223±29	1600–1430 cal BC
	(3B-0127), fill of ring-ditch [3B-0125]	SUERC-58510	Charcoal: Hazel	3183±29	1500–1420 cal BC
	(3B-0016), upper fill of ring-ditch [3B-0015]	SUERC-58514	Charcoal: Willow	3136±29	1490–1310 cal BC
	(3B-0127) fill of ring-ditch [3B-0125]	SUERC-58515	Charcoal: Hazel	3134±29	1490–1310 cal BC
Gairnhill	Gairnhill 7 (4B-0013), fill of ring-ditch [4B-0002]	SUERC-58518	Nutshell: Hazel	3124±29	1490-1300 cal BC
Nether Beanshill	(3B-0303), deposit within cremation urn 03-V03	SUERC-58844	Bone: Burnt bone	3105±30	1430–1290 cal BC
Gairnhill	Gairnhill 7 (4B-0039), basal fill of pit [4B-0040]	SUERC-58496	Charcoal: Hazel	3084±29	1420–1270 cal BC
Chapel of Stoneywood	Charcoal dump in curvilinear gully [1C-0007]	SUERC-57933	Charcoal: Birch	3074±29	1410–1270 cal BC
Nether Beanshill	(3B-0004) fill of cremation pit [3B-0003]	SUERC-59290	Charcoal: Hazel	3059±29	1410–1240 cal BC
Chapel of Stoneywood	Basal deposit of post-hole [1C-0087]	SUERC-49725	Charcoal: Hazel	3035±32	1400–1210 cal BC
Gairnhill	Gairnhill 6 (4D-0514), fill of hearth [4D-0512]	SUERC-58035	Charcoal: Birch	2986±30	1370–1120 cal BC
	Gairnhill 3 (4D-0550), fill of ring-ditch/ hearth [4D-0551]	SUERC-58036	Charcoal: Alder	2876±30	1190–940 cal BC
	Gairnhill 2 (4D-0210), fill of ring-ditch [4D-0204]	SUERC-58031	Charcoal: Alder	2867±30	1120–930 cal BC
	Gairnhill 6 (4D-0538), fill of post-hole [4D-0537]	SUERC-68141	Charcoal: Birch	2864±29	1120–940 cal BC
Gairnhill	Gairnhill 1 (4D-0050), fill of post-hole [4D-0049]	SUERC-68134	Charcoal: Hazel	2857±29	1110–930 cal BC
	Gairnhill 3 (4D-0403), fill of ring-ditch [4D-0433]	SUERC-58033	Charcoal: Hazel	2852±30	1110–930 cal BC
	Gairnhill 1 (4D-0030), fill of hearth [4D-0013]	SUERC-58030	Charcoal: Hazel	2850±30	1110–930 cal BC
	Gairnhill 4 (4D-0067), fill of ring-ditch [4D-0065]	SUERC-68136	Charcoal: Hazel	2841±29	1100–920 cal BC
	Gairnhill 5 (4D-0213), fill of pit [4D-0212]	SUERC-58032	Charcoal: Hazel	2819±30	1050–900 cal BC
	Gairnhill 2 (4D-0103), fill of post-hole [4D-0102]	SUERC-68135	Charcoal: Hazel	2792±29	1010–850 cal BC
	Gairnhill 4 (4D-0502), fill of post-hole [4D-0501]	SUERC-58034	Charcoal: Pomaceous fruit wood	2772±30	990–840 cal BC
	Gairnhill 5 (4D-0018), fill of ring-groove [4D-0017]	SUERC-68140	Charcoal: Birch	2760±29	970–840 cal BC
Gairnhill	Gairnhill 5 (4D-0361), fill of pit [4D-0381]	SUERC-68142	Charcoal: Alder	2746±29	970–830 cal BC
Chapel of Stoneywood	Basal fill, pit/hearth [1C-0001]	SUERC-57932	Charcoal: Hazel	1878±26	cal AD 70–220

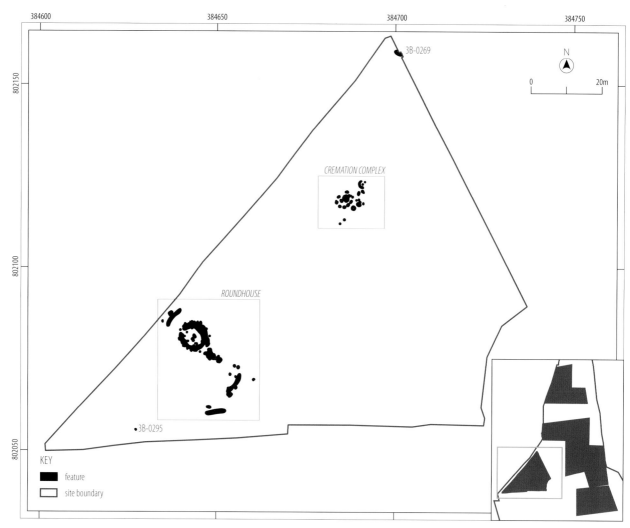

Illus 3.03 Plan of archaeological features at Nether Beanshill

To the south-east of the core of the structure, an elaborate entrance was formed by two parallel gullies [3B-0049] and [3B-0050] with post-holes located at either end. Within each gully a large stone had been placed at the point they intersected with the post-holes. It was unclear if these relate to the structure of the porch, but they were unlikely to have been post-pads owing to their irregular shape. It is possible that they were deposited after the abandonment of the building, and indeed the disturbance to the metalled surface of the entrance way (see below) caused by the removal of the south-eastern post suggests that it was disturbed after its use. The gullies seem likely to have been beam slots holding upright timber panels forming the walls of the entranceway.

The entranceway was metalled, with a surface formed of small pebbles pressed into the natural deposits (see Illus 3.05C, Illus 3.06). Small amounts of pottery and flint were recovered from the two gullies, the surface and the post-holes of the porch. A fragment of charcoal from the fill (3B-0060) of gully [3B-0049] was submitted for radiocarbon dating and returned a date of 1600–1430 cal BC (SUERC-58495).

The fills of the post-holes across the structure did not vary and were homogeneous, suggesting that the posts most likely rotted *in situ* rather than being removed or burnt down, with the exception of the south-eastern post of the entrance way discussed above. Two post-holes contained packing stones *in situ*. Only two post-holes – [3B-0130] and [3B-0138] – at the north of the structure contained abundant charcoal, which could be from the remnants of charred posts. Post-hole [3B-0287] contained abundant well-preserved barley along with a small number of weed seeds, and small amounts of barley were recovered from three other post-holes on the north-west side.

3.4.1.2 Internal features

A hearth lay just off-centre of the roundhouse and consisted of a poorly defined cut and area of heat-affected subsoil, filled by a deposit containing charcoal and bone inclusions. The pits to the south-west of the hearth were shallow (up to 0.06 m deep) and undiagnostic in terms of function, although are thought to be contemporary with the structure. A copper-alloy object was found within a

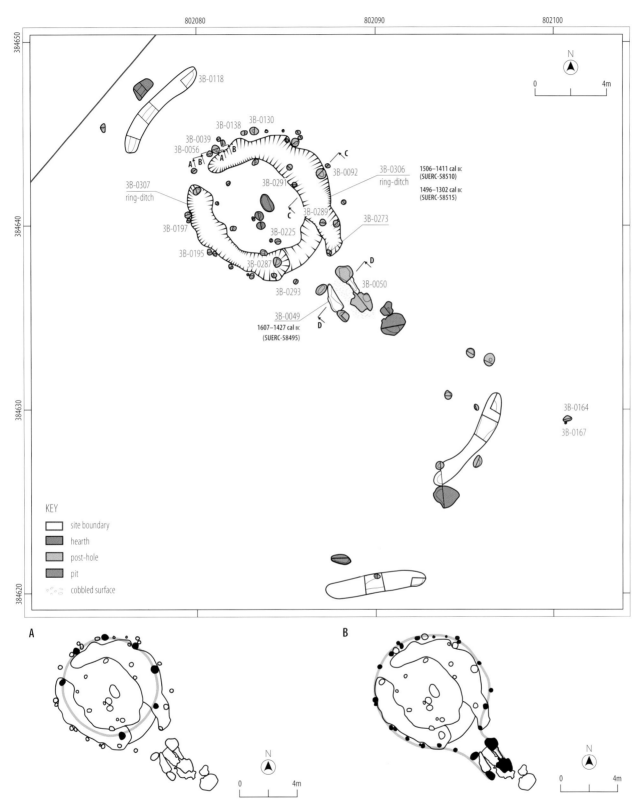

Illus 3.04 Nether Beanshill roundhouse A. Inner post-ring B. Outer post-ring and porch

turbated layer above the hearth (see 3.8.7 below) but is of limited significance and may not even relate to the structure.

Opposing ring-ditches [3B-0306] and [3B-0307] were formed through wear (rather than being deliberately cut features) and conform to the lines of the outer post-ring (Illus 3.04 and 3.05). The ring-ditch was shallower and narrower on the south-west and deeper and wider (up to 2 m) on the north-eastern arc, consistent with truncation

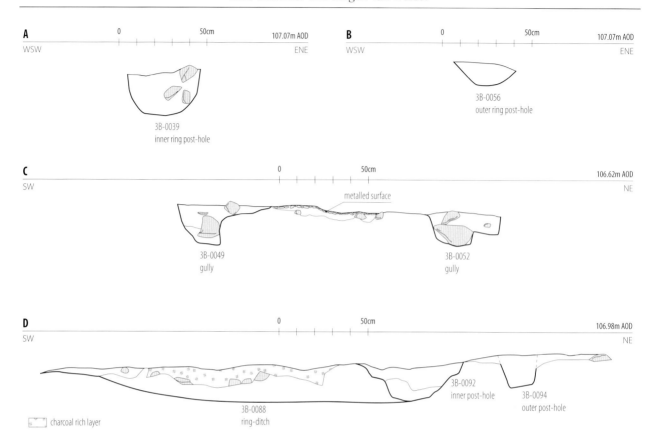

Illus 3.05 Selected sections from roundhouse

observed across the structure. In general, there was a steeper slope on the outside edge of both ring-ditches (Illus 3.05D). The southern terminals of the two ring-ditch sections were conjoined by a further wear hollow formed at the entrance to the structure.

The ring-ditch contained a spread of uncoursed medium to large granite stones sitting directly on the base (Illus 3.07). Overlying the stones was a black loamy sand containing abundant charcoal, with far greater concentrations in the eastern ring-ditch (Illus 3.08). The charcoal was principally hazel and alder with occasional oak and birch. Most appeared to be locally gathered twigs and small branches, some of which would have been dead wood, indicating that much of the charcoal derived from hearth rakings. Heather thatching to the structure is suggested by charcoal of this species recovered from the upper deposit of the ring-ditch. Radiocarbon dating of two samples of hazel charcoal from ring-ditch [3B-0306] placed it in the Middle Bronze Age with a date range of 1500–1420 cal BC and 1490–1310 cal BC (SUERC-58510 and SUERC-58515 respectively).

Small quantities of struck flint and pottery were recovered from lower fills throughout the ring-ditches. Little of the assemblage was diagnostic and, in combination with the charcoal, it is likely that these lower deposits represent hearth rakings and general domestic waste. An overlying homogeneous sandy deposit represented the silting up of the ring-ditches following their disuse.

3.4.1.3 External features

Approximately 7 m beyond the entrance and lying on the same alignment were four small post-holes forming a rectangle measuring roughly 3 m × 1.5 m. One of the post-holes [3B-0140] contained a sherd of undiagnostic prehistoric pottery and a small number of lithics. This post-hole also showed evidence of post-removal in the form of disturbed packing stones. These features were too distant from the building to form part of the porch itself but may have formed a separate structure or avenue leading to the entrance of the building. A similar four-post structure showing evidence of post removal was seen at Thainstone, Inverurie (Murray & Murray 2006), although that example dates to the 1st or 2nd century AD.

Two sections of a very shallow curvilinear ditch to the north-west [3B-0118] and south-east [3B-0172] of the roundhouse may be the remnants of an enclosure surrounding the building. A number of fragments of pottery were recovered from the northern ditch segment that were prehistoric in date. One vessel (03-V09; Illus 3.47) had a distinctive ridged shape, which was also seen on a vessel from Chapel of Stoneywood (see 3.6 below).

3.4.1.4 Roundhouse summary

The roundhouse was constructed from two post-rings; an inner post-ring of larger posts providing support for the roof of the building, most likely by utilising a ring-beam at the top of the posts, and an outer post-ring representing

Illus 3.06 Metalled surface within Nether Beanshill roundhouse entrance facing north-west

supports for the outer walls. The overall size of the building would have been approximately 8.3 m in diameter. The porch structure, orientated towards the south-east, would have had walls bedded in foundation cuts on either side. The porch would also have extended out approximately 3 m from the outer walls of the building. There is limited evidence of occupation activities, but the ring-ditches represent repeated wear by either people or animals around the periphery of the building.

3.4.2 Nether Beanshill cremation complex. Middle Bronze Age: 1550–1150 BC
(with contributions from Dave Henderson)

The cluster of features to the east of the roundhouse (Illus 3.09) included the remains of three urns from different pits and cremated human bone from multiple features. The primary cremation context was a pit enclosed by a small ring-ditch and surrounded by a number of associated pits and an oval structure defined by eight posts. Two further small ring-ditches were also identified in close proximity, one containing the highly truncated remains of a third cremation burial. The features appear to have suffered heavily from truncation and it is likely that much of the original assemblage has been lost.

Cremation Pit [3B-0104] was 0.35 m in diameter and only survived to a depth of 0.11 m (Illus 3.10A and 3.11). A barrel-shaped cremation urn (03-V03, Illus 3.12 and 3.50) had been placed upright in the pit, sat atop a small stone plinth. The cremation urn contained 191 g of fragmented burnt human bone of which 160 g was unidentifiable. The upper portion of the urn (and presumably a large part of the cremated material) had been lost. The presence of only unfused cranial sutures and of unworn enamels from the premolar teeth, combined with the observation that all the molar root tips seen were fully developed, suggests a young individual, probably in their twenties.

Although human cranial bone is inherently more identifiable than the rest of the skeleton, the absence of almost any other recognisable fragment may indicate that the remains were gathered from the pyre from the head end and placed directly into the vessel. This must remain speculative, as so much of the upper part of the deposit was absent. Radiocarbon dating of a fragment of bone was undertaken and returned a date of 1430–1290 cal BC (SUERC-58844).

The cremation pit was surrounded by a small and shallow ring-gully which served both to demarcate the extent of the cremation burial and also to provide material for forming a mound over the urn in the centre (Illus 3.11). The presence

Illus 3.07 View of Nether Beanshill roundhouse from south-west

Illus 3.08 Stones on base of ring-ditch of Nether Beanshill roundhouse

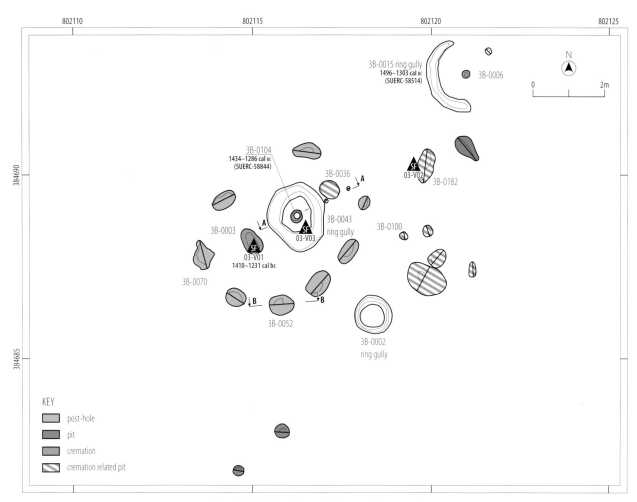

Illus 3.09 Nether Beanshill cremation complex

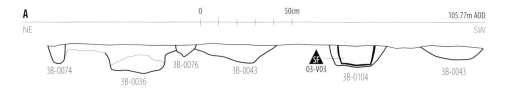

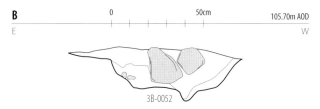

Illus 3.10 Selected sections from cremation complex

of a mound is no longer directly detectable; however, the level of truncation of the cremation urn in the centre suggests such a mound would have been required to fully cover the urn. The fill of the ring-gully included small fragments of bone and pottery in the western portion that was most likely disturbed from the central cremation by ploughing.

Directly to the south-west of the ring-gully was a small sub-oval pit [3B-0003] that also contained the remains of an urn and cremated bone. Two flat stones had been placed on the base of the pit and a single vessel (03-V01, Illus 3.48) had been placed on the stones. All that remained of the urn, however, was part of the base and a few fragments of the

Illus 3.11 Cremation complex looking south

Illus 3.12 Cremation urn (03-V03) prior to lifting

body and less than 50 g of cremated bone were recovered from the pit fill. The identifiable bone was from an adult, with fragments of jaw, skull and vertebral joints, but no further age or sex-determining features were noted. A fragment of hazel charcoal from this fill was radiocarbon dated to 1410–1240 cal BC (SUERC-59290). A single piece of flint was also recovered from this deposit.

To the north-east of the central ring-gully, a pit [3B-0036] filled with decayed and fragmented charcoal and bordered by two stake-holes also contained a small amount of burnt bone. The quantity of charcoal suggests the pit contained the remnants of pyre material.

These features were surrounded by an oval structure of post-holes, several of which contained dislodged packing stones, suggesting post removal. Six sherds of undiagnostic pottery were recovered from post-hole [3B-0070], and [3B-0052] (Illus 3.10B) is notable in containing charcoal that can be identified as conifer although it is unclear if this derived from the original post. If pit [3B-0003] is to be interpreted as a separate cremation to that found within the ring-gully it is possible that these posts acted as the visual marker for that pit and that collectively they represent a different phase of activity.

A second ring-gully [3B-0015] of similar size to the first lay 5 m to the north-east of the enclosure, with evidence of posts or wooden uprights lining the gully. Willow charcoal from this fill was radiocarbon dated to 1490–1310 cal BC (SUERC-58514). A heavily truncated pit in the centre of this ring-gully contained very small fragments of burnt bone (16 g in total) but no traces of pottery to suggest an urn. Despite its fragmentary nature, this may represent the highly truncated remains of another cremation burial. A third small ring-gully [3B-0002] lay to the south-east of the main group and may represent either contemporary activity or another phase. The absence of a central pit or of any burnt bone in the fill of the gully excludes this from being interpreted as a further cremation, although truncation may have removed any evidence here.

Two further pits in this group contained material related to the cremation burials. Pit [3B-0100] contained abundant charcoal and burnt bone, but at only 41 g still less than about 3% of the weight expected from a complete adult cremation (McKinley 2000, 407). There were 26 g of fragments of limb-bone, one skull fragment and 15 g of non-identifiable

fragments. No age or sex characteristics were observed. A fragment of flint was also recovered from this fill. Pit [3B-0182] contained multiple sherds of pottery from a single vessel (03-V02, Illus 3.49), most likely an urn similar to those from pits [3B-0104] and [3B-003]; however, no cremated bone was recovered from the fill. Given the proximity of these two pits to the other cremations it is entirely possible that they represent ancillary features to the main cremations and contained pyre sweepings and additional votive vessels.

Other small pits along the eastern and southern edges of the cluster contained small amounts of burnt bone, but this most likely originated from the disturbed cremation burials. Given the poor overall preservation of this cluster, it is difficult to judge how many cremated individuals were originally present. The quantity of cremated bone from across all of the features was not sufficient to establish this, as all the material could have come from a single funeral pyre. Likewise, the presence of three vessels does not dictate that we have three individual burials. The strongest argument for more than one burial being present is in the form of the ring-gullies and post-holes that serve to enclose or demarcate certain features. Unfortunately, the radiocarbon dates recovered from the cluster are very closely grouped, which makes phasing the features impossible. It is likely that most if not all of the features are roughly contemporary and would have appeared as a series of small mounds surrounded by gullies. It is notable that the pits [3B-0003], [3B-0104], [3B-0036] and [3B-0006] form a rough south-west to north-east alignment. This could be used to argue that they are all part of the same single burial activity. However, as two of the three likely cremations are defined by ring gullies, the fact that the third one is not would point to it being either slightly earlier or later. The oval-shaped arrangement of posts represents a separate phase of activity and served as markers for the cremation in pit [3B-0003], which was not marked by a ring-gully.

3.4.3 Other features at Nether Beanshill

In the very northern corner of the excavation area, a small section of gully contained fragments of prehistoric pottery. The pottery could not be more accurately dated, and no other features were found in close proximity; however, it attests to a wider spread of prehistoric activity.

3.4.4 Post-medieval remains at Nether Beanshill

A single fragment of rig and furrow aligned north-east to south-west was uncovered in the south-western corner of the site. Despite these limited remains the furrow is evidence of later medieval or post-medieval agricultural activity at the site.

3.5 Gairnhill

The site at Gairnhill was located 2.3 km to the north of Nether Beanshill on a relatively steep south-westerly facing slope from 140 m AOD in the north-eastern corner to 110 m AOD in the south-western, spread over an area c470m from south to north. The remains included a Neolithic pit, an Early Bronze Age burnt mound, and seven Middle to Late Bronze Age roundhouses (Illus 3.13). During excavation the roundhouses were numbered 1 to 7 from north to south, but radiocarbon dating has since shown Gairnhill 7 to be the earliest structure.

Topsoil, uniformly a dark grey sandy clayey silt, varied in depth from 0.65 m in the south to around 0.2 m in the north. Geological subsoils consisted of glacial till that varied between orange-brown sandy clays and yellow-brown sandy gravels. Frequent angular stones and boulders were encountered within the geological subsoil and the topsoil, especially at the edges of fields indicating agricultural clearance throughout the area.

3.5.1 Gairnhill: Neolithic: 4000–2400 BC

A shallow pit represents the earliest activity recovered from the excavations (Illus 3.13). It contained a small piece of flint and sherds of pottery (04-V01) that were dated to the Neolithic period (see 3.8 below). Although isolated and relatively insignificant, this find places the later settlement activity within an earlier, Neolithic, context of landscape use, though relatively limited.

3.5.2 Gairnhill: Early Bronze Age: 2200/2000–1550 BC

3.5.2.1 Construction of the burnt mound

The southernmost excavation area uncovered the remains of a burnt mound dated to the late third and early second millennium BC (Illus 3.14), close to a small water course in a boggy field corner at around 110 m AOD. Excavations revealed a buried ground surface into which a rectangular wood-lined trough had been cut. Analysis of the plant macrofossils in the buried soil indicated that peat had already begun to form prior to the construction of the trough (see 3.7.2.1 below). Around the trough were three arrangements of stones, and other features related to water management. The mound was formed of burnt material and heat-affected rocks and was later covered over by angular boulders related to agricultural field clearance.

The trough comprised a rectangular cut lined with roughly squared alder planks (Illus 3.15, 3.16) on its base and sides, sealed with clayey sand. The timber forming the northern edge was a single radially-cut trunk segment of oak rather than alder (Appendix 2.1.14). The internal dimensions of the trough measured 1.8 m × 0.42 m × 1.0 m giving it an overall volume of 0.75 m³ (Illus 3.17). A modification to the trough was made by the insertion of a stone upright that shortened the internal space (Illus 3.18). Fragments of possible wattle-like timbers were found beneath planks placed to the south of the stone upright. Timber from the central base plank was radiocarbon-dated to 2130–1930 cal BC (SUERC-58026).

A water channel extended for around 1 m from the south-eastern end of the trough, presumably to either feed water in or drain away excess from the trough. A roughly V-shaped, possibly stone-lined, water channel also ran from the southern edge of the mound, beyond the limit of excavation of the site. The channel base sloped to the south, presumably draining water to the nearby burn. Four stake-holes to the south-west of the trough (Illus 3.17 & 3.18) may have provided support for a wind break or drying rack.

A series of three stone features were located to the east, south and south-west of the trough (Structures 1, 2 and 3). Although described as structures, they are not upstanding walls; rather, they appear to delineate the arrangement of the subsequent burnt mound material.

Structure 1 consisted of a shallow stone-filled curvilinear cut curving round the south-east corner of the trough. The channel to the south of the trough was bordered by a rough stone surface on both sides. Structure 2 consisted of a rough L-shaped wall foundation or edging stones of large unfaced granite field-stones set in a linear cut (Illus 3.19). This channel, surface and structure suggest another focus of activity at the site, not directly tied to the trough.

Structure 3 formed the western boundary of the burnt mound and consisted of an alignment of unfaced, large granite field-stones, some of which were glacial boulders that had been left *in situ* and utilised to form this structure.

3.5.2.2 Evidence for activity and use

The trough, ditches and structures were all overlain by the mound, formed from a dark silty sand containing abundant charcoal fragments and medium sub-angular stones discoloured and cracked by heat. This material covered an area roughly 11.5 m by 11 m and survived up to a thickness of 0.4 m. Despite the presence of heat-affected material, no hearth was discovered. Presumably multiple small bonfires were lit, and the remains of these bonfires mixed into the expanding burnt mound material. The mounded material was generally homogeneous throughout (Illus 3.20A and B) and no evidence of separate phases of firings could be discerned. Fragments of hazel and alder twigs were identified from the charcoal showing that locally available species were being utilised (Illus 3.21). Charcoal from the burnt mound deposit was submitted for radiocarbon dating and returned a range of 2130–1910 cal BC (SUERC-58025). The accumulation of this material most likely derives from heating stones to be placed into the trough. Used stones, blackened and cracked from the heating, were then discarded immediately around the

Illus 3.13 Plan of archaeological features at Gairnhill

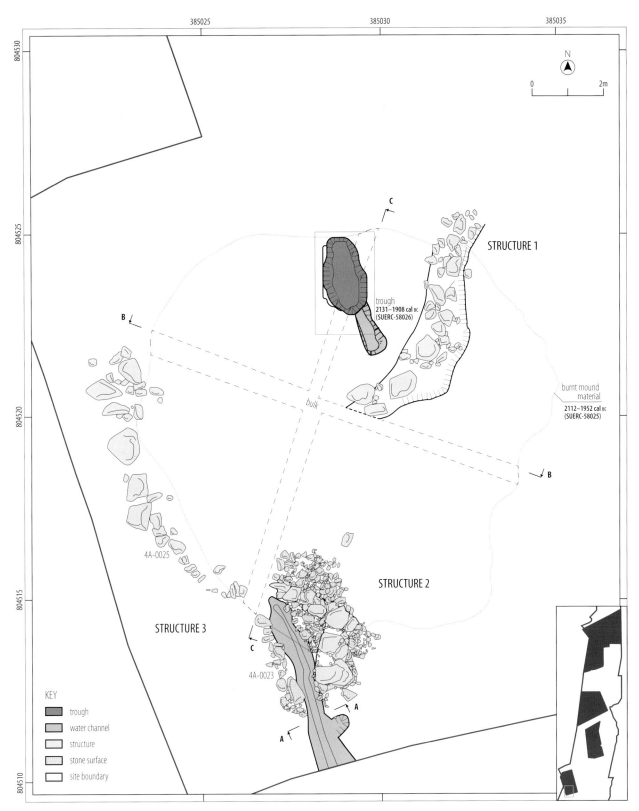

STRUCTURE 1

trough
2131–1908 cal BC
(SUERC-58026)

burnt mound
material
2112–1952 cal BC
(SUERC-58025)

bulk

B

4A-0025

STRUCTURE 2

STRUCTURE 3

C

4A-0023

A

A

KEY

trough
water channel
structure
stone surface
site boundary

N

0   2m

Illus 3.14 Plan of Gairnhill burnt mound

Matt Ginnever and Jürgen van Wessel

Illus 3.15 Photo of trough with wood lining and later stone upright facing north-east

Illus 3.16 Photo of trough with wooden planks at base

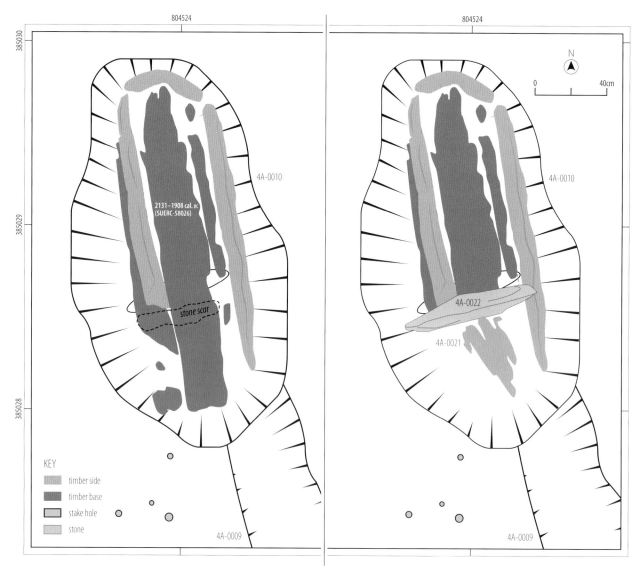

Illus 3.17 Detail of trough – primary phase

Illus 3.18 Detail of trough – secondary phase

Illus 3.19 Photo of Structure 2 [4A-0018] facing north

trough, most likely with sweepings from the undiscovered hearth or bonfire used to heat them.

3.5.2.3 Abandonment and disuse

The trough was infilled with silt-rich deposits containing heat-affected stones and charcoal on abandonment. The upper fill had a high peaty/organic content suggesting peat formation continued following the trough falling out of use.

During this abandonment phase, the south-western flank of the burnt mound became covered by a colluvial deposit of mid-reddish brown silty sand. The eastern part of the mound was overlain by a mid-brown sandy silt containing abundant large and medium sub-angular stones that derived from field clearance relating to much later agricultural activity.

3.5.3 Gairnhill: Middle Bronze Age: 1550–1150 BC

3.5.3.1 Gairnhill Building 7

Gairnhill 7 was located 135 m to the north-east of the burnt mound on a plateau at around 123 m AOD (Illus 3.13). The structure was formed by a ring of post-holes with an entrance porch facing south. The remains had been severely truncated by later agricultural activity. The most prominent feature of the structure was a substantial paved internal ring-ditch forming an arc along the inner eastern edge of the structure. An internal post-ring, most likely for the support of the roof, was apparent within the western arc of the building but was masked by the ring-ditch to the east (Illus 3.22).

Eight post-holes defined the limits of the structure (Illus 3.22A) and represent the location of the outer walls of the building; however, the posts are too far apart to have held timber or wooden panelling and are likely to be outer supports for where the roof timbers rested on a turf or earth wall that has not survived. The surviving depth of post-holes was greater along the eastern side (up to 0.2 m deep) and it seems likely some are lost on the western side. Post-holes [4B-0017] and [4B-0019] to the south of the ring formed a south-facing porch.

A possible inner post-ring consisted of five post-holes and two post-pads within the western arc of the building (Illus 3.22B). The absence of similar posts in the east is likely because the ring-ditch on the same alignment masked any traces.

A small hearth was situated slightly off-centre in the interior (Illus 3.22), defined by stones and containing a series of charcoal-rich silts and undiagnostic sherds of pottery. Hazel charcoal from the basal fill of the hearth was submitted for radiocarbon dating and returned a date of 1420–1270 cal BC (SUERC-58496).

A large ring-ditch, roughly paved with sub-rounded to sub-angular stones, was present on the eastern side of the structure. A smaller section of ring-ditch was also visible along the western arc of the building but contained no paving. The main ring-ditch was formed by a series of intercutting depressions that give the ditch an undulating outline in plan (Illus 3.22). The profiles of these depressions were shallow with very gently sloping sides (Illus 3.23A–C) and appeared to have been formed from erosional processes. The stones forming the paving had been deposited within the series of conjoining hollows in an attempt to level out the uneven surface (Illus 3.24).

The paving was overlain by a series of charcoal-rich sandy clay silts containing small undiagnostic sherds of pottery evenly distributed throughout. These deposits are likely to have accumulated within the ring-ditch during the use of the building from general refuse and hearth sweepings. Hazel charcoal from the basal fill of the ring-ditch was submitted for radiocarbon dating and returned a date of 1490–1300 cal BC (SUERC-58518). The final upper deposit was an abandonment or post-abandonment fill closely resembling topsoil.

Within the porch was an irregular depression with steep sides and a flat base. This was interpreted as an erosion hollow formed from the traffic of people and animals through the entrance way.

In summary, the building appears to have been constructed sometime between 1600–1300 BC, with an inner post-ring supporting the roof and the outer walls represented by the outer post-ring, which would give an overall diameter of just under 10 m, and a protruding, south-facing entrance. The walls themselves were most likely formed from a bank of earth or turf subsequently lost to ploughing rather than stone; despite the presence of stones in the ring-ditch to the east, none were found in the western portion.

3.5.4 Gairnhill: Late Bronze Age: 1150–c800 BC

Six roundhouses from the northernmost excavation area have been dated to the Late Bronze Age. An isolated building (Gairnhill 6) at the south returned the earliest date from the six. Four of these structures were clustered in an east to west line in the north-western corner of the site (Illus 3.25). Radiocarbon dates from all four are too close to provide a sequence of construction (Illus 3.02, Table 3.01). A further structure was found on the same alignment

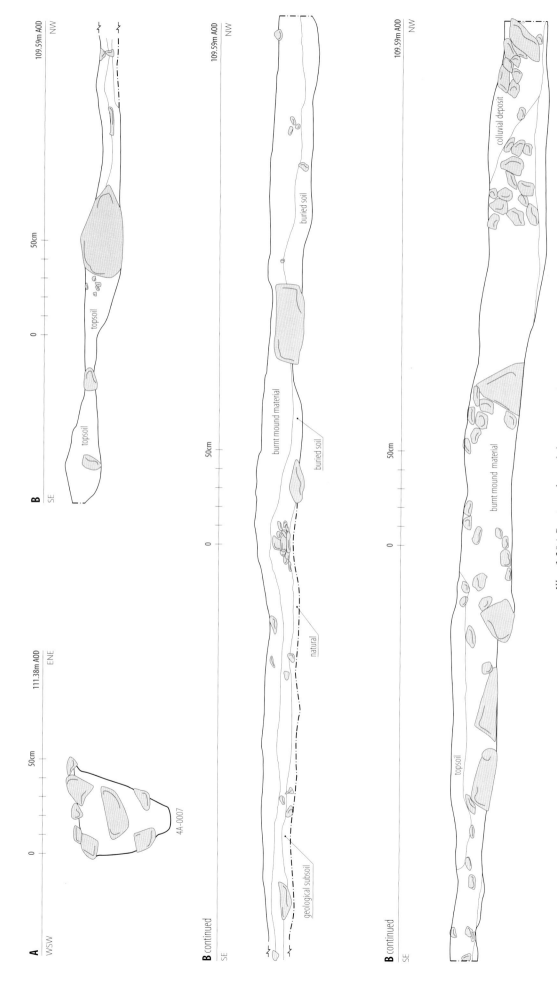

Illus 3.20A Sections through burnt mound

A
WSW
ENE
111.38m AOD
50cm
0
4A-0007

B
SE
NW
109.59m AOD
50cm
0
topsoil
topsoil

B continued
SE
NW
109.59m AOD
50cm
0
burnt mound material
buried soil
buried soil
natural
geological subsoil

B continued
SE
NW
109.59m AOD
50cm
0
colluvial deposit
burnt mound material
burnt mound material
topsoil

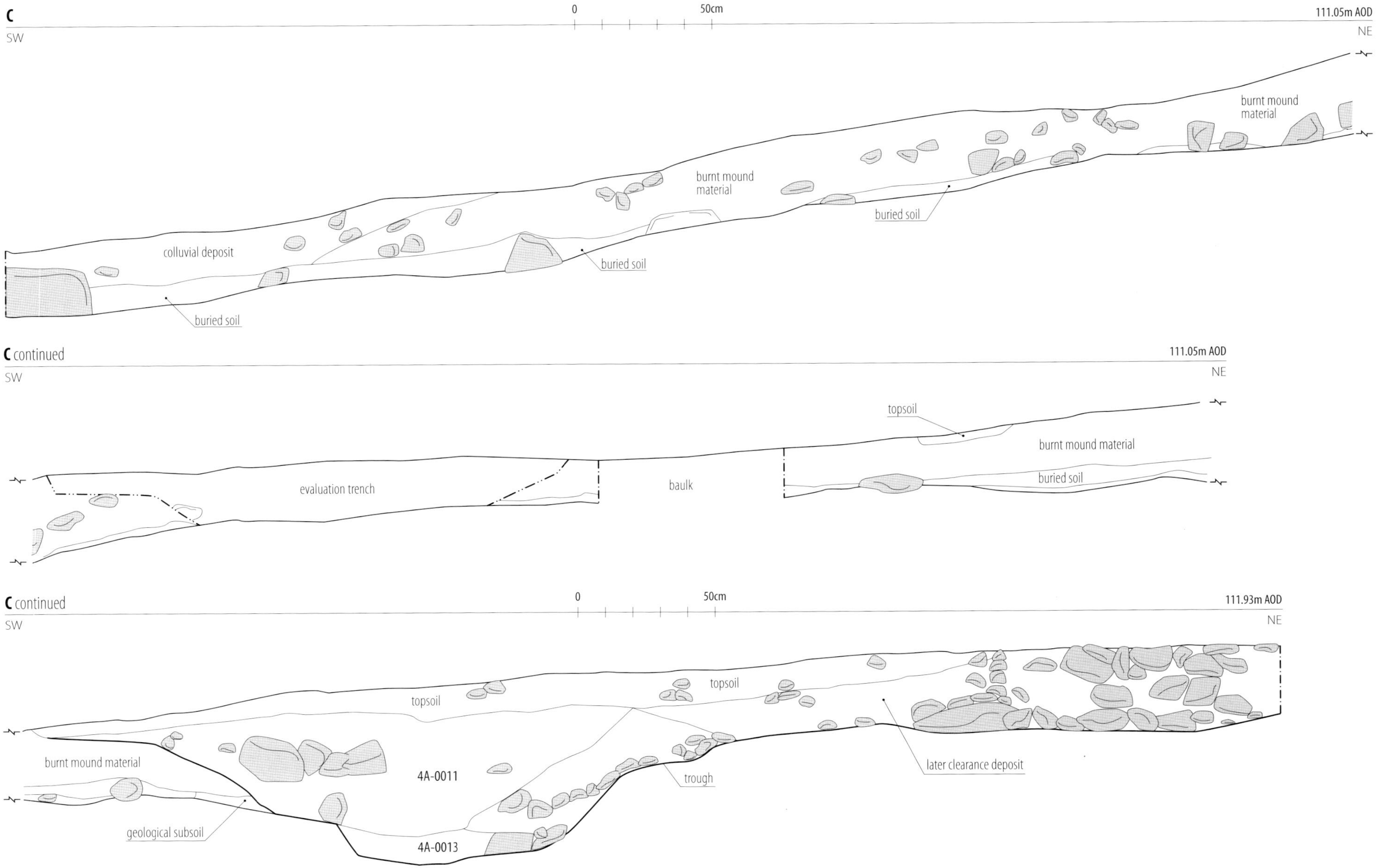

Illus 3.20B Sections through burnt mound

C

SW / NE — 111.05m AOD

- burnt mound material
- buried soil
- buried soil
- burnt mound material
- colluvial deposit
- buried soil

C continued

SW / NE — 111.05m AOD

- burnt mound material
- buried soil
- topsoil
- baulk
- evaluation trench

C continued

SW / NE — 111.93m AOD

- topsoil
- later clearance deposit
- trough
- topsoil
- 4A-0011
- 4A-0013
- burnt mound material
- geological subsoil

50cm 0

Illus 3.21 Photo of burnt mound facing south-west

around 25 m to the east of this group, and although broadly contemporary, also produced the latest date from site. Some structural variations were apparent among these roundhouses although the majority were defined by post-rings and had south-east facing entrances. Ring-ditches were present in four of them. The site as a whole appears to have suffered from truncation owing to later agricultural practices. This truncation was especially noticeable on the western, downslope, side of most structures. *In situ* burnt timbers were present within the ring-ditches of three of the buildings. These remains indicate that either they had burnt down or that the buildings had been deliberately fired upon abandonment. A possible four-post structure was also associated with this group. A single pit, outwith any of the buildings, also contained substantial quantities of oats, which are of an Iron Age or later date (see 3.7.2.3 below).

3.5.4.1 Gairnhill 6

Gairnhill 6 was situated some 75 m to the south of the other Late Bronze Age buildings at Gairnhill. It was also at the lowest altitude and appears to have suffered the greatest level of truncation owing to the relatively thin topsoil covering in this area of the site. It comprised a partially complete post-ring, an internal hearth and a narrow curvilinear ring-groove (Illus 3.26).

The post-ring contained eight post-holes and had an approximate diameter of 8 m. The post-holes were between 0.2 m and 0.4 m in diameter and were up to 0.29 m deep. A single post-hole [4D-0543] to the south-east of the post-ring could represent the remains of an entrance post. A fragment of birch charcoal from post-hole [4D-0537] was submitted for radiocarbon dating and returned a date range of 1120–940 cal BC (SUERC-68141).

The outer curvilinear feature [4D-0511] extended approximately 7 m but was only 0.08 m deep, surviving as a scar in the underlying geology for a further 4 m towards the south and west (not illustrated). The feature is interpreted as a possible ring-groove foundation based on the alignment with the post-holes to the west, or possibly a drainage gully close to the outer wall of the building.

Internal features included a hearth and a single stake-hole. The hearth was located within the north-eastern portion of the building and comprised a charcoal-rich layer with a stony layer above this (Illus 3.27). Birch charcoal from the basal fill was submitted for radiocarbon dating and returned a date of 1370–1120 cal BC (SUERC-58035), earlier but broadly consistent with the date recovered from the post-hole. The date from the hearth is probably a more reliable indicator of the date of use of the structure.

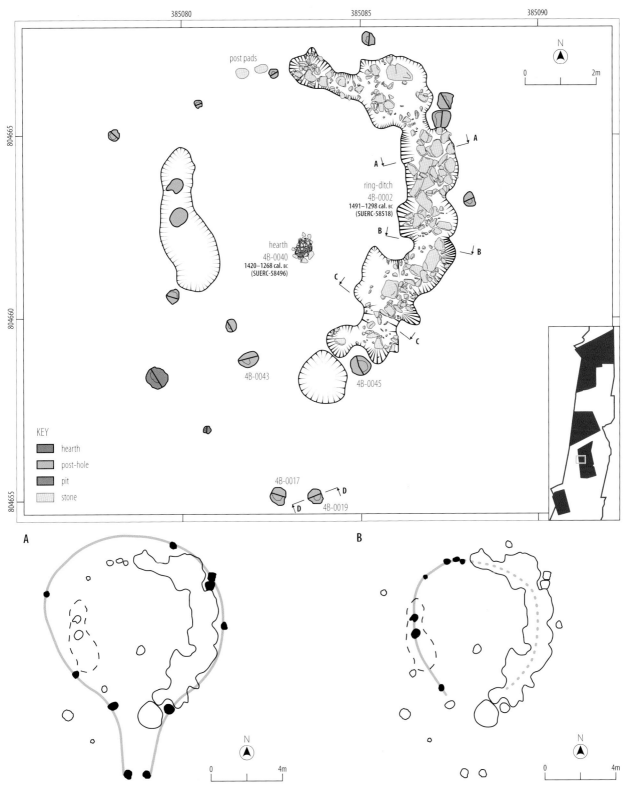

Illus 3.22 Plan of Gairnhill 7 A. Outer post-ring B. Inner post-ring

In summary the structure of Gairnhill 6 consisted of a partial ring-groove indicating the original position of the outer walls. An estimated diameter of the building can be extrapolated from this of approximately 11 m. Preservation of this structure was poor, and it is assumed that many features have been lost to truncation. The roof was supported by an inner post-ring that would have held a ring-beam. The entrance orientation was not established due to the level of preservation, though is hinted at by a post-hole to the south-east. The date from the hearth in particular suggests that this is the earliest of the Late Bronze Age buildings at Gairnhill.

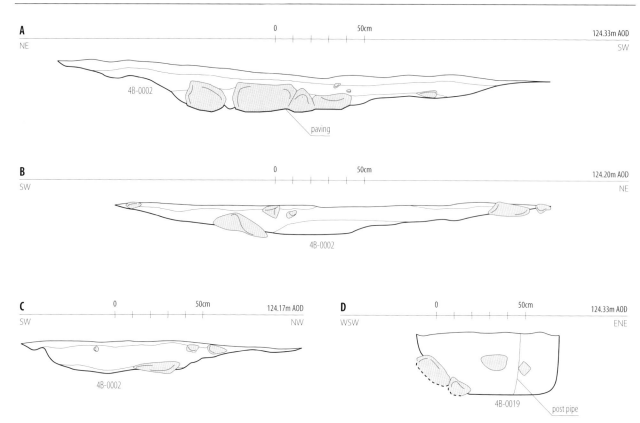

Illus 3.23 Sections of Gairnhill 7

Illus 3.24 Photo of Gairnhill 7 facing south-west

3.5.4.2 Gairnhill 1

Gairnhill 1 was found in the north-western corner of the site (Illus 3.28). This building consisted of a small ring-groove foundation trench with an internal hearth. The ring-groove was only present along the eastern edge of the structure. The shape suggests a series of straight sections arranged to form a roughly hexagonal or octagonal building (Illus 3.28A). It is also possible that the western side of this structure was always open and that this was not a completely enclosed building. The ring-groove was

irregular in width and depth, curving approximately 8.0 m from south-west to north-west, and was between 0.7 m and 1.4 m wide. The base undulated owing to the stony nature of the geological subsoil and was a maximum of 0.2 m deep. Up to six post settings were identified within the ring-groove and a seventh post-hole was located on the same alignment. Hazel charcoal from the basal fill of the ring-groove was submitted for radiocarbon dating and returned a date range of 1110–930 cal BC (SUERC-68134).

The central hearth was filled with heat-affected stones and soil. Charcoal from the basal fill was identified as predominantly oak and hazel, utilising both medium-size branches as well as small twigs. The upper deposits appeared to have been fire rakings of heat-affected soil, burnt bone and charcoal dumped in the cut together with a large stone (Illus 3.29). Sherds of pottery from a single vessel (04-V02) was recovered from the upper fill but were too small to be diagnostic. Hazel charcoal from the basal fill of the hearth was submitted for radiocarbon dating and returned a date range of 1110–930 cal BC (SUERC-58030).

In summary, Gairnhill 1 was a small structure, no more than 6 or 7 m in diameter formed of timber or wattle panels that resulted in the building having an angular rather than circular appearance. The roof of the building, if present, would have been supported directly on the walls as no further evidence for roof supports were seen.

To the south-west of the roundhouse, a series of post-holes formed the possible remains of another structure,

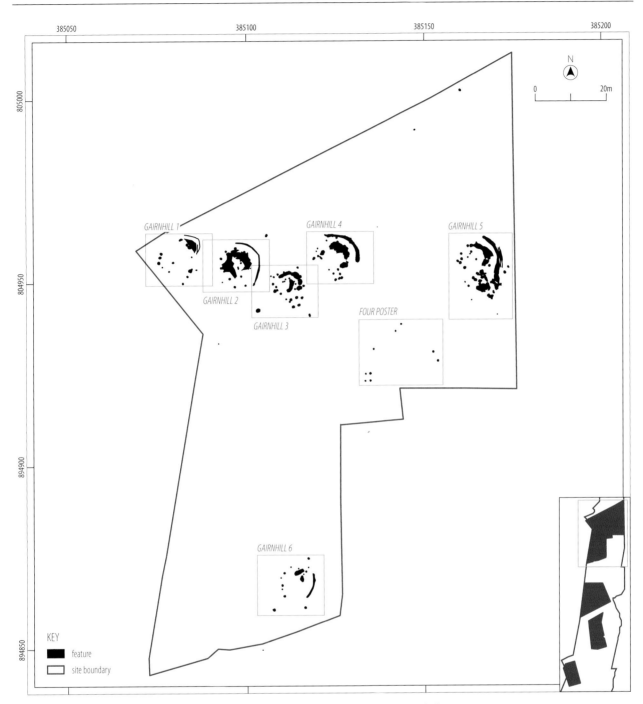

Illus 3.25 Late Bronze Age features at Gairnhill

the form of which was not readily identifiable. Post-holes [4D-0042] and [4D-0051] contained sherds of prehistoric pottery, with portions of a single vessel in each (04-V03 and 04-V04 respectively). It is possible that these post-holes are the truncated remains of out-buildings or ancillary structures such as animal pens, potentially relating to Gairnhill 1.

3.5.4.3 Gairnhill 2
Gairnhill 2 was defined by the remains of a post-ring with a south-east facing entrance and a narrow gully around

the eastern arc; most likely the truncated remains of a ring-groove for the outer walls (Illus 3.30). Internally a ring-ditch was present within the eastern arc of the building.

Nine post-holes formed the post-ring (Illus 3.30A), spaced 2 m to 2.3 m apart and all roughly 0.5 m diameter. The overall diameter of the post-ring was 8.7 m, and would have supported a ring-beam, in turn supporting the roof. There was a high degree of variability in survival of the post-holes; post-hole [4D-0145] only survived as the impression of the base of the cut. Post-holes [4D-0114] and [4D-0136] contained *in situ* packing stones, suggesting the

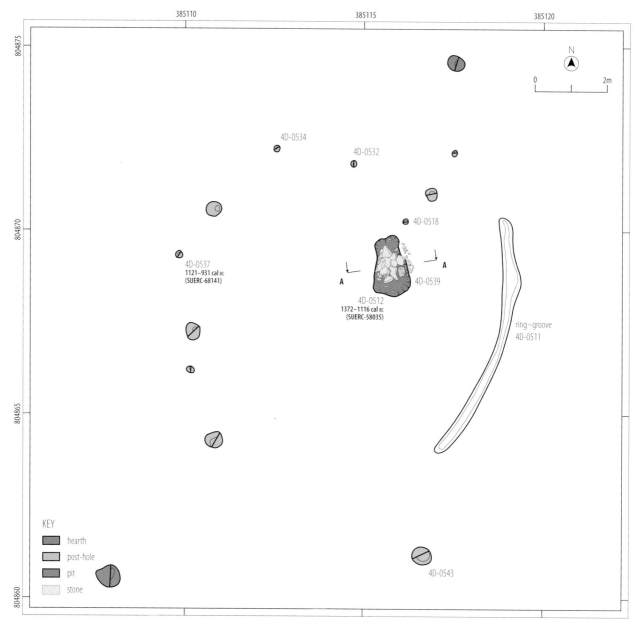

Illus 3.26 Plan of Gairnhill 6

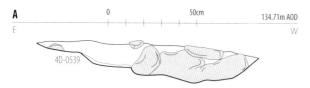

Illus 3.27 Gairnhill 6 section through hearth

posts were between 0.2 m to 0.25 m in diameter. Four post-holes appear to have had posts removed, with disturbed packing stones within their backfill. Post-hole [4D-0102] contained a significant number of small and medium sherds of a pottery vessel (04-V05, Illus 3.51), which seemed to have been deliberately placed into the void created by the removal of the post. Hazel charcoal from the fill of post-

hole [4D-0102] was submitted for radiocarbon dating and returned a date range of 1010–850 cal BC (SUERC-68135). Two post-holes lay to the south-south-east of the structure and formed an entrance 2.1 m wide.

A narrow curvilinear gully enclosing the eastern arc of the building represents the remains of the outer walls. A series of stake-holes to the east of the centre of the building most likely supported wattle hurdles or panels serving as internal divisions, and further evidence of these partitions was seen in the form of carbonised timbers with the structure of staves and withies found at the base of the ring-ditch immediately to the east of the stake-holes (Illus 3.31). The preservation of these timbers was good enough in a few cases to identify tool marks, although the wood had largely not been modified (see 3.7.2.4 below). The ring-ditch had

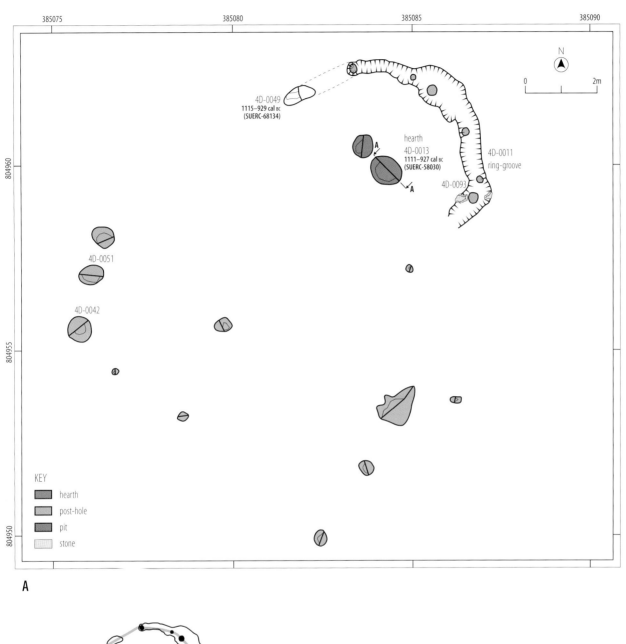

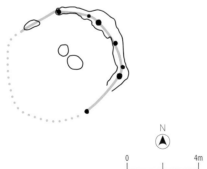

Illus 3.28 Plan of Gairnhill 1 A. Proposed extent of Gairnhill 1

formed through erosion or wear and, similar to Gairnhill 7, there was a concentration of stones roughly laid in the centre of the base, possibly as paving or levelling material (Illus 3.32). A surface find of a saddle quern in close proximity to the roundhouse may well be contemporary.

The later deposits within the ditch relate to the abandonment or demolition of the structure; carbonised wattle remains were dated to 1120–930 cal BC (SUERC-58031), giving a broad date of abandonment for the building. Overlying this were further ashy deposits

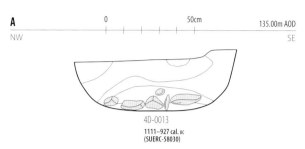

Illus 3.29 Section through hearth in Gairnhill 1

overlain by heat-affected soil. Some of these deposits may be the degraded remains of further structural components of the building collapsed from above.

The structure of Gairnhill 2 consisted of a ring-groove construction, with an estimated original size of approximately 12.3 m (extrapolating the line of the ring-groove to the west). The fact that it only survived on the upslope side of the roundhouse suggests that the building may have been partially terraced in order to create a flat platform for construction. The roof was supported by a post-ring that would have held a ring-beam. The entrance was orientated towards the south-east and would not have protruded beyond the limits of the outer walls. Internal divisions were suggested by a series of stake holes on the interior of the building. A ring-ditch on the north-eastern interior of the structure was formed through erosion related to the use of the building.

3.5.4.4 Gairnhill 3

Gairnhill 3 was defined by a post-ring and a south-east facing entrance (Illus 3.33). The post-ring (Illus 3.33A) was c7.5 m in diameter, consisting of ten post-holes with a maximum depth of 0.13 m. Two further post-holes were situated to the south of the ring and formed an entrance approximately 1.5 m wide. No remains of the outer walls (which may have been of turf or stone construction) were observed; however, the presence of a ring-ditch extending beyond the post-ring suggests that the wall lay beyond this feature. Three post-holes to the north-west of the post-ring may be evidence for its replacement or repair; alternatively these might represent an annexe or lean-to feature.

Because of the lack of direct archaeological evidence for the external diameter of Gairnhill 3, an estimate must be made. A circle with a diameter of 11.4 m encompasses the two entrance posts. Similar to Gairnhill 2, the interior of the structure contained a number of small post- or stake-holes relating to internal divisions or features within the structure. These were arranged in a semi-circle along the eastern side of the building and may have held wattle hurdles, evidence for which was contained within the lower fills of the ring-ditch.

The ring-ditch consisted of four separate irregular depressions formed through wear. Attempts to partially level these out with stones were seen in the larger central depression. Above the stones lay a heavily turbated charred

deposit, which contained very few charred wood fragments, suggesting an oxygen-rich fire, capable of reducing wooden remains almost completely to ash. Tentatively drawn lines of former structural timbers were noted during the course of the excavation that suggested wattle panelling similar to that seen in Gairnhill 2 (see 3.5.4.3 below), and a probable bone pin, burnt by fire, was recovered from this deposit. A fragment of hazel charcoal was submitted for radiocarbon dating and returned a date range of 1110–930 cal BC (SUERC-58033). Above this deposit a brown-grey sandy silt represented partial mixing of the topsoil with the ditch deposits through plough action.

In the centre of the building was a curvilinear pit containing heat-affected material that appeared to be formed through erosion. This could be related to the building's hearth, ie a rake out pit, although the location of the hearth is not known. Alder charcoal from fill (4D-0550) of the pit was submitted for radiocarbon dating and returned a date range of 1190–940 cal BC (SUERC-58036), similar to that from the ring-ditch.

In summary, Gairnhill 3 consisted of a post-ring measuring 7.5 m in diameter, which would have held a ring-beam to support the roof. Two posts formed a south-east facing entrance. Internal divisions were suggested by a series of stake-holes on the north-eastern side of the interior. A segmented ring-ditch was formed through erosion related to the use of the building and a scooped pit in the centre was probably formed in a similar way and might relate to a hearth.

Located immediately outside of the post-ring of Gairnhill 3 was a pit containing the remains of approximately 60% of a bucket-shaped urn (04-V08) of Bronze Age date. A number of heat-affected stones, including two coarse stone polishers possibly used for leather working, were recovered from the upper fill. The function of the pit is not clear though the pottery recovered is from a type of vessel associated with cremation burials rather than domestic situations (see 3.8 below). Organic residue indicating use in cooking or preparing foodstuffs was recovered from the interior face of the vessel, and no burnt bone was observed from any of the fills in this feature. A similar feature from near Gairnhill 5 (see 3.5.4.6 below) returned a date range of 970–830 cal BC (SUERC-68142) and both features may represent either foundation or abandonment deposits for the building.

3.5.4.5 Gairnhill 4

Gairnhill 4 was defined by a post-ring and a partial ring-groove (Illus 3.34). This structure also contained the best-preserved examples of carbonised wood in the fill of its internal ring-ditch.

Eight post-holes formed the remnants of an internal post-ring, 8.1 m in diameter (Illus 3.34A), with post-holes between 2 m and 2.5 m apart. Paired (eg [4D-0322] and [4D-0430]) and intercutting post-holes ([4D-0497] and [4D-0498]) indicate the possibility of repair

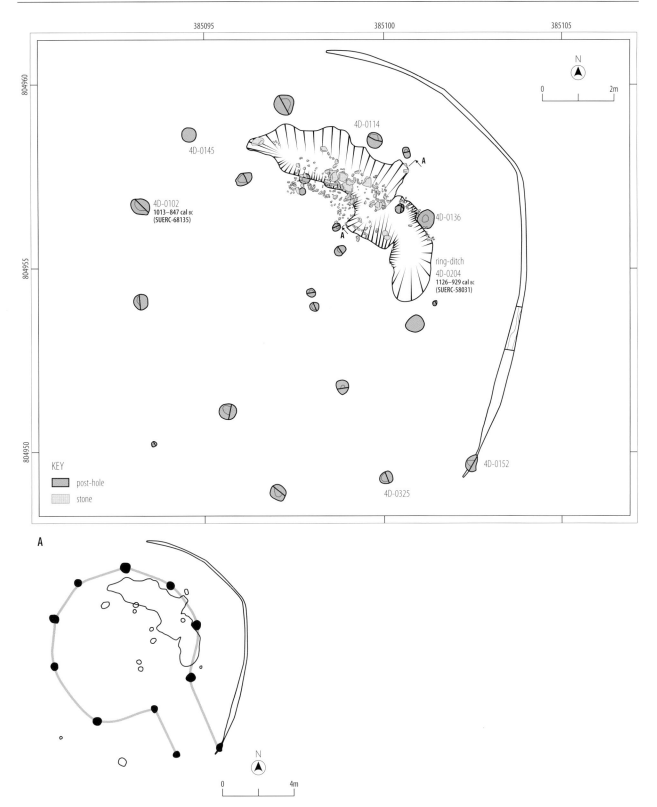

Illus 3.30 Plan of Gairnhill 2 A. Ring-beam post-ring

or replacement. The entrance of the roundhouse was on the south-east. Post-hole [4D-0501] contained a stone packing deposit encircling the remains of a post, 0.26 m in diameter, which appeared to have been burnt *in situ*. Charcoal from this burnt post was submitted for radiocarbon dating and returned a date range of 990–840 cal BC (SUERC-58034).

The internal post-ring was surrounded by a partially surviving ring-groove or foundation gully, a maximum of 1 m wide with gently sloping sides. Hazel charcoal from

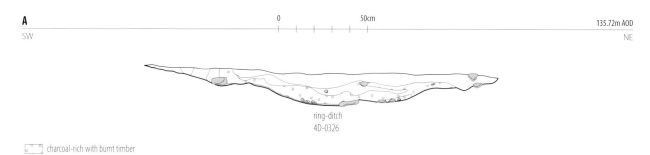

A

0   50cm   135.72m AOD

SW   NE

ring-ditch
4D-0326

charcoal-rich with burnt timber

Illus 3.31 Section from Gairnhill 2

Illus 3.32 General post excavation photo of Gairnhill 2 facing south-west showing stones in base of ring-ditch

its basal fill was submitted for radiocarbon dating and returned a range of 1100–920 cal BC (SUERC-68136). Two post-holes were found within the ring-groove and a series of post-holes to the south of the building, including [4D-0190], [4D-0276], [4D-0273], were on the same circular alignment and are likely also to belong to the structure of the outer walls (Illus 3.34B). As with other buildings the level of truncation appears to be greater downslope and the western portion of the ring-groove did not survive.

An inner ring-ditch was formed from erosion and only survived to a depth of 0.16 m (Illus 3.35). Unlike other ring-ditches on site, there appears to have been no attempt to level out the base with stone paving. Feature [4D-0074] was 0.15 m deep and most likely represents a truncated continuation of the ring-ditch. The lower deposits within

the ring-ditch were predominantly formed of burnt and heat-affected material and contained well-preserved timber remains (Illus 3.36). The lowest identifiable wooden remains were all of narrow diameter roundwood and most likely originated from stakes and wattle panelling. A row of twelve stake-holes extending for around 6 m were present in line with the interior of the ring-ditch, showing the original location of the panels.

In places, overlying these wattle fragments were the remains of more substantial oak timbers, which given the distance of the ring-ditch from the outer walls most likely fell in from the collapsing roof. Overlying these was a mid-orange red heat-affected deposit that is interpreted as either turf or degraded daub material. Again, this may have originated from roofing material.

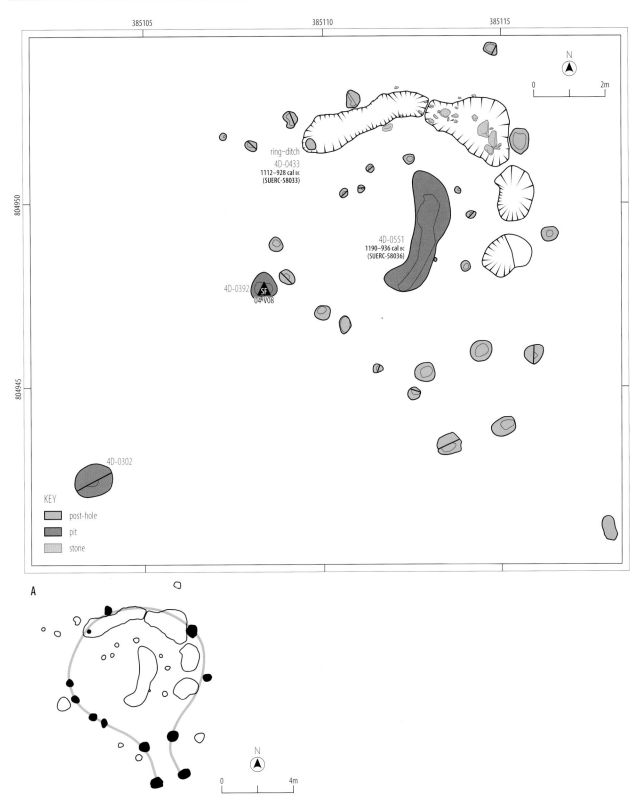

Illus 3.33 Plan of Gairnhill 3 A. Ring-beam post-ring and porch

Multiple sherds of coarseware pottery were found throughout the upper and lower deposits of both sections of ring-ditch (Illus 3.52 and 3.53). Some of these were conjoining although found in different deposits, strengthening the likelihood that these were all hollows within the building open at the same time. The lack of carbonised timbers from [4D-0074] suggests the wattle partitions were only present towards the rear of the structure.

A mid-greyish-brown sandy loam overlying and extending beyond the bounds of the ring-ditch represented

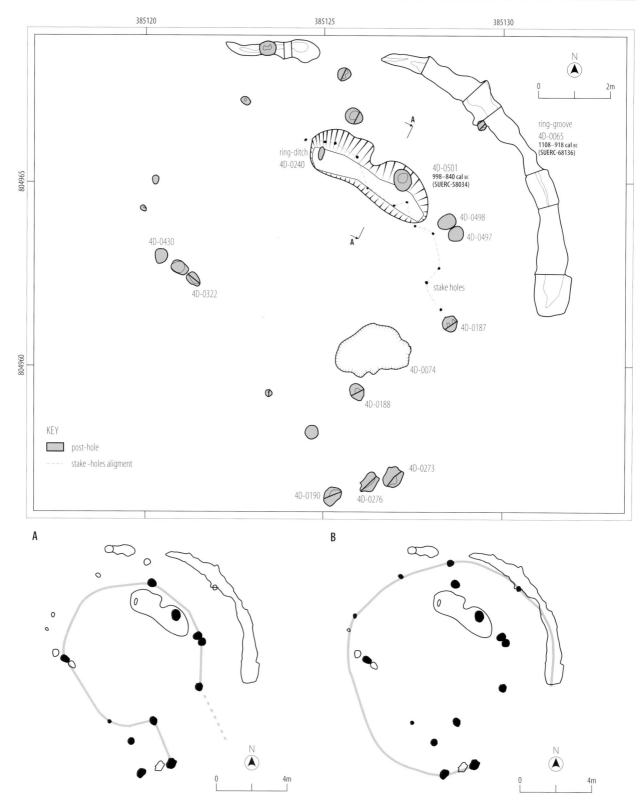

Illus 3.34 Plan of Gairnhill 4 A. Ring-beam post-ring B. Possible line of outer walls

an interface horizon with the overlying topsoil and appeared heavily mixed, most likely from later ploughing. A possible Late Neolithic or Early Bronze Age plano-convex flint knife was recovered from this deposit, as was a small fragment of burnt human bone, but both were most likely residual.

A fragment of dolphin or whale bone was also recovered from this mixed deposit.

In summary, Gairnhill 4 consisted of a partial ring-groove and outer post-ring indicating the position of the outer walls. An estimate of the original building size based

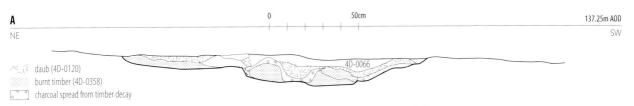

daub (4D-0120)
burnt timber (4D-0358)
charcoal spread from timber decay

0   50cm   137.25m AOD
NE   SW   4D-0066

Illus 3.35 Section though ring-ditch in Gairnhill 4

Illus 3.36 Detail of burnt timbers in ring-ditch of Gairnhill 4

on the ring-groove is approximately 12.3 m. The partial survival of the ring-groove might indicate terracing of the building into the slope. The roof was supported by an inner post-ring, probably supporting a ring-beam. The entrance was orientated towards the south-east and would not have protruded beyond the limits of the outer walls. Internal divisions were present, and a ring-ditch on the north-eastern interior of the structure formed through erosion contained charred timbers, possibly related to the internal divisions. The carbonised remains also indicate that the building either burnt down or was deliberately fired on abandonment.

3.5.4.6 Gairnhill 5

Gairnhill 5 was the best-preserved structure at the site. The building comprised a post-ring, an outer curvilinear ring-groove ditch and an internal ring-ditch. The building also had an elaborate south-east facing entrance structure (Illus 3.37).

The eastern perimeter of the structure was defined by a ring-groove, similar to Gairnhill 2 and 4. The ring-groove had an extrapolated diameter of approximately 13 m. The ring-groove had relatively steeply sloping sides and a narrow flat base and was a maximum of 0.3 m deep (Illus 3.38). A continuation to the ring-groove defined the eastern side of the entrance porch. Birch charcoal from the upper fill was submitted for radiocarbon dating and returned a date range of 970–840 cal BC (SUERC-68140). The upper fills of the ring-groove are derived from natural erosional deposits after the demolition or abandonment of the building but are thought to incorporate material from its construction.

The internal post-ring measured approximately 8 m in diameter and was formed of 14 post-holes (Illus 3.37A). Packing stones were evident within some of the post-holes that had been disturbed or backfilled, indicating the removal of the posts. Although the post-ring is not complete, the surviving post-holes were relatively evenly spaced between 1.8 m and 2 m apart. Some post-holes were present in pairs, which may suggest post replacement during the life of the roundhouse, although it is equally possible that two posts were present as supports either side of heavy roof beams.

The entrance to the building was defined by two rows of intercutting post-holes that narrow as they approach the interior of the building (see Illus 3.37). The intercutting nature of these post-holes suggests repair and replacement of the porch structure over time. The interior of the entranceway was metalled with small stones and fragmentary patches of the metalled surface existed further south, potentially indicating an area some 5 m in diameter had originally been metalled. A spread of material overlying the metalled surface contained a number of fragmentary sherds of pottery and has been interpreted as an occupation layer. A number of internal post-holes were present, which may indicate internal features or structural components. No hearth was identified.

The abandonment of the building was represented by a series of burnt deposits in the entranceway, overlying the metalled surface. Hazel charcoal from this layer was submitted for radiocarbon dating and returned a date range of 1050–900 cal BC (SUERC-58032). The deposits appear to have related to a discrete episode of burning within the area defined by the entrance. It is possible that, as with Gairnhill 2 and 4, the whole structure or parts of it were deliberately fired upon its abandonment.

Within the interior of the structure was a shallow spread (4D-0098) curving from the south-west to north-west and truncated by a furrow towards its southern extent. The deposit consisted of heat-affected silty sand and charcoal within a silty sandy clay matrix. Again, this burnt material most likely relates to the abandonment of the building and may have been sitting in a hollow left by a very shallow ring-ditch, the cut of which was not apparent at the time of excavation. A small fragment of human bone, possibly originating from a humerus, was recovered from this spread but is likely to be residual.

In summary, Gairnhill 5 consisted of a partial ring-groove indicating the original position of the outer walls and a south-east facing porch. The overall size of the

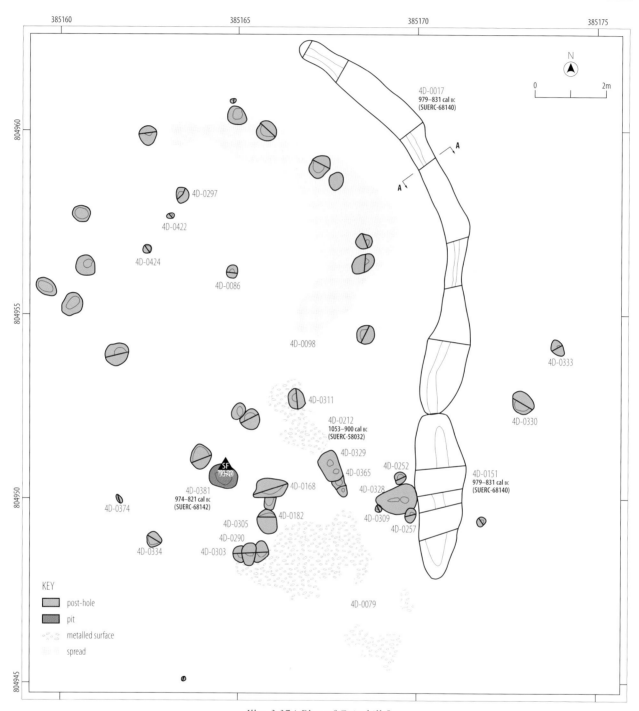

Illus 3.37A Plan of Gairnhill 5

building is estimated at approximately 13 m. The ring-groove only survived along the eastern, upslope side and might suggest that the structure was partially terraced. The roof was supported by an inner post-ring that would have supported a ring-beam. The entrance was orientated towards the south-east and would have had a porch with a metalled surface extending up to 4 m beyond the building. Internal divisions were present and a spread of material on the north-eastern interior of the structure may have been the remains of an erosional ring-ditch.

A small pit [4D-0381] measuring under a metre in diameter and 0.14 m deep lay to one side of the entrance area. The truncated remains of an inverted urn (04-V20, Illus 3.39 and 3.55) were recovered from this deposit. The deposit within the urn was a dark greyish-brown sandy silt with large amounts of charcoal. A fragment of alder charcoal from within the urn was submitted for radiocarbon dating and returned a date range of 970–830 cal BC (SUERC-68142). This date range placed the pit as roughly contemporary with Gairnhill 5 and was similar to pit

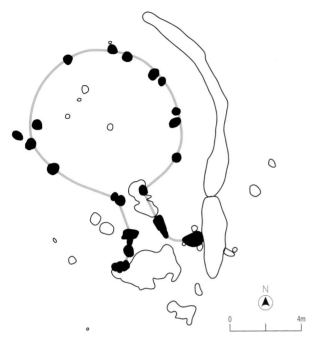

Illus 3.37B Ring beam post-ring and entrance porch

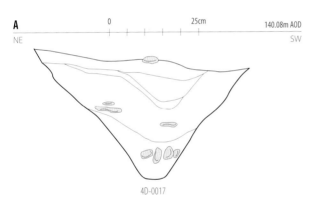

Illus 3.38 Section though ring-groove in Gairnhill 5

[4D-0392] found within Gairnhill 3. It may represent a foundation or abandonment deposit.

3.5.4.7 Four-poster structure and miscellaneous features

Situated approximately 25 m to the south of Gairnhill 4 lay four post-holes that formed the remains of a rectangular structure measuring 2.15 × 1.45 m (Illus 3.40). They were very shallow with maximum depths of 0.07 m and contained no datable material. Four-post structures are commonly found on later prehistoric settlement sites and are frequently interpreted as the remains of agricultural features such as elevated grain storage platforms. Further scattered post-holes were present to the north and east of the four-poster structure and were similarly undatable but likely relate to further prehistoric activity.

To the south-west of Gairnhill 3, an ovoid pit [4D-0302] (Illus 3.33) was filled with a dark greyish-brown silty clay

Illus 3.39 Pottery from possible foundation deposit [4D-0381]

that appeared to be quite sticky and suggestive of a former organic content. The relationship between this pit and the roundhouses is unclear; however, the presence of large amounts of oat grains within the fill (see 3.7.2.3 below) suggests that this pit is unlikely to have originated before the Iron Age as this crop is not thought to have been widely cultivated until then.

3.3.5 Post-medieval Gairnhill

At Gairnhill an extensive system of furrows aligned north-east to south-west were recorded across the excavation areas. These represent agricultural field systems with a north-east to south-west alignment that roughly conforms to modern field boundaries. The furrows were more common across the northern extent of the site where they had truncated some of the archaeological remains associated with the later Bronze Age roundhouses. Their presence in greater numbers in the north is indicative of the better general survival of features further upslope, which mirrored the survival of archaeological remains. No furrows were noted at the southern extent of the site where the burnt mound was discovered; this boggier area may not have been used for agrarian activities.

3.6 Chapel of Stoneywood

Jurgen van Wessel

The excavation at Chapel of Stoneywood covered an area of 2,864 m² on a south-east facing grassy slope at an elevation of between 104–109 m AOD.

The topsoil was up to 0.4 m thick and directly overlay geological subsoil, which comprised coarse sandy gravels with occasional bands of cleaner sand and frequent medium to large angular stones. The remains of a roundhouse consisting of a large segmented ring-ditch, associated pits and post-holes, and an outer curvilinear feature and a series of peripheral pits were discovered (Illus 3.41). Three linear features were interpreted as post-medieval furrows, which were found to truncate the earlier archaeological remains.

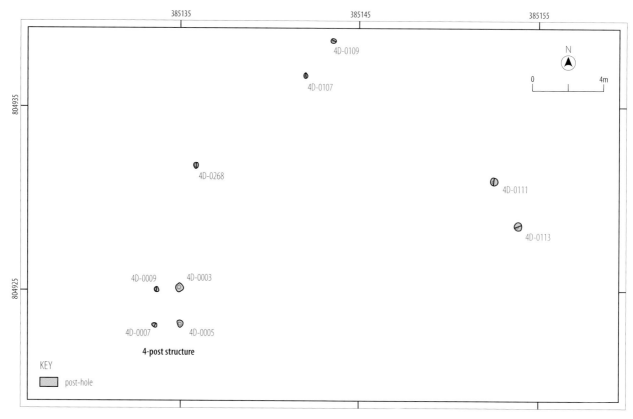

Illus 3.40 Four-poster structure at Gairnhill

3.6.1 Chapel of Stoneywood roundhouse. Middle Bronze Age: 1550–1150 BC

The Chapel of Stoneywood roundhouse comprised an inner and outer post-ring, a series of ovoid pits and a small number of additional pits, a ring-ditch, and possible post-holes and gullies (Illus 3.42). The north-eastern portion of the structure was best preserved, with little evidence of truncation (Illus 3.43). Little survived of the south-western part, probably as a result of later ploughing. A single furrow cut across the roundhouse, although some features still survived beneath it.

Six post-holes with a diameter of approximately 6.5 m formed the post-ring (Illus 3.42A); however, five of the post-holes were masked by later deposits infilling a later curvilinear ring-ditch. Four of these were truncated by later ovoid pits and survived only as very shallow features at their bases, barely discernible during excavation. Based on this proxy, two further post-holes are suggested, located on the flat bases of ovoid pits [1C-0114] and [1C-0113]. The original diameter of the post-holes is somewhat unclear, but a reasonable estimation of 0.4–0.5 m can be extrapolated from their relatively flat bases. The post-holes were spaced 2–2.5 m apart, suggesting that there may originally have been ten post-holes in this ring, with the four missing features likely to have been completely removed by truncation to the south-west side of the structure. The surviving depth of these features was generally 0.15 m or

less. Where visible, the post-holes were filled with a dark brown-black sandy silt or the same fill as the features that truncated them. A radiocarbon determination from the sealed fill of post-hole [1C-0087] returned a Middle Bronze Age date of 1400–1210 cal BC (SUERC-49725). There was no indication of post-packing or post-pipes in any of these features. However, the relatively regular spacing, size and position of these features still suggest a structural function, and most likely represent the footings of a load-bearing post-ring supporting the roof.

A further inner post-ring (Illus 3.42B) had a diameter of around 4.2 m and comprised ten post-holes measuring between 0.2–0.4 m in diameter and up to 0.26 m deep. These were spaced fairly regularly, although there was a gap to the western side. This fell within the deepest part of the furrow that cut through the structure, so any post-holes may not have survived. One of the post-holes showed dark staining in the section indicative of a post-pipe; possible packing stones were noted in several others. A single sherd of prehistoric pottery recovered from the fill of one of these features, however, provides little additional information. The size of these post-holes suggests that they did not hold load-bearing posts and are most likely supports for an internal partition.

A number of post-holes were found on the periphery of the building. The distribution of post-holes appears to be clustered in three locations, separated approximately into

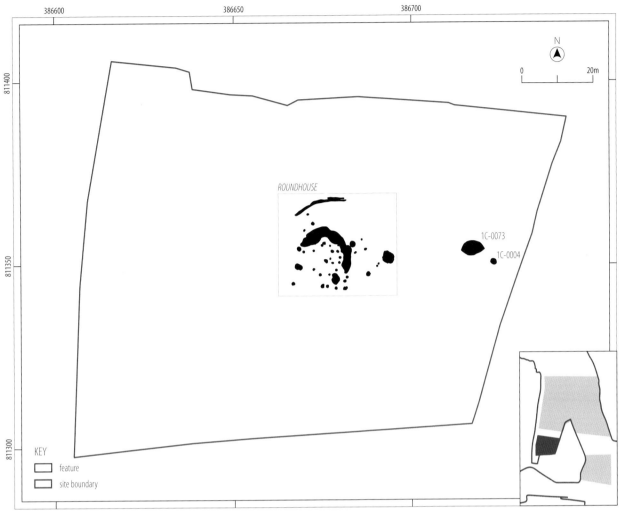

Illus 3.41 Plan of archaeological features at Chapel of Stoneywood

quadrants (north-west, north-east and south-east). It could be that these are the remains of earth-fast roof supports, possibly marking the outer extent of the buildings walls. The lack of a continuous outer post-ring suggests that the building would have had a turf or earth bank wall.

Two narrow gullies were recorded to the north of the structure. They respected the curve of the roundhouse and were only found upslope of it. These may have served to divert rainwater around the structure where the roof was closest to the ground.

Four of the post-holes from the outer load-bearing post-ring had been heavily truncated by large, ovoid pits (Illus 3.44). These pits measured between 1.6 m and 1.9 m long, 1 m and 1.5 m wide and survived to a depth of 0.2 to 0.3 m. The longer axis of each pit was in line with the circumference of the outer post-ring, and each was broadly centred on one of the post-holes. Three of the ovoid pits [1C-0114], [1C-0105] and [1C-0113] were filled with substantial sub-angular stones (Illus 3.45), set in a matrix of charcoal-rich material. In pit [1C-0105], these stones

sealed the post-hole [1C-0087] at its base. Two saddle querns (Illus 3.46) were recovered from [1C-0114]. They appeared to have been placed as part of the stone infill rather than for use *in situ*. The fourth ovoid pit [1C-0119] did not contain stones and was instead filled with material from the curvilinear gully above.

One further pit was recorded on a similar alignment, to the south-west of [1C-0112]. It was irregular in plan and survived to 1.55 m long, 0.96 m wide and 0.1 m deep. The basal fill comprised a mid-greyish-brown loamy sand with a distinct charcoal lens. The upper fill was of reddish, possibly burnt, sand. A radiocarbon determination of cal AD 70–220 (SUERC-57932) was obtained from the basal deposit, dating the use of this pit to the Middle Iron Age. This is considerably later than the likely abandonment of the structure (see below) and must represent later activity or intrusive material. This was also the only feature within the roundhouse from which burnt animal bone was recovered (see 3.7 below). It is possible that this feature represents a fifth ovoid pit used as a hearth during the Iron Age.

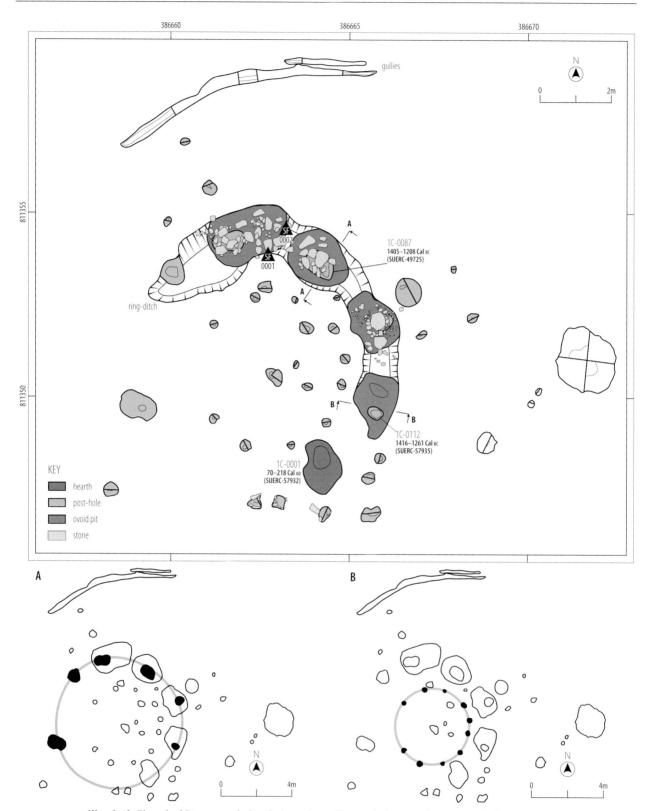

Illus 3.42 Chapel of Stoneywood, detail plan of roundhouse A. Structural post-ring B. Inner post-ring

Overlying and truncating the tops of the ovoid pits was a curvilinear ring-ditch. In plan, the ring-ditch connects and extends the ovoid pits, measuring 7.45 m long, up to 1.7 m wide and 0.3 m deep. The fill of the ring-ditch comprised dark greyish-brown loamy sand containing abundant charcoal. Concentrations or dumps of charcoal were recorded sealing the stone fill of ovoid pit [1C-0113] and may relate to the abandonment of the structure. Forty-two sherds of prehistoric pottery dated typologically to the Bronze Age were retrieved from these charcoal-rich deposits, concentrated in the south-eastern part of the ring-ditch (see 3.8 below) and are highly abraded, consistent with these deposits representing dumped refuse material. A radiocarbon determination of 1410–1270 cal BC (SUERC-57933) was obtained from one of the charcoal dumps, confirming a Middle Bronze Age date for the abandonment of the structure. A further thin deposit of silty material was encountered overlying the charcoal dumps.

3.6.2 Observations on the truncated post-ring

The most perplexing element of the Chapel of Stoneywood roundhouse is the stratigraphic relationship between the structural post-ring, the ovoid pits and the ring-ditch. The post-ring is the most substantial ring of post-holes present, and it is reasonable to suggest that these supported the roof at some stage. However, at some point the post-holes were substantially truncated by larger ovoid pits, which in turn were infilled with stone. These were then further truncated by the later ring-ditch, thought to relate to the occupation phase of the roundhouse. For this sequence of events to take place during the active life of the structure, it would have required the removal or partial removal of the main load-bearing posts and possibly the roof.

It is possible that the earth-fast portions of the posts degraded and were removed or replaced at some point. The ovoid pits could represent the removal in order to replace these posts – by excavating to the base of the original post-holes, they could be swung out from under the ring-beam and taken away. Slope is an additional factor here – in order to generate a level ring-beam with standard-length posts, those post-holes furthest upslope would need to be deeper than those further down, perhaps explaining better their survival here. The shape of the ovoid pits matches this hypothesis well. The pits are elongated, which would allow the posts to be 'swung' out from under a ring-beam – there would be more room to do this along the line of the ring-beam than radially. The replacement posts may then have been placed on post pads rather than made earth-fast again to avoid further

Illus 3.43 Chapel of Stoneywood, pre-excavation view of round-house, facing north-west

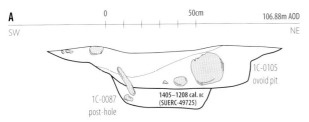
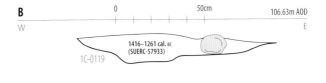

Illus 3.44 Chapel of Stoneywood, sections through curvilinear ditch [1C-0007]

Illus 3.45 Chapel of Stoneywood, general view of stone spreads in pits (from foreground) [1C-0113], [1C-0105] and [1C-0114], facing north-west

Illus 3.46 Chapel of Stoneywood, detail of quernstones set in pit [1C-0114], facing north

degradation of the posts. The simple need to level the ground would explain the stone infill in three of the pits. It is possible that these were the only three deep enough to really require infilling.

3.7 Environmental synthesis

Tim Holden, Anne Crone and Richard Tipping

There are no pollen records that can describe the high ground between the Dee and the Don in later prehistory. Some have been recorded 40 km to the west, in the Howe of Cromar, at Loch Davan and Braeroddach Loch (Edwards 1979a; 1979b; Edwards and Rowntree 1980), which are situated in a landscape with woodland that contained some Scots pine, in contrast to more coastal areas (Durno 1957; Bennett 1989; Tipping 1994; 2007) and, today at least, significantly higher amounts of rainfall (Glentworth and Muir 1963, 30). Parallels with the Dee–Don high ground should not be drawn too closely. The pollen core recovered from Hare Moss as part of the AWPR/B-T scheme (Timpany 2012c) only covers the period from the Mesolithic to the Early Bronze Age and relates more directly to the uplands south of the Dee.

Bronze Age human activities around Lochs Davan and Braeroddach (Edwards 1979a) appear to have been small in spatial scale and seemingly short lived, a pattern in common with other areas at this time (Tipping 1994; 2015), although some soil erosion indicators increased at Braeroddach Loch from c2000 BC. Clearance events, given the imprecision of radiocarbon assays, persist for, perhaps, 100–300 years and were for both crop-growing and grazing. More extensive and more sustained agriculture is suggested ('major woodland reduction': Edwards & Whittington 2003, 75) to have developed in the later Bronze Age, affecting particularly birch and hazel trees, dated at Braeroddach Loch to 1611–1001 cal BC. Cereal pollen (barley type) is recorded from this time at Braeroddach Loch (Edwards 1979b). Lake sediments at Braeroddach also record from this time radiocarbon age reversals, indicating significant transfers of old organic matter to the lake from eroding soils (Edwards 1979b; Edwards & Rowntree 1980; Edwards & Whittington 2001), and this instability is most readily ascribed to comparatively intense settlement and arable agriculture.

At Nether Beanshill the roundhouse and cremation complex were found on a gentle (6°) south-facing slope. The substrate immediately around the structure is a very sandy and bouldery till laced with glaciofluvial sand and gravel that behaves pedologically and agriculturally like a very well-drained glaciofluvial sand and gravel. The soil today is a podsol of the Counteswell Series, and this was probably so in the Middle Bronze Age (Lancaster *et al.* 2005). The farm of Nether Beanshill, a few tens of metres away, is on a low bedrock knoll. At Gairnhill the roundhouses are found on a comparable 7° south-west

facing slope, and again the substrate is a free-draining sand and gravel till, supporting a Dess Series podsol, close to a bedrock knoll.

Though the structures at Gairnhill and Nether Beanshill are on dry well-drained soils, each had around them soils that are and probably were more waterlogged, gley soils in shallow valleys and below springs. They may have shared access to the same valley floor of the Silver Burn. The valley is bordered by dry soils on glaciofluvial gravel and is floored by alluvium and peat, in places shown by civil engineering boreholes to be over 2.5 m deep, and though no attempt was made in excavation to date when they formed, comparison with fluvial development along the River Dee (Chapter 2) would suggest that both were present by the Middle Bronze Age. They would have provided good grazing and, if needed, hay meadow. The excavated site at Chapel of Stoneywood was also on sandy till and is beneath a thin free-draining podsol of the Counteswells Series. This is an isolated site along the road-line yet there is nothing marginal about the setting, facing south-east on soils that warm well in the spring.

As part of the environmental sampling strategy for the three excavations, a total of 301 ten litre bulk soil samples were taken from the three excavated sites on the Dee–Don high ground. All were processed by flotation and wet sieving and assessed by appropriate specialists. Further environmental analyses for each site were undertaken and the full reports are included in the appendices for this volume (Appendix 2.2). The results of the analyses are discussed below in relation to each of the three sites.

3.7.1 Nether Beanshill

The archaeological excavations at Nether Beanshill recovered a limited environmental assemblage. The wood charcoal assemblages from both the roundhouse and the cremation complex were primarily composed of alder and hazel with rare occurrences of birch, oak, heather, willow and Maloideae (a subfamily that includes rowan, apple, hawthorn and whitebeam). The alder collected seems to have included some larger branches. Some dead wood was also collected.

Natural woodland on dry soils in the Bronze Age is likely to have been dominated by birch and hazel, with lesser amounts of oak, and other minor species like rowan and ash. Alder, birch and willow will have typified wetlands along river margins and on valley floors. The wood charcoal from Nether Beanshill supports the general nature of local woodland. The presence of *Calluna* (ling heather) in the assemblage is also perhaps of note in that it confirms the presence of at least small areas of heath, but since ling has traditionally been used for many purposes in the past (eg thatch: Walker *et al.* 1996; Holden 1998a) this may have been collected and transported from some distance.

There are very few, if any, primary deposits of charcoal, ie exhibiting *in situ* burning, so it is not possible to separate wood used specifically as fuel from that burned either accidentally or for other purposes. It is very difficult to make definitive comments regarding the source and selection of the fuel wood or structural timber. In fact, structural timber would undoubtedly have been used as fuel once it had served its purpose, thereby confusing the picture further. In any event there is nothing from this dataset that indicates selective use of wood for one purpose or another.

Cereal grain was comparatively rare but present in thirteen contexts, all within or closely related to the ring-ditches of the roundhouse. Barley (*Hordeum vulgare*), primarily naked barley, was the most common grain, although only one post-hole contained a significant number. Cereal grain was being consumed on site and similar small assemblages have been recovered from other Late Neolithic/Early Bronze Age sites in Aberdeenshire, including Midmill (Timpany & Masson 2009). In a Scottish context, barley has been a common element on settlement sites since the Neolithic period, with the hulled variety gradually replacing the naked form from the Bronze Age (Boyd 1988). The Nether Beanshill assemblage is entirely in keeping with the dating evidence for the roundhouse structure. The presence of nutshell also indicates that hazel was not only a common element in the environment but also utilised as a wild food.

3.7.2 Gairnhill

Environmental remains were recovered from a variety of features at Gairnhill including an Early Bronze Age burnt mound, and Middle and Late Bronze Age roundhouses. Samples of the buried soil from beneath the burnt mound were analysed to establish environmental conditions prior to construction of this monument. The preserved wooden trough was also analysed for species identification. Species identification of charred wood was undertaken from across the site, including the burnt mound and the roundhouses. Specialist analysis of the best-preserved carbonised timbers from Gairnhill 4 was also undertaken (see 3.7.2.4 below; Appendix 2.1.15) to try and determine the structural function of the timbers.

3.7.2.1 Burnt mound

The trough related to the burnt mound comprised roughly squared alder planks (see 3.5.2.1 above and 3.8.6 below). This was set into a ground surface of herb peat, dominated by monocotyledon species, typically species of sedge and grass. The original extent of the peat is not known. Its position on a slope suggests it to have been blanket peat. Whether it formed naturally or as a result of anthropogenic activities such as woodland clearance or cultivation is also unknown. Alder is unlikely to have grown on this peat, and so had to be collected, but the wide marshy floor of the Silver Burn, only hundreds of metres to the south, is one likely source. Alder decays quite readily in other than waterlogged environments, and its good preservation at Gairnhill indicates that this location has remained at or below the soil water table since the Bronze Age.

Few charred remains other than wood charcoal were recovered, conforming to a pattern noted by O'Néill (2000), though few burnt mounds in Scotland have been examined in any detail (ScARF 2012c, 3.3.1). No hearth was identified at Nether Beanshill, though the abundance of unabraded charcoal in the fired debris indicates that burning took place nearby and therefore probably relates directly to activities taking place around the burnt mound. Three samples from the firing debris (4A-0003) were composed of hazel and alder. The ring curvature of the fragments suggests the use of smaller branches and twigs of both species. Those from the basal deposits of the trough (4A-0027) were largely similar but also contained a small proportion of oak.

3.7.2.2 Gairnhill 7

Wood charcoal was present in most samples but concentrated in two post-holes and within the ring-ditch. The majority of charcoal in the post-holes was non-oak. Little of the charred material is thought likely to have been burnt *in situ* and is therefore probably not directly related to the original function of the features. The only exception to this is charcoal from the fill of the hearth.

Rare weed seeds, fragments of hazel shell and poorly preserved cereal grains were recovered from several negative features. Identified weed seeds included cleavers (*Galium aparine*), docks (*Rumex* sp), goosefoots (*Chenopodium* sp) and common hemp nettle (*Galeopsis tetrahit*), all common seeds associated with acidic, sandy loam soils and cultivated and disturbed ground.

A small number of burnt animal bone fragments were recovered from features, including the hearth. These were very heavily fragmented, but some were thought to have been sheep or goat (D. Henderson pers comm).

The assemblage from Gairnhill 7 offers some low-level insights into site economy. The presence of hazelnut shell, rare cereal grains together with burnt mammal bone, particularly in the hearth, suggests a low level of food waste. Although little can be said regarding the function of the features on the basis of the charred plant and bone assemblage, the plant remains undoubtedly reflect the local flora in some way. The majority of the plant remains are typical of disturbed ground so would have been common around human settlement and in agricultural fields. Small quantities of oak may indicate the burning of material brought to site for structural purposes.

3.7.2.3 Gairnhill 1 to 6

The focus of the environmental analysis in relation to the six Late Bronze Age buildings was primarily concerned with the carbonised timber recovered from the buildings. Three of the roundhouses (Gairnhill 2, 3 and 4) show evidence that they may have been destroyed by fire and some of the better preserved ring-ditches contained carbonised structural timbers. The structural remains suggested that the superstructure from Gairnhill 2, for example, contained elements of hazel wattle hurdle. Gairnhill 4 comprised a wide range of species including hazel withies, birch, members of the Maloideae family and alder together with some larger oak structural timbers. Comparatively few structural elements were recovered from Gairnhill 3, but alder and oak fragments were identified.

Having burnt down or been deliberately burnt, these structures would inevitably incorporate elements of structural material together with elements of the contents of the building and other traces of material discarded or charred in the house in previous years. In many cases large fragments of unabraded charcoal was recovered and in some (Gairnhill 2) the condition was sufficient to identify tool marks but not enough to undertake detailed analyses.

A small quantity of cereal grain was recovered from 17 features. The largest number of grains (oat) was from the fill (4D-0301) of pit [4D-0302], located in close proximity to Gairnhill 3. The abundance of oats in the fill of feature [4D-0302] suggests it is unlikely to be earlier than the Iron Age in date and is probably medieval or later, therefore not related to the nearby roundhouses. The majority of cereal grain in other contexts was hulled barley (*Hordeum vulgare*). It was present in 15 features but with little evidence that it had been burnt *in situ*. Just two grains of bread wheat (*Triticum aestivo-compactum*) were present in the ring-ditches of Gairnhill 3 and 4. The quantities recovered are considered very unlikely to have come from the burning of storage features (sacks, racks etc) and tends to support the suggestion that the houses may have been cleared before being set alight or before accidental fire was able to spread to stores. The character of the cereal and 'weed' seed assemblage appears more likely to derive from incidental losses around hearths or processing areas over a period of time.

Apart from the cereal grain, small quantities of hazel nutshell and animal bone were recovered. The condition of neither category of material was good but some of the bone from unidentified animals exhibited chop marks. Together with the cereal grains, the overall suggestion is that these represent evidence for food preparation.

3.7.2.4 The carbonised wood assemblage from Gairnhill 4
Anne Crone with Laura Bailey

Carbonised wood was recovered from throughout the ring-ditch of Gairnhill 4. Carbonised remains that visibly resembled wattle hurdles were also observed in the ring-ditch of Gairnhill 2 but were not preserved well enough for detailed analysis. The full report can be found in Appendix 2.1.15.

Two distinct groups of timber remains were observed. The first were pieces of a wickerwork panel (4D-0314) found throughout the ring-ditch. This consisted of two surviving stakes or verticals, averaging 34 mm in diameter,

one of alder and one oak. The horizontals, or withies, were all of hazel rods on average 15 mm in diameter. A single chopmark was observable on one of the withies.

The second group were of larger timbers not related to the wattle hurdle, which were grouped together and appeared to represent the same structural group. The first of these groups (4D-0358) was recovered from the base of the ring-ditch and consisted of six timbers, five of alder and one of oak. These were the largest timbers recovered, with some of the fragments having estimated minimum diameters of 90 mm and the largest at least 300 mm.

Three further groups – (4D-0484), (4D-0487) and (4D-0488) – represented clusters of roundwood found around the periphery of the ring-ditch. The lengths were a mixture of alder and hazel, although a single piece of birch and one of oak were also present. They range in diameter from 16 mm to 77 mm and did not exhibit any evidence of working.

The final group, comprised of contexts (4D-0491) and (4D-0492), in plan consisted of a bundle of roundwood overlain by two lengths of roundwood, situated towards the centre of the ring-ditch. All the Maloideae in the assemblage came from these contexts, and there were also a small number of lengths of alder, hazel and one of birch. The Maloideae roundwood had an average diameter of 32 mm, and eight had been shaped. The roundwood displayed evidence of being pared along their lengths, and many displayed knife or axe facets around the entire circumference. The best-preserved example displayed nine thin facets, reducing the diameter of the rod from 35 mm to 12 mm, so that it resembles a peg.

There was no evidence to suggest that any of the carbonised wood that survived the burning event in Gairnhill 4 had been shaped beyond the round, ie it is all invariably roundwood. The only clear evidence for modification is that of the Maloideae in (4D-0491/0492). The assemblage can be characterised as comprising small (10–30 mm) to medium (30–50 mm) diameter roundwood, most suitable for wickerwork panels and stakes (Crone 2008, 273). Apart from the larger oak roundwood in (4D-0358) there was nothing present that represented more substantial structural timbers.

The wickerwork panel (4D-0314) survives best along the back of the ring-ditch where it is most suggestive of a collapsed wall screen. Carbonised wickerwork panelling in the same position have been found in the Middle Iron Age roundhouse RH23 at Kintore (Crone 2008, 281–3), where it could represent the outer wall of the house. The inner face of the bank in the Bronze Age hut circle 10/1 on Tormore, Arran was also lined with withies (Barber 1997, 11, 15). However, at both these sites the wickerwork panelling would have formed the lining of the outer wall, whereas at Gairnhill the wickerwork panel lies within an internal ring-ditch. Evidence for internal concentric wickerwork screens have been found on the Iron Age wetland site of Black Loch of Myrton (Crone & Cavers 2015). Wickerwork panels have also been found used as sub-floors at that site, so it is equally possible that (4D-0314) could be the remains of flooring, though it remains unclear as to whether there was wood lying above or below (4D-0314).

It is difficult to determine the function of the rest of the carbonised wood given that most of the material was mixed, so it is impossible to say whether the wood represents internal structural elements, walling or roofing. The experimental burning of an, admittedly, rectangular house at Lejre, Denmark, showed that the roof collapsed first, the walls falling in afterwards so that stratigraphically, the roof timbers would have been found under the wall components (Rasmussen 2007, 77). However, in Gairnhill 4 the ring-ditch lies some 2–2.5 m inside the ring-groove that would have housed the wall timbers, so it seems unlikely that any of the surviving wood in the ring-ditch came from the walling. It is more likely therefore to represent either internal fittings or roof timbers.

The homogeneity of some of the clusters of wood suggests that they might represent a discrete structural element, for example, all but two of the oak in the assemblage occur in (4D-0358) and all the Maloideae in (4D-0492/0492). The degree of shaping displayed by some of the roundwood in (4D-0492/0492) would not have been necessary in most structural elements, such as wickerwork panels, roofing or flooring, and suggests that some care has been taken in its construction. The selection of species is also unusual; Maloideae most often occurs as a relatively small component of fuel debris (cf Crone 2008, 283, table 31); the fruit species in particular are good fuel woods. Interestingly, the only concentration of Maloideae in the roundhouses at Kintore was in the ring-ditch of RH09, where it was identified as cf rowan (*ibid.*, 277).

If we exclude the hazel used in (4D-0314) and the clusters of oak and Maloideae described above, as examples of deliberate selection for a particular function, then hazel and alder, with a small amount of birch and oak were used for general construction in Gairnhill 4. Only one post-hole yielded charcoal, which was birch.

The site that invites the closest parallels with Gairnhill 4 is Kintore, where several of the Late Bronze Age and Middle Iron Age roundhouses had burnt down and rich assemblages of charcoal had been preserved. Like Gairnhill, very little (ie 2%) of the assemblage was greater than 50 mm in diameter prompting the suggestion that the larger structural elements might have been removed pre-conflagration (Crone 2008, 286). The species used in construction throughout the Bronze Age at Kintore varied very little (*ibid.*, table 30 and fig 190); there it was primarily a mixture of birch, hazel and oak, with smaller amounts of alder and willow. Unlike Gairnhill, evidence for the modification of timbers had survived in the form of squared willow and alders (*ibid.*, 277). At Birnie, where several Iron Age roundhouses had burnt down, oak overwhelmingly dominates, comprising between 70% and 92.5% of the assemblages from the roundhouses; there was evidence for some radially split

oaks but like Gairnhill the assemblage was primarily unconverted roundwood (Crone & Cressey 2014).

3.7.2.5 What can the botanical remains tell us about the environment around Gairnhill?

The charred remains recovered provide limited evidence with respect to the local or wider environment. There is no reason to believe that the crops (barley, oats and wheat) or collected resources such as hazelnuts were not grown/procured locally. Perhaps the absence of wheat is a reflection of the poor soils in this area. It is not possible to comment on the scale of production nor how this interfaced with the pastoral side of the economy.

Across the site small numbers of charred 'weed' seeds were recovered. These are, almost exclusively, common species of cultivated and disturbed ground including knotgrasses (*Polygonum* sp), pale persicaria (*Polygonum lapathifolium*), docks (*Rumex* sp), sedges (*Carex* sp), nettle (*Urtica diocia*), ribwort (*Plantago lancelota*), common hemp nettle (*Galeopsis tetrahit*) and corn spurrey (*Spergula arvensis*). One can envisage these growing around the settlement, on dung heaps and path sides, with perhaps the taller species up against fences and structures away from the trample of feet and hooves. Many of them would have been equally at home in agricultural fields and may have been inadvertently harvested and brought to site along with the cereal crop.

All of the species represented by the wood charcoal would undoubtedly have been commonplace in Bronze Age Scotland, as they are still today; alder in the valley bottoms or close to water courses and hazel, birch and oak on dryer ground. Smaller stands of members of the Maloideae family (which includes, crab-apple, hawthorn, rowan and whitebeam) were also present.

Hazel and birch make up much of the small diameter wood in both the burnt mound and roundhouses. The larger diameter timbers tend to be of alder and particularly oak. It is possible that coppicing of hazel proved a regular source of small diameter withies for wattle and roofing while alder and oak were used more as supporting/weight-bearing timbers.

3.7.3 Chapel of Stoneywood

Organic remains from Chapel of Stoneywood were principally preserved by charring and small amounts of wood charcoal, cereal grain, hazel nutshell as well as burnt bone were all recovered. The provenance of most of this material is uncertain and only survives through incidental inclusion in negative features. It does, however, provide a general indication of activity across the site.

Small numbers of barley grains (*Hordeum vulgare*) and a single bread wheat grain (*Triticum aestivo-compactum*) were recovered from several features, as was a small amount (ie >1 g) of heavily fragmented hazel (*Corylus avellana*) nutshell. These, together with a number of quernstones identified on the site indicate that both cultivated and wild resources were used. Other remains preserved by charring include undiagnostic fragments of animal bone and a small number of weed 'seeds'. These included cleavers (*Galium aparine*), docks (*Rumex* sp), chickweed (*Stellaria media*) and corn spurrey (*Spergula arvensis*). All are common seeds associated with acidic, sandy loam soils and cultivated and disturbed ground.

One feature [1C-001], a pit possibly used as a hearth, was suspected as containing material burnt *in situ*. This feature contained traces of hazel shell, barley grain, weed seeds and fragments of burnt bone. A representative sample of the charcoal was analysed and oak (*Quercus* sp) and small diameter hazel wood were identified as the principal species, but they offer little information regarding wood selection or the character of the local environment. A radiocarbon assay from this feature returned a date range of cal AD 70–218, which would make it considerably later than the Middle Bronze Age roundhouse. The oak charcoal appeared 'vitrified' and may therefore have been heated at a high temperature, while mineral deposits suggest post-depositional leaching of minerals possibly indicating some fluctuation in the water table.

3.8 Materials synthesis

Julie Lochrie

3.8.1 Introduction

Material types recovered from the excavations across the three Dee–Don sites varied little, mostly consisting of fragmentary sherds of prehistoric pottery, stone tools and lithics related to Bronze Age domestic activity. Exceptions to this include the cremation urns from Nether Beanshill and a significant amount of vitrified material from Gairnhill, which also produced the only worked wooden remains. A copper-alloy item was also recovered from the roundhouse at Nether Beanshill and a bone pin from Gairnhill 4. Detailed analysis reports of each material type are included in the appendices to this volume (Appendix 2.2).

3.8.2 Pottery

3.8.2.1 Nether Beanshill

The prehistoric pottery assemblage from Nether Beanshill numbers 247 sherds from 27 features, representing up to 22 vessels (03-V01 to 03-V22; Table 3.02; Illus 3.47–3.50). The assemblage from the roundhouse numbered 203 sherds with 44 from the cremation cluster. Some outlying features also yielded pottery numbering a total of 12 sherds.

The cremation vessels would have been placed complete into a pit or a shallow scoop and covered over with soil or stones. Small sherds were present through many contexts and had clearly come from smashed or crushed vessels that were also abraded, indicating some movement caused by later agricultural disturbance. In many instances the pottery sherds did not appear to be deliberately placed in the contexts they were found. For this reason, caution

has been exercised when assigning how many vessels were actually present. The only contexts that contained substantial quantities were [3B-0003], [3B-0104] and [3B-0182]. It is likely these were the only contexts originally containing urns although the sherds from [3B-0182] were not found in association with cremated material. The better rate of survival for base sherds indicates the vessels were interred upright. Dating of cremated bone held within urn 03-V03 from [3B-0104] returned a date of 1430–1290 cal BC (SUERC-58844).

The pottery from the Nether Beanshill roundhouse was spread out in low, very fragmented quantities with thick undiagnostic body sherds dominating. Dates for the building are between 1607–1302 cal BC (see 3.3 above).

The fabric is very similar across all the vessels from both the cremation cemetery and the roundhouse assemblages. The walls are thick, with a sandy fabric containing moderate and very coarse angular rock inclusions; granite and what looks like a pink-coloured quartzite seem to be the most common.

Vessel 03-V01 (Illus 3.48) is mostly represented by a base of 110 mm diameter and many very small sherds and fragments that are practically ground to dust. The base is flat but uneven on the interior, thickening towards the middle. The exterior corners of the base have been pinched into shape giving an almost footed appearance; the pinching has left little folds of clay and the whole vessel has a coarse and unfinished appearance. The walls are substantially thinner than the base (6 mm versus 16.5 mm). The only other detail came from a very small everted body sherd, which suggests some kind of feature on the upper body such as ridges or cordons.

Vessel 03-V02 (Illus 3.49) comprised conjoining base sherds and some body sherds. The basal sherds provided a diameter of 170 mm. Along the very edge of the base are pinch marks and nail marks for where the clay has been squeezed to the correct angle. A clear clay join can be seen in the section that begins on the interior base and carries on diagonally to the very foot of the exterior. The efforts to join these two sections together can be seen in the shallow finger-smoothing groove around the interior basal circumference. This pushing has made the base thicker on the interior and convex in section. The manufacturing process for this likely involved the initial creation of a large, thick, flat, circular 'puck' to which the walls were then connected. This also explains the subsequent breakage pattern of 03-V01 and 03-V03, which were probably made in a similar way.

The largest surviving urn was Vessel 03-V03 (Illus 3.50), which included the entire base and a few rim sherds. The base has a diameter of 180 mm, the largest of the three, and it must have been a sizeable urn. The urn was lifted complete, but shortly after excavation the walls broke away from the base in the same manner as the other vessels and this is almost certainly the original point at which the clay was joined. This vessel has a smooth surface and a little

Table 3.02 Nether Beanshill summary of vessels

Area	Feature	Context	Vessel #	Sherd count	Fragment count (unless otherwise stated)
Cremation Complex	[3B-0003]	[3B-0004], [3B-0007], [3B-0023], [3B-0046]	03-V01	118	200g
	[3B-0104]	[3B-0071], [3B-0105]	03-V03	75	90
	[3B-0182]	[3B-0048], [3B-0134], [3B-0183], [3B-0184]	03-V02	15	23
	[3B-0202]	[3B-0203]	–	1	–
Roundhouse	[3B-0039]	[3B-0040]	03-V04	2	7
	[3B-0049]	[3B-0059]	03-V05	1	1
	[3B-0056]	[3B-0057]	03-V06	1	1
	[3B-0094]	[3B-0095]	03-V07	-	1
	[3B-0111]	[3B-0112]	03-V08	1	-
	[3B-0123]	[3B-0122]	03-V09	6	–
	[3B-0140]	[3B-0141]	03-V10	1	1
	[3B-0150]	[3B-0149]	03-V11, 03-V12	7	–
	[3B-0159]	[3B-0160]	03-V13	–	1
	[3B-0164]	[3B-0165]	03-V14	1	1
	[3B-0195]	[3B-0196]	03-V15	–	1
	[3B-0199]	[3B-0200]	03-V16	2	–
	[3B-0218]	[3B-0220]	03-V17	1	–
	[3B-0219]	[3B-0221]	03-V18	–	2
	[3B-0231]	[3B-0232]	03-V19	–	2
	[3B-0285]	[3B-0286]	03-V20	–	1
	[3B-0291]	[3B-0292]	03-V21	1	3
Other	[3B-0269]	[3B-0270]	03-V22	12	3

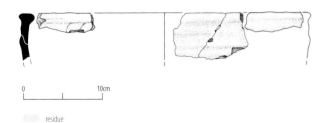

0   10cm

░░ residue

Illus 3.47 Vessel 03-V09 from Nether Beanshill roundhouse

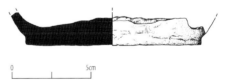

0   5cm

Illus 3.48 Vessel 03-V01 from cremation pit [3B-0003]

more care seems to have been taken in its appearance. The base is smooth with rounded corners and the walls flare out gently.

Other small sherds were scattered around the cremation cemetery, including a very small rim sherd from feature [3B-0070]. This sherd is likely to belong to one of the three urns described above; it was squared and slightly lipped on the interior.

The Nether Beanshill roundhouse contained similarly fragmented pottery and in only two cases is it possible to say anything about the vessels. Vessel 03-V05 was represented

by a small upright rounded rim sherd, whereas Vessel 03-V09 is the best represented from the roundhouse vessels and comprises six sherds including three rim sherds, two of which conjoin. Vessel 03-V09 has a T-shaped rim that has a convex top, giving a 'pillowed' appearance. On the exterior, directly below the rim, are two shallow grooves that give a ridged appearance. The shaping and smoothing of the rim has been carried out with a small tool that must have been flat with a squared end, like a small spatula. It has been used in two ways; firstly it has been pushed into the exterior of the rim directly below the horizontal arms of the 'T'. This makes a sharp and well-defined lip on the exterior. The individual lines where the tool has

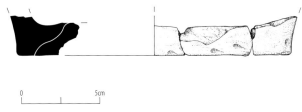

Illus 3.49 Vessel 03-V02 from pit [3B-0182]

Illus 3.50 Vessel 03-V03 from cremation pit [3B-0104]

Table 3.03 Gairnhill summary of vessels

Area	Feature	Context	Vessel #	Sherd count	Fragment count (unless otherwise stated)
Neolithic Pit	[4C-0001]	[4C-0002]	04-V01	1	–
Gairnhill 1	[4D-0013]	[4D-0014]	04-V02	3	1
	[4D-0042]	[4D-0043]	04-V03	2	20
	[4D-0051]	[4D-0052]	04-V04	5	–
Gairnhill 2	[4D-0102]	[4D-0103]	04-V05	109	155g
Gairnhill 3	[4D-0348]	[4D-0358]	04-V06		2
	[4D-0386]	[4D-0549]	04-V07	1	1
	[4D-0392]	[4D-0390]	04-V08	5	2
	[4D-0433]	[4D-0412]	04-V09	1	–
	[4D-0444]	[4D-0420]	04-V10	2	–
Gairnhill 4	[4D-0065]	[4D-0067], [4D-0238]	04-V11	56	18
	[4D-0074]	[4D-0186]	04-V12		
	[4D-0240]	[4D-0066]	04-V13		
Gairnhill 5	[4D-0017]	[4D-0018], [4D-0045]	04-V14	9	–
	Layer in entrance	[4D-0026]	04-V15	14	–
	[4D-0121]	[4D-0126]	04-V16	2	–
	[4D-0138]	[4D-0161]	04-V17	2	–
	[4D-0151]	[4D-0164], [4D-0226], [4D-0227]	04-V18/04-V19	12	3
	[4D-0381]	[4D-0360]	04-V20	38	7
Gairnhill 7	[4B-0002]	4B-0003], [4B-0011], [4B-0013]	04-V21/04-V22/04-V23	32	9
	[4B-0006]	[4B-0007]	04-V24	1	–
	[4B-0040]	[4B-0037]	04-V25	2	–

been pushed in can still be seen. Its second use has been employed on the interior where the tool has been smeared down vertically from right to left, leaving overlapping impressions. This has not been smoothed over in any further way to hide these marks, but finger smoothing has been carried out between the exterior ridges and may even be how it was created.

3.8.2.2 Gairnhill

The pottery assemblage from Gairnhill numbers 297 sherds and a high quantity of fragments (summarised in Table 3.03) A total of 25 vessels are estimated to be present, in various states of preservation and fragmentation. Excepting an Early Neolithic sherd, the entire assemblage is Middle or later Bronze Age.

The Neolithic pot sherd was found in pit [4C-0001] along with a flint flake. It likely relates to broader Neolithic activity; however, no other evidence was discovered.

The 24 remaining vessels were found across six Middle to Late Bronze Age buildings (Gairnhill 1–5 and 7). The pots are typically represented by a small quantity of abraded sherds that feature organic residues from foodstuffs. Two examples do not conform to this pattern; 04-V08 from [4D-0392] in Gairnhill 3 and 04-V20 from [4D-0381] in Gairnhill 5. In both these instances partially complete sections from the circumference of the rim survived, although the bases were missing. They may have been deposited complete and inverted, perhaps as a ceremonial/votive offering.

The pottery from fill (4C-0002) of pit [4C-0001], located in the south-west, is a burnished rim sherd from a small uncarinated cup of the carinated bowl tradition. This pot type dates between c3950–3650 BC.

GAIRNHILL 7

Gairnhill 7 is the earliest of the Bronze Age houses, with a Middle Bronze Age radiocarbon date (1490–1310 cal BC; SUERC-58515). Thirty-five sherds representing five vessels (04-V21 to-V25) were associated with this building. The vessels are highly fragmented small to medium thickness body sherds (up to 14 mm thick). The only sherd from this sub-group that provides information on the shape of the vessel is a base sherd from 04-V22. This has a very straight-sided wall that is unlike most of the assemblage where the walls tend to kick out, creating a wider body. There are not enough vessels to confirm whether this indicates a chronological preference at the site; bucket and barrel shapes are prevalent through the Middle and later Bronze Age with no evidence to suggest straighter sided vessels date to the middle of the period.

GAIRNHILL 1

Sherds from this building account for vessels 04-V02 to 04-V04. Vessels 04-V03 and 04-V04 were from post-holes external to the building and 04-V02 is from a hearth. Vessels 02-V02 and 02-V03 are fairly undiagnostic small body sherds. Vessel 04–04 includes five medium sherds including a base sherd. The base sherd is flat with visible undulations from finger pinching around its edge. The base is too small to provide a diameter, but it shows walls that kick out.

GAIRNHILL 2

The single vessel (04-V05; Illus 3.51) discovered from Gairnhill 2 comprised a large quantity of mostly small and some medium sized sherds, almost entirely from the upper body. The vessel is bucket-shaped, with a slight shoulder and an obliquely angled internal bevel. Almost none of the basal sherds remain but two small abraded sherds were found from the very corner of the base and show little detail. The vessel has both exterior and interior

organic residue. It also has a surface treatment rare within the assemblage. It has been smoothed over with a clay slurry, providing a slip-like appearance.

GAIRNHILL 3

The sherds from Gairnhill 3 represent five vessels, 04-V06 to 04-V10. All except 04-V08 are small undiagnostic body sherds. At least 50–60% of Vessel 04-V08 remains; its base is missing but around 75% of its circumference is intact. The base has broken off along a distinctive elongated S-shaped clay join. An identical join to this was noted on another vessel (04-V11) from Gairnhill 4. The rim of 04-V08 is internally bevelled and slightly lipped on the exterior. It appears almost shouldered in shape although the rim is still the widest point. The urn has a 145 mm rim diameter and would have been quite small when complete. The sherds are all large and conjoin well with no edge abrasion. They likely broke *in situ* with the base lost to ploughing and this scenario indicates it was inverted in the pit. The urn has interior organic residue indicating it has been used to cook or prepare foodstuffs.

GAIRNHILL 4

The remains of three vessels (04-V11 to 04-V13) were recovered from this building, all from within the ring-ditch. Every vessel has a rim sherd present. Vessel 04–11 (Illus 3.52) is represented by the most sherds and took the form of a bucket-shape with gently curving walls. The rim has a very oblique internal bevel that has folded down on the interior to variable degrees around the vessel. This gives the appearance that the potter has gone around the edge in a hurried manner, pushing down and inwards to create the bevel, leaving excess clay patted down on the interior. The walls are thick, and finger smoothed unsystematically with patchy areas including vertical and horizontal smoothing; at some points the marks are so evident the clay appears fluted. All these manufacturing marks give the impression of a crude and fast hands-on approach that is not overly concerned with refinement. The vessel has broken along an almost identical S-shaped clay join that appeared on Vessel 04-V08 from Gairnhill 3. Much less remains of the other two vessels, both from ring-ditch [4D-0240]. One, 04-V12, is a straight bodied and squared rim sherd of quite a fine, sandy but ungritty fabric. The second, 04-V13 (Illus 3.53), is a quite coarse sand with few large inclusions but gritty with fine sub-rounded rock particles. This vessel is shouldered and much thinner than most vessels from site (7–8 mm). It has an exterior lip and an internal bevel which is concave.

GAIRNHILL 5

This building contained seven vessels, 04-V14 to 04-V20. Vessels 04-V16, 04-V17 and 04-V19 are body sherds providing limited information. Vessel 04-V19 is unusually thick at 16 mm but could be from a base. The other vessels all include rim or base sherds and diameter estimates were achievable in three cases.

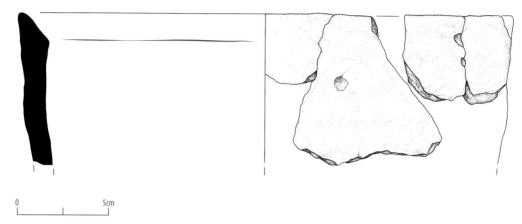

Illus 3.51 Vessel 04-V05 from Gairnhill 2

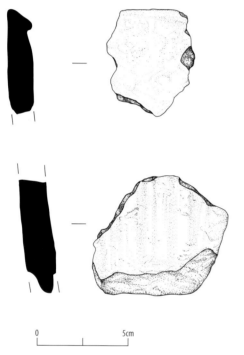

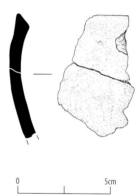

Illus 3.53 Vessel 04-V13 from Gairnhill 4

The form of vessel 04-V20 (Illus 3.55) from [4D-0381] is unusual for a domestic context and, aside from 04-V08, for the entire assemblage. A long conjoining section of the rim is present, with fresh breaks indicating recent post-depositional loss of further sherds. The vessel is very thin, and it is difficult to estimate an accurate diameter, but it appears to be between c280–320 mm and must have been very large in size. The rim is very irregular and uneven with a slight lip that varies across the sherds. The body is very gently shouldered but as lower body sherds are missing it is impossible to reconstruct fully.

3.8.2.3 Chapel of Stoneywood

The pottery from Chapel of Stoneywood numbers 43 sherds and 21 fragments from four vessels. There were also four small abraded fragments of fired clay, possibly daub, weighing 3 g, from (1C-0099). Forty-two of the sherds were recovered from charcoal-rich deposits in curvilinear gully [1C-0007], which are likely to relate to the abandonment of the building. These sherds represented up to three vessels, one of which (01-V04) was found spread across two deposits (1C-0095) and (1C-0099), suggesting it may have been dragged or trampled. A single sherd was found within possible post-hole [1C-0065] and may have slumped in during or after abandonment.

Illus 3.52 Vessel 04-V11 from Gairnhill 4

Vessel 04-V15 is from a possible occupation layer located within the entrance to the building where 14 sherds had survived. The rim sherds indicate a base diameter of c150 mm. The base and wall are of uniform thickness, the external basal corner is nicely rounded, and the sherd generally gives the impression of a well-made and finished vessel. The wall gradually angles outwards. Vessel 04-V14 is similar in thickness and its walls straighter. Five of the nine sherds from 04-V14 (Illus 3.54) are rim sherds and three of these conjoin to provide a diameter of c275 mm, a sizeable vessel. The rim is gently squared, and the body of the vessel is gently barrelled in shape. The exterior surface has been wiped and the overall appearance is smooth and even. Vessel 04-V18 includes a small rounded rim sherd with thick interior residue, which other than being used for cooking does not provide much more information.

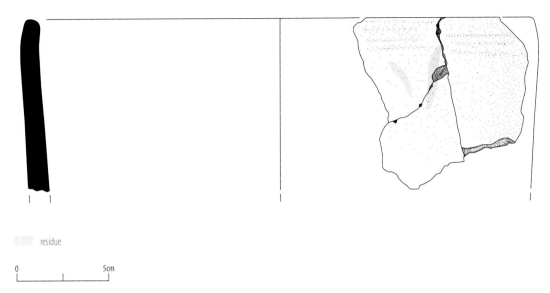

residue

0   5cm

Illus 3.54 Vessel 04-V14 from Gairnhill 5

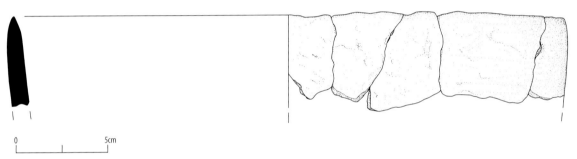

0   5cm

Illus 3.55 Vessel 04-V20 from Gairnhill 5

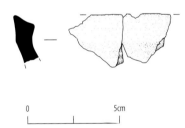

0   5cm

Illus 3.56 Vessel 01-V04 from Chapel of Stoneywood roundhouse

The pottery is in a highly fragmented and abraded condition, consistent with refuse debris. The fabric of the vessels is generally gritty, and the addition of large angular granite and quartz gives a very coarse appearance. The thickness of the walls goes some way to disguise this on the surface of the sherd but some of the inclusions do protrude. Very little can be said about vessels 01-V01 to 01-V03 other than a description of their fabric; Vessel 01-V04 on the other hand has a distinctive shape (Illus 3.56). The 38 sherds reveal an internally bevelled rim with two exterior finger-smoothed cavettos, creating a ridged upper body. The interior also has a shallower, less pronounced finger-smoothed hollow. There is not much indication

of manufacturing techniques other than the ridges being created by horizontal finger smoothing.

3.8.3 Coarse stone

3.8.3.1 Gairnhill

The coarse stone assemblage from Gairnhill, comprising two querns, two polishers and a pounder/hammerstone, was found from Gairnhill 3 and Gairnhill 5, with an unstratified quern recovered from topsoil near Gairnhill 2.

The querns are both saddle type and would have been used for grinding foodstuffs, primarily grain. These querns require a secondary stone, a rubber, to be ground against them but none were recovered. The two querns are very similar in manufacture and use; both could be termed 'slug' querns. They are broadly plano-convex in shape and are dressed. Peck marks remain visible around the convex underside. The overall plan of each is a little different; one is sub-oval the other is sub-triangular, likely reflecting the original shape of the stone. The grinding surface of each is fairly flat with grinding occurring right to the edge, which must have pushed whatever was being ground off the edge of the stone. In fact, on the quern from Gairnhill 3, the smooth wear is greatest at one edge where the wear carries round and down its edge. The sub-triangular quern has a similar feature but is much more pronounced, with a raised edge upon which the smooth wear continues up and over. No satisfactory explanation can be made for the wear on the sub-triangular quern other than the stone may have either been re-modified during its life or it may have been used as a rubber; at 370 mm maximum length this is not wholly unreasonable. These type of plano-convex 'slug querns' were found at Kintore where wear extending to their edges was also noted (Engl 2008, 215). Engl also makes the point that these stones are more portable than other querns.

The polishers are unmodified hand-sized, sub-spherical and sub-ovoid cobbles. They are of a stone that is already naturally fine-grained and very smooth. Both stones have a naturally flatter face and upon this face is a dark black-brown stain. The most likely explanation for their use is in leather working. The pounder/hammerstone has seen much use; almost 90% is covered in pitmarks. It fits in the hand but is a little larger than the polishers and would have had a bit more weight. The type of action that must have caused the pit-like marks would be a steady pounding, with occasionally movement of the stone for better grip, resulting in larger areas of wear on the surface. The specific activity cannot be identified with certainty but is likely to be the grinding down of something hard or the use of the hammer against an intermediate percussor. One small circular section of the stone has deeper wear and it is likely this was from repeated, stronger force in the same localised position. This is more akin to the type of wear expected from hammering and the strength of force applied suggests the purpose was to drive one object into another.

3.8.3.2 Chapel of Stoneywood

Two saddle querns were found in the Chapel of Stoneywood building, among other large stones, infilling ovoid pit [1C-0114]. One of the querns has been deliberately shaped while the other is an unworked natural stone. The worked quern has been pecked to a roughly plano-convex shape and is oval in plan. The grinding surface is gently convex and deepest at the centre, suggesting a short movement with most pressure applied halfway through the action. The unworked quern is wedge-shaped and sub-rectangular in plan. The grinding surface is naturally concave with much of its natural irregular texture remaining, pointing towards non-intensive use. The focus for most of the wear on the unworked quern is towards one end, suggesting it was positioned near the body and the natural angle and wedge shape was used to advantage.

3.8.4 Chipped stone

The chipped stone resource from all three sites is small and mostly consists of chips and flakes with very few tools. Three cores were recovered from Nether Beanshill and a single core, two blades and a plano-convex knife from

Gairnhill. The whole Chapel of Stoneywood assemblage consisted of chips and flakes with a single blade.

3.8.4.1 Nether Beanshill

The Nether Beanshill assemblage numbers 50 pieces of flint. The assemblage is mostly populated by chips, accounting for 64%; the remaining assemblage, amounting to 18 pieces, are mostly characterised by flake fragments. In addition to the debitage the assemblage also includes three cores and an edge-retouched flake. The characteristics within the assemblage all fit with a Middle Bronze Age date, namely hard and bipolar reduction and a lack of more formalised blanks or tools. The three cores are bipolar cores, a type of reduction where a hammer on anvil technique is used. This reduction strategy can be an expedient way to produce sharp flakes. The three bipolar cores from Nether Beanshill are fairly typical; they are bifacially reduced and in two cases have been worked along two different axes. The single retouched piece is a secondary flake with retouch along its right lateral that would have been useable in a variety of tasks.

Table 3.04 provides a summary of the lithic distribution. Most pieces were found in contexts relating to the roundhouse. Three pieces are associated with the cremation cemetery, one of which, from cremation pit [3B-0104] is clearly burnt. There are 16 burnt pieces in total. During the Middle Bronze Age stone technology begins to wane and become more simplistic (Ballin 2010). Complex reduction strategies and formalised tools are eschewed for simpler, ad hoc, reduction that presumably complemented other material available at the time. Looking at the Nether Beanshill roundhouse, which must have been extensively cleaned out before its abandonment, it is clear that the use of stone tools was still an essential component of domestic lifestyles at this point.

3.8.4.2 Gairnhill

The Gairnhill chipped stone assemblage is small, numbering 20 pieces of flint. The datable lithics are earlier than the Middle to Late Bronze Age structures, which mean that some, if not most, are residual.

The assemblage is mostly populated by chips, accounting for 45% of the total. Once chips and an indeterminate piece are excluded from analysis the assemblage consists of nine pieces. The most diagnostic of these are a bipolar core, a soft-hammer blade and a plano-convex knife. The bipolar core is the only core in the assemblage. It is bifacial reduced along two different planes of direction. Bipolar cores can be found during most periods but their popularity soars in the Middle Neolithic, from which point onwards they remain a fairly popular reduction method (Chapter 6).

One of the two blades in the collection is a soft-hammer blade. It is long with a trapezoidal section and some edge damage, perhaps indicative of use wear. Soft hammer percussion is more prevalent in the periods pre-dating the

Table 3.04 Quantity and distribution of lithics at Nether Beanshill

Feature	Chips	Flakes	Indet. pieces	Bipolar cores	Edge retouch	Total
Unstratified				1	1	2
Cremation Complex						
3B-0100	1					1
3B-0104	1					1
3B-0151	1					1
Roundhouse Complex						
3B-0025	1	2		1		4
3B-0032	1					1
3B-0039				1		1
3B-0049	3	1				4
3B-0050	3					3
3B-0063	1					1
3B-0092	1					1
3B-0111	1	1				2
3B-0130	1					1
3B-0140	1		1			2
3B-0150	2					2
3B-0180	1					1
3B-0189	1	1	1			3
3B-0212			1			1
3B-0218		1				1
3B-0219	1					1
3B-0233	1					1
3B-0241	1	2				3
3B-0281		1				1
3B-0285	1	1				2
3B-0287	1					1
3B-0291	4	1				5
3B-0302	2					2
3B-0293	1					1
Total	32	11	3	3	1	50

Middle Neolithic and, although only one example, this piece cannot date to the Middle to Later Bronze Age. The remaining pieces of debitage showed seven flakes of hard-hammer percussion and a single bipolar flake.

The most diagnostic retouch seen in the collection is in the form of a plano-convex knife. These knives are typically synonymous with the Late Neolithic to Early Bronze Age and have most commonly been found in funerary or cinerary contexts. This piece is broken and extensively burnt. In total few pieces were visibly burnt – only four, including the plano-convex knife and a chip that has fractured from it. The level to which the knife has been burnt has left it with no dorsal surface, potlid fractures, crazing and a glassy vitrified appearance.

Table 3.05 summarises the distribution of the material. Most of the chips were retrieved from soil samples and their distribution will likely be biased towards the sampling collection strategy. Added to this, the chips are small and easily transportable making their distribution unlikely to reveal areas of knapping activity and or lithic use. The typologically earliest piece in the assemblage, the soft-hammer blade, is from rig and furrow. The bipolar core and an edge-retouched piece are both from Gairnhill 5 and the knife is from Gairnhill 4.

3.8.4.3 Chapel of Stoneywood

The Chapel of Stoneywood assemblage is small and fragmentary, numbering 48 pieces. Absolute dating of the

Table 3.05 Quantity and distribution of lithics at Gairnhill

Area	Feature	Chips	Flakes	Blades	Indet. pieces	Bipolar core	Edge retouch	Piercer	Plano-convex knife	Total
U/S								1		1
Neolithic Pit	4C-0001		1							1
Rig & furrow	4D-0020			1						1
Gairnhill 1	4D-0011			1						1
	4D-0028		1							1
Gairnhill 2	4D-0102	1								1
Gairnhill 4	4D-0120	1							1	2
	4D-0320	1								1
	4D-0240				1					1
Gairnhill 5	4D-0026						1			1
	4D-0017	1				1				2
	4D-0211	1								1
Gairnhill 7	4B-0002	1	1							2
	4B-0019	1	1							2
	4B-0040	2								2
Total		9	1	2	1	1	1	1	1	20

industry they belong to is not possible and they reveal very little about activities at the site.

The assemblage is dominated by chips (62.5%), followed by small broken flakes (14.6%) and indeterminate pieces (12.5%). The single blade discovered is not a true blade but the edge of a bipolar core that, while twice as long as it is wide, is as thick as it is wide. There are three bipolar cores that are essentially the remains of three small pebbles that have been struck on either opposing end, and all have bifacial fractures. The single retouched piece is a burnt and broken flake with some edge retouch to the right lateral, near the proximal end. Burnt pieces number 14 but the presence of so many small pieces in the assemblage means this number is likely to be an underestimate. The highest concentration of lithics occurs in the ring-ditch where 22 pieces were found, most likely related to the building's occupation.

3.8.5 Vitrified material

Dawn McLaren

3.8.5.1 Nether Beanshill

A small quantity (43.5 g) of heat-affected and vitrified material was retrieved from Nether Beanshill. The majority of the material was found to be a heat-affected material known as cinder or clinker, which though indicative of high-temperature pyrotechnic processes is not diagnostic of metalworking. Despite this, a very small number of fractured pieces of prill-like magnetic vitrified residues were present indicative of ferrous metalworking. These include two fragments of micro-debris – known as slag spheres – that are considered to be diagnostic of bloom- or black-smithing activities. No 'bulk' slags were present,

Table 3.06 Summary of the vitrified material from Gairnhill by type and weight

Type	Mass (g)
Metalworking waste	
Plano-convex slag cake fragment (PCSC)	108.4
Unclassified iron slag (UIS)	53.4
Runned slag (RS)	337.4
Magnetic vitrified residues (MVR)	1.51
Undiagnostic vitrified/heat-affected material	
Fuel ash slag/low-density slag (FAS)	882.8
Cinder	54.9
Magnetic residue	6.2
Stone (vitrified and non-vitrified)	72
Total	1516.7

nor were there any fragments of magnetic vitrified residue suggestive of iron smelting activities.

The quantities of potential ferrous metalworking waste from Nether Beanshill is too limited to suggest it derived from *in situ* metalworking features but does imply, at the very least, that small-scale ironworking was taking place in the vicinity of the excavated features. Their incorporation into these features is almost certainly intrusive as the radiocarbon dating programme has shown the site dates to the Middle Bronze Age.

3.8.5.2 Gairnhill

A total of 1516.7 g of vitrified and heat-affected material was recovered from Gairnhill (Table 3.06). The majority of

Table 3.07 Distribution summary of vitrified material from Gairnhill

Area	Contexts	Material	Metalworking debris	Total weight (g)
Gairnhill 1	(4D-0011), (4D-0013), (4D-0056)	cinder, fuel ash slag/low-density slag, undiagnostic magnetic residues	no	20
Gairnhill 2	(4D-0148)	unclassified iron slag	yes	0.4
Gairnhill 3	(4D-0245), (4D-03810, (4D-04330, (4D-0386), (4D-0444), (4D-0468)	cinder, fuel ash slag/low-density slag, undiagnostic magnetic residues, Unclassified iron slag, a single flake of hammerscale and a single slag sphere	yes	28
Gairnhill 4	(4D-0065), (4D-0151), (4D-0089), (4D-0074), (4D-0240)	cinder, fuel ash slag/low-density slag, undiagnostic magnetic residues, unclassified iron slag, vitrified stone	Yes	642
Gairnhill 5	Unstratified, (4D-0017), (4D-0025), (4D-0083), (4D-0138), (4D-0190), (4D-0196), (4D-0235), (4D-0338), (4D-0433), (4D-0439), (4D-0444), (4D-0468)	cinder, undiagnostic magnetic residues, unclassified iron slag, runned slag, vitrified stone, small slag sphere and a small flake of hammerscale	Yes	708
Gairnhill 6	Unstratified, (4D-0512), (4D-0523), (4D-0537), (4D-0539), (4D-0554)	cinder, plano-convex slag cakes, undiagnostic magnetic residues		112
Four-post structure	(4D-0021)	magnetic residue		1

the assemblage is composed of low-density fuel ash slags, cinder and other heat-affected residues. A total of 501 g of waste associated with ferrous metalworking was recovered, comprising a single fragment of a plano-convex slag cake (108.4 g), fractured pieces of runned slag (337.4 g) and unclassified iron slag pieces (53.4 g). In addition, a small quantity of magnetic residues came from sample processing (1.51 g) that contained a very limited number of possible hammerscale flakes and slag spheres.

The plano-convex slag cake is incomplete, but the size, density and texture are suggestive of smithing waste. This is also implied by the small number of hammerscale flakes and slag spheres recognised within the assemblage. The quantity of micro-debris is so limited that it is not possible to argue for *in situ* metalworking waste as these small flecks could be easily disturbed as the result of bioturbation and are likely to represent intrusive later material.

The bulk of the assemblage comprises amorphous fragments of partially vitrified, low-density material (882.8 g), which are porous and friable, and range in colour from pale to dark brown. Some areas of the slags are heat-affected, brittle and fused, with a granular texture and pockets or inclusions of a light-grey/green, vesicular, glassy vitrified material. These glassy inclusions and patches are similar in appearance and texture to fuel ash slag or clinker (also known as cramp; Bayley 1985, 41–43; Bayley *et al.* 2001, 21; Spearman 1997, 165; Photos-Jones *et al.* 2007). This suggests a high siliceous and organic content but lacks the porous structure expected of fuel ash slag and the high organic content typical of clinker/cramp.

A single sample of this low-density material was selected for further analysis to determine its chemical and

structural composition. The mounted and polished sample was examined using a Scanning Electron Microscope (SEM) and the microstructure recorded using a back-scattered electron detector. The chemical composition of discrete areas of the sample was determined using an Energy Dispersive X-ray spectrometer (EDS) attached to the SEM.

The microstructure of the high-temperature residue indicates that it was largely formed from rock (or possibly soil). The low levels of iron, copper and other metals suggest that it was not formed during the manufacture or fabrication of metals. The chemical composition of the matrix suggests that this was formed at least in part by the vitrification of plant ashes. Given the uncertain extent to which the composition of the matrix has been altered by the dissolution of quartz and feldspar, there is no certain way to determine the identity of the plant ash. While this material might represent the vitrification of rock, soil and/or plant ashes as a result of deliberate human action, it could also have been produced unintentionally or even as the result of natural processes.

The majority of the vitrified material from Gairnhill is not metalwork-related in origin but rather appears to be the by-product of household hearths in use within and in association with the timber-built roundhouse structures. A summary of the distribution can be seen in Table 3.07. Material was found in every building, with concentrations in Gairnhill 4 and 5.

A small quantity of ferrous metalworking waste was also present but is likely to be secondary intrusive material post-dating the occupation of the roundhouses. Although it is fairly common for small fractured pieces of fuel ash slag and non-metalwork related vitrified materials to be recovered from later prehistoric structures associated with hearths, kilns and other pyrotechnic activities, the formation processes that lead to the creation of this material are not always well understood. Small quantities of similar material are known from other Late Bronze Age settlements, such as those at Oldmeldrum, Aberdeenshire (McLaren 2010), Kirtaraglen, Isle of Skye (McLaren 2013, 47) and Northton, Harris (Heald 2006, 171). These fuel ash slags and other low-density slags are typically thought to represent debris from domestic hearths but the fact that not every hearth of later prehistoric date produces fuel ash slag indicates that specific constituents, in terms of fuel type, soil type, temperature and perhaps other materials added to the fire while lit, are key components in the formation of this partially vitrified material. The formation processes that lead to the production of these slags is not well understood but may be the result of the fire within the hearths being continuously fed and maintained over an extended period of time, allowing underlying soils, stones and ash from the fuel to partially melt and fuse together. The small quantity of ferrous metalworking waste within the slag assemblage from Gairnhill represents a spread of unstratified and intrusive later debris relating to metalworking activities of an unknown date and provenance.

3.8.6 Wooden artefact

Anne Crone

The trough from the burnt mound at Gairnhill is the only evidence for wood that has been modified into an object other than the remains of wattle (see 3.7.2.4 above). Timber from a base plank was radiocarbon dated to 2130–1930 cal BC (SUERC-58026). The construction of the trough itself shows techniques of inner and outer tangential conversion. The basal, eastern and western sections were made of alder timbers while the northern wall is oak. The different wood species were approached in two different ways. The alder had been cleaved in half then the outer chord cleaved away to leave a roughly rectangular cross-section. This kind of plank conversion is known as inner tangential. The oak, on the other hand, is outer tangential as the outer surface of the original log has not been removed. This manner of converting logs into planks is a technique that had been practised from the Neolithic (ie O'Sullivan 1996, 304, 327 and fig 427). Other than the splitting of the logs the only other evidence for woodworking is that some of the edges have been dressed square. The base has been chopped flat on one of the oak chords and the toolmarks have survived well; blade jambs up to 40 mm wide are visible.

3.8.7 Other finds

Julie Lochrie

Additional finds include a copper-alloy object from Nether Beanshill and a bone pin from Gairnhill. The copper-alloy object was found lying on the surface of the interior of the Nether Beanshill roundhouse; it takes the form of a small ovoid lump in poor condition with no identifiable features. The bone pin is from Gairnhill 3 where it was recovered from the ring-ditch. It is burnt and broken, comprising the mid-section of a pin shaft, broken into pieces. No traces of use wear can be seen but it has been very well worked, has a circular cross-section and is very smooth.

3.8.8 Discussion

Julie Lochrie

The earliest artefacts were found in a single pit from Gairnhill. Within the pit a sherd from a small uncarinated cup and a single burnt flake were found. The vessel sherd, which had been burnished to a leather-like finish, belongs to the Carinated Bowl tradition of Britain's Early Neolithic. The presence of these at Gairnhill is remarkable as so little archaeology of Neolithic date has been discovered in this area. The small assemblage likely represents domestic refuse.

Following the deposition of the carinated bowl there is no artefactual evidence for occupation until the Early Bronze Age at Gairnhill. The finds from this period include a wooden trough (see 3.9.2.2 below) and a plano-convex knife. The plano-convex knife was discovered further north near Gairnhill 4. This type of artefact is Late Neolithic to Early Bronze Age in date and the most interesting aspect is that it is extensively burnt from a very high-temperature fire. These knives are very commonly found in cinerary contexts and although it is tempting to suggest this as a potential provenance no other remains relating to cremations were found.

The practice of cremation and the use of cremation urns arose in the Early Bronze Age and were still prevalent in the Middle Bronze Age, as shown at the small cremation complex at Nether Beanshill. Three cremation urns, probably bucket-shaped (Illus 3.48–3.50), have been identified but all are in very fragmentary condition. The extreme truncation of the pots indicates that over 80% of the pots have been destroyed; two of the bases that survived were *in situ*. The higher survival of basal portions points towards upright positions when interred, with one vessel actually positioned on a stone plinth. The way the pots have broken by truncation indicates that either a substantial depth of topsoil has been removed or that the pots were covered by a mound or cairn. As so little survives of the cremation urns it is not possible to compare them in detail to other vessels. The chipped stone from the cremation complex was 31% burnt. The most probable scenario for their burnt condition is that they were present on the funeral pyre. It is not possible to say whether the flint was deliberately placed upon the body, was already present upon the individual, or originally lay on the surrounding ground where they were cremated. The unburnt flint, however, if not already present in the area must have been deliberated added to the cremated bone after the pyre.

Table 3.08 Chronological roundhouse assemblage summary

Building	Sherd count	MNI vessels	Other finds	Radiocarbon date
Nether Beanshill	247	18	Copper-alloy object	1600–1430 cal BC (SUERC-58495)
				1500–1420 cal BC (SUERC-58510)
				1490–1310 cal BC (SUERC-58515)
Chapel of Stoneywood	42	4	Two saddle querns	1410–1270 cal BC (SUERC-57933)
				1400–1210 cal BC (SUERC-49725)
Gairnhill 7	73	5	–	1490–1300 cal BC (SUERC-58518)
				1420-1270 cal BC (SUERC-58496)
Gairnhill 3	9	5	two polishers, a bone pin	1190–940 cal BC (SUERC-58036)
				1110–930 cal BC (SUERC-58033)
Gairnhill 2	109	1	saddle quern	1120–930 cal BC (SUERC-58031)
				1010–850 cal BC (SUERC68135)
Gairnhill 1	10	3	–	1110–930 cal BC (SUERC-58030)
				1110–930 cal BC(SUERC-68134)
Gairnhill 5	39	7	pounder/hammerstone saddle quern	1050–900 cal BC (SUERC-58032)
				970–840 cal BC (SUERC-68140)
Gairnhill 4	56	3	–	1100–920 cal BC (SUERC-68136)
				990–840 cal BC (SUERC-58034)

More interesting is the ridged vessel from the Nether Beanshill roundhouse. The distinctive shape of Vessel 03-V09 (Illus 3.47) from Nether Beanshill and 01-V04 from Chapel of Stoneywood (Illus 3.56) are both from a broadly comparable period during the Middle Bronze Age. At the site of Old Meldrum, Aberdeenshire, located around 17 km north, two pots also demonstrated similar ridges (P86 and P89, Johnson 2010, 13), both pots being from a Middle Bronze Age building (White & Richardson 2010, 22). Applications of ridges, cordons and finger grooves to Middle Bronze Age vessels seem to be an even further widespread trend and could potentially have developed from cordoned urns. There was one present at Echline Fields, South Queensferry, which dated to 1370–1130 cal BC SUERC-39754 (Robertson *et al.* 2013, 122) and looking south-west to the Bronze Age unenclosed platform settlements of Lanarkshire there are examples of ridged and cordoned vessels at both Lintshie Gutter (Terry 1995) and Green Knowe (Jobey 1978, 80).

The roundhouse finds assemblages are summarised in Table 3.08. These all point to clearance of the structures when they went out of use. The remains likely represent a few dropped fragments, some mixed rubbish and a couple of deliberate interments (eg 04-V08 and 04-V20). The rubbish has collected in post-holes and ring-ditches which may indicate middens were in use and subsequently slumped and spread over features post-abandonment. This is even more probable as it appears that Gairnhill 2, 3, 4 and perhaps 5 were burnt down; however, none of the pottery shows signs indicative of the high temperatures suggested by the burnt timbers. If the pottery is from middens that have later spread across the buildings it would explain the lack of burnt pottery, its high fragmentation and abrasion. If we compare the roundhouse assemblage to some other significant middle to later Bronze Age assemblages it becomes clear how little is represented. Cobble tools in particular are under-represented, especially as stone survives better than organics and pottery. The two querns from Gairnhill weigh 12.8 kg and 14.8 kg each; they certainly could be managed short distances, but they are at the heavier side of portability. They may have deliberately been left as too heavy to transport. At Kintore the coarse stone assemblage numbered 93 artefacts (Engl 2008) while the Old Meldrum pottery assemblage represented a minimum of 111 vessels (Johnson 2010). Apart from the low quantity of finds, other aspects of the assemblage such as organic containers or textiles are completely unrepresented, either through post-depositional deterioration or by removal from the complex. The presence of two polishers in a pit from Gairnhill 3 is not quite enough to be termed a cache but these tools are likely to have been stored together for a similar purpose. This strongly suggests that the activity or the person using them were located very close by. The presence of a burnt and fragmentary bone pin from the same building would appear to fit best with textile or leatherworking.

Some of the artefacts may have been deliberately placed. The quernstones from Chapel of Stoneywood appear to be deliberately levelling the ring-ditch. It is worth noting that the combined weight of the stones is 27.6 kg, a substantial quantity to have carried to the building. This could suggest that the stones have not travelled far and relate to domestic activity within the building. Their reuse in this sense then may have been entirely practical but a sense of meaning in their deposition cannot be discounted. This type of meaningful addition has been discussed at other sites including Culduthel, Inverness (McLaren forthcoming), North Kessock, Inverness (Lochrie pers comm), and Kintore, Aberdeenshire (Engl 2008). In these examples it is usually theorised that the querns imbue the new home with 'luck' in some form or another (*ibid.*). Such deposits have also been seen as related to abandonment or closing rituals. It is worth emphasising here the presence of vessels 04-V08 from Gairnhill 3 and 04-V20 from Gairnhill 5, which may have fulfilled a similar purpose as foundation or closing tokens.

The assemblages from these sites may show only partial representation of the material culture in use at the time but they still provide valuable information when reconstructing Bronze Age domestic settlements. If we also considered the assemblage alongside the life cycle of the roundhouses we gain further understanding of the site itself. The buildings were likely cleared before they were burnt down, which suggests a deliberate act. As most of the artefacts found in or around the buildings show no traces of being in a fire, the likeliest explanation is that they derived from associated middens that spread across the site many years after its abandonment.

3.9 Discussion

3.9.1 The archaeology between the Dee and the Don: the chronology

The archaeological assemblage recovered from the 10 km stretch of road line between Nether Beanshill and Chapel of Stoneywood included a single Neolithic pit, an Early Bronze Age burnt mound, a Middle Bronze Age cremation cemetery and nine Middle and Late Bronze Age buildings with associated pits, post-holes and ancillary features.

The very earliest activity, the Neolithic pit at Gairnhill, appears typically domestic in style (see 3.8 above). There is no excavated evidence of settlement from the Neolithic in the immediate vicinity. This may be a result of the limited scope of the linear scheme (see Chapter 7); the long cairn at West Hatton (NJ80NE 13) as well as Binghill stone circle (NJ80SE 16) are indicative of further early prehistoric activity in the general area. However, in comparison to the discoveries made at Milltimber (Chapter 2), Blackdog and Wester Hatton (Chapter 6) in particular, the lack of Neolithic archaeology in this landscape seems notable and this feature, though small, is a significant addition to the known Neolithic archaeology of this area.

Visible traces of settlement remains do not appear until the Bronze Age. The activity is episodic rather than continuous; the radiocarbon determinations from all three sites contain gaps in the chronology. The artist's impression of activity at Gairnhill gives a good indication of this spasmodic sequence of events (Illus 3.57). Bronze

Age activity starts at the bottom of the slope with the burnt mound sometime between 2100 and 1900 BC. After this the site appears to be abandoned and between 300 and 500 years later the roundhouse and cemetery at Nether Beanshill were established. At roughly the same time buildings were constructed and inhabited at Gairnhill 7 and Chapel of Stoneywood. We also see the establishment of the earliest Bronze Age settlement at Wester Hatton at this time. The sites at Nether Beanshill and Chapel of Stoneywood were abandoned by 1200 BC. This coincides with the earliest dates from Gairnhill 1 to 6, further up the slope from Gairnhill 7. These houses probably formed a small settlement rather than non-contemporary single structures. There is no architectural reason why all six buildings could not have been occupied at the same time, although the proximity of Gairnhill 1 to 4 may argue against this.

It is difficult to estimate the duration of the later Bronze Age settlement at Gairnhill. Radiocarbon dates from the structures are roughly contemporary and span a period from 1370 to 820 BC. The dates might suggest that Gairnhill 6 was the earliest and Gairnhill 5 the latest.

By 800 BC, on the basis of the evidence from the AWPR/B-T works, this landscape is once more relatively empty. Hints of Iron Age activity are seen at Chapel of Stoneywood with a single radiocarbon date suggesting limited visits. In the wider landscape the unexcavated hut circles at Beanshill (NJ80SW 50) could easily be later prehistoric in date. Subsequent activity in the landscape is sparse; evidence of the local population effectively disappears until the post-medieval period when field clearance begins to take place and evidence for rig and furrow agriculture is seen at all three of the excavation sites. Evidence from the trial-trenching phase (Dingwall 2013, 8.3.5) revealed that furrows in general were only seen around Gairnhill and Nether Beanshill and only patchily in the landscape otherwise.

3.9.2 Early Bronze Age burnt mound

The burnt mound consisted of a spread of firing debris, a rectangular wood-lined trough with structural wooden elements preserved through waterlogging, and peripheral structural elements related to the activities occurring at the site (Illus 3.57). It is generally accepted that burnt mounds are formed by heating stones that are then placed into a container in order to heat the water in it. This process leads to the stones cracking and being discarded along with the charred material from the hearth. The debate over what the hot water or steam produced was used for remains unresolved.

Recent estimates suggest that there are at least 1900 examples in Scotland (ScARF 2012c, 3.3.1). Most are known from surface surveys and are concentrated in the Northern Isles, with a second concentration in southern and south-western Scotland. Very few have been excavated, with the majority that have located in the Northern

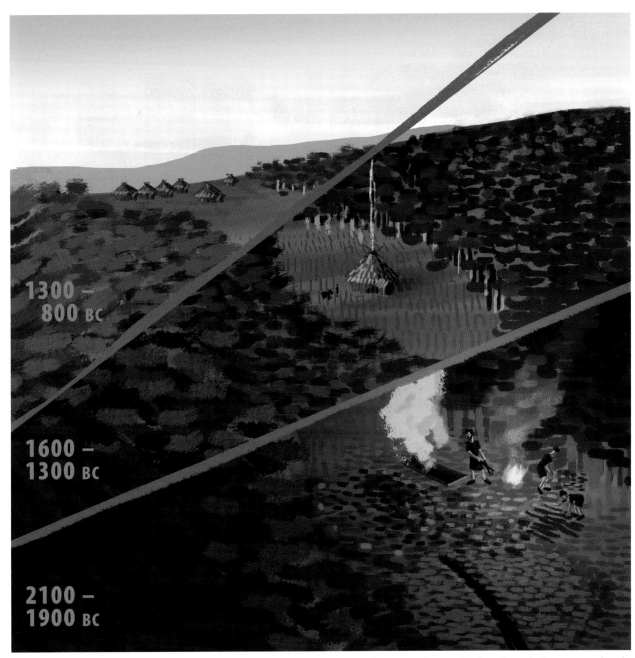

Illus 3.57 Artist's impression of Gairnhill at three points in the Bronze Age. Activity at the site develops from the burnt mound at the base of the hill, to an isolated roundhouse, to a nucleated settlement by the end of the period

Isles. It is likely that the true number may far exceed this estimate, given the increasingly frequent discoveries from developer-funded work (ScARF 2012c, 53). Local excavated examples are limited to two burnt mounds found by Strachan & Dunwell (2003, 166–67) during the monitoring of a gas pipeline at East Dens near Peterhead and a burnt mound with a wood-lined trough encountered during monitoring of a cable route in Moray (Jenorowski & Sludden 2016). The East Dens examples (not visible on the surface and partly plough-truncated) consisted of little more than spreads of heat-affected stones and charcoal with no associated structures or troughs. The burnt mound at Gairnhill is another demonstration that these sites can often

be undetectable in surface surveys and are only discovered during programmes of soil stripping, although usually in predictable locations near watercourses.

3.9.2.1 Location of the burnt mound

Burnt mound sites tend towards isolation; O'Néill's study of over 500 excavated burnt mounds in Ireland demonstrated that it is very rare that a burnt mound can be related to a contemporary settlement in the landscape (O'Néill 2009, 199). Surveys in Shetland also note that while there appears to be some association between settlement areas and burnt mounds, these are often some distance from the settlement (Moore & Wilson 1999, 233).

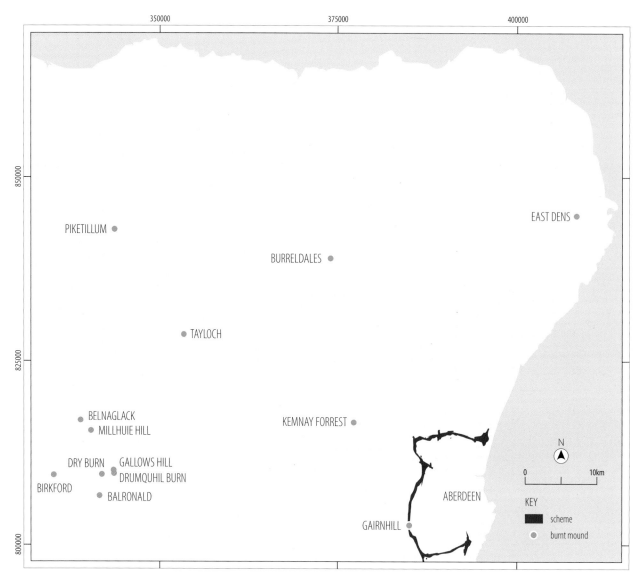

Illus 3.58 Distribution plan of burnt mounds in north-east Scotland

The site is relatively isolated in relation to other known examples in Aberdeenshire (Illus 3.58), most of which are clustered around the eastern fringes of the Cairngorms. One was identified by survey in Kemnay Forest near Kintore (NJ71NE 106) 25 km to the north-west of Gairnhill and a scattering of sites are known further to the north, including those from East Dens near Peterhead. With the exception of the Peterhead example, most remain unexcavated.

The positioning of the burnt mound at Gairnhill was obviously important; a relatively isolated spot, towards the foot of a slope, in wet and boggy ground near a small watercourse. There is no reason to believe that these conditions were not the same in the Early Bronze Age. Peat had already begun to form prior to the construction of the trough in a local environment dominated by grass and sedge (see 3.5.2.1 above). The two gullies found close to the trough also suggest that water management

was an important activity on site. The presence close to the surface of many readily available stones needed for heating the water may have been another factor in the choice of this location.

At Gairnhill, domestic structures were found a few hundred metres away from the burnt mound, but they are later in date. The absence of excavated contemporary settlement does not necessarily mean it did not exist; the relatively narrow width of the scheme excludes known sites to the east (Chapter 7.1.8). Excavated and dated Early Bronze Age settlement sites are rare in north-east Scotland in general (Pope 2015, 160, Illus 9.1) and no dated structures contemporary with the burnt mound are currently known from the region. A typologically Early Bronze Age plano-convex knife recovered in proximity to the Late Bronze Age Gairnhill buildings is a tantalising glimpse of further activity but provides little concrete evidence of settlement.

3.9.2.2 The form of the burnt mound and its features

There was evidence for most of the typical processes associated with burnt mounds at Gairnhill. The site consisted of the wood-lined trough with its associated drainage gully and cluster of stake-holes, the drainage gully at the southern end of the area and the three stone structures. A contemporary hearth or multiple hearths is presumed, although no formal hearth structure was found. It may have lain beyond the limit of excavation, possibly to the south, as suggested at the excavated burnt mound at Coarhamore in Ireland (Sheehan 1990). On the other hand, hearths at burnt mounds, where recorded, tend to be informal and difficult to discern from the surrounding burnt mound material. In some cases, usually at the more complex burnt mound sites, the hearth area may be more formalised, as at Ballyvourney (O'Kelly 1954, 110) and Beaquoy (Hedges 1975, 53).

The plank construction of the rectangular pit trough places the Gairnhill burnt mound into O'Néill's Type 4 (O'Néill 2009, 86). Rectangular pit troughs have a date range in Scotland of 2500 BC to AD 220 (*ibid.*, 86). Wood linings are rare in Scotland, with only five examples of wood-lined troughs. Three of these, Cleuchbrae in Dumfries and Galloway, Dervaird, East Rhins (Russell-White & Barber 1990), and Beechwood Farm, Inverness (Cressey & Strachan 2003), were composed of oak planks or hollowed oak trunks. Chapeldonan in South Ayrshire is reported as possessing a rectangular pit with a non-specific wood lining (Speller *et al.* 1997). The wood-lined trough from Beechwood Farm, Inverness was very similar in appearance to that from Gairnhill and returned similar late third to early second millennium BC dates (Cressey & Strachan 2003). A more recent excavation from Moray (Jenorowski & Sludden 2016) is unpublished but was also lined with wooden planks and was similar in size and construction to both Beechwood Farm and Gairnhill. Perhaps the closest example to the Gairnhill example in terms of date and construction is that from Garlands Hospital, Carlisle, where a tangentially converted alder plank in the base of a pit under a burnt mound produced a date of 2300–1985 cal BC (GU-8007; Neighbour & Johnson 2005). More common in Scotland are stone-lined troughs in various pit shapes, but this probably results from the emphasis on burnt mound research in the timber-poor Western Isles.

Post-holes and stake-holes are often found in and around burnt mounds but rarely form a coherent pattern. The most likely interpretation for those at Gairnhill is that they were possible firebreaks, or racks (Grogan *et al.* 2007, 89). The stake-holes at Gairnhill, assuming all were found, were not numerous enough or dispersed widely enough to represent a larger structure such as a tent.

The stone structures located around the trough are less easily assigned a function. Structure 3, formed of large rough field-stones, including some *in situ* boulders, may have acted to retain or demarcate some of the burnt mound material during its use. Structure 2 to the south of the trough appeared more substantial. Here, an L-shaped line of stones and a stone surface may have defined an area of activity associated with the trough. Surfaces such as these can be either wooden or stone and are often located near or around the trough to provide a stable working area in boggy ground or they can be located to facilitate access to the burnt mound site (Grogan *et al.* 2007, 89; O'Néill 2009, 47). The gully, which drained water away to the south, may have functioned to keep this work area dry, or may have supplied water for a secondary activity taking place away from the trough.

The associated stone structures are less common. O'Néill estimates only 5% of excavated mounds are furnished with structures that in general are not visible on the surface. This figure may be an inflation of the proportion of burnt mounds with structures, as it derives mainly from research-driven settlement excavation in the Western Isles, which tend towards greater elaboration than isolated burnt mounds from the mainland. The evidence from Gairnhill perhaps attests to less formal construction in relation to isolated burnt mounds.

3.9.2.3 Duration of use of the burnt mound

The radiocarbon determinations from the burnt mound provide a broad period of use for the structure of between 2130 and 1900 BC. There are few other clues as to more precise duration of use. The lack of a structured hearth or fire-place at Gairnhill compounds the problem. Although a comparison of the volume of the trough to the volume of the firing debris can be made (roughly 1:67), this is an arbitrary observation as we have no indication about the volume of firing debris created during a single period of use. Experimental archaeology has attempted to address this question but requires many assumptions to be made, such as the required temperature of the water and the duration of the process that was being carried out (O'Néill 2009, 55–67).

Grogan (Grogan *et al.* 2007, 91), in summarising the multitude of burnt mounds uncovered during the construction of a pipeline in Ireland estimated that, on average, sites were used at least 100 times, with the largest estimate being 340 uses and the lowest 67. Grogan used a simplistic methodology of looking at the volume of the trough in comparison to the volume of burnt stone recovered. Using figures derived from Buckley's work on the thermodynamics of different stone types (Buckley 1990), Grogan settled on the average number of reuses of a stone at approximately six before the stones would shatter and become unusable. The maximum number of uses of a burnt mound, therefore, could be estimated by dividing the mound size by the trough size and multiplying the result by six. Such a methodology would place a rough maximum number of uses at Gairnhill at 402, which is a considerably higher number than in Grogan's Irish examples.

The above estimate is simplistic at best and a more detailed one would require a far greater range of information to be available or for greater assumptions to be made on the process taking place. Water may have been heated to different temperatures and for different durations depending on the process required, be that cooking or bathing or any number of crafts that might utilise heat or steam. The stone recovered from the trough at Gairnhill was too intermixed with the rest of the overlying burnt mound stones to assume that it was the remainder of a final heating process. We do not know how long the water in the trough was heated for in each instance, or even if the process was a long continuous one. For example, O'Néill, examining the excavated mound at Broadlough, used O'Kelly's observation from an experiment at Ballyvourney where stone equal to half of the volume of the trough needed to be added every fifteen minutes to maintain temperature. Using this, O'Néill calculated that the amount of stone excavated from the Broadlough mound could have been used in a continuous process taking 22 hours (O'Néill 2009, 189). O'Néill used other data sources such as estimated hearth temperatures and the amount of stone recovered from the trough: such estimates are beyond the limits of the dataset from Gairnhill.

The trough at Gairnhill had been subject to some modification in that it was shortened by the insertion of the stone upright. Troughs recorded at other burnt mound sites also show modifications and reuse over time, such as at Cahiracon 122a (Grogan *et al.* 2007, 92) where a platform had been placed over one end of the trough at a later date. Modifications such as this might suggest a change in use of the trough or slight alterations to make the process being carried out easier or more efficient. As such it is not necessarily an indicator that the trough was in use for any great amount of time.

The homogeneity of the burnt mound deposit at Gairnhill also yields few clues to the duration or number of uses. The absence of lenses in the burnt mound material suggests that the burnt mound was continually in use for an indeterminate period before being abandoned. No evidence for soil formation within or over the firing debris was observed except after the final abandonment deposits. These deposits appear to relate to later, agricultural clearance, phases.

3.9.2.4 The function(s) of the burnt mound

Burnt mounds form from the by-products of heating water through the application of hot stones. The end purpose of this is still a matter of much debate. Burnt mounds were traditionally understood to be a locus of cooking and feasting, particularly in reference to hunting parties preparing deer (O'Kelly 1954). However, this interpretation has fallen from favour owing to the absence of food remains or domestic refuse at many sites. More recent studies have favoured a variety of functions beyond cooking, including sweat lodges or saunas (Barfield & Hodder 1987; Armit &

Braby 2002); textile and leather production (Coles 1979; Jeffrey 1991), wood working, including boat building (Rausing 1984) and, most recently, brewing (Quinn & Moore 2007).

The Gairnhill burnt mound provides only absences of evidence for these many interpretations, as at many other excavated sites. The absence of faunal remains can be explained through their decay in acid soils. Gairnhill provides little evidence to support wood working, but such evidence is likely to have decayed, save within the trough. The arrangement of stake-holes to the south of the trough is not sufficiently substantial to suggest a structure. Other excavated examples of simple burnt mounds in Scotland have similar absences of evidence (eg Strachan & Dunwell 2003; Suddaby 2009). It is likely that individual burnt mounds were multi-functional or changed function (Barber 1990).

3.9.3 Bronze Age settlement patterns and roundhouse construction

The excavations at Nether Beanshill, Gairnhill and Chapel of Stoneywood uncovered nine previously unknown Middle to Late Bronze Age roundhouses spread across the lower slopes of the higher ground between the Dee and Don valleys. Single and clustered roundhouse sites are becoming more commonly discovered in north-east Scotland, with several large developer-funded excavations building a more detailed picture of settlement patterns during this period. These include sites at Wester Hatton (Chapter 6), Ednie, Aberdeenshire (Strachan & Dunwell 2003), Oldmeldrum, Aberdeenshire (White & Richardson 2010), and Hatton Farm, Angus (Gray & Suddaby 2010). The sites of Deer's Den (Alexander 2000) and Forest Road, Kintore, Aberdeenshire (Cook & Dunbar 2008) currently comprise the largest assemblage of prehistoric roundhouses in the region, numbering over 30 between them. More recently, Pope (2015) has summarised the structural forms of the dated Scottish Bronze Age roundhouse assemblage.

3.9.3.1 Roundhouse construction and form

Pope (2015) highlights three principal architectural forms for the dated Scottish Bronze Age roundhouse assemblage; ring-bank, post-built and ring-groove roundhouses. Upstanding examples of ring-banks are still seen throughout Scotland, mostly in upland areas that have escaped modern cultivation although many are also known from the lowlands. Ring-banks utilised mass walls, which were low and wide and constructed of earth, stone or turf that could support and distribute the weight of the roof, which would typically rest on top (Pope 2015, 163).

Post-built structures provide a frame of uprights onto which timber or wattle panels and roof beams could be attached. The earth-fast ends of the posts distribute the weight of the roof directly into the ground. These could be made using individual post-holes or alternatively with a continuous foundation trench known as a ring-groove.

Pope (2015, 173) has argued that trench foundations would have been easier to excavate than individual post-holes, especially in harder ground. Ring-grooves also allow the use of sill beams and pre-fabricated wattle or timber panels, evidence for which can be seen when the ring-groove takes on a sub-circular and more angular appearance (eg Gairnhill 1).

In the smallest of houses, it is generally supposed that the outer walls would have been sufficient to take the weight of any roof structure on their own (Pope 2003, 110). Rafter beams may also have been made earth-fast at their ends in a 'wig-wam' fashion, or supported on earthen banks, as suggested by Cook & Dunbar (2008, 324), which might not leave any physical remains in the ground once the banked material had been ploughed away. In larger structures additional supports would have been required both to support the weight of the roof and prevent the rafters from splaying. In these cases, additional rings of beams were attached to the roof to protect against vertical and lateral movement. These 'ring-beams' were supported in their construction by rings of earth-fast posts.

While these structural distinctions are broadly useful, it is possible for all three structural techniques to be utilised in a single building. Pope (2015) has also demonstrated that all of the building techniques have their origins in the Bronze Age and have a wide geographical distribution. As such the structural remains presented above do not alter our understanding of roundhouse construction but add to the growing corpus of excavated sites from the region.

3.9.3.2 Settlement in the Middle Bronze Age

Given the date ranges recovered from the three Middle Bronze Age sites on the AWPR/B-T, the proximity of these settlements and the degree to which they may have interacted is of note. The similarity of pottery vessels from both Nether Beanshill and Chapel of Stoneywood (see 3.8.8 above) suggests that these two settlements may have been linked in some way either through trade, shared cultural tradition or even by the movement of people between the two locations. While the sites would not have been inter-visible the distance between them, especially Nether Beanshill and Gairnhill, is negligible (eg an hour's walk). That three previously unknown sites of this period were discovered along this relatively narrow road corridor is also important. Given the sparsity of evidence for earlier prehistoric settlement (see 3.2.4 above) in this landscape, the Middle Bronze Age can be seen as a period in which settlement becomes, if not more common, at least significantly more visible in the archaeological record. The Middle Bronze Age roundhouses were broadly similar in their construction and add to the growing corpus of dated roundhouses from this period in north-east Scotland. The roundhouse at Nether Beanshill was the earliest, dating to between 1607–1302 BC. It was also the smallest of the three, at slightly over 8 m in diameter. The construction of the

outer walls at Nether Beanshill appears to be formed from a post-ring onto which timber or wattle could have been attached. The main roof support appears to have been at the outer walls. External ring-banks are suggested for the other two Middle Bronze Age buildings; Gairnhill 7 and Chapel of Stoneywood. The outer post-rings at both sites are spaced too far apart and are too irregular to be related directly to wall structures (Pope 2015, 171). These may have been supports for roof timbers at the point they crossed the walls. Inner post-rings supporting ring-beams were present in Gairnhill 7 and Chapel of Stoneywood.

Entrances, where identifiable, appear to have been to the south or south-east. South-east facing entrances maximise both light and shelter from prevailing winds in Scotland and the northern parts of England, and are the most common orientation in prehistoric buildings in this region. Nether Beanshill had an unusually elongated entranceway or porch-type structure. A similar entrance with an eroded surface was seen at Deer's Den House 3 (Alexander 2000, 20) which also had a south-east orientated entrance passage with a sunken floor. At Deer's Den, dated between 1890 and 1100 BC, the excavator has suggested that this passage may have run between the termini of a large external bank, in which case the 'porch' would not have appeared to extend from the building at all (*ibid.*, 67). A similar interpretation at Nether Beanshill is tempting but speculative at best in the absence of any evidence for an outer bank.

3.9.3.3 Settlement in the Late Bronze Age

Late Bronze Age settlement was confined to Gairnhill (Gairnhill 1–6). Gairnhill 6 produced the earliest dates (1120–940 cal BC, SUERC-68141) and Gairnhill 5 the latest (1050–830 BC) but all could have been roughly contemporary. As such it is tempting to imply a change in settlement patterns from the Middle to the Late Bronze Age, with multiple isolated single building sites being replaced by a single multi-building settlement. This has to remain largely speculative, however, owing to the general lack of excavated sites in the local area. If the buildings were not contemporary the builders of new houses were aware of and actively avoided constructing new buildings in the same place as the old.

By the later Bronze Age, the outer walls at Gairnhill were set into foundation trenches (ring-grooves) with the exception of Gairnhill 3. That these ring-grooves only partially survive along the northern and eastern edges of the structures is most likely to do with the angle of slope at these sites. For a level construction the buildings would have had to be partially terraced into the slope, which is suggested for Gairnhill 2 and possibly for most of the buildings here. The downslope edges have likely been lost to later ploughing. The greater survival of the Middle Bronze Age structures at Nether Beanshill and Gairnhill 7 probably result from their positioning on more level ground.

Gairnhill 1 was the most unusual of the Later Bronze Age structures. Its diameter was considerably smaller than the others and its shape was very angular in appearance. A similarly small ring-groove building was identified at Ednie, Aberdeenshire (Strachan & Dunwell 2003, 146). Structure 3 from Ednie was radiocarbon dated to the 9th century BC and measured no more than 7 m in diameter. It had a very similar angular shape to its ring-groove, most likely the result of the use of straight sections of wattle or timber panelling to form the outer walls. That this structure was potentially unroofed should also be considered and hints at non-domestic activities taking place in the north-western corner of the site.

The other Late Bronze Age buildings were all considerably larger than Gairnhill 1 and contained inner post-rings, most likely for roof supports. Similarly sized ring-groove houses dating to the Late Bronze Age have been seen at Wester Hatton (Structure 5: Chapter 6), Arid Quarry, Dumfriesshire (Cook 2006), and Structures 1 and 2 at Ednie, Aberdeenshire (Strachan & Dunwell 2003, 141–42), all of which were in excess of 12 m in diameter. The ring-grooves in themselves do not exclude the possibility that the buildings also had some form of banked walls. The large gaps between the internal ring-ditches and the outer ring-grooves in Gairnhill 2, 4 and 5 might be partially explained by the presence of a wide mass wall with the wattle or timber set in the ring-groove acting as a form of external cladding. Gairnhill 3 would certainly fit with this construction method, in the absence of any ring-groove or outer post-ring.

3.9.4 Living in the houses – evidence for use, function and meaning

As seen from the environmental and material synthesis (see 3.7 & 3.8 above), none of the roundhouses displayed evidence for anything beyond routine or low-level exploitation of readily available local food and common domesticates. However, it is still possible to tease out evidence of daily life.

3.9.4.1 Ring-ditches and internal divisions

Ring-ditches were present in all roundhouses except for Gairnhill 1 and 6. In all cases they appeared to have formed through a process of erosion. In two cases – Nether Beanshill and Gairnhill Building 7 – the ring-ditches were observed enclosing the entire inner circumference of the building. In Gairnhill 2, 3, and 4 the ring-ditches were only observed within the north-eastern arc, an observation also made for most of the ring-ditches at Kintore (Cook & Dunbar 2008, 331) though as suggested above (see 3.9.3.2) this might be due to truncation at Gairnhill. The spread observed within the north-eastern arc of Gairnhill 5 may have been the remains of a heavily truncated ring-ditch or indicate that a lower level of erosion had taken place within this building.

A common interpretation for the formation of erosion ditches is either through the footfall of the inhabitants or livestock stalled within the building, seasonally or overnight (eg Jobey and Tait 1966, 14; Reynolds 1982, 53). Through a combination of the trample of animals and soil removed along with manure when being mucked out, these ring-ditches would have formed as a by-product of function. The lack of ring-ditches in Gairnhill 1 and Gairnhill 6 suggests that animals may not have been housed in these smaller structures, which again suggests a possible specialist or ancillary use of these two buildings. Two distinct forms of ring-ditch were observed across the sites. The first was formed by a series of depressions that linked together to create the full ring-ditch shape (seen at Gairnhill 3 and 7). The second and more common consisted of a more or less regular wear gully, not displaying this segmented nature (eg Nether Beanshill). A possible origin of the segmented form could be that the ring-ditch area was partitioned in a radial fashion (as suggested by Reid 1989), leading to deeper grooves developing within the middle of each partition. This explanation was also suggested for the segmented nature of the ring-ditch in Deer's Den Structure 3 (Strachan & Dunwell 2003, 68).

Evidence for radial partitions at Gairnhill 3 and 7 were not present, however, and the stake-holes that did survive in the ring-ditch roundhouses (most obviously at Nether Beanshill, Gairnhill 3 and 4, and Chapel of Stoneywood) tended to follow the inner arc of the ring-ditch suggesting concentric partitions instead. Concentric partitions have also been noted at Black Loch of Myrton (Crone & Cavers 2015) where they have survived *in situ*. As discussed above (see 3.7.2.4), the wattle remains from the ring-ditches were thought likely to originate from these internal partitions. A small amount of possible wattle fencing, thought to be internal partitioning relating to the stalling of animals, was also recovered from a Middle Iron Age roundhouse at Kintore (Crone 2008, 281–83).

A layer of stones was placed at the base or in the deepest sections of most ring-ditches. In most cases these stones were not laid with the intention of providing flat surfaces to walk upon, except at Gairnhill 7 which displays the most complete attempt at 'paving'. Later agricultural truncation might explain the haphazard nature of the stones in most of the ring-ditches. Alternatively, the stones may not have acted solely to fill the bulk of the hollows and straw or turf might have formed a surface above these. If this was the case the stones beneath the organic surface may have helped to drain away some of the more liquid by-products of stalled animals.

At Rattray in Aberdeenshire (Murray *et al.* 1992) a 2.5 m long line of wattle fencing was uncovered in conjunction with a field system in the form of ard marks and was interpreted as a possible field boundary. This fence was constructed from rowan, willow and hazel and returned a radiocarbon date of 1180±50 BC (*ibid.*, 120). How this presumably external fence burnt down remains unexplained. The excavators have suggested it may have actually served as a trackway rather than a fence owing to the lack of structural post-holes found in association with it. It is possible that the charred remains of wattle hurdles found within the ring-ditches at Gairnhill may also have served as a surface or flooring to level out the wear hollows.

3.9.4.2 Hearths and pits

Only four of the buildings at Gairnhill and Nether Beanshill had evidence of internal hearths; the Middle Bronze Age structures at Nether Beanshill and Gairnhill 7, and Late Bronze Age Gairnhill 1 and 6. Across the archaeological record one in three ring-ditch roundhouses have a central hearth (Pope 2007, 255). This observation holds true here as only Gairnhill 7 and Nether Beanshill were seen to have both a ring-ditch and a hearth, with none observed in the Late Bronze Age ring-ditch roundhouses at Gairnhill. However, the analysis of fuel ash slag from Gairnhill shows hearth debris was present within most of the buildings (see 3.8.5 above). While it is possible that hearths may have been lost to later truncation, they were found in Gairnhill 1 and 6, which did not contain ring-ditches. Another possibility is that hearths may have been placed on raised structures that do not survive, or even that they were placed on a first-floor living space, separating the agricultural space below from the domestic space above.

Pit digging was mostly absent as a phenomenon at Gairnhill with the exception of Gairnhill 3 and 5 where pits containing stone tools and pottery were recovered. Quernstones were also found reused in the ring-ditch at Chapel of Stoneywood. At Kintore, pit digging within roundhouses was most frequent in the Middle to Late Bronze Age, though it was not at all common. Where significant quantities of artefacts were recovered, it was seen as an act enriching or enhancing the buildings either at foundation or abandonment (Cook & Dunbar 2008, 334–35). The presence of these artefact-rich pits in Gairnhill 3 and 5 is similarly unusual and is presumed to have held some significance and meaning. These could also have been foundation deposits for the buildings, although there is no evidence that they pre-date the construction of the buildings. Conversely, they could easily have been deposited at any time during the use of the building or on abandonment.

3.9.5 Abandonment by fire

Given that three of the buildings (Gairnhill 2, 3 and 4) displayed the remains of charred wattle hurdle and small structural timbers in the ring-ditches we can surmise that at least three were destroyed by fire. Charcoal forms through combustion in either anaerobic (carbonisation) or limited oxygen conditions (charring). The range of charcoal present and its varying survival suggests that the buildings burnt down, with perhaps the roof or outer walls collapsing to smother the internal wattle panels and prevent complete combustion, or that the fire was doused before the wood

was turned to ash. Since the wattle was then left undisturbed within the ring-ditches it suggests there was no attempt made to clean up after the fire and rebuild. Potentially an accidental fire got so out of control as to cause irreparable damage to these buildings, or, perhaps more likely, the firing was deliberate.

Destruction by fire is an uncommon occurrence for Bronze Age roundhouses in the archaeological record. Pope states that across northern and central Britain only 39 out of over 1100 structures suffered such an event and at least one in three of those were rebuilt (Pope 2003, 369), suggesting unintentional firing. The presence of so many burnt buildings here, and at the excavations at Kintore, where at least five of the Bronze Age roundhouses were destroyed by conflagration (Crone 2008, 286), may point to a regional practice in north-eastern Scotland in the Late Bronze Age.

A very close comparator with Gairnhill 4 is Carn Dubh House 5 in Perthshire (Rideout 1995, 164) where carbonised roof timbers were recovered from an upper layer of an erosional gully. As at Gairnhill these were small and narrow diameter lengths of wood and did not include larger structural rafters. Rideout suggested that the roof had been partially dismantled prior to the house being burnt (*ibid.*, 167). This structured form of abandonment is also suggested for Gairnhill. Analysis of the carbonised timbers at Gairnhill (see 3.7.2.5 above) shows that most of the charred remains derive from smaller branches and twigs of hazel, alder and oak and that large structural timbers were generally missing. This would be consistent with the posts being removed for reuse in other buildings, which suggests deliberate and planned abandonment rather than loss to accident or arson.

Wooden housing is certainly prone to accidental fire, as with the case of Tormore on the Isle of Arran (Barber 1997, 15) or Must Farm Timber Platform, Cambridgeshire (Knight 2012). At the site of Tormore, a wattle fence lining the inner bank wall of a Late Bronze Age building was preserved by a fire that ended a long period of occupancy. In this instance, it appears that the fire was accidental as a large store of grain and even a tethered cow appear to have been lost to the flames. At Must Farm (as yet unpublished) the settlement was suspended above a watercourse, and upon burning down the remains fell into the water and were preserved in the soft sediment. The number of artefacts recovered from the excavations, including tools, pottery and organic remains, has been a revelation on the richness of possessions that could have been present in a Bronze Age house. While it is not assumed that a similar abundance of artefacts would have been present at Gairnhill, the relative lack of artefactual and environmental remains, and especially of large structural timbers, suggests a level of clearance either before or after the fire. That the wattle remains in the ring-ditches appeared relatively undisturbed suggests that the clearance took place before the buildings were burnt.

Illus 3.59 Artist's impression of the Nether Beanshill cremation complex and roundhouse. As the cremation is placed in the ground, the roundhouse can be seen just beyond the bedrock outcrop. Possible earlier cremation mounds surround the monument

3.9.6 The cremation burials at Nether Beanshill

3.9.6.1 The cremation complex – mounds, markers and miniature ring-gullies

The cremation complex at Nether Beanshill can be dated between 1490–1240 BC and is therefore seen as roughly contemporary with the roundhouse approximately 50 m away (dated between 1600–1300 BC). The complex consisted of three cremations, two within miniature ring-gullies and one marked by a horseshoe-shaped arrangement of posts. Related pits, some of which contained fragments of pottery and cremated bone, are likely to be ancillary features for the three main cremations. A fourth cremation

was hinted at by a third miniature ring-ditch, but no burial was found in the centre.

The ring-gullies resemble traditional round-barrows from southern England, in form if not in size. Similar 'miniature barrows' have been found elsewhere in northern England, Scotland and Northern Ireland. Miniature ring-gullies dating to the Bronze Age were identified in Yorkshire, at the site of Ferry Fryston during works ahead of the construction of the A1 (M) (Brown *et al.* 2007, 27–35). Two of the cremations from this site were surrounded by miniature ring-ditches. At Ballintaggart, Northern Ireland, a group of eight ring-ditches ranging in size from 2 m to 6 m in diameter with cremation pits in the centre were interpreted as a barrow cemetery (Porter 2009, 39–43). The nearest example from Scotland is from Midmill, Kintore, which consisted of a central cremation pit enclosed by six small pits with shallow slots between, forming a ring up to 2.9 m in diameter. An outer ring of post-pits surrounding the central cremation was thought to be related (Murray & Murray 2008, 24–5). Two miniature ring-ditches interpreted as barrows, one of which was dated to the Middle Bronze Age, were also recovered from Greenbogs to the north of Monymusk, Aberdeenshire (Noble *et al.* 2012, 137). These ring-ditches, both under 3 m in diameter, were found in association with contemporary cremation burials but did not themselves contain cremated remains, although the author suggests that plough truncation may have removed any evidence for this (*ibid.*, 166). It is possible, given the lack of cremated remains from the third ring-gully at Nether Beanshill, that these features served purely as markers and may not have held burials themselves.

The presence of two confirmed cremations in immediate proximity, one in a simple pit and one covered by a mound and surrounded by a ring-ditch, does point to two separate phases of use for the monument. Alternatively, the difference in burial structure might be a reflection of less tangible differences such as social status or gender. An artist's impression of the complex suggests the first (unmounded) burial being marked by the oval post arrangement (Illus 3.59)

3.9.6.2 Living beside the dead – proximity of cremations and settlement

Nether Beanshill was the only site to recover evidence for human burial. Their location so close to a roundhouse raises questions as to the significance of this arrangement. The cemetery and the house were certainly inter-visible at the time of excavation, although a low rocky outcrop between the two would have partially obscured a full view. It should also be considered that tree cover may have been more extensive in the Bronze Age and could have restricted the line of sight.

Cremation burials are not common in close association with dated Middle Bronze Age buildings. At Greenbogs, also in Aberdeenshire, timber structures were found

together with cremation burials dating to between 1490 and 1120 BC (Noble *et al.* 2012, 137–39). Topsoil stripping of a ridge revealed three gravel knolls, one of which was occupied by two cremation pits and two very small ring-ditches. The typological similarities between these two sites are quite striking and both are very similar in date, which might suggest a regional practice in north-east Scotland of burying the dead close to settlements during the Middle Bronze Age. It is tempting to interpret this as a small family cemetery directly linked to the adjacent roundhouse. The presence of the burials so close to the house also suggests a certain concern with permanence in the landscape, not often associated with roundhouses that are increasingly interpreted to have been in use for a few decades or a generation (Halliday 2007b). This may reveal a different attitude to the dead than in later periods in this region, with burials close to the living areas and showing a regard for the dead as part of everyday life. The use of miniature ring-gullies or barrows as markers may also be part of shared tradition in this region.

3.9.7 After the Bronze Age – post-medieval and historic remains

Subsequent to the conflagration events at Gairnhill, there follows an apparent gap in activity. No evidence for later prehistoric settlement on the Dee–Don high grounds was encountered, nor any other types of activity until the advent of more extensive farming techniques in the medieval and post-medieval periods. Rig and furrow agricultural remains were found at all three sites and are widely recorded on the Aberdeenshire Sites and Monuments Record, following the same distribution as later prehistoric domestic structures. It is not possible to define the age of these cultivation traces: they have a currency from the 9th century AD to the last few centuries. However, not all areas of excavation showed evidence of historic agriculture. At Gairnhill the large excavation area around where the Neolithic pit was recovered contained considerably more boulders than the other areas of excavation. This was also true for large swathes of Nether Beanshill where *in situ* boulders were present as well as numerous stone holes likely related to recent field clearance.

Chapter 4

Standingstones, an Upland Camp

Jürgen van Wessel

4.1 Introduction to the circumstances of discovery at Standingstones

4.1.1 At the edge of the woods – the background to the archaeological work

This chapter will discuss the results of a small excavation (formerly NL/003B; Illus 4.01) undertaken at Standingstones on the eastern edge of Kirkhill Forest, covering the section of the road line traversing the east-facing slopes of Tyrebagger Hill, overlooking Aberdeen Airport at Dyce. Although this fits within the landscape described in Chapter 3 (Don–Dee uplands), the site is of a different date and at a higher elevation; 146–147 m AOD rather than 136–139 m AOD of the roundhouses at Gairnhill.

The site aimed to explore the full extent of potential Mesolithic activity encountered during the earlier trial-trenching phase (Robertson 2014, 28). Prior to the trial trenching the site had been investigated through geophysical survey (Bartlett & Boucher 2012d, Illus 74). The environmental statement identified a number of cultural heritage sites, primarily to the north of Standingstones. The most prominent was the recumbent stone circle at Tyrebagger (ES site 134; NJ81SE 11), which lay outside the scheme.

The geophysical survey provided negative results for the area around Standingstones although the area available to survey in this upland landscape was limited owing to the surrounding forestry. The forestry also limited the amount of trial trenching undertaken in this landscape; however, on the results of the trial trenching, areas were stripped of topsoil at NL/002, NL/003A and NL/003B and investigated further.

4.1.2 Site location and extents of mitigation

The site of the Standingstones excavation was situated to the east of Kirkhill forest, approximately 300 m west of the modern Standingstones farm. The Tyrebagger recumbent stone circle is about 300 m north-east of the excavation. The excavation covered a triangular area of 1689 m², centred on NJ 85780 12950, on a south-west sloping hay field at an elevation of 143–155 m OD (Illus 4.02). It comprised a series of pits in a circular arrangement, apparently overlain by a spread contained within a hollow. Topsoil was up to 0.65 m in depth and directly overlay geological subsoil of light yellow-brown sand and gravels. A spread of sandy silt was encountered near the middle of the excavation area and, prior to excavation, appeared to be masking several cut features. Similar material was found filling a number of shallow natural hollows nearby. It is likely that this material formed a larger spread that has been latterly truncated, and so survived only in depressions.

4.2 Archaeological context

Only a limited amount of archaeological investigations had taken place along the eastern edge of Kirkhill Forest prior to the work associated with the AWPR/B-T scheme. A recent survey of this area recorded several possible hut-circles and cairns (Shepherd 2010) within the forested area approximately 100 m east of Standingstones. Other than Tyrebagger recumbent stone circle (NJ81SE 11), most of the remaining sites identified in the ES generally comprised cairns, potential cairn fields, clearance cairns, consumption dykes and land divisions. Of these, only sites at Bogenjoss 1 cairns (ES Site 136; NJ81SE 5), Bogenjoss 2 cairns (ES site 129; NJ81SE 4), and a number of consumption dykes (ES-137–139) were within the footprint of the road scheme. The cairn fields proved to have been disturbed by forestry activities and none were found to be extant when works for the AWPR/B-T began. The post-medieval field dykes that remained in the area were investigated during the construction phase of the road programme (Wilson 2017; Appendix 1.4) but are not reported further here.

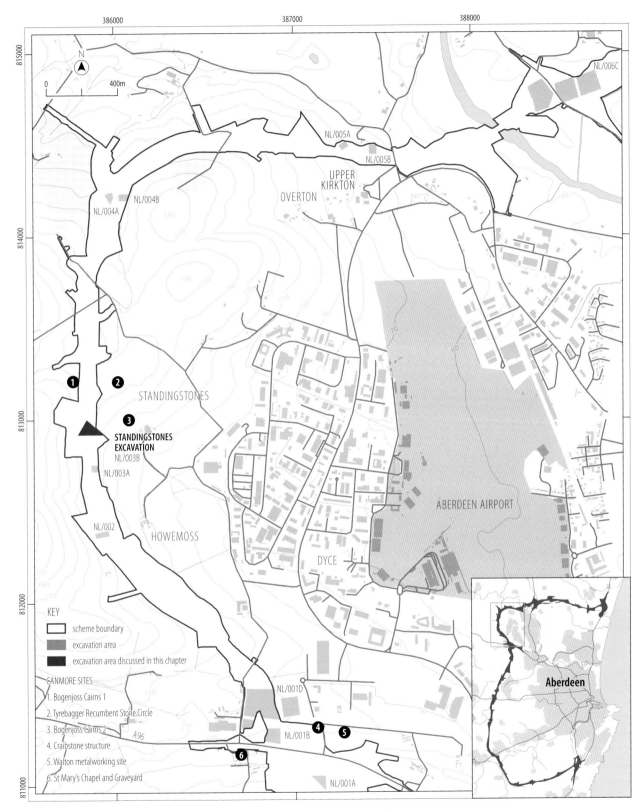

Illus 4.01 Location of site at Standingstones

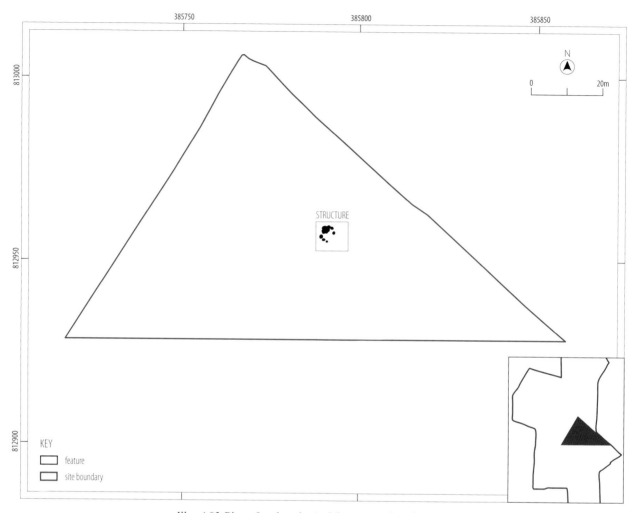

Illus 4.02 Plan of archaeological features at Standingstones

4.3 Environmental context

The Standingstones site lies on a featureless, quite steep but uniform east-facing slope (Illus 4.03), close to a geological boundary between two sequences of Aberdeen Formation meta-sediments, more clay-rich on the lower ground and coarser, sandier psammite on higher ground. The psammite outcrops immediately above the site, in Standingstones Wood. The shallow valley the archaeological site is set within was deepened slightly by a glacial meltwater stream during deglaciation (Munro 1986, fig 33). Civil engineering boreholes along the road-line around Standingstones record between 1.2 m and 1.9 m of a poorly sorted sand with cobbles over bedrock variously described as schist, gneiss and amphibolite. The many stones in the 'natural' are angular, and the deposit the pits were excavated into might be a Late Devensian solifluctial (slopewash) sediment with local stones moved only a short distance and so unabraded. This is the parent material to what today are podsols of the Counteswells Series, which by c7000 BC had, by comparison with Warren Field, become acidic. Standingstones is, however, just downslope of the pedological boundary between

Illus 4.03 General view of site after topsoil strip

peaty podsols of the Charr Series and Counteswells Series free-draining podsols. Charr Series soil cloaks the summit plateaux of the Hill of Marcus, uncultivated today because of its imperfect drainage, with a tendency to gley, which slows organic matter decay and creates today a c20 cm thick peaty A horizon (Glentworth &

Muir 1963, 118–19), and which would have been much thinner at c7000 BC. This impeded drainage is a physical reason for the location of the site.

The hillside today is probably artificially drained below this as part of an enclosure field system. A spring issues within Standingstones Farm, some 270 m due east and 25 m lower down the slope, and below the farm the soil is a poorly drained gley (Terryvale Series) because of this. The nearest flowing water lies at the crest of the rock ridge, a headwater of an unnamed stream that falls to the north-east and then east, on the north side of a shallow valley past the Tyrebagger recumbent stone circle, inset within mounded heaps of the Blairdaff Moraine Formation.

4.4 Radiocarbon results and dating

Dating of the Standingstones site is provided by a combination of radiocarbon determinations from selected features (Table 4.01; Illus 4.04), along with evidence of the flint manufacturing processes taking place. This revealed

that the site likely had a very short duration, somewhere in the first half of the seventh millennium BC, clearly placing the site in the Mesolithic.

4.5 Standingstones
4.5.1 Pits

Eight pits lay in a broad arc enclosing a space of just over 3 m diameter (Illus 4.05). The pits were roughly oval in plan and had steeply sloping or near-vertical sides, and generally had flat bases. They were generally c0.8 m long and 0.6 m wide, with the longest axis following the curve of the arc. The pits were deeper towards the north (upslope), where they were up to 0.6 m in depth, but only survived to around 0.15 m downslope. The AOD height of the bases of the features is within 0.2 m of each other, suggesting a common purpose; that they were cut into the slope to create a level base. Three of the largest pits [3B-0023], [3B-0025] and [3B-0031] were intercutting (Illus 4.06), but no stratigraphic relationship between them could be determined.

Table 4.01 Radiocarbon determinations from Standingstones

Context	Lab no	Material	Radiocarbon age BP	Calibrated age 98.4% probability
(3B-0004), fill of pit [3B-0003]	SUERC-49726	Nutshell: *Corylus avellana*	8026±38	7070–6820 cal BC
(3B-0017), fill of pit [3B-0016]	SUERC-68125	Nutshell: *Corylus avellana*	7988±29	7040–6780 cal BC
(3B-0028) basal fill of pit [3B-0025]	SUERC-57938	Nutshell: *Corylus avellana*	7985±25	7040–6780 cal BC
(3B-0026), upper fill of pit [3B-0025]	SUERC-68126	Nutshell: *Corylus avellana*	7967±30	7040–6710 cal BC
(3B-0019), spread within hollow [3B-0007], north-east quadrant	SUERC-68124	Nutshell: *Corylus avellana*	7960±29	7030–6710 cal BC
(3B-0018), spread within hollow [3B-0007], south-west quadrant	SUERC-57937	Nutshell: *Corylus avellana*	7825±30	6740–6600 cal BC

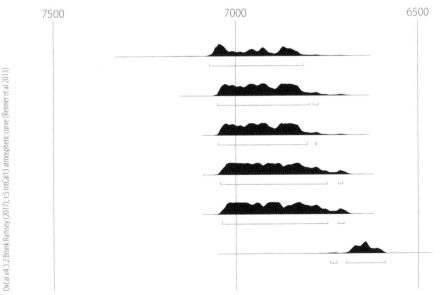

Illus 4.04 ¹⁴C graphs from Standingstones

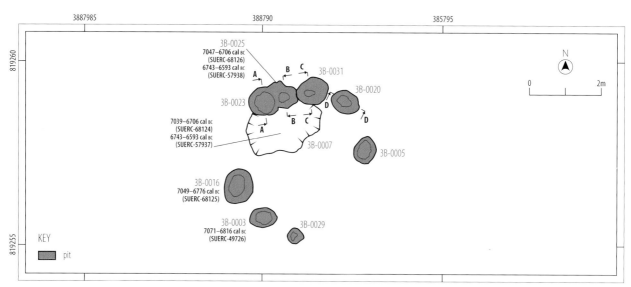

Illus 4.05 Detail plan of hollow [3B-0007] and pits

Illus 4.06 General view of intersecting pits and hollow, facing north-east

The same sequence of deposition was seen in all the pits (Illus 4.07A–D, Illus 4.08). At the base was a concentration of charcoal, mixed with small burnt stones. This was overlain by a firm mid-greyish-brown sandy silt, within which were occasional larger stones, possibly dislodged packing stones. Worked flint and burnt hazel nutshell was common throughout the fills of the pits. The two shallowest pits [3B-0003] and [3B-0005] contained only charcoal-rich material, suggesting later truncation.

Despite the presence of extensive burnt material in the bases, there was no evidence for burning or staining of the surrounding geological subsoil. The charcoal and nutshell recovered was generally unabraded and had likely not moved far from the source of burning. The pits also appeared to have been open only for a short time; no slumping or silting was visible, with the exception of pit [3B-0031] where a thin layer of redeposited geological subsoil was encountered below the charcoal.

Pit [3B-0029] was smaller than the others and had a pointed base. The fill was different, and it contained no lithics (although charcoal and nutshell were still present). It is suggested that while this feature may be contemporary, it was certainly peripheral to the activity taking place, in particular the working of flint.

Four radiocarbon determinations from fills of the pits provide a tight cluster of Mesolithic dates (Illus 4.04). The upper and lower fills of pit [3B-0025] produced dates of 7040–6710 cal BC (SUERC-68126) and 7040–6780 cal BC (SUERC-57938) respectively; this corresponds well with the date of 7070–6820 cal BC (SUERC-49726) obtained from pit [3B-0003], and another from pit [3B-0016] of 7040–6780 cal BC (SUERC-68125). This gives a broad range in the first few centuries of the seventh millennium BC when this site was in use.

The lithics recovered from the pits form 82% of the total lithic assemblage from the site and are consistent with a Mesolithic date. They are discussed in more detail in 4.7 below.

4.5.2 Hollow [3B-0007]

Hollow [3B-0007] was roughly oval in plan, with an uneven base and very gently sloping sides (Illus 4.09). It measured 1.7 m by 1.9 m in plan and was up to 0.13 m deep. It did not appear to have been deliberately created and was defined more by the presence of a burnt deposit, which may originally have extended beyond the limits of the hollow. The deposit masked the three pits immediately to the north; however, the relationship between the two categories of feature could not be confidently ascertained during excavation.

The deposit filling the hollow comprised a thin layer of compact mid-reddish-brown sandy silt, containing frequent charcoal and nutshell, and an assemblage of 470 lithic artefacts (18% of the total assemblage). There were no signs of *in situ* burning around or below the deposit but

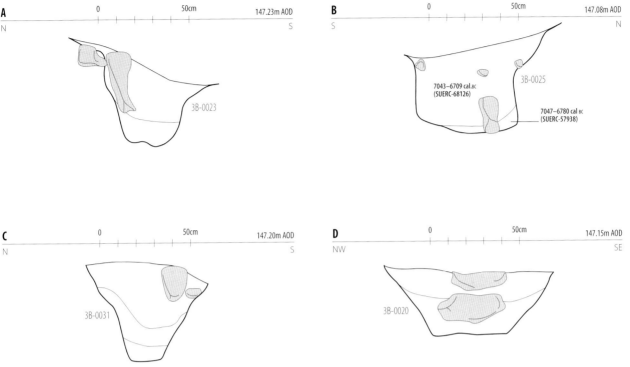

Illus 4.07A-D Section of pits [3B-0023], [3B-0025], [3B-0031], [3B-0020]

Illus 4.08 Pit [3B-0020] showing basal charcoal layer

Illus 4.09 Hollow during excavation, facing south-east

the reddish hue and presence of charcoal and burnt lithics imply that burning had taken place during its formation. It is suggested that this represents geological subsoil burnt and loosened by a hearth set above it, into which charcoal and other debris has become incorporated. It follows that the hollow is not a cut feature as such, but merely a delimiter of the extent of heat-affected subsoil.

Two radiocarbon determinations from burnt nutshell retrieved from this deposit provide dates of 7030–6710 cal BC (SUERC-68124) and 6740–6600 cal BC (SUERC-57937) provide a date range in the first half of the seventh millennium BC (Illus 4.04). The first of these dates (from the north-east quadrant of the hollow) fits well with the other dates obtained from the pits. The other date,

from the south-west quadrant, appears to be an outlier. This could represent a second distinct period of activity but, taken alongside the evidence from the lithics analysis (see 4.7 below), it seems more likely that there is only one phase of activity, somewhere between 7000 and 6700 BC.

In summary, the morphological and depositional evidence at Standingstones describes a process of pit digging centred on a small hearth (Illus 4.10). The size and shape of the pits makes it almost certain that these were used as post-holes or post supports in some fashion, although the sequence of deposits does seem unusual for this interpretation. The time span over which this activity occurs is short and is likely to represent a single or low number of visits.

4.6 Environmental synthesis

Tim Holden

Soil conditions at Standingstones were such that the only organic material to survive was through charring. Charred wood, seeds and hazel nutshell were recovered from the samples. Charcoal from the fills of pits [3B-0023] and [3B-0025] comprised small-diameter fragments (<10 mm) of hazel, bird cherry (*Prunus avium*), pomaceous fruitwood (*Sorbus* type) and small amounts of oak. Many of the fragments also showed evidence of fungal hyphae (Appendix 2.1.6). This evidence indicates the collection and burning of readily available small-diameter branches of hazel and bird cherry, some in a state of decay, as would be the case if picked from the woodland floor (eg Salisbury & Jane 1940). This is in keeping with other evidence indicating short, but possibly repeated, visits to the site. From the two pits examined in detail, there was no evidence for the use of larger diameter timbers, despite the large size

of the pits with the appearance of post-holes. Perhaps this is not surprising given the nature of the Mesolithic 'toolkit' from the site, which is dominated by microliths unsuitable for the working of sizeable timbers, although this is not to say that such tools did not exist in this period.

Rare charred weed 'seeds' were recovered from a number of features. All are common seeds of cultivated and disturbed ground and include corn spurrey (*Spergula arvensis*), cleavers (*Galium aparine*), sun spurge (*Euphorbia helioscopia*), clover (*Trifolium* sp) and small grass seeds. Unfortunately, the small number of seeds (ie never over five) makes interpretation problematic. Later material of this size can easily be introduced into deeper deposits through invertebrate activity – a single cereal grain was, for example, recovered from a Mesolithic pit at Milltimber (Chapter 2). In the case of Standingstones, it is clear that the area has been subject to later agriculture and stubble burning or manuring using domestic midden material, which could have introduced charred weed seeds into the sequence, and these are therefore of limited significance.

4.6.1 Hazel consumption and hazel nutshell

Hazel nutshell was recovered from nearly all features with up to 7.7 g of charred nutshell per litre of sediment (Illus 4.11). Most of the nutshells were broken or fragmentary, pointing to some level of processing taking place on site. The consumption of hazel nuts is considered a common activity at Mesolithic sites across Scotland, and it has been suggested that they were routinely and deliberately roasted in pits (Mithen *et al.* 2001, 228). From experiments conducted by those authors, this process can lead to as much as 25% loss through burning. This seems unsustainable and should result in the charring of large numbers of whole nuts, which are generally not recovered archaeologically.

As part of this project and in an effort to clarify some of the conventionally stated uses of hazel nuts, an

Illus 4.10 Standingstones fully excavated, facing north-west

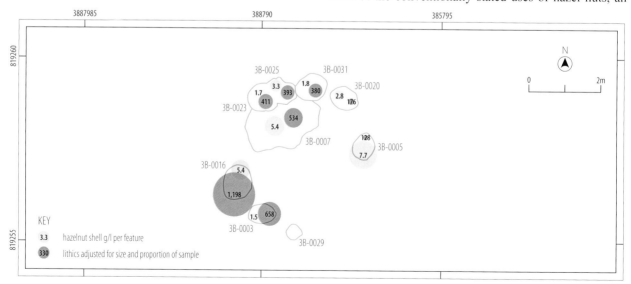

Illus 4.11 Plan showing relative distributions of charred hazelnut shell and lithics (adjusted for size and proportion of sample)

ethnographic review of their use in traditional societies was undertaken, together with other taxa having similar physical properties (Mason forthcoming; Appendix 2.1.11). Of relevance to the current project are those examples from environments analogous to those in Scotland, particularly North America, where issues of storage, processing and carrying capacity are potentially similar.

In their reviews both Mason (*ibid.*) and Bishop *et al.* (2013) discuss the issue of storage and survival of hazel nuts. Some data seem to suggest that roasting might extend storage duration, but others suggest it is in fact shortened; however, both authors note that drying rather than roasting is potentially more important to extend palatability. Also noted is that shelling significantly reduces storage life but that it improves ease of transport.

The practicalities of nut collection are touched upon, with the point made that the European species of the nuts in question, *C avellana,* is found on shrubs or trees that might reach heights of 6–12 m (Mason in prep, 6; Appendix 2.1.11), not an easily accessible resource. However, they also shed from the branches more readily than other varieties once ripe. This would mean that practices such as shaking trees to aid collection would be highly beneficial. It might also suggest a greater need for a more mobile and time-focused collection strategy, potentially ranging fairly widely to find bushes with nuts ripening at different times.

To some extent, a key result of the study is that it is difficult to be conclusive about the use of hazel nuts, given the current range of evidence; however, an over-reliance on assumptions regarding the presence of abundant charred nutshell and the significance thereof seems to have emerged. Ethnographic evidence would not support the assertion that roasting nuts is both beneficial for consumption or for storage, and roasting pits could equally have been used for other root-type foods that would have formed an important resource. Alternative explanations for the routine discovery of charred hazel nutshell in Mesolithic contexts must be prioritised. The most obvious is that after hazel nuts were shelled, the shell was simply disposed of in the hearth as it would burn readily and help fuel the fire.

The fact that in all probability hazel represented only a part of the Mesolithic diet should not be under-estimated. It would have been complemented by a broad range of plant foods, from acorns and leaves to the underground storage organs of aquatic plants (Clarke 1976; Zvelebil 1994). Remains of this type of material rarely survive in archaeological contexts in comparison with hazel nutshell (eg Mason *et al.* 2002). This disparity of survival was recognised throughout the present project and every attempt was made to identify the 'missing' plant foods by the recovery and identification of vegetative plant parts, for example. All samples assessed from these early sites were scanned for charred plant parenchyma following,

for example, Hather's (2000) recommendations for the recovery and identification of starch-rich plant tissues. The absence of any positive results, even of hazel nut kernels, reinforces the difficulty of this type of research.

4.6.2 Plant communities and their disturbance at Standingstones c7000 BC
Richard Tipping

The pollen analysis by Davies *et al.* (2009) from Pit 5 at Warren Field, Crathes (Chapter 2.2) provides a very strong analogy for Standingstones. Pit 5 at Warren Field is statistically indistinguishable in date from the Standingstones pits, the soils are and probably were similar, and they lie at the same altitude. Birch–hazel woodland covered the Dee–Don upland in the Mesolithic period, dynamic and changing through disturbance at different spatial scales, but mostly evolving by gap-phase replacement of individual trees (Chapter 2.6).

If not contaminants (and the oak charcoal retrieved suggests some contamination), the seeds of a few herbs at Standingstones suggest adventitious colonisation of disturbed and bare ground: corn spurrey (*Spergula arvensis*) produces seeds prolifically that are long lived in soil seedbanks, and is suited to the dry sandy soil at Standingstones but not to the trampling that would have accompanied intense or persistent human activities; goosegrass (*Galium aparine*) is also at home on dry soils and dispersed by clinging to people and animals; sun spurge (*Euphorbia helioscopia*) is rare today in eastern Scotland. Clover (*Trifolium* sp and probably *T. repens* from its current range) is the only perennial, living in grassland and tolerant of disturbance. None of these need imply more than their occurrence in a gap-phase, though human disturbance, not necessarily more than ephemeral or brief, is also likely in this instance. It is possible that this disturbance led to some erosion and redeposition of soil near the pits, within the spread (see 4.2 above).

Hunter-gatherers disturb landscapes and vegetation. Though this degree of disturbance has usually been thought of as small in scale (Simmons & Innes 1996a–c), there have been arguments that larger-scale ecosystem restructuring was possible, 'human niche construction' (Bishop *et al.* 2015), either inadvertently or with purpose (Serjeantson 1990; Simmons 1996; 2003, 42–43; Warren *et al.* 2014; Bishop *et al.* 2013; 2015). No new telling evidence has been forthcoming, however, to suggest that the abundance of hazel in the early Holocene woodland was in any way induced by people. Hunter-gatherers liked to eat hazel nuts and went to considerable efforts to harvest and, possibly, to store them (Mithen *et al.* 2001; Holst 2010). The presence of nutshell and evidence of fire at Standingstones is not conclusive proof of processing, and while it was probably one of the reasons the camp is here, it is far from likely that it was the sole or main reason for the location.

Table 4.02 General lithics artefact list

Debitage	No.	Cores	No.	Tools	No.
Chips	1553	Split pebbles	2	Microlith preforms	2
Flakes	357	Core rough-outs	2	Scalene triangles	9
Blades	156	Single-platform cores	16	Crescents	3
Microblades	313	Cores with two platforms at angle	1	Edge-blunted microliths	3
Indeterminate pieces	48			Backed bladelets	5
Crested pieces	5			Frags of microliths	6
–				Frags of microliths/backed bladelets	29
				Krukowski microburins	6
				Microburins	59
				Short end-scrapers	5
				End-/side-scrapers	1
				Truncated pieces	3
				Pieces w edge-retouch	7
Total debitage	2432	Total cores	21	Total tools	138
TOTAL			2591		

4.7 Materials synthesis

Torben Bjarke Ballin

The only artefactual evidence recovered from Standingstones was a substantial lithic assemblage (Appendix 2.2.12); 2591 lithic artefacts were recovered. In total, 94% of this assemblage is debitage, 1% being cores and 5% tools (Table 4.02). Please see the Glossary for an explanation of technical terms used in this analysis.

4.7.1 Raw materials – types, sources and condition

The lithic assemblage from Standingstones consists entirely of flint. Similar to the assemblage from Nethermills Farm from Banchory (Ballin 2013a), the resource includes a multitude of varieties, with the two most common being of reddish-brown and light-grey mottled type, dominated by the light grey. It seems that sites along the Don and the Dee and further south in Aberdeenshire may include less flint of the reddish-brown forms than those further north, with the border between the two groups of sites running immediately north of Aberdeen (including among others the Kingfisher site; Ballin 2008b). The bulk of flint from sites in the Scottish north-east is of high quality, as is the flint from Standingstones. Although a considerable resource, the data from the Standingstones site (along with that from Milltimber, Chapter 2) did not allow detailed understanding of the range of Mesolithic people in collecting flint nodules and pebbles.

The flint cortex suggests it was most likely collected at a local pebble source such as the beaches of Aberdeenshire, where it was washed ashore from deposits in the North

Sea (Harker 2002), with the River Don functioning as the area's main transport route for the pebbles. This is further supported by the abraded character of the cortex of the site's primary and secondary flakes and blades, which points to local procurement. The size of the intact cores and refitted burnt pebble suggests the collected pebbles had maximum dimensions of c40–70 mm.

Some 20% of the assemblage (520 pieces) had been exposed to fire, causing crazing, splitting and discolouration. The highest proportion of burnt flint came from pit [3B-0005] at the east, and the lowest from the hollow and pits [3B-0003] and [3B-0016] in the west. In all features, the basal deposits had the highest proportion of burnt pieces. It should be noted that most of the site's indeterminate pieces are burnt (94%). Burning can cause flakes and blades to shed their faces, and many of the indeterminate pieces from Standingstones are probably flakes and blades that have lost their ventral faces, making it impossible to identify them as flaked pieces.

In the vast majority of cases burning was probably accidental, but there is evidence that heat treatment was taking place to make the most of the relatively small pebbles available in Aberdeenshire. Two burnt flint pebbles found in the base of pits [3B-0023] and [3B-0025] had split owing to the application of heat and were crazed, dried out and discoloured (pink), with their abraded cortex displaying scorched, blackened areas. It is possible that attempts to improve the flaking properties of the two pebbles by heat-treating them (eg Olausson & Larsson 1982; Eriksen 1997) resulted in 'over-roasting' (as indicated by the scorch-marks) and they disintegrated.

Thirteen pieces were characterised as having a notable sheen; several others display a lighter sheen.

4.7.2 Technological summary

Generally, the assemblage appears very homogeneous, and this, in conjunction with the fact that the finds were recovered from a small number of closely situated features, with refits possible across those features, suggests that the flints were left at the location within a short space of time and by the same group of people.

The shape of the cores, together with their mostly plain surfaces, make it likely that the nodules were opened by simply splitting them across rather than detaching a primary 'opening flake'. This is supported first and foremost by the fact that it has been possible to conjoin two cores platform-to-platform, re-establishing most of the original pebble to a length of 61 mm (core rough-out CAT2428 and single-platform core CAT2448). This approach made it unnecessary to shape or adjust platforms, as the splitting of a pebble created two core preforms with immediately usable striking platforms.

As noted above, heat treatment is a possibility (Olausson & Larsson 1982; Griffiths *et al.* 1987; Eriksen 1997; Coles 2009; 2011). It is also interesting to note that many cores and flakes have shiny surfaces, which is usually considered an indicator of heat treatment (*ibid.*). Heat treatment is thought to be used to allow more blades and microblades to be detached from the small flint pebbles available (Mike Cook, American knapper, pers comm).

The cores generally seem to have received little or no core preparation before the initiation of blank production, as shown by the two core rough-outs CAT2428 and CAT2445. In both cases, blank production started with trimming of the platform edges but without forming any crests (guide ridges), and in both cases the rough-outs were abandoned shortly after commencement of production, as the cores did not perform as the knapper(s) had hoped. No platform rejuvenation was carried out, as indicated by the character of the platforms and the absence of core tablets. This is probably largely a function of the small size of the nodules and the cores.

Two sets of blanks were produced, namely squat, mainly hard-hammer flakes (357 pieces) and elongated regular soft-hammer blades/microblades (469). The fact that 40% of the flakes were produced by the application of soft percussion indicates that many flakes may be failed blades, which simply turned out slightly shorter than intended. Apart from dual-platform core CAT2439, all surviving cores are single-platform cores, and predominantly (15 of 16 pieces) neat conical microblade cores. There is little doubt that the purpose of the lithic reduction at Standingstones was to produce microblades and narrow macroblades (widths c3–11 mm), most likely for the manufacture of microliths.

The tools include two main groups, namely microliths and microlith-related implements (63 pieces, supplemented

by 59 microburins) and scrapers (six pieces). Three truncated pieces are relatively 'flimsy' expedient knives, and seven pieces with edge-retouch are probably fragments of pieces with varying functions; two of these (CAT2449, CAT2450) may, for example, be broken off scraper-edges.

The microliths are generally based on regular soft-hammer microblades or narrow macroblades. As indicated by the approximate numerical parity between microliths and microburins, at Standingstones most microliths were clearly manufactured by the application of microburin technique (using either the notch or the lamelle à cran approach). The resulting microliths were either geometric scalene or crescentic forms or simpler edge-blunted pieces, as well as Krukowski pieces, supplemented by a handful of backed bladelets.

Apart from one end-/side-scraper, all scrapers are based on robust cortical hard-hammer flakes with a convex, steep scraper-edge at one end.

4.7.3 Debitage

In total, 2432 pieces of debitage were recovered from the site (Table 4.03). The proportion of chips is high, typically a result of the consistent sieving strategy undertaken and collection of very small chips from the processed samples. Forty-eight pieces were defined as indeterminate pieces, and 94% of these mostly flat pieces are fire-crazed.

Although large numbers of flakes were recovered from Standingstones (357 pieces), the debitage is dominated by blades and microblades, totalling 513 pieces. As shown above, the industry responsible for the Standingstones lithic assemblage is clearly a microblade industry, with microblades being this industry's main, or 'target', blanks. This is demonstrated by the regular appearance of most blades/microblades, the squat nature of most flakes and the proportional use of soft percussion (Table 4.04; 68% of all definable unmodified flakes and blades).

In Illus 4.12, the width of all Standingstones' intact blades and microblades are indicated by the diagram's blue curve. This curve is neat (a statistically 'normal', or bell-shaped, distribution), indicating that the location's blades may represent a single visit to the site, or at least represent one relatively narrow chronological period. It does, however, have a fairly long 'tail' towards the diagram's right side of broad blades. It was thought that these pieces

Table 4.03 Relative composition of the debitage

Type	N	%
Chips	1553	64
Flakes	357	15
Blades	156	6
Microblades	313	13
Indeterminate pieces	48	2
Preparation flakes (all crested pieces)	5	trace
Total debitage	2432	100

Table 4.04 Applied percussion techniques: definable unmodified flakes and blades

Technique	N	%
Soft percussion	321	68
Hard percussion	83	17
Indeterminate platform technique	21	4
Platform collapse	41	9
Bipolar technique	8	2
Total	474	100

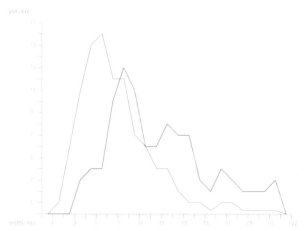

Illus 4.12 Width of all unmodified blades and microblades from Standingstones (blue); width of all cortical, hard percussion, crested and overpassed blades (orange)

could be larger specimens produced at the beginning of the site's operational schema by the application of more robust approaches, and to test this, all cortical, hard percussion, crested and overpassed blades were measured separately, forming the red curve. In summary, comparison of red and blue curves suggest that the site's broad blades are generally a form of preparation blades, and the narrower ones are intentional 'target' blanks. The former pieces have widths of c7–22 mm, and the latter c3–11 mm.

Only five crested pieces were recovered from the site, and no core rejuvenation flakes (Illus 4.13). Three of the crested pieces are broad (CAT2462, CAT2465, CAT2470) and probably relate to the initial preparation of cores, whereas two (CAT2459, CAT2468) are narrow, most likely relating to core adjustment during the reduction process.

4.7.4 Artefact types

4.7.4.1 Cores

In total, 21 cores were recovered during the excavation at Standingstones. They include the following core types: two split pebbles, two core rough-outs, 16 single-platform cores, and one core with two platforms at an angle.

Two split pebbles (CAT2440 and CAT2441–2) were recovered from the basal layers of pits [3B-0023] and [3B-0025]. CAT2441–2 is an 'exploded' core, which had disintegrated into several irregular angular bits, found in

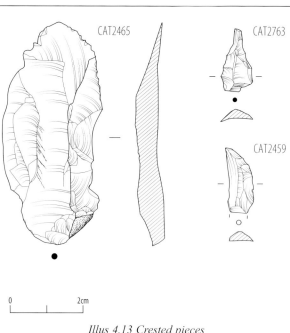

Illus 4.13 Crested pieces

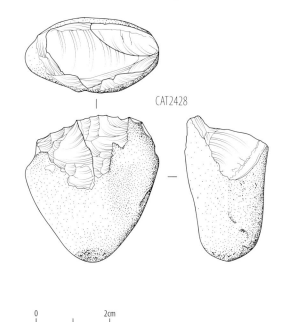

Illus 4.14 Core rough-outs

fragments spread between both pits. The original pebbles would have had sizes of c50–70 mm.

The assemblage includes two core rough-outs (Illus 4.14; CAT2428, CAT2445) of approximately the same size (Greatest Dimension, hereafter GD = 31–36 mm). CAT2428 had been used as a small hammerstone or percussor at some stage, although it is unclear if this was as the original pebble, or after abandonment of the core rough-out. A corner of the platform broke off at some point, and the surface of this fracture is distinctly 'greasy' looking, indicating that this piece may have been heat-treated. CAT2445 was part of the same pebble as CAT2428, was split along its long axis, and the surface of the irregular surface produced in this manner was subsequently used as a striking platform. For both core rough-outs, cresting was not carried out, no proper blanks were produced, and the two rough-outs were subsequently discarded.

Single-platform cores dominate the site's cores (76%), with most pieces being highly regular. These cores were clearly intended for the production of microblades and, subsequently, microliths. Fifteen of the 16 single-platform cores have been defined as regular conical specimens, whereas one (CAT2444) is an irregular flat piece.

With regard to conical cores (Illus 4.15), it was possible to refit conical core CAT2448 with rough-out CAT2445, platform-to-platform, re-establishing most of the original pebble (from the middle and upper fills of pit [3B-0031]). It was probably common practice to split pebbles into two halves and transform these halves into two single-platform cores, with the contact surfaces becoming the cores' striking platforms. No cores have any remaining whole or partial crests, suggesting that cresting may not have been commonly practised at Standingstones (as also indicated by the two rough-outs). However, the cores' apices were carefully shaped when needed (CAT2429, CAT2434, CAT2444, CAT2446), although left cortical when the apices were naturally regular (most cores). Platform-edge trimming was carried out, probably before any attempt to detach a microblade, or a series of microblades. In most cases (ten pieces), the cores' 'back-sides' were left cortical.

Three cores have what appears to be slightly scorched cortical surfaces (CAT2433, CAT2435, CAT2438), and six of the site's conical cores are crazed and have clearly been burnt, but it is not possible to determine whether this relates to heat treatment or accidentally falling into the fire. CAT2433 (Illus 4.15) is crazed, suggesting that in this case the scorching may be due to secondary firing. CAT2430 represents six conjoined parts of one burnt 'exploded' conical core.

Although some of the smallest conical cores have clearly been exhausted completely, many seem to have been abandoned owing to the development of deep step or hinge fractures (eg CAT2432), whereas a series of circular impact scars on some cores' platforms (CAT2437, CAT2448) are evidence of robust (hard-hammer) attempts to rejuvenate the cores by detaching entire flaking-fronts. These efforts were clearly unsuccessful, probably a result of these particular cores being too dense.

One core with two platforms at an angle was recovered from the site (CAT2439, Illus 4.16). This core is a fairly large piece (compared to the location's single-platform cores), measuring 42 × 40 × 37 mm. Owing to the presence of numerous internal impurities (chalk balls and fossils), this piece did not flake well, and the core was eventually abandoned.

4.7.4.2 Tools

The 138 tools (Table 4.03) include a small number of separate implement categories, such as 63 microliths and microlith-related implements, 59 microburins, six scrapers, three truncated pieces, and seven pieces with edge-retouch. With approximately nine out of ten implements belonging to the category 'microliths and microlith-related implements', this formal group clearly dominate the tools. This category embraces a number of formal types, including two microlith preforms, nine scalene triangles, three crescents, three edge-blunted microliths, five backed bladelets, 35 fragments, and six Krukowski microburins.

The evidence from Standingstones suggests that microliths were predominantly produced in two ways, namely 1) by producing a lateral notch and then breaking the microblade blank in the notch to create a microlith preform; or 2) by producing a usually shouldered linear retouch along one lateral side and then breaking the microblade blank towards the (most commonly) proximal end of the piece (called lamelles à cran). The evidence from Standingstones suggests that, at this site, only one microlith was produced from each blade or microblade blank (cf Albarello 1987).

Two microlith preforms were recovered during the excavation, namely CAT2471 and CAT2525 (Illus 4.17). The latter is a lamelle à cran with shouldered retouch along its left lateral side (16.3 × 8.1 × 2.6 mm).

The scalene triangles, crescents and edge-blunted microliths are all defined by their blank forms and dimensions as later Mesolithic pieces. The nine scalene triangles measure on average 13.5 × 3.4 × 1.9 mm, varying in length between 9.9 mm and 16 mm. Three of the scalene triangles have ancillary retouch of their longest side (CAT2534, CAT2538, CAT2590; Illus 4.17), and in two cases the original piquant triédre is identifiable, although in slightly modified form.

The assemblage includes three crescentic microliths, which are all highly regular pieces. These pieces have average dimensions of 14.6 × 3.0 × 1.5 mm, varying in length between 10.8 mm and 18.4 mm, and have their left lateral side blunted. CAT2586 (Illus 4.17) has ancillary retouch of the cutting-edge. Its left lateral side was modified by the application of sur enclume retouch.

The three intact edge-blunted microliths measure on average 12.8 × 2.9 × 1.1 mm, varying in length between 11.4 mm and 14.4 mm. They all have their retouched lateral side towards the left. The fact that edge-blunted microlith CAT2591 had its bulb of percussion removed by retouch diagonally through the bulbar area, rather than by microburin technique, also indicate that edge-blunted microliths and backed bladelets form a continuum. This is in contrast to, for example, Nethermills Farm near Banchory, where nine of 30 edge-blunted microliths had surviving microburin facets at their proximal ends, usually adjusted by very fine retouch (Ballin 2013a).

Five backed bladelets are probably functionally related to the edge-blunted microliths. However, where the latter have had their proximal ends removed by microburin technique, the backed bladelets display intact proximal

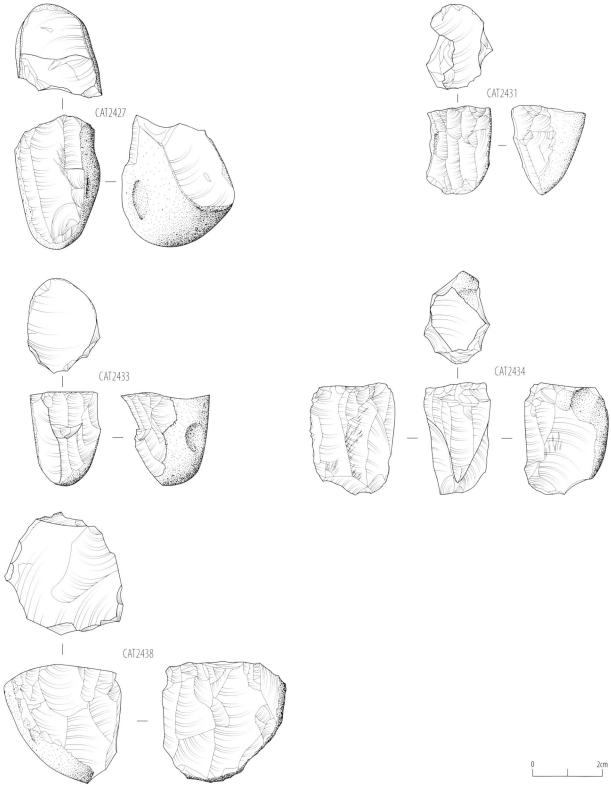

Illus 4.15 Conical cores

ends. They measure on average 14.4 × 2.8 × 1.4 mm, varying in length between 13 mm and 15.7 mm. The pieces are roughly equally distributed across backed bladelets with the blunted edge orientated towards the left (three) and towards the right (two). CAT2563 has additional fine retouch of the cutting-edge, whereas CAT2541 (Illus 4.17) has additional basal retouch at the proximal end.

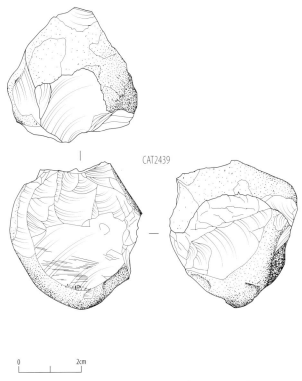

CAT2439

0   2cm

Illus 4.16 Core with two platforms at angles

Edge-modified fragments, microliths and microlith-related implements were subdivided into two groups, namely 1) fragments of microliths, and 2) fragments of microliths or backed bladelets. In total, six fragments of microliths were recovered, and 29 fragments of microliths or backed bladelets. The pieces included in these two categories have an average width of 3.3 mm; 26 of these fragments have a retouched left lateral side, seven have a retouched right lateral side, and two have bilateral retouch.

Of the Krukowski pieces from Standingstones, two (CAT2544, CAT2592; Illus 4.17) have a scalene outline, and may be pieces used as microliths without further adjustment of the microburin facet. Two (CAT2573, CAT2592) have additional retouch of the lateral side opposite the modified edge, which also supports the interpretation of the Krukowski pieces from Standingstones as microliths, rather than waste products or production failures. It seems likely that this group type as a whole includes waste material as well as production failures, and each assemblage should be considered on its own merits.

Fifty-nine microburins were recovered from Standingstones. Two fragments could not be characterised in detail, but of the remaining 57 pieces, 46 (81%) are proximal and 11 (19%) distal. The proximal forms are slightly broader than the distal forms, which is a function

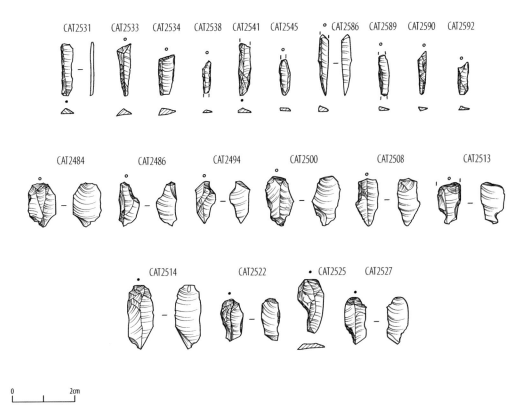

0   2cm

Illus 4.17 Microliths

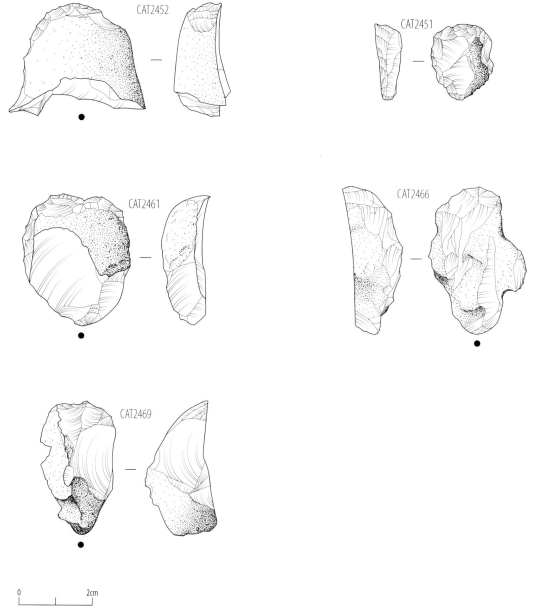

0   2cm

Illus 4.18 Scrapers

of the generally tapering shape of most blades/microblades. The average width of the proximal microburins is 6.6 mm, and that of the distal pieces 4.9 mm.

Examination of the width also indicates that the microburins include two sub-groups, and the proximal and distal specimens both include a narrow group (peak c3.1–4.5 mm) and a broad group (peak c7.1–7.5 mm). This split may indicate either the production of two functionally different groups of microliths, or a minimum of two visits to the site.

Microburins were mainly recovered from the hollow and pits [3B-0003] and [3B-0023] but only small numbers were retrieved from pit [3B-0016], which held relatively large numbers of microliths. Interestingly, all proximal microburins have the microburin notch in the left-hand

side, whereas all distal specimens (bar one) have the notch in the right-hand side. This would usually be considered indicative of the work of one knapper with one set of motoric habits; in contrast, the microliths include 83% LHS variants, 14% RHS variants and 3% with bilateral retouch, which would be more in tune with the composition of a 'normal' human population with most people being right-handed, and a proportion left-handed (cf Andersen's 1982 discussion of right- and left-handedness among people in the Danish Maglemosian).

Six scrapers were recovered from the site, namely five short end-scrapers and one end-/side-scraper (Illus 4.18). Two of the end-scrapers (CAT2452, CAT2461) are fairly large pieces, with CAT2452 being the detached proximal working-edge of an oval scraper (GD 37 mm), and

CAT2461 is an intact oval scraper with a distal working-edge (35 × 30 × 12 mm). CAT2466 and CAT2469 are two almost identical, elongated, expedient pieces with slightly irregular scraper-edges (av dim: 36 × 23 × 17 mm); the former has a dorsal crest. They are based on a dense, medium-grained form of flint, characterised by large inclusions of very soft chalk, and although they do not conjoin directly, they were almost certainly struck from the same pebble. All end-scrapers are based on either primary or secondary, hard percussion waste flakes, and they all have convex, steep scraper-edges.

End-/side-scraper CAT2451 (Illus 4.18) is based on a fairly small bipolar flake (20 × 17 × 7 mm), and it has two straight to slightly convex, steep working-edges – one at the distal end, and one along the left lateral side. Three of the scrapers have been burnt (CAT2451, CAT2452 and CAT2469) and three are clearly used specimens (CAT2451, CAT2452 and CAT2467).

Three truncated pieces appear to be expedient implements, and their modification is generally very fine. CAT2453 has a concave truncation, whereas the truncation of CAT2454 is oblique (Illus 4.19), and that of CAT2458 straight. The blanks are either small flakes (CAT2458 has

a GD of 12 mm) or small blades (CAT2454 measures 19 × 8 × 4 mm), and these pieces are most likely small knives, where one edge was rubbed slightly to blunt it and protect the user's fingers.

Seven lithic artefacts display various forms of edge retouch. Three are based on flakes, two are blades, one is a microblade, and the blank of one is indeterminate. These pieces differ considerably in shape and size (GD 12–34 mm), and it is thought that this tool group includes artefacts, or fragments of artefacts, with different functions. The modification of CAT2457 may be hafting retouch, and CAT2449 and CAT2450 may be broken off scraper-edges.

4.7.5 Distribution and on-site activities

A number of conjoining artefacts shed light on the relationship between the various features (for a discussion of refitting as an analytical tool, see Cziesla *et al.* 1990; Ballin 2000). In some cases, it was possible to refit breakage fragments of the individual flakes, blades, or microblades found within the same feature, but the following refit complexes are the most revealing (Illus 4.20):

- Refit Complex 1 (RC1: overpassed blade CAT2381 and conical microblade core CAT2427). Although these two pieces do not conjoin directly, the character of the flint strongly suggests they are from the same original pebble.
- Refit Complex 2 (RC2: split pebble CAT2441–2). Five fragments of this pebble, possibly representing unsuccessful heat treatment (see above).
- Refit Complex 3 (RC3: core rough-out CAT2428 and conical microblade core CAT2448). These two pieces conjoin platform-to-platform, re-establishing most of the original parent pebble.
- Refit Complex 4 (RC4: short end-scrapers CAT2466 and CAT2469). Although these two pieces do not conjoin directly, the character of the flint suggests with

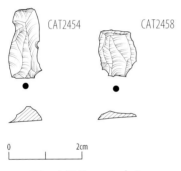

CAT2454   CAT2458

0   2cm

Illus 4.19 Truncated pieces

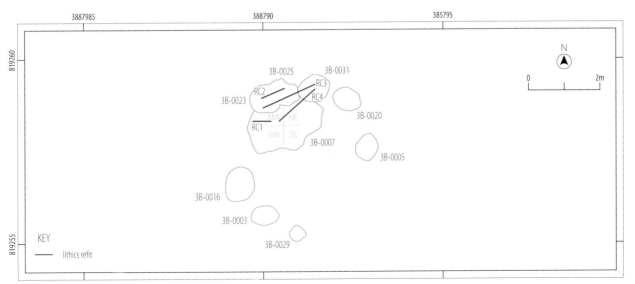

Illus 4.20 Lithics refits between features

a high degree of probability that they are from the same original pebble.

These connections suggest that the lithic artefacts from the features form a unit, and that the assemblage was deposited over a very short time-span. The stratigraphy of the site is not entirely clear, but the presence of refitting parts and of knapping debris in the basal deposits of probable post-holes, overlain by the infilled hollow, would suggest a sequence comprising some level of knapping prior to the erection of any structure, and knapping continuing once the structure was erected.

A general picture of the distribution also emerges (Illus 4.11). Most of the lithics were recovered from the hollow and pits [3B-0003], [3B-0016], [3B-0023], [3B-0025] and [3B-0031] towards the north-west, with pits [3B-0020] and [3B-0005] towards the east containing relatively few finds and [3B-0029] none. The concentration of lithic finds indicates that the hollow may represent the focus of the site, unsurprising as the probable location of a hearth, where knapping would usually take place. It may also suggest the toss zone of debitage was towards the west. Pits with lower densities are on the periphery. The complete absence of lithic material from pit [3B-0029] may be an indication it does not form part of the structure at all.

Many of the microliths are probably damaged ones that were removed from composite hunting implements and replaced at the site. The discarded microliths may to some extent have been manufactured elsewhere, whereas new microliths were produced at Standingstones, and the microburins represent on-site production. This replacement of microliths is partly demonstrated by the fact that the microliths (55 pieces) have a higher burnt ratio (16.4%) than the microburins/preforms (61 pieces) representing on-site production (9.8%). Some of the former group may have been shot into prey, for example, and so entered the hearth when they were subsequently roasted with the meat, whereas the burnt microburins were only burnt when they accidentally fell into the fireplace during production. This hypothesis may be challenged by the use-wear analysis below, which suggests that hunting is not a primary use for the microliths from Standingstones.

4.7.6 Dating

The only diagnostic artefact types recovered from the site are microliths and microburins. The microliths are all narrow-blade forms, including scalene triangles, crescents and edge-blunted pieces, and as such they suggest a date in the later Mesolithic period. Generally, the Scottish Mesolithic is subdivided chronologically into two main parts which, as a rule of thumb, define early sites as those including isosceles triangles based on broad blades (W >8 mm), and later sites including scalene triangles based on microblades (W ≤8 mm).

Technologically, the assemblage from Standingstones clearly represents a microblade industry, where microblades

and narrow macroblades were produced from conical single-platform cores. The reduction of these cores followed a strict, but relatively simple operational schema, and a number of idiosyncratic details (such as the apparent absence of initial cresting) indicate the deposition of the assemblage within a very narrow chronological band.

Technological approaches related to the one defined for Standingstones (usually involving initial cresting) characterises other parts of the later Mesolithic period, but also the earliest part of the Early Neolithic, with the main aim of these industries being the production of regular microblades and narrow macroblades (cf Garthdee Road, Aberdeen; Ballin 2016b). Within the region, similar approaches were identified in connection with the analysis of the Mesolithic site at Nethermills Farm on the Dee (527 microlith-related implements and 620 microburins; Ballin 2013a), but this site also includes a significant Early Mesolithic sub-assemblage, as well as some later finds, and it was not possible to associate any of the assemblage with any of the site's radiocarbon dates.

4.7.7 Use-wear analysis
Karen Hardy

A sample comprising 32 pieces was taken from the Standingstones lithics assemblage for analysis, on the basis of an initial rapid assessment looking for evidence of use-wear (Table 4.05).

Out of the 32 pieces selected, six pieces had no evidence of use, including a blade, a core, two microliths and two flakes. The unused artefacts were removed from future analyses except for general morphological comparisons. They have been carefully made, and were clearly intended to be used, so the assumption is that they were accidentally lost. Most of the artefacts that were used had more than one used edge, most commonly both lateral edges.

As a general point, when examining an assemblage from the perspective of use, it becomes apparent that there is a great deal of flexibility in how tools were used. There is no formality and they appear to be used in the best way possible according to their size and shape. Most usable edges are taken advantage of, meaning small artefacts with lower edge angles were used largely on lighter materials and for cutting rather than scraping. It should also be noted

Table 4.05 Artefacts examined for use-wear

Type	No
Blades/backed blades	8
Cores	1
End scrapers	3
Unretouched flakes	11
Microliths	7
Truncations	2
Total	32

that artefacts that are formal types are not necessarily used in the expected way or exclusively on the prepared edge.

Possibly the most surprising feature of the Standingstones assemblage is that there are very few artefacts with evidence for extensive use in the form of well-developed polish. It is particularly surprising that tools such as the end-scrapers have so little evidence for use. This suggests that there was ready access to abundant raw materials and that manufacturing was swift and easy.

The microliths proved the exception to this rule. In many cases their use-wear is relatively intensive, and they are likely to have been used for a relatively hard material. To gain the traction required for them to be used in this way suggests that they must have been hafted, and it is notable that pieces with possible evidence for hafting are all very small.

Though the use-wear analysis cannot suggest precise tasks or worked materials, it is important to note that many studies, both of use-wear on archaeological assemblages and of ethnographic material, have emphasised the role of lithic artefacts in the manufacture and maintenance of other tools (Hayden 1979; Hardy & Sillitoe 2003). It is generally accepted that the importance of stone tools is exaggerated because of their survival. The central role of plants in the pre-agrarian world is highlighted by Adovasio *et al.* (2007), who point out that in archaeological contexts with exceptional survival of plant materials, fibre artefacts outnumber stone tools by a factor of 20 to 1, while in anaerobic conditions 95% of all artefacts are either made of wood or fibre. Any prehistoric tool kit will no doubt have incorporated artefacts of many different materials of which stone was but a part.

4.7.7.1 Unretouched edges

The majority of used tools are unretouched flakes and blades, and formal tool types represent a tiny proportion of the overall use of an assemblage (Table 4.06).

The use-wear features were divided into 'hard' and 'soft'. The exact use cannot be determined, but they can be represented as heavy use, such as scraping or a on a medium-hard material, and soft use, such as cutting or on a soft material. The analysis demonstrates that indeed there is a clear distinction, with two major groups emerging. Simple blades formed the artefact group with the most abundant 'soft' features and least 'hard' features. Examination of flakes suggests they were used in a range of different ways.

4.7.7.2 Retouched edges

There are three used end scrapers in the assemblage and, overall, they display very little evidence of use. In every case, the edges are sharp, and the polish is either on the tips of the retouching flakes or only on the extreme edges. One piece (CAT2461) also has evidence of being used along its lower left lateral (unretouched) edge. This short edge has intensive fracturing, but the polish development is only on the tips of the fracture ends. Why these pieces have been so little used is unclear, but the small amount of evidence that is present, largely the restricted polish distribution, suggests they were used very lightly, on relatively hard materials, most probably wood.

One backed blade has evidence of heavy flake and snap fractures and parallel polish lines. Together this suggests transversal motions, probably cutting. The polish is largely edge only, suggesting a harder material. Examination of microliths from other Scottish Mesolithic and Northumbrian sites (Finlayson 1990; Finlayson & Mithen 2000; Hardy & Sillitoe 2003), confirm that their use may be as cutting implements and that they have rarely been found to have use-wear traces that link them to projectile use. This is in contrast to traditional assumptions regarding microliths, ie to be hafted and used as spears or arrows.

A single microlith from Standingstones has possible evidence for hafting. At Camas Daraich the only pieces with possible evidence for hafting are two microliths (both backed bladelets). The lack of evidence for hafting of microliths again conflicts with traditional assumptions of their use as spears or arrows. Their small size makes other methods of use functionally difficult.

4.7.7.3 Milltimber and Standingstones: a comparison

The presence of assemblages of Mesolithic date from two sites across the AWPR/B-T route allows more extensive comparisons to be made, which is useful in furthering our understanding of how lithic artefacts were used in reality.

Illustration 4.21 demonstrates that indeed there is a clear distinction, with two major groups emerging. The

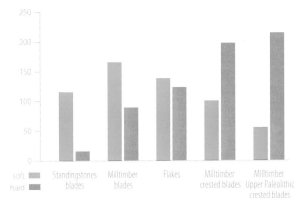

Illus 4.21 Comparison of use-wear at Milltimber and Standingstones

Table 4.06 Unretouched edges

Type	No
Blades	9
Microliths	5
Flake	14
Truncations	2
Total	30

artefacts that are 'softest' are the blades, and blades from Standingstones are shown to have the most abundant 'soft' features and least 'hard' features. These are followed by the blades from Milltimber, which are also predominantly 'soft' though with a slightly higher number of hard features. Flakes are roughly equally split between soft and hard. Crested blades have strong 'hard' features and fewer 'soft' features while Upper Palaeolithic blades are almost entirely 'hard'.

The retouched artefacts were considered separately, to determine whether there are any use-wear features that suggest these might have been used differently from the unretouched artefacts. There is, once again, a clear separation between the groups' edge-retouched pieces and truncated pieces, which have a greater proportion of 'soft' use-wear traces, while the blade scraper and the core fall into the 'hard' category. Size and edge angle once again correlate well with these groupings and shape does not. It should be remembered that these groups are very small and, in the case of the core and the blade scraper, represent only one artefact each.

Taking all the features together, for both the unretouched and retouched artefacts, two clear clusters emerge. The first cluster comprises blades, edge-retouched pieces, serrations and truncated pieces. These all have a predominance of 'soft' features, are all relatively small artefacts with relatively small edge angles. This group represents pieces that were most likely used for cutting soft materials, such as plant matter, and activities such as skinning animals. The second cluster comprises crested blades and large retouched pieces with wide edge angles. These pieces have edge wear correlated with heavy use or use on hard materials. They were more likely to have been used in a scraping motion or in cutting hard materials such as wood or bone.

4.7.8 Discussion of lithic assemblage
The typo-technological repertoire of Standingstones is exceptionally limited, being heavily dominated by knapping debris related to the production of microblades and narrow macroblades, numerous microburins from the production of scalene, crescentic and edge-blunted microliths, and a small number of scrapers and expedient truncated pieces. In comparison, the assemblage from the sturdy and probably more sedentary Howick house (Waddington & Pedersen 2007, 81) includes many more scrapers in relation to the microliths than Standingstones (microlith: scraper ratio of 72:28 and 91:09, respectively).

The dense concentration and homogeneous nature of the lithic assemblage makes it likely these pieces were deposited at Standingstones by the same group of people in a short space of time. There may be a minimum of two knappers active, as attributes belonging to both right- and left-handed people are present.

Microliths are generally perceived as having been produced as tips and edges/barbs in composite hunting gear (hundreds of slotted bone points with *in situ* inserts have been recovered from southern Scandinavia and the Baltic region; eg Lidén 1942), and the main activity taking place could have been the production of microblades and new microliths, with the intention of replacing damaged microliths from used hunting equipment. The small number of scrapers and truncated pieces may represent either the processing of prey or subsistence-related activities. However, caution should accompany any interpretation of tool types being used in only one fashion – the use-wear analysis shows that many pieces with sharp edges would have been used as expedient tools, and there is limited evidence of hafting such microliths. Further detailed use-wear analysis on similar assemblages in the future will assist in understanding the specific use of microliths.

Although the microliths may have been intended as inserts in composite bone tools, some of the pieces recovered from Standingstones are exceptionally small (the smallest intact scalene triangle CAT2538 measures 9.9 × 2.4 × 2.2 mm). It should be considered whether such pieces may have been used in a slightly different way, as a correspondingly small shaft would have been needed to insert these into. In terms of the production of microliths, at Standingstones, as well as Nethermills Farm 25 km towards the south-west (Ballin 2013a), microburin technique was clearly the standard approach (both assemblages are characterised by approximate numerical parity between microliths and microburins), although small numbers were produced in different ways. The reason why some Mesolithic assemblages from Scotland are almost devoid of microburins may be that, while processing of the finds from Standingstones and Nethermills included inspection of all chips with a magnifying glass (8×), allowing the minuscule microburins (some as small as GD = 2 mm) to be identified; in other assemblages (particularly from older excavations) some microburins may still hide among the chips.

The presence of burnt flint pebbles and pieces with scorched cortex and shiny surfaces points to the use of heat-treatment, probably to increase the yield of microblades from the small nodules available along the Aberdeenshire North Sea shores.

In the larger Scottish perspective, heat treatment of lithic raw materials is a phenomenon that deserves greater consideration. Although certain evidence of heat treatment in Scottish prehistory has not yet been made available, it is highly likely that it took place. Roasting of lithic raw material was undertaken for a number of reasons; among others, to increase the yield of blades and microblades from small pebbles, to allow the detachment of thinner flakes during bifacial production, and to improve the flaking properties of coarse or flawed lithic raw materials (Olausson & Larsson 1982; Griffiths *et al.* 1987; Eriksen 1997; Coles 2009; 2011). In some parts of Scotland only small pebbles or coarse/flawed raw materials were available, and heat treatment would have been an attractive option in some places and at some points in time. We should begin looking for the evidence.

The lithic assemblage from Standingstones represents a form of analytical baseline for the investigation of more complex sites, or palimpsests. To understand and 'unlock' the more complex sites and their assemblages, it is necessary to know how assemblages from single-occupation sites appear (also see Ballin 2013b), and an attempt has been made above to gain an understanding of Standingstones through attribute analysis of its lithic assemblage. Basically, simple diagrammatical and tabular representations indicate short-term single-occupation sites. In terms of 'unlocking' and gaining an understanding of the larger Milltimber assemblage (Chapter 2), the approaches applied to the analysis of Standingstones were very helpful.

4.8 Discussion

The above analysis has generated a list of specific activities that we can be confident were undertaken at Standingstones: pit digging, use of a hearth, microlith manufacture and (to some extent), use of hazel nuts as a resource. There are other activities implied: deliberate selection of the site as an attractive spot, probable provision of shelter, and gathering of firewood and food, whether through collection of nuts, berries and tubers or through actively hunting or trapping animals. The reasons for the size of the pits present at the site and the sequence of deposition within them is more ambiguous; however, there seems little doubt they are directly related to the other activities taking place.

4.8.1 Structure or shelter?

The layout of the arc of pits quickly leads to the consideration of structures. The last decade has revealed increasing numbers of early round or oval buildings. Wickham-Jones (2004) describes evidence for at least 23 Mesolithic buildings or shelters in Scotland, and several significant additional discoveries can be added to that list, including Howick, Northumberland (Waddington *et al.* 2003; Waddington 2007); East Barns, East Lothian (Gooder 2007); and two separate structures at Echline Fields, Fife (Robertson *et al.* 2013). The structures that have received the most attention (or perhaps, publicity) are those that form definite structures, however temporary, with post- or stake-holes, often lying within a fairly well-defined hollow. However, not all of those discussed by Wickham-Jones are such regular structures. Around half are circles or part-circles in plan, most feature a hearth and other occupation deposits filling a shallow depression. The definition of post-holes or structural elements within these arrangements is far from certain.

The arrangement of the pits at Standingstones matches well with the layout of sites such as Fife Ness, Fife (Wickham-Jones & Dalland 1998) and Structure 519 at Echline Fields (Robertson *et al.* 2013), in terms of both size and layout (Illus 4.22). At both these sites, the arrangement was interpreted as being representative of the location of uprights.

The pits at Standingstones appear to have been cut to provide a level base into the gentle south-west-facing slope; with the better preserved (upslope) pits surviving to a greater depth than those downslope, but all having a base around the same level AOD.

The plan of the pits suggests a structural origin. However, this interpretation is not without problems, primarily with the sequence of deposits within each feature, but also with the size of the features in comparison to the presumed sizes of timbers available and duration of occupation. The basal deposit of charcoal-rich material, present in every single one of the pits, suggests the pits were lying open and the material was placed or washed in, which does not fit with the concept of them supporting upright timbers.

The diameter and depth of the features is also troublesome; not far off 1 m in diameter and as much as 0.6 m in depth. This is in comparison to the pits of around 0.4 m diameter and 0.3 m depth at Fife Ness (Wickham-Jones & Dalland 1998) or those of a similar size or smaller at Echline Fields (Robertson *et al.* 2013, 81). Without the presence of clear post-pipes, it is merely speculation to suggest the size of timbers that might be present, but the large holes at Standingstones could lead the excavator to assume timbers of equally large size (eg half a metre or similar). None of this is in keeping with a small, lightweight tent or windbreak-like structure proposed for the comparator sites.

There would certainly have been some trees growing in the broader vicinity that could reach reasonable diameters. Equally, it has been shown that antler mattocks would be capable of chopping birch of a reasonable size (Saville 2004). This, combined with the use of fire to weaken the base of trees for ease of chopping down and removal of branches, or use of wind-blown trees, means it is not impossible that the structure was larger and sturdier than the Fife and Queensferry examples.

Without further evidence it is difficult to say conclusively that the pit arrangement is a structure; however, this was the preferred interpretation of the excavator. Other possible interpretations were considered (and generally discarded) in writing this publication. The most likely would have to involve the use or deposition of some form or range of organic material that has not survived down the years. It is easy to forget that flint, while providing important evidence of the materials and ultimately tools available to Mesolithic peoples, is likely to be only a tiny proportion of the range of resources available. Baskets made of plant material, wooden objects, bone tools and other items would routinely have been used and perhaps some organic material was present here that would clarify the function.

4.8.2 Microlith manufacture and use

The lithic assemblage from Standingstones is small but significant. The secure context, extensive sampling and careful identification of microburins and other small fragments gives a high degree of confidence in the results of the analysis.

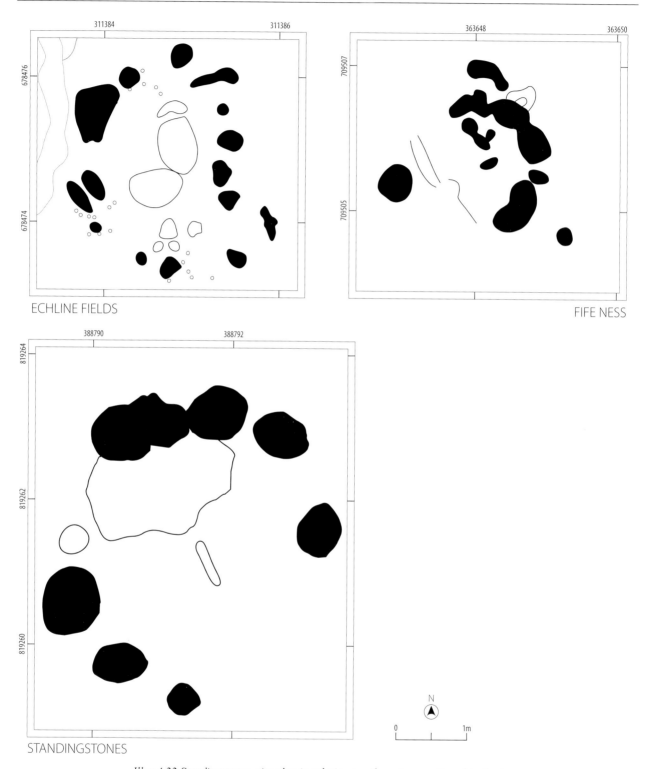

Illus 4.22 Standingstones, site plan in relation to other sites mentioned in the text

This describes a very homogeneous assemblage and suggests that it was created by one group of people, possibly as few as two individuals, in a very short period of time. The knappers were experienced, demonstrated by the care with which the tools were crafted and potentially the understanding of heat-treatment to improve yield. The incorporation of lithic material into the pits suggests this activity took place both before and after the erection of any structure.

At least some of the new microliths could have been used to replace worn ones hafted in bone or wooden hunting equipment. Indeed, there is the suggestion that some of the burnt microliths had become lodged in prey and became roasted with the cooking of the meat, much like lead shot. Hunting of specific prey is a plausible reason to leave the coastal areas and river valleys. It is noted in the analyses above that hunting may not be the main use of such microliths, and here we have little evidence in terms of use-wear on the artefacts themselves. It may still be reasonable to expect that *some* of the assemblage was used for hunting. The few scrapers recovered would be appropriate for the skinning of killed animals, or similar tasks – although the very limited evidence for actual use indicates that they may also have been used on wood. The higher proportion of scrapers found at Howick (Waddington & Pedersen 2007, 81) is interesting as that site is considered sturdier and probably longer-lived.

Sands of Forvie provides an alternative comparator: a coastal site in Aberdeenshire where there is evidence for the manufacture of a range of tools unlikely to be used in the same location (Warren 2005, 102). This suggests a 'settled' system of manufacturing, close to flint resources and with a degree of planning for anticipated activity. The assemblage from Standingstones gives more the impression of 'running repairs' or 'on demand' creation for the activities specific to the locale. Interestingly, the level of skill in lithic manufacture does not seem to differ greatly between the sites. It must also be noted that the evidence from use-wear indicates that many of the debitage pieces were also being used in some fashion as expedient tools.

4.8.3 Hearths, hazelnuts and hunting/gathering of resources

A hearth is suggested by localised deposits of charcoal and burnt sand, roasted hazel nutshell and flint, and a gentle hollow containing more burnt sand that probably indicates the position of the fire itself. The fact that the occupants appear to have been mostly burning small sticks and branches indicates they would have been collecting them from the woodland floor. As well as providing warmth and a means to cook food, the hearth may have been used for the heat treatment of flint pebbles to improve the yields during microlith production (Olausson & Larsson 1982; Griffiths *et al.* 1987; Eriksen 1997; Coles 2009; 2011). This seems to have achieved mixed success, as there are at least two examples of split or exploded pebbles that may have been over-heated.

A further potential use for the fire is for hazelnut roasting. However, some have questioned both the rationale for roasting and the archaeological features associated with the process, and alternatives are also suggested (Cunningham 2011, 140; Mithen & Finlay 2000, 435; Bishop *et al.* 2013; Lopez-Doriga 2013). Mason points out that roasting of hazelnuts is a common feature of historic European cookery but the ethnographic record from North America (Mason forthcoming) gives very few indications of the cooking of hazelnuts *in situ*ations likely to be analogous with Mesolithic Europe. The majority of examples simply suggest they were eaten, sometimes after drying and storing. In conclusion, Mason suggests that the

ethnographic data and studies of the storability of shelled and roasted nuts make interpretations based on 'roasting' open to question. There is no evidence from this site that the pits at Standingstones, the most significant features, had anything to do with the processing of hazel nuts. The simplest explanation for the quantities of charred hazel shell is that they were simply burnt on the settlement hearths as a complementary and readily available fuel; a by-product of food production.

Hunting has been proposed as one of the possible activities represented at the site, and it seems certain that in some part the lithic manufacture must relate to repair of the typical tools of the trade – composite spears and arrows formed of numerous microliths. However, the use-wear analysis has highlighted the problem with such simplistic interpretations (that microliths = hunting), and it is undoubtedly the case that activities were more complex. The presence of some burnt lithic tools does permit the possibility that they were lodged in an animal being cooked on a fire, but equally, they could be the result of accidental loss.

Understandably, excavation reports focus on the evidence that is present; what can be said with confidence. However, it is also important to remember that other actions must also have taken place, less visible to us now. The 'soft' actions that dominate at Standingstones could include cutting up plant material, including below-ground tubers or above-ground plants such as nettles or other leaves, which would have formed at least some part of the Mesolithic diet (Mears & Hillman 2007, 105–09). Use-wear analysis at an upland site in the Cairngorms has revealed activities such as scraping hides, cutting up animals, and cutting a variety of plants. Only two out of 12 artefacts analysed appear to have been used as projectiles (Graeme Warren, pers comm). At Standingstones, other resources such as birds' eggs, berries, specific types of vine/leaves may all have formed part of the overall mix. To call this site purely a hunting camp is simplistic and probably incorrect.

4.8.4 Site selection and the people of Standingstones

The relatively upland location of Standingstones does not seem to be typical for the Mesolithic period, but may be compared to sites such as Daer Valley Site 84 in South Lanarkshire (Ward 2005; Wright nd) or Caochanan Ruadha in the Cairngorms (not yet published; Graeme Warren pers comm), although both sites lie at a considerably higher elevation than Standingstones. There are no obvious topographical reasons for the specific location of the site – good views to the south and east would easily be obscured with the lightest tree cover. Resources such as flint would have come from the coast, and it is likely that hazelnuts were widely available along the river valleys. Perhaps the location was directed by the presence of some other resource for which we have no evidence; either game trails similar to the site at Milltimber (Chapter 2), or the location of a particularly fruitful patch of tubers

Illus 4.23 Artist's impression of Mesolithic people setting up camp at Standingstones. Erecting a shelter, collecting fuel and setting a fire, tool repair and flint knapping were all activities taking place at the site

or berries. Broadly, the location of the site indicates that groups in the Mesolithic were ranging from the valley floors (Milltimber on the River Dee) up into the higher ground (Standingstones) and even far into the hills and mountains. The short-lived nature of the site indicates that the movement around these locations was probably fairly regular, speedy, and would probably be dictated by the duration of availability of specific resources.

It is useful to consider what minimum equipment and resources would result in the remains found during the excavation, either from direct evidence, or through inference. This might include: a digging stick or antler mattock for site clearance and pit digging (and possibly

timber preparation); some form of shelter or tent; flint pebbles and a small toolkit for knapping; resin for hafting; some means of starting a fire including dry kindling; hazelnuts (and most likely other gathered food); hunting equipment (arrows or spears); and food preparation tools (scrapers/knives). Although we do not have direct evidence of antler mattocks, resin or any of the other food that might have been gathered, or of any animals that may have been hunted and were being processed here, it seems entirely reasonable to assume these were present.

With this range of activities and equipment, the site seems to represent a small handful of individuals, maybe between 3 and 5 people, rather than a larger group and wider settlement encampment (Illus 4.23). At the East Barns structure in East Lothian, it has been suggested that it may have been suitable for up to 6 people (Wickham-Jones 2004). This was undoubtedly a more substantial construction than that at Standingstones. The area of the structure is c14.5 m², and some comparative models suggest hunter-gatherer buildings may have an average area of between 5–7 m² per person (Belfer-Cohen & Goring-Morris 2013, 553), although it should be noted that this is specifically in the context of the consideration of 'base-camp hamlets' versus 'hunting camps' within the periphery or in more upland zones. For Standingstones, this would point to 2–3 individuals.

The evidence also hints at some level of spatial arrangement of activities within the structure. The general distribution of lithics against hazel nutshell highlights the fact that although the hearth and resulting hollow might be the focus, the front of the shelter was where the debris ended up, with lithics seemingly on one side and nutshell on the other.

4.8.5 Standingstones in context

A broad picture of the nature of activity at Standingstones has emerged. Wickham-Jones (2004, 241) discusses how our relatively limited dataset of Mesolithic structures is insufficient basis for generating typologies, and individual site interpretations are still the most important aspect of these sites. In the case of Standingstones, it is a short-lived camp, probably used for a variety of activities (including but not restricted to hunting), for which a trip uphill and away from the rivers was necessary.

The site adds to the growing body of sites with possible structural remains of houses or shelters, which at present can be subdivided into three groups, namely: 1) sturdy post-built houses of a semi-permanent nature (eg, Howick, Northumberland, Waddington 2007; East Barns, East Lothian, Gooder 2007; Echline Fields, Fife, Robertson *et al.* 2013); 2) relatively 'flimsy' post- or stake-built structures, which have been interpreted as temporary shelters or wind-breaks (eg the present site; Fife Ness, Fife, Wickham-Jones & Dalland 1998; Garvald Burn, Scottish Borders, Ballin & Barrowman 2015); and 3) potential dwellings or shelters surviving as hollows or turf-banked structures and which may or may not have been supported by posts or stakes (eg, Staosnaig, Colonsay, Mithen *et al.* 2000; Littlehill Bridge, South Ayrshire, Macgregor *et al.* 1994; Glentaggart, South Lanarkshire, Ballin & Johnson 2005). The latter group may include the poorly preserved remains of structures belonging to the former two categories. For a more detailed discussion of Mesolithic houses and dwellings in Scotland, see Robertson *et al.* (2013).

Possibly the best comparative material for Standingstones and its assemblage is Fife Ness (Wickham-Jones & Dalland

1998), which closely resembles the present site on a number of points. In terms of chronology, the two sites both date to the Mesolithic period, with the occupation of Fife Ness taking place several centuries earlier (7680–7080 cal BC [AA-25202–25215]; Waddington *et al.* 2007, table 15.1) than that of Standingstones (7036–6614 cal BC). The sites are both associated with a semi-circular setting of pits or post-holes, possibly relating to slight structures or shelters/wind-breaks with diameters of a few metres (Illus 4.22; also see Wickham-Jones & Dalland 1998, Illus 2). Both assemblages are relatively small, with that from Fife Ness numbering 1518 pieces and that from Standingstones 2591 pieces. Most of the pieces are chips from the production of microblades, some of which were subsequently transformed into microliths. Both assemblages also include some scrapers and informal cutting implements (pieces with informal retouch, or blades and flakes used without modification). It is presently uncertain whether the dominance of the Fife Ness microliths by crescents and the dominance at Standingstones of scalene triangles relate to chronology, function or personal or regional preferences. Further discovery and excavation of sites within the two regions will assist in clarifying these issues.

An important difference between the two is the coastal location of Fife Ness as opposed to the upland location of Standingstones, c12km from the coast and several kilometres from the River Don. Although the on-site activities at both locations involved the production of microblades, and subsequently microliths, the focus may have been on different prey. At Fife Ness, sea birds or migrating birds are the likely target, whereas at Standingstones this is less convincing.

The site at Standingstones offers a valuable contribution to our knowledge of the Mesolithic of Scotland and, in particular, eastern Scotland. It remains unusual to find such small, upland sites of this date, where lithic assemblages are neatly matched to negative features and other signs of specific activity, especially where the specific location cannot be tied to any currently visible landscape or resource factors. However, the odds are improving. Besides Standingstones, many more of the most interesting recent Mesolithic discoveries have been found through (initially) un-targeted developer-funded archaeological work, including East Barns, Fife Ness, Echline Fields and Littlehill Bridge. All are a direct product of the somewhat 'steamroller' approach of large programmes of trial trenching or monitoring, where areas are not targeted or ignored due to the lack of known sites in the vicinity. The importance of these types of scheme are discussed in more detail in Chapter 7, but it is undoubtedly the case that this approach was key in identifying a single example of a type of site that must have been present in their thousands across the northern part of this island in the Mesolithic.

Chapter 5

Goval: Intermittent Settlement Activity on the Banks of the Don

Jürgen van Wessel

5.1 Introduction to the circumstances of discovery at Goval

5.1.1 Background to the archaeological works

This chapter will discuss the results of the mitigation excavation at Goval (Illus 5.01), covering the section of the road line between the north bank of the River Don and the A947 Dyce-Old Meldrum road. This section traverses the southern flank of the Hill of Goval, an area of undulating rough pasture overlooked by Goval Farm.

The ES (Jacobs UK 2007) identified several cultural heritage sites in the area of Goval, some of which were located within the road corridor (see 5.2 below). The geophysical survey identified two clusters of potential archaeological anomalies (Bartlett & Boucher 2012d). These were targeted during the trial trenching, which revealed several features of archaeological interest (Robertson 2014). From this evidence, four mitigation areas (NL/006A-D) were investigated, covering a total area of around 4.2 ha (van Wessel 2015; Appendix 1.1). As part of the same programme of mitigation work, an orthostat just to the east of the A947 was also investigated but was concluded to be of modern origin (Site NL/014; *ibid*, 41).

5.1.2 Site locations and extent of mitigation

Areas NL/006A and NL/006B contained significant archaeological remains and were subject to further investigation and analysis and are discussed in detail below. The features identified in area NL/006C were found to relate to post-medieval field clearance (van Wessel 2015, 51–2) and did not warrant further analysis. At NL/006D a localised colluvial (hillwash) deposit contained a number of undiagnostic flint chips and fragments of coarseware that offered little scope for interpretation but demonstrated broader prehistoric activity in the area (*ibid*, 40–1). No further work was undertaken on NL/006C or NL/006D and they are not discussed further in this chapter.

Area NL/006A covered 16,700 m² centred on NJ 8832 1477, at 38–43 m OD. It was irregular in plan, having been extended to the south-west to expose the full extent of activity, and contracted to the north-west to avoid disturbing a known badger sett. The archaeology identified in the south-west corner extended beyond the limit of the land made available for the AWPR/B-T scheme. Area NL/006B was broadly rectangular, with a small extension to the north to expose the full extent of activity. The excavation covered 11,327 m² centred on NJ 8846 1480 at 39–44 m OD.

The topsoil across both areas was between 0.3 m and 0.85 m thick, being deepest at the base of a significant slope to the south-west of area NL/006A. Below the topsoil in this area, a deposit of loose dark brownish-black silty sand up to 0.2 m thick was observed across the southern third of the site, although it was patchy and most likely heavily truncated by ploughing. This was the base of a remnant topsoil, and during stripping charcoal-rich features were visible, cut through this deposit. In NL/006B a peaty layer up to 0.2 m thick had formed in parts below the topsoil, concentrated in the low-lying central part of the area. The geological subsoil consisted mainly of sands with a substantial band of stony gravel aligned north-west to south-east across the site, and in general becoming more gravel rich to the north.

Eighty-four cut features and four spreads were recorded across both areas, with NL/006A having the greater concentration. Prehistoric activity is represented primarily by several isolated Neolithic pits, the remains of a Middle Bronze Age roundhouse, a second roundhouse, metalworking furnace and a grain-drying kiln of Middle Iron Age date. Four features were recorded in area NL/006B, comprising a curvilinear gully dated to the Early Historic period, and three undated pits containing residual prehistoric material. Evidence of medieval/post-medieval activity comprised a system of rig and furrow cultivation and several

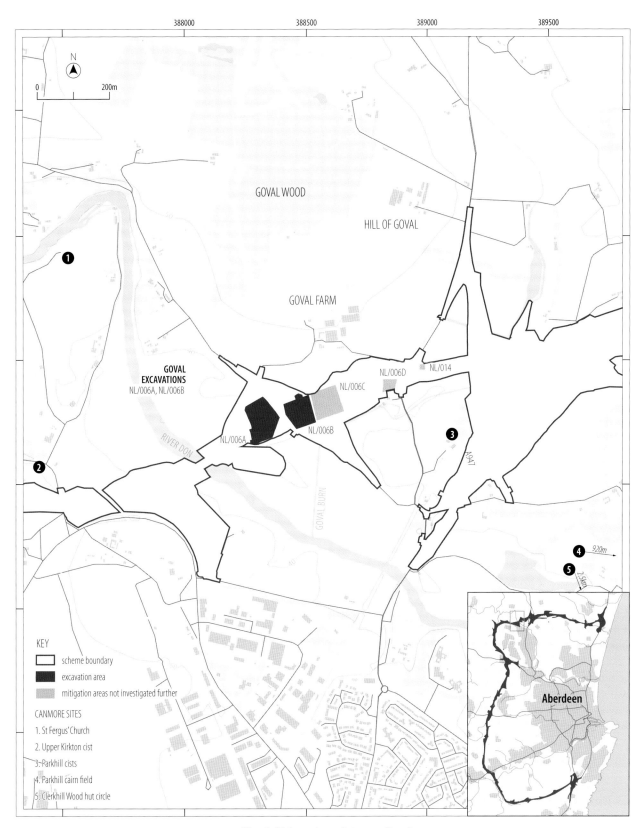

Illus 5.01 Location of sites at Goval

rectilinear features that may be contemporary. These later period features are not discussed in detail below, although the significance of this landscape in the more recent past is discussed in more detail in Chapter 7. Ten features could not be confidently assigned to either prehistoric or later activity.

5.2 Archaeological context and past settlement patterns

The ES (Jacobs UK 2007) identified eighteen sites in the immediate area. Known prehistoric remains from the area around Goval are few and are limited to antiquarian discoveries. Two cists, both including beakers, were found to the east of Goval at Parkhill (NJ81SE 13) between 1867 and 1881. To the south of the River Don at Upper Kirkton, an earthenware urn containing ashes was recovered in 1853 (NJ81SE 1). The remainder of the identified sites from the ES consist of relatively recent activity primarily related to 19th and 20th-century quarrying, railway and military emplacements, all located to the north side of the Don. To the south of the river the remains of the Aberdeenshire Canal were also identified.

Further to the north and east of Goval the low number of sites listed in the National Record of the Historic Environment (NRHE) suggests human activities to have been no more prominent than along the road-line. Neolithic monuments are absent. Bronze Age funerary monuments are very few and recorded only on well-drained soils. The cairn field at East Lodge, Parkhill (NJ91SW 38) is on glaciofluvial gravel, as is the Stoneyhill Wood hut circle (NJ91SW 43). The gravel occurs as a thin spread between large expanses of till, on which stands the Clarkhill Wood hut circle (NJ91SW 58). Such dry soils attracted farmers, but they also favour the preservation of cropmarks, and yet few cropmarked sites have been found (Halliday 2007a, fig 6.15). Even the Early Historic symbol stones, such as at St. Fergus Church (NJ81NE 8) on the southern bank of the Don, line the southern side of the River Don from St. Fergus up-river to Inverurie, and later medieval parish boundaries follow the line of the Don from St. Fergus to Kintore. From this apparent lack of human activity on the northern side of the river it seems clear that this area has long been seen as separate from the Dee–Don upland. Dating from the more recent past, a late 19th-century pumping station and lade at Parkhill was recorded as an early example of the use of metal-reinforced concrete in Scotland (van Wessel 2012a, 16).

5.3 Environmental context

Richard Tipping

The Hill of Goval is dry, with free-draining podsols on sandy till and a series of glaciofluvial gravel terraces, each narrow and most with no morphological expression today. The excavated slope faces south, which at this latitude is important for agricultural soils (O'Dell & Walton 1962). The concentration of archaeological remains discovered lie on the lowest and youngest fragment of Lochton Formation glaciofluvial gravel, a clearly delineated terrace, maybe 8 m above the present surface of the River Don. Whether the setting on well-drained gravel was intentional is unclear: the other excavated areas to the east on this hillside are on till, but no less sandy. The soil at the eastern area of Goval is Corby Series podsol, which has a mean thickness of 1.1 m in typical profiles (Glentworth & Muir 1963, table 3), suggesting some truncation of them in excavated areas (Illus 5.02). The multi-period occupancy of this hillside might surprise, given the meagre archaeological evidence for settlement elsewhere in this landscape but the Hill of Goval is among the best, of generally poor, agricultural land north and east of the Don. It is also located on the favoured south-facing sunny dry slope of the Don valley. This impression of predominantly marginal land to the north and east side of the river is, however, built on fragmentary information. With so little detailed archaeological work undertaken in this region, there is no benchmark for 'normal' distributions and densities of human activity or patterns of survival in any period.

5.4 Radiocarbon results and dating

Eight samples were submitted for AMS dating from Goval – one from pottery residue and seven from charcoal. The results are presented in Table 5.01 and Illus 5.03. Where possible, charcoal from short-lived species or small branch wood was used to date features, to achieve as precise a date-range as possible. Proxy dating for the Neolithic pits was provided by pottery typology (see 5.11.2 below) and lithics (see 5.11.3 below). Iron Age radiocarbon dates from the roundhouse, furnace and kiln are corroborated by the relative abundance of hulled barley in those features, a common crop in the Iron Age. Although not corroborated by radiocarbon, lithic evidence indicative of possible Mesolithic or Early Neolithic activity was also recovered.

The dates illustrate very clearly the extensive time-span over which Goval attracted people. Importantly, they also highlight the episodic nature of that activity – there is no indication of long-term or continual occupation. As will be shown below, the duration of each occupation is also likely to have been short – at most the life-span of a single roundhouse.

5.5 Neolithic pits

Four pits containing diagnostic Neolithic material were encountered in area NL/006A (Illus 5.04). Potentially the earliest was an isolated pit [6A-0006] containing a substantial quantity of modified Carinated Bowl, dated typologically to the Early-Middle Neolithic. The fill of the pit also contained hazel nutshell, and flint chips indicative of knapping. The purpose of the pit is unclear although

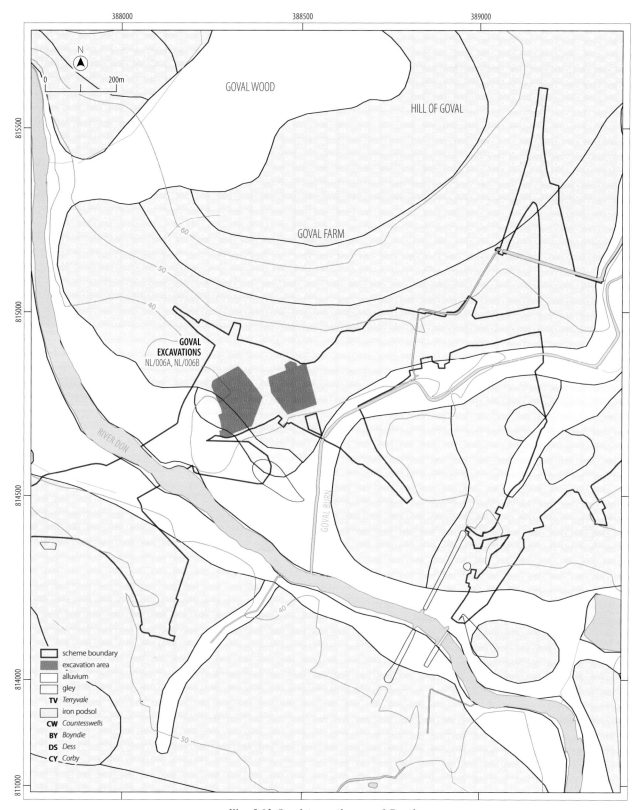

Illus 5.02 Overlying soils map of Goval

the slightly abraded edges on the pottery may imply it represents domestic refuse.

To the south-east of NL/006A were two adjacent sub-circular pits [6A-0036] (Illus 5.05) and [6A-0041], both with similar profiles. Pit [6A-0036] was approximately 0.5 m in diameter and [6A-0041] around 0.9 m. The pits were 0.15 m deep and contained large quantities of prehistoric pottery, as well as charcoal, hazel nutshell

Table 5.01 Radiocarbon determinations from Goval

Area	Context	Lab no	Material	Radiocarbon age BP	Calibrated age 98.4% probability
NL/006A	(6A-0042), pottery residue from pit [6A-0041]	SUERC-68133	Pottery residue	4619±29	3510–3350 cal BC
Structure A	(6A-0069), fill of post-hole [6A-0068]	SUERC-57929	Charcoal: Hazel	3035±29	1390–1220 cal BC
Furnace B	(6A-0124), peripheral deposit	SUERC-57930	Charcoal: Hazel	1930±26	cal AD 10–130
Structure B	(6A-0050), hearth [6A-0049]	SUERC-57928	Charcoal: Cherry	1908±29	cal AD 20–210
	(6A-0157), post-hole [6A-0156] (outer ring)	SUERC-68131	Charcoal: Hazel	1894±29	cal AD 50–220
	(6A-0177), post-hole [6A-0176] (inner ring)	SUERC-68130	Nutshell: Hazel	1885±29	cal AD 60–220
Kiln A	(6A-0101) central pit [6A-0096]	SUERC-68132	Charcoal: Hazel	1725±29	cal AD 240–390
NL/006B	(6B-0004), Curvilinear gully [6B-0003]	SUERC-57931	Charcoal: Alder	1336±29	cal AD 640–770

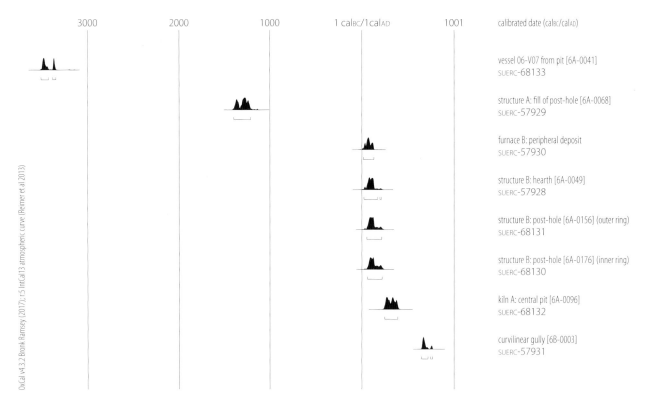

Illus 5.03 ¹⁴C graphs from Goval

and lithic debitage. The pottery included large parts of five Impressed Ware vessels, two of which were spread across both pits, and several fragments of coarseware. One vessel showed evidence for damage from use, and had been repaired at least once. These are indicative of domestic activities occurring nearby. The pottery appears to have been placed directly into the pits, with no indication of wear identified. This may represent more purposeful deposition of material, often seen in Neolithic contexts (see 5.12 below).

The Impressed Ware vessels have been typologically dated to the middle to later Neolithic. Residue from the vessel in pit [6A-0041] returned a radiocarbon determination of 3510–3350 cal BC (SUERC-68133), which matches well with this hypothesis, tending towards the Middle Neolithic. This date overlaps with the general date range for Carinated Bowl pottery, and may well indicate the two pits are contemporary. The final pit [6A-0032], located a short way to the east, contained a small quantity of similar pottery and is therefore also thought to be contemporary.

Six flint cores were recovered during the topsoil strip and from several features at Goval. None could be considered to be *in situ*, but they do demonstrate several approaches

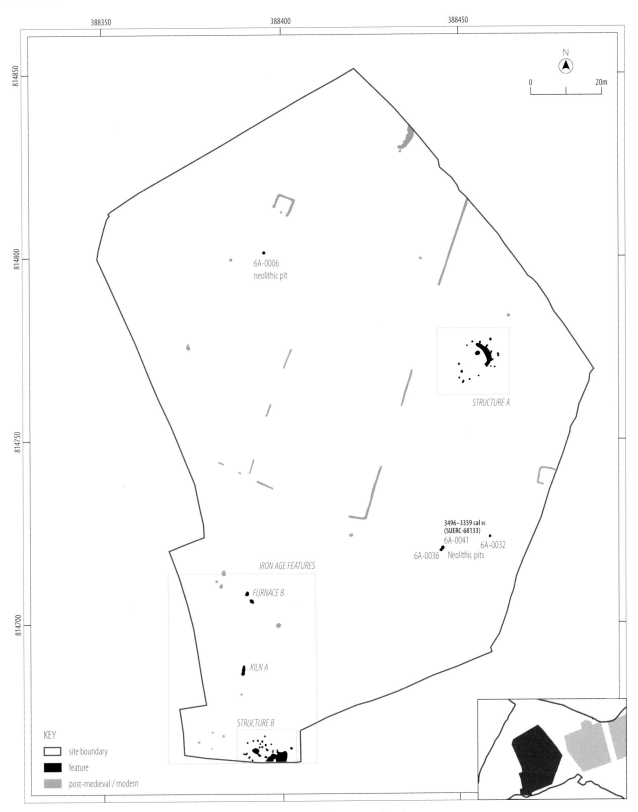

Illus 5.04 Plan of archaeological features at Goval in western area

to reduction identified throughout the Mesolithic to Middle Neolithic periods (see 5.11.3 below). Their presence further attests to sporadic activity from these periods for which we have limited evidence.

5.6 Bronze Age roundhouse – Structure A

Structure A was located near the eastern edge of the site, adjacent to a broad band of geological gravel (Illus 5.06). It comprised 23 post-holes, a hearth, a curvilinear gully and two pits (Illus 5.07). A partial ring of post-holes was recorded with an approximate diameter of 9.5 m (Illus 5.07A). The post-holes ranged between 0.1 m and 0.4 m in diameter and between 0.04 m and 0.3 m deep. They were typically filled with compact brown loamy sand with occasional charcoal flecks and lacked evidence for post-pipes or packing. These posts may have supported a ring-beam, which in turn supported the roof, similar to that suggested for a number of the structures at Gairnhill (Chapter 3). Three post-holes on the eastern side of the

Illus 5.05 Neolithic pit [6A-0036] showing location of pottery

structure appear to have either been replacements or used as additional support for the ring-beam. One post-hole [6A-2059] contained two sherds of prehistoric pottery and post-hole [6A-0062] contained a fragment of burnt bone recovered from the environmental sample. A fragment of hazel charcoal from post-hole [6A-0068] was submitted for radiocarbon dating and returned a date range of 1390–1220 cal BC (SUERC-57929), placing the structure in the Middle Bronze Age.

Six shallow post-holes were encountered south-west of the projected line of the structure, which may be the heavily truncated remains of a south-west facing entrance (see Illus 5.07A). Four further post-holes identified to the east and north-east are also likely to be related to the structure but their function is unclear.

The curvilinear gully measured up to 1.40 m wide and 6.8 m long with a maximum depth of 0.15 m, although its southern end may have been truncated. The gully had gently sloping sides and a slightly rounded stony base (Illus 5.08) and is more likely a result of erosional wear than intentional excavation. It was filled with a loose clayey silt containing occasional pebbles, charcoal fragments and a small quantity of hazel nutshell, indicative of general domestic debris. A single small post-hole [6A-0105] was cut into this deposit and contained a heat-affected silt with frequent charcoal inclusions. This suggests that a post had been inserted through the gully and burnt down at some point during use

Illus 5.06 Structure A – facing west

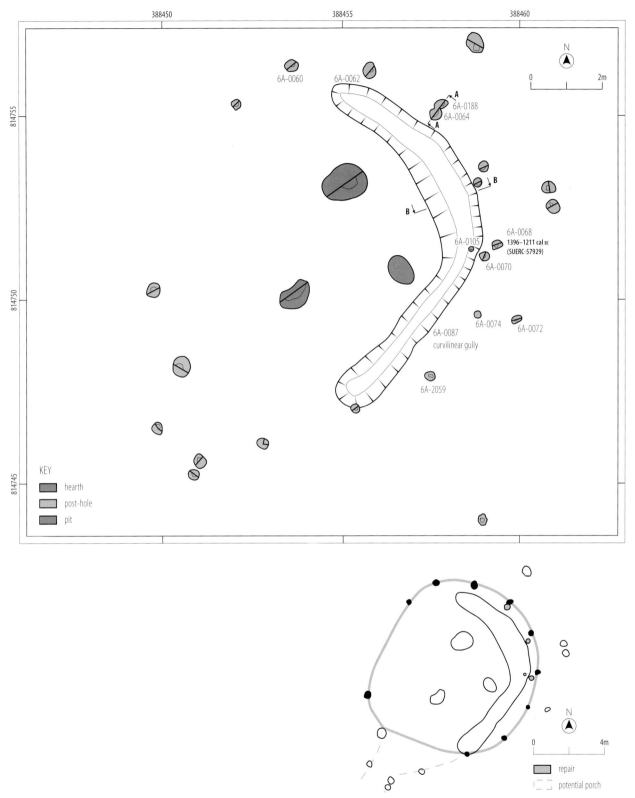

Illus 5.07 Plan of Structure A A. Post-ring

or abandonment of the structure. The position of the feature close to a post that was replaced or repaired suggests that this may have been a further attempt to stabilise this part of the structure. Internal features included a pit containing lithic fragments, charcoal and burnt bone and interpreted as a hearth, plus two undiagnostic shallow pits.

Structure A is interpreted as a Middle Bronze Age domestic roundhouse, with evidence for structural

Illus 5.08 Structure A – section through curvilinear gully [6A-0087] showing stony base

Illus 5.09 Structure B – facing north-west

maintenance indicative of a prolonged period of use. The low volumes of artefactual or ecofactual indicators for specific activities may be a factor of preservation, but may also suggest clearing out prior to disuse. There is no evidence for rapid destruction of the structure by fire, as interpreted at Gairnhill (Chapter 3) and Wester Hatton (Chapter 6), or other catastrophic collapse, and it may imply the abandonment was planned, with the occupants leaving little behind.

5.7 Iron Age activity at Goval

5.7.1 Iron Age roundhouse – Structure B

Structure B was a roundhouse located in area NL/006A (see Illus 5.04). It comprised 28 post-holes arranged around a central hearth (Illus 5.09 & 5.10), two areas of stone paving and a number of nearby pits. The interpretation of individual features was made more difficult by significant burrowing and bioturbation, as well as horizontal truncation.

The main structural feature was an inner post-ring (Illus 5.10A), comprising nine post-holes with a diameter of approximately 5.7 m. These post-holes were between 0.2 m and 0.6 m in diameter and up to 0.6 m deep. On the western side of the structure, three further post-holes may be indicative of repair. Two post-holes contained small quantities of iron slag; another contained nutshell and another burnt animal bone. A fragment of hazel charcoal from post-hole [6A-0176] was submitted for radiocarbon dating and returned a date range of cal AD 60–220 (SUERC-68130).

The remains of a possible outer post-ring were represented by four post-holes (Illus 5.10B), forming an arc of 9.8 m diameter around the eastern side of the structure, and may indicate the line of an outer wall. The post-holes were between 0.2 m and 0.3 m in diameter, up to 0.25 m deep and filled with loose silty sand. One also contained burnt animal bone. A radiocarbon date of cal AD 50–220

(SUERC-68131), obtained from hazel charcoal from the fill of post-hole [6A-0156], indicated it was contemporary with the inner post-ring.

No convincing evidence of an entrance to the roundhouse was encountered, with the most likely position being south-facing, beyond the limits of excavation. A cluster of four post-holes and a pit were recorded east of the outer ring. The post-holes were shallow and it is not clear what structural role they may have played. The pit contained no significant anthropogenic material.

Seven internal features were identified in Structure B. The hearth was roughly central to the post-rings, sub-oval in plan and measuring 1.7 m × 1.25 m and up to 0.15 m deep (see Illus 5.10 & 5.11). It contained a loose silty sand fill with lenses of burnt sand, frequent charcoal fragments, burnt animal bone, a flint flake, several fragments of iron slag and four sherds of prehistoric coarseware. The presence of several lumps of iron slag in the hearth may indicate metalworking activity. Three post-holes set in a triangular shape to the north-east of the hearth may have supported a small structure that may also have related to the use of the hearth (Illus 5.10C). A fragment of cherry charcoal from the hearth was submitted for radiocarbon dating and returned a date range of cal AD 20–210 (SUERC-57928), which is roughly contemporary with the post-rings and places the structure in the Middle Iron Age.

Two areas of stone paving were encountered immediately to the east of Structure B (Illus 5.12). Paving [6A-0040] was closest to the structure, overlying part of the outer post-ring and another external post-hole. The western edge of the paving had been truncated slightly during machining but would have aligned well with the inner post-ring. The southern edge continued beyond the limit of land made available to the scheme. The exposed area of paving measured 3.7 m by 2.7 m and was laid directly onto the remnant topsoil. It consisted of sub-angular stones of various shapes and sizes, up to 0.6 m × 0.7 m × 0.2 m, with smaller packing stones in between. The surface was quite irregular but it is likely that stones had been dislodged somewhat by later agricultural activity.

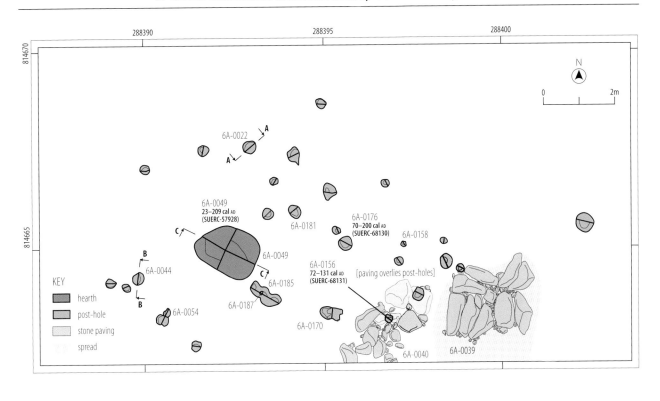

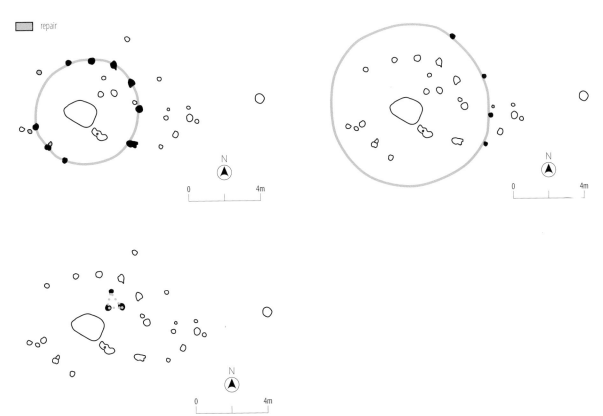

Illus 5.10 Plan of Structure B A. Inner post-ring B. Outer post-ring C. Possible internal structure

Paving [6A-0039] was located half a metre east of [6A-0040]. It measured 2.6 m by 2.3 m and was set on a bedding deposit, which in turn overlay the remnant topsoil. The paving itself was quite different to [6A-0040], consisting of nine large irregular elongated stone blocks measuring up to 1.1 m × 0.4 m × 0.2 m. The gaps between these had been packed with much smaller, more rounded stones and a single roughly rectangular block of quartz-rich stone had

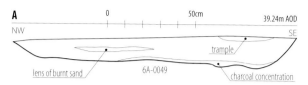

Illus 5.11 Structure B – section through hearth [6A-0049]

been placed in the middle. It is likely that some of the outer stones had been dislodged by later agricultural activity.

The space between the two areas of paving appeared to have been intentional, perhaps serving as a drainage gully. The stratigraphy and method of construction of the two surfaces differ sufficiently to suggest they represent two distinct surfaces, but their proximity and common surface level indicates that they are contemporary. No artefactual evidence was recovered from either surface.

Structure B is interpreted as a Middle Iron Age domestic roundhouse. The inner structural post-ring appears to have been repaired at least once, indicating a degree of extended use. A posited outer wall appears to have been at least partially superseded by a substantial raised stone surface immediately outside the structure. As with Structure A, evidence for the specific use of the building is limited, although it is likely that the occupants were involved with the metalworking activity described below. We have little information about the abandonment of this building.

5.7.2 Metalworking Furnace B

Furnace B was recorded 38 m north of Structure B (Illus 5.13). It consisted of a sub-oval pit [6A-0118] 0.85 m × 0.45 m and 0.2 m deep (Illus 5.14). The deposits within comprised a central dark grey-black silty sand overlying a peripheral ring of mid-brown silty sand. Both deposits were rich in iron slag, ironworking residues, daub and charcoal. A radiocarbon determination of cal AD 10–130 (SUERC-57930) was obtained from hazel charcoal retrieved from the outer deposit, providing a Middle Iron Age date contemporary with Structure B.

Analysis of the vitrified material from this feature confirms that it is likely to represent the remains of an iron-smelting furnace (see 5.11.4 below). These typically take the form of an upright clay cylinder in which charcoal and ore were burnt to produce an iron bloom. Evidence for this sort of construction at Goval is found in a fragment of daub shaped as a coil and suitable for a thick, stacked clay superstructure (see 5.11.5 below). The iron bloom would have collected in the base or run out of a hole near the base to surround the furnace (Tylecote 1986, 123). Since no clear tapped slag was identified, in this case, it is likely that the bloom was allowed to collect internally. It is suggested that the inner deposit represents the internal waste material of the furnace, with the surrounding deposits representing either external waste or material formed from the destruction/collapse of

Illus 5.12 Structure B – stone paving, facing west

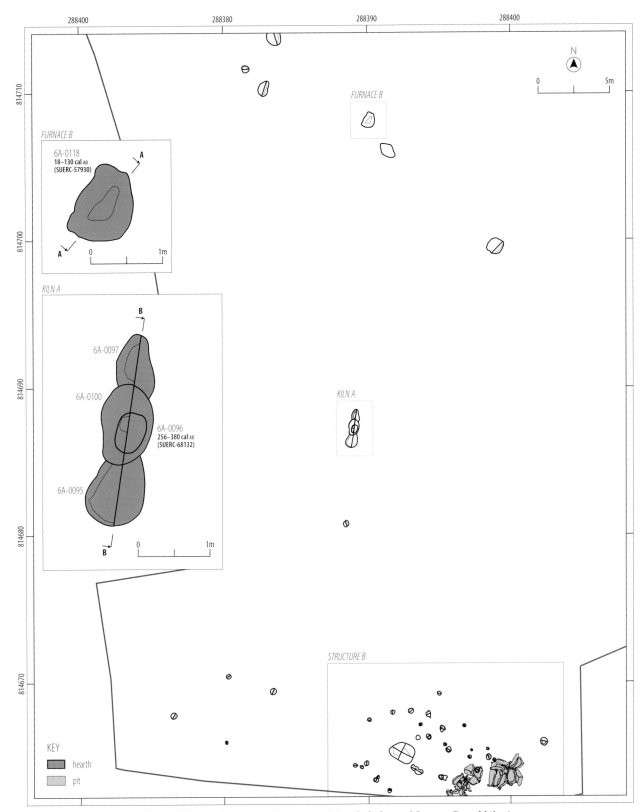

Illus 5.13 Plan of Iron Age features and detailed plans of furnace B and kiln A

the structure. A possible hole for extracting the bloom was orientated to the south-west, where the base of the cut had been left somewhat higher. The geological subsoil below the furnace had been extensively heat affected, which would be consistent with *in situ* metalworking taking place rather than the deposition of waste materials. Chemical analysis of the vitrified material suggests that the slags were typical of Iron Age smelting in Scotland, and that iron-rich bog ore was used as the raw material (see 5.11.4 below).

A deposit of metalworking waste, with no clear evidence for a cut or *in situ* burning was recorded to the south-east of the furnace. The composition of this material and its inclusions were similar in character to (6A-0126) and is likely to have resulted from the same activity.

5.7.3 Kiln A

A small kiln was recorded 18 m north of Structure B (Illus 5.13). It consisted of three intercutting shallow sub-oval pits arranged on a north–south axis (Illus 5.15). The middle pit [6A-0096] appeared to be stratigraphically later than the others, with a clear halo of burnt sand overlying or cutting the pits to the north and south. This sand may have been redeposited inside a clay superstructure (perhaps for levelling) prior to being burnt. The two flanking pits were of a similar size and form as the central pit. The central pit showed evidence for *in situ* burning and contained possible metalworking waste; the outer pits contained fragments of daub. On detailed inspection, two pieces of the daub appear to have impressions of organic withies, perhaps suggesting a wattle and daub screen (see 5.11.5 below). One piece may be part of a kiln lining or superstructure.

All three pits contained charcoal, iron slag and significant quantities of hulled barley grain, a cereal that predominates in the Iron Age (Boyd 1988). A fragment of hazel charcoal from the upper fill of the central pit was submitted for radiocarbon dating and returned a date range of cal AD 240–390 (SUERC-68132). This dates Kiln A later than

the other Middle Iron Age remains, perhaps by around two hundred years.

In the absence of any related domestic activity, this feature must be treated as representative of an isolated process. Metallurgical analysis (see 5.11.4 below) of the waste concluded this was likely to be intrusive material, possibly from Furnace B, and therefore the presence of significant quantities of hulled barley grain imply it was more likely used for drying barley.

5.8 Early Historic gully

In area NL/006B four features were encountered (Illus 5.16). Three of these were irregular undiagnostic pits and the fourth was a shallow curvilinear gully. Only the southern part of this gully survived, the remainder perhaps having succumbed to plough truncation, which may have had a more severe effect further upslope owing to the decreasing thickness of the topsoil here (Illus 5.17). For the same reason, neither end of the gully as recorded is likely to represent a genuine terminal. It was also further truncated by modern field drainage. The gully measured 13 m long, 0.25 m wide and up to 0.2 m deep, with steep, sloping sides leading to a flat base.

The basal fill was a compact grey silty sand that contained wheat, oat and barley grains, weed seeds, nutshell and frequent charcoal fragments, as well as a single flint core typologically dated to the later Neolithic. A radiocarbon determination of cal AD 640–770 (SUERC-57931) was obtained from alder charcoal retrieved from this deposit, providing an Early Historic date and implying that the flint is intrusive. The upper fill comprised longitudinal bands of charcoal with pink heat-affected lenses of sand and clay (Illus 5.18). This deposit may represent the remains of *in situ* burning of longitudinal timbers. It also contained oat and barley grains, weed seeds and nutshell.

The presence of longitudinal timbers at the base of this feature suggests a structural function. The slight inward curve at the north-eastern end of the gully may suggest a small enclosure or building of approximately 5 m in length. The purpose of the structure cannot be derived from the archaeological evidence. Whether its destruction by fire was intentional or otherwise is also unclear.

5.9 Medieval and post-medieval agriculture

A system of rig and furrow cultivation was recorded in area NL/006A, aligned north-east/south-west and visible across most of the site (not illustrated). A slight curve was visible at the south-western end of some of these furrows,

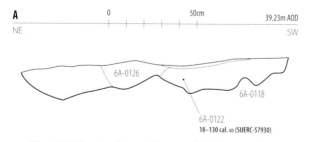

Illus 5.14 Section through furnace B, facing south-east

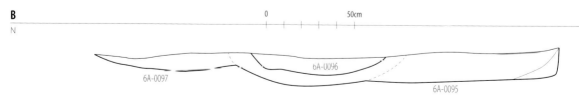

Illus 5.15 Section through kiln A, facing east

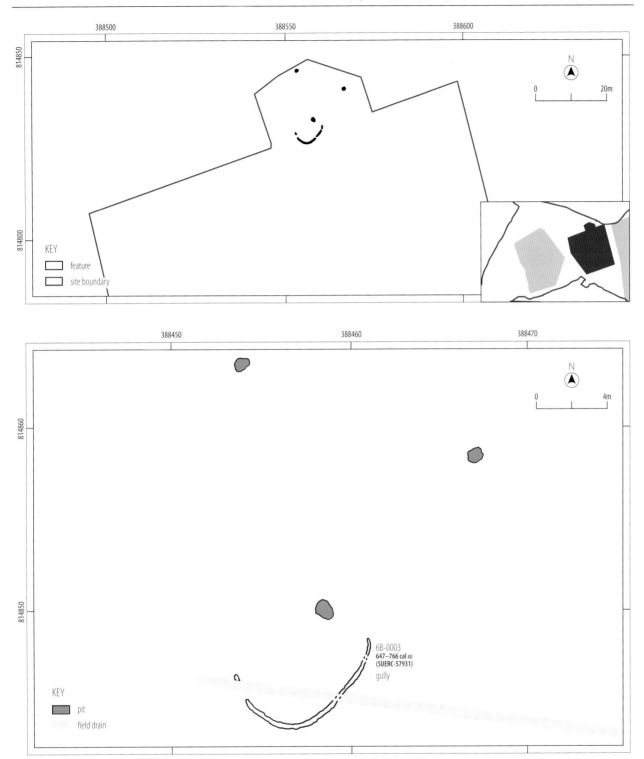

Illus 5.16 Plan of archaeological features at Goval in eastern area

indicative of the turning of the plough-team at the edge of the field. In area NL/006B, a fragmentary system of furrows was aligned broadly north/south down the slope. The spacing of both sets of furrows is typical of pre-improvement broad rig (Dixon 1994, 38).

Two enclosure gullies were encountered in NL/006A, on the same alignment as the furrows (see Illus 5.04).

However, the furrows extended beyond the gullies, implying they were not contemporary. Two smaller rectilinear gullies, measuring approximately 4 m square were also encountered. They were also on the same alignment and are likely related to the same agricultural system, although their specific function is not clear.

Illus 5.17 General view of curvilinear gully [6B-0003], facing north

Illus 5.18 Detail of burnt timbers in curvilinear gully [6B-0003]

5.10 Environmental synthesis

Tim Holden

5.10.1 Introduction

Eighty-seven soil samples of up to 40 l were taken in line with the overall sampling strategy for the project. Twenty samples were selected for full processing, based on potential for ecofactual survival and the significance of the contexts represented. It had been noted during the fieldwork phase that the typical quantities of visible ecofacts

(such as charcoal) appeared low, and this was reflected in a relatively small environmental assemblage comprising plant remains preserved by charring and a small collection of mostly fragmentary animal bone. In order to extract the maximum value from a limited resource, cereal grain from fourteen samples was quantified, and charcoal from eight samples was analysed in more detail to identify the species.

5.10.2 Environmental evidence

The environmental assemblage, though modest, does offer some insight into the site economy. The Neolithic pits contained the greatest concentrations of hazel (*Corylus avellana*) nutshell, which is in keeping with the routine and persistent use of hazel throughout the Mesolithic and Neolithic (see Chapters 2, 5 and 6). Early crop-growing is indicated by small amounts of naked barley and bread wheat (*Triticum aestivo-compactum*), both common before the Iron Age (Boyd 1988).

The majority of evidence relates to Iron Age occupation. Hulled barley (*Hordeum vulgare*) was the most abundant grain. A concentration in Kiln A is the clearest indicator of function for this feature, possibly representing the incidentally burnt waste from a drying process. The wood used in Kiln A comprised small diameter hazel, with no oak charcoal present. This may demonstrate a requirement for a lower temperature of burning that these fuels provide. At Furnace B, oak charcoal was dominant, although willow, alder, hazel, birch and heather were also recovered. Oak is often associated with metal smelting owing to its superior burning properties (Tylecote 1986). Most of the fragments had evidence of fungal hyphae, which suggests that dead wood was collected, as opposed to recently felled wood (Salisbury & Jane 1940). A specific preference for fallen oak demonstrates specialist knowledge and an understanding of the importance of certain resources. The charcoal from the hearth in Structure B indicated the use of small diameter alder (*Alnus glutinosa*) and bird cherry (*Prunus avium*), with lesser quantities of oak (*Quercus* sp), showing little evidence of selection in the wood species used.

Low numbers of weed seeds were recovered from the fills of various features, with a small concentration of hemp nettle (*Galeopsis tetrahit*) seeds from the hearth in Structure B. It is difficult to comment on the significance of this but the most likely explanation is that it represents a single plant brought to site along with fuel or field crops. Other weed seeds identified, including docks (*Rumex* sp), fat hen (*Chenopodium* sp) chickweed (*Stellaria media*), nettle (*Urtica diocia*) and sedges (*Carex* sp), are commonly associated with cultivated and disturbed ground. Common hemp nettle typically grows on sandy soils.

The taxa present indicate that both valley floor/carr as well as dry woodland existed in the vicinity during the Iron Age. Alder, willow and birch would probably have been gathered from along the banks of the River Don unless this extensive, wide, well-drained and fertile haughland was by the Iron Age cleared for grazing and meadow (cf Chapter 2), or still grew along the smaller Goval Burn to the east. Dryland taxa such as hazel, oak, bird cherry and heather were collected from further up the valley side.

5.10.3 Discussion
Richard Tipping and Jürgen van Wessel

The Hill of Goval represents some of best agricultural land to the north and east of the Don (see 5.3 above). Well-drained substrates are argued to have been very important for founding farming communities next to the River Dee (Chapter 2.10.1), and the gravels at Goval offer similar opportunities. Furthermore, the slope faces south and is not so steep as to be unworkable. It is surprising, therefore, unless a product of poor preservation, that excavation produced so little evidence for agriculture of any significant scale. Small quantities of barley in varieties common to the Bronze and Iron Ages were recovered, as well as a grain-drying kiln dating to the latter period. If the conditions for growing did not limit occupation, perhaps other factors were more significant. The stoniness of the ground (clearly visible in Illus 5.6 & 5.17) may have been a factor, hindering the excavation of foundations for structures. This is demonstrated by the positioning of Structure A, just avoiding a band of particularly gravel-rich subsoil.

The environmental evidence from Goval perpetuates the sense of marginality described above (see 5.3) for the wider region. The conditions to the north and east of the Don appear to have been so unfavourable that they did not support significant habitation. Settlements (or fermtouns) in 1696 (Walton 1950; Tyson 1985; Dixon & Fraser 2008, fig 8.61) lay along the glaciofluvial gravel terraces bordering the Don, next to the Elrick Burn around Newmachar, and near the North Sea coast. This is the setting of Goval. The broad 8 km wide ridge of the upland from the Don north to Udny seems always, in its bogginess, to have supported low population densities, and yet, as a likely source of bog ore, was perhaps one reason for settlement activity at Goval in the Iron Age. Against this backdrop, the presence of small-scale, but long-term and repeated human activity at Goval is even more significant.

5.11 Materials synthesis
Julie Lochrie

5.11.1 Introduction
The artefact assemblage from Goval comprises prehistoric pottery, lithics, vitrified materials and fired clay dating from the Neolithic to the Iron Age. Each material type is described below followed by a general discussion of the overall assemblage. Detailed analysis reports of each material type are included in the digital appendices to this volume (Appendices 2.2).

5.11.2 Prehistoric pottery
The assemblage of prehistoric pottery comprises 111 sherds and 70 fragments, weighing 2.7 kg. Of the nine vessels present (06-V01 to 06-V09, Table 5.02), seven are of Neolithic type, with only two representing Bronze Age or Iron Age activity. The predominance of the Neolithic pottery and the near-total absence of later prehistoric pottery is surprising, particularly given the presence of Bronze Age and Iron Age structures on site and the absence of any Neolithic structures.

Vessels 06-V01 and 06-V02 were recovered from an isolated pit [6A-0006]. They are both round-based vessels from the early Middle Neolithic and belong to the modified Carinated Bowl (CB) tradition. Vessel 06-V01 (Illus 5.19) is in many small, delaminated sherds and fragments. They belong to a round-bellied vessel with a slightly everted rim. The frequent large and granular rock inclusions probably account for the delamination of the sherds. Despite the very coarse temper, the sherds look finer and smoother than expected owing to thorough wiping of the interior and exterior surface. Vessel 06-V01 has comparatives from Kintore in Aberdeenshire (V403; MacSween 2008, 175) and further afield at Meadowend Farm, Clackmannanshire (P20; Jones *et al.* 2018). Both these examples and that from Goval exist only as rim sherds but the curvature of all sherds points towards a round-based vessel with no carination. Vessel 06-V02 is represented by one rim sherd and five body sherds. The body sherds have a slight curvature and

Table 5.02 Summary of vessels from Goval

Area	Feature	Context	Vessel #	Sherds	Frags	Weight (g)	Type
NL/006A	Pit [6A-0006]	(6A-0007)	06-V01	53	23	120	Modified Carinated Bowl
	Pit [6A-0006]	(6A-0007)	06-V02	5	–	56	Modified Carinated Bowl
NL/006A	Pit [6A-0032]	(6A-0033)	06-V03	2	2	3	Impressed Ware
	Pit [6A-0036]	(6A-0037)	06-V04	7	–	79	Impressed Ware
	Pit [6A-0036]	(6A-0037)	06-V05	2	10	165	Impressed Ware
	Pit [6A-0041]	(6A-0042)					
	Pit [6A-0036]	(6A-0037)	06-V06	8	2	48	Impressed Ware
	Pit [6A-0041]	(6A-0042)					
	Pit [6A-0041]	(6A-0042)	06-V07	30	30	2246	Impressed Ware
Structure A	Post-hole [6A-2059]	(6A-2060)	06-V08	2	1	11	Undiagnostic Coarseware
Structure B	Hearth [6A-0049]	(6A-0050)	06-V09	2	2	2	Undiagnostic Coarseware

the rim is fairly upright with an expanded T-shaped rim. The curvature of the body sherds along with the upright rim may suggest the presence of a carination which does not survive. These sherds are thinner than vessel 06-V01 and they do not have the same coarse and granular temper. They do, however, have similar wipe marks and surface appearance.

All that remains of Vessel 06-V03 from pit [6A-0032] are two small body sherds and two small fragments. They are fairly undiagnostic except from a small circular depression, which may be impressed decoration indicative of Impressed Ware.

The pottery from pits [6A-0036] and [6A-0041] can be considered as a group, as sherds of almost identical thickness and fabric from two vessels (V05 and V06; see below) were found in both pits. Vessel 06-V04 (Illus 5.20) comprises seven conjoining sherds. The breaks are post-depositional and this would have formed one large sherd. The vessel would originally have been quite small, the curve of the rim indicating a diameter of around 190 mm. There is a concave strip directly below the rim exterior and the walls gently curve inward. The rim itself expands on the exterior and interior and is gently squared down on top (a rough T-shape). The walls undulate slightly in thickness, being thinnest at the points where sections of clay were joined together. Clay folds are visible along the interior lip where the clay was flattened down, and while the interior wall has been smoothed no attempt has been made to disguise the clay fold at the rim. The interior shows horizontal finger/hand smoothing. Three shallow stab marks appear to have been accidentally caused by fingernails. On the exterior, there are similar folds where the rim has been pushed down and the concave band has been finger-smoothed, as once again there are traces of horizontal lines and possible fingernail marks. An entirely different technique has been used to finish the vessel exterior which has resulted in vertical lines created.

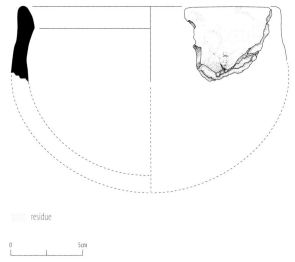

residue

0   5cm

Illus 5.19 Vessel 06-V01 from pit [6A-0006]

Vessel 06-V05 (Illus 5.21) includes a decorated rim sherd from [6A-0036] and a large body sherd of almost identical fabric and thickness from [6A-0041] although they do not conjoin. The rim sherd indicates a very narrow vessel of 120 mm diameter, which must have had a saggy or baggy base. The rim has been initially rounded then gently pushed out from the interior to create a slight lip. The base of the lip on the exterior has been smoothed by the fingers to enhance and refine the shape. The rim itself is very thin in comparison to the walls. Like Vessel 06-V04, there is evidence for the use of tooling during manufacture, in this case possibly a small smoothing spatula which has left three lines on the interior wall. The decoration takes the form of a row of deep finger pinching. The lower finger has pushed as far as the nail while the upper finger has pushed deeper into the clay, pulling out and downwards to create a raised effect.

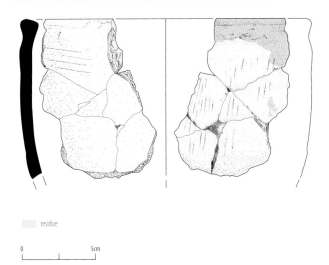

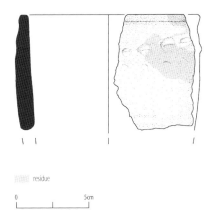

Illus 5.20 Vessel 06-V04 from pit [6A-0036]

Illus 5.21 Vessel 06-V05 from pit [6A-0036] and pit [6A-0041]

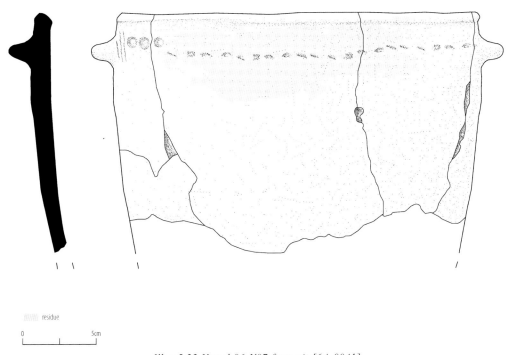

Illus 5.22 Vessel 06-V07 from pit [6A-0041]

Vessel 06-V06 is the only vessel from these pits with no feature sherds. Eight small body sherds were identified in both pits owing to the similarity in the appearance of the fabric itself. The sherds are friable and have delaminated. They have a smoothed buff exterior, sandy quartz-rich fabric and grey toned interior with strong mica sheen as a result of several large mica platelets and frequent small micaceous particles.

Vessel 06-V07 (Illus 5.22) from pit [6A-0041] is missing its base but it would have been very large and baggy shaped in profile. The vessel has a rim diameter of 240 mm and the two small handles on either side would have helped

facilitate handling. The rim has been flattened and bevels internally although varies around the vessel, with one half having a slight exterior lip and the other half showing a slight interior lip. The decoration also takes two different forms. One side is decorated with fingernail impressions; they are bordered at one end by three diagonal slashes. Much of the other half of the vessel is missing but it shows the diagonal slashes continuing beyond the lugs. The vessel has extremely undulating walls where the clay rings used in its creation have been joined. The thin joins have left the vessel very weak at these points and they

Table 5.03 Summary of lithic assemblage

Area	Feature	Chips	Flakes	Blades	Indet pieces	Cores	Tools	Total
Unstratified	(6A-0000)			2		2	2	6
	Pit [6A-0006]	21	5		3			29
NL/006A								
NL/006A	Rectilinear gully [6A-0016]	1						1
NL/006A	Pit [6A-0018]					1		1
NL/006A	Pit [6A-0036]	3	1					4
NL/006A	Pit [6A-0041]	1	2					3
	Hearth [6A-0049]		1					1
Structure B								
NL/006A	Tree bole [6A-0132]					1		1
NL/006A	Linear [6A-0134]	2						2
NL/006B	Curvilinear gully [6B-0003]					1		1
	Pit [6B-0010]					1		1
Total		28	9	2	3	6	2	50

correspond to several pre- and post-depositional breaks. The join can be viewed in section and shows the clay was pushed down on the interior and up on the exterior. The horizontal bands where the clay has been joined have been excessively finger-smoothed, leaving deep channels on the interior. Like other vessels from these two pits, 06-V07 has diagonal lines to its body that result from a small spatula-like device, most likely used to smooth and even out the walls. This large vessel was probably a cooking pot and the residue adhering to the interior lower two-thirds and exterior upper third clearly shows it has been used for this purpose. It is also likely to have been repeatedly used as there are signs of repair. Two post-firing perforations (and a failed third attempt) are positioned either side of a crack that would have allowed binding to hold it together and prevent further damage.

The sherds from Structures A and B are undiagnostic. The former comprises two, small, thick, coarsely rock-tempered sherds. They give no indication of form but fit with the Bronze Age date of the structure. The pottery from the hearth in Structure B comprises two small, abraded sherds, compatible with the Iron Age date from this building.

5.11.3 Lithics

The Goval assemblage numbers 50 pieces of flint and is summarised in Table 5.03. The greatest concentrations were retrieved from pits also containing Neolithic pottery (see 5.12.2 below). Seven of the lithics were unstratified and the remainder found in small numbers in other features across both areas of the site.

The assemblage is small and dispersed but does offer some useful insights into activity at Goval. Abraded pebble cortex on several pieces indicates that the flint

at Goval has very likely been sourced from local gravel outcrops or stream banks. The greatest concentration of lithics was from pit [6A-0006]. The small chips and flakes found here indicate nearby knapping, and suggest a degree of domestic activity. Although in themselves undiagnostic, the lithics from this pit are compatible in date with the associated early Middle Neolithic pottery from the feature.

The small scattering of lithics from the other contexts do not reveal any other occupational information but do indicate that low levels of prehistoric activity were spread over a large area. The two tools collected from the topsoil are unstratified and are not formal tool types. The fine retouch on one of these is similar to Mesolithic techniques of modification.

The most interesting aspect of the assemblage is the collection of six cores, which demonstrates two different percussion techniques and several different approaches to reduction. Three of the cores show platform reduction, two of which are single platform cores. One of these shows soft and hard percussion characteristics and is oval in plan, with one cortical critical and one reduced side (Illus 5.23a). This core could broadly be termed conical and the blank removals would have comprised blades and some flakes. These types of core are most commonly seen in the Mesolithic and Early to Middle Neolithic. The second single-platform core has been reduced around 75% of its platform and at some point the apex has been removed and further flakes have been struck from the platform edge. These would have been very short and this may be an attempt to fashion the flint into a tool, most likely a scraper.

The final core to show platform reduction is the most interesting and is made from the best quality of flint

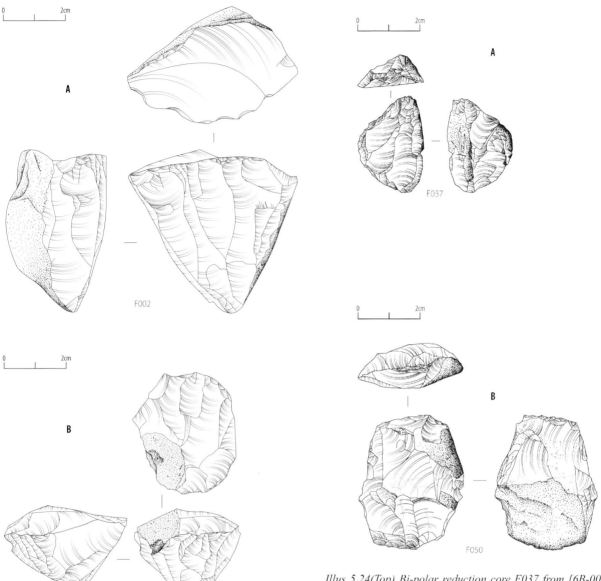

*Illus 5.24(Top) Bi-polar reduction core F037 from [6B-0010];
(bottom) Bi-polar core F050 from [6B-0010]*

Illus 5.23 (Top) Single platform core F002 from [6A-0132]; (bottom) Single platform core F049

found in the assemblage (Illus 5.23b). Two platforms are identifiable and many orientations of removal can be seen. The general shape of the core looks like a squat conical but the apex is in fact the edge of a previous platform. The main platform from which most of the removals have been made is sub-circular in plan and is covered in previous flake scars around a 360 degree orientation. The point of impact for most of these no longer remains, having been removed by subsequent flakes, although one section could be a third platform.

Bipolar reduction is present on two examples (Illus 5.24). Both cores have two opposing axes of removals and in both case the removals are bifocal. The combination of platform and bipolar reduction is a very common assemblage

characteristic from the Middle Neolithic onwards, as it is at this point that traditional platform techniques give way to bipolar reduction and Levallois-like reduction. In fact, one platform-reduced core from Goval shows the emphasis during this period of orientating the core in specific ways to maximise yield. This very strategic method of reduction has a similar motivation to the more strictly Levallois-like approach.

5.11.4 Vitrified material

Dawn McLaren and David Dungworth

A total of 2370.6 g of vitrified material was recovered during excavation and from soil sample processing. Visual examination of the individual pieces, complemented by

Table 5.04 Summary of quantity and range of vitrified and heat-affected materials The following abbreviations have been used: runned slag (RS), unclassified iron slag/runned slag (UIS/RS), magnetic vitrified residue (MVR), vitrified ceramic (VC) and fuel ash slag (FAS). Measurements are in grams

Area	Feature	RS	UIS/RS	MVR	VC	FAS	Cinder	Ore	Other	Total
–	Rectilinear gully [6A-0016]						0.2			0.2
–	Pit [6A-0036]						0.1			0.1
Structure B	Post-hole [6A-0022]			1.1						1.1
	Post-hole [6A-0024]			0.1						0.1
	Post-hole [6A-0046]								39.6	39.6
	Hearth [6A-0049]		27.7	1.8	6.9		0.1			36.5
	Post-hole [6A-0170]			1	5.7					6.7
Kiln A	Pit [6A-0095]			13.4						13.4
	Pit [6A-0096]		3.5	0.8						4.3
	Pit [6A-0097]			0.3						0.3
Furnace B	Furnace [6A-0118]	115.5	604.9	542	3.6					776
–	Boundary [6A-0134]			0.1						0.1
–	Boundary[6A-0136]			0.1						0.1
–	Deposit [6A-0151]		19.8	108.2	3.4					131.4
–	Post-hole [6A-0181]							28		28
–	Mixed	414.9		361.6	36.4					812.9
–	Unstratified	4.3	24			1.5				29.8
Sub-total mass (g)		534.7	679.9	1030.5	56	1.5	0.4	28	39.6	2370.6

chemical and microstructural analysis of selected samples, indicates that the ferrous metalworking slags are fragments of waste from iron smelting. No debris indicative of bloom- or blacksmithing were recognised amongst the assemblage. The greatest concentration of vitrified material was found in Furnace B. Table 5.04 shows the breakdown of vitrified and heat-affected materials from Goval.

The largest concentration of ferrous metalworking slags were recovered from Furnace B. In total 1266 g of vitrified material came from the various fills of this feature and comprise runned slag, a mixture of small fractured fragments of unclassified iron slag and small runned fragments, magnetic vitrified residues and vitrified ceramic (Illus 5.25). The slags are dominated by fragments of waste indicative of primary iron smelting including runned and amorphous rake-out material, and small granular magnetic residues. Chemical and microstructural analysis has confirmed these are mostly pieces of roasted bog ore that must have fallen to the base of the smelting furnace while in operation. Modelling of the chemical composition of the bog ore has confirmed that the slags are derived from that source. The presence of bog iron ore at Goval confirms that this was an important (and possibly dominant) source of iron ore at this time.

0   2cm

Illus 5.25 Slag from furnace B

Vitrified material was also recovered from Kiln A and Structure B, albeit in much smaller quantities. Only 18 g of vitrified material was retrieved from Kiln A, comprising small quantities of runned and unclassified iron slags and magnetic vitrified residues. Macroscopic analysis alongside detailed chemical and microstructural analysis of a sample of these residues confirm that they are likely to have been produced during iron smelting. However, the

Table 5.05 Summary of the fired clay by feature

Area	Feature	Quantity	Mass (g)	Condition	Heat-affected	Shaped	Impressions
NL/0006A	Pit [6A-0004]	1	0.1	fractured	Y	N	N
NL/0006A	Rectilinear gully [6A-0034]	1	0.1	abraded	Y	N	N
NL/0006A	Pit [6A-0096]	1	0.2	fractured	Y	N	N
Kiln A	Pit [6A-0095]	4	8.1	abraded/ fractured	Y	N	N
	Pit [6A-0097]	1	0.1	abraded	Y	N	N
NL/0006A Structure A	Post-hole [6A-0105]	3	0.3	abraded	Y	N	N
NL/0006A Furnace B	[6A-0118]	85	132.9	Fractured, some abraded	Y	N	Varies: some with grass/rush stems; some with withy (21 mm diam); some with concave impression – possible withy notch or junction between two moulded strips of clay
NL/0006A	Pit [6A-0150]	17	37.3	fractured	Y	N	N
NL/0006A	Mixed	47	132.3	abraded/ fractured	Y	Y (×1)	N

quantities of waste are so small and restricted in range that Kiln A is unlikely to relate directly to metalworking. The hearth in Structure B produced only a scatter of vitrified waste (36.5 g). It is likely that the material from these two features is residual waste deriving from smelting activities close by that has become incorporated incidentally within the fills.

The remaining 1030 g of waste represents a residual scatter of material incorporated in pits, post-holes, linear features, and deposits across the excavated area.

Overall the Goval slag samples share similar chemical compositions with other early bloomery slags from Scotland, being distinct from early bloomery slag from England (cf Paynter 2006). The differences between the Scottish and the English slags also suggests that the Scottish ore sources were distinct from the English ones.

5.11.5 Fired clay
Dawn McLaren

A total of 306.5 g of heat-affected clay was recovered during soil sample processing from 15 contexts across the site and are summarised by weight and quantity by context in Table 5.05. The majority of the 158 individual pieces are small fractured fragments with no original surfaces surviving, making it impossible to draw any useful conclusions about their original form or provenance. Sixty-six fragments were associated directly with Furnace B. These fragments are likely to represent degraded pieces of furnace lining. A further five fragments of fired clay

were recovered from the various fills of Kiln A, which also appear to be the focus of a high-temperature process.

Only three pieces among this small group of fired clay are worthy of further note. The first, from the outer, peripheral deposit of Furnace B, preserves a thin elongated sub-circular notch on one fractured surface suggesting that the clay had been packed around an organic withy, perhaps part of a wattle and daub screen. The second comprises a small fractured piece from the inner deposit of Furnace B, which preserves a concave impression on one face. It is possible that this is an abraded surface of a withy impression, as already described, but the slightly uneven surface suggests that this may be a junction between two moulded strips of clay and could be a fragment of the hearth or furnace lining. A further fragment from this feature is very similar to that just described, retaining distinct evidence of shaping. It comprises two re-joining pieces of a curving sub-rectangular rod of clay, probably prepared as a coil for a thick, coil-constructed pottery vessel or structure of stacked clay construction such as the shaft superstructure of a furnace. This matches well with the metallurgical evidence for Furnace B and conforms to structural norms for Iron Age smelting furnaces in Scotland (Tylecote 1986, 132–33).

5.11.6 Finds discussion
The artefactual evidence from Goval indicates low levels of activity throughout prehistory, with particular emphasis on the Neolithic and Iron Age. There is a hint of possible Mesolithic or Early Neolithic activity in the lithic

assemblage, although these unstratified pieces could be later examples of their types. This would fit with the more substantial evidence for early Middle Neolithic activity.

The dating of the two main Neolithic pottery types found at Goval is interesting. The 'style drift' of traditional carinated bowls can occur as early as c3800 BC with north-eastern style carinated bowls (CBNE) dated to this time and discussed in more detail in Chapter 2.14.3.1. There is no associated dating for the modified Carinated Bowl from Goval so the date range for the vessel type cannot be refined any further, but it is likely that this activity post-dates 3600 BC.

The dating of Impressed Ware in Scotland has been under scrutiny recently, with an increasing number of early dates (Kinbeachie, 3500–2920 BC, MacSween 2001, table 1, 63; Kintore, 3530–3340 BC, MacSween 2008, 181) compared to the more traditional range of 3300–2900 BC (for example at Meadowend Farm, 3350–2900 BC, Jones *et al.* 2018). At least one Impressed Ware vessel from Goval falls within the earlier part of this group, with a secure radiocarbon determination of 3510–3350 cal BC (SUERC-68133). This date compares well with the modified Carinated Bowl pottery. The dating implications for Goval are that the modified Carinated Bowl and the Impressed Ware all belong to the same date bracket of 300 years between 3600–3300 BC. The two types were found some distance apart and it does not necessarily follow that the pottery and features relate to the same period of activity but, equally, it does not rule this out. Similar assemblages of both pottery types were also recorded at Wester Hatton (Chapter 6).

The lugged vessel from Goval has comparatives from the early to later Neolithic. The appearance of lugs on Neolithic Carinated Bowl pottery are one of the earliest variations to Carinated Bowl pottery and are specifically seen as defining the CBNE variant. Lugged modified CB at Kintore had dates spread through the Middle Neolithic (P50 3810–3650 BC, P21 3710–3620 BC and ST12 3130–2920 BC and 3030–2880 BC; Macsween 2008). In addition to this a lugged and decorated Impressed Ware vessel from Kintore was associated with the date 3530–3340 cal BC (SUERC-1322). Further examples of CBNE were also recorded at Milltimber (Chapter 2), Blackdog and Wester Hatton (Chapter 6).

The lithic and ceramic evidence for Neolithic activity at Goval is indicative of domestic occupation where knapping, cooking, serving and collection of refuse were taking place. The isolated pit containing abraded pottery and small lithics points towards discard of unwanted items and nearby knapping. The Impressed Ware and associated lithics also appear to be domestic in origin. This includes the large section of vessel 06-V07; given its poor construction joins, weight and large size it is highly likely that the base broke off in its entirety and the remainder was directly discarded. It is highly probable there was a domestic structure in the vicinity which has either left no trace or was located beyond the excavation areas.

The very low quantity of pottery relating to the Bronze Age and Iron Age occupation at Goval could be explained in two ways: either the site was cleared prior to abandonment; or containers were primarily organic in composition (leather or wood). A similar lack of finds was noted at the Gairnhill roundhouses (Chapter 3.8.2). The Iron Age activity is most clearly illustrated by the iron-smelting debris originating from Furnace B, but found in lesser concentrations incorporated into the other Iron Age features. The quantity and range of slag recovered is limited and suggests only small-scale metalworking activities. Intriguingly, there is no evidence of blacksmithing to complement the smelting at the site. However, the remains of smithing are typically slighter than those of smelting and could easily be destroyed through truncation of soils, as has been noted across the excavated area.

Looking at the importance of the evidence of ferrous metalworking from the site more broadly, the metalworking waste and the processes this material represents provide a valuable addition to the growing corpus of Iron Age iron-smelting sites in the north-east of Scotland, including the A96 Park & Choose, Dyce (Woodley forthcoming), Culduthel, Inverness (Murray 2007; 2008; McLaren & Dungworth 2012), East Beechwood Farm, Inverness (McLaren & Engl in prep), Grantown Road, Moray (McLaren & Dungworth 2016) and Bellfield, North Kessock (Murray 2011; McLaren 2012).

5.12 Discussion

The excavations at Goval offer a starting point for re-evaluating the relationship between both the marginal land to the north and east of the site and the more favourable land close to the river here. A large proportion of the area may indeed have been marginal, showing very little evidence for use prior to larger scale medieval/post-medieval agriculture. However, it also demonstrates that small pockets of better quality ground would have been repeatedly identified and targeted by humans during various periods in the past.

5.12.1 Neolithic pit digging

Although there are indications of background Mesolithic/Early Neolithic activity at Goval (see 5.10.3 above), the earliest activity is in the early part of the Middle Neolithic. The small number of Neolithic features at Goval imply this may have been a single phase of activity, or at most two or three discrete ones. No structural remains were encountered during the excavation, and indeed the area north and east of the Don is devoid of any evidence for Neolithic settlement (see 5.2 above). At Goval, the Neolithic activity is indicated primarily by the deposition of cultural material into small pits, a pattern also recorded at Gairnhill (Chapter 3), Blackdog (Chapter 6) and Wester Hatton (Chapter 6). Indeed, the practice of pit digging is a recognised phenomenon of the Neolithic and is discussed in more detail in Chapter 6.11.2.

The word 'pit' is not an interpretation but rather a term used for any negative feature to which a more specific function (ie post-hole, hearth) cannot be ascribed. The discovery of negative features containing pottery, lithics and plant remains has become synonymous with much of prehistory but it is important to be more critical of this interpretation. Two basic types can be identified – pits that had been cut for an original unknown purpose that had subsequently become filled with domestic debris or those cut for the intentional deposition of cultural material, either in a ritual manner or as a more mundane practice.

How this difference in deposition practices can be identified is far from clear. One pit at Goval contained pieces of modified Carinated Bowl, the condition of which suggests that it could have been domestic waste that had become incorporated into an earlier open pit. Although this is possible, the quantity of pottery recovered from this pit points to more purposeful deposition of this material, possibly within a pit cut for this purpose.

The pits containing Impressed Ware at Goval showed clearer evidence for deposition of largely complete (albeit non-functional) and less abraded vessels in pits that seem to have no prior use. This phenomenon in the Neolithic of placing material into pits in specific ways has led to much debate. This debate is as complex as any attempt to understand an ancient culture, but some general points have emerged. It is now clear that interpreting pits as either domestic or ritual is an overly simplistic duality. The nature of these actions is now more popularly considered on a spectrum, the interpretation of which should include consideration of the 'contents, contexts and setting' (Brophy & Noble 2011). Ritual activity is a repeated action performed regularly in a defined way. This activity is often something that defines cultural norms and accepted behaviour. It can be repeated so many times that the original reasons behind them fade while they continue to be held as accepted social practice.

This idea can be simply expressed at Goval. A large ceramic vessel fell apart during use, and has been disposed of by placing it directly into a pit. This was likely to be a recognised and 'normal' way to dispose of such material – a domestic ritual and no more. The origins or initial purpose of this routine may very well not have been known by those practising it.

This further strengthens the argument for Neolithic domestic activity at Goval, and again draws attention to the lack of matching structural evidence. This pattern of 'missing' Neolithic structures has been suggested at Gairnhill, Blackdog and Wester Hatton and is discussed further in Chapter 7.

5.12.2 Middle Bronze Age isolated settlement

Middle Bronze Age roundhouses from the wider area are characterised in Chapter 3 as post-built, non-specialised and isolated structures. Structure A at Goval fits neatly within this pattern. It was broadly contemporary with the

roundhouses at Chapel of Stoneywood, Nether Beanshill, Gairnhill 6 and 7 (Chapter 3) and Wester Hatton (Chapter 6).

The structure itself was simple and comprised a single post-ring serving as roof support and outer wall, with a possible south-west facing entrance. The internal area can be considered typical for structures of this period (Pope 2015, 171). A worn internal ring-ditch was evident to the north and east sides of the structure, a pattern seen at Chapel of Stoneywood, Gairnhill and Nether Beanshill and also at Kintore (Cook & Dunbar 2008, 324). Overall, the structure aligns well with the morphology and size of the Kintore Type 1A/1B roundhouses (Cook & Dunbar 2008, 324), three examples of which have also been dated to the Middle–Late Bronze Age (RH 24, 25 and 26). Other similar structures in Aberdeenshire have been excavated at Hatton Farm (Gray & Suddaby 2010) and Oldmeldrum (House 2; White & Richardson 2010, 5–7).

There is limited evidence for specific activities during the Bronze Age at Goval – the lithics, charcoal and burnt bone represent typical domestic refuse. Pastoralism is indicated by the internal ring-gully, and there is some ecofactual evidence of a barley crop. Combined with the isolation, this reinforces the suggestion that such structures were multi-purpose, and non-specialised (see Chapter 3.9.4).

There is presently no evidence for any further Middle Bronze Age activity near Goval, despite the substantial size of the mitigation areas. This is perhaps not surprising, for two reasons. The trend for Middle Bronze Age roundhouses to stand alone (as opposed to the clustering seen later in the period) was encountered at Gairnhill and Nether Beanshill (Chapter 3.9.4). Similar degrees of isolation are recorded at other sites in the north-east of Scotland, for example Structure 3 at Deer's Den (Alexander 2000, 67). It is not clear if this represents social organisation (small family groups living self-sufficiently), or perhaps seasonal movement. This is discussed further in Chapter 7. Structure A shows evidence for structural repair, which could support arguments for both continual or episodic use. The second reason is the location at Goval itself. Each period of activity here is fairly short-lived and small-scale. Structure A is a perfect example – it has been in use long enough to require repair, but no replacement structures are evident. There is no sign of industrial activity or burials, and only limited evidence for agriculture. This supports the idea that Goval was visible as a small pocket of better quality land offering enough of an advantage over its surroundings to entice periodic settlement.

5.12.3 Middle Iron Age metalworking and domestic activity

There were two phases of Middle Iron Age activity at Goval, separated by perhaps 200 years. Early activity was focused on iron smelting, with evidence for a furnace and an associated roundhouse. The metalworking activity is small in scale, and typical of smelting in Scotland at this time (see 5.10.4 above). The roundhouse conforms

Illus 5.26 Artist's impression of the Iron Age settlement at Goval. The furnace in the foreground was likely just for domestic use, serving the single roundhouse which lay closer towards the River Don

to the description of a Type 4, 5 or 6 structure (Cook & Dunbar 2008, 324) and the dating is in the same range as for similar types at Kintore.

The Iron Age building at Goval appears to have seen a degree of alteration during its lifespan. There is evidence for routine replacement or repair of posts, but also the addition of a substantial external stone surface that has required the removal of at least part of an earlier external wall. This could be an example of 'dual flooring' as identified by Pope (2003, 254). This refers to the practice of selectively paving only parts of a roundhouse, and is particularly common around the entrance. In this instance, the thickness of the stone seems likely to have resulted in a raised surface, perhaps as grain-drying platforms or a form of working surface, although no specific evidence for either was recovered. The function of the roundhouse as a whole

appears to have been domestic, with an internal hearth and evidence for barley growing and the keeping of goats/sheep (Illus 5.26). It is suggested that this period of occupation is primarily domestic – the scale of metalworking, probably representing a single use furnace, is so small that it is unlikely to have been the focus of activity.

Detailed interpretation of Furnace B is derived largely from the material evidence. Illus 5.14A, which shows the feature during excavation, illustrates how the feature was relatively unprepossessing in the field, and without the survival of the metalworking waste, could easily have been dismissed as an insignificant rubbish pit.

The second phase of Iron Age activity at Goval comprised a small kiln, most likely for grain drying. Although apparently isolated, it is likely that the stone surface encountered at Structure B (only 18 m away) was still visible, despite a time gap of potentially 200 years. The availability of such a surface could have been a specific reason to come to Goval to grow and process grain.

The presence of an Iron Age phase of any sort is unique for the sites reported in this volume. Indeed, the nearest remains identified from this period are at Kintore (Cook & Dunbar 2008), some 8 km west along the Don. In some cases this period is conspicuous by its absence. Recent excavations at a park and ride facility near to Chapel of Stoneywood have evidence for concentrated activity throughout the 2nd–4th centuries BC, then nothing further until the 5th century AD (Thomson 2015; Woodley forthcoming). Potential reasons for such 'gaps' are discussed further in Chapter 7.

5.12.4 Early Historic enclosure

The only feature relating to the Early Historic period was a single curvilinear gully of the mid-7th to mid-8th centuries AD. Although shallow, evidence of burning longitudinal timbers suggests an originally structural function. This was most likely in the form of a rectilinear building or enclosure approximately 5 m wide. The only other features found within this area comprised three undated pits. As such the function of the enclosure cannot be derived from the present archaeological evidence. Whether its destruction by fire was intentional or otherwise is also unclear.

While the limited scale of the remains makes interpretation problematic, there is broadly contemporary evidence for similar construction methods. A horizontal timber 'antenna' setting of a similar scale was revealed at Rhynie (Gondek & Noble 2012, 13). This formed an offshoot from a much larger enclosure ditch (itself dated to the 5th–6th century AD) and most likely divided the space between the ditch and an outer palisade. While we cannot infer any such function for the remains at Goval, this does show that similar construction methods were in use locally.

The problem of identification and excavation of domestic/agricultural remains of this period is discussed in Chapter 2.15.8. Although some comparative enclosures have been found at sites such as Rhynie and Portmahomack (Carver *et al.* 2016), the comparative lack of datable examples of these kind of features is apparent. The importance of radiocarbon dating not just the 'understood' features but also those that do not easily fit into a site's narrative is crucial and should form part of the excavation and post-excavation strategy on schemes such as this.

Chapter 6

The coastal plain

Jürgen van Wessel and Don Wilson

6.1 Introduction to the circumstances of discovery at Blackdog, Wester Hatton and Middlefield

6.1.1 Background to the archaeological works

This chapter presents the results of the mitigation excavations at Blackdog, Wester Hatton and Middlefield (Illus 6.01). These are the only ones set in a coastal landscape, approximately 1 km from the modern shoreline. Wester Hatton was the only site identified in the Environmental Statement from the area (Jacobs UK 2007; Site 362). It had been recorded from aerial photography as a roughly circular cropmark (NJ91NE 36) measuring approximately 10 m in diameter. A geophysical survey of the road corridor found nothing of archaeological potential at Middlefield (Bartlett & Boucher 2012b; 2012d) and was not completed at Blackdog (owing to the steepness of slope) and Wester Hatton (because of access issues).

The sites at Blackdog and Middlefield were identified during trial trenching and were subsequently targeted for further mitigation in the form of a programme of strip, map and record. Access to the Wester Hatton site was eventually gained during the construction phase of the road scheme. As part of the Construction Joint Venture's (CJV) archaeological works, trial trenching was undertaken across the area. This identified several surviving prehistoric archaeological features and led to a controlled topsoil strip of the area followed by full excavation.

6.1.2 Site locations and extent of mitigation

At Blackdog (formerly NL/012), the excavation targeted a pit containing large sherds of Neolithic Carinated Bowl, initially identified during the trial trenching (Robertson 2013, 40–1). The excavation area was situated north of a modern housing development at Blackdog, and immediately south of the Blackdog Industrial Centre. The excavation covered an area of 1,735 m², centred on NJ 9584 1427 on a steep, south-facing grassy slope at an elevation of 28–36 m AOD.

The topsoil was generally 0.3–0.45 m in depth but up to 1.2 m near the south-western corner, likely the result of bunding during construction activity in the wider area. A hillwash deposit 0.05 m deep was identified at the base of the slope near the south-western corner of the site and an assemblage of 20 flint and pitchstone lithics were recovered from this deposit. This deposit was found to directly overlay the geological subsoil with no further features identified. The geological subsoil itself comprised a loose reddish-yellow sand with stony patches, frequently affected by rabbit burrows and bioturbation. Two substantial areas of modern disturbance were encountered to the west and north of the site and most likely related to recent house building.

Six archaeological features were recorded at Blackdog, all containing prehistoric material (van Wessel 2015, 56–60). Three were very substantial circular pits of broadly similar form and sequence of infilling. Two contained Neolithic pottery and worked lithics were found in all three. Three smaller pits also contained lithic assemblages.

The excavation area at Wester Hatton (CJV site AMA22) revealed the remains of five structures and a series of small and large pits. These produced pottery and lithic assemblages pointing towards Neolithic and Bronze Age domestic occupation across the site (Wilson 2017; Appendix 1.4). It was located south of Wester Hatton farm and defined by the A90 (Aberdeen to Peterhead) to the east, the minor Potterton/Belhelvie road to the south and a landfill site to the west. The excavation area was situated on a south-facing slope within a rectilinear parcel of land measuring approximately 9000 m² and centred on NJ 9568 1505 (Illus 6.01).

The ground within the land parcel rose from 35 m AOD at the Potterton/Belhelvie road intersection to 44 m AOD at its highest point in the centre of the site. The ground sloped from this high point down toward the A90 to the

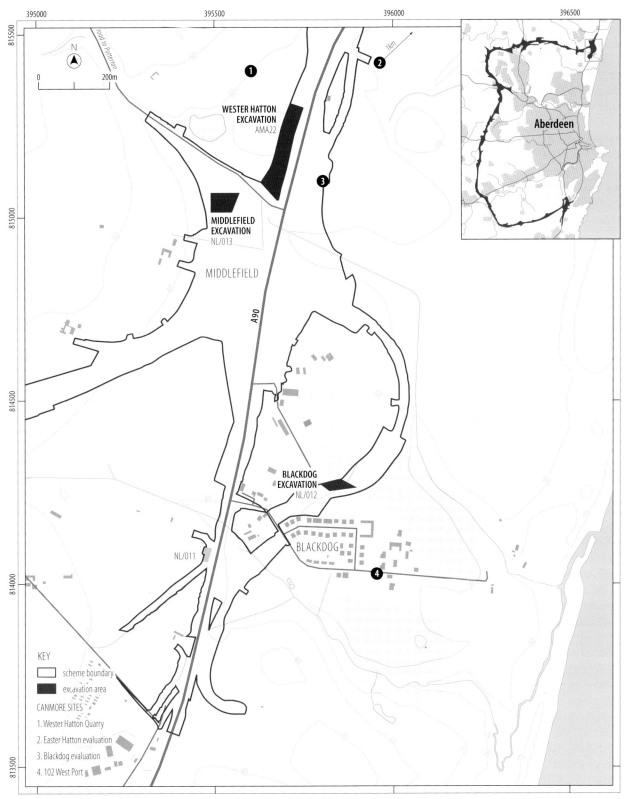

Illus 6.01 Location of sites at Middlefield, Blackdog and Wester Hatton

east as well as to the north and south. The topsoil was generally 0.3–0.45 m in depth but became shallower at the top of the slope and deeper at the base (up to 0.6 m near the south end of the site). This increase in depth may have been the result of hillwash and post-medieval ploughing.

The Middlefield excavation (formerly NL/013) aimed to explore the full extent of activity indicated by a single lithic-rich pit discovered during trial trenching (Robertson 2014, 42). The site was situated north-east of Middlefield Farm, south of the Potterton/Belhelvie road (Illus 6.01).

The excavation covered a trapezoidal area of 3,636 m² centred on NJ 95530 15040, on relatively flat pasture at an elevation of 32–34 m AOD.

The topsoil was up to 0.4 m deep and directly overlay the geological subsoil, which comprised compact stony sands and gravels, with patches of looser stony sands, particularly to the west of the site. Six pits were recorded at Middlefield, four of which were found to contain lithic assemblages, including indicators of nearby knapping and Mesolithic activity (van Wessel 2015, 60–1). Towards the south of the area, the two largest pits had clearly defined cuts but did not contain any visible anthropogenic material. An extensive system of rubble and ceramic field drains was concentrated to the western side of site.

6.2 Archaeological context and past settlement patterns

Jürgen van Wessel

The ES (Grontmij and Natural Capital 2007) identified eleven cultural heritage sites within the vicinity of the three sites. The majority relate to post-medieval agriculture, industry and boundary marking. The only site that represented potential archaeological remains was that of Wester Hatton (Site 362).

The surrounding coastal area has been well scrutinised by archaeologists in recent years. This includes trial trenching for the present road scheme (Robertson 2014), and an evaluation at Easter Hatton (NJ91NE 58, Holden 1998b) that resulted in the investigation of a substantial flint scatter. Other recent works include a large scheme to the north and west of Blackdog (NJ91NE 69, Clements & Cook 2009; NJ91SW 206, Lenfert & Cameron 2016). This recorded a possible Early Bronze Age funerary ring-ditch, a post-hole constructed roundhouse and a number of isolated pits with a lithic assemblage relating to the Late Bronze Age or Iron Age, which are presently subject to further investigation (Martin Cook pers comm). A watching brief undertaken as part of the evaluation work revealed patches of hillwash material just downslope from the Blackdog excavation, from which a small assemblage of lithic material was gathered. Other work has produced little or no evidence for prehistoric activity, including the evaluation of another large site at Wester Hatton quarry (NJ91NE 64, Halliday 2000), a watching brief at 102 West Port, Blackdog (NJ91SW 193, Cook 2008) and the excavation of a small area south-west of Blackdog (van Wessel 2015, site NL/011).

The wider area includes a number of prehistoric archaeological sites indicating a rich and diverse prehistoric landscape. These include a recumbent stone circle (Temple Stones; NJ91NE 17) north-east of Potterton, a single cropmark (NJ91NE 37) interpreted as a probable souterrain to the north of Wester Hatton and a prehistoric burial cairn (Shepherd 1984) further to the north revealing a small quantity of cremated bone and flint flakes. This cairn had subsequently been enlarged and a food vessel cremation inserted (NJ91NE 11). Further inland, prehistoric activity has been evidenced from sites at Belhelvie and Overhill with gold torcs and chains, cist burials, food vessels, stone and bronze axes reportedly found.

6.3 Environmental context

Richard Tipping

6.3.1 The formation of the landscape

Most of the hills along the coast are made of gravel and sand, and with the same NNE–SSW lineation: temporary shallow sections in the southern flank of Fife Hill show the sediment here to be dominated by sand, with little gravel. The elongated ridges fade into more rounded forms only a couple of kilometres inland, making the coastal plain distinctive. The sand and gravel is glaciofluvial, deposited by flowing water at the end of the last glaciation in a series of eskers and kames (Murdoch 1975) and deltas filling glacio-lacustrine lakes (Merritt *et al.* 2003).

Illus 6.02 uses the distribution of soils to indicate changes in sub-surface geology and in drainage because soil mapping is more detailed than geological mapping. The glaciofluvial sand and gravel unsurprisingly gives rise to free-draining soils, the Corby Association, and the Corby Series (Glentworth & Muir 1963), formed also on the gentler slopes around Fife Hill. Countesswells Series soils are also comparatively free-draining but are formed on glacial till.

6.3.2 Changing soils and plant communities

The varied parent materials produce soils of different drainage and chemistry. The Corby and Countesswells Series are iron podsols. The Tipperty Series soil is a brown forest soil, though not well drained. At Blackdog, Middlefield and Wester Hatton in the Mesolithic and Early Neolithic, the soils were probably nutrient-rich. Drainage properties differed because parent materials differed and, in a world before field drains, we can imagine that some soils, like the patches of Blackhouse and Tipperty Series soils and especially the patches of poorly drained Terryvale Series gleys (Illus 6.02), were marshy, providing different resources to people. The sites at Middlefield and Wester Hatton were beside what may have been a small marsh or fen.

Peats buried by rising sea level on the Ythan estuary are our only source of pollen data on the coastal plain (Smith *et al.* 1983; 1999), and this estuarine setting may make their data untypical. Nevertheless, the same tree taxa that colonised inland soils colonised the coast and seemingly with no less vigour. By the later Mesolithic, all tree taxa we see today had colonised (Tipping 1994; 2007) and there was a degree of stability to the woodland. The patchiness of the soils was probably not matched by patchiness in the

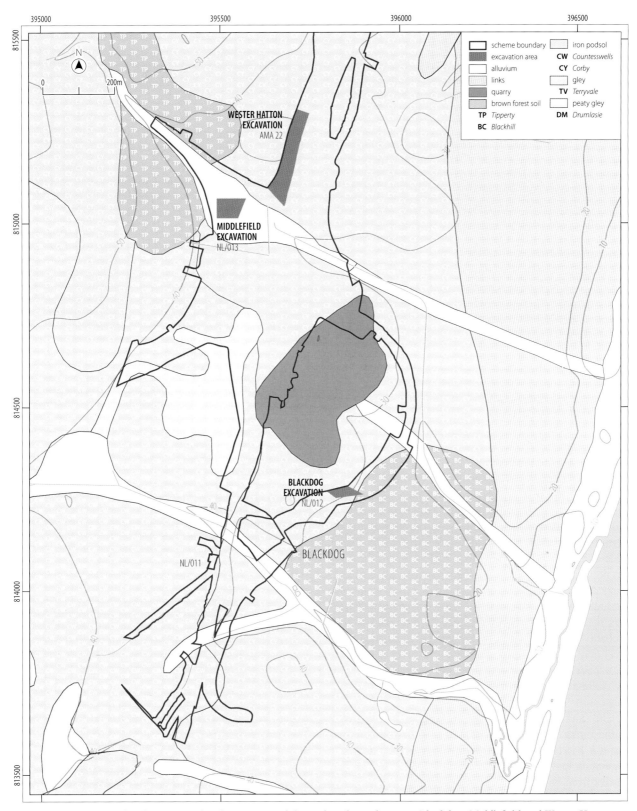

Illus 6.02 Topography, drainage and soil types around the archaeological sites at Blackdog, Middlefield and Wester Hatton

woodland because soils of the Corby and Countesswells Series provide similar niches. Free-draining soils will probably have been covered in a deciduous woodland of oak and elm, with hazel as an under-storey shrub and as a tree of the natural edges of the woodland, on the wind-pruned coast and around wetlands. Birch, ash, aspen and holly will also have sought light along these edges and colonised gaps in the wood where big trees fell by decay or wind. Brambles and berries would also have responded to these gap-phases for a few decades before moving on as the canopy grew back, as would grasses and bracken. Most grassland herbs will have grown at woodland edges and on the coast. We think of these woodlands as having closed canopies because the proportions of grasses in pollen records are so low, but this is partly because trees produce enormous amounts of pollen. When this imbalance is adjusted mathematically, the woodlands appear to have been more open (Fyfe *et al.* 2013) but openness only encourages thorns and brambles. Perhaps the only variation might have been seen around what are now poorly drained soils, the Blackhouse and Terryvale Series, strongholds for alder, birch and willow.

6.3.3 The changing coastline

The Neolithic pits at Blackdog were only 800 m from the present coast and the settlement activity at Wester Hatton approximately 1 km away. The distance may have been greater in the Neolithic because the sediments on the coast, glacial till and glacio-lacustrine clays, are soft and easily eroded. There appear to be no estimates of long-term cliff retreat for this coast, but drawing on change since the mid-19th century the coast-line may have lain some 1.4 km east of its present position. A higher sea surface, +3.38 m AOD by c4800 BC (Smith *et al.* 1999), flooded into the deepened Blackdog Burn, pushing inland some 250 m west of the present coast-line and creating a drowned valley filled to around 4 m AOD by marine sediment. This would have been an environment and a resource different from the open coast, a place of restricted salt marsh, sheltered and protected by the hills on either side. This sediment remains uneroded, because the present small stream is too weak, keeping the floor of Blackdog Burn wide and marshy still. This process of sediment infilling has not happened, however, to the unnamed canalised and ditched burn immediately to the north that passes close to the archaeological site, implying that this shallow valley was inactive for much of the present interglacial, and probably dry after glacial meltwater was exhausted. Sea level may have remained at around 4 m AOD until some time, poorly defined, before the Early Bronze Age c2200 BC, falling thereafter with one significant though undated pause to its present level.

The sand dunes at the coast are mapped in Illus 6.02 as the Links Series, a free-draining soil, so free-draining that it is barely soil at all, with little to hold the thin grass vegetation together. The dunes form a continuous coastal barrier from within Aberdeen itself on the Old Town or King's Links, to the River Don and to the Ythan estuary in the north, and beyond. They are no more than one dune wide south of the Blackdog Burn, but they become markedly wider at the Blackdog Links, east of the archaeological sites. When they began to form is unclear, but it may have been after 2200 cal BC (Smith *et al.* 1999).

6.4 Radiocarbon results and dating

A total of 14 radiocarbon determinations were obtained from the coastal sites. The results are presented in Table 6.01 and Illus 6.03. Where possible, charcoal from short-lived species or small branch wood was used to date features, to achieve as accurate a date-range as possible. At Wester Hatton both hazel nutshell and pottery residue was also utilised. Proxy dating for many of the features was also provided by pottery and lithic typologies (see Table 6.02, 6.9.2 below, Tables 6.05–6.06 and 6.9.4 below)

The Bronze Age date from Middlefield does not correspond with the Mesolithic lithic assemblage recovered from that site. The Neolithic date for the pottery from the Bronze Age ring-ditch features at Wester Hatton also fails to correspond, although in both cases they suggest a prolonged period of low-level land use and activity. There is a very late Mesolithic date (SUERC-68123) from a large pit at Blackdog, although it is from a deposit above one dated to the Early Neolithic (SUERC-68122). This stratigraphic issue is discussed further below (see 6.5.1). An Early Neolithic date (SUERC-58955) from the upper fill of a second large pit that corresponded stratigraphically with a deposit of Carinated Bowl North-East (CBNE) pottery could suggest an early date for that type of pottery, although this date is from oak charcoal, and could be subject to the old oak effect. The Neolithic pottery recovered from the Bronze Age structures at Wester Hatton is probably the result of disturbance of existing Neolithic features during the Bronze Age.

6.5 Mesolithic/Neolithic activity at Blackdog

Jürgen van Wessel

6.5.1 Large Mesolithic/Neolithic pits at Blackdog – 4300–3400 BC

A cluster of three large pits were aligned broadly east–west along the base of a short east–west aligned slope, spaced approximately 12 m apart (Illus 6.04, 6.05). The pits displayed similar properties to the numerous large pits recorded at Milltimber (Chapter 2). As at Milltimber two types of pit seem to be present, although in this instance the difference was not as marked. Two of the pits [12–0001] and [12–0002] had rounded bowl-shaped profiles with a maximum depth of 1.3 m. Pit [12–0034] in comparison was steeper with a flat base 1.9 m deep. The three pits were circular to sub-circular in plan measuring up to 3 m diameter and included multiple fills with potential episodes of recutting although this was much less prevalent in pit [12–0034].

The fills of pits [12–0001] (Illus 6.06) and [12–0002] had been interpreted as having been recut up to four times, although the sequence of this activity was not always clear (Illus 6.07, 6.08). The multiple fills were very similar to those recorded at Milltimber and will not be repeated

Table 6.01 Radiocarbon determinations from Blackdog, Wester Hatton and Middlefield

Site	Context	Lab no	Material	Radiocarbon age BP	Calibrated age 98.4% probability
Blackdog Mesolithic and Neolithic pits	(12-0007) fill of Mesolithic pit [12-0001]	SUERC-68123	Nutshell: *Corylus avellana*	5373±29	4330–4070 cal BC
	(12-0018) final fill in Mesolithic pit [12-0034]	SUERC-58599	Charcoal: *Quercus sp*	5111±28	3970–3810 cal BC
	(12-0019) fill of small Mesolithic pit [12-0001]	SUERC-68122	Charcoal: *Corylus avellana*	4996±29	3930–3710 cal BC
	(12-0025) fill of Neolithic pit [12-0023]	SUERC-58600	Charcoal: *Alnus glutinosa*	4744±28	3630–3390 cal BC
Wester Hatton Pit Clusters	PC1 fill (AMA-6052) of Neolithic pit cut [AMA22-6051]	SUERC-74400	Nutshell: *Corylus avellana*	4492±27	3340–3100 cal BC
	PC5 Fill (AMA-6271) of Neolithic pit cut [AMA22-6269]	SUERC-74399	Nutshell: *Corylus avellana*	4416±29	3310–2920 cal BC
Wester Hatton Bronze Age features	WH2 fill (AMA-6239) of ring-ditch [AMA22-6238]	SUERC-73583	Pottery residue	3372±31	1740–1570 cal BC
	Upper fill (AMA-6187) of large BA pit cut [AMA22-6188]	SUERC-74401	Cereal grain: barley	3203±29	1520–1430 cal BC
	Fill (AMA-6166) of BA pit cut [AMA22-6167]	SUERC-73591	Cereal grain	3037±31	1400–1210 cal BC
	WH 3 base fill (AMA-6181) of ring-ditch cut [AMA22-6179]	SUERC-73584	Cereal grain	2995±31	1370–1130 cal BC
	WH4 primary fill (AMA-6029) of ring-ditch [AMA22-6030]	SUERC-73586	Pottery residue	2946±31	1260–1050 cal BC
	WH4 sSpread (AMA-6025) over ring-ditch [AMA22-6030]	SUERC-73585	Pottery residue	2916±31	1210–1020 cal BC
	WH5 primary fill (AMA-6119) of post-hole [AMA22-6050]	SUERC-73587	Charcoal: non-oak	2851±31	1110–930 cal BC
Middlefield Bronze Age pit	(13-0012) Fill of small BA pit [13-0011]	SUERC-68121	Charcoal: *Corylus avellana*	3744±29	2270–2040 cal BC

here in full. Both pits had evidence of slumped geological subsoil at the base and more anthropogenic layers above. The potential recuts observed are open to interpretation, although the final recut in both pits do appear real.

One of the middle layers of pit [12–0001] was a compact, charcoal-rich deposit mixed with some geological subsoil. None of the surrounding deposits or stones appeared heat-affected, suggesting a process of dumping rather than *in situ* burning. Small quantities of nutshell and weed seeds were recovered from this material. A radiocarbon date of 3930–3710 cal BC (SUERC-68122) from hazel charcoal provides an Early Neolithic date for this material. The final recut included charcoal-rich deposits containing weed seeds, nutshell and a near-complete, but broken, north-eastern style modified Carinated Bowl (12-V01; see 6.9.1 below) along with a heavily abraded sherd of prehistoric pottery, a broken flint pebble and a single flint flake. Hazel charcoal from the basal deposits of this recut returned a

carbon date of 4330–4070 cal BC (SUERC-68123). This date does not sit well with the stratigraphic sequence as it lies above the Neolithic material from the lower deposit. The layers had no direct interface, being separated by a layer of charcoal-rich burnt sand, although this was thin and it is possible that even a modest degree of mixing could cause such an issue. It is also possible that the Mesolithic date (not having any direct support from other evidence) has come from residual material that has become incorporated into the Neolithic pit, given the slightly random mix of flint and abraded pottery within the fill of the later pit. It must also be noted that the pit had been partially excavated during the trial-trench evaluation.

The secondary use of pit [12–0002] included a mixed deposit of grey sand, ash and charcoal. This represents either *in situ* burning or dumping of burnt material. Two subsequent burnt sand and charcoal deposits may indicate further *in situ* burning. A single flint blade and significant

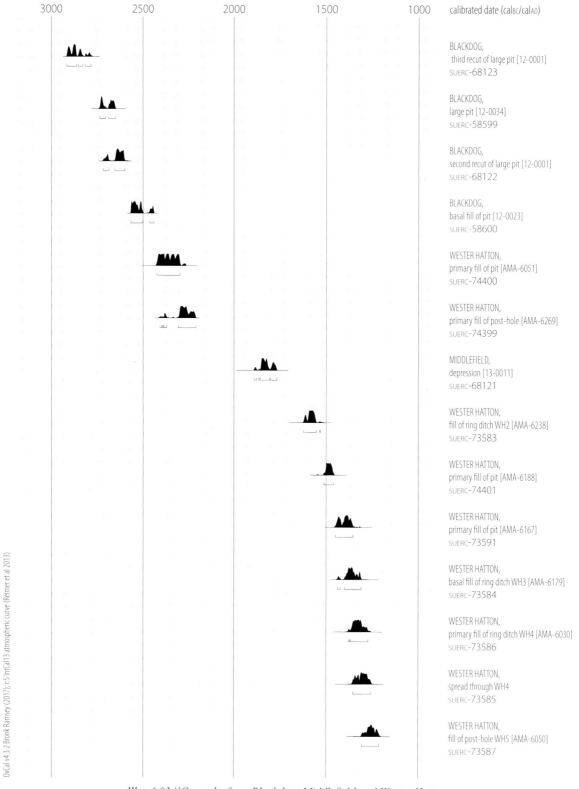

Illus 6.03 ¹⁴C graphs from Blackdog, Middlefield and Wester Hatton

quantities of charcoal and nutshell were retrieved from these deposits, as well as two fragments of modern redware. The latter is likely to be intrusive – a degree of disturbance, possibly animal burrowing, was encountered above and although there were no obvious signs in section that this had penetrated lower deposits this must remain a possibility.

The final recut [12–0048] of pit [12–0002] was partially filled with a concentration of sub-angular granite and quartz stones in the southern half of the pit along with a

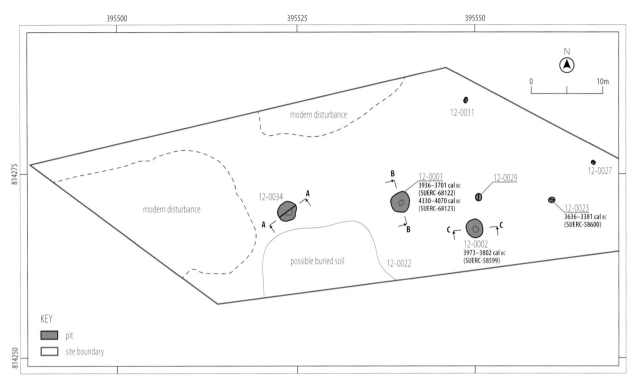

Illus 6.04 Plan of archaeological features at Blackdog

deposit derived from the geological subsoil. A single flint flake and a significant quantity of charcoal and nutshell were retrieved from this deposit, as well as two fragments of modern pottery, which may have been introduced by animal burrowing. A radiocarbon date of 3970–3810 cal BC (SUERC-58599) from charcoal recovered from this upper deposit indicates an Early Neolithic date, although this may be subject to the 'old-oak' effect (see 6.8.1 below).

The sequence of deposition in pit [12–0034] (Illus 6.09) was somewhat different. Here at least two potential episodes of *in situ* burning were evident, comprising lenses of heated grey sand and charcoal. A small quantity of nutshell was retrieved from each of these contexts. The upper deposits in the pit appear to represent further *in situ* burning. A single flint chip, a single grain of barley and a small quantity of nutshell were recovered from these upper layers.

No dating material was recovered from the lower fills of these pits and there is a stratigraphic issue with the Mesolithic date obtained from pit [12–0001]. This was from one of the upper fills although it was considered to be intrusive. Given this, even if it was intrusive it does signify a potential for Mesolithic activity in the area and may even represent the period these pits were first excavated. Although the pits at Milltimber were very similar in size and fill composition, the majority of those were dated to the earlier Mesolithic. This may provide a clue as to why the Blackdog pits in particular show such clear evidence of recuts. If the pits had initially been cut c4300 BC they were more likely to have still been visible in the Early

Neolithic. Perhaps these partially filled pits were useful and easily re-excavated or held some known or even unknown cultural significance. Certainly there seems to be differences between the pits at the two sites, although this variation may not necessarily imply different uses. At Milltimber these were considered to represent animal traps (see discussion in Chapter 2) and there is no reason to suggest anything different occurring at Blackdog in the Mesolithic.

As with the Milltimber pits, the reuse of the pits at Blackdog was not fully understood, although it clearly involved either *in situ* burning or the deposition of burnt material within the tops of the earlier cut. At both sites Neolithic pottery was recovered from these later deposits, providing dating evidence for the final phase of activity related to these pits. The specific local style of the Carinated Bowl in pit [12–0001] gives a broad possible date range from c3800 to 2880 BC although there is a tendency towards earlier Neolithic dates for this style of vessel (see 6.9.1 below). These recuts may provide further evidence of what seems like a pit-digging tradition in the Neolithic that is represented at Blackdog and Wester Hatton.

6.5.2 Smaller Neolithic pits at Blackdog – 4000–3400 BC

Four smaller pits were recorded at Blackdog (see Illus 6.4). These were located to both the north and east of the large pits. Pits [12–0023] and [12–0029] were 0.75 and 0.95 m in diameter and 0.08 m and 0.16 m deep respectively. The homogeneous sand fills contained frequent charcoal

Illus 6.05 General view of excavations at Blackdog showing slope of underlying subsoil

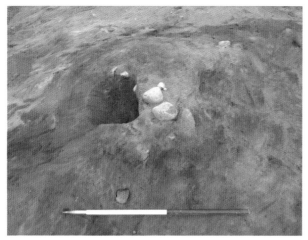

Illus 6.06 Pit [12–0001] under excavation

fragments, small quantities of nutshell, small lithic assemblages, including a pitchstone scraper, and several fragments of prehistoric pottery (see 6.9 below). A radiocarbon date of 3630–3390 cal BC (SUERC-58600) from charcoal recovered from the base of [12–0023] dates the infilling of this feature to the Early to Middle Neolithic. None of the finds proved diagnostic for dating (other than

being prehistoric) and it was not clear whether the charcoal was the result of *in situ* burning (later disturbed) or waste deposition. Pits [12–0031] and [12–0027] to the north and east were slightly larger and also contained charcoal and a small lithic assemblage, with [12–0031] including a flint core.

The purpose of the pits was not identified and apart from the similarity of the fills nothing was identified to suggest the four pits were contemporary. Given this, the absence of any later phases of activity plus the similarity of the fills implies they likely represented the same phase of Neolithic activity. The presence of pitchstone may also suggest trading from as far away as Arran (see 6.9.2.1 below). Similar pits were recorded at Wester Hatton (see 6.6.1 below); however, these had a slightly later Neolithic date (see 6.10.2 below).

6.6 Occupation at Wester Hatton

Don Wilson

Wester Hatton presented a spread of archaeological features across the south-facing slope of a rise that formed the main topographic feature of the area (Illus 6.10). The scientific dating evidence in conjunction with the

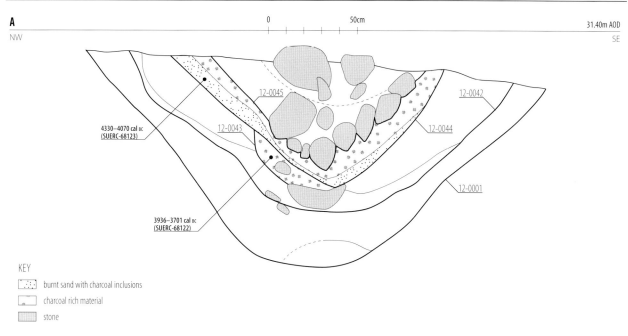

Illus 6.07 Section of pit [12–0001] facing south-west

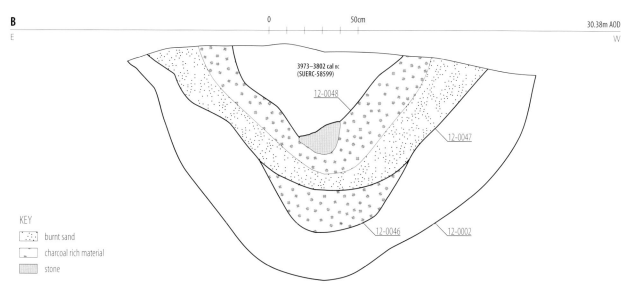

Illus 6.08 Section of pit [12–0002] facing north

material culture pointed to two broad phases of activity on the site, although additional low-level Mesolithic activity was identified in the shape of a small residual lithic assemblage. The Neolithic activity comprised the remains of a series of small pits forming five clusters (Pit Clusters 1–5). This was followed by intermittent Bronze Age settlement activity comprising a series of five roundhouse structures. Four of these (Wester Hatton 1–4) included stone-filled curvilinear ring-ditches and arcs of post-holes. A fifth structure (Wester Hatton 5), comprising an arc of post-holes and an outer ring-groove, was found partially truncating the south side of Wester Hatton 4. There were also four large pits and a spread of charcoal-rich material.

Cultivation rig-and-furrow was prevalent across the site, representing post-medieval agricultural activity. To the south-east corner of the area a tarmac road was also exposed that formed an earlier alignment of the Aberdeen to Fraserburgh road and potentially originated in the mid- to late 18th century.

6.6.1 The Neolithic pits at Wester Hatton – 3300–2900 BC

The Neolithic activity primarily comprised five clusters of small pits (PC1–5). These clusters were generally formed of three or four closely arranged pits, although in the case of PC4 these had a slightly wider spread. PC1 to PC3 were

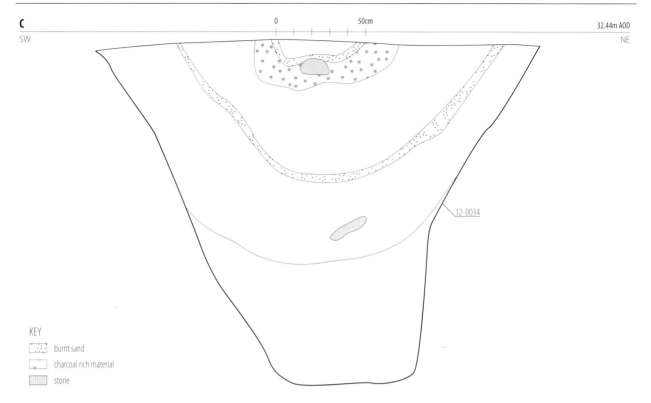

Illus 6.09 Section of pit [12–0034] facing south-east

located to the south-western quarter of the site (Illus 6.11) with PC4 roughly 20 m to the north (Illus 6.12). The only anomaly to this was PC5 that formed a more random spread of pits located close to the eastern side of structure Wester Hatton 2 (see Illus 6.12).

The phasing of these pits is primarily based upon the recovered ceramic and lithic assemblages, which were predominantly Neolithic in date, comprising fragments of modified Carinated Bowls and Impressed Ware vessels (see 6.9.1 below) plus a small assemblage of Levallois-like cores and flakes (see 6.9.2.2). This material corresponds well to the two radiocarbon dates of 3340–3100 cal BC and 3310–2920 cal BC returned from pits [AMA22–6051] (PC1) and [AMA-22–6269] (PC5) respectively (SUERC-74400 and SUERC-74399).

Each of the four pit clusters to the south (PC1–PC4) was formed of three or four small pits, although the spread of these pits varied within each cluster. The majority of the pits were between 0.5 m and 0.6 m diameter with a general depth of 0.1 m to 0.2 m. Most pits had a single homogeneous sand fill with only two pits – [AMA22–6063] and [AMA22–6066] – containing a secondary fill, with a third pit [AMA22–6075] containing three diffuse fills. Each cluster included a significant quantity of pottery fragments, lithic debitage, cores and tools, occasional nutshell fragments and, in some cases, charred plant remains.

Pit Cluster PC5 (Illus 6.13) was formed of two roughly parallel east–west aligned rows approximately 0.5 m apart with an additional small spread of pits immediately south of these. The pits ranged in size and depth but were generally

0.30 m to 0.45 m diameter with depths between 0.05 m and 0.24 m. The majority had a single fill with only three pits found to include secondary deposits. Of note was pit [AMA22–6266]. This truncated pit with [AMA22–6273] formed the only example of intercutting pits identified (Illus 6.14). The fill of both these pits included burnt bone with pit [AMA22–6273] also containing vitrified lithic pieces. The burnt bone was not abundant and not diagnostic. The likelihood is that this material represents domestic waste. The pottery assemblage from these two pits also represented the bulk of the material found in this cluster. They contained the remains of at least eight separate vessels (Table 6.02 and see 6.9.2 below) with sherds of two of these vessels also being recovered from pit [AMA22–6278]. One of the vessels (06-V30) from pit [AMA22–6266] comprised 74 sherds and 99 fragments of a single vessel, signifying a substantial part of the pot was deposited in this pit. Could this represent more votive depositional practices taking place here? This is certainly a possibility, although one that is difficult to positively identify. The overall domestic nature of the pottery assemblage would imply a more mundane practice occurring.

One other anomaly was pit [AMA22–6282]. This seemed to be cut within a much larger and irregularly shaped pit [AMA22–6284], although the exact sequence was unclear. The pottery and lithics here were all recovered from the darker fill of pit [AMA22–6282] and it is possible that the larger pit may actually represent a tree-bowl. Certainly the mixed light yellow sand fill of this pit would be commensurate

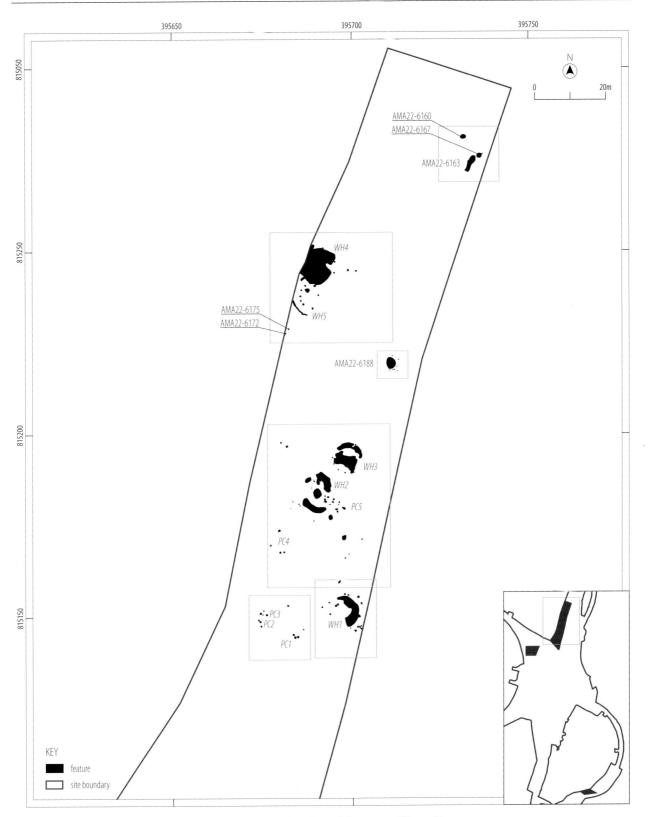

Illus 6.10 Plan of archaeological features at Wester Hatton

with this conclusion. The pottery from pit [AMA22–6282] also represented a further eight separate vessels that were predominantly Middle Neolithic in date. Fragments and sherds of multiple vessels were also recovered from pits [AMA22–6269] (seven vessels) and [AMA22–6287] (two vessels; Table 6.02 and see 6.9.2 below).

In general the pit clusters seem to represent a period of Middle Neolithic activity although the basis of this activity

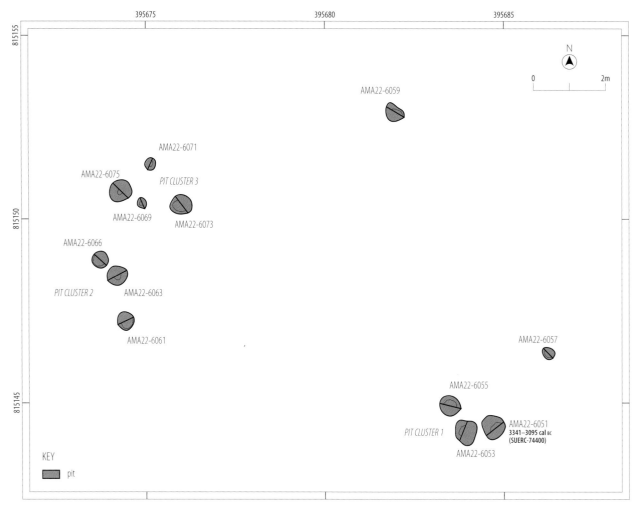

Illus 6.11 Plan of pit clusters 1–3

is unclear. Whether this represents a short-lived but busy period of activity or the result of longer term intermittent activity is difficult to pinpoint (Illus 6.15).

6.6.2 Bronze Age settlement activity – 1700–900 BC

Five separate structures (WH1–WH5) were recorded at Wester Hatton along with a number of large pits, mainly located to the northern end of the site. Four of these structures (WH1–WH4) were represented by outer post-rings and ring-ditches, although variances in this basic design were identified. The final structure (WH5) comprised the partial remains of an outer ring-groove and an inner post-ring. The pits varied in size and shape with no two features the same.

Not all the structures were scientifically dated, although of the four that were, the earliest proved be WH2. This structure was significantly earlier than the other three dated structures (WH3, WH4 & WH5), all of which formed a relatively tight, although not overlapping, grouping of Middle Bronze Age dates. The pits provided further evidence of Middle Bronze Age activity but again with no overlapping dates established.

6.6.2.1 Wester Hatton 2 – Early Bronze Age 1700–1600 BC

Two opposing ring-ditches, one of which was poorly defined (Illus 6.16, 6.17), formed the main features associated with WH2. These two ring-ditches enclosed a large but very shallow circular scoop with a heat-affected sand. Evidence of further structural elements such as internal or external post-holes was very limited. The diameter of the structure as defined by the ring-ditches was 10.5 m. However, since these are internal features, the diameter of the structure was likely to have been larger. The eastern side of the ring-ditches was also the location of a Neolithic pit cluster (PC5).

Ring-ditch [AMA22–6243] defined the north-eastern side of the structure and was roughly curvilinear in plan, although slightly irregular to the north-west side. The moderately steep uneven sides were up to 1.55 m wide leading to a concave base with a maximum depth of 0.23 m. The fills presented a sequence of poorly sorted but compact stone cobbles (Illus 6.18), intermixed and overlain by a dark grey mottled fine sand that spread beyond the limits of the cut, particularly to the outer north-east edge.

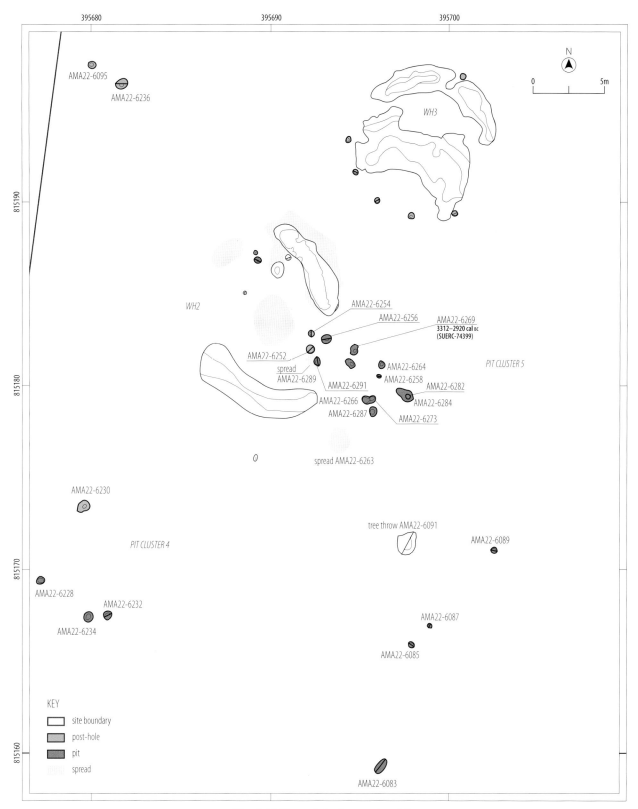

Illus 6.12 Plan of pit clusters 4 and 5

This fill included occasional patches of orange and black sand indicating potential areas of burning. The spread also masked a number of internal features including pits [AMA22–6294] and [AMA22–6295]. The masking of these features by this deposit could imply that it represents a burning event at the abandonment of the structure. A small amount of Neolithic pottery was recovered from the fills of the ring-ditch among a larger assemblage

Illus 6.13 View of pit cluster 5 showing the excavated pits

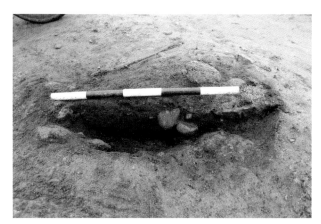

Illus 6.14 Mid-excavation of pits [AMA22–6266] and [AMA22–6273]

Illus 6.15 Mid-excavation shot of pit clusters 2 and 3 facing north-west

of Bronze Age material. A small lithic assemblage was also recovered that included Mesolithic/Early Neolithic material. It is likely that the earlier dated pottery and lithics were residual, representing material that originated from PC5. The construction of WH3 would certainly have disturbed this pit cluster. The deposit also produced one of the most abundant concentrations of cereal grain from the site (see 6.8.2 below).

To the south side of the structure, ring-ditch [AMA22–6238] was generally much shallower than the opposing ring-ditch and also displayed a more gradual slope. The fills again (Illus 6.19) comprised a basal deposit of rounded cobble stones although these were significantly less predominant than those recorded in the opposing ring-ditch. These were overlain by a charcoal-rich sand that may represent evidence of burning. The upper horizon of the fill produced a large quantity of lithic and pottery fragments that included residual Middle Neolithic Impressed Ware.

A shallow scoop [AMA22–6240] in the centre of the structure, 2.4 m in diameter with a maximum depth of only 0.16 m, included a charcoal-rich spread of sand. This also produced a moderate volume of cereal grain and a small assemblage of prehistoric pottery and lithic

debitage, possibly indicating the location of a central hearth or an occupation deposit. Further activity within WH2 was evidenced by two small spreads of heat-affected sand [AMA09–6277] and [AMA09–6289], the second of which overlies an earlier pit [AMA9–6291], plus a small pit [AMA09–6248] and three post-holes [AMA09–6246], [AMA09–6261] and [AMA09–6276]. Residue from pottery recovered from the fill of the southern ring-ditch was submitted for radiocarbon dating and returned a date range of 1740–1570 cal BC (SUERC-73583).

6.6.2.2 Wester Hatton 3

A post-ring with a single ring-ditch formed the remains of WH3 (Illus 6.20). An unusual internal spread of material was also recorded within a poorly defined cut. The post-ring was formed of eight post-holes, though two of these; [AMA22–6183] and [AMA22–6184], located to the outer edge of the ring-ditch, were poorly defined and potentially represented post-pads located on the stepped extent of the ditch. None of the post-holes were particularly deep although the ground surface in this area was predominantly a firm gravel, unlike the softer sand encountered in the areas to the north and south.

The cut of the crescent-shaped ring-ditch was broken close to its central point, almost forming two smaller ditches. Both sides of the cut were generally steep, leading to an occasionally uneven but generally concave base 0.34 m deep (Illus 6.21). The basal fill was a compact black friable sand with frequent charcoal lump inclusions and evidence of daub, although this was too small to collect. This charcoal-rich fill was predominantly found to the sides and base of the cut with a small amount of carbonised roundwood, thought to be potential evidence of wattle, identified on the outer edge of the cut. The basal layer was overlain by a thick deposit of dark grey sand that probably represents a natural silting up of the cut. A small and undiagnostic prehistoric pottery and lithic assemblage was recovered from this fill. This proved to be the only structure at Wester Hatton that had a charcoal-rich layer at the base of the ring-ditch cut, rather than overlying a

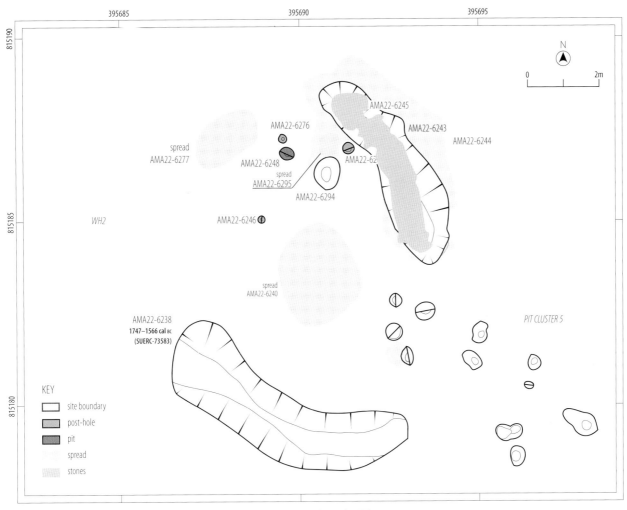

Illus 6.16 Plan of WH2

Illus 6.17 View of WH2 from the south-east

Illus 6.18 View of the sections through [AMA22–6244] of WH2 from the east

stone-rich deposit. There was also an almost complete absence of stones within the fill of this ring-ditch, which in comparison to the other structures seemed unusual. Cereal grain recovered from the basal fill of the ring-ditch produced a radiocarbon date of 1370–1130 cal BC, placing the structure in the Middle Bronze Age.

Within the extents of the post-ring to the south was a large irregular-shaped shallow cut [AMA22–6193]. The edges of this cut were poorly defined and the profile had gradual sloping sides and an uneven concave base (Illus 6.22). The dark grey silty sand fill overlay two thin

Illus 6.19 View of the sections through [AMA22–6238] of WH2 from the west

deposits of silt possibly representing slumping events at the base of the cut. The three fills were sterile apart from a single sherd of prehistoric pottery and a single lithic fragment.

In summary, WH3 consisted of an outer post-ring measuring approximately 8.5 m diameter and an inner ring-ditch. The post-ring probably held a ring-beam for the support of the roof. It is thought that the ring-ditch formed through erosion related to the use of the building in a similar way to that suggested for the roundhouses at Gairnhill (Chapter 3). The carbonised roundwood identified at the base of the ring-ditch along with the burnt daub and the charcoal-rich basal deposit may be indicative of a burning event, probably representing the abandonment of the structure. Whether this burning was accidental or deliberate is not known. The large irregular-shaped ditch [AMA22–6193] within the post-ring to the south possibly represents an additional area of erosion within the roundhouse. The lack of environmental evidence in this ditch is a concern. It did not include any evidence of charcoal-rich deposits and the homogeneous fill was also similar to the topsoil overlying the site, suggesting it may represent more recent activity that just happened to respect the post-ring that surrounded it.

6.6.2.3 Wester Hatton 1

Located to the south end of the site, WH1 comprised the partial remains of a post-ring with an internal ring-ditch

occupying the east side (Illus 6.23). A limited number of post-holes were also identified to the west of the ring-ditch forming a potential post-ring. The remains of the building had been truncated by both plough furrows and a modern water pipe that had removed the southern terminal end of the ring-ditch.

An outer ring of up to seven post-holes defined the limits of the visible structure. These were mainly to the eastern side of the structure and were generally relatively shallow with depths between 0.15 m and 0.25 m recorded. The fills were also on the whole fairly homogeneous with occasional stone inclusions. A small assemblage of prehistoric pottery was recovered from the fills of two of these post-holes although these were undiagnostic. A saddle quern (06-CS8) was also recovered from post-hole [AMA-6115] and may have been used as packing for the post.

The ring-ditch [AMA22–6096] had uneven and poorly defined sides, formed by a series of depressions resulting in an uneven outline in plan. The profiles through this ring-ditch varied indicating steep to gradual sloping sides leading to a relatively flat base with a maximum depth of 0.25 m. This was predominantly filled with a single homogeneous sand fill that included frequent large rounded and sub-rounded stones (Illus 6.24) that were more common towards the central area of the ditch. A localised deposit of darker orange sand was recorded at the base of the ditch to the north end, possibly indicating a burning

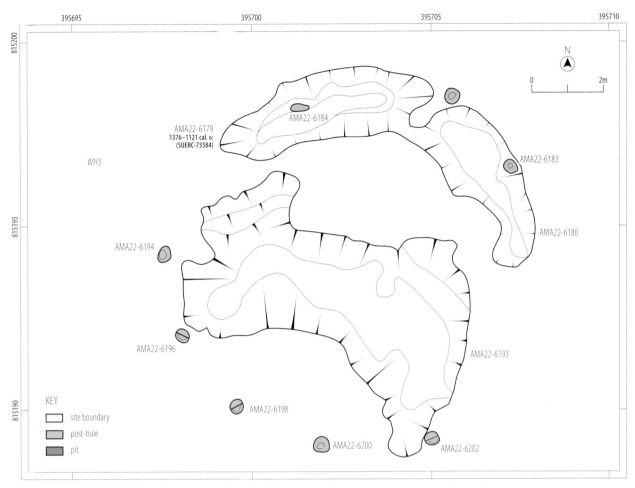

Illus 6.20 Plan of WH3

Illus 6.21 Post-excavation view of ditch [AMA22–6193] of WH3

Illus 6.22 Post-excavation view of the sections excavated through [AMA22–6179] of WH3

event. A second saddle quern (06-CS11) was recovered from the main fill along with further prehistoric pottery from at least two vessels (06-V78 and 06-V79) and a small undiagnostic lithic assemblage. The pottery included two small, soft sherds that have some slight interior vitrification indicating these may belong to a crucible for use in metal casting. The pits and post-holes recorded to the west side of the ring-ditch potentially relate to both the post-ring and internal features although this could not be proven. Only pit [AMA22–6102] provided any diagnostic evidence, in the form of three sherds of prehistoric pottery from a single vessel (06-V74).

It is fairly common for roundhouses to have a south to south-eastern facing entrance. To the south-east of the ring-ditch of WH1 are a group of closely packed post-holes; [AMA22–6008], [AMA22–6079], [AMA22–6081],

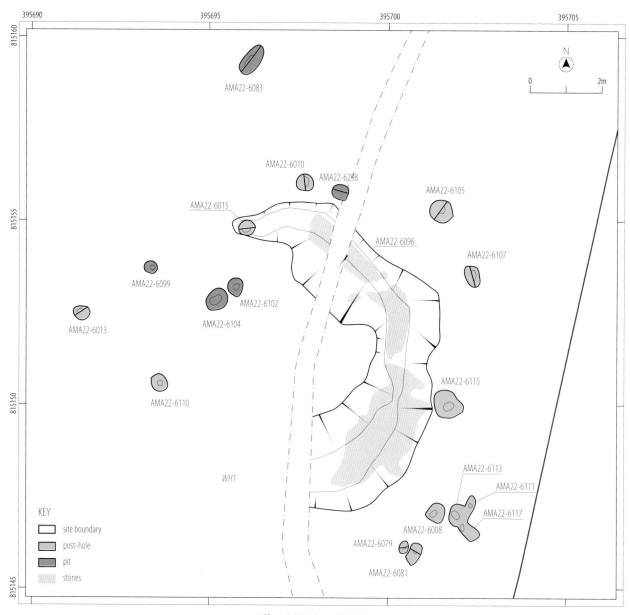

Illus 6.23 Plan of WH1

Illus 6.24 Section view of ditch [AMA22–6096] of WH1 facing north

[AMA22–6111], [AMA22–6113] and [AMA22–6117]. The location and grouping of these may indicate something slightly more complex occurring here. Although the evidence for this being the location of an entrance is not convincing it cannot be discounted. These multiple post-holes may also indicate an area of repair or consolidation to the structure. No dating evidence was recovered from this structure though a date between c1700 and c1100 BC can be assumed based on proximity and similarity to WH2 and WH3. The post-ring has a diameter of about 10 m. The walls themselves were most likely formed from a bank of earth or turf and would probably have been some way outside the post-ring.

6.6.2.4 Wester Hatton 4

The western extent of WH4 was not fully exposed as the structure continued beyond the site boundary (Illus 6.25). It comprised a penannular ring-ditch [AMA22–6030], a limited number of external post-holes and a small number of internal pits. The structure had an east-facing entrance and the ring-ditch had been partially truncated to the south side by a later phase structure (WH5; see 6.6.2.6 below).

The cut of the ring-ditch [AMA22–6030] varied in profile along its length. To the north side it had steep sides and a concave base, forming a cut 3.3 m wide and up to 0.4 m deep. To the south side a vertical 0.1 m deep cut to the outer edge was recorded, leading to an uneven and slightly concave base 4.3 m wide (Illus 6.26). This vertical cut did not continue around the full circumference of the southern edge but turned inwards at right-angles before it reached the southern terminal end. The ditch here was only 2.4 m wide. The inner edge of the cut in general was much more gradual and poorly defined, particularly along the southern side. The terminal ends to the east also become increasingly shallow towards the end points.

The primary fill was a fairly homogeneous dark grey-brown sand up to 0.3 m thick that included a substantial quantity of sub-rounded and sub-angular stones (Illus 6.27), some up to 0.3 m across. These were generally poorly sorted but in places, particularly to the north side, they seemed to form a level surface within the cut. An almost formal

inner edge to this stone fill was noted on both the north and south sides of the ditch. This edging provides evidence that the stones represent structural remains as opposed to collapsed or randomly sorted fills. At the terminal ends the stones within the fill were less frequent and poorly sorted. Two quernstone fragments and a stone rubber were recovered from this deposit, along with an assemblage of Middle to Late Bronze Age pottery with up to six separate vessels represented (Table 6.3, see 6.9.2 below). Pottery residue from the primary fill was submitted for radiocarbon dating and returned a date range of 1260–1050 cal BC (SUERC-73586).

Within the stone fill on the northern side of the ditch was potential evidence of a small pit cut [AMA22–6155] (Illus 6.28). This measured 0.6 m by 0.3 m with a maximum depth of 0.15 m. The exact sequence of events was not understood and it may have been incorporated into the stone surface during its construction. It certainly did not cut the overlying layer. An amount of burnt bone and pottery recovered from this cut had been thought to represent a cremation deposit although it is more likely this was accumulated domestic waste, based on the small amount of bone.

A spread of heat-affected sand [AMA22–6142] was identified close to the entrance, potentially representing an area of burning associated with the final destruction of the structure. Two pits [AMA22–6141] and [AMA22–6144] were also present within the entrance. The first of these was poorly defined and the second was irregular in shape and measured 1.2 m diameter with steep sides 0.3 m deep. The fills of both these pits produced small assemblages of Middle to Late Bronze Age pottery (06-V57 and 06-V58, see 6.9.2 below) and lithic fragments, with two stone tools (06-CS6 and 06-CS6; see 6.9.3 below) and burnt bone also recovered from [AMA22–6144].

The remains of an outer post-ring seem to be represented by three pairs of post-holes ([AMA22–6036], [AMA22–6292], [AMA22–6133], [AMA22–6135], AMA22–6136] and [AMA22–6138]) identified to the south side of the ring-ditch. Evidence to the north side was very limited with only one post-hole identified [AMA22–6031]. It was not apparent if the lack of post-holes to the north side was in some way related to the presence of the stone surface in this area. Perhaps the post-ring here sat over the stones. The limited number of post-holes forming an outer post-ring may indicate that the majority of the roof supports were placed within an earthen bank. This may even have been formed from turves removed during the construction of the roundhouse, or even up-cast from the excavation of the ring-ditch. It seems six of the identified outer post-holes were set in three pairs to the south side of the ditch, although at least one of these may have been part of the WH5 inner post-ring. The positioning of these pairs of post-holes to the outer edge of the ditch at its widest point where the vertical cut was present may be indicative either of alterations to the structure or, more likely, evidence of partitioning of the internal space. Two further

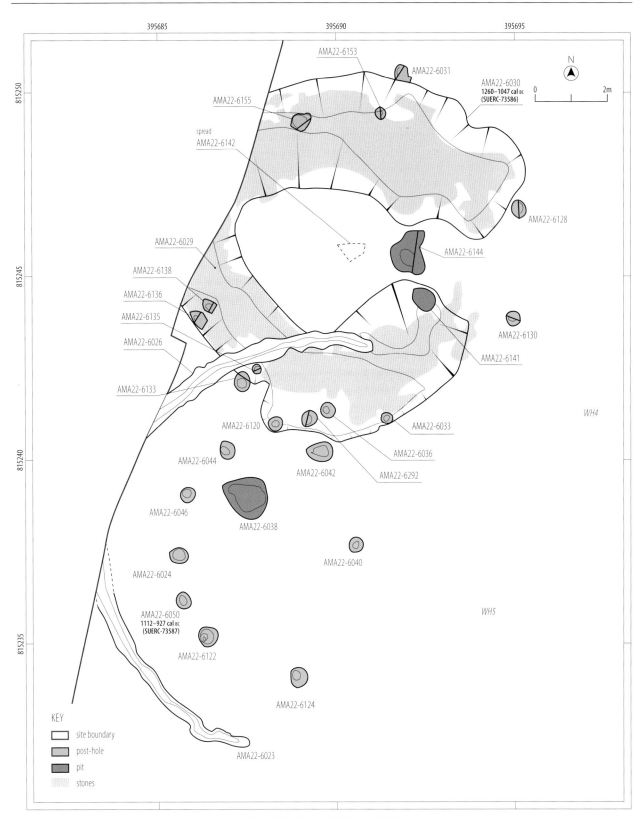

Illus 6.25 Plan of WH4 and WH5

post-holes – [AMA09–6128] and [AMA22–6130] – were recorded close to the terminal ends of the structure and may represent the remains of an entrance. Both post-holes were very shallow with homogeneous fills that included sherds of Bronze Age pottery (06-V59 and 06-V60).

The final deposit that covered the entire area of the structure comprised a thin layer of compact dark grey-brown charcoal-rich sand with lenses of burnt orange sand and burnt clay (Illus 6.29). This layer seems to represent a final destruction event. A moderate quantity of Middle

Illus 6.26 Mid-excavation view of the sections to the south side of [AMA22–6030] showing the vertical edge cut to the outer side of the feature

Illus 6.27 Mid-excavation shot showing the cobbled stone fill of ring-ditch [AMA22–6030]

Illus 6.28 Pre-excavation view of the potential cremation [AMA22–6155] to the north side of ring -ditch [AMA22–6030] facing south

Illus 6.29 Pre-excavation view of ring-ditch [AMA22–6030] of WH4 facing north-east

to Late Bronze Age pottery amounting to six separate vessels (Table 6.03, see 6.9.2 below) was recovered from this layer, along with a moderate lithic assemblage and two fragments of saddle quern (see 6.9.3 below). Residue from one of these pottery fragments provided a radiocarbon date of 1210–1020 cal BC (SUERC-73585) that was commensurate with the pottery recovered.

In summary, the penannular ring-ditch contained a substantial stone fill with evidence of an inner edging. These stones seem to have been deliberately placed within an excavated cut rather than being used as in-filling of an eroded area. Certainly the stone surface would have provided a well-drained and dry surface to place straw or bedding material over. This structure also presents a slight change in form of construction compared to WH1–WH3, although the same basic elements are present. Given the slightly later date of this structure it may just signify improvements to a familiar construction design. The charcoal-rich deposits across the top of the remains seem to suggest the structure was destroyed by fire.

6.6.2.5 Wester Hatton 5

A narrow curvilinear ring-groove [AMA22–6023/6026] and an inner post-ring formed the remains of WH5. Most

of the eastern side of the structure was missing and the western edge ran into the edge of the excavation area (see Illus 6.25). The increasing shallowness of the ring-ditch towards the east suggests that the remainder was truncated away. The ring-groove, along with three of the internal post-holes [AMA22–6120], [AMA22–6036] and [AMA22–6033], cut the upper fill of WH4 (Illus 6.30), which therefore must have been abandoned by the time WH5 was constructed.

The ring-groove was up to 0.6 m wide and 0.3 m deep with generally steep sides and a rounded base. It was filled with a homogeneous firm dark grey sandy silt. The nine post-holes of the post-ring were all of similar form, with steep sides and a flattish base and all contained a single homogeneous fill. Charcoal recovered from post-hole [AMA22–6050] presented a radiocarbon date of 1110–930 cal BC (SUERC-73587), c65 radiocarbon years after the apparent demolition deposit at WH4 (SUERC-73585).

There were three internal features within the post-ring. Two were interpreted as post-holes [AMA22–6040] and [AMA22–6042] and the third as a shallow pit [AMA22–6038]. A small assemblage of lithic fragments was recovered from post-hole [AMA22–6040]. Pit [AMA22–

Illus 6.30 Ring-gully [AMA22–6026] of WH4 during excavation, facing north-west

6038] was filled with a mid-brown firm sand that included frequent well-sorted stone inclusions and charcoal flecks. Given its location it is possible that this may represent occupation debris associated with the roundhouse.

In summary the structure was represented by a ring-groove and post-ring with no inner ring-ditch. This was in contrast to earlier structures that were represented by post-rings and ring-ditches. The ring-groove presumably represents the location of the outer wall, giving the building an overall diameter of 10.7 m. The internal post-ring measured approximately 7 m diameter. No entrance was apparent in the surviving western half of the structure and thus this was presumably on the eastern side.

6.6.2.6 The Bronze Age pits – 1500–1200 BC

Four large pits were recorded that appear to be broadly contemporary with the roundhouses, their dates falling between those for WH2 and WH3. The largest pit [AMA22–6188] was located 30 m south-east of WH4. It was circular in plan and 2.8 m diameter (Illus 6.31 & 6.32) with a maximum depth of 0.2 m, containing a complex sequence of five fills. At the base of the pit cutting the geological substrate were two pits and a post-hole. Immediately south-east of the pit an arc of eight post-holes was recorded.

The sterile basal layer was a spread of sand found predominantly in the south-east quadrant of the pit. This fill showed no signs of being affected by heat although the geological subsoil below was orange and heat-affected. This may imply the fill represented wind-blown sand that entered the pit prior to a secondary activity as represented by the later fills. The sequence of fills in the centre of the pit and overlying the primary fill comprised three thin layers of differing coloured sand. It was unclear if these layers represented multiple use of the pit, as the interfaces between them were fairly diffuse. A small amount of burnt bone, prehistoric pottery (06-V80) and lithic pieces were recovered from the middle layer (AMA22–6190) of this sequence, the remaining two being sterile. The upper fill (AMA22–6187) formed

the bulk of the material within the cut. This contained a small assemblage of prehistoric coarseware pottery (06-V81) along with burnt bone, lumps of daub and a small amount of charred cereal grain. A charred barley grain collected from the upper fill was submitted for radiocarbon dating and returned a date range of 1520–1430 cal BC (SUERC-74401). The upper fill must represent a closing deposit of this pit.

The two smaller pits [AMA22–6221] and [AMA22–6223] and a post-hole [AMA22–6225] cut the geological substrate within the base of the larger pit, indicating they either represent an earlier phase of activity or are structural elements of the pit. Both pits included charcoal fleck inclusions and a small amount of abraded daub was recorded in pit [AMA22–6223].

A series of six post-holes (Illus 6.31) formed an arc around the southern and eastern sides of the pit. An additional post-hole was recorded lying outside of this arc. In general these had steep sides and either flat or conical bases and were no more than 0.14 m deep. The fills were predominantly sterile with the exception of post-hole [AMA22–6219], which included occasional charcoal fleck inclusions. The post-holes may represent the remains of a wind-break. Alternatively, it is possible that they represented the remnants of a larger series of posts, the rest of which had been truncated by later ploughing, possibly representing a small post-ring structure 4–5 m diameter. In this context, outlying post-hole [AMA22–6215] looks like part of an entrance on the south-eastern side of the structure.

Three further pits were grouped in the north-east corner of the site. These comprised a large sub-oval pit, two smaller circular pits and two post-holes (Illus 6.33). Pit [AMA22–6163] measured 5.00 m × 1.43 m and its profile exhibited uneven steep sides leading to a concave base 0.24 m deep. It contained two fine soft dark-grey sand fills. The lower contained occasional charcoal flecks and stones; the upper was lighter in colour although the interface between the two was very diffuse. A small assemblage of prehistoric pottery (06-V82 and 06-V83) was recovered from both fills. It was unclear what this unusual feature represented.

Pit [AMA22–6167] was bowl-shaped and measured 1.33 m in diameter and 0.23 m deep. The homogeneous dark grey-brown sand fill contained charcoal fleck inclusions and a few flakes of lithic debitage plus a very small quantity of cereal grain. A radiocarbon date of 1400–1210 cal BC was obtained from the cereal grain (SUERC-73591). A post-hole [AMA22–6171] was found at the base of the pit, positioned off-centre. It was not clear if this post-hole was contemporary or an earlier feature disturbed by the cutting of the pit. A second post-hole [AMA22–6169] was recorded immediately north-east of the pit. Given the spatial proximity of the post-holes to the pit it was considered they were contemporary with this feature.

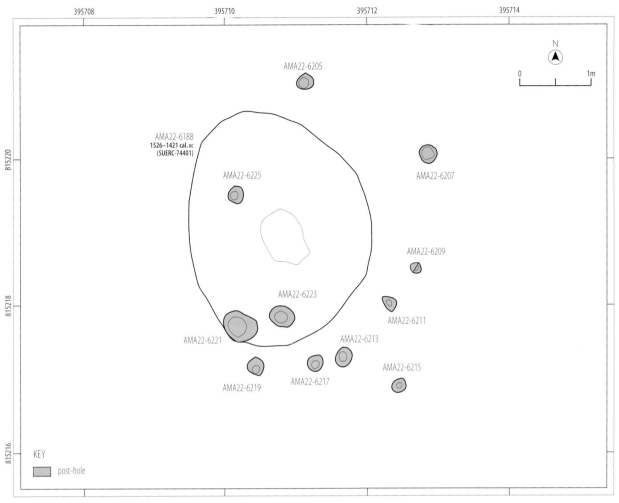

Illus 6.31 Plan of pit [AMA22–6188] and associated post-holes

Illus 6.32 Mid excavation view of the sections through pit [AMA22–6188]

A little further to the north there was a shallow oval pit [AMA22–6160] measuring 1.7 m × 1.3 m. The pit was concave in profile and 0.2 m deep. It included a charcoal-rich upper fill but no artefacts. The diffuse basal deposit was a light grey sand potentially indicating a degree of burning, although the natural sand below this had not been heat-affected. This may indicate that the burning event did not produce a lot of heat and may imply this was just a single use fire pit.

The function of these features was not identified although the presence of charcoal, pottery and lithic debris suggests a certain domestic presence and it might be that these pits relate to the settlement activity represented by the structures. Only two of these pits were dated and thus it was not proven they were all contemporary.

6.6.3 Undated features at Wester Hatton

Across the site as a whole, there were a number of features that could not confidently be assigned to a phase either by absolute or relative dating or even by association or form. Many of these were isolated pits or post-holes. Little can be said about the majority of these features but a small number are of interest.

In particular, there was a row of three pits ([AMA22–6085], [AMA22–6087] and [AMA22–6089]) located south-east of WH2 (see Illus 6.12). The fills of these contained charcoal fleck inclusions although no artefacts.

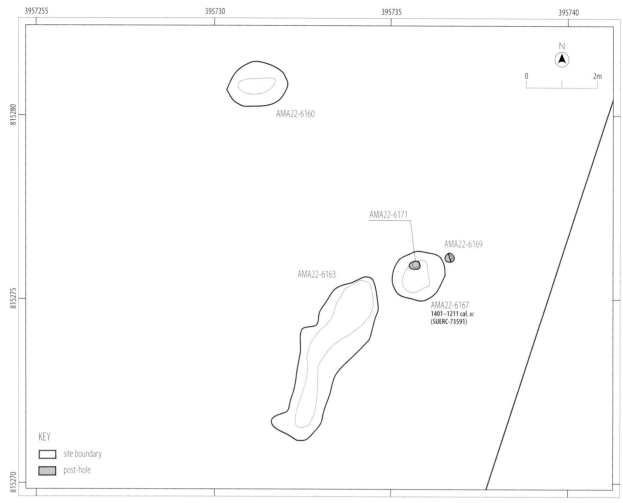

Illus 6.33 Plan of pits to the north-east of the site

They may represent a fenceline or other features associated with the structure.

Two post-holes [AMA22–6172] and [AMA22–6175], located to the south of WH5 (see Illus 6.10) contained evidence of post-pipes and one [AMA22–6172] included a small undiagnostic prehistoric pottery (06-V84) and lithic assemblage. The proximity of these features to the western edge of the excavation areas could imply they are part of a larger undiscovered structure to the west.

6.7 Bronze Age Activity at Middlefield

Jürgen van Wessel

6.7.1 Pit digging – Chalcolithic 2300–2000 BC

A short distance south of Wester Hatton further prehistoric activity was identified. A cluster of three small pits was excavated on the eastern side of the site at Middlefield (Illus 6.34 & 6.35). An additional pit 10 m to the north was also excavated (as part of the trial trenching; Trench NL978) with two further pits investigated 15 m to the south. They were broadly similar in size, measuring approximately 0.5 m diameter and between 0.1 m and

0.25 m in depth. Each was irregular in both plan and section and had a single homogeneous fill.

The primary indication of anthropogenic activity at Middlefield was the lithic assemblage. This comprised some 122 pieces, including cores and tools, two pieces of which may date to the Mesolithic (see 6.9.2.3 below). The pits also contained occasional charcoal inclusions, one of which returned a Chalcolithic/Early Bronze Age radiocarbon date of 2270–2040 cal BC (SUERC-68121). Small quantities of magnetic residue, slag, fuel ash slag and modern redware was also recovered from these pits, although this is likely to be intrusive.

It is possible that the pits represent stone-holes, and were the result of stone clearance, perhaps in advance of setting up a camp or field system at some point (or points) between the Mesolithic period and Early Bronze Age. In this instance the lithic assemblages and charcoal present in the fills would have been the product of an accumulation of waste from activity taking place in the immediate vicinity. These pits could also represent evidence of purposeful pit digging, the fills representing the remains of the activity occurring at this location. Similar pit digging activity had clearly taken place just 100 m to the north at Wester

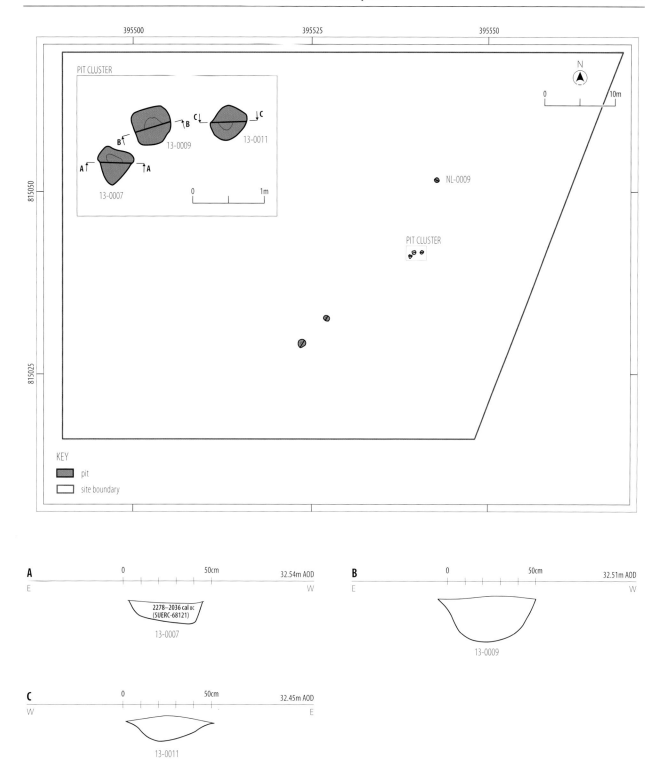

Illus 6.34 Plan and sections of archaeological features at Middlefield

Hatton. There the pits also contained rich lithic assemblages although in many cases they were associated with Late Neolithic activity, thus are unlikely to be contemporary with the activity at Middlefield. The Middlefield pits also seem to be considerably earlier than the Bronze Age occupation activity at Wester Hatton (1740–930 cal BC).

The area, particularly to the north of Middlefield, was clearly the focus of occupation activity in both the Neolithic and the Bronze Age, with earlier low-level Mesolithic activity also present. The location of the pits at Middlefield, being situated on the low-lying ground to the south of an area of more frequent occupation activity, may provide clues as to their provenance, possibly to clear the area in advance of crop cultivation. This could imply that the pits indeed represent stone-holes rather than deliberate pit-digging.

Illus 6.35 General view of Cluster A at Middlefield, facing east

6.8 Environmental synthesis

Tim Holden and Angela Walker

6.8.1 Blackdog

Excavations at Blackdog revealed seven cut features. All except one contained prehistoric material, including lithics and Neolithic pottery. One provided a late Mesolithic date. Thirty-four bulk soil samples of up to 40 l were taken during excavation and processed by flotation and wet sieving.

Single heavily abraded barley grains (*Hordeum vulgare*) were present in two pits, [12–0002] and [12–0034]. The presence of a Mesolithic date from one feature clearly shows some mixing and with such small concentrations of cereal grains it is impossible to be certain that they are contemporary with the features themselves.

Fragments of hazel nutshell (*Corylus avellana*) came from 23 contexts. These never exceeded 1 g in any one context but it seems likely that they were the remains of food processing of some sort. Together with the cereals they demonstrate both crop cultivation and the collection of wild resources, but the concentrations do not enable any detailed interpretation.

A relatively small number of 'weed' seeds were recovered from 12 samples, with no significant concentrations. The species identified included cleavers (*Galium aparine*), corn spurrey (*Spergula arvensis*), knotweed (*Polygonum* sp) and common hemp nettle (*Galeopsis tetrahit*). These taxa are commonly associated with cultivated and disturbed ground around fields and settlements. Occasional seeds of vetches or wild peas (*Vicia/Lathyrus*) were also present in small numbers and would be more indicative of hedgerows and field edges. These could potentially have been brought to site with crops or fuel.

Specialist charcoal analysis was undertaken on samples from three of the pits that contained evidence for *in situ* burning interspersed with periods of backfilling (by either human or natural agencies). None of the features, however, contained sufficient diagnostic material to suggest a function.

In all cases oak and hazel were the dominant species, with much smaller quantities of heather and alder. Most of the wood was small to medium diameter wood and could all have been collected close to the site, with the oak and hazel on the valley sides, alder from the valley floor and heather from more open areas. The charcoal data is in keeping with that from pollen (Timpany 2012b) and regional reviews by Tipping (1994, and this volume, Chapter 1).

6.8.2 Wester Hatton

The Neolithic wood charcoal assemblage from Wester Hatton was principally alder, which is comparable to the presence of alder recorded in the Mesolithic/Neolithic pit [12–0002] at Blackdog.

The charcoal assemblage from the Bronze Age structures and associated pits was of mixed diameter alder with larger calibre oak wood and small hazel branch wood. Evidence for these three species was noted in all structures selected for analysis (WH1–WH4) as well as in pits [AMA22–6160] and [AMA22–6188]. This suggests continuity in the availability of these species types throughout the Bronze Age occupation phases at Wester Hatton.

The charcoal assemblages also contain evidence for the presence of birch, plum/cherry, beech and willow/poplar. As with Middlefield and Blackdog the charcoal from Wester Hatton is in keeping with the data from pollen analyses and regional reviews (Timpany 2012b; Tipping 1994).

At Wester Hatton the dominant crop in both the Neolithic and Bronze Age was barley. Naked 6-row barley and possible occasional hulled barley was identified in a number of the Bronze Age features. The three largest concentrations of cereals were from ring-ditch [AMA22–6243], ring-ditch [AMA22–6238] and pit [AMA22–6240], all three of which relate to elements of WH2. The grains were heavily abraded and it was not possible to determine how they became incorporated in these features. Most likely it was through the accumulation of waste material generated in and around the building during use.

The dominance of barley, particularly naked barley, is common on Bronze Age sites in Scotland (Boyd 1988) but the presence of the hulled form is not. The Bronze Age site at Oldmeldrum, Aberdeenshire (White & Richardson 2010) also demonstrated a similar pattern of dominance of naked barley grains with occasional hulled barley, but the assemblage from that site dated to the Late Bronze Age and not the Early/Middle Bronze Age as at Wester Hatton.

The wild plant assemblage at Wester Hatton was similar in composition to other Scottish Bronze Age sites with common agricultural weeds such as corn spurrey and chickweed possibly being brought in with the barley crop during harvest. The presence of abundant grasses alongside the barley grains suggests that crop processing was undertaken at the site; this was further alluded to via the presence of barley chaff and smaller weed seeds in the wider vicinity.

Fragments of hazel nutshell were recovered from 32 features; five dating to the Neolithic, 25 from the Bronze Age and two from undated features. The features with abundant hazel nutshell from both periods were predominantly pits and, as with those recovered from Blackdog, are likely to be the remains of food processing.

6.8.3 Middlefield

The site comprised five pits, some of which contained lithics and industrial waste. Three samples, ranging in volume from 20 to 40 litres were taken during excavation and were processed by flotation and wet sieving.

The only environmental remains of significance were small fragments of wood charcoal that were present in the fills of pits [13–0007], [13–0009] and [13–0012]. Wherever preservation allowed, the charcoal was categorised as oak and this would be in keeping with the data from pollen analyses such as that by Timpany (2014) and regional reviews by Tipping (1994; see also Chapter 1).

6.8.4 Discussion

By the later Mesolithic, all tree taxa we see today had colonised (Tipping 1994; 2007) and there was a degree of stability in the woodland. As mentioned above (see 6.3.2) the patchiness of the soils was not matched by patchiness in the woodland, which comprised a deciduous woodland of oak and elm with hazel as an under-storey shrub. Birch, ash, aspen and holly will also have sought light along the edges and colonised gaps in the wood. Perhaps the only variation might have been seen around what are now poorly drained soils, the Blackhouse and Terryvale Series (see Illus 6.02), strongholds for alder, birch and willow.

The ecofactual assemblage from Blackdog, Wester Hatton and Middlefield is modest but fits in well with our current understanding of the environment in this coastal area. The indications of disturbed ground and settlement at Blackdog and Wester Hatton adds support to the notion of some Neolithic occupation on or near the site, for which we have no direct structural evidence.

6.9 Materials synthesis

Julie Lochrie

The artefact assemblage from Blackdog and Wester Hatton comprises lithics, pottery and course stone, while that from Middlefield comprises lithics only. Each material type from each site is described below followed by a general discussion of the overall assemblage. Full versions of the individual finds reports can be found in Appendix 2.2.

6.9.1 Pottery

6.9.1.1 Blackdog

The assemblage is small, numbering 50 sherds and 19 fragments and weighing 803 g (Table 6.02). The majority belongs to vessel 12-V01 (Illus 6.36), but a further four vessels were also present, in various states of preservation and fragmentation. All the pottery was Neolithic in date with an earlier group dated c3950–3700 BC and a later group dated c3600–3300 BC.

The context and condition of the pottery is perhaps the most important thing to acknowledge before attempting to interpret their date and meaning. There is stark contrast in vessel condition and fragmentation from pit [12–0001] compared to the rest of the assemblage. Discovered within this feature was 60% of a well-made fluted Carinated Bowl (12-V01) and a few sherds from a second round-based vessel (12-V02). The condition of the two vessels suggests different biographies. The edges of the former include both modern and antiquated breaks, indicating that a portion of the vessel has been lost in recent years to plough or machine truncation; it may have been largely complete, if not complete during original deposition. Vessel 12-V02 is mostly composed of poor-quality delaminated sherds broken in antiquity. These vessels are centrally located in an older, much larger pit. It is highly implausible that they were not consciously located. Similar Neolithic deposits located in the tops of larger pits are recognised at other sites (eg Milltimber, this volume; Warren Field, Murray *et al.* 2009, Chapelfield, Squair & Jones 2002; Port Elphinstone, Lochrie 2013). In all these examples the earlier features were Mesolithic in date. We also have a Mesolithic date (4330–4070 cal BC, SUERC-68123) from one of the upper deposits in pit [12–0001], although this is tempered by the fact that a later date 3930–3710 cal BC (SUERC-68122) was obtained from a lower deposit.

Three other deposits contained pottery but in such negligible quantity that their inclusion cannot be considered deliberate. Pit [12–0023] contained two fragments (one from each fill). These are undatable but radiocarbon dating from the pit suggests they are from between 3630–3390 cal BC (SUERC-58600). Spread (12–0022) also contained

Table 6.02 Summary of pottery assemblage

Feature	Context	Vessel	Sherd count	Fragments	Weight (g)
Large pit [12-0001]	(12-0002), (12-0003), (12-0004)	12-V01	27	–	747
	(12-0003), (12-0006)	12-V02	15	–	38
Hillwash (12-0022)	–	12-V03	–	2	11
Small pit [12-0023]	(12-0024), (12-0025)	12-V04	1	2	<1
Small pit [12-0029]	(12-0030)	12-V05	7	15	7

12-V01

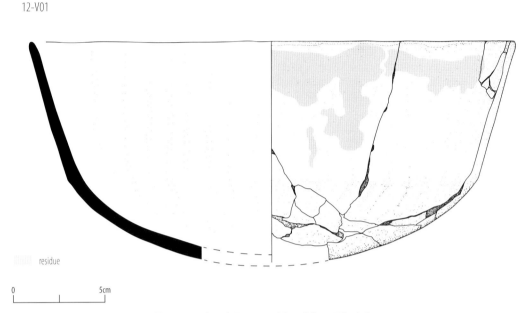

residue

0   5cm

Illus 6.36 Fluted Carinated Bowl from Blackdog

a single, small, sherd of pottery. The fabric and surface treatment of these three fragments are similar to 12-V01 and point towards a Neolithic date. The sherds from pit [12–0030] are more numerous but have delaminated beyond identification.

Vessels 12-V01 and 12-V02 are the only ones with discernible form and belong to the Carinated Bowl tradition's earliest style drift. This is a very well made open carinated bowl with a flaring neck, gentle carination and shallow belly. The fabric is hard and thin and burnished to a leather-like finish. This is hidden behind a thin layer of organic black residue that is adhering to the exterior of the rim and neck area. The manufacture of the vessel is effectively hidden by how well it has been made and burnished. A series of breaks occurring shortly below the carination may indicate the point of coil joins. The fluting to the vessel would have been created with the fingers and is placed around the carination and the very top of the rim. The overall effect is a fine, thin elegant bowl. It would have most likely been used for several different purposes but the residue shows it was certainly used for cooking. The form of the vessel makes it suitable for a variety of uses; the open neck would have allowed pouring (helped further by the decorative fluting to the rim) and aided with handling. When used for cooking the rounded base would have been nestled into the embers of the fire. The fact the vessel was valued is shown by two repair holes, and a third abandoned attempt, which would have allowed binding on either side of a crack. This also suggests the vessel was not newly made and would have had a longer history of use.

Fluted Carinated Bowl pottery has been found at many sites in north-east Scotland, including Milltimber (Chapter 2), Garthdee Road (Murray & Murray 2014), Port Elphinstone (Lochrie 2013), Westgate (Lochrie 2010a),

Mosstodloch (Johnson 2012), Warren Field (Sheridan 2009), Deer's Den (Alexander 2000), Boghead (Henshall 1984) and Midtown of Pitglassie (Henshall 1996). What is most striking is the range of features the pot is found in, which bearing in mind its versatility for storage, cooking, drinking and serving, may not be so unusual. The Blackdog pot is closest to Vessel 1 from Garthdee Road (Murray & Murray 2014) and V16 at Warren Field (Sheridan 2009). Both of these pots have quite shallow hemispherical bellies and long open necks.

Vessels 12-V03 to 12-V05 are represented by rather poor remains. The small quantity, lack of features or even original surfaces precludes any discussion of form.

6.9.1.2 Wester Hatton

The pottery assemblage at Wester Hatton includes 858 sherds and 790 fragments collected during excavation and sample flotation. The sherds belong to an estimated 84 vessels. Out of these 43 have been dated to the Neolithic, the remainder are likely to date from the Early to Middle Bronze Age.

The high number of fragments almost matches the same quantity of sherds. The reason for the high number of fragments could have several origins. The first is that the site has been occupied through several periods and phases, which would have disturbed and further fragmented previous remains. The pottery itself, excepting some specific examples of the finer Neolithic fabrics, is coarsely tempered with large rock inclusions that add to the fragmentation and higher number of small body sherds. Finally, the fact that all the pottery appears to represent domestic debris means it was discarded when no longer needed, or when already broken, without the care you would associate with structured deposition and burial.

In addition to the pottery there is also a small quantity of fired clay, weighing 271 g found in small quantities in the following contexts, (AMA22–6025), [AMA22–6188], [AMA22–6223], [AMA22–6266/6273] and [AMA22–6278]. Much of the fired clay has impressions that indicate they were likely part of daub superstructures such as wattle walls.

The site has been divided into several areas formed of pit/post-hole clusters and buildings. The dating in Table 6.03 is, in the first instance, based on the pottery identification. When the pottery could not be identified the radiocarbon dating programme for the site has been used to find its likeliest date.

Only in one instance was a full profile present, Vessel 06-V12, a bipartite, collared vessel. Most of the pottery was represented by small sherds and lots of fragments. All the pottery was abraded to some degree and it all appears to be from domestic occupation. This is not only surmised by its condition but by frequent remains of carbonised organic material on the interior of the vessels, indicating cooking and serving of food.

The pottery from PC1 includes Early to Middle Neolithic pottery types while PC2 and PC4 includes Middle Neolithic pottery types. The dating of individual pottery types will be discussed further below but they are

Table 6.03 Wester Hatton Vessel Summary

Dates	Area	Feature	Context	Vessel no.	Vessel qty	Sherd count
Early to Middle Neolithic	PC1	[AMA22-6051]	(AMA22-6052)	06-V1 to 06-V4	4	21 + 11 fragments
	PC1	[AMA22-6053]	(AMA22-6054)	06-V6	1	19 + 2 fragments
Middle Neolithic	PC1	[AMA22-6055]	(AMA22-6056)	06-V5	1	9 + 2 fragments
	PC2	[AMA22-6063]	(AMA22-6064)	06-V7	1	3
	PC2	[AMA22-6061]	(AMA22-6061) (AMA22-6062)	06-V8	1	15 + 26 fragments
	PC2	[AMA22-6073]	(AMA22-6074)	06-V9	1	34 + 35 fragments
	PC2	[AMA22-6075]	(AMA22-6076)	06-V10	1	3 + 11 fragments
	PC2	[AMA22-6066]	(AMA22-6067) (AMA22-6068)	06-V11	1	11 + 36 fragments
	PC4	[AMA22-6228]	(AMA22-6227)	06-V12	1	65 + 30 fragments
	PC4	[AMA22-6234]	(AMA22-6235)	06-V13	1	29 + 69 fragments
	WH2	[AMA22-6238]	(AMA22-6239)	06-V14	1	
	WH2	[AMA22-6243]	(AMA22-6253)	06-V15	1	3
	WH2	[AMA22-6263]	(AMA22-6263)	06-V16	1	11
	PC5	[AMA22-6273]	(AMA22-6268)	06-V17 to 06-V18	2	13 + 31 fragments
	PC5	[AMA22-6278] [AMA22-6273]	(AMA22-6279) (AMA22-6281)	06-V19 to 06-V20	2	104 + 86 fragments
	PC5	[AMA22-6273]	(AMA22-6281)	06-V21	1	1
	PC5	[AMA22-6273]	(AMA22-6274)	06-V22	1	15 + 21 fragments
	PC5	[AMA22-6269]	(AMA22-6270)	06-V23 to 06-V24	2	5 + 3 fragments
	PC5	[AMA22-6269]	(AMA22-6271)	06-V25 to 06-V28	4	26 + 16 fragments
	PC5	[AMA22-6278]	(AMA22-6279)	06-V29	1	8
	PC5	[AMA22-6266]	(AMA22-6272) (AMA22-6280)	06-V30	1	74 + 99 fragments
	PC5	[AMA22-6266] [AMA22-6273]	(AMA22-6267) (AMA22-6280)	06-V31	1	3
	PC5	[AMA22-6266]	(AMA22-6280)	06-V32	1	1
	PC5	[AMA22-6282]	(AMA22-6283)	06-V33 to 06-V40	8	108 + 176 fragments
	PC5	[AMA22-6284]	(AMA22-6285)	06-V41	1	10 + 8 fragments
	PC5	[AMA22-6287]	(AMA22-6288)	06-V42 to 06-V43	2	24 + 21 fragments

Table 6.03 Wester Hatton Vessel Summary (Continued)

Dates	Area	Feature	Context	Vessel no.	Vessel qty	Sherd count
Early Bronze Age	WH2	[AMA22-6238]	(AMA22-6239)	06-V44 to 06-V46	3	
Early Bronze Age/ undated	WH2	[AMA22-6243]	(AMA22-6244)	06-V47	1	2 + 4 fragments
	WH2	[AMA22-6240]	(AMA22-6241)	06-V48	1	1
	WH2	[AMA22-6258]	(AMA22-6259)	06-V49	1	1
	WH2	[AMA22-6261]	(AMA22-6260)	06-V50	1	1 + 1 fragment
	WH2	–	Surface	06-V51	1	1
	WH2	[AMA22-6264]	(AMA22-6265)	06-V52	1	3 + 2 fragments
Middle Bronze Age/ undated	Pits	[AMA22-6188]	(AMA22-6187)	06-V80	1	1 + 1 fragment
	Pits	[AMA22-6188]	(AMA22-6190)	06-V81	1	3
	Pits	[AMA22-6163]	(AMA22-6165)	06-V82	1	1
	Pits	[AMA22-6163]	(AMA22-6164)	06-V83	1	7
Middle to Late Bronze Age/undated	WH3	[AMA22-6179]	(AMA22-6179)	06-V53 to 06-V54	2	3
	WH3	[AMA22-6193]	(AMA22-6180)	06-V55	1	1
	WH3	[AMA22-6200]	(AMA22-6201)	06-V56	1	1
	WH4	[AMA22-6144]	(AMA22-6149)	06-V57	1	2 + 2 fragments
	WH4	[AMA22-6141]	(AMA22-6140)	06-V58	1	5 + 5 fragments
	WH4	[AMA22-6128]	(AMA22-6129)	06-V59	1	2
	WH4	[AMA22-6130]	(AMA22-6131)	06-V60	1	1 + 2 fragments
	WH4	[AMA22-6025] [AMA22-6030]	(AMA22-6025) (AMA22-6028)	06-V61	1	10
	WH4	[AMA22-6030]	(AMA22-6028)	06-V62, 06-V64, 06-V66 to 06-V67, 06-V69	5	9 + 3 fragments
	WH4	[AMA22-6025]	(AMA22-6025)	06-V63, 06-V65, 06-V68, 06-V70 to 06-V72	6	55 + 28 fragments
	WH5	[AMA22-6122]	(AMA22-6127)	06-V73	1	1
	WH1	[AMA22-6102]	(AMA22-6101)	06-V74	1	2 + 1 fragment
	WH1	[AMA22-6105]	(AMA22-6106)	06-V75	1	4 fragments
	WH1	[AMA22-6298]	(AMA22-6299)	06-V76	1	1
	WH1	[AMA22-6079]	(AMA22-6080)	06-V77	1	1 fragment
	WH1	[AMA22-6096]	(AMA22-6097)	06-V78 to 06-V79	2	81 + 46 fragments
	–	[AMA22-6172]	(AMA22-6174)	06-V84	1	2 + 3 fragments
	WH4	[AMA22-6025] [AMA22-6030] [AMA22-6155]	(AMA22-6025) (AMA22-6151)	n/a		6

broadly in line with a radiocarbon date retrieved from PC1, pit [AMA2–6052] 3340–3100 cal BC (SUERC-74400).

The pottery from structure WH2/PC5 represents two different date ranges, the earliest is Middle Neolithic and the later date is Early Bonze Age. These are reflected by two radiocarbon dates, one from pit [AMA22–6269], 3310–2920 cal BC (SUERC-74399) and one from ring-ditch [AMA22–6238], 1740–1570 cal BC (SUERC-73583). The ring-ditch included Middle Neolithic pottery alongside Early Bronze Age pottery. As mentioned above (see 6.6.2.1), the Neolithic pottery had residually become mixed into its deposits and was likely to have been associated

with PC5 to the east that contained exclusively Neolithic pottery.

Much of the remaining pottery could not be easily dated. This was not the case for 06-V44, 06-V50, 06-V57, 06-V61, 06-V63, 06-V64, 06-V69, 06-V70, 06-V87 and 06-V79, which are recognisable flat-rimmed ware forms, dating to the Bronze Age. However, it is acceptable to assume that the pottery found in each of the various structures and areas has a similar date to that indicated by the radiocarbon dating programme. Pits AMA22–6188 and AMA22–6163 are Middle Bronze Age and structures WH3, WH4 and WH5, Middle to Late Bronze Age (Table 6.01).

NEOLITHIC POTTERY FROM WESTER HATTON

Vessels 06-V1 to 6-V43 are all Neolithic in date (Table 6.03; Illus 6.37 & 6.38A, 6.38B). They mostly include Impressed Ware with a few modified Carinated Bowls. The dating of Impressed Ware, previously termed 'Later Neolithic Impressed Wares', has changed dramatically over the

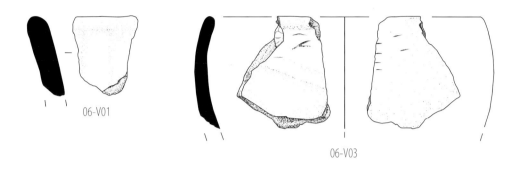

06-V01   06-V03

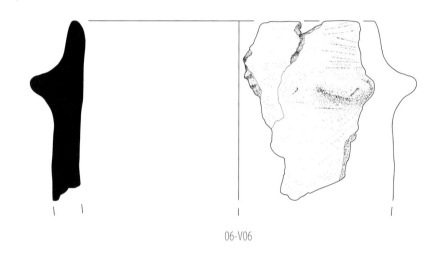

06-V06

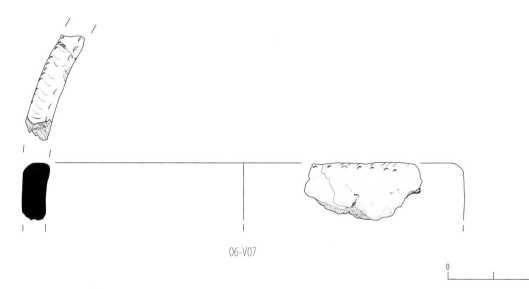

06-V07

0   5cm

Illus 6.37 Early to Middle Neolithic pottery from PC1 and PC2

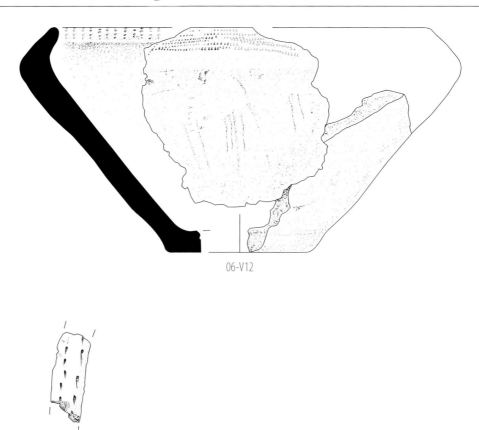

06-V12

06-V13

0   5cm

Illus 6.38A Middle Neolithic Pottery from PC4

last couple of decades. Radiocarbon dates have made it clear that it first appears in the mid-fourth millennium BC and this is now accepted as a type of middle to later Neolithic ware (Kinbeachie, 3500–2920 BC, MacSween 2001, table 1, 63; Kintore, 3530 BC–3340 BC, MacSween 2008, 181; Meadowend Farm, 3350 BC to 3000/2900 BC, Jones et al. 2018). These earlier dates have also led to a consideration of the links between Impressed Wares and modified Carinated Bowl pottery. There are common features between the two: lugs; baggy shapes; bipartite forms; and decoration confined to the upper zone. It may be that a continuity of regionalisation can be seen between Henshall's 'north-eastern' style of the Carinated Bowl tradition (Henshall 1984; 1996) and the Impressed Wares of eastern Scotland (MacSween 2007, 369; 2008, 181).

The remains of up to three vessels could all be termed modified Carinated Bowl of Henshall's 'north-east' style (CBNE). The first and only one of its kind are represented by three sherds comprising Vessel 06-V01, from pit [AMA22–6051], which is a fluted Carinated Bowl. Very little remains but a fluted, everted rim sherd make its form clear. It is thick at 11 mm and is unfortunately too small to give a reliable indication of vessel diameter. Fluted

Carinated Bowl pottery has been found in the north-east at many sites, including Blackdog and Milltimber (this volume). Dates for CBNE suggest its appearance at c3800 BC at the earliest (eg OxA-8132, OxA-8131, Oxa-8133, Deer's Den, Alexander 2000, 17; GU-9155, Dubton Farm, MacSween 2002, 41; Warren Field, Sheridan 2009, 92). At Port Elphinstone and Kintore dates range from 3700 to 3640 cal BC (SUERC-42979; Murray & Murray 2013) and 3810–3650 cal BC to 3710–3620 cal BC (MacSween 2008, 179), which suggest a long period of use. Interestingly an outlying date of 3030–2880 cal BC was associated with one at Kintore (MacSween 2008, 179) and the nearest associated radiocarbon date from Wester Hatton is 3310–2920 cal BC (SUERC-74399). That aside, the lithics report suggests evidence for earlier Neolithic activity and this vessel is still likeliest to date between c3800–3600 BC.

The other two vessels that fit within this group are two lugged vessels, 06-V05 and 06-V06, from pits [AMA22–6055] and [AMA22–6053] respectively. Vessel 06-V05 was incomplete and the lug from this was a completely detached, applied lug, measuring 8 × 8 × 10 mm. This lug was different in shape from that on 06-V06, which was longer and flatter, measuring 36 × 19 × 17 mm. Both

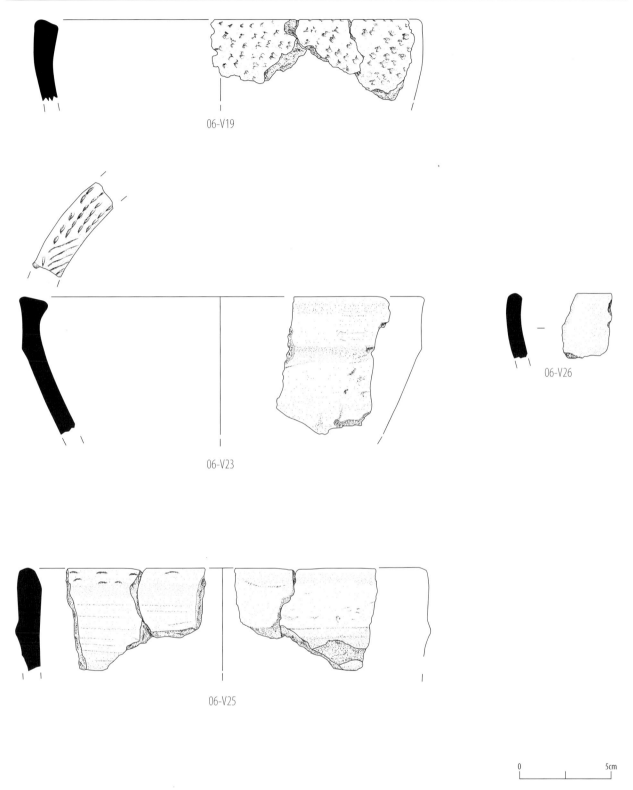

06-V19

06-V23

06-V26

06-V25

0   5cm

Illus 6.38B Middle Neolithic Pottery from PC5

these lugs would have helped aid the grip of the vessels but, especially in the case of the smaller example, could not have been held by these alone. More remains of Vessel 06-V06, providing a rim diameter of c180–190 mm and a vessel form with gently curving sides and an upright, rounded rim. There were no basal sheds for either, but they are likely to have been baggy-based. The addition of lugs to vessels is another early modification to Carinated Bowl pottery, a trend that continues into the Impressed Ware tradition. A lugged, decorated example was found at Goval (Chapter 5), which was associated with a radiocarbon date of 3510–3350 cal BC (SUERC-68133). At Kintore

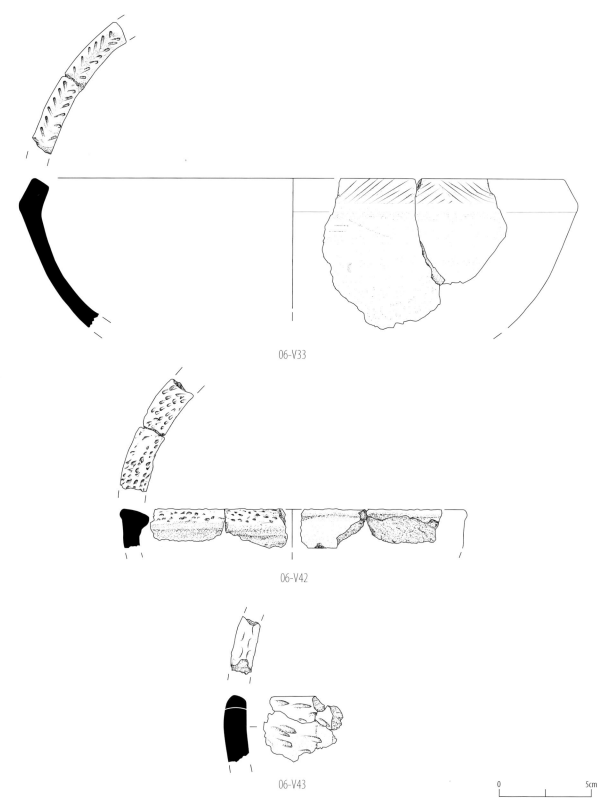

06-V33

06-V42

0   5cm

06-V43

Illus 6.38C Middle Neolithic Pottery from PC5

lugged vessels classified as modified Carinated Bowls were associated with a spread of dates between 3810 and 2880 cal BC (P50 3810–3650 cal BC, P21 3710–620 cal BC and ST12 3130–2920 cal BC and 3030–2880 cal

BC) and lugged impressed Ware associated with the date 3530–3340 cal BC (SUERC-1322).

Sherds from two very similar profiles from PC5, post-hole [AMA2–6269] and pit [AMA2–6282] may be small uncarinated cups. Both vessels, 06-V26 and 06-V38, have small gently squared rim sherds with curvature that suggests they are round-based. Another uncarinated cup, 06-V03, may come from PC1; this one is a little different as it may have decoration. It comprises a medium rim and body sherd, the rim is gently curving and quite thin, with rows of fingernail marks that may be decorative or accidental and appear on the interior and exterior. It could be round, saggy or baggy based.

The remainder of the Neolithic vessels are likely to be Impressed Ware, numbering a total of 37 vessels, 06-V02, 06-V07 to 06-V25, 06-V27 to 06-V42 and 06-V43. The very few instances where large portions of the vessels survive show mostly bipartite forms. The rims themselves are either rounded or with internal bevels, often expanded on the interior and exterior to a T-shaped section. The vessel forms, rim types and decoration appear in different combinations throughout the assemblage and seemingly show no correlation with where or how the decoration

is applied. Table 6.04 summarises the rim forms, overall forms and decoration. Since decoration was typically on the rim or upper half of the vessels there are few decorated examples that are not included in Table 6.03.

The only vessel in the whole assemblage that provides a full profile is vessel 06-V12 from pit [AMA22–6228]. This vessel is bipartite, standing 115 mm tall, but with a very trunconic shape. It has a short collar around 28 mm in length and inturned neck, which leads down to a small flat base of c70–80 mm. The vessel's rim diameter could not be estimated as very little of the rim remains, but the carination is around 240 mm in diameter. This vessel is decorated with comb-impressed lines in panels around the collar. They alternate between horizontal and vertical lines. The very edge of the rim has short vertical impressions, made from the same implement. A second bipartite vessel, 06-V33, with inturned collar, was found in [AMA22–6282]. In this instance not as much remained, the collar is enhanced by a slightly stepped carination and

Table 6.04 Impressed Ware rim forms and decoration summary

Vessel	Overall form	Rim form	Rim diameter (mm)	Decoration	Decoration location
06-V2	–	Rolled, T-shaped	–	n/a	–
06-V7	–	Upright, flattened	c230–240	fingernail and sub-circular impression	Top of rim
06-V9	–	Rounded	–	n/a	–
06-V12	Bipartite, collared	Rounded	–	comb-impressed	Collar and edge of rim
06-V13	–	T-shaped, internally bevelled	–	stab and drag, sub-circular impressions	Bevel and body
06-V16	–	Internal bevel	–	Fingernail	–
06-V18	–	Internal bevel	–	Stab	bevel
06-V19	–	Internal bevel	c210	Bid-bone	Bevel and body
06-V20	–	Internal bevel	–	Fingernail	Bevel
06-V21	–	Internal bevel	–	Stab	Bevel
06-V23	Bipartite, sharp carination	T-shaped, internal bevel	215–220	Stab and drag (panelled)	Bevel
06-V25	Bipartite, rounded carination	Oblique internal bevel	c210	Fingernail	Bevel
06-V30	–	Internal bevel	–	Stab	Bevel
06-V31	–	Internal bevel	–	Fingernail	Bevel
06-V33	Bipartite, collared	Internal bevel	290	Herringbone, incised (panelled)	Collar and bevel
06-V34	–	Internal bevel	–	Fingernail	Bevel
06-V35	–	Rounded	–	–	–
06-V37	–	Rounded	–	–	–
06-V42	–	T-shaped internal bevel	190	Stab	Bevel
06-V43	–	Rounded	–	Stab, fingernail, incised	Exterior and top of rim

this vessel may have had a round base. The rim is internally bevelled and decorated with short diagonal impressions in a herringbone motif and the collar is incised in panels of alternating directional linears. The shape of these vessels is similar to vessel 02-V45 found at Milltimber (Chapter 2). Parallels were drawn between this vessel and the Proto-Unstan vessels from Peterhead, which are dated to 3370–3090 cal BC but these vessels have round bases. A closer comparison are pots with decorated collars and trunconic forms and flat bases found elsewhere within the Impressed Ware repertoire (eg Meadowend Farm, Clackmannanshire, c3350–3000/2900 cal BC, Jones *et al.* 2018; and Deer's Den, Aberdeenshire, 3130–2910 cal BC, OxA-8177 and 3360–3030 cal BC, OxA-8176, Alexander 2000, 64). Panel-decorated collars similar to 06-V33 were found at Spurryhillock, Aberdeenshire (Alexander 1997) and Culduthel, Inverness (Sheridan forthcoming).

The other bipartite vessels in the assemblage include two vessels with carinations. They are each different from the other – 06-V23 has a well-rounded carination, very oblique internal bevel and soft rounded edges; the bevel is decorated with fingernail impressions. Vessel 06-V23 has a very sharp, well-angled carination, a T-shaped internal bevel and panel-decorated stab and drag. Vessel 06-V19 is unique in the assemblage and may be all-over decorated and is unlikely to be bipartite in form.

The most common form of decoration is fingernail impression and the second is stab or stab and drag. The most common location of this is on the rim, either on a bevel or along the very top. Table 6.02 summarises the rim decoration, vessel shape and vessel size. It was rare in the assemblage to have a combination of decoration where more than one tool was used, but this was present on 06-V13, 06-V33 and 06-V43. Decorated sherds from vessels with no rim sheds surviving, include stab marks on 06-V15, small sub-circular impressions on 06-V17 and probable comb-impressions on 06-V36. One interesting impression appears on sherd 06-V24; it may be decorative or could be from a tool mark. The impression is in the shape of a small, shallow square that has been driven in from one side, with two appearing on the sherd. This could be decorative from a small spatula used to help form the vessel, such as the marks seen on the vessel from Goval (Chapter 5).

Rim diameters could be estimated on seven of the Neolithic vessels and show sizes ranging from c180 mm to c290 mm, which is a good repertoire of sizes. The overall capacity of the vessels would have been dependent on the overall vessel form, but a range of sizes tends to suggest a mixed range of uses within cook and service ware. Most of the vessels were wiped or gently smoothed horizontally and few other manufacturing details were evident other than a few clay joins. Vertical finger-smoothing on 06-V12 was visible on its lower portion; these marks were fairly deep and as this was the only one of these vessels to have a surviving base it is not clear if this technique was unusual in the assemblage. On vessel 06-V16 there was a clay

join to the internal angle of a rim bevel, indicating a strip of clay was used to enhance the bevelled effect. The only other clay joins noted were all in relation to the very tops of rims (06-V18 and 06-V20), suggesting the emphasis on the larger, decorated rims of this period were created by adding small strips to the top that allowed more customisation.

BRONZE AGE POTTERY FROM WESTER HATTON

The Bronze Age pottery (Illus 6.39) is in a much poorer state of preservation and for the bulk of the assemblage, 31 vessels, consists of small to medium, abraded, body sherds only.

From WH2 there are two vessels with identifiable forms. Vessel 06-V44 is bucket-shaped with an internal bevel that has been folded on the interior. It is quite small at only 170 mm rim diameter. The second vessel is a small, slightly inturned rim sherd that is flattened on top and creates a very subtle P-shape. This rim is too small to indicate the vessel size. It is very similar to the rim sherds from Vessel 06-V61 from WH4.

The most vessels with recognisable forms were recovered from WH4 but despite the survival of six rim types (06-V57, 06-V61, 06-V63, 06-V64, 06-V69 and 06-V70), only one possible basal sherd was identified (06-V63). Vessels 06-V57 and 06-V70 are both primarily comprised of an internally bevelled rim and a few small body sherds. All that survives of 06-V69 is a corner sherd from a rim of uncertain form. The two vessels for which more remains are Vessel 06-V61 and Vessel 06-V63. The former is comprised of two conjoining rim sections that indicate a vessel of around 220 mm rim diameter. The rims are slightly inturned and flattened on top but with a rounded exterior edge and sharper interior edge, like the rim sherd from WH2 (06-V50). Vessel 06-V63 is bucket-shaped with an upright rounded rim of 125–145 mm diameter and a possible flat base sherd. This vessel is very irregular and has lots of organic surface impressions.

Vessel 06-V64 is a single rim sherd but is a recognisable Middle Bronze Age form also found at Gairnhill and Chapel of Stoneywood (Chapter 3). The rim is upright and very gently squared, like many of the other Bronze Age pots, but this one has the addition of two finger grooves to the exterior, located 17 mm apart and beginning 12 mm from the rim. At the site of Oldmeldrum, Aberdeenshire, located around 17 km north, two pots from a Middle Bronze Age building also had similar ridges (P86 and P89, Johnson 2010, 13). Ridges, cordons and finger grooves to Middle Bronze Age vessels seem to be an even further widespread trend and could potentially have developed from cordoned urns (Echline Fields, South Queensferry, Robertson 2013; Lintshie Gutter, Lanarkshire, Terry 1995; and Green Knowe, Jobey 1978).

No scientific dating was carried out on WH1 but Bronze Age settlement activity is clearly represented. Two vessels were found here, one of which is so vitrified with such a

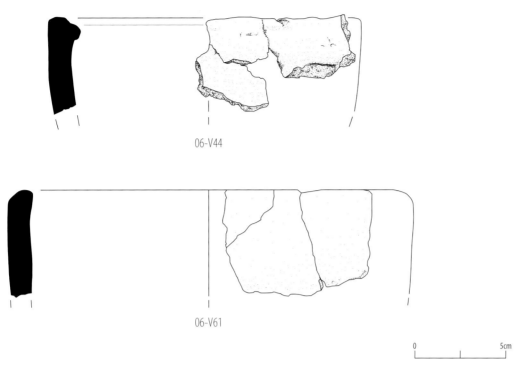

06-V44

06-V61

0   5cm

Illus 6.39 Early Bronze Age pottery from WH2 (06-V44) and Middle Bronze Age pottery from WH4 (06-V61)

Table 6.05 Blackdog lithic assemblage summary

Feature	Chips	Flakes	Blades	Indet pieces	Bipolar cores	Single platform core	Flat uni-facial core	Scrapers	Edge retouch	Total
Mesolithic pit [12-0001]		2		1						3
Mesolithic Pit [12-0002]			2							2
Hillwash deposit [12-0022]	7	10				1		3	1	22
Neolithic pit [12-0023]	38	10	4	2	1					55
Neolithic pit [12-0029]	11	8	2				1			22
Neolithic pit [12-0031]		2		1	1					4
Mesolithic pit [12-0034]	1									1
Total	57	32	8	4	4	1	1	3	1	109

small rim it may be a crucible rather than pottery. The other vessel is a large bucket-shaped pot with a rim diameter of 210 mm. It has a rounded very irregular rim and straight walls that kick out from a flat base. This vessel is a very typical form of 'flat-rimmed ware' dating to this period. Its featureless shape makes any chronological refinement problematic.

6.9.2 Lithics

6.9.2.1 Blackdog

Julie Lochrie

This report covers all lithics retrieved from the site during excavation and sample flotation. The assemblage is small,

totalling 109 pieces. Table 6.05 provides a summary of the assemblage by feature. Interestingly, pit [12–0001] contained an almost complete Early Neolithic bowl but some of the lowest quantity of lithics from the whole site. The greatest quantities were from an overlying subsoil deposit [12–0022], and pit [12–0023].

All but a pitchstone scraper (F024: Illus 6.40) and a quartz flake is of flint. The pitchstone has very few, small probable phenocrysts and is likely porphyritic. Pitchstone was not available locally and was imported from the island of Arran in the Firth of Clyde. The trade and exchange of this stone was at its height in the Early Neolithic period (Ballin & Faithfull 2009, 31). Pitchstone found at Warren Field (Murray *et al.* 2009) is associated with a Neolithic

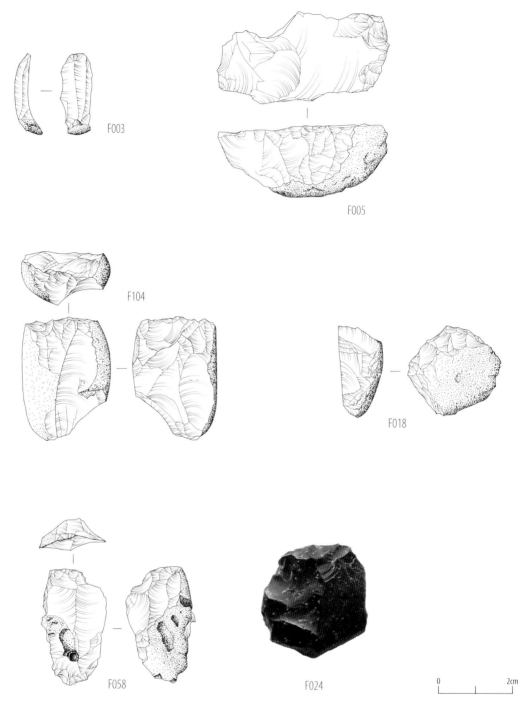

Illus 6.40 Blackdog lithics

timber hall and Carinated Bowl pottery. The flint from Blackdog is present in a range of colours, which is to be expected from the north-east of Scotland. Chapter 2.14.2 provides a more detailed account of raw material resources in Aberdeenshire.

The cores include three different types, a flat uni-facial core, a single platform core and two bipolar cores. The flat uni-facial core has been barely worked but it looks like the beginnings of a Levallois-like core, which would place its date within the Middle to Late Neolithic (Ballin 2011a). The single platform core is quite squat and most

of the removals are flakes. The two bipolar cores are very similar, with bifacial removals and pillowed profiles. The debitage represents the main bulk of the assemblage and mostly comprises small flakes and chips. Very little information is revealed by these, although they do include some examples of both bipolar and platform reduction. Scrapers are the dominant tool type and may relate to the types of activities taking place.

The high quantity of chips and the presence of cores indicate knapping took place at the site. The debitage ratios are as expected for a flake-focused industry with some blade production. However, it is possible that there is a mix of industries rather than one. The blade-based material and single platform core is more likely to belong to the Mesolithic or Early Neolithic phase. One particular example likely to be Mesolithic or very Early Neolithic in date is an overshot blade from a single platform blade core, which retains the apex of the core at its distal end, found in pit [12–0002]. The flat uni-facial core and the two bipolar cores are more likely to be Middle to Late Neolithic, tentatively assigning pits [12–0029] and [12–0031] to this period. Deposit (12–0022) contains evidence for both periods, although it was identified as hillwash and so would be expected to include a mixed finds assemblage.

6.9.2.2 Wester Hatton
Torben Bjarke Ballin

Excavations at Wester Hatton recovered 1839 lithic artefacts (Appendix 2.2.16), listed in Table 6.06. In total, 96% of this assemblage is debitage, whereas 3% is cores and 1% tools. These appear to date predominantly to the Middle Neolithic period, with a supplement of Early Bronze Age lithic material. These sub-assemblages generally have a domestic appearance, representing knapping floors disturbed by the construction of later Bronze Age houses and pits in the area.

RAW MATERIALS

Apart from three flakes in white milky quartz from ring-ditch [AMA22–6238] (WH2), all lithic artefacts from Wester Hatton are flint. The colour of the flint varies, with most being mottled-grey, and with relatively few belonging to the honey-brown variety known from many Aberdeenshire sites. As shown in Chapters 2 and 4, prehistoric sites from the region include a substantial number of other colours, such as buff, cream, beige, black and olive, and these colours are also present in the Wester Hatton assemblage.

The main difference between the present assemblage and, for example, Mesolithic (eg, Nethermills Farm on the Dee; Ballin 2013a) and Early Neolithic (eg, Garthdee Road, Aberdeen; Ballin 2016) assemblages from Aberdeenshire is that these tend to be defined mostly by homogeneous, fine-grained, vitreous flint, whereas the present collection includes much medium- to coarse-grained, more opaque flint with impurities like chalk balls, fossils and clusters of micro-crystals. It is generally thought that the flint from the early prehistoric sites from the region was collected from beach walls along the North Sea shores, whereas it is likely that a proportion of the later Neolithic and Early Bronze Age Wester Hatton material was procured from the later Neolithic flint mines in the Buchan Ridge area near Peterhead, just over 30 km towards the north.

The flint from the Buchan Ridge Gravels includes different forms of flint, with some sources being dominated by one type and other sources by other types (Bridgland *et al.* 1997; Bridgland & Saville 2000), such as fine-grained

honey-brown forms and coarser varieties characterised by other colours. The impure medium- and coarse-grained flint from Wester Hatton is not unlike some of the flint from Stoneyhill Farm (Suddaby & Ballin 2010), which is situated on top of the Buchan Ridge Gravels, and Wester Clerkhill north of Peterhead (Ballin pers comm), which is thought to be based on glacially transported flint from the area around Den of Boddam.

The mining operations at Den of Boddam and Skelmuir Hill are thought to have taken place during the later Neolithic period, a date supported by the recovery of a chisel-shaped arrowhead during the excavations at Den of Boddam (Bridgland 2000, fig 53), and the waste material from the mining area is characterised by numerous Levallois-like and bipolar cores (Saville 2005; 2006). The assemblage from Wester Hatton, as well as those from Stoneyhill Farm and Wester Clerkhill, is distinguished by the presence of the same types of core, and these sites are probably contemporary with the Buchan Ridge mining operations.

The flakes and blades are mostly cortical (c60%, with as much as 13% being primary flakes), and the cortex is generally smooth and abraded (Table 6.07). The high cortex ratio, and the character of the cortex, suggest that flint may have been imported from the Buchan Ridge area in the form of raw pebbles, rather than prepared cores. This impression is supported by the retrieval of several abandoned early-stage core rough-outs at Wester Hatton. Although relatively large pebbles and cobbles are available in the Buchan Ridge area – on top of the gravels as well as below ground – the size of the Wester Hatton cores indicate that pebbles of up to c60 mm were selected for transport.

In total, 139 pieces are burnt, with nine specimens being vitrified. The lightly burnt pieces indicate that a number of hearths were likely to be present in the area (see discussion of artefact distribution, below), but the vitrified pieces were probably affected by higher temperatures than those commonly experienced in connection with domestic fireplaces, such as in cremation pyres. Two vitrified pieces were found in WH4 and PC1 and PC2, with most deriving from PC5. Four of the vitrified specimens from the latter derive from pits [AMA22–6266] and [AMA22–6273].

CORES

In total, 30 cores were recovered with the following core types present: three single-platform cores (including one rough-out); eight Levallois-like cores (including three rough-outs); and 19 bipolar cores (including one split pebble).

The Wester Hatton material sheds light on the development of the Levallois-like cores during the reduction process, from rough-outs, over single-platform variants, to opposed-platform variants. The most notable effect of the redefinition of a Levallois-like core, from one form to another, is a drop in length of c15–20% between the different stages. Bipolar core CAT1783 from the PC4 furthermore links Levallois-like cores and bipolar cores within one common operational schema. This relatively large bipolar core ($41 \times 37 \times 22$ mm)

Table 6.06 Wester Hatton lithic assemblage summary

	PC1 & PC 2	PC4	WH1	WH2 & PC 5	WH3	WH4	WH5	AMA22-6188	AMA22-6163	Other	Total
Debitage											
Chips	85	264	9	570	9	56	6	8		1	1008
Flakes	41	143	12	364	7	57	3	9	3	1	640
Blades	2	17		30	1	2					52
Microblades	5	11		24		1		2			43
Indeterminate pieces		2		13		3		2	1		21
Crested pieces		3		7							11
Platform rejuvenation flakes		1									
Total debitage	*133*	*441*	*21*	*1,008*	*17*	*119*	*9*	*21*	*4*	*2*	*1775*
Cores											
Single-platform cores, rough-outs				1							1
Single-platform cores		1		2							3
Levallois-like cores, rough-outs		1		3							4
Levallois-like cores		3		5							8
Split pebbles (early-stage bip cores)				1							1
Bipolar cores	5	2	1	18		7					33
Total cores	*5*	*7*	*1*	*30*		*7*					*50*
Tools											
Leaf-shaped arrowheads	1										1
Short end-scrapers				1		1					2
Side-scrapers				1							1
Scale-flaked knives						1					1
Serrated pieces				4							4
Polished-edge implements				1							1
Edge-retouch		2		2							4
Total tools	*1*			*9*		*2*					*12*
Total	139	450	22	1047	17	128	9	21	4	2	1839

Table 6.07 Reduction sequence of all unmodified and modified flakes and blades

	Quantity					%				
	WH2/PC5	WH4	PC4	PC1 and PC2	Total	WH2/PC5	WH4	PC4	PC1 and PC2	Total
Primary	102	15	11	7	135	14	24	6	15	13
Secondary	365	22	84	20	491	48	36	48	41	47
Tertiary	291	25	82	21	419	38	40	46	44	40
Total	758	62	177	48	1045	100	100	100	100	100

has a crushed terminal at either end, but at one end it also retains a small part of an original faceted platform.

CAT1812 is a rough-out for a single-platform core (34 × 33 × 24 mm). It had a primary flake removed at one end to create a platform, followed by the detachment of a single flake. The removal of this flake revealed a relatively large internal cavity, and the core was immediately discarded. Two 'proper' single-platform cores include a relatively cubic piece (CAT1827), measuring 32 × 31 × 32 mm, and a broad piece (CAT1816), measuring 27 × 41 × 37 mm. The former has a plain platform and the latter a faceted platform, and they are both untrimmed, with a cortical 'back-side'. They were discarded when the development of deep hinge and step fractures dug into the flaking-front, making further systematic blank production impossible. Incipient circular impact scars on the platforms show that both cores were reduced by the application of hard percussion.

The Levallois-like cores include three rough-outs (CAT1824, CAT1832–33), and five smaller exhausted specimens (CAT1813, CAT1829, CAT1835–36, CAT1843). CAT1824 is a highly irregular rough-out, which was abandoned when internal impurities made the piece flake in an uncontrolled manner (GD 40 mm). CAT1832 and CAT1833 have surviving cortex on either face, showing that these pieces are based on flat pebbles. The former is a relatively large specimen (59 × 53 × 30 mm). It has a neat faceted platform at one end, and a small number of flakes were detached in an attempt to shape the first lateral crest and the flaking-front, but without completing these tasks. It is difficult to say why this piece was abandoned, but the flint appears to be impure and dense and may have been difficult to control. CAT1833 is slightly smaller (47 × 42 × 23 mm) and has a faceted platform at either end. It was attempted to develop a flaking-front on either face by detaching flakes from either platform, but this rough-out was also abandoned, possibly owing to impurities and the development of deep hinge fractures.

The five Levallois-like cores embrace three single-platform variants (CAT1835–36, CAT1843) and two opposed-platform variants (CAT1813, CAT1829). They all have either one single or two opposed faceted platforms, and they all have a domed cortical lower face. Table 6.08 shows how the Levallois-like cores from WH2 gradually grew smaller as they developed from rough-outs to single-platform variants, and then finally to opposed-platform variants.

Single-platform core CAT1835 was simply abandoned when it became too small (thin) for further reduction to take place, whereas all the other Levallois-like cores were discarded due to the development of deep hinge- or step-fractures.

The 19 bipolar cores include a number of different sub-types. One piece (CAT1815) is a small pebble (33 × 31 × 22 mm) from which one flake was removed by bipolar technique; eight pieces are unifacial cores (with one cortical face); whereas ten are bifacial cores (with two opposed flaked faces). Seventeen of the cores have one reduction axis (one set of opposed terminals), whereas only one has two (two sets of opposed terminals). The average size of the seven cores is 37 × 24 × 13 mm. The bipolar cores from WH2/PC5 are considerably larger than those from WH4, which may reflect the application of different operational schemas. At WH4, the reduction clearly focused on bipolar technique, and although some platform flakes are present, it appears that flakes were mainly produced by reducing pebbles entirely by anvil technique. In contrast, some of the bipolar cores from WH2 may represent the final exhaustion of Levallois-like cores by bipolar technique. This hypothesis is supported by the cores from PC4, where Levallois-like technique was also practised. Two bipolar cores from this area have average dimensions of 41 × 34 × 19 mm.

It was possible to conjoin a number of bipolar cores and bipolar flakes, shedding light on several interesting issues. In Refit Complex (RF) CAT1793–94 it was obvious that both pieces were created at the same time, namely when a pebble was held on an anvil and violently struck with a hard hammerstone.

In RF CAT1795–99 a number of flakes fragments and indeterminate pieces make up the entire original pebble. This complex demonstrates the poor quality of some of the flint used at WH2, as the weaknesses of the flint simply caused the pebble to disintegrate the moment it was placed on an anvil and struck. These weaknesses were also seen in RF CAT1805–06 with internal impurities and irregular flaking properties causing the complex to collapse.

DEBITAGE

The 1008 pieces of debitage embrace 570 chips, 364 flakes, 30 blades, 24 microblades, 13 indeterminate pieces and seven crested pieces. As shown in Table 6.09, the flakes and blades consist of roughly equal numbers of hard-hammer and bipolar pieces (44% and 41%, respectively), supplemented by some soft-hammer specimens (6%). A total of 29 flakes, blades, microblades and crested pieces have finely faceted platform remnants, showing that they were detached from Levallois-like cores. In Scotland, the Levallois-like technique was in use during the Middle and

Table 6.08 The average dimensions of all Wester Hatton's Levallois-like rough-outs, single-platform variants, and opposed-platform variants

Levallois-like core variants	Length (mm)	Width (mm)	Thickness (mm)
Rough-outs	47	39	21
Single-platform variants	41	34	19
Opposed-platform variants	34	35	18

Table 6.09 Applied percussion techniques: definable unmodified and modified flakes and blades from the four main areas within Wester Hatton

Technique	WH2/ PC5	WH4	PC4	PC1 & PC2	Total
Soft percussion	17		15	2	34
Hard percussion	131	5	74	11	221
Indet platform technique	13		11		24
Platform collapse	14	3	10	1	28
Bipolar technique	121	35	6	15	177
Total	296	43	116	29	484

Late Neolithic periods (Ballin 2011a). Thirteen flakes (4%) display split-bulb fractures testifying to the application of robust reduction techniques.

Compared to other later Neolithic assemblages, such as Stoneyhill Farm and Midfield in Aberdeenshire (Suddaby & Ballin 2010; Ballin 2010), the blades from Wester Hatton are quite small and include a fair number of microblades. However, the blades as well as the microblades include Levallois-like pieces, and most of these are clearly contemporary. There is a tendency for the larger blades to have pronounced bulbs of percussion, whereas the smaller ones have more discrete bulbs. Two delicate soft percussion microblades (probably produced by the application of pressure-technique) form a small separate group (CAT1045, CAT1763) – they probably date to the later Mesolithic to Early Neolithic period.

The 13 indeterminate pieces are generally fragments of objects that disintegrated, either owing to exposure to fire (one-third of these pieces are burnt) or due to internal impurities. One piece (CAT1798), for example, was conjoined with other bits of debris and a bipolar core (RF complex CAT1795–99), and the original pebble simply fell apart when it was placed on an anvil and struck.

Seven crested pieces were recovered from the site, but no core rejuvenation flakes. Two (CAT1839–40) are bilateral, with small flakes detached to either side of the dorsal ridge, whereas five (CAT1804, CAT1814, CAT1817, CAT1837, CAT1841) are unilateral, with small flakes detached to one side of the ridge only. The former may relate to the initial shaping of the Levallois-like cores, and the latter to adjustments made during blank production. CAT1814 is a blade (37 × 18 × 12 mm), whereas the others are elongated flakes (av dim: 30 × 18 × 8 mm). CAT1804 has retained parts of the corner where a faceted platform meets the lateral crest, showing that this piece was detached from a Levallois-like core.

TOOLS

A total of 12 tools were retrieved from Wester Hatton (Table 6.06). These include one short end-scraper, one side-scraper, a leaf-shaped point, a scale-flaked knife, four serrated pieces, one polished-edge implement and two pieces with edge-retouch.

The serrated pieces form a heterogeneous group, with the blanks including one large bipolar flake (CAT1823), two blades (CAT1825, CAT1838) and one microblade (CAT1819; Illus 6.43B). Size-wise, the two extremes are CAT1823 (51 × 33 × 10 mm) and CAT1819 (24 × 7 × 3 mm). The serration usually only covers part of one lateral side, but that of CAT1823 covers the entire left lateral side. In two cases (CAT1823, CAT1825) the teeth are so worn that it was not possible to calculate a 'teeth-per-centimetre' ratio, but CAT1819 has six teeth per cm, and CAT1838 has 16 teeth per cm. It was possible to refit the serrated microblade CAT1819 dorsal-ventrally with

another microblade – CAT1820. The blank of CAT1825 (Illus 6.43B) is a Levallois-like blade. Serrated flints ('micro-denticulates') are generally relatively rare in Scottish prehistoric assemblage, and most seem to be Neolithic. The best comparison for the serrated pieces from Wester Hatton are those from the Neolithic settlements at Stoneyhill Farm in Aberdeenshire (Suddaby & Ballin 2010), where several finely serrated narrow blades were recovered (up to 17 teeth per cm). Several of these pieces were found in Middle Neolithic contexts.

One polished-edge implement was retrieved from the site (CAT1828). It is based on an elongated indeterminate flake (48 × 28 × 8 mm), and it has notable abrasion along both lateral sides, proximal end. The abraded areas are associated with edge-retouch. The abrasion corresponds more to the rough abrasion noticed on many pieces from the Milltimber Zone 5 scatter (see 2.14.2) than to the smooth, mirror-like polish noticed on pieces from the later Neolithic sites Overhowden and Airhouse in the Scottish Borders (Ballin 2011b).

One tool was recovered, namely the basal fragment of a leaf-shaped arrowhead (CAT1774; Illus 6.41) from pit [AMA22–6066] (PC2). The arrowhead broke into

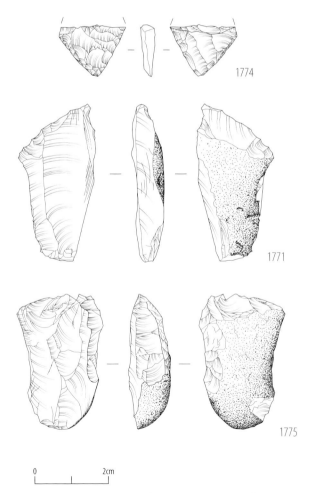

Illus 6.41 Lithics from Wester Hatton PC4

two halves and the fact that the recovered fragment (13 × 18 × 3 mm) has a tiny surviving part of a lateral angle allows the original piece to be identified as a kite-shaped arrowhead with a pointed base.

TECHNOLOGICAL SUMMARY OF PIT CLUSTERS 1 AND 2

With 139 pieces, the sub-assemblage PC1 and PC2 includes 133 pieces of debitage, five cores, and one tool (Illus 6.42A&B). The debitage embraces 85 chips,

41 flakes, two blades, and five microblades. The flakes from the pit clusters include roughly equal numbers of hard-hammer and bipolar specimens (ratio 42:58). The debitage also includes two soft percussion microblades, both of which are thought to date from the Mesolithic/ Early Neolithic period. In contrast to the sub-assemblages from WH2, WH4 and PC4, the ones from PC1 and PC2 contain no Levallois-like flakes at all. The five cores (CAT1771–73, 1775–76) are all bipolar specimens, two

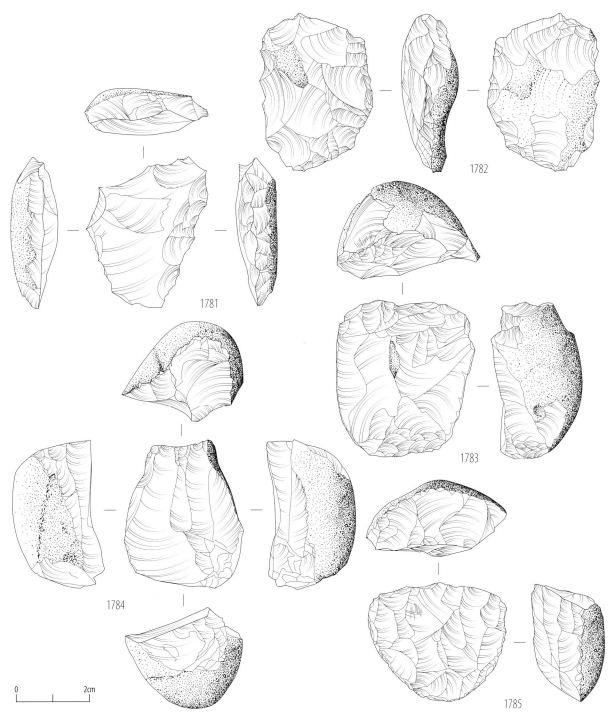

Illus 6.42A Lithics from Wester Hatton PC1 and PC2

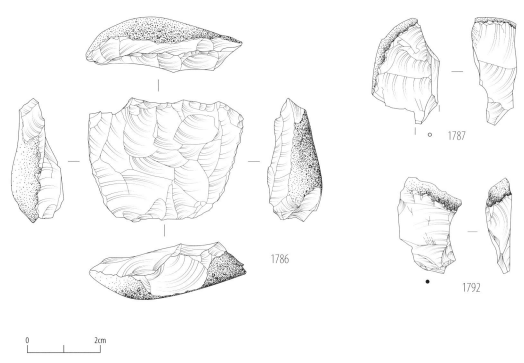

0   2cm

Illus 6.42B Lithics from Wester Hatton PC1 and PC2

of which are fragmented. Three are uni-facial, and one bifacial, and they all have one reduction axis.

In addition, this sub-assemblage includes a kite-shaped arrowhead from pit [AMA22–6066], a type generally dated to the latest part of the Early Neolithic (Green 1980). It is quite possible that the flint used to make the arrowhead is from north-east England. British leaf-shaped points (or other Neolithic/Bronze Age lithic points) have not been dealt with in any detailed general studies and the precise dating of the points and their sub-types is still uncertain. Most leaf-shaped points from the main prehistoric sites in the Biggar area, South Lanarkshire (Ballin 2011b), are informative in the sense that a relationship between sub-type and raw material is implied: the chert arrowheads are apparently all drop-shaped, whereas the flint arrowheads include a significant number of kite-shaped pieces. The flint seems to be mottled grey Yorkshire flint, and this material is generally associated with the Scottish Middle and Late Neolithic periods. As the Modified Carinated Pottery/ Impressed Ware pottery from this pit also belongs to the Middle Neolithic it is highly likely that the kite-shaped point similarly dates to this period.

The number of pieces recovered from the two clusters varied between one or two pieces up to a maximum of 34 pieces from pit [AMA09–6066]. Pit [AMA22–6053] contained 27 pieces of debitage and two bipolar cores. A few fragments of highly regular microblades were also recovered from both clusters. Apart from the small number of probably later Mesolithic to Early Neolithic microblades, these two clusters also yielded Modified Carinated Bowls and Impressed Ware. This suggests that most of the flint (apart from the microblade fragments) may date to the

same Middle Neolithic period. As most of the debitage is in the form of minuscule chips it is most likely to represent a knapping floor. It is possible that the knapping floor pre-dates the pits and the lithic assemblage entered the features with the backfill.

PIT CLUSTER 4

The sub-assemblage from PC4 amounted to 450 pieces. Its composition suggests that it may be contemporary with parts of this site (Illus 6.41). The collection embraces 441 pieces of debitage, seven cores, and two tools. The debitage includes 264 chips, 143 flakes, 17 blades, 11 microblades, two indeterminate pieces, three crested pieces, and one platform rejuvenation flake.

All finds derive from three roughly equal-sized pits, [AMA22–6228], [AMA22–6232] and [AMA22–6234]. Almost the entire sub-assemblage (95%) was recovered from pit [AMA22–6234], including all the cores and tools. As almost 60% of all finds from the latter pit is in the form of minuscule chips, it is almost certain that the flint is residual knapping debris, and that it entered the features with the backfill. Considering the large number of finds retrieved from this pit, including seven cores (four of which are Levallois-like), it is beyond doubt that the knapping floor dug through by the pit diggers was of notable magnitude.

The seven cores comprise five platform cores and two bipolar cores. The former are a single-platform core (CAT1784) and four Levallois-like cores (CAT1780–81, CAT1785–86). The sub-assemblage is dominated by hard-hammer flakes, supplemented by soft-hammer specimens, with bipolar flakes being rare. Seventeen of the flakes (12%) are Levallois-like pieces with finely faceted platform remnants. Five flakes (4%) display split-bulb fractures, testifying to the application of robust reduction techniques. The 28 blades and microblades include soft-hammer and hard-hammer specimens (soft:hard ratio c1:2), showing that more delicate approaches were generally applied when detaching these blanks than when flakes were manufactured. The Levallois-like cores, flakes and blades are all datable to the later Neolithic period.

PIT CLUSTER 5 AND WESTER HATTON 2

The diagnostic lithics in the area of PC5 and WH2 (Illus 6.43A–D) mainly date to the later Neolithic. However, a radiocarbon-sample from ditch [AMA22–6238] returned an Early Bronze Age date (1740–1570 cal BC; SUERC-73583), indicating that the structure and possibly some of the lithics date to this period. This is supported by the distribution patterns, where the finds from ditch [AMA22–6238] and from the pit cluster differ notably in typo-technological terms. It is suggested that the finds from the pit cluster are largely Middle Neolithic, whereas those from ditch [AMA22–6238] are largely Early Bronze Age. Most other parts of WH2 and its surroundings were almost entirely devoid of lithic artefacts.

The only strictly diagnostic types recovered at the structure are eight Levallois-like cores, which are all datable to the Middle to Late Neolithic. Apart from the polished-edge implement (CAT1828), none of the tool types is strictly diagnostic. Polished-edge implements are generally found in later Neolithic contexts (cf Ballin 2011a). So far, the only exception to this rule is the concentration of heavily abraded flints recovered from the Zone 5 scatter at Milltimber (see 2.14.2), where they were associated with Mesolithic finds.

Four finely serrated pieces ('micro-denticulates') were also retrieved from PC5 (CAT1819, 1823, 1825, 1838), and although in Scotland individual serrated pieces may be found throughout the post Mesolithic period, they are most commonly found in later Neolithic contexts. At Stoneyhill Farm (Suddaby & Ballin 2010) two of the serrated pieces were dated to the later Neolithic period by the presence of Levallois-like cores and flakes/blades. Side-scraper CAT1821, also from PC5, is not typologically diagnostic, but the fact that it is based on a very large blade suggests that it may form part of this group of later Neolithic objects.

The composition of the sub-assemblages from PC5 and WH2 differ considerably (Table 6.10). The former includes eight Levallois-like cores and 19 bipolar cores (including the solitary split pebble), reflecting the combined technological approach one would expect from a later Neolithic site (cf Suddaby & Ballin 2010). In addition, this area also includes a number of likely later Neolithic implements, such as a side-scraper on a very large blade; four serrated pieces (cf Suddaby & Ballin 2010); and a polished-edge implement (cf Ballin 2011a). In contrast, all 11 cores from the southern ditch of WH2 are bipolar cores, and the technologically

definable blanks from this feature are heavily dominated by bipolar specimens: 85% of the flakes are bipolar; 89% of the blades are bipolar; and 100% of the microblades are bipolar. This sub-assemblage includes no formal tools.

The most sensible interpretation of events at this location is that there were two knapping floors in this area – a later Neolithic one towards the east (PC5) and a Bronze Age one, indicated by two ditches (WH2). Two microblades from the northern ditch, produced by pressure-technique, and two soft percussion microblades (CAT1045, CAT1763) probably represent a very brief visit to the site in later Mesolithic to Early Neolithic times. This certainly corresponds well to both radiocarbon dates provided for these features and the pottery types recovered from the fills.

WESTER HATTON 4

A modest sub-assemblage of 128 pieces was recovered from WH4 (Illus 6.44), including 119 pieces of debitage, seven cores, and two tools. The debitage includes 56 chips, 57 flakes, two blades, one microblade, and three indeterminate pieces. Most of the flakes are bipolar specimens, whereas five are hard-hammer flakes. Two of the latter are Levallois-like pieces, indicating a later Neolithic presence at the location. Only one of the two blades was technologically definable, and it is a bipolar piece.

The seven cores are all bipolar specimens. Three pieces are unifacial cores, whereas four are bifacial cores. Six of the cores have one reduction axis, whereas one has two. The average size of the seven cores is 29 × 18 × 9 mm.

In addition, this sub-assemblage includes two tools, namely one short end-scraper (CAT1770) and one scale-flaked knife (CAT1844). CAT1770 is the broken-off scraper-edge of a vitrified implement (24 × 20 × 8 mm), and its working-edge is highly regular, convex and steep. Overhanging areas along this edge indicates that the piece is well used. It was found within the general fill of ring-ditch [AMA22–6030). The scale-flaked knife is unstratified, and its date is uncertain. The scale-flaking only indicates a date within the Early Neolithic to Early Bronze Age period (Clark 1936, 47). The ditch was dated to the Middle Bronze Age and it is likely these tools represented part of occupation debris of this structure.

6.9.2.3 Middlefield
Julie Lochrie

The assemblage at Middlefield is small, totalling 122 pieces, with the vast majority retrieved during sample processing. Two pieces in the assemblage point towards a Mesolithic date. The assemblage was retrieved from four small pits [13–0007], [13–0009], [13–0011] and [NL-0009]. The small size of most of the lithics means they would not have been visible during excavation.

Assemblage quantity and composition is summarised in Table 6.11. Apart from a chalcedony microblade, the

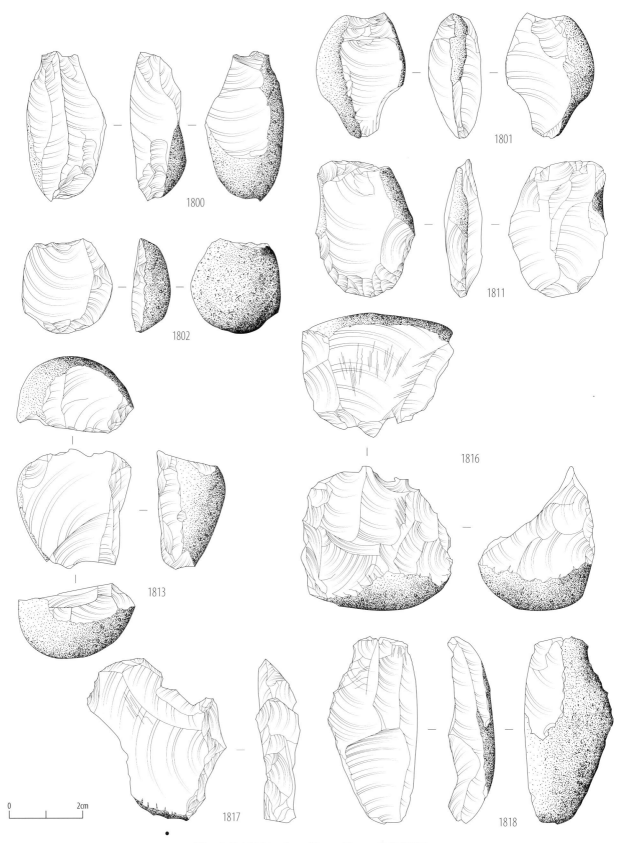

Illus 6.43A Lithics from Wester Hatton PC5/WH2

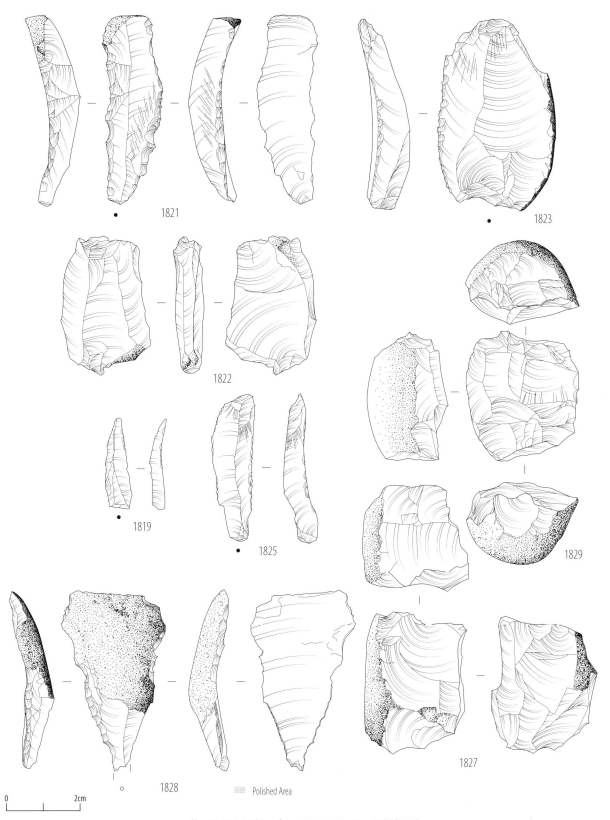

1821

1823

1822

1829

1819

1825

1828

1827

Polished Area

0   2cm

Illus 6.43B Lithics from Wester Hatton PC5/WH2

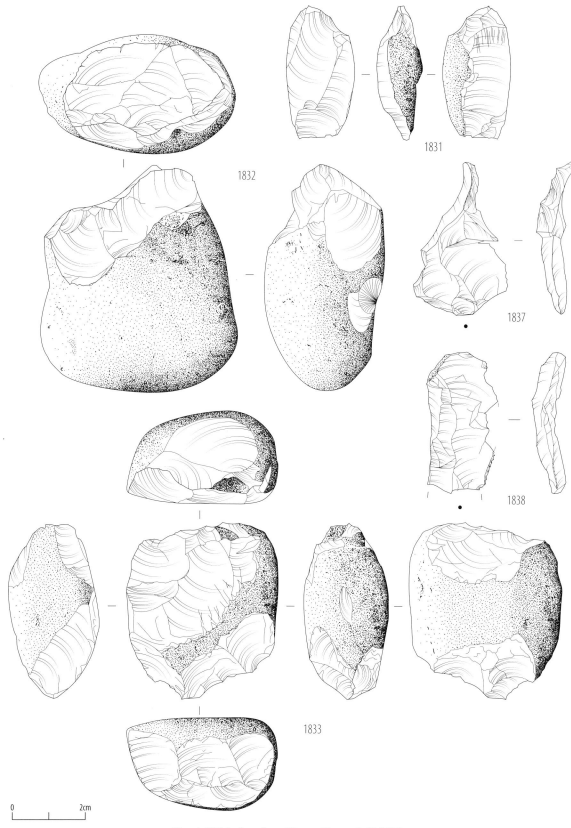

Illus 6.43C Lithics from Wester Hatton PC5/WH2

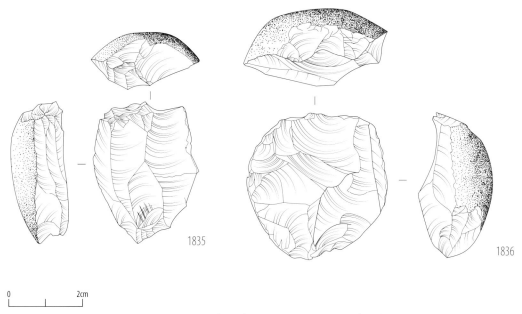

Illus 6.43D Lithics from Wester Hatton PC5/WH2

Table 6.10 The distribution of diagnostic elements across WH2/PC5

WH2/PC5 features		Debitage	Crested pieces	Single-platform cores	Levallois-like cores	Levallois-like flakes	Bipolar cores	Serrated	Polished-edge imps	Burnt	Vitrified	Total
Central pit	[AMA22-6240]	7										7
South ring-ditch	[AMA22-6238]	279	1			1	11			8		300
North ring-ditch	[AMA22-6243]	16								3		19
	[AMA22-6294]	1										1
Pit cluster 5	[AMA22-6252]	8										8
	[AMA22-6254]	5										5
	[AMA22-6258]	1										1
	[AMA22-6264]	37	1	1	1		1					41
	[AMA22-6265]		1									1
	[AMA22-6266/73]	166	1	1	1	8	2		1	12	4	196
	[AMA22-6269]	15								2		17
	[AMA22-6278]	99			1	6	2	3		8	1	120
	[AMA22-6282/84]	332	4		4	8	1	1		14	2	366
	[AMA22-6287]	18				1	1			3		23
	Surf/top				1		1					2
Total		984	7	3	8	24	19	4	1	50	7	

assemblage is exclusively yellow-brown and red-brown coloured flint. The abraded character of the cortex of the site's primary and secondary flakes is indicative of local procurement of pebble flint. The cores have an average size of 36 × 20 mm, although three of the cores all measure 27 mm maximum length. The largest core is 46 mm in length, and it is probable the original pebble size would not exceed a maximum dimension of 50 mm.

In all instances chips are the most numerous finds. When small flake and chips are present it shows that knapping has been occurring nearby. The presence of cores alongside this knapping debris points towards an area of

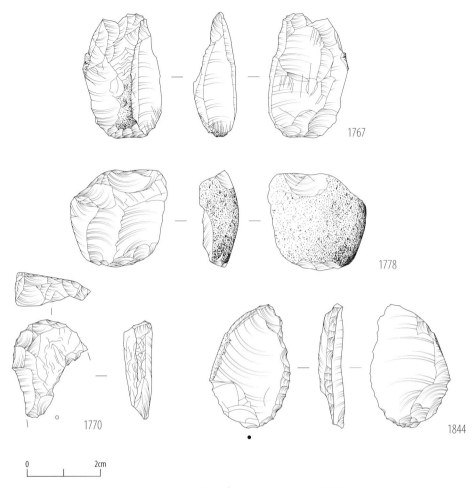

Illus 6.44 Lithics from Wester Hatton WH4

Table 6.11 Middlefield lithic assemblage summary

Feature	Chips	Flakes	Blades	Micro-blade	Indet pieces	Bipolar cores	Edge retouch	Notched	Total
[13-0007]	13	1					1		15
[13-0009]	25	7		1		3			37
[TT-0009]	31	11	2		2	5			51
[13-0011]	16	1				1		1	19
Total	85	21	2	1	2	9	1	1	122

low-level knapping. The composition of the assemblage shows a high percentage of chips (69%). This is likely due to the sampling strategy employed on the sites. As demonstrated in Ballin (1999), the chip ratio of sieved assemblages usually varies between c30% and 55%. There are more flakes than blades although a small microblade with triangular cross-section is present.

The cores are bipolar and have usually been worked along one plane, with one face the focus of removals while the reverse still retains cortex. There is no evidence for the preparation of the cores in any way. There are two flakes with retouch. The edge retouched piece from pit [13–0007] is an atypical piece. This thick bipolar flake has a small section of abrupt retouch to the right of the distal, most likely to enhance a natural point. This type of non-formal tool could have been made for a specific purpose in the vicinity. The character of the retouch and the soft hammer percussion all point towards a Mesolithic date. As well as the retouched piece being Mesolithic in character, the small chalcedony microblade is also likely to be Mesolithic, both in terms of its technology and evidence of convenient use of local materials.

The pits were dated to the Bronze Age (Table 6.01) and were thought to represent evidence of stone clearance in the area for growing crops. The lithic assemblage clearly pre-dates this period and has likely entered the features with the backfill. The assemblage probably represents evidence of a knapping floor in the general area.

Table 6.12 Coarse stone summary

Area	Feature	Context	No	Weight (g)	Summary
PC2	[AMA22-6075]	(AMA22-6004)	1	28800	Saddle quern, 06-CS12
PC4	[AMA22-6234]	(AMA22-6235)	1	176	Pounder/Hammerstone, 06-CS7
WH4	–	(AMA22-6025)	1	287	Grooved stone, 06-CS1
WH4	[AMA22-6030]	(AMA22-6028) (AMA22-6029)	5	63566	Four saddle querns and one rubber 06-CS2, 06-CS3, 06-CS4, 06-CS9 and 06-CS10
WH 4	[AMA22-6144]	(AMA22-6149)	2	900	Grinder and possible hammerstone. 06-CS5 and 06-CS6
WH1	[AMA22-6096]	(AMA22-6097)	1	31700	Saddle quern, 06-CS8
WH1	[AMA22-6115]	(AMA22-6116)	1	10000	Saddle quern, 06-CS11

0   10cm

Illus 6.45 Saddle quern 06-CS12 from PC 2

6.9.3 Coarse stone

Julie Lochrie

The coarse stone assemblage numbers 12 pieces (Table 6.12), which includes seven saddle querns, a rubber, a grinder, a pounder/hammerstone, a possible hammerstone and a grooved stone. Most of the saddle querns are particularly large and heavy and would have been intended for stationary use, with the exception of two smaller slug querns from WH4 ditch [AMA22–6030].

The dating of coarse stone is usually reliant on contextual dating as there is no clear chronological typology and unlikely to ever be one. The reason for this is that coarse stone, and saddle querns in particular, do not change much throughout their period of use from the Neolithic into the Iron Age. The range of quern types found here from the Bronze Age can be compared to the range from Kintore, which include large stationary querns, portable 'slug' querns and saucer querns (Engl 2008).

The area of PC2 and PC4 has no associated radiocarbon dates but from the pottery evidence is thought to be Middle Neolithic. A saddle quern (Illus 6.45) was found in pit [AMA22–6075] and is a long, flat, sub-oval stone at a slight incline. It has the largest surface area than any of the saddle querns, measuring 582 × 310 mm, but is one of the thinnest at 45–121 mm. Its underside has been roughly dressed and its grinding surface is smooth with very slight central dishing.

Pit [AMA-6234] in PC4, contained an ovoid cobble that has been used as both a pounder and a hammerstone (06-CS7; Illus 6.46). It has bifacial flaking at one end and a pounding facet, measuring 7 × 2.5 mm on the other.

The four saddle querns from WH4 (Illus 6.47) were all retrieved from ditch [AMA22–6030]. Two are small portable slug querns and the other two are large stationary querns. The large querns are both more or less wedge shaped, one natural (06-CS10) and the other roughly shaped (06-CS9). The wedge shape helps in two ways; it can allow the user to rest their knees under the quern if they wish and, whether they did or not, the natural angle allows an easier downward thrust when grinding. The

06-CS7

Illus 6.46 Pounder/hammerstone 06-CS7 from PC4

small slug querns (06-CS2 and 06-CS4) are typical of their type, both being plano-convex in shape, the grinding surface being almost flat to the very edges. The broken one has a dressed concave side and the complete one is natural. A rubber was also found in this group that is not much larger than the slug querns. The difference between the slug querns and rubber is that the ground face on the rubber is convex. A fragmentary grinder (06-CS5) (Illus 6.48) and a large fractured, soot stained cobble possibly used as a hammerstone (06-CS6) was also found at Wester Hatton 4.

Two of the saddle querns came from WH1, one being partial, of an unknown form and the other a large saucer quern. The saucer quern (06-CS8) is sub-circular in plan with a deep central dish (Illus 6.49); it appears that it hasn't been shaped but the base has worn a little smooth. The base is slightly convex but is stable enough not to rock on its base. The fragmentary quern is shaped, with peckmarks along one edge, but the very base of it is also exceptionally smooth. The grinding surface on this quern is very deep and well-used.

6.9.4 Finds discussion

Very little artefactual evidence remains from the Mesolithic presence in this area but we know limited activity during this period took place. We have a Mesolithic radiocarbon date from one of the large pits at Blackdog and Mesolithic lithics from Middlefield and Wester Hatton (Table 6.13). The Middlefield and Wester Hatton lithics are in a mixed assemblage of later date and both were probably formed

Illus 6.47 Saddle querns from WH 4: 06-CS2, 06-CS4, 06-CS9 and 06-CS10

part of a spread or random discard. The large pit at Blackdog, however, contains *in situ* deposits of Mesolithic date and, most interestingly, it seems to have been reused in the Early Neolithic when a CBNE vessel was deposited in its upper fills.

06-CS5

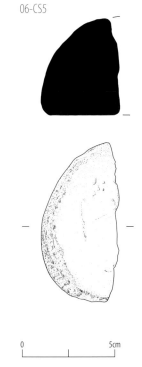

Illus 6.48 Grinder 06-CS5 from WH4

The pot had been used for cooking and had been in use long enough to show evidence of repair. It has not derived from midden material and was certainly found in the location it was originally placed. The deposition of most of a single vessel suggests a single act or event. Interestingly the majority of the vessel comes from one side and this is also the case at Milltimber (see 2.14.1) Port Elphinstone (Lochrie 2013) and Chapelfield (Squair & Jones 2002). It was theorised at Chapelfield that specific parts of the pot were selected for deposition (*ibid*, 162). There certainly appears to be something more complex occurring than simple deposition of rubbish – perhaps this represents the closing and clean-up ceremony after an event or feast. The presence of one large section of the vessel could be explained if the pot was deliberately broken before placing it in the ground. Perhaps the part that was held in the hand was retained and deposited while the pieces that broke away were left behind. The importance behind deliberately breaking a vessel is that it could not be used again, providing meaning to its final use. The placing of the pot into the top of an existing pit also suggests a degree of purposefulness behind the deposition. This reuse of large pits was also evidenced at Milltimber and the issues around this are discussed in more detail in Chapter 2.

Fluted carinated bowl was also found at Wester Hatton. There are no associated radiocarbon dates for this pottery at this site, or indeed Blackdog, but a date range of 3970–3700 cal BC from other features at Blackdog suggests an Early Neolithic date. Examples mentioned above (see 6.9.1)

Illus 6.49 Saucer quern 06-CS8 from WH1

Table 6.13 Wester Hatton pottery and lithics summary and date range

Area	Pottery date range	Lithic date range	Radiocarbon dates
PC1	3800–3600 BC;	Later Mesolithic to Early Neolithic;	3340–3100 cal BC, SUERC-74400
	3600–2900 BC	Middle to Late Neolithic	
PC2	3600–2900 BC	Later Mesolithic to Early Neolithic;	–
		Middle to Late Neolithic	
PC3	3600–2900 BC		–
PC4	3600–2900 BC	Middle to Late Neolithic	–
PC5	3600–2900 BC	Later Mesolithic to Early Neolithic;	3310–2920 cal BC SUERC-74399
		Middle to Late Neolithic	
WH1	Bronze Age		–
WH2	Bronze Age	Bronze Age	1740–1570 cal BC, SUERC-73583
Pit [AMA22-6188]	Bronze Age	Later Mesolithic to Early Neolithic	1520–1430 cal BC, SUERC-74401
Pit [AMA22-6167]	Bronze Age		1400–1210 cal BC, SUERC-73591
WH3	Bronze Age		1370–1130 cal BC, SUERC-73584
WH4	Middle Bronze Age	Middle to Late Neolithic	1260–1050 cal BC, SUERC-73586;
		Bronze Age	1210–1020 cal BC, SUERC-73585
WH5	Bronze Age		1110–930 cal BC, SUERC-73587

provided evidence it was a long-lived type. Tantalising evidence from Blackdog suggests that there was more going on in the Early Neolithic than is immediately evident from the sparse features. Pitchstone from a nearby spread of material, an overshot blade and a platform core are also dated to this period. Similarly, at Wester Hatton the fluted bowl was not found in isolation. In the same Pit Cluster, lugged bowls of CBNE style were found and evidence for Early Neolithic lithics in the form of small blades were spread across the site. No Early Neolithic radiocarbon dates were found at Wester Hatton and the site chronology is complex owing to several artefact types being long-lived.

While the Early Neolithic assemblage at Blackdog and Wester Hatton is small the residues identified on the pottery along with the knapping debitage points towards domestic Neolithic activity. This is tempered by the fact that no settlement activity was identified at either site, and the placing of pots into pits has ritual connotations and may have been the product of some sort of symbolic end process for the pot. Interestingly, Ballin (2016, 33–35) made a connection between small lithic assemblages and special sites (eg timber halls) when compared with the larger assemblages of domestic sites such as the sunken-floored building at Garthdee Road. That certainly isn't reflected here and the precise nature of their presence is not clear. The pits at Wester Hatton are discussed in more detail below (see 6.10.2).

The Middle Neolithic is represented at all three of the sites but predominantly at Wester Hatton, where evidence for substantial domestic activity comes in the form of an assemblage of a minimum of 38 vessels and a substantial Levallois-like lithic assemblage. The dating of Impressed Ware has changed dramatically over the last couple of

decades and it clearly first appears in the mid-fourth millennium BC, making it a Middle to Late Neolithic ware (Kinbeachie, 3500–2920, MacSween 2001, table 1, 63; Kintore, 3530 BC–3340 BC, MacSween 2008, 181; Meadowend Farm, 3350 BC–3000/2900 BC, Jones et al. 2018). One of the more complex elements of dating the pottery assemblage is the fact that Henshall's 'north-eastern' style of the Carinated Bowl (CBNE) clearly has an ancestral relationship to Impressed Ware. The bipartite shapes of both are clearly related and some of the first modifications to Carinated Bowl pottery were changes to the rim shapes, additions of minor decoration and the appearance of lugs. This change did not happen overnight and there is a clear overlap in the dates for both styles. The implications of this for Wester Hatton is that despite the identifications of two different pottery wares, they could all relate to the same broad period.

A chronological model has been produced (see 2.14.1), analysing typo-technological compositions of prehistoric lithic assemblages. The suggested sequence of industries should be perceived as a working hypothesis in need of corroboration. The scheme includes five techno-complexes, covering the Mesolithic–Bronze Age period. Wester Hatton has been invaluable in understanding the Levallois-like/ bipolar approach practised during the Middle and Late Neolithic periods. It has also aided understanding of typical Early Bronze Age assemblages, which are characterised by the almost exclusive use of bipolar technique. An assemblage from the recently excavated later Bronze Age site of Blackdog (Clements & Cook 2009), a few kilometres from Wester Hatton, shows a different form of bipolar approach, which is less schematic and could be described as simple 'bashing'.

The Bronze Age activity at Wester Hatton is also identifiable in the pottery assemblage. Flat-rimmed ware is the term commonly given to pottery of this period, which tends to lack features, decoration or much variation. The usual appearance of this type is as fairly coarse bucket- and barrel-shaped pots. One exception to this is a ridged vessel from WH4, which appears to be most commonly associated with the Middle Bronze Age and may be an evolved form of cordon, seen on Early Bronze Age types (see above). Ridged vessels were also found at Chapel of Stoneywood and Gairnhill (Chapter 3). As at Gairnhill, the Bronze Age pottery assemblage is not large. Despite five structures dating to the Bronze Age, the pottery assemblage includes around 41 vessels, a similar quantity to the Neolithic assemblage. It was suggested at Gairnhill that the site was deliberately cleared before abandonment and reusable domestic material transferred with the occupants. This could also be an explanation for the large number of querns found abandoned in WH4, two of which were large stationary querns. Overall the coarse stone would not have been easily moved to another location.

6.10 Discussion
Jürgen van Wessel and Don Wilson

6.10.1 Mesolithic and/or Neolithic large pits at Blackdog

The site at Blackdog and, to a lesser extent, Wester Hatton and Middlefield provide further evidence of Mesolithic activity in Aberdeenshire. These latter two sites included small lithic assemblages representing small scale tool making using local beach flint pebbles, as seen at a number of other nearby coastal locations, such as Forvie and Menie (Hawke-Smith 1978–80) and Foveran Links (Shepherd 1983). The Mesolithic radiocarbon date from the pit at Blackdog seems to signify more intensive activity taking place here, although not on the same scale at that recorded at Milltimber (Chapter 2).

Although the dating of the pit at Blackdog is suspect, owing to issues with the stratigraphy, there is no doubt that the three large pits here correspond closely in form and patterns of deposition to the pits at both Milltimber and Warren Field, Crathes (Murray *et al.* 2009). Several of the pits at both sites were radiocarbon dated to the Mesolithic, and by proxy the others were attributed to this period. At Milltimber some may have been left open for an extended period of time. At least six had also seen the introduction of burnt material, stones and Carinated Bowl pottery in their latter phases, indicating a level of reuse of the pits in the Early Neolithic. These characteristics were all mirrored at Blackdog, suggesting they were part of a similar pattern of events. At Milltimber, there was insufficient dating information to understand whether individual features were deliberately reused hundreds or even thousands of years after their initial excavation, or if the large pits are simply

a type common to both periods. These interpretations are not mutually exclusive.

Both the spacing and size of the pits at both Milltimber and Blackdog was also variable, although this is harder to characterise at Blackdog, with only three pits present. These variabilities were also noted and discussed in depth at Warren Field (*ibid*, 25). The authors suggested a possible woodland setting to explain the irregularity in the spread of these pits. Although this is not demonstrated at Blackdog the area would certainly have been wooded (see 6.3.2 above). The potential function of the pits at Warren Field is also discussed, suggesting they appear poorly sited to have been hunting traps, that there was no raw material found within that could not be gathered more easily elsewhere and that there was no evidence for cremated bone or other funerary remains. All these factors are similarly true at Blackdog, although on a much smaller scale.

Issues relating to both the original purpose of these pits and the reuse have been discussed in more detail in 2.15.2 and owing to their similarities will not be repeated here. The number of these features excavated in Scotland over the last 10 years or so has certainly increased, partly due to the increase in commercial excavation but also because of the increasing awareness of these types of features. Large pits of this sort are more commonly recorded in Neolithic contexts, for example Pit VII at Chapelfield (Atkinson 2002, 139–92). This may be due in part to the easier visibility of the burnt upper deposits, and the presence of material that can be dated on site by specialists (as opposed to through radiocarbon dating completed during post-excavation analysis).

6.10.2 Neolithic pit clusters at Wester Hatton

The Neolithic pit clusters, incorporating both pottery fragments and lithic assemblages, at Wester Hatton were intriguing, although far from unusual. Pit digging in the Neolithic, and to a lesser extent in the Bronze Age, seemed to be common practice across Britain. No overriding theories for this activity predominate, although a number of studies (Carver 2012; Anderson-Whymark & Thomas 2011; Noble *et al.* 2016) have attempted to make sense of this phenomenon. In general it seems that the digging of these pits and the practice of depositing cultural waste/ domestic debris was at once a recognisable tradition and yet extremely variable (Carver 2012, 128). This activity also amounted to a coherent and long lived tradition with its origins in the Mesolithic (Darvill 2011, 37).

The Wester Hatton pits themselves are quite variable in size and shape with no overriding patterns identified. They have been found in small clusters, in linear alignments and as single features. Many contained Impressed Wares and modified Carinated Bowls, plus flint assemblages covering all aspects of the knapping sequence. Charred hazel nutshell and charcoal also seem to be common inclusions, with burnt bone less predominant.

Along the route of the AWPR/B-T the presence of Neolithic pits has also been identified at Blackdog, Milltimber (Chapter 2) and Goval Farm (Chapter 5). In a wider context similar features have been recorded at Forest Road, Kintore (Cook & Dunbar 2008), Grantully, Perthshire (Simpson & Cole 1990), Deer's Den (Alexander 2000), Knocknagael Farm, Inverness (Kilpatrick 2016), Meadowend Farm, Clackmannanshire (Jones *et al.* 2018) and Granton Road, Forres (Cook 2016). At Deer's Den at least 20 pits were identified with Carinated Bowl pottery and lithic assemblages recovered. At Knocknagael Farm, Meadowend Farm and Granton Road further pits and pit clusters with similar pottery types and lithic assemblages were found. These sites are all securely dated to the Middle Neolithic. Further afield similar pits have been identified at Milfield, Northumberland (Waddington 2011), across East Yorkshire (Carver 2012) and further south at North Fen, Cambridgeshire (Tabor 2016), and Kilverstone, Norfolk (Brophy & Noble 2011).

At Wester Hatton each of the pit clusters to the south end of the site comprised three or four closely placed pits. The inference of this is that each cluster of pits represented a single event. Whether each of the five clusters was contemporary was less certain. At Milfield (Waddington 2011) multiple phases of activity were identified and at Kilverstone, (Brophy & Noble 2011, 70) it was suggested that people were digging small clusters at each visit and returning seasonally or periodically over centuries. It is possible that this is what was occurring at Wester Hatton. Certainly the pottery and lithic assemblages recovered from the fills here are of relatively long-lived traditions, but without more precise dating the episodic nature of this activity or lack of it is uncertain.

The linear spread of fairly equidistant pits recorded in PC5 might imply they were part of a single event, or at least occurred a period of time that meant the location of the earliest pits was either still visible or known. There is some evidence to suggest that the pits were reused. Pits [AMA22–6266] and [AMA22–6273] intercut each other and pit [AMA22–6291] seems to have been inserted into an earlier pit [AMA22–6289]. This reuse may have been accidental, perhaps indicating a lack of visibility although at the same time implying that the activity was occurring periodically.

At Forres Road (Cook 2016), a number of clusters containing pottery and lithic assemblages were thought to be domestic in nature, although it was suggested that the deposition of the artefacts was deliberate. At Milfield (Waddington 2011) two types of pits, burning pits and midden pits, were identified. No evidence of structured deposition was recognised in these pits, although it was stated that it was not clear how this would be identified. At Kilverstone (Tabor 2016) it was suggested that the bulk of the material within the pit clusters was from surface deposits/middens. Of note was that pottery from the same vessel was found in separate pit clusters, showing a degree of connectivity/contemporaneity. This was also observed at Wester Hatton, where on two occasions pottery from the same vessel was found in separate pits. In both cases the same two pits were involved. This could imply that not only were the pots being deliberately deposited in the pits but that the two pits were contemporary.

The motivation behind pit digging and deposition was investigated as part of a study in East Yorkshire (Carver 2012). Here it was noted that very few pits contained whole vessels and that the remains were more generally from several vessels. This was also seen to an extent at Wester Hatton. Carver suggested that the pits appeared to form a common practice that took place in the everyday living sphere (2012, 129), available to and comprehended by all members of the community rather than as a specialised practice carried out by elites. At Grantully, Perthshire (Simpson & Cole 1990) it was suggested that pits were associated with a whole range of activities and symbolic associations, from ending activities in a particular locale to marking that place for future visits (Brophy & Noble 2011, 74). Certainly Noble *et al.* (2016a, 172) realised that pits can no longer be characterised as either 'domestic' or 'ritual' and that they generally display characteristics that fall between these two seemingly opposing spheres of interpretation.

Importantly, it was realised that when looking at the function/reason for the pits they had likely been truncated both through later activity and the excavation process itself (Darvill 2011, 38) changing the context and appearance. Further to this, Becket & MacGregor (2011, 61) suggested that the fills of the pits represent the deposition of only a small proportion of materials that were used and broken on the sites. They represent distinct choices about when it was socially required or appropriate to deposit materials that are typically categorised as refuse. Whatever the motivations for pit digging and deposition, it shows the existence of a shared knowledge that was widespread.

In summary, the Neolithic pits at Wester Hatton seem to represent similar activities taking place in a diverse number of contexts from isolated single-use pits, pit clusters and multiple-use pits. These are seemingly associated with both domestic and ceremonial activities. Also the quantity of domestic and lithic-working debris found with the pits implies that they relate to substantial and reasonably long-lived domestic occupation in the area, in structures that are otherwise archeologically invisible.

6.10.3 Neolithic activity in the coastal zone

One interesting factor not yet considered is the location of Blackdog and Wester Hatton in relation to other sites with Neolithic activity. Much of the Early Neolithic activity in this area focuses on major rivers and good potential farmland (ScARF 2012b). While both Milltimber and Goval (Chapters 2 and 5) fit this pattern, being sited next to the Rivers Don and Dee respectively, Blackdog and Wester Hatton are coastal. This may simply be a factor of discovery, as both sites provide recent examples that differs from the norm, although neither site provided evidence for occupation.

At both sites there appears to be no direct evidence for structures in the vicinity of the pit clusters. It has been suggested that the pattern of pit groups and spreads is not random but is in fact activity surrounding the main domestic buildings that have themselves left no trace owing to truncation (Wellbrae; Alexander & Armit 1993, 37–41), or the structures are represented by low impact turf and beam houses (Meadowend Farm, Jones *et al.* 2018). This may also speak to the idea of the 'mobile Neolithic' (Brophy 2006, 7–46). Carver surmised that particular places were gaining a developed sense of permanence. This could be seen in the repetition of digging pits in similar locations over long periods of time without the older deposits being disturbed. At Wester Hatton in particular it seems we are seeing levels of activity that represent familiarisation with the site over a prolonged period. The fact that we have so much domestic debris here must represent a certain level of permanence, be it on a short-term seasonal basis or longer term permanence.

6.10.4 Bronze Age settlement activity at Wester Hatton

The Bronze Age settlement activity was based around five large circular structures and a small number of large pits. Although the pits were poorly understood, the remains as a whole pointed to sustained settlement activity across the site. The dating evidence and stratigraphy implied at least three clear phases of occupation, although in actual fact each structure could represent a different phase. It is also likely that the settlement activity extended beyond the limited excavation area.

Not surprisingly, a number of similarities exist between the sites at Wester Hatton and Gairnhill (Chapter 3). Both sites have a series of roundhouses aligned down a south-facing slope, the structural elements of the buildings are similar and they cover a similar period of occupation. While these similarities existed, the sites were certainly not identical. Variability of structural elements was seen at Gairnhill although certainly not to the degree seen at Wester Hatton. Of the seven roundhouse structures recorded there the earliest (Gairnhill 7) was dated to the Middle Bronze Age. This included a substantial stone fill within the ring-ditch. The six later Bronze Age structures (Gairnhill 1–6) all included aspects of ring-grooves and internal post-rings similar to WH5, although three also included evidence of internal ring-ditches. The dating of these structures was also compatible with WH5, with a spread of dates covering 1110–930 cal BC.

In comparison, at Wester Hatton more variability was identified between the structures and none were contemporary. Indeed WH2 (1740–1570 cal BC) was found to be much earlier than the slightly tighter framework of dates obtained for the remaining four structures (1370–1130 cal BC to 1110–930 cal BC), although even these failed to provide any overlapping dates. The truncation of WH4 by WH5 also clearly represented later re-occupation of the site after the former structure had gone out of use. It seems at Wester Hatton a more intermittent level of occupation was taking place, with the likelihood that the site was only occupied by a single structure at any one time.

The structures may represent the same people moving up and down the hill (and further away) as each house wears out. Halliday (2000, 61; 2007b, 53–4) suggested that the Bronze Age farm land was in continuous use but was being rotated between cultivation and pasture. With this in mind he suggested that the roundhouses would have followed the farming and were placed where necessary to take care of the tasks in hand at the time. This movement over large areas could explain the discontinuous settlement patterns that have not only been widely noted in Bronze Age archaeology but also expressed to a degree at Wester Hatton and to a lesser extent at Gairnhill.

The main structural form of the roundhouses is discussed in Chapter 3 and will not be repeated here, although the ring-ditches at Wester Hatton provide a number of anomalies that are worthy of discussion. These features are generally thought to be the product of erosion through general wear within the roundhouses caused by general footfall, or even the stalling of livestock. The inclusion of so much stone within the fill of these features is also a common occurrence. The addition of these large stones may have been both to ease drainage and to form a more solid surface. At Wester Hatton four of the structures (WH1–WH4) presented variable designs of this element. The slightly irregular shape of the two opposing ditches at WH2 certainly suggested patterns of wear, although the moderate depth may indicate a level of purposeful clearance, possibly to enable the inclusion of the stone infill. The depth of the ditch at WH3 was also moderate, although the lack of a stone fill was telling. A further noteworthy aspect of this ditch was the presence of a charcoal-rich layer at the base of the cut. This contrasted with the other ring-ditches, all of which had stone fills with an overlying charcoal-rich deposit. A sequence also recorded on the majority of the roundhouses at Gairnhill. Could the cobbles have been removed from WH3 prior to its destruction? Or maybe it just represents abandonment after the floor had been worn down.

The ring-ditch of WH4 provided potential evidence of changes to the way these structures were being constructed. The large continuous penannular ring-ditch here included the purposeful digging of a vertical cut edge and the construction of a more compact and substantial stone infill with signs of inner stone edging. This suggests the ring-ditch had become part of the construction of the building rather than an element of its use. Although the stone fill was more extensive in WH4, the stones probably formed a similar function to that suggested for ring-ditches at Gairnhill, primarily as drainage. They would also have provided a much dryer surface over which straw or bedding material could be spread.

The final phase of occupation at Wester Hatton was represented by WH5. The remains of this roundhouse provided evidence of a slightly different set of structural elements, although the general form of the house was probably fairly similar. It is possible that the absence of a ring-ditch was due to short-lived occupation or even a change in use. As only half of the post-holes survive there is clearly a case for significant horizontal truncation to have taken place. This may also explain the absence of familiar elements found more commonly on the other structures.

Abandonment is generally the most prominent aspect of the archaeological record related to these structures. A common characteristic of the structures at Wester Hatton was the presence of clearly defined charcoal-rich layers. This was particularly evident at WH2, WH3 and WH4 and may be indicative of destruction by fire for these buildings. In WH2 this layer overlies the stone cobble fills of the ring-ditches and in WH4 formed a spread across the footprint of the whole structure. The charcoal-rich layer in WH3 was found at the base of the ring-ditch, although this probably resulted from the absence of a stone fill in this ditch. Whether the conflagration of these structures was the result of a deliberate or purposeful act or just accidental was not identifiable, although given the majority of the structures show evidence of burning it seems more likely to be the former. At least three of the roundhouses at Gairnhill also displayed evidence of destruction by fire. This was particularly the case for Gairnhill 4, which included carbonised wattle at the base of the ring-ditch. As discussed in 3.9.5, destruction by fire is generally an uncommon occurrence (Pope 2003, 369) and the anomaly seen in north-east Scotland is potential evidence for a regional practice of deliberate destruction of the structures by fire.

It is worth mentioning the large number of sites excavated in this area that revealed prehistoric archaeology (Easter Hatton flint scatter, Wickham-Jones & Holden 1998; Blackdog, Clements & Cook 2009; Blackdog, Lenfert & Cameron, 2016). The bounty that the coast can provide is clearly shown by its enduring popularity throughout prehistory; not only a place for food such as fish, shellfish and marine mammals but an area rich in fresh water. These streams, rivers and coastal paths would not only have been an important transport network but they would have also helped carry local sources of pebble flint into the area.

6.10.5 Hiatus and agricultural activity

After the abandonment of the site in the Late Bronze Age we see a hiatus in activity across all three sites, considered further by Tipping in 7.1.9. At Wester Hatton the site eventually became part of agricultural land associated with the farm at Wester Hatton. This is mapped in the mid-18th century, although may have earlier origins. This agricultural activity was evidenced across the site by the remnants of plough furrows. These were generally 1 m wide and spaced 9 m to 10 m apart and broadly aligned north-west/south-east. The furrows survived variably, partially because of differential machine stripping and later ploughing activity.

To the south end of Wester Hatton site, the remains of a tarmac road were also exposed. This represents the remains of the original trunk road leading from Aberdeen north to Fraserburgh and Peterhead. A road in this location is first depicted on Taylor and Skinners 1776 'Survey and maps of the roads of North Britain; the road from Aberdeen to Fraserburgh' and more clearly on Robertson's later 1822 'Topographical and military map of the counties of Aberdeenshire, Banff and Kincardine'. This may also be the same road depicted on Roy's Military map c1745, although the detail on this map is not accurate enough to confirm this. The tarmac road surface exposed during the excavations was clearly of modern 19th/20th century construction, although in all probability followed the line of earlier roads.

Chapter 7

Spaces, places and finding the traces; concluding thoughts on the context of discoveries of the AWPR/B-T

*Kirsty Dingwall, Matthew Ginnever,
Richard Tipping and Jürgen van Wessel*

The preceding chapters have illustrated the wealth of archaeological remains along the AWPR/B-T route. By any measure the discoveries have major implications for our understanding of north-east Scotland and, beyond that, for the British Isles as a whole. The timespan and range of sites present means that not only have we pushed back the boundaries for human occupation but also massively increased the archaeological resource for the locale. The importance of the project in advancing archaeological knowledge should not be underestimated.

This concluding chapter provides an overview and synthesis of the significance of the discoveries; however, it also teases out some of the recurring themes that have emerged. The issue of mobility and permanence or otherwise in the landscape across time is highlighted at different sites, with multi-phase aspects at some and single-phase duration at others. There was a progression of societies intimately linked to the landscapes around them at the most detailed and most expansive levels. There are sites across the scheme where, despite the advancing millennia, there seem to be identical behaviour patterns taking place again and again. Contrasting with this appreciation of how communities in the past moved through the various landscapes and utilised them differently, there is also a recognition of the presence of gaps in the record where we might have expected evidence of activity. In fully comprehending the importance of the discoveries made during the AWPR/B-T, the implications and importance of these themes must be examined.

At a much more practical level, the process of identification, discovery, excavation and even analysis of the dataset merits a critical analysis. Linear schemes such as this are both relatively rare in terms of the total number of excavations carried out each year across the country, and yet are often one of the largest originators for increasing the number of known sites. Consideration is given to some

of the practical aspects of undertaking large infrastructure projects and the methodologies used to collect and make sense of the data.

7.1 A chronological examination of significance

Kirsty Dingwall

7.1.1 Late Upper Palaeolithic

The discovery of material of Late Upper Palaeolithic (LUP) date within the lithics scatter at Milltimber was quite simply the most unexpected of all the artefactual remains from the scheme (Illus 7.01). The fact that it was only identified during detailed analysis, long after the excavation works were complete, only makes it more remarkable. The post-excavation analysis process can often (wrongly) be regarded as the point at which the assumptions made in the field are merely confirmed or refined, but rarely altered significantly, particularly in terms of the periods of activity.

The existence of a Scottish Late Upper Palaeolithic, although perhaps long suspected, has only very recently come to be confirmed in a substantive manner. In their reassessment of the early prehistory of the Scotland published in 1996, Pollard and Morrison make clear that convincing evidence for the earliest periods in this region had yet to be identified (1996, x). Somewhat over a decade later, Saville & Ballin's (2009) examination of presumed Mesolithic material from Kilmelfort Cave in Argyll confirmed the presence of hunter-gatherers of the Late Upper Palaeolithic in the western region. This followed work by Biggar Archaeology Group at Howburn in the later 2000s, where a field-walking project identified a great many flints of comparatively large size (Ballin *et al.* 2010). Early consultation with Torben Ballin and Alan Saville

Illus 7.01 Selection of Late Upper Palaeolithic material from Milltimber

again confirmed what they were seeing in the Kilmelfort assemblage; the presence of lithics of definite Late Upper Palaeolithic date.

The discoveries from Milltimber are in many respects similar to that from Howburn; they are found within an assemblage that contains material of Mesolithic and even Neolithic date (both from lithics and from pottery). Although full analysis is still forthcoming, the early interpretation of Howburn was that it related to hunter-gatherers of around 12,000 BP following reindeer herds through the river valleys to the north of the Southern Uplands (Ward 2010, 21).

The frustrating aspect of the Milltimber Late Upper Palaeolithic assemblage is that there are no obvious features that can be related to it or evidence of the people of the time, beyond the artefacts. In many respects this is not dissimilar to our understanding of the Mesolithic in Scotland a few decades ago, where artefacts were being identified, but structures, temporary or otherwise, were unknown. Fast forward 30 years and structures of the Mesolithic, although still rare, are being added to the records all the time; the camp at Standingstones is one of those discoveries. It would be hoped that our knowledge of the Late Upper Palaeolithic in Scotland would follow a similar track; initially a recognition that the period is present and artefacts exist, then a concerted effort made to identify sites with typical characteristics of the period and then ultimately the discovery of structural and activity-related features that allow us to put flesh on the bones about what life would have been like.

To some extent and on the basis of the artefacts, the evidence from the LUP phase points to an existence potentially not that different from the Mesolithic. The river is a key route, not only into the interior of the country but also likely as a way of following prey. Human presence is probably focused on the river, but permanent settlement is unlikely. Until more is understood about lifestyles and the range of activities in both periods, little more can be said about the Late Upper Palaeolithic. Despite this,

the recognition of the existence of these artefacts will significantly alter how we view this period on the east coast of Scotland, and how lithics scatters of potentially mixed date might be dealt with in the future.

7.1.2 Mesolithic

Against the backdrop of the discovery of even earlier material, it might seem that the *in situ* Mesolithic material also found as part of the lithics scatter at Milltimber would be considered of lesser significance. This is not the case. Mesolithic sites within Scotland are still relatively rare, and the opportunity to fully excavate and analyse an assemblage such as this is not routinely available. However, even given the interest in the Mesolithic assemblage, it could be argued that the other features of similar date across the scheme are of more interest in terms of broadening our understanding of the period. The camp at Standingstones is still one of only a handful of excavated domestic sites, however temporary that activity might be. The location of the site at a relatively high elevation, away from a typical river- or loch-side setting has until recently been thought of as unusual. Discoveries such as the 'little house in the mountains' as described by Warren *et al.* (2018) indicate the presence of equally small and potentially temporary encampments at an elevation well above what would normally be expected. At Caochanan Ruadha, the site lay at nearly 550 m AOD, and the excavators were able to tease out evidence of specialist zoning of activities within the structure, something that could not be identified at Standingstones. No longer can we rule out highland/upland zones as being barren with respect to early prehistoric remains and, in fact, these may be the areas where investigation might prove most fruitful (Illus 7.02), being less subject to later disturbance from development.

Discovery of confirmed structures are still few and far between, so that the tent/camp at Standingstones makes a major contribution to the architectural traditions (if they can be defined as such) of the Mesolithic. The other aspect of the Mesolithic discoveries at Milltimber are also what make it stand out; beyond structures, we have evidence of the activities that are long assumed to have taken place, but which can be so difficult to tie down in tangible form. We see the hunter aspect of the hunter-gather community and from this we can begin to investigate the practicalities of how these groups used their territories.

7.1.3 Neolithic

The transition between the Mesolithic and Neolithic and how this came about is a subject still under discussion to some extent. Much focus is placed on the question of the origin of the Neolithic traditions; were these adopted by the existing communities on the British Isles, taking what they found attractive of the Neolithic culture they saw on the European mainland, or was there some form of wholescale population movement that resulted in the new practices for which evidence was found on the scheme (Noble 2006, 24)? Some focus has been placed on the islands of the

Illus 7.02 Mesolithic structures. Typically, these have been found in coastal locations. However, discoveries such at the structure at Standingstones (Chapter 4) are challenging this assumption

west of Scotland as the starting point for the incoming changes; however, the dates of hearth deposit activity at both Milltimber and Blackdog not only indicate activity in the very first centuries of the fourth millennium BC, but also from the last few centuries of the fifth millennium BC, within what would be termed the Mesolithic period but from features typologically similar to the features of the Neolithic.

It is also of note that although there are increasing numbers of monumental structures of Early Neolithic date in Scotland, there are very few that would be confirmed as domestic in nature and dating to the first few hundred years of the fourth millennium. The closest stylistic comparator at Garthdee Road, around 6 km further downstream but in a similar topographic location, was more precisely dated through Bayesian analysis to the first half of the 38th century cal BC (Murray & Murray 2014, 14). Analysis of that site made much of the potential relationship between it and the monumental timber halls further upstream from both Garthdee and Milltimber at Crathes and Balbridie, but the evidence from Milltimber is simply not stratigraphically complex enough to stand up to such interrogation. Certainly

the structure, the further hearth deposits across the site to the west of the structure, and the presence of possible drying racks would suggest a settlement of at least some permanence, rather than fitting the longer-lived hunter-gatherer lifestyle which is sometimes posited for the Early Neolithic in Scotland (Illus 7.03).

As the Neolithic period progresses, the evidence returns to a more familiar form; pits filled with apparent waste material, fragments of pottery and lithics, sometimes forming pit clusters (eg Wester Hatton) but equally common as single or isolated features (Milltimber, Gairnhill, Goval). These fragments of evidence from the Middle Neolithic can be taken as some form of proxy for settlement, but whether they directly represent the location of shallow foundations or temporary structures that leave no mark within the geological subsoil is less clear. The importance of radiocarbon dating in clarifying the division between Early/Middle/Late Neolithic and indeed the distinction between the earlier periods and the Bronze Age was well illustrated at Milltimber where an extensive suite of radiocarbon dates of pit features thought to relate to one period or another quickly challenged the

Illus 7.03 Neolithic structures are still a relatively rare occurrence. The structure from Milltimber (Chapter 2) was also of note due to its early date in the very first centuries of the 4th millennium BC

assumptions of the excavators during the post-excavation analysis process.

Although not much touched on here, as the evidence is too inadequate to do more than offer it up as an archaeological quandary, the curved ditch found in the south of the Milltimber site is another aspect of the Neolithic evidence that may prove to fundamentally change our understanding of the typologies of the north-east (Illus 7.04). Stylistically, it appears similar to Late Neolithic henges, but the sequence of geoarchaeological changes to the River Dee valley floor mean that if it was originally oval or circular in plan and has been partially eroded away by the river, it must pre-date c3300 BC. A possible causewayed enclosure was suggested by Smith at Sprouston in the Borders for a similar feature; this may also have been subject to erosion by the River Tweed (Smith 1991, 266). If the prehistoric ditch is an enclosure of early date, could it be a causewayed enclosure of some description, a site type rarely found in a Scottish context? As before, the significance of the data is in adding new sites that do not fit the accepted story.

7.1.4 Chalcolithic

The arrangement of timber settings found on the higher Camphill Terrace at Milltimber is only briefly touched upon in this monograph, and yet is a hugely important discovery in its own right. The south-west to north-east alignment of post-holes is a fairly unusual arrangement, and the discovery of an intact Beaker pot at the base of one of the post-holes is unique in terms of survival. A tight array of radiocarbon dates for at least two of the rows of between 2400 and 2200 BC places the settings in the Chalcolithic period; with the Beaker this is neatly representative of the new cultures and attitudes that were to emerge in the Bronze Age.

Excavated examples of timber settings of this type are few and far between; the discussion of comparators for the site in Chapter 2 makes this clear. Despite the extensive area investigated around the setting, it is difficult to argue

Illus 7.04 Undated features. This curved ditch from Milltimber (Chapter 2) is undated, but likely to date to the Early or Middle Neolithic period

that the monument lies within a landscape where such features are common. Discovering these kinds of sites, where they do not form part of a larger suite of ceremonial structures, broadens our understanding of what might be considered a 'typical' location for them. The survival of the Beaker undamaged is also quite remarkable and raises questions about how well such pottery might survive in buried contexts.

7.1.5 Bronze Age settlement patterns and progressions

To some extent, of the periods present, the evidence from the Bronze Age (and Chalcolithic leading into it) gives the roundest and most comprehensive sense of what life was like at the time. The types of sites range from large-scale ceremonial (Milltimber timber settings), to more familial burial practices and attitudes to life and death (Nether Beanshill), to the first stirrings of proto-industrial practices (Gairnhill Burnt Mound), to a wealth of information about the development and progression of roundhouse architecture and settlement formation (Nether Beanshill, Gairnhill, Chapel of Stoneywood and Wester Hatton) as the period advances. Not only that, but in this period we are able to talk with more confidence about the relationship between sites on the scheme of the same date, with connections between the settlements at Gairnhill and Chapel of Stoneywood represented through the artefacts.

Without question, the key type of evidence from the Bronze Age is the roundhouse (Illus 7.05), illustrating the changes in settlement patterns. A total of 13 roundhouses of Bronze Age date were identified across four different sites (Nether Beanshill, Gairnhill, Chapel of Stoneywood and Wester Hatton). To a great extent the structures support the proposition that in the north of the country, there is a lack of domestic construction of Early Bronze Age date (ScARF 2012c, 3.3); the roundhouses present generally date from the Middle and Late Bronze Ages. That some level of domestic activity is taking place is represented by the Early Bronze Age (c2000 AD) burnt mound at Gairnhill, but the overall evidence reinforces the apparent gap in domestic construction contemporary with this.

The exception to this is WH2 from Wester Hatton, dated to between 1740–1570 cal BC, which is notably earlier than any of the other roundhouses, both on that site and across the scheme as a whole. The date was obtained from residue from pottery collected from the ring-ditch of the structure. On the one hand, this provides a more accurate provenance for the date; however, the ring-ditch

also contained pottery of Middle Neolithic date, and the structure overlay an area occupied by an earlier pit cluster of Neolithic date. Although it could be a fairly rare example of the development of the roundhouse in the Early Bronze Age, caution must be applied to the date, as the origin of the pottery cannot be conclusively confirmed. Beyond this Wester Hatton roundhouse, the remaining structures fit well with the ever-increasing number of roundhouse settlements known from the north-east of Scotland.

7.1.6 Roman

Similar to the discovery of the Late Upper Palaeolithic material, the presence of an extensive military encampment (whether defended by ditches or not) has massive potential for altering our understanding of both the tradition of Roman temporary camps, and for how the Roman army were moving around the north-east region.

The excavations at Kintore (Murray & Cook 2008) are one of the only examples of an extensively investigated interior to a known temporary camp, where defences along with large parts of the enclosed area have been examined. To some extent the remains at Milltimber are the poorer relation to this; without 'finding' the ditch which it is assumed must be there, there will always be uncertainty from some quarters about the interpretation of

Illus 7.05 Middle and Late Bronze Age roundhouses were the most frequently identified feature type across the scheme. This structure from Wester Hatton (Chapter 6) had a ring-ditch filled with stone, which was also seen in some other examples

it as a camp. This is not seen as an issue by the current authors; the evidence confirms an encampment of the Roman military, whereas the details and implications of this may be up for some discussion. The very fact it does not fit the typical examples known and recorded to date, and that it challenges the fairly accepted status quo means the archaeology from the site will contribute to our comprehension of all sites of this date, not just in Britain but across the Roman Empire.

7.1.7 Early Historic

The handful of features that date to the post-Roman first millennium AD could easily be lost against the catalogue of stand-out remains from the preceding 14,000 years. The features themselves are generally isolated, unrelated to other features of similar date and do not provide a particularly coherent 'story' of activity in this period.

Despite this, they provide fragmentary indications of the Picts in locations where such evidence has previously not been seen. The period between around 400 and 900 AD in north-east Scotland is dominated by this group. However, the archaeological evidence is heavily biased in favour of symbol stones, Early Christian sites, forts and other religious or monumental site types that bear little relation to the grain-drying kiln at Milltimber or even the small enclosure at Goval.

Finding evidence of the more mundane aspects of daily life from the Pictish period is equally as important as understanding how a power centre such as Burghead (Shepherd 1996, 142) or Rhynie (Noble & Gondek 2016, 30; Noble *et al.* 2017, 22) would have functioned and the relationship between them and their surrounding territories. However, to do this, features need to be identified and, crucially, dated by scientific means to this period.

7.2 Gaps, mobility and connection to landscapes

Kirsty Dingwall, Matthew Ginnever and Richard Tipping

The large and diverse range of landscapes investigated during the road scheme has produced a wealth of archaeology spanning the whole of human history in north-east Scotland. At most sites this activity was observed to be periodic rather than continuous, but periodic throughout the millennia. The work has also enabled us to identify blank areas where no archaeology is present. The gaps are infrequently discussed in volumes such as this, possibly because of the perceived notion that they tell us little about a site. In this instance they are as instructive as the archaeology itself. Naturally, it is not just the landscapes that determine the capacity for anthropogenic activity but also the environment. Having a good understanding of the general environmental conditions across both time and place is integral to understanding the gaps.

Also included in this thematic review is the concept of mobility and a sense of place. This can be a difficult aspect of the archaeological record to define. The term mobility here is used for a diverse range of past movements including hunter-gatherer territorial dynamics, migration, trade and dissemination of ideas. Despite the relatively large scope of this project (archaeologically speaking), most past societies could have traversed the route in a relatively short amount of time even without transportation, and in many cases would have regarded the limits of the route as easily within their 'territories'. As such, connections between contemporary sites are probably easier to assume than to physically prove.

This concept is not restricted to a simple understanding of how people moved between one site and another. On a linear scheme such as this it can become easy to focus on relationships between one excavated site and the next, rather than considering how humans from a specific time span would have related to the location itself. How would they have viewed that spot? Would they have had any appreciation of thousands of years of activity before them and would that have been important? In some cases, it seems that the people living in the north-east had a very clear understanding that things had gone before; in others, the story and relationship with 'the place' was probably of limited value. At the multi-phase sites we certainly see repetition of behaviours across the millennia. This presumably is in large part down to basic needs such as shelter, food and warmth, but there are also elements that seem to contribute to their appreciation of a sense of place. On the basis of the AWPR/B-T, what is also particularly interesting is that the evidence from the scheme is not restricted to local inhabitants; the Roman ovens represented invaders in the most literal sense. As a mass of bodies passing through these landscapes, to what extent would they have been aware of and engaged with those landscapes, or were they merely seen as hostile environments and resource-rich territories?

What emerges is a picture of a landscape where the inhabitants or incomers were making choices about location. Where they lived, whether they settled, to what degree they wanted to alter their surroundings and the extent to which that might have been a permanent or temporary choice all contributes to our overall grasp of life in north-east Scotland over the last 15,000 years. That those decision-making processes may have resulted in areas absent in archaeology is key to understanding settlement patterns and predicting areas of potential in the future. Selected sites and time periods are considered in the following sections.

7.2.1 Temporal gaps and a sense of place in the Mesolithic

Developer-funded excavation has added considerably in recent years to the corpus of Mesolithic archaeological sites in the north-east (Alexander 1997; Cameron 2002;

Johnson & Cameron 2012; Murray & Murray 2014; Noble *et al.* 2016a; and Balneaves Cottage, Broom Lodge, Skilmafilly and Aden Arboretum in the Aberdeenshire SMR). To this list can now be added the Mesolithic pits and gridded excavation of lithics at Milltimber (Chapter 2) and Blackdog (Chapter 6), and the pit-defined structure at Standingstones (Chapter 4). Research excavations at Warren Field, Crathes, produced a pit-defined alignment (Murray *et al.* 2009; Gaffney *et al.* 2013) and activities high in the Cairngorms have been recently identified (Fraser *et al.* 2015), demonstrating a radical geographical shift in the locations of Mesolithic activity. Of the recently discovered sites, only those at Spurryhillock, Garthdee Road, Middlefield and Blackdog are close to the coast, and the hills and lowlands of north-east Scotland are rapidly being filled with Mesolithic activity. With the increased dataset, patterns may emerge.

Single pits from Milltimber, Warren Field and Broom Lodge (Noble *et al.* 2016a) are broadly contemporary with each other and with the structure from Standingstones (in the early seventh millennium BC). The gap or cessation in pit-digging following c6700 BC seen at Milltimber is replicated in calibrated radiocarbon date age estimates compiled for the Mesolithic period in the Aberdeenshire SMR by Bruce Mann. A similar gap in age estimates for activity in northern Britain at around this time (Wicks & Mithen 2013; Waddington & Wicks 2017) has been suggested to have been due to the 'collapse' of populations in response to what is known as the 8 ka BP climatic 'event'; the most severe climatic deterioration in the Holocene epoch (Alley & Ágústdóttir 2005; Seppä *et al.* 2007). Despite the similarity, in north-east Britain there are comparatively few archaeological assemblages and too few radiocarbon age estimates (Williams 2012), and the population 'collapse' is not coincident with the 8 ka BP event (Waddington & Wicks 2017, 708). The case remains unproven from their data. The gap in activity more broadly between around 6700 and 5700 BC at Milltimber in the later part of this period could also be linked to the impact of the Storegga slide, occurring in the early centuries of the sixth millennia BC (ScARF 2012a, 3.4.2). Although the assumption is that settlement was not occurring at Milltimber the resulting changes to the coastline, the impacts of the tsunami and the rising sea levels at the time may all have played their part in Mesolithic people abandoning the river bank and valley edges at Milltimber for a period as a place for hunting.

A modest increase in radiocarbon-dated activities after 4800 BC is detected in northern Britain (Wicks & Mithen 2013; Waddington & Wicks 2017). Whether this rise is related to increasing population size is unclear. In lowland Aberdeenshire and Angus, a potential increase in later Mesolithic activities after around 5000 BC could be argued as the result of improved visibility to modern-day archaeologists (Noble *et al.* 2016a, 187; Blackdog and Milltimber this volume), owing to increased radiocarbon

dating of material from developer-funded projects. At Milltimber, this trend confirms that issue; following a gap of several thousand years, the latest example of one of the hunting pits has a fifth millennium BC date from an upper deposit. Rather than confirming without question continuity of activity or social memory, the date merely offers up a range of questions regarding what it represents.

The north-east region is, perhaps, also beginning to offer evidence of a more complex, experiential Mesolithic. The Warren Field pit alignment is one of only two sites in Britain of this period that might be described as monumental (Thomas 2013, 178–80). Further comparative sites are starting to emerge through the cropmark records of the north-east and certainly could be targeted for investigation in the future (eg Wester Fintray NJ81NW 38, Pittengardner NO77NW 189) and Mesolithic post-pits may also not be as rare as was once thought. However, the most convincing interpretation for the contemporary large pits at both Milltimber and Blackdog is as hunting features (Illus 7.06). This is in sharp contrast to the interpretations offered for those further up the River Dee. This difference is not necessarily problematic and, in fact, may assist in appreciating how people saw the land at the time. In later periods, the interaction and connectivity between the sacred and the profane has been much examined (for example in the ritualised deposition in pits in the Neolithic period, Noble *et al.* 2016a). The fact that the examples at Warren Field appear to be more deliberately laid out means that offering an alternative, more specialised, function for them is not at odds with features that may be similar in form but appear to be used in a different fashion at Milltimber or at Blackdog. The possibility that one site represents a day-to-day functional process and the other represents a more spiritual representation of that activity is one that could be tested, if further examples of such features were discovered.

Ethnographic studies have shown that hunter gatherer societies can and most frequently do cover vast distances annually (ScARF 2012a, chapter 6.1). Evidence of active hunting (Milltimber and Blackdog), tool repair (Milltimber and Standingstones), the implied seeking out of resources (Standingstones) and consistent but occasional 'overnighting' at locations (Standingstones and Milltimber) all provide concrete evidence for a group or groups who are moving from location to location, carrying out a range of activities at each one. While it is impossible and indeed unlikely to state this is a single group moving between these, particularly given the wide range of dates across the sites, it gives an indication of the complex way in which those group(s) would have appreciated the landscape around them. Until recently, the paucity of known sites of this period might have suggested that it was solely the coastal plains and the river valleys that were being exploited and explored. By expanding our expectation of sites up into higher ground, into the hinterland (eg at sites such as Caochanan Ruadha, Warren *et al.* 2018) and within the forests we know to have been present, life in

Illus 7.06 A functional Mesolithic. The distribution of at least some of the hunting pits at Milltimber (Chapter 2) is best represented by the orange fencing surrounding the deep holes

the Mesolithic can be described as being in some respects fairly indistinguishable from that in the Early Neolithic.

7.2.2 The earliest farming communities along the River Dee

Chapter 2 described in detail the archaeological evidence for the earliest Neolithic activity at Milltimber (see 2.6). Whitehouse *et al.* (2013) argued that agriculture was introduced 4000–3600 BC in a favourable climate (cf Bonsall *et al.* 2002 and contra Tipping 2010a). The meta-data on radiocarbon-dated human activities compiled by Collard *et al.* (2010) and Stevens & Fuller (2012) show a very large peak, which is taken to represent a very rapid increase in population size. This peak may instead reflect the great interest in refining the chronology of the introduction of agriculture. Woodbridge *et al.* (2013) attempted to explore the pollen record of the British Isles in the light of this purported rapid population rise. While some landscape reconstructions stress that Early Neolithic landscapes were forested, pollen diagrams conventionally under-estimate the degree of landscape openness because the pollen of most trees swamps that of grasses and herbs. However, corrections for this bias are possible. Applied to the landscape immediately around the Warren Field timber hall, Tipping *et al.* (2009) showed that the land cleared,

though perhaps 2 km across, was still subsumed in a region full of trees. Woodbridge *et al.* (2013) employed a different, less sophisticated correction procedure (Fyfe *et al.* 2010). They found that woodland loss in the Early Neolithic was detectable across the British Isles, with significant areas of grassland, arable land and heath (Woodbridge *et al.* 2013), and in Scotland in particular, from 3850 to 3450 BC, but their Scottish palynological data-set (n = 17) is heavily skewed towards pollen records from the Northern and Western Isles and north-west Scotland (n = 13) where woodland has, through oceanicity, exposure and the growth of blanket peat, always been more open (Crawford 1997; Fenton 2008; Tipping 2008; Fyfe *et al.* 2010, 1168).

The evidence from the scheme in the Early Neolithic is strongly focused at Milltimber, although features are also present at Gairnhill, Blackdog and Wester Hatton. At Milltimber, the domestic nature of the evidence points to the progression of the location from a 'visiting spot' in the Mesolithic, to a location where settlement was taking place, however brief that might have been, eg a single generation. Although this cannot be used to signify land clearance and the beginnings of agriculture it does provide clues to a less nomadic existence. Although the palynological evidence may not be conclusive, the types of feature found do seem to support a more settled approach to life.

The relationship between the monumental timber halls further upstream (and increasingly being found elsewhere in Scotland) and the more obviously domestic evidence from the Early Neolithic is discussed in detail in Chapter 2 but is worth revisiting here. The monumental timber halls such as those at Warren Field and Balbridie could still be described as relatively rare; however, evidence of formal structures in this period are rarer still. Despite some uncertainty regarding the dating of Balbridie, all currently known and dated timber halls fit within the 3800–3600 BC timeframe (Millican 2016, 146).

The structure at Milltimber may well still be described more toward the 'short-lived' end of permanence, but the presence of a range of contemporary features further to the west on the slope, including possible drying racks and further hearths, along with an extensive accumulation of lithic material surely is an indication that this comprises something that could almost be described as settlement.

7.2.3 Returning to the pits; Neolithic domestic and structured activity

The concept of reuse (and revisiting) the sites at Milltimber and Blackdog are represented by upper deposits in the earlier hunting pits that can clearly be dated to the first part of the Neolithic. At Milltimber this was seen as a coincidental occurrence, while at Blackdog it may have been more deliberate (Illus 7.07). However, this kind of revisiting/reusing activity is also seen from the pits at Warren Field (Murray *et al.* 2009, 6) and something of the same type of behaviour is also seen at Spurryhillock (Alexander 1997) where a Neolithic structure was placed over an earlier Mesolithic pit.

At first glance, it is not easy to square the two contrasting interpretations – on the one hand that the pits were known about through the millennia, their location remembered, and to some extent revered, on the other that they were simply part of the background of the landscape for the Early Neolithic society and happened to have had material washed into them. Each seems to point to a very different appreciation of the surrounding environment for the contemporary inhabitants. Having said that, it is not impossible that both could be feasible.

As has been discussed above, there is some evidence to suggest that the Warren Field site is something exceptional or unusual; not necessarily representing the day-to-day activities of the Mesolithic. Meanwhile, we have fairly concrete evidence at Milltimber of the domestic; a structure, hearths, tool repair. Does the evidence actually add support to the notion that from the early phases on the site through into the fourth millennium BC, people were very acutely aware of the fact that the Milltimber location was part of the 'normal' world, and that further upstream was a location seen as special and separate. Even though the same types of feature could be present at both, they might have been viewed very differently.

Illus 7.07 Evidence of reuse. The upper deposits in the Mesolithic hunting pits from Blackdog (Chapter 6) are interpreted differently from those at Milltimber (Chapter 2). This may be an indication of people at the time viewing the same type of feature differently at different locations

7.2.4 What happened in the north-east after 3700 BC?

There is no radiocarbon-dated human activity at Milltimber, or any of the other sites on the scheme between, conservatively, around 3100 and 2500 BC (see 2.6.3 & 2.7.1). The features from the mid-to-later Neolithic are no more than transitory, sporadic visits, and moving beyond this period, the Late Neolithic/Chalcolithic structures are non-domestic in character. The temporal gap in archaeological evidence for settlement specifically at Milltimber extends through the Iron Age. Although there may have been infrequent flood events, fluvial processes will not have been hostile to human occupation on the Camphill Terrace surface. Equally, following the lateral erosion by the river to form the younger Maryculter Terrace, it could have been attractive for activity in the mid- to Late Neolithic, but excavation widely exposed these and found nothing. The gap in activity is real.

Taken alongside other sites (Marshall & Cook 2014), the likelihood is that Milltimber, Balbridie, Warren Field and Garthdee Road, and perhaps Wardend of Durris above the Dee (Russell-White 1995), were unoccupied after the mid-fourth millennium BC. A prolonged hiatus was defined by Rees (1997) from 3331–2679 cal BC to 1491–1130 cal BC at the ring-cairn at Cairnwell, Portlethen, east of Wardend of Durris.

In the middle-course of the River Don, Cook & Dunbar (2008, 394) identified a possible hiatus in activity at Forest Road, Kintore, between 3350 and c3100 BC. Two roundhouses (RH27 and RH13) might represent settlement, although are not conclusively domestic, and in general the activity on the site is seen as insubstantial and transitory. An absence of activity after the mid-fourth millennium BC can be suggested for nearby Deer's Den (Alexander 2000). Closer to the coast, this project identified a mid-Neolithic presence (between 3300 and 3000 BC) at Wester Hatton, but no structures were identified and again the pits could represent transitory episodic behaviour.

Does this point to a real gap in activity in the centuries following 3700 BC? Recent analyses have argued for significant population declines across Britain and north-west Europe after the Early Neolithic (Stevens & Fuller 2012; Shennan *et al.* 2013; Whitehouse *et al.* 2013; Woodbridge *et al.* 2013: see also Ashmore 2004). The abandonment of Milltimber may, then, have been part of a much larger pattern. Stevens & Fuller (2012) thought climatic deterioration after 3350 BC the most likely driver, as did Whitehouse *et al.* (2013) for Irish data, and greater adaptability to this was thought by Bishop *et al.* (2009) to lie behind the shift to barley cultivation. The 5.2 ka BP climatic event (Roland *et al.* 2015) marks this deterioration, commencing around 3550 BC and ending c3300 BC, but it impacted most on western Britain: north-east Scotland is unlikely to have been directly affected. The increased vulnerability of crops in the later Neolithic to pests and diseases (Dark and Gent 2001) remains intriguing yet still speculative.

Stevens & Fuller (2012) defined a later decline in radiocarbon-dated resource consumption, at 2900 BC, and while some structures in north-east Scotland are of this date (Noble *et al.* 2012; Brophy 2016) they are as yet rare. As intriguing is a second temporal gap in radiocarbon-dated human activity from 2500 to 1800 BC at Forest Road, Kintore (Cook & Dunbar 2008, 169), when the nearby ceremonial monuments at Broomend of Crichie (Bradley 2011) were in use. This mirrors the erection of the timber settings at Milltimber in the same period, with no associated evidence of domestic activity.

7.2.5 An 'empty' Dee–Don upland in later prehistory?

Excavation in the upland areas along the road-line between the Rivers Dee and Don recorded one Neolithic feature, a shallow pit (see 3.5.1). Otherwise there is an apparent absence of evidence in this landscape specifically. The RCAHMS survey of the Don region (Gannon *et al.* 2007, 47–8) identified one Early Neolithic monument, the long cairn at, fittingly, Longcairn. New finds (Leivers *et al.* 2000; Brophy 2016; Noble *et al.* 2016a) are non-domestic in character. Even portable finds are very few (Gannon *et al.* 2007, fig. 5.1), despite being in an upland (and close to a University town) that was 'improved' in the 19th century when antiquarian interest was extraordinarily high (Welfare 2007). The contrast between the sparseness of the archaeological record of the Dee–Don upland and the richness of the record in Garioch in Donside, and across the Dee and The Mounth, is striking. There are also no later prehistoric roundhouses or cairnfields recorded in the NRHE across the Dee–Don upland between Gairnhill and Chapel of Stoneywood. The sites presented in Chapter 3

might suggest many more remain undiscovered, but what is interesting is that it is possible to predict the location of these new sites using the distribution of known monuments. The gap between Gairnhill and Chapel of Stoneywood, however, remains a gap despite intensive and extensive mitigations along the road-line.

Survival and destruction of archaeological monuments are important themes in any understanding of later prehistoric landscapes (Stevenson 1975; Gannon 2007). While destruction might explain the near-absence of later prehistoric sites on the Dee–Don upland, it is possible to explain the absence in terms of avoidance, in seeking reasons why people did not want to settle in this terrain. There are two threads to this argument: the implications for water availability of the gravel-rich glacial till, and the observation that a great many stones and boulders were not cleared by late prehistory, as might be expected (and is the case in other parts of Scotland) and had still to be cleared as late as the mid-19th century.

The till covering the Dee-Don upland (see 1.4.3) is pierced by 'islands' of granite, which are impermeable and result in water being retained in the overlying deposits. Around these are expanses of very free-draining, acid podsols of the Countesswells and Dess Series, which form on very thick, very well-drained sandy and gravelly glacial till (Auton & Crofts 1986, 8; Munro 1986, 104). Meltwater channels that might line valleys with less permeable alluvium are few (Chapter 1). These properties affect surface drainage. The density of present-day drainage, assessed from the blue-line network in 1 km² Ordnance Survey grid squares, shows that wetter areas with drainage densities >3.0 are west of Peterculter, west of Gairnhill Wood and at Craibstone, south of Chapel of Stoneywood. Dryer areas with drainage densities <1.0 are extensive across the upland.

Granite and granodiorite boulders are abundant in the till (Illus 7.08), loosened by deep chemical weathering in pre-glacial climates (Auton & Crofts 1986; Hall 1986; 1987; Munro 1986, 104), then transported east and concentrated by glacier flow and along meltwater streams. Interrogation of civil engineering boreholes on Geoindex (2016) suggests that south of Kingswells, boulder and cobble-rich gravelly till is in general buried beneath 1.5–3 m of sand and gravel, too deep to demand stone clearance. Across the Dee–Don upland, weathered bedrock is much closer to the ground surface. There were still enormous numbers of these on the ground surface in the later 19th century (Illus 7.09), in comparison to most upland landscapes in Scotland, where extensive stone clearance was a later prehistoric activity (Carter 1993; Halliday 1993; McCullagh & Tipping 1998). William Alexander described the effort of one crofter, George Carr, on a farm close to the Loch of Park, constructing dykes 'some 1900 yards … from five to fifteen feet in width, and from five to eight feet in height' (Alexander 1886, 87) from cleared boulders. Consumption dykes

Illus 7.08 The geology of north-east Scotland. An aerial shot looking over Gairnhill shows the frequency of very large erratic boulders within the geology of the area. This found to be the case at almost every area subject to large-scale topsoil stripping

swallowed in exaggerated form the prodigious number of boulders needing to be cleared (O'Dell & Walton 1962). One 440 m long example at Kingswells to the south of the AWPR/B-T road-line was begun in 1854 and is two metres high and 10.5 m wide, wide enough to support a path along its axis. It is now a Scheduled Monument (NJ80NE 17, SM 108). Other consumption dykes are concentrated around Kingswells, Westhill, Echt and Charlestown (NHRE; Aberdeenshire SMR), and some examples were investigated as part of the road scheme works (see 1.2).

The need for consumption dykes in the 19th century and the implied fact that the fields had not been previously cleared may indicate that the density of later prehistoric settlement across the Dee–Don upland was very low, because of the scarcity of surface water away from areas of bedrock (the permeable substrate). Arable farming was thwarted by a quality of ground only able to be cleared using 19th century incentives and technology. These already acid, impoverished and unattractive soils are also susceptible to salt deposition from easterly winds, most notably as haar which persists for days (Glentworth & Muir 1963, 37). This possibility allows us to evaluate archaeological landscapes at the scale they were experienced; entities to be walked across. It allows the possibility that patches of landscape were unoccupied, by choice, and that pressure to expand into empty spaces was not irresistible, if they existed at

all. Towards the end of their report on the dense pattern of human activities at Forest Road, Kintore, Cook & Dunbar (2008, 371–3) asked whether what they had found was typical or untypical. They concluded, optimistically, that they were typical. Our extensive area investigation of a landscape only 10 km away would suggest that the Forest Road assemblage is untypical, or at least only typical of those soil conditions, and not to be expected everywhere. Understanding the underlying soil conditions in detail at specific locations in the north-east may go a great way to helping predict settlement patterns without excavation.

7.2.6 The end of Bronze Age settlement

Chapter 3 (see 3.9.1) suggests that the settlement at Gairnhill was abandoned by around 800 BC. This also seems to have been the case at Wester Hatton (Chapter 6), with no dated features after 930 BC. Three structures are thought to have burnt down, either accidentally or as an act of closure (see 3.9.5) at Gairnhill with similar evidence also suggested at Wester Hatton (see 6.7.2). At Gairnhill it is possible, though it cannot be demonstrated, that all the houses were destroyed at the same time. We do not know what happened next at Gairnhill. However, the absence of Iron Age archaeology across the Dee-Don upland (see 7.2.7 below) might suggest that they did not move too far uphill and the dearth of hut circles along the

Illus 7.09 Stony geological subsoil. In addition to large boulders, many stripped areas revealed dense patches of smaller stones. It would be assumed that such areas would be unattractive for settlement, but it is worth noting evidence of stake-built structures would be nearly impossible to identify against this kind of geological subsoil

Dee alluvial corridor on the NHRE provides no indication that settlement moved downhill.

No Bronze Age domestic structures at Deer's Den date after 800 cal BC. One assay (OxA-8182: 810–520 cal BC) may be influenced by the Hallstatt plateau (Alexander 2000), but settlement continued a short distance away at Forest Road, Kintore (Cook & Dunbar 2008). Excavation at Goval (Chapter 5) suggests that the isolated mid-Bronze Age roundhouse there was followed only after a long gap by metalworking activity and small-scale settlement in the early centuries AD. There are other temporal gaps in the archaeological record of north-east Scotland at this time (Carter 1993; Armit *et al.* 2011). Cook's model of hill fort construction between 800 and 400 BC (2013a; 2013b) is unsupported by the dating evidence. Ashmore (2004) showed for Scotland an abrupt fall in the numbers of radiocarbon-dated charred barley grains around 800 BC. There is no indication in the pollen record from Braeroddach Loch (Edwards 1979b) for woodland regeneration in the Late Bronze Age but the loch was then receiving eroding sediment throughout this period, which might include reworked and non-contemporary pollen (cf Tipping 2010a, 58); it is not clear whether the record from Loch Davan (Fyfe *et al.* 2013) has this problem.

Interpretation of these sites as representing meaningful gaps in the Early Iron Age is fraught with uncertainties. Is this a real gap? Radiocarbon 'plateaux' not only stretch calibrated radiocarbon assays within them but also 'compress' them on either side (Williams 2012). The gap has most commonly been explained through population collapse (Barber 1998; Dunbar 2007; Amesbury *et al.* 2008) or strategic agrarian restructuring (Tipping 2010b; Pope 2015, 179) in upland landscapes. Another cause is sought in climatic deterioration tied to fluctuations in solar activity that also created the Hallstatt radiocarbon plateau (van Geel *et al.* 1998). Climatic deterioration was real and significant in north-east Scotland (Blundell & Barber 2005; Dalton *et al.* 2005), and may actually have affected lowland regions more (van Geel *et al.* 1998). Parts of lowland Aberdeenshire contain large spreads of soils equally susceptible to water-logging as The Netherlands (see Tipping 2007, fig 4.4) such as the plateaux south of the Dee and east of the Don, but these were always unattractive to farmers (Chapter 1). The settlements at Forest Road, Deer's Den, Goval, Gairnhill and Wester Hatton were on free-draining gravels or gravelly till. Climatic change after 800 BC may have restricted agricultural expansion rather than actively threatening their survival. Our data are poor though, compared to that from Ireland used by Armit *et al.* (2015) to dismiss climate change as causal in population decline. Instead, the adoption of iron technology is argued to have destabilised existing power structures that depended for their wealth on long-distance trade in metals. In lowland Aberdeenshire, we might see this in a shift from the central places, best captured by the distribution of recumbent stone circles (Ruggles 1999, 99), to smaller, more independent communities of the later Iron Age invoked by Hunter (2007).

7.2.7 The paucity of Mid- to Late Iron Age evidence on the road-line

Structure B at Goval (see 5.8) is seen as a domestic settlement, a single roundhouse, though altered over time, in a farmed local landscape, dated to the early first millennium AD. Furnace B may be contemporary and Kiln A slightly later. The sites at Goval represent the only Iron Age structures encountered during excavation along the road-line. In their analysis, Cook & Dunbar (2008, 320) suggested an absence of settlement at Forest Road, Kintore, from perhaps the 3rd century BC to the 5th century AD. This dearth of evidence in the region was recognised by Halliday (2007a, 79), who argued for their heavy attrition from recent ploughing, leading to rare survival (Russell-White 1995; Alexander 2000) of what was originally extensive settlement activity. There is no evidence along the road-line for monuments now reduced to sub-soil remnants. Some hillforts in lowland Aberdeenshire are now dated, though from keyhole trenches. The inner defences of the Barmekin of Echt, Wester Fintray and Suttie on the Dee–Don upland are of Middle Iron Age date (Cook 2013a; 2013b). Forts and other enclosures are largely confined, however, to Donside and there are very few along Deeside (Halliday 2007a, fig 6.26), so we might argue that the hinterland to Aberdeen was very different in population density and human activity at this time to the Garioch, as earlier in prehistory. Cook (2013a; 2013b) argued that defended enclosures emerged from competition for resources, and in particular the generation of an agricultural surplus that drove extensive woodland clearance in southern and central Scotland (Tipping 1997; 2010b), but the distinctive signature of this horizon in pollen records has not so far been found in pollen records north of the Midland Valley (Tipping pers comm).

Ralston (1997), Halliday (2006) and Hunter (2007) all indicated the paucity of evidence for Iron Age settlement in eastern Scotland after the mid-2nd century or early 3rd century AD, recognising it as of regional significance, with Hunter (2007, 49) considering the period AD 250–400 to have been a time of crisis, possibly provoked by Roman manipulation of local elites. The rarity of later Iron Age settlements is seen elsewhere in Scotland (Haselgrove 2009, 231).

7.2.8 Passing through: a Roman appreciation of 'foreign lands'

An invading army, by its very nature, is unlikely to have a long-standing and in-depth appreciation of the land it moves through. Its purpose is much more tied up with rapid advance, with moving on, with exploitation of available resources. Having said that, an army must take note of surrounding territory, to ensure they are not ambushed or trapped somewhere they do not want to be. The encampment at Milltimber presents an interesting strand of evidence in relation to this. The military are present, but apparently unconcerned enough about the local tribes to bother with substantial defences. From many documentary sources, and from camps across the Roman Empire, it was standard practice to dig a defensive ditch, and to the Roman Army on campaign this would not have been seen as a particular inconvenience. The implication is that an active decision was made not to dig defences; the army felt comparatively safe in their surroundings and secure enough to take the opportunity to bake bread and resupply their food stores.

As is noted in Chapter 2, there are a group of Roman temporary camps that are thought to date to the Agricolan campaigns, which run up the eastern side of the Grampian Mountains (Jones 2011). The Romans' mark on the north-east of Scotland was not inconsiderable, but it might be assumed that beyond their route of advance and their formal camps, they would have limited impact. Until now we have assumed that the army was entirely fixated on ditch-digging but in truth their appreciation of the landscape in which they found themselves may have been much more focused on rapidly taking advantage of the opportunities it afforded them (Illus 7.10).

The question of why the ovens are at this specific location perhaps cannot be answered in this volume – the possibility of the Roman navy has been offered up, but it is acknowledged that this is far from conclusive. An alternative explanation might revolve around a fordable point on the River Dee; however, this is not known at this point from historic mapping or documentary evidence.

Prior to the Roman presence, throughout the prehistoric period one of the continuing themes relates to the transitory and temporary nature of the majority of the evidence. The existence of post-hole repair and some minor alteration to the roundhouse at Goval perhaps suggests an increased longevity of settlement at that location. However, even when settlement proper can be identified, the structures show little evidence of a society intimately linked to a single location for an extended duration. The arrival of the Romans merely continues this theme; from the evidence of the AWPR/B-T it could be argued that there is no marked difference between the attitudes, activities and behaviours of the long-term inhabitants and the comparatively fleeting visits of the invaders. In both cases, in a variety of periods, a group of people arrive at this point on the River Dee,

Illus 7.10 The Roman ovens (Chapter 2) would have been located roughly at the division between the second and third field in the distance, overlooked by the slope from which this photo is taken. A defensive position may not have been a priority

stay for a few nights, gathering supplies, lighting fires and feeding themselves, and presumably repairing and maintaining their weapons. There is little difference in these activities, and those carried out by the first visitors to Milltimber 13,000 years before.

7.2.9 Historic Period settlement patterns

Were archaeological data the only source of evidence for settlement and human activities in the centuries after AD 400, it would seem that the landscape explored along the road line was almost empty. At Milltimber there is little archaeological evidence save for a corn-drying kiln of 5th to 6th century AD date, a similarly dated pit, and an enclosure and possible structure of 7th to 8th century AD date. A single fragmentary structure dating to the 7th to 8th century AD from Goval forms the only evidence from the northern part of the scheme.

Kilns are the key monument type for the period (Alexander 2000, 31–34; Cook & Dunbar 2008, 149–57). Rig-and-furrow was recorded at both Nether Beanshill and Gairnhill Wood (Chapter 3). Across the Dee–Don upland (Chapter 3), and across the plateau between the River Don

and the coast (Chapters 5–6) there were no significant finds. Very few structures of this period were excavated at Forest Road, Kintore, and those present were rather scrappy; Cook (2013b) thought the evidence amounted to little more than transient occupation, or that the area had become marginal to urban development (Cook & Dunbar 2008, 357). A suite of small enclosures (ringforts) in and around Donside are now dated to the 6th century AD (Cook 2013a; 2013b) but these lie to the north and west of the road-line, as does the 5th to 6th century AD fortified complex at Rhynie (Noble *et al.* 2013). The Hill of Kier, above Westhill, may be of this period but is undated. Enclosed sites seem not to have been constructed after the 7th century AD. Distinctive domestic settlements of 7th to 9th century AD date have recently emerged in the hills of Perthshire south of The Mounth – the Pitcarmick houses (RCAHMS 1990; Carver *et al.* 2012; Strachan *et al.* in press) – but these have not been found in eastern Aberdeenshire. Recent work at Sands of Forvie, on the River Ythan have identified at least one small potential building, unfortunately undated but within an area with extensive shell midden deposits of the 1st millennium AD (Noble *et al.* 2016b, 141).

Cook (2013b, 330) argued that Class 1 Pictish symbol stones can be used as a proxy for population and activity; however, this need not have been the case (Whittington 1975, 109). That at St. Fergus (see 1.4.1) is the only one on or near the road-line; all others in the region are to the north-west. There are four Early Historic 'Pit-'place names near the road-line close to Dyce, but these would form part of the thanage of Kintore (Fraser & Halliday 2007, 135) with their areas of interest looking more to the west. Achadh- names are found on the high ground of the Dee–Don upland north west of Westhill (Fraser & Halliday 2007, fig 7.17), but they usually denote use of less fertile soils. A high proportion of 'Pit-' names near the road-line have associations with natural features or wild animals (Whittington 1975, 103), but interpretations of what this means are many. What is clear is that the Early Historic period in particular is almost exclusively represented in the north-east by a combination of place name evidence and high-status sites, neither of which is borne out by the evidence seen during the AWPR/B-T works, again highlighting the importance of these discoveries (Illus 7.11).

By the end of the 12th century, the road-line formed part of the royal thanage of Aberdeen, except the northern valley sides and 'wooded farmland' of the River Dee. Aberdeen became a burgh under David I. Gilbert (1979, 360–61) depicted a 13th-century hunting reserve south of Aberdeen at Nigg, and the royal forest of Aberdeen straddled the River Don from Dyce along the string of plateau wetlands (see 1.4.4) towards the North Sea coast. Tyrebagger Hill and the Hill of Marcus became the Forest of Cordyce, first recorded in 1316 (Dixon & Fraser 2007, 147), and it and the Forest of Aberdeen may have been coterminous where Dyce Airport is today. The road-line runs through the former Forest of Cordyce between Chapel of Stoneywood and Overton. To the south-east, the north-western border of the former Stocket Forest may have been nearly coterminous with Cordyce around the Chapel of Stoneywood (Coull 1963), itself a 14th-century chapel of ease.

A ring of forests practically surrounded the city of Aberdeen, forming large tracts of uncultivated land. This is surely significant; even in early documents, this upland was (still) empty of settlement and cultivation. Later medieval and early modern colonisation of Stocket Forest – the 'freedom lands' – after 1319 is clear (Cruickshank & Gunn 1929). The northern march went west from the coast between Old and New Aberdeen to the gap between Brimmond and Tyrebagger Hills, the southern march following the hills above the River Dee. Though Lynch & Dingwall (2002, 188) inferred a 'landscape of power' from the pattern of baronies, estates and tower-houses drawn by Timothy Pont in the 1590s, what separated these was still wilderness, almost empty in 1696, and described as a 'poor infertile boulder-covered waste' (Walton 1950, 21). Settlements (or fermtouns) recorded in the 1696 poll tax returns (Walton 1950; Tyson 1985; Dixon & Fraser 2007,

Illus 7.11 The Early Historic period kiln on the south side of the River Dee at Milltimber (Chapter 2) is an unprepossessing feature. Consideration needs to be given to ensuring features such as these are radiocarbon dated to pick up the less commonly-found periods of activity

fig 8.61) were around Dyce and north of Brimmond Hill, but not to the south of these. All this is suggestive, at least, that what is preserved in the prehistoric archaeological record on the Dee–Don upland is not simply what survives, but is representative of past settlement patterns, determined in part by the soil.

7.2.10 Post-Improvement settlement and agriculture

Although not forming part of the main records presented here, the works in relation to the AWPR/B-T involved an extensive programme of recording and, in some cases, investigation of sites of much more recent date (Chapter 1.2). The changes in agricultural practices of the mid-18th century (Dixon & Gannon 2007, 218f) resulted in enclosure of fields and creation of consumption dykes, one of the most visible type-sites of the north-east for many modern viewers. It also resulted in the incorporation of new areas not previously farmed into agricultural use (eg Auchintoul Croft; Dingwall 2013, 90; Illus 7.12). Excavation at Auchintoul revealed some complexity of phasing within what would be considered a fairly typical ruinous farmstead prior to excavation. The location of this excavated croft, within the section of road to the south of the River Dee, between it and the A90, highlights the contrast

Illus 7.12 Excavation of Auchintoul Croft. This was a valuable example of how the targeted sample excavations allowed investigation of a normally somewhat neglected period in the archaeological records

between the prehistoric and the most recent periods. By the post-medieval period, settlement, agriculture and evidence of everyday life was no longer restricted to the north of the River Dee and beyond. Lands that once might have been considered marginal and unattractive for almost any kind of activity now come into play, and the estates of Kingcausie and Culter bear further witness to this.

7.3 Traces in the field: lessons from infrastructure methodologies

Kirsty Dingwall and Jürgen van Wessel

Too infrequently do volumes such as this analyse the success or otherwise of the methods chosen to find and mitigate the archaeology they describe. The strategy for identifying and excavating previously unknown sites across the country is seen as fairly routine and accepted practice, often from the smallest privately funded development, up to large-scale infrastructure projects such as the AWPR/B-T. To some extent this is because the approaches commonly used do produce beneficial and wide-ranging results. However, it is vital that with projects as unique as this, the opportunity to analyse, compare and debate the strategies and techniques used is grasped. The overall objective of contributing to meaningful archaeological knowledge generation requires a critical approach and implications

of such a review in planning further work should not be brushed over.

7.3.1 Non-intrusive techniques

The non-intrusive and intrusive works across the scheme were part of an iterative approach to identify the nature, complexity, extent and potential significance of archaeological remains and to maximise the opportunity to complete archaeological fieldwork before construction work started.

An initial comprehensive desk-based assessment and walkover survey were completed for the cultural heritage chapters of the Environmental Statement (Jacobs UK 2007) for the scheme. For a study area around the scheme, the cultural heritage chapter identified known cultural heritage assets and areas of potential, assessed impacts and identified measures to further evaluate or mitigate these impacts. Nearly 400 cultural heritage assets were identified, the majority of which were post-medieval agricultural features and historic buildings. Some prehistoric sites were noted, and these tended to be monumental in nature, such as cairns or stone circles, and chance finds such as stone balls, arrowheads or cist burials, or untested sites in the form of cropmarks. On both the Northern and Southern Legs, there was an apparent lack of sites from the later prehistoric period. However, the Mesolithic potential of the River Dee in particular was noted, as was the background of a Roman presence across the region in the form of marching camps.

To some extent, this is perhaps a typical mix for a desk-based assessment of this sort of area. The Environmental Statement did state that 'the number of known archaeological sites of earlier date is unusually low for such a relatively large study area' (*ibid*, 13–17). The distribution and types of site reflected relatively limited archaeological fieldwork and a general lack of recent development within the study area of development in recent years. The record of known sites was somewhat biased towards visible remains that might be described as rarer in nature, eg funerary monuments, and post-medieval upstanding structures.

A route-wide programme comprising nearly 460 ha of geophysical survey using magnetometry was commissioned, with the aim of identifying previously unknown sites (Bartlett & Boucher 2012a; 2012b). This was one of the largest geophysical surveys completed for a road scheme in Scotland. There has been a belief that the geology in Scotland is unfavourable for this methodology, and the nature of likely archaeology (more often pits and discrete features than linear features) is not well suited to these means. This was noted in the southern section of the route, in particular the difficulty in identifying archaeological pits against the background of strong responses from drift deposits containing metamorphic/igneous boulders (Bartlett & Boucher 2012b, 20). There was greater confidence in the identification of linear features, although with the exception of cultivation marks there were few strong correlations between geophysical responses and genuine archaeological ditches.

The survey covered an initial 40 m-wide corridor along the centre line of the scheme, and this was expanded where potential geophysical features of archaeological interest might be identified, along with targeting known archaeological remains. For future schemes it may be worth considering a different approach to bring greater benefits. Sample testing of areas of differing geology and use of alternative methods such as resistivity or GPR could be considered. Data obtained for sample areas could be ground-truthed using an initial targeted programme of trial-trenching or test-pitting to allow better calibration of the results. Only after gaining a more detailed understanding of the local conditions would a scheme-wide survey begin.

It is worth noting that other non-intrusive approaches may also be useful in providing background information for later stages of work – LiDAR data are now commonly available for urban areas and watersheds and can be commissioned relatively cost-effectively for larger areas. Detailed analysis of such data could provide a very useful baseline dataset of upstanding earthworks (including overgrown areas otherwise difficult to access), corroborate cropmarks and provide some of the raw data required for subsequent archaeological topographic surveys. In addition, availability of a recent aerial photographic layer as well as LiDAR would have tremendous value for planning the logistics of large archaeological programmes such as this, a not inconsiderable undertaking that can then impact on the process of investigation.

7.3.2 Other mitigation works

Alongside the geophysical survey, a programme of topographic and historic building surveys built a permanent record of upstanding remains that would be affected by the construction work (van Wessel 2012a; 2012b; 2014; Wilson 2017). For selected sites, this was further complemented by sample excavation. Many of the sites targeted related to post-medieval agricultural practice, especially the consumption dykes, a very distinctive Aberdeenshire boundary feature that resolved simultaneously the need for field divisions and clearance of characteristically stony ground (see 7.2.10 above). In total 42 were identified by the ES as being directly affected by the scheme, of which 16 were surveyed and described in detail, and five subsequently investigated by trial excavations (Illus 7.13). Aside from broader surveys undertaken by Croly (2001; 2004), this is one of the larger recent programmes of recording work undertaken on this class of feature. On occasion recording and excavating these features can be dismissed as being routine parts of the project and less 'interesting' or attractive to the archaeologist on the ground than discovery of sites of prehistoric date. However, they

Illus 7.13 Section excavated through the consumption dyke at West Charlestown (SLEX-02)

provide an important resource for understanding the context of earlier sites and how the landscape has changed in the last few centuries, which then impacts on our current appreciation of the survival of archaeology of the earlier periods.

The topographic and historic building surveys, along with the targeted mitigation works, make a valuable contribution to archaeological knowledge generation; they have provided detailed insights into post-medieval agricultural life in this area. This is a period and subject that has received sustained attention (ScARF 2012d, 115), and may often be considered as 'well enough' understood, and worthy of little effort. Perhaps in a general sense this is defensible, but the generation of detailed empirical evidence for local traditions and practices is surely an important legacy when the greatest impact of a development is to those who live along its route. The surveys of upstanding archaeology provided a robust record, which could make a very useful contribution to ongoing or new studies into this period of Aberdeenshire's past (*ibid*). Although not included in any detail in this publication, the records have been made fully available as part of the digital appendix for the volume (Appendix 1.1 and 1.2).

7.3.3 Trenching to identify sites

Trial trenching, as with any other large-scale infrastructure, formed the main method of establishing the extent and character of archaeological deposits in order that the impact of the scheme on the archaeological resource could be further understood. Mitigation excavations aimed to offset those impacts on the resource through the acquisition of a full archaeological record and an evidence-based interpretation of that record (Jacobs 2013, 97–8). Trial-trenching evaluation also plays a major role in establishing the likely time and resources required for mitigation work, and allows programming of that work to have the lowest possible impact on construction deadlines.

Main design factors affecting the success of evaluation by trial trenching include the size and layout of trenches, the density or sample percentage, and the means of reacting to concentrations of activity. An extensive study (Hey & Lacey 2001) of the early 2000s examined the effectiveness of different patterns and layouts of trenching schemes to establish what the best approach in any specific situation might be. While there is no intention to revisit old ground, given the advances and changes in the intervening decades, it is worth examining the results from the AWPR/B-T to establish if alternative approaches might have been appropriate, more cost-effective and have succeeded in gaining the same level of information.

In this case, trenches were generally set at 25 m × 2 m in a regular pattern with alternate trenches perpendicular to each other; they were also located to evaluate known archaeological sites and anomalies identified by geophysical survey. This pattern is considered one of the more effective available (Hey & Lacey 2001, 59). While shorter trenches were necessary on the AWPR/B-T in an attempt to minimise the disturbance to land still being farmed, the experience of the authors in undertaking trenching where the total length is several kilometres would also support the value of longer trenches for efficiency and effectiveness. Longer trenches mean less setting out, rationalised recording and plant movement and could offer reductions in time required for the works, but resulting in potentially similar results. Clearly, the efficiencies of the project need to be balanced with ensuring good relationships with local communities are maintained.

On the AWPR/B-T, a 5% sample size was selected (not including any targeted trenches). Percentages of this order have been found to be effective when the evaluation acts primarily as a trigger for full excavation, most commonly of a single, clearly defined development area, and particularly in areas where linear features are likely to characterise a site. Hey & Lacey suggest that a larger percentage, in the 6–10% range, is much more effective at locating discrete, pit-like archaeological features (2001, 59). Was there a risk that with the smaller sample size, sites characterised by such discrete features might be missed? In practice, the mitigation design on this scheme was such that if even modest archaeological features were revealed in the evaluation, a large excavation area (often the full width of the Land Made Available) was specified for mitigation. Once sites were identified, overburden was stripped well beyond the limits of the site, ensuring a buffer between it and the 'blank' areas beyond (Illus 7.14). This greatly improved the chances of catching the full extent of activity and ensured that potential sites were unlikely to be missed. It also provided a useful degree of local context and confirmed the limits of activity where possible. Furthermore, some of the most valuable results from this scheme came from areas where little further archaeology was revealed – absence is a very useful contributor to our understanding of population density and pressure for land.

Illus 7.14 Large area excavations. Stripping sufficient buffers around any identified archaeology ensured there was minimal risk of missing significant archaeological features

Designing large mitigation areas from the outset reduces the potential for delays to the construction programme caused by small trial-trench sample size – by allowing time for large sample areas from the start, the proportional effect of small extensions and additional work is minimal compared to a tentative, 'start small and keep growing' approach.

All archaeology, however tentatively identified at trial trenching stage, was explored further during the next phase of mitigation. This proved a very effective approach – in some cases resulting in a useful, negative result, but also discovering wholly unanticipated sites. Standingstones was only discovered because a single, unprepossessing pit encountered in the trial trenching was found to contain microliths during sample processing. It was subsequently targeted for excavation and has offered considerable insights into Mesolithic life in the area. Even at Middlefield, a collection of stone-holes that possibly relate to prehistoric stone-clearance gave useful context for sites nearby at Blackdog and Wester Hatton.

7.3.4 Alternative and additional techniques

The trial-trenching phase established that the flat valley floor at Milltimber contained a small handful of features, likely discrete pits, a small number of ditches that were interpreted as being agricultural in origin, and confirmed the presence of some level of ancient river activity. What it did not establish at this stage of the mitigation process was the presence of a complex, multi-period site, the existence of an *in situ* flint scatter or the presence of pits of the size and type previously identified at Warren Field, further upstream.

As has been outlined above, the approach of trial trenching followed by wide area stripping of all areas of even supposedly low archaeological potential resulted in ensuring the discovery of a multitude of sites. However, it is also the case that the full extent and significance of the archaeology at Milltimber was only recognised in the midst of the mitigation excavation stage. Would alternative strategies have allowed a better understanding of the site prior to excavation, or have ensured that the excavation strategy was honed to the site type?

One possibility on future projects would be to consider the use of test-pitting and sieving to complement trial trenching where relevant finds are made or there is a high potential for such finds, for instance with lithics scatters. Traditionally, the presence of lithics scatters can be targeted by utilising fieldwalking, as was done in the field to the west of the Milltimber site in the 1970s (NJ80SE 36), and has been undertaken to great success as part of the Mesolithic Deeside project (Mesolithic Deeside 2018). This would have been appropriate at Milltimber but can only be carried out on ploughed fields. At the time of evaluation (and for many years previously) the land was used for pasture and horse paddocks; there would be no opportunity to walk the area as part of a programme of evaluation. The narrow periods of time when farmland is available for such methods can be difficult to fit into a large-scale scheme of works; fieldwalking simply may not be a viable option.

Potentially, test-pits could have been used as an alternative, alongside trial trenching. Test-pits are more flexible when environmental or other constraints have to be taken into account, are less damaging (a real consideration when works are undertaken prior to land purchase), take little time and could even be done by machine in a development context, which would speed up the process considerably. This approach would be most appropriate in areas where interesting topsoil finds have been recovered or been reported previously, especially lithics, or where full-sized trenches are not practical owing to the depth of deposits present. Linear trenching becomes problematic where the depth of deposits means that trenches must be benched to get to the underlying geological material or archaeological layers; benching is both disproportionately time-consuming in a trial-trenching schedule and has the potential to cause extensive damage to land that may not yet be owned by the developer. Clearly, in a situation where there were extensive riverine deposits spread across the southern part of the Milltimber site, the depth of trenches was an issue. Test-pitting should not replace trial trenching wholesale and would need to have clear objectives to be worthwhile; for example, in areas of potential lithics scatters the aim would be retrieval of material for sieving to confirm and hopefully categorise the scatter.

An alternative might be to tie in with existing geotechnical test-pitting programmes more proactively. As part of the AWPR/B-T works, monitoring of geotechnical works was undertaken; however, the archaeological involvement was limited to recording the sequence of deposits present, and flagging up potential archaeological deposits. Working more closely with geotechnical teams may allow at least some archaeological input or guidance into the location and methods of test pit excavation. Requirements to include sieving of deposits or geoarchaeological analysis may also be possible. A more integrated approach might form

a relatively cost-effective and worthwhile element of the data-gathering exercise, which would then greatly benefit the planning of a full mitigation programme.

In the presentation of data on the hunting pits from Milltimber (see 2.6.2), it was stated that these were largely invisible immediately following topsoil stripping (Illus 7.15). Where pits contained an upper charcoal-rich deposit, they were flagged up as likely features, but most only started to appear after several weeks or months of weathering. Clearly, on a scheme where there is a tight schedule of construction deadlines, it is unrealistic to suggest that all stripped areas could be left to weather for several months. However, it is not unreasonable to allow for at least a few weeks between stripping finishing and excavation commencing, particularly on sand or gravel sites where features might be difficult to identify and weathering is of benefit. As with other approaches, if such procedures were standard they could be worked into the overall programme of excavation without undue delay to completion.

Although not strictly speaking an excavation technique, there is an opportunity within this section to examine the success of the programme of radiocarbon dating across all sites on the scheme. As might be expected on such a large scale project, it was always intended that post-excavation analysis would allow for extensive dating of features. In total, 152 dates were obtained for samples from deposits, ranging from pits to post-holes to hearths to ovens, and everything in between. Contrary to the approaches that might be taken on some equivalent projects, features that did not necessarily fit into the sequence or form part of the comprehensible story of the site were still targeted for dating. Not only did this produce some unexpected results (eg the Early Historic features at Milltimber and Goval) it also highlighted the presence of what would otherwise be considered 'missing' periods in the development of individual sites. The lesson from this should be that as extensive a dating programme as possible should be allowed for on multi-phase sites, particularly where features of differing periods have similar morphology. In addition, it may be beneficial to place some focus on dating selections of features that do not adequately fit the layout of structures or patterns of features already reasonably well understood.

7.3.5 Cross-disciplinary approaches

It should be apparent from each of the preceding chapters that tying each site into its local and wider environment was vital in making sense of the individual discoveries. It allowed interpretation of the sites to move beyond site types and accounts of periods of activity to look at the evidence from a regional and broad temporal basis.

Linear schemes in particular provide special circumstances to examine environments on both a micro and macro scale. Peat coring at specific locations formed part of the work specifications and provided useful

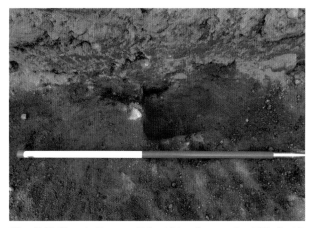

Illus 7.15 The challenge of identifying features backfilled with gravel. These images show the same feature: A. A hunting pit [2D-1003] from Milltimber as it was identified during trial trenching as a small charcoal patch with very indistinct edges, and B. fully excavated having been left to weather for several months

palaeoenvironmental information that has helped inform our understanding of archaeological 'gaps' in the route (discussed above). However, it was only the identification of complex fluvial evidence at Milltimber that prompted the involvement of a geoarchaeological specialist during site works and as part of the post-excavation process. Potentially, this could have been incorporated as an option from the outset of the site works; having access to such expertise would undoubtedly help excavators to understand the sites, and allows a more detailed and targeted set of research questions relating to the environment to be posed and revised as necessary during the excavation process.

In summary, a review of the methodologies used has established that they were largely successful, and that hand-wringing over percentages of samples and layout of trenches is largely unnecessary, particularly where the ultimate intention is for large area stripping as mitigation. However, it is also the case that there are a handful of less frequently considered approaches which it would be worth having as options for future schemes of similar scale. In many cases, these approaches could have been suggested on the AWPR/B-T scheme at the time, but the pressure of the average excavation schedule makes it less likely that they are considered and are feasible within timescales already agreed. By including them as options within the specification for works, they would be kept at the forefront of the minds of those curating, planning and running the sites in question.

7.4 Conclusions

The techniques for prospecting for archaeology on linear schemes have been developed since the 1970s, as the national motorway construction programme was building up to full steam. A whole-landscape approach was developed in response and is 'perhaps the single clearest contribution of road-related archaeology to the discipline'

(Alexander 2011, 95). It cannot be denied that the close archaeological scrutiny over vast areas such as this (over 400 ha, 11 times bigger than Kintore, by way of example) makes an incredible contribution to the overall body of archaeological knowledge about a given area. That such schemes do not select for good-quality agricultural land or proximity to settlement offers a much more diverse range of landscape units and preservation potential. Linear archaeological projects are a highly effective means of identifying what is still categorised as unusual; the Palaeolithic, the hunting pits, the hill sites, the ritual sites, the Romans. However, the more we find, the less unusual such sites become.

To some extent, that is the real value of the archaeology discovered on the Aberdeen Western Peripheral Route/Balmedie-Tipperty project. An area apparently relatively devoid of archaeological remains has been shown to be, if not a hotbed of sites, certainly host to numerous complex, extensive and wide-ranging typological discoveries. Any single one of the sites presented here would be a significant contribution to our understanding of the archaeology of north-east Scotland. In many cases, evidence from single periods is argued to be of national significance and will undoubtedly form the basis of extensive future discussion and research. It is not an underestimation to say that the archaeology of the AWPR/B-T has fundamentally changed the story of the region, and that it will impact well beyond the publication of the data.

Few projects can rival a well-planned and deliberately targeted research programme in producing tangible results that advance the discipline of archaeology. However, research can only progress when there is a body of data against which to test theories, to provide material and to allow theoretical kites to be flown. There can be little question that archaeological works on large-scale infrastructure projects such as the AWPR/B-T scheme are vital in providing a large part of that body of data, and in pushing the limits of what we know of the region.

References

Aberdeenshire, S. M. R. (2013) NE *Scotland Research Framework – Resource assessment: Section 2 Mesolithic (8000 BC– 4000 BC)* https://www.aberdeenshire.gov.uk/media/10166/ resourceassessment-mesolithic-listofsitesv1–1.pdf.

Adovasio, J. M., Soffer O. and Page J. (2007) *The Invisible Sex* New York

Aitken, J. F. (1995) 'Lithofacies and depositional history of a Late Devensian ice-contact deltaic complex, northeast Scotland' *Sedimentary Geology* 99, 111–30

Albarello, B. (1987) 'Technique du 'coup du microburin' par pression' *Bulletin de la Société préhistorique française* 84 (4), 111–15

Alexander, D. (1997) 'Excavation of pits containing decorated Neolithic pottery and early lithic material of possible Mesolithic date at Spurryhillock, Stonehaven, Aberdeenshire' *Proceedings of the Society of Antiquaries of Scotland* 127, 17–127

Alexander, D. (2000) 'Excavation of Neolithic pits, later prehistoric structures and a Roman temporary camp along the line of the A96 Kintore and Blackburn Bypass. Aberdeenshire' *Proceedings of the Society of Antiquaries of Scotland* 130, 11–75

Alexander, M. (2011) *A Look in the Rear-view Mirror: Twentieth Century road building and the development of professional archaeology* Portsmouth

Alexander, D. and Armit, I. (1993) 'Unstratified stratigraphy: methodologies for interpreting and presenting cropmark sites' in Barber, J. (ed) *Interpreting Stratigraphy: conference proceedings, 25th November 1992*, 37–41, Edinburgh

Alexander, W. (1886) 'The Aberdeenshire Crofter' in Alexander, W. (1992) *Rural Life in Victorian Aberdeenshire*, 76–122, Edinburgh

Alley, R. and Ágústdóttir, A. M. (2005) 'The 8k event: cause and consequences of a major Holocene abrupt climate change' *Quaternary Science Reviews* 24, 1123–49

Amesbury, M. J., Charman, D. J., Fyfe, R. M., Langdon, P. G. and West, S. (2008) 'Bronze Age upland settlement decline in southwest England: testing the climate change hypothesis' *Journal of Archaeological Science* 35, 87–98

Andersen, K. (1982) 'Mesolitiske flækker fra Åmosen, Sjælland' *Aarbøger for Nordisk Oldkyndighed og Historie* 5–18

Andersen, S. (1970) 'The relative pollen productivity and pollen representation of North European trees, and correction factors for tree pollen spectra' *Danmarks Geologiske Undersøgelse II* 96, 1–99

Anderson-Whymark, H. and Thomas, J. (eds) (2011) *Regional Perspectives on Neolithic Pit Deposition: Beyond the Mundane* Oxford

Armit, I. (1997) *Celtic Scotland* London

Armit, I. and Braby, A. (2002) 'Excavation of a burnt mound and associated structures at Ceann nan Clachan, North Uist' *Proceedings of the Society of Antiquaries of Scotland* 132, 229–58

Armit, I., Schulting, R., Knüsel, C. J. and Shepherd, I. A. G. (2011) 'Death, decapitation and display? The Bronze and Iron Age human remains from the Sculptor's Cave, Covesea, North-east Scotland' *Proceedings of the Prehistoric Society* 77, 251–78

Armit, I., Swindles, G. T., Becker, K., Plunkett, G. and Blaauw, M. (2015) 'Rapid climate change did not cause population collapse at the end of the European Bronze Age' *Proceedings of the National Academy of Sciences* Dec 2 2014 111 (48) 17045–49 https://doi.org/10.1073/pnas.1408028111

Ashmore, P. J. (1996) *Neolithic and Bronze Age Scotland* London

Ashmore, P. (2004) 'Absolute chronology' in Shepherd, I. A. G. and Barclay, G. (eds) *Scotland in Ancient Europe. The Neolithic and Early Bronze Age of Scotland in their European Context,* 125–38, Edinburgh

Atkinson, J. A. (2002) 'Excavation of a Neolithic occupation site at Chapelfield, Cowie, Stirling' *Proceedings of the Society of Antiquaries of Scotland* 132, 139–92

Auton, C. A. and Crofts, R. G. (1986) *The sand and gravel resources of the country around Aberdeen, Grampian Region. Description of 1:25 000 sheets NJ 71, 80, 81 and 91, parts of NJ 61, 90 and 92 and with parts of NO 89 and 99* Mineral Assessment Report of the British Geological Survey No. 146

Ball, D. F. (1964) 'Loss-on-ignition as an estimate of organic matter and organic carbon in non-calcareous soils' *Journal of Soil Science* 15, 84–92

Ballantyne, C. K. (2010) 'Extent and deglacial chronology of the last British-Irish Ice Sheet: implications of exposure dating using cosmogenic isotopes' *Journal of Quaternary Science* 25, 515–34

Ballin, T. B. (1998) Steinbustølen. 'Quartzite reduction in the Norwegian High Mountains' *Universite tets Oldsaksamling Årbok 1997/1998*, 83–92

Ballin, T. B. (1999) 'Bipolar cores in Southern Norway – classification, chronology and geography' *Lithics* 20, 13–22

Ballin, T. B. (2000) 'Relativ datering af flintinventarer (Relative Dating of Flint Assemblages)' in Eriksen, B. V. (ed) *Flintstudier – en håndbog i systematiske analyser af flintinventarer (Flint Studies – a Handbook in Systematic Analyses of Flint Assemblages)*, 127–40, Aarhus

Ballin, T. B. (2001) *Shieldaig, Wester Ross: The quartz assemblage.* (Unpublished report)

Ballin, T. B. (2002a) *The lithic assemblage from Dalmore, Isle of Lewis, Western Isles.* Unpublished report commissioned by Historic Scotland

Ballin, T. B. (2002b) *Shieldaig, Wester Ross: The flint and bloodstone assemblage* (Unpublished report)

Ballin, T. B. (2008a) 'Quartz technology in Scottish prehistory' *Scottish Archaeological Internet Reports (SAIR)* 26. [http://www.sair.org.uk/sair26/index.html]

Ballin, T. B. (2008b) *The lithic assemblage from the Kingfisher Industrial Estate, Aberdeen* (Unpublished client document)

Ballin, T. B. (2010) 'Lithic artefacts' in Suddaby, I. and Ballin T 'Late Neolithic and Late Bronze Age lithic assemblages associated with a cairn and other prehistirc features at Stoneyhill Farm, Longhaven, Peterhead, Aberdeenshire, 2002–03' *Scottish Archaeological Internet Reports* 45, 21–43

Ballin, T. B. (2011a) 'The Levallois-like approach of Late Neolithic Britain: a discussion based on finds from the Stoneyhill Project, Aberdeenshire' in Saville, A. (ed) *Flint and Stone in the Neolithic Period*, 37–61, Neolithic Studies Group Seminar Papers 11, Oxford

Ballin, T. B. (2011b) *Overhowden and Airhouse, Scottish Borders. Characterization and interpretation of two spectacular lithic assemblages from sites near the Overhowden Henge* British Archaeological Reports British Series 539 Oxford

Ballin, T. B. (2012a) 'Lithic artefacts' in Johnson, M. and Cameron K 'An Early Bronze Age unenclosed cremation cemetery and Mesolithic pit at Skilmafilly, near Maud, Aberdeenshire' *Scottish Archaeological Internet Reports (SAIR)* 53, 23–26. [http://www.sair.org.uk/sair53].

Ballin, T. B. (2012b) *The lithic assemblage from Donich Park, Lochgoilhead, Argyll* (Unpublished report)

Ballin, T. B. (2013a) *The lithic assemblage from Nethermills Farm, Banchory, Aberdeenshire* (Unpublished client report)

Ballin, T. B. (2013b) 'Lundevågen 31, Vest-Agder, SW Norway. The spatial organization of small hunter-gatherer sites – a case study (or: Binford in practice)' Online academic repository: *Academia.edu* (https://independent.academia.edu/TorbenBjarkeBallin) accessed 29 May 2017.

Ballin, T. B. (2014a) 'Moray's lithics – impressions from local museums and excavations. Research from Elgin Museum, Moray' (http://elginmuseum.org.uk/l/wp-content/uploads/2014/07/Morays-lithics2.docx) accessed 29 May 2017.

Ballin, T. B. (2014b) 'The provenance of some Scottish lithic raw materials – identification, terminology and interpretation', Stonechat 1: 4–7, (http://implementpetrology.org/wp-content/uploads/2014/04/2014–03-stonechat.pdf) accessed 29 May 2017.

Ballin, T. B. (2016a) 'Rising waters and processes of diversification and unification in material culture: the flooding of Doggerland and its effect on north-west European prehistoric populations between ca. 13000 and 1500 cal BC' *Journal of Quaternary Science* 32 (2), 329–39.

Ballin, T. B. (2016b) 'The lithic assemblage' in Murray, H. K. and Murray JC 'Mesolithic and Early Neolithic activity along the Dee: excavations at Garthdee Road, Aberdeen' *Proceedings of the Society of Antiquaries of Scotland* 144, 20–35

Ballin, T. B. and Barrowman, C. (2015) 'Chert artefacts and structures during the final Mesolithic at Garvald Burn, Scottish Borders' *Archaeology Reports Online* 15 vhttp://www.archaeologyreportsonline.com/PDF/ARO15_Garvald_burn.pdf

Ballin, T. B. and Bjerck, H. B. (2016) 'Lost and found twice: Discussion of an early post-glacial single-edged tanged point from Brodgar on Orkney, Scotland', *Journal of Lithic Studies* 3 (1), 31–50 https://doi.org/https://doi.org/10.2218/jls.v3i1.1393

Ballin, T. B. and Faithfull, J. (2009) Gazetteer of Arran pitchstone sources, presentation of exposed pitchstone dykes and sills across the Isle of Arran, and discussion of the archaeological relevance of these outcrops, *Scottish Archaeological Internet Reports (SAIR)* 38 https://doi.org/10.5284/1017938

Ballin, T. B. and Johnson, M. (2005) 'A Mesolithic chert assemblage from Glentaggart, South Lanarkshire, Scotland: chert technology and procurement strategies' *Lithics* 26, 57–86

Ballin, T. B. and Saville, A. (2003) 'An Ahrensburgian-type tanged point from Shieldaig, Wester Ross, Scotland, and its implications', *Oxford Journal of Archaeology* 22 (2), 115–31

Ballin, T. B. and Wickham-Jones, C. (2017) 'Searching for the Scottish late Upper Palaeolithic: a case study of early flints from Nethermills Farm, Aberdeenshire' *Journal of Lithic Studies* 4 (1) https://doi.org/https://doi.org/10.2218/jls.v4i1.1907

Ballin, T. B., Saville, A., Tipping, R. and Ward, T. (2010) 'An Upper Palaeolithic flint and chert assemblage from Howburn Farm, South Lanarkshire, Scotland: first results', *Oxford Journal of Archaeology* 29 (4), 323–60.

Ballin, T. B., Saville, A., Tipping, R. and Ward, T. (forthcoming) 'An Upper Palaeolithic flint and chert assemblage from Howburn Farm, South Lanarkshire, Scotland: final results', *Proceedings of the Prehistoric Society*

Ballin Smith, B. (2014) 'The Beaker vessel' in Ballin Smith, B. (ed) *A Highland Funeral: Portrait of an Early Bronze Age Beaker Burial at West Torbreck, south-west Inverness.* Archaeology Reports Online, No. 8–10

Barber, J. (1990) 'Scottish burnt mounds: variations on a theme' in Buckley, V. (ed) *Burnt Offerings: International Contributions to Burnt Mound Archaeology,* 98–101, Dublin

Barber, J. (1997) *The Archaeological Investigation of a Prehistoric Landscape: Excavations on Arran 1978–1981* Edinburgh

Barber, J. (1998) *The Archaeological Investigation of a Prehistoric Landscape: Excavations on Arran 1978–1981* Edinburgh

Barber, J. and Crone, B. A. (2001) 'The duration of structures, settlements and sites: some evidence from Scotland' in Raftery, B. and Hickey, J. (eds) *Recent Developments in Wetland Research,* 69–86, Dublin

Barclay, G. (1983) 'Sites of the third millennium BC to the first millennium AD at North Mains, Strathallan, Perthshire' *Proceedings of the Society of Antiquaries of Scotland* 113, 122–281

Barclay, G., Carter, S., Dalland, M., Hastie, M., Holden, T., MacSween, A. and Wickham-Jones, C. (2001) 'A possible Neolithic settlement at Kinbeachie, Black Isle, Highland'

Proceedings of the Society of Antiquaries of Scotland 131, 57–85

Barfield, L. and Hodder, M. (1987) 'Burnt mounds as saunas and the prehistory of bathing' *Antiquity* 61, 370–79

Barrett, J. and Gourlay, R. (1999) 'An early metal assemblage from Dail na Caraidh, Inverness-shire, and its context' *Proceedings of the Prehistoric Society* 129, 161–87

Bartlett, A. and Boucher, A. (2012a) *A96 (T) Dyce Drive Park and Choose and Associated Link Road (Dyce). Geophysical Survey* (Unpublished client report) Headland Archaeology (UK) Ltd

Bartlett, A. and Boucher, A. (2012b) *A90 Balmedie to Tipperty Scheme. Geophysical Survey* (Unpublished client report) Headland Archaeology (UK) Ltd

Bartlett, A. and Boucher, A. (2012c) *Aberdeen Western Peripheral Route Package (Fastlink). Geophysical Survey* (Unpublished client report) Headland Archaeology (UK) Ltd

Bartlett, A. and Boucher, A. (2012d) *Aberdeen Western Peripheral Route Package (Northern Leg). Geophysical Survey* (Unpublished client report) Headland Archaeology (UK) Ltd

Bartlett, A. and Boucher, A. (2012e) *Aberdeen Western Peripheral Route Package (Southern Leg). Geophysical Survey* (Unpublished client report) Headland Archaeology (UK) Ltd.

Bayley, J. (1985) 'What's what in ancient technology: an introduction to high-temperature processes' in Phillips, P. (ed) *The Archaeologist and the Laboratory* CBA Research Report 58, 41–44, London

Bayley, J., Dungworth, D. and Paynter, S. (2001) *Archaeometallurgy* Swindon

Bayliss, A. (2009) 'Rolling out revolution: using radiocarbon dating in archaeology' *Radiocarbon* **51**, 123–47

Bayliss, A. (2015) 'Quality in Bayesian chronological models in archaeology' *World Archaeology* 47, 677–700

BBC (2003) *Aberdeen gets road bypass* http://news.bbc.co.uk/1/hi/scotland/2697305.stm accessed 21 September 2017

BBC (2009) *Aberdeen bypass given green light by ministers* http://news.bbc.co.uk/1/hi/scotland/north_east/8424142.stm accessed 21 September 2017

Becket, A. and MacGregor, G. (2011) 'Big pit, little pit, big pit, little pit… Pit practices in Western Scotland in the 4th millennium BC' in Anderson-Whymark, H. and Thomas, J. (eds), *Regional Perspectives on Neolithic Pit Deposition: Beyond the Mundane,* 51–62, Oxford

Belfer-Cohen, A. and Goring-Morris, A. N. (2013) 'Breaking the mould: phases and facies in the Natufian of the Mediterranean Zone' in Bar-Yosef, O. and Vall, F. R. (eds) *Natufian Foragers in the Levant. Terminal Pleistocene Social Changes in Western Asia,* 544–61, Michigan

Bell, J. N. B. and Tallis, J. H. (1973) 'Biological flora of the British Isles. *Empetrum nigrum L.*' *Journal of Ecology* 61, 289–305.

Bennett, K. D. (1989) 'A provisional map of forest types for the British Isles 5000 years ago' *Journal of Quaternary Science* 4, 141–44

Bennett, K. D. and Birks, H. J. (1990) 'Postglacial history of alder (*Alnus glutinosa (L.)* Gaertn.)' *British Isles Journal of Quaternary Science* 5 (2), 123–33

Bergstøl, J. (2015) 'Trapping pits for reindeer – a discussion on construction and dating' in Indrelid, S., Hjelle, K. L. and Stene, K. (eds) *Exploitation of Outfield Resources – Joint Research at the University Museums of Norway,* 49–54, Bergen

Binford, L. R. (1983) *In Pursuit of the Past. Decoding the Archaeological Record* London

Birks, H. J. B. (1973) *The Past and Present Vegetation on the Isle of Skye – a palaeoecological study* Cambridge

Birks, H. J. B. (1988) 'Long-term ecological change in the British uplands' in Usher, M. B. and Thompson, D. B. A. (eds) *Ecological Change in the Uplands* Oxford, 37–56

Birks, H. J. B. (1989) 'Holocene isochrone maps and patterns of tree-spreading in the British Isles' *Journal of Biogeography* 16, 503–40

Bishop, R. R., Church, M. J. and Rowley-Conwy, P. A. (2009) 'Cereals, fruit and nuts in the Scottish Neolithic' *Proceedings of the Society of Antiquaries of Scotland* 139, 47–104

Bishop, R. R., Church, M. J. and Rowley-Conwy, P. A. (2013) 'Seeds, fruits and nuts in the Scottish Mesolithic' *Proceedings of the Society of Antiquaries of Scotland* 143, 9–71

Bishop, R. R., Church, M. J. and Rowley-Conwy, P. A. (2015) 'Firewood, food and human niche construction: the potential role of Mesolithic hunter-gatherers in actively structuring Scotland's woodlands' *Quaternary Science Reviews* 108, 51–75

Bjorck, S. and Clemmensen, L. B. (2004) 'Aeolian sediment in raised bog deposits, Halland, SW Sweden: a new proxy record of Holocene winter storminess variation in southern Scandinavia?' *The Holocene* 14, 677–88

Blundell, A. and Barber, K. (2005) 'A 2800-year palaeoclimatic record from Tore Hill Moss, Strathspey, Scotland: the need for a multi-proxy approach to peat-based climate reconstructions' *Quaternary Science Reviews* 24, 1261–77

Bogaard, A. and Jones, G. (2007) 'Neolithic farming in Britain and central Europe: contrast or continuity?' *Proceedings of the British Academy* 144, 355–75

Bohncke, S., Vandenberghe, J. and Wijmstra, T. A. (1988) 'Lake level changes and fluvial activity in the Late Glacial lowland valleys' in Lang, S. and Schluchter, C. (eds) *Lake, Mire & River Environments in the Past 15,000 Years,* 115–21, Rotterdam

Bonsall, C., Macklin, M. G., Anderson, D. E. and Payton, R. W. (2002) 'Climate change and the adoption of agriculture in north-west Europe' *European Journal of Archaeology* 5, 9–23

Boyd, W. E. (1988) 'Cereals in Scottish antiquity' *Circaea* 5, 101–10

Boyd, W. E. and Dickson, J. H. (1986) 'Patterns in the geographical distribution of the early Flandrian *Corylus* rise in southwest Scotland' *New Phytologist* 102, 615–23

Boyd, W. R. and Kenworthy, J. B. (1982) 'The use of wood as a natural resource at a Scottish mesolithic site' *Glasgow Archaeological Journal* 17, 11–19

Bradley, R. (2005) *The Moon and the Bonfire: an investigation of three stone circles in north-east Scotland* Edinburgh

Bradley, R. (2007) *The Prehistory of Britain and Ireland* Cambridge

Bradley, R. (2011) *Stages and Screens: an investigation of four henge monuments in northern and north-eastern Scotland* Edinburgh

Bradley, R. (2017) *A Geography of Offerings. Deposits of valuables in the landscapes of ancient Europe* Oxford

Bradley, S. L., Milne, G. A., Shennan, I. and Edwards, R. (2011) 'An improved glacial isostatic adjustment model for the British Isles' *Journal of Quaternary Science* 26 (5), 541–52

Bremner, A. (1921) 'Limits of valley glaciation in the basin of the Dee' *Transactions of the Edinburgh Geological Society* (xi) 61–8

Bremner, A. (1935) 'The lochs of the Dee Basin' *The Deeside Field* 7, 25–36

Bridgland, D. R. (2000) 'Flint-rich gravels in Aberdeenshire' in Merritt, J. W., Connell, E. R. and Bridgland, D. R. (eds) *The Quaternary of the Banffshire Coast & Buchan. Field Guide*, 96–101, London, Quaternary Research Association

Bridgland, D. R. and Saville, A. (2000) 'Den of Boddam' in Merritt, J. W., Connell, E. R. and Bridgland, D. R. (eds) *The Quaternary of the Banffshire Coast & Buchan. Field Guide*, 102–15, London, Quaternary Research Association

Bridgland, D. R., Saville, A. and Sinclair JM 1997 'New evidence for the origin of the Buchan Ridge Gravel, Aberdeenshire', *Scottish Journal of Geology* 33 (1), 43–50

British Geological Survey (http://www.bgs.ac.uk/geoindex/)

Bronk Ramsey, C. (2017) *OxCal 4.3 manual.* http://c14.arch.ox.ac.uk/oxcalhelp/hlp_contents.html

Brooks, A. J., Bradley, S. L., Edwards, R. J. and Goodwyn, N. (2011) 'The palaeogeography of northwest Europe during the last 20,000 years' *Journal of Maps* 7 (1), 573–87

Brooks, S. J., Matthews, I. P., Birks, H. H. and Birks, H. J. B. (2012) 'High resolution Lateglacial and early-Holocene summer air temperature records from Scotland inferred from chironomid assemblages' *Quaternary Science Reviews* 41, 67–82

Brophy, K. (2006) 'Rethinking Scotland's Neolithic: combining circumstance and context' *Proceedings of the Society of Antiquaries of Scotland* 136, 7–46

Brophy, K. (2007) 'From big houses to cult houses: early Neolithic timber halls in Scotland' *Proceedings of the Prehistoric Society* 73, 75–96

Brophy, K. (2016) 'On ancient farms: a survey of Neolithic potentially domestic locations in Lowland Scotland' in Brophy, K., Macgregor G and Ralston, I. (eds) *The Neolithic of Mainland Scotland* Edinburgh

Brophy, K. and Noble, G. (2011) 'Within and beyond pits: deposition in lowland Neolithic Scotland' in Thomas, J. and Anderson-Whymark H *Regional Perspectives on Neolithic Pit Deposition: Beyond the Mundane*, 63–76, Oxford

Brown, A. G. (1995) 'Holocene channel and floodplain change: a UK perspective' in Gurnell, A. and Petts, G. (eds) *Changing River Channels*, 43–64, Chichester

Brown, A. G. (1997) 'Clearances and clearings: deforestation in mesolithic/neolithic Britain' *Oxford Journal of Archaeology* 16, 133–46

Brown, F., Howard-Davis, C., Brannand, M., Boyle, A., Evans, T., O'Connor, S., Spence, A., Heawood, R. and Lupton, A. (2007) *The Archaeology of the A1 (M) Darrington to Dishforth DBFO Road Scheme* Lancaster

Brown, I. M. (1993) 'Pattern of deglaciation of the last (Late Devensian) Scottish ice sheet: evidence from ice-marginal deposits in the Dee valley, northeast Scotland' *Journal of Quaternary Science* 8, 235–50

Brown, I. M. (1994) 'Former glacial lakes in the Dee valley: origin, drainage and significance' *Scottish Journal of Geology* 30, 147–58

Bryant, S. (1942) Complete Works of Tacitus. New York. Available online as http://data.perseus.org/citations/urn: cts: latinLit: phi1351.phi001.perseus-eng2:25, accessed 19 March 2018

Buckley, V. (ed) (1990) *Burnt Offerings. International Contributions to Burnt Mound Archaeology. Academic Publications* Dublin

Bunting, M. J. and Tipping, R. (2000) 'Sorting dross from data: possible indicators of post-depositional assemblage biasing in archaeological palynology' in Bailey, G., Charles R and Winder, N. (eds) *Human Ecodynamics*, 63–69, Oxford

Burl, H. A. W. (1970) 'The recumbent stone circles of north-east Scotland' *Proceedings of the Society of Antiquaries of Scotland* 102, 56–81

Burl, A. (1976) *The Stone Circles of the British Isles* London

Burl, H. A. W. (1984) 'Report on the excavation of a Neolithic mound at Boghead, Speymouth Forest, Fochabers, Moray, 1972 and 1974' *Proceedings of the Society of Antiquaries of Scotland* 114, 35–73

Butler, C 2005 *Prehistoric Flintwork*. Stroud: Tempus.

Cameron, A. D. and Ives, J. D. (1997) 'Use of hemispherical photography techniques to determine the association between canopy openness and regeneration of Scots pine (*Pinus sylvestris* L.) and downy birch (*Betula pubescens* Ehrh.) in Ballochbuie native pinewood, north-east Scotland' *Scottish Forestry* 51, 144–49

Cameron, K. (2002) 'The excavation of Neolithic pits and Iron Age souterrains at Dubton Farm, Brechin, Angus' *Tayside & Fife Archaeological Journal* 8, 19–76

Cameron, K., Rees, A., Dunwell, A. and Anderson, S. (2007) 'Prehistoric pits, Bronze Age roundhouses, an Iron Age promontory enclosure, Early Historic cist burials and medieval enclosures along the route of the A92, Dundee to Arbroath' *Tayside and Fife Archaeological Journal* 13, 39–73

Carter, S. (1993) 'Tulloch Wood, Forres, Moray: the survey and dating of a fragment of a prehistoric landscape' *Proceedings of the Society of Antiquaries of Scotland* 123, 215–33

Carver, G. (2012) 'Pits and place-making: Neolithic habitation and deposition practices in East Yorkshire c.4000–2500 BC' *Proceedings of the Prehistoric Society* 78, 111–134

Carver, M. (1999) *Surviving in Symbols: a Visit to the Pictish Nation* Edinburgh

Carver, M., Barrett, J., Downes, J. and Hooper, J. (2012) 'Pictish byre-houses at Pitcarmick and their landscape: investigations 1993–5' *Proceedings of the Society of Antiquaries of Scotland* 142, 145–200

Carver, M., Garner-Lahire, J. and Spall, C. (2016) *Portmahomack on Tarbat Ness* Society of Antiquaries of Scotland Monograph

Chaix, L. (2009) 'Mesolithic elk (*Alces alces* L.) from Zamotje 2 (Russia)' in McCartan, S. (ed) *Mesolithic Horizons* Vol 1, 190–97, Oxford

Chapman, W. D., Riley, C. F. and Riley, C. F. (1952) *The Granite City: a Plan for Aberdeen* Corporation of the City and Royal Burgh of Aberdeen

Clapperton, C. M., Gunson, A. R. and Sugden, D. E. (1975) 'Loch Lomond readvance in the eastern Cairngorms' *Nature* 253, 710–12

Clark, C. D., Hughes, A. L. C., Greenwood, S. L., Jordan, C. and Sejrup, H. P. (2012) 'Pattern and timing of retreat of the last British-Irish Ice Sheet' *Quaternary Science Reviews* 44, 112–46

Clark, J. G. D. (1936) 'Report on a Late Bronze Age Site in Mildenhall Fen, West Suffolk' *The Antiquaries Journal* XVI, 29–50

Clarke, D. (1976) 'Mesolithic Europe: the economic basis' in Sieveking, G., Longworth, I. H. and Wilson, K. E. (eds) *Problems in Economic and Social Archaeology*, 449–81, London

Clarke, D. (1978) *Mesolithic Europe: the Economic Basis* London

Clements, V. and Cook, M. (2009) *Blackdog, Aberdeenshire Evaluation: Data Structure Report* (Unpublished client report) AOC Archaeology Group

Coleman, R. and Photos-Jones E 2008 Early medieval settlement and ironworking in Dornoch, Sutherland: excavation at the Meadows Business Park *Scottish Archaeological Internet Reports (SAIR,* 28 https://doi.org/10.5284/1017938

Coles, B. (2001) 'The impact of Western European beaver on stream channels: some implications for past stream conditions and human activity' *Journal of Wetland Archaeology* 1, 55–82

Coles, D. (2009) 'The fire in the flint: arrowhead production and heat treatment' *Internet Archaeology* 26 http://intarch.ac.uk/journal/issue26/coles_index.html

Coles, D. (2011) 'A welter of flint chips: experimental knapping to investigate local flint from Luce Sands, Wigtownshire' *Lithics* 32, 22–28

Coles, J. (1979) *Experimental Archaeology* London

Collard, M., Edinborough, K., Shennan, S. and Thomas, M. G. (2010) 'Radiocarbon evidence indicates that migrants introduced farming to Britain' *Journal of Archaeological Science* 37, 866–70

Cook, M. L. (2006) 'Excavations of a Bronze Age roundhouse and associated palisaded enclosure at Aird Quarry, Castle Kennedy, Dumfries and Galloway' *Transactions of the Dumfriesshire and Galloway Natural History and Antiquarian Society* 80, 9–28

Cook, M. (2008) *Blackdog, Bridge of Don, Watching Brief: Data Structure Report* (Unpublished client report) AOC Archaeology Group

Cook, M. (2011) 'New evidence for the activities of Pictish potentates in Aberdeenshire: the hillforts of Strathdon' *Proceedings of the Society of Antiquaries of Scotland* 141, 207–29

Cook, M. (2013a) 'Open or enclosed: settlement patterns and hillfort construction in Strathdon, Aberdeenshire, 1800 BC–AD1000' *Proceedings of the Prehistoric Society* 79, 327–52

Cook, M. (2013b) 'Paradigms, assumptions, enclosure and violence: The hillforts of Strathdon' *Journal of Conflict Archaeology* 8 (2), 77–105

Cook, M. (2016) 'Prehistoric settlement patterns in the north-east of Scotland; excavations at Grantown Road, Forres 2002–2013' *Scottish Archaeological Internet Report* 61 https://doi.org/10.9750/issn.1473–3803.2016.61

Cook, M. and Dunbar, L. (2008) *Rituals, Round houses and Roman: Excavations at Kintore, Aberdeenshire 2000–2006* Vol 1, Edinburgh

Cook, M., Ellis, C. and Sheridan, A. (2010) 'Excavations at Upper Largie quarry, Argyll and Bute, Scotland: new light on the prehistoric ritual landscape of the Kilmartin Glen', *Proceedings of the Prehistoric Society* 76, 165–212

Coppins, A. M. and Coppins, B. J. (2010) *Atlantic Hazel* Edinburgh

Coull, J. R. (1963) 'The historical geography of Aberdeen' *Scottish Geographical Magazine* 79 (2), 80–94

Crawford, R. M. M. (1997) 'Oceanicity and the ecological disadvantage of warm winters' *Botanical Journal of Scotland* 49, 205–22

Cressey, M. and Strachan, R. (2003) 'The excavation of two burnt mounds and a wooden trough near Beechwood Farm, Inshes, Inverness, 1999' *Proceeding of the Society of Antiquaries Scotland* 133, 191–203

Crew, P. and Rehren, T. (2002) 'High temperature workshop residues from Tara: iron, bronze and glass', in Roche, H. (ed) 'Excavations at Ráith na Ríg, Tara, Co. Meath, 1997', Discovery Programme Reports 6, 83–102. Dublin

Croly, C. (2001) *Consumption Dykes in Aberdeen* (Unpublished)

Croly, C. (2004) *'the fences are built immoderately thick…': Consumption Dykes in Aberdeen, c. 1750–2004* (Unpublished document)

Crone, A. (2008) 'The carbonised wood assemblage' in Cook, M. and Dunbar L *Rituals, Roundhouses and Romans; excavations at Kintore 2000–2005* Vol 1, 238–42, Edinburgh

Crone, A. and Cavers, G. (2015) *Black Loch of Myrton 2015; Data Structure Report* (Unpublished client report)

Crone, A. and Cressey, M. (2014) *Birnie charcoal analysis (Phase 1)* (Unpublished client report)

Cruickshank J and Gunn, D. B. (1929) *The Freedom Lands and Marches of Aberdeen* Aberdeen

Cummings, V. and Whittle, A. W. R. (2003) 'Tombs with a view: landscape, monuments and trees' *Antiquity* 77, 255–66

Cunningham, P. (2011) 'Caching your savings: the use of small-scale storage in European prehistory' *Journal of Anthropological Archaeology* 30, 135–44

Cziesla, E., Eickhoff, S., Arts, N. and Winter, D. (eds) (1990) 'The big puzzle. International Symposium on Refitting Stone Artefacts, Montrepos, 1987' *Studies in Modern Archaeology* 1, 45–60, Holos, Bonn

Dalland, M. (2013a) *Third Don Crossing: Archaeological Trial Trenching* (Unpublished client report) Headland Archaeology (UK) Ltd

Dalland, M. (2013b) *A96 Park & Ride Scheme: Archaeological Evaluation* (Unpublished client report) Headland Archaeology (UK) Ltd

Dalland, M. and Wickham-Jones, C. R. (1998) 'A small Mesolithic site at Craighead Golf Course, Fife Ness, Fife' *Tayside and Fife Archaeological Journal* 4, 1–19

Dalton, C., Birks, H. J. B., Brooks, S. J., Cameron, N. G., Evershed, R. P., Peglar, S. M., Scott, J. A. and Thompson, R. (2005) 'A multi-proxy study of lake development in response to catchment changes during the Holocene at Lochnagar, north-east Scotland' *Palaeogeography Palaeoclimatology Palaeoecology* 221, 175–201

Dark, P. and Gent, H. (2001) 'Pest and diseases of prehistoric crops: a yield "honeymoon" for early grain crops in Europe?' *Oxford Journal of Archaeology* 20, 59–78

Darvill, T. (2011) 'Sounds from the underground: Neolithc ritual pits and pit-clusters on the Isle of Man and beyond' in Anderson-Whymark, H. and Thomas, J. (eds) *Regional Perspectives on Neolithic Pit Deposition: Beyond the Mundane,* 30–42, Oxford

David, B and Thomas, J. (2012) *Handbook of Landscape Archaeology* London.

Davidson, JM 1939–40 'Notes on some antiquities from Sutherland' *Proceedings of the Society of Antiquaries of Scotland* 74, 13–23.

Davidson, D. A., Carter, S., Boag, B., Long, D., Tipping, R. and Tyler, A. (1999) 'Analysis of pollen in soils: processes of incorporation and redistribution of pollen in five soil profile types' *Soil Biology & Biochemistry* 31, 643–53

Davies, A., Tipping, R. and McCulloch, R. (2007) Crathes, Warren Field: *Assessment, analysis and interpretation of pollen contents from Pots 5, 16 and 30* (Unpublished report)

Davies, A., Tipping, R. and McCulloch, R. (2009) 'Pollen analyses' in Murray, H. K., Murray, J. C. and Fraser, S. M. (eds) *A Tale of the Unknown Unknowns. A Mesolithic pit alignment and a Neolithic timber hall at Warren Field, Crathes, Aberdeenshire,* 43–44, Oxford

Davis, B. A., Brewer, S., Stevenson, A. C. and Guiot, J. (2003) 'The temperature of Europe during the Holocene reconstructed from pollen data' *Quaternary Science Reviews* 22, 1701–16

Denton, G. H., Alley, R. B., Comer G and Broecker, W. (2005) 'The role of seasonality in abrupt climate change' *Quaternary Science Reviews* 24, 1159–82

Dictionary of the Scots Language (2004) (http://www.dsl.ac.uk/): accessed November 2016.

Dingwall, K. (2013) *Aberdeen Western Peripheral Route/ Balmedie-Tipperty Lot 3 – Southern Leg, Volumes 1–3* (Unpublished client report) Headland Archaeology (UK) Ltd

Dingwall, K. (2015) *Aberdeen Western Peripheral Route/ Balmedie-Tipperty Lot 3 – Southern Leg: Sites SL/001 and SL/002A-D, Milltimber, Aberdeenshire: Post-Excavation Assessment and Mitigation Excavation Assessment Report* (Unpublished client report) Headland Archaeology (UK) Ltd

Dixon, P. (1994) 'Field systems, rig and other cultivation remains' in Foster S and Smout, T. C. (eds) *The History of Soils and Field Systems* Edinburgh

Dixon, P. and Fraser, I. (2007) 'The medieval and later landscape' in RCAHMS *In the Shadow of Bennachie. A Field Archaeology of Donside, Aberdeenshire,* 137–214, Edinburgh

Dixon, P. and Gannon, A. (2007) 'The transformation of the rural landscape' in RCAHMS *In the Shadow of Bennachie. A Field Archaeology of Donside, Aberdeenshire* 2nd edition, 215–244, Edinburgh

Dunbar, E., Cook, G. T., Naysmith, P., Tripney, B. G. and Xu, S. (2016) 'AMS 14C dating at the Scottish Universities Environmental Research Centre (SUERC) Radiocarbon Dating Laboratory' *Radiocarbon* 58, 9–23

Dunbar, L. (2007) 'Fluctuating settlement patterns in Bronze Age Sutherland: excavation of a roundhouse at Navidale, Helmsdale' *Proceedings of the Society of Antiquaries of Scotland* 137, 137–168

Dunbar, L. (2017) 'Unenclosed prehistoric settlement and early medieval pits at Macallan Distillery, Craigellachie, Highlands' *Scottish Archaeological Internet Report* 66 https://doi. org/10.9750/issn.2056-7421.2017.66

Duncan, J. S. and Halliday, S. (1997) 'Paddy's Rickle Bridge to Johnstonebridge (Kirkpatrick-Juxta; Johnstone parishes), watching brief' *Discovery and Excavation in Scotland,* 25

Dungworth, D. and Wilkes, R. (2009) 'Understanding hammerscale: the use of high-speed film and electron microscopy', *Historical Metallurgy* 43 (1), 33–46

Durno, S. E. (1956) 'Pollen analysis of peat deposits in Scotland' *Scottish Geographical Magazine* 72, 177–87

Durno, S. E. (1957) 'Certain aspects of vegetational history in north-east Scotland' *Scottish Geographical Magazine* 73, 176–84

Durno, S. E. (1970) 'Pollen diagrams from three buried peats in the Aberdeen area' *Transactions of the Botanical Society of Edinburgh* 41, 43–50

Edwards, K. J. (1978) *Palaeoenvironmental and archaeological investigations in the Howe of Cromar, Grampian region, Scotland* Unpublished PhD thesis, University of Aberdeen

Edwards, K. J. (1979a) 'Environmental impact in the prehistoric period' *Scottish Archaeological Forum* 9, 27–42

Edwards, K. J. (1979b) 'Palynological and temporal inference in the context of prehistory, with special reference to the evidence from lake and peat deposits' *Journal of Archaeological Science* 6, 255–70

Edwards, K. J. (1981) 'The separation of *Corylus* and *Myrica* pollen in modern and fossil samples' *Pollen et Spores* 23, 205–18

Edwards, K. J. (1993) 'Models of mid-Holocene forest farming for north-west Europe' in Chambers, F. M. (ed) *Climate Change and Human Impact on the Landscape,* 133–45, London

Edwards, K. J. and Ralston, I. B. M. (1984) 'Postglacial hunter-gatherers and vegetational history in Scotland' *Proceedings of the Society of Antiquaries of Scotland* 114, 15–34

Edwards, K. J. and Rowntree, K. M. (1980) 'Radiocarbon and palaeoenvironmental evidence for changing rates of erosion at a Flandrian Stage site in Scotland' in Cullingford, R. A., Davidson, D. A. and Lewin, J. (eds) *Timescales in Geomorphology,* 207–23, Chichester

Edwards, K. J. and Whittington, G. (2001) 'Lake sediments, erosion and landscape change during the Holocene in Britain and Ireland' *Catena* 42, 143–73

Edwards, K. J. and Whittington, G. (2003) 'Vegetation change' in Edwards, K. J. and Ralston, I. B. M. (eds) *Scotland After the Ice Age. Environment, Archaeology and History, 8000 BC–AD 1000,* 63–82, Edinburgh

Eeles, F. C. (1899) 'Note on a cist and urn found at Glasterberry, near Peterculter, Aberdeenshire' *Proceedings of the Society of Antiquaries of Scotland* 36, 627–28

Engl, R. (2008) 'Coarse stone' in Cook, M. and Dunbar L *Rituals, Roundhouses and Romans; excavations at Kintore 2000–2005* Vol 1, 210–25, Edinburgh

Eriksen, B. V. (1997) 'Implications of thermal pretreatment of chert in the German Mesolithic' in Schild, R. and Sulgostowska Warszawa, Z. (eds) *Man and Flint. Proceedings of the VIIth International Flint Symposium,* 325–29

Ewan, L. (1981) *A Palynological Investigation near Banchory: Some Local and Regional Implications, Aberdeen* O'Dell Memorial Monograph No. 11

Fairweather, A. D. and Ralston, I. B. M. (1993) 'The Neolithic timber hall at Balbridie, Grampian Region, Scotland: the building, the date, the plant macrofossils' *Antiquity* 67, 313–23

Food and Agriculture Organisation of the United Nations (2006) *World Reference Base for Soil Resources 2006: a framework for international classification, correlation and communication* World Soil Resources Report 103, Rome

Fenton, J. (2008) 'A postulated natural origin for the open landscape of upland Scotland' *Plant Ecology and Diversity* 1, 115–27

Ferguson, J. (1842) 'Report of the improvement of the Muir of Altens' *Transactions of the Highland and Agricultural Society of Scotland* 7, 163–79

Finlayson, B. (1990) 'The function of microliths, evidence from Smittons and Starr SW Scotland' *Mesolithic Miscellany* 11 (1), 2–6

Finlayson, B. and Mithen, S. (1997) 'The microwear and morphology of microliths from Gleann Mor' in Knecht, H. (ed) *Projectile Technology,* 107–29, New York, London

Finlayson, B. and Mithen, S. (2000) 'The morphology and microwear of microliths from Bolsay Farm and Gleann Mor: a comparative study' in Mithen, S. (ed) *Hunter-gatherer Landscape Archaeology,* 589–98, Cambridge

Finsinger, W., Tinner, W., van der Knaap, W. O. and Ammann, B. (2006) 'The expansion of hazel (*Corylus avellana* L.) in the southern Alps: a key for understanding its early Holocene history in Europe?' *Quaternary Science Reviews* 25, 612–31

Fleming, A. (2005) 'Megaliths and post-modernism: the case of Wales' *Antiquity* 79, 921–32.

Franklin, J. (2012) *Aberdeen Western Peripheral Route Package (Fastlink) Metal-Detector Survey: Hill of Muchalls Battlefield (Site 411)* (Unpublished client report) Headland Archaeology (UK) Ltd

Fraser, GK and Godwin, H. (1955) 'Two Scottish pollen diagrams: Carnwath Moss, Lanarkshire, and Strichen Moss, Aberdeenshire' *New Phytologist* 54, 216–21

Fraser, I. and Halliday, S. (2007) 'The early medieval landscape' in RCAHMS *In the Shadow of Bennachie. A Field Archaeology of Donside, Aberdeenshire,* 115–35, Edinburgh

Fraser, S., Knecht, R., Noble, G., Warren, G., Wickham-Jones, C. (2015) 'Aberdeenshire, Upper Dee Tributaries Project, excavation and fieldwalking' *Discovery and Excavation in Scotland* New series, 16, 20–21

Fyfe, R., Roberts N and Woodbridge, J. (2010) 'A pollen-based pseudobiomisation approach to anthropogenic land-cover change' *The Holocene* 20 (7), 1165–71

Fyfe, R. M., Twiddle, C., Sugita, S., Gaillard, M. J., Barratt, P., Caseldine, C. J., Dodson, J., Edwards, K. J., Farrell, M., Froyd, C. and Grant, M. J. (2013) 'The Holocene vegetation cover of Britain and Ireland: overcoming problems of scale and discerning patterns of openness' *Quaternary Science Reviews* 73, 132–48

Gaffney, V., Fitch, S., Ramsey, E., Yorston, R., Ch'ng, E., Baldwin, E., Bates, R., Gaffney, C., Ruggles, C., Sparrow, T., McMillan, A., Cowley, D., Fraser, S., Murray, C., Murray, H., Hopla, E. and Howard, A. (2013) 'Time and place: a luni-solar "time-reckoner" from 8th millennium BC Scotland' *Internet Archaeology* 34 http://dx.doi.org/10.11141/ia.34.1

Gannon, A. (2007) 'Survival, destruction and discovery' in RCAHMS *In the Shadow of Bennachie. A Field Archaeology of Donside, Aberdeenshire,* 17–24, Edinburgh

Gannon, A., Halliday, S., Sherriff, J. and Welfare, A. (2007) 'The Neolithic and Bronze Age landscape' in RCAHMS *In the Shadow of Bennachie. A Field Archaeology of Donside, Aberdeenshire,* 45–78, Edinburgh

Gear, A. J. and Huntley, B. (1991) 'Rapid changes in the range limits of Scots Pine 4000 years ago' *Science* 251, 544–47

Geoindex http://www.bgs.ac.uk/geoindex/accessed 2016

Gibson, A. (2004) 'Visibility and intervisibility: some thoughts on Neolithic and Bronze Age sites' in Shepherd, I. A. G. and Barclay, G. (eds) *Scotland in Ancient Europe. The Neolithic and Early Bronze Age of Scotland in their European Context,* 155–69, Edinburgh

Gibson, A. and Taverner, N. (1989) 'Excavations at Dundee High Technology Park, Tayside', *Proceedings of the Society of Antiquaries of Scotland,* 119, 83–9

Gilbert, J. M. (1979) *Hunting and Hunting Reserves in Scotland* Edinburgh

Gilliver, K. (1999) *The Roman Art of War* Oxford

Giorgi, J. (2017) 'Milltimber (AMA09) Environmental assessment' in Wilson D *Construction Phase Archaeological Monitoring Areas for the Aberdeen Western Peripheral Route (AWPR): Results of Archaeological Monitoring & Mitigation during Post-Excavation Assessment and Assessment Report* [unpublished client report] Headland Archaeology Ltd

Glentworth, R. and Muir, J. W. (1963) *The Soils of the Country round Aberdeen, Inverurie and Fraserburgh* Edinburgh

Golledge, N. R. (2010) 'Glaciation of Scotland during the Younger Dryas Stadial: a review' *Journal of Quaternary Science* 25, 759–64

Gondek M and Noble, G. (2012) *Excavation of a palisaded and ditched enclosure and timber buildings in association with the Craw Stane, Rhynie* (Unpublished Data Structure Report), http://reaparch.blogspot.co.uk/p/more-information.html

Gooder, J. (2007) 'Excavation of a Mesolithic House at East Barns, East Lothian, Scotland: an interim view' in Waddington C and Pederson, K. (eds) *Mesolithic Studies in the North Sea Basin and beyond,* 49–59, Oxford

Goransson, H. (1982) *The utilization of the forests in North-west Europe during Early and Middle Neolithic PACT* 7, 207–21

Goransson, H. (1986) 'Man and the forests of nemorial broad-leaved trees during the Stone Age' *Striae* 24, 143–52

Gradziński, R., Baryła, J., Doktor, M., Gmur, D., Gradziński, M., Kedzior, A., Paszowski, M., Soja, R., Zieliński, T. and Żurek, S. (2003) 'Vegetation-controlled modern anastomosing system of the upper Narew River (NE Poland) and its sediments' *Sedimentary Geology* 157, 253–76

Graves, D. (2011) 'The use of predictive modelling to target Neolithic settlement and occupation activity in mainland Scotland' *Journal of Archaeological Science* 38, 633–56

Gray, H. and Suddaby, I. (2010) 'An early Neolithic pit, a Middle Bronze Age roundhouse and other features at Hatton Farm, Elliot, Angus' *Tayside & Fife Archaeological Journal* 16, 8–29

Green, H. S. (1980) *The Flint Arrowheads of the British Isles: A detailed study of material from England and Wales with comparanda from Scotland and Ireland.* BAR British Series 75 (i) Oxford

Greig, J. (1991) 'The British Isles' in van Zeist, W., Wasylikowa, K. and Behre, K. (eds) *Progress in Old World Palaeoethnobotany,* 299–334, Rotterdam

Griffiths, D. R., Bergman, C. A., Clayton, C. J., Ohnuma, K., Robins, G. V. and Seeley, N. J. (1987) 'Experimental investigation of the heat treatment of flint' in Sieveking G de, G. and Newcomer, M. H. (eds) *The Human Uses of Flint and Chert. Proceedings of the fourth international symposium held at Brighton Polytechnic 10–15 April 1983,* 43–52, Cambridge

Grigson, C. (1986) 'Bird-foraging patterns in the Mesolithic' in Bonsall, C. (ed) *The Mesolithic In Europe,* 60–72, Edinburgh

Grimm, E. C. (1987) 'CONISS: a FORTRAN 77 program for stratigraphically constrained cluster analysis by the method of incremental sum of squares' *Computers and Geosciences* 13, 13–35

Grogan, E., O'Donnell, L., Johnston, P. and Gowen, M. (2007) *The Bronze Age landscapes of the Pipeline to the West – An integrated archaeological and environmental assessment* Bray

Grontmij and Natural Capital (2007) 'Chapter 12: Archaeology and Cultural Heritage' in *A90 Dualling – Balmedie to Tipperty Environmental Statement*

Gurnell, A. (2014) 'Plants as river system engineers' *Earth Surface Processes and Landforms* 39 (1), 4–25

Hall, A. M. (1986) 'Deep weathering patterns in north-east Scotland and their geomorphological significance' *Zeitschrift fur Geomorphologie* 30, 407–22

Hall, A. M. (1987) 'Weathering and relief development in Buchan, Scotland' in Gardiner, V. (ed) *International Geomorphology* Vol, I. I., 991–1005, Chichester

Hall, A. M. and Jarvis, J. (1989) 'A preliminary report on the Late Devensian glaciomarine deposits around St Fergus, Grampian Region' *Quaternary Newsletter* 59, 5–7

Halliday, S. P. (1990) 'Patterns of fieldwork and the distribution of burnt mounds in Scotland' in Buckley, V. (ed) *Burnt Offerings: International Contributions to Burnt Mound Archaeology,* 60–61, Dublin

Halliday, S. P. (1993) 'Marginal agriculture in Scotland' in Smout, T. C. (ed) *Scotland Since Prehistory. Natural Change and Human Impact,* 64–78, Aberdeen

Halliday, S. (2000) 'Wester Hatton Quarry, Potterton (Belhelvie parish), evaluation' *Discovery and Excavation in Scotland* New series, 1, 8

Halliday, S. P. (2006) 'Into the dim light of history: more of the same or all change?' in Woolf, A. (ed) *Landscape and Environment in Dark Age Scotland* (11), 11–28, St. Andrews

Halliday, S. P. (2007a) 'The later prehistoric landscape' in RCAHMS *In the Shadow of Bennachie. A Field Archaeology of Donside, Aberdeenshire,* 79–114, Edinburgh

Halliday, S. P. (2007b) 'Unenclosed round-houses in Scotland: occupation, abandonment and the character of settlement' in Burgess, C., Topping, P. and Lynch, F. (eds) *Beyond Stonehenge. Essays on the Bronze Age in honour of Colin Burgess,* 49–56, Oxford

Halliday, S. P. (2015) 'Scotland in Europe' in Ralston, I. and Hunter, F. (eds) *Scotland in Later Prehistoric Europe,* 281–94, Edinburgh

Hamilton WD and Krus, A. M. (2017) 'The myths and realities of Bayesian chronological modeling revealed' *American Antiquity,* (doi:10.1017/aaq.2017.57) (Early Online Publication) accessed 24 May 2017

Hannon, G., Bradshaw, R. H. W., Nord J and Gustafson, M. (2008) 'The Bronze Age landscape of the Bjäre peninsula, southern Sweden, and its relationship to burial mounds' *Journal of Archaeological Science* 35, 623–32

Hanson, W. S. (2003) 'The Roman presence – brief interludes' in Edwards, K. J. and Ralston, I. B. M. (eds) *Scotland: Environment & Archaeology, 8000BC–AD1000,* 195–216, Chichester

Hardy, K. and Sillitoe, P. (2003) 'Material perspectives: stone tool use and material culture in Papua New Guinea' *Internet Archaeology* 14 available: <http://intarch.ac.uk> accessed 31 August 2017

Harker, S. (2002) 'Cretaceous' in Trewin, N. H. (ed) *The Geology of Scotland,* 351–60, London

Harkness, D. D. and Wilson, H. W. (1979) 'Scottish Universities Research and Reactor Centre Radiocarbon Measurements III' *Radiocarbon* 21, 203–56

Harwood, K. and Brown, A. G. (1993) 'Fluvial processes in a forested anastomosing river: flood partitioning and changing flow patterns' *Earth Surface Processes and Landforms* 18, 741–48

Haselgrove, C. (2009) *The Traprain Law Environs Project* Edinburgh

Hather, J. G. (2000) *Archaeological Parenchyma* London

Hawke-Smith, C. F. (1978–80) 'Two Mesolithic sites near Newburgh, Aberdeenshire' *Proceedings of the Society of Antiquaries of Scotland* 110, 497–534

Hayden, B. (1979) *Palaeolithic Reflections: Lithic Technology of the Western Desert Aborigines* New Jersey

Heald, A. (2002) 'Metalworking objects and debris', in Cook M 'Excavations of an Early Historic settlement within a multi-period landscape at Dolphinton, South Lanarkshire' *Scottish Archaeological Journal* 24 (1), 61–83

Heald, A. (2006) 'Ferrous objects and slag' in Simpson, D. D. A., Murphy, E. M. and Gregory RA *Excavations at Northton, Isle of Harris* BAR British Series 408, 170–1, Oxford

Heald, A. (2008) 'Metalworking by-products' in Cook, M. and Dunbar L *Rituals, Roundhouses and Romans. Excavations at Kintore, Aberdeenshire 2000–2006. Volume 1 Forest Road* STAR Monograph 1, 206–9

Heald, A., McDonnell, G. and Mack, I. (2011) 'Ironworking debris', in Cressey, M. and Anderson S 'A Later prehistoric settlement and metalworking site at Seafield West, near Inverness, Highland', *Scottish Archaeological Internet Reports (SAIR)* 47, 20–24

Hedges, J. (1975) 'Excavation of two Orcadian burnt mounds at Liddle and Beaquoy' *Proceedings of the Royal Society of Antiquities of Scotland* 106, 39–98

Heggie, D. C. (1981) *Megalithic Science. Ancient mathematics and astronomy in northwest Europe.* London

Henderson, J. A. (1982) *Annals of Lower Deeside* Aberdeen

Henshall, A. (1984) 'The pottery' in Burl, H. A. W. 'Report on the excavation of a Neolithic mound at Boghead, Speymouth Forest, Fochabers, Moray, 1972 and 1974' *Proceedings of the Society of Antiquaries of Scotland* 114, 59–66

Henshall, A. (1996) 'The pottery' in Shepherd A 'A Neolithic ring-mound at Midtown of Pitglassie, Auchterless, Aberdeenshire' *Proceedings of the Society of Antiquaries of Scotland* 126, 29–33

Hey, G. and Lacey, M. (2001) *Evaluation of Archaeological Decision-making Processes and Sampling Strategies* Oxford

Hill, P. H. (1984) 'A sense of proportion: a contribution to the study of double-ring roundhouses' *Scottish Archaeological Review* 3 (2), 80–86

Hodder, M. A. (1990) 'Burnt mounds in the English West Midlands' in Buckley, V. (ed) *Burnt Offerings: International Contributions to Burnt Mound Archaeology,* 13–17, Dublin

Hoek, W. M. and Bos, J. A. A. (2007) 'Early Holocene climatic oscillations – causes and consequences' *Quaternary Science Reviews* 26, 1901–6

Holden, T. (1998a) *The Archaeology of Scottish Thatch* Historic Scotland Technical Advice Note 13

Holden, T. (1998b) 'Easter Hatton, Belhelvie' *Discovery and Excavation in Scotland,* 6

Holden, T. (2012) *Access from the North Proposal (The Third Don Crossing) Building Recording Survey: Danestone Walled Garden (Site L1)* (Uunpublished client report) Headland Archaeology (UK) Ltd

Holden, T., Hather, J. G. and Watson, J. P. N. (1995) 'Mesolithic plant exploitation at the Roc del Migdia, Catalonia' *Journal of Archaeological Science* 22, 769–78

Holst, D. (2010) 'Hazelnut economy of early Holocene hunter-gatherers: a case study from Mesolithic Duvensee, northern Germany' *Journal of Archaeological Science* 37, 2871–80

Hughes, P. D. M. and Barber, K. E. (2004) 'Contrasting pathways to ombrotrophy in three raised bogs from Ireland and Cumbria, England' *The Holocene* 14/1, 65–77

Hunter, F. (2007) *Beyond the edge of the Empire – Caledonians, Picts and Romans* Rosemarkie

Hunter, F. (2017) 'Roman Britain in 2016: 2. Scotland' *Britannia* 48, 322–27

Huntley, B. (1993) 'Rapid early Holocene migration and high abundance of hazel (*Corylus avellana* L.): alternative hypotheses' in Chambers, F. M. (ed) *Climate Change and Human Impact on the Landscape,* 205–15, London

Huntley, B. (1994) 'Late Devensian and Holocene palaeoecology and palaeoenvironments of the Morrone Birkwoods, Aberdeenshire, Scotland' *Journal of Quaternary Science* 9, 311–36

Jackson, G. (2002) 'The economy: Aberdeen and the sea' in Dennison, E. P., Ditchburn, D. and Lynch, M. (eds) *Aberdeen Before 1800. A New History,* 159–80, East Linton

Jacobi, RM 2004 'The Late Upper Palaeolithic lithic collection from Gough's Cave, Cheddar, Somerset, and human use of the cave', *Proceedings of the Prehistoric Society* 70, 1–92.

Jacobs, U. K. (2007) 'Chapter 28 – Cultural Heritage' in Jacobs UK *Aberdeen Western Peripheral Route Environmental Statement*

Jeffrey, S. (1991) 'Burnt Mounds, fulling and early textiles' in Hodder, M. and Barfield, L. (eds) *Burnt Mounds and Hot Stone Technology,* 97–108, Sandwell

Jenorowski, T., Sludden, K. (2016) *Caithness-Moray-Shetland HVDC Link: Moray Section Archaeological Watching Brief* (Unpublished client report) CFA Archaeology Ltd

Jervise, A. (1875) *Epitaphs and inscriptions from burial grounds and old buildings in the north-east of Scotland, with Historical, Biographical, Genealogical and Antiquarian notes, also, an Appendix of Illustrative papers* Edinburgh

Jobey, G. (1978) 'Green Knowe unenclosed platform settlement and Harehope cairn, Peebleshire' *Proceedings of the Society of Antiquaries of Scotland* 110, 72–113

Jobey, G. and Tait, J. (1966) 'Excavations on palisaded settlements and cairnfields at Alnham Northumberland' *Archaeologia Aeliana* 4th series, 44, 5–48

Johnson, M. (2010) 'Prehistoric pottery' in Suddaby, I. and Ballin, T. B. (2010) 'Late Neolithic and Late Bronze Age lithic assemblages associated with a cairn and other prehistoric features at Stoneyhill Farm, Longhaven, Peterhead, Aberdeenshire, 2002–03', *Scottish Archaeological Internet Reports (SAIR)* 45, 18–21

Johnson, M. (2012) 'The finds' in Gray, H. and Suddaby I 'Early Neolithic pits, an Iron Age ring-ditch house and associated features at Coul Brae, Mosstodloch, Moray' *Scottish Archaeological Journal 38,* 25–70.

Johnson, M. (2016) 'Excavation of two Early Bronze Age short cists and a prehistoric pit at Lindsayfeild, near Stonehaven, Aberdeenshire' *Scottish Archaeological Internet Report* 63 https://doi.org/10.9750/issn.1473–3803.2016.63

Johnson, M. and Cameron, K. (2012) 'An Early Bronze Age unenclosed cremation cemetery and Mesolithic pit at Skilmafilly, near Maud, Aberdeenshire', *Scottish Archaeological Internet Reports (SAIR)* 53 https://doi.org/10.9750/issn.1773–3808.2012.53

Jones, A. F., Lewin, J. and Macklin, M. G. (2010) 'Flood series data for the later Holocene: available approaches, potential and limitations from UK alluvial sediments' *The Holocene* 20 (7), 1123–35

Jones, E. and Atkinson, D. (2006) Upper Forth Crossing, Kincardine (Unpublished client report) Headland Archaeology (UK) Ltd

Jones, E., Sheridan, A., Smith, A. and Franklin, J. (2018) 'Pots, pits and roundhouses at Meadowend Farm' *Scottish Archaeological Internet Reports (SAIR)* Edinburgh.

Jones, R. H. (2009) 'Troop movements in Scotland: the evidence from marching camps' in Morillo, A., Hanel, N. and Martín E *Limes XX: Estudios Sobre la Frontera Romana, Anejos de Gladius 13, Madrid*, 867–77

Jones, R. H. (2011) *Roman Camps in Scotland* Edinburgh

Jones, R. H. (2012) *Roman Camps in Britain* Stroud

Jones, R. H. (forthcoming 2018) 'Soldiers and sailors in the conquest of Scotland' in Sommer, CS et al (eds) *Limes XXIII: Proceedings of the International Congress of Roman Frontier Studies, Germany*

Juel Jensen, H. (1994) *Flint Tools and Plant Working: Hidden Traces of Stone Age Technology: a use wear study of some Danish Mesolithic and TRB implements* Århus

Keith, G. S. (1811) *A General View of the Agriculture of Aberdeenshire* Aberdeen

Keeley, L. H. (1982) 'Hafting and retooling: effects of the archaeological record', *American Antiquity* 47 (4), 798–809

Kenney, J. (1993) *The Beginnings of Agriculture in Britain: a critical assessment* Unpublished PhD thesis University of Edinburgh

Kenworthy, J. B. (1975) 'The prehistory of north east Scotland' in Gemmell, A. M. D. (ed) *Quaternary Studies in North East Scotland,* 74–81, Aberdeen

Kilpatrick, M. C. (2016) 'Relieving floods, revealing history: early prehistoric activity at Knocknagael Farm, Inverness' *Scottish Archaeological Internet Reports* 64 https://doi.org/10.9750/issn.2056–7421.2016.64

Kirby, M. (2014) *Aberdeen Western Peripheral Route/ Balmedie-Tipperty. Lot 4 – Fastlink. Invasive Archaeological Investigations* (Unpublished client report) CFA Archaeology Ltd Report No. 3089

Kirby, M. (2015a) *Aberdeen Western Peripheral Route/ Balmedie-Tipperty. Lot 4 – Fastlink. Invasive Archaeological Investigations: Mitigation Excavation AWPR/B-T/FL/001* (Unpublished client report) CFA Archaeology Ltd Report No. 3185

Kirby, M. (2015b) *Aberdeen Western Peripheral Route/ Balmedie-Tipperty. Lot 4 – Fastlink. Invasive Archaeological Investigations: Mitigation Excavation AWPR/B-T/FL/003A* (Unpublished client report) CFA Archaeology Ltd, Report No. 3187

Kirby, M. (2015c) *Aberdeen Western Peripheral Route/ Balmedie-Tipperty. Lot 4 – Fastlink. Invasive Archaeological Investigations: Mitigation Excavation AWPR/B-T/FL/005* (Unpublished client report) CFA Archaeology Ltd, Report No. 3190

Knight, M. (2012) *Must Farm Must Read, Articulating Britain's Lost Prehistoric Landscape* http://www.mustfarm.com/wp/ wp-content/uploads/MustRead-June2012.pdf Accessed May 2016

Lancaster, S. (2009) 'Palaeoenvironmental synthesis' in Murray, H. K., Murray, J. C. and Fraser, S. (eds) *A Tale of the Unknown Unknowns: a Mesolithic pit alignment and a Neolithic timber hall at Warren Field, Crathes, Aberdeenshire*, 43–50, Oxford

Lancaster, S., Davidson, D. A. and Simpson, I. A. (2005) 'Soil micromorphology' in Bradley R *The Moon and the Bonfire: An Investigation of Three Stone Circles in North-east Scotland*, 42–46, Edinburgh

Lauder, T. D. (1830) *An Account of the Great Floods of August 1829 in the province of Moray and adjoining district* Elgin

Ledingham, J. (1874) 'Notice of the discovery of cists on the farm of Slap, near Turriff, Aberdeenshire', *Proceedings of the Society of Antiquaries of Scotland* 10, 739–40

Leivers, M., Roberts, J. and Peterson, R. (2000) 'The cairn at East Finnercy, Dunecht, Aberdeenshire' *Proceedings of the Society of Antiquaries of Scotland* 130, 183–95

Lelong O and MacGregor, G. (2007) *The Lands of Ancient Lothian: interpreting the archaeology of the A1* Edinburgh

Lenfert, R. and Cameron, A. (2016) *Report on an Archaeological Evaluation for Land at Blackdog, Aberdeenshire, AB23 8BT Site Code CA266–2015* (Unpublished client report) Cameron Archaeology

Lewin, J. and Brindle, B. J. (1977) 'Confined meanders' in Gregory, K. J. (ed) *River Channel Changes*, 221–33, Chichester

Lewin, J. and Macklin, M. G. (2003) 'Preservation potential for Late Quaternary river alluvium' *Journal of Quaternary Science* 18, 107–20

Lewin, J., Macklin, M. G. and Johnstone, E. (2005) 'Interpreting alluvial archives: sedimentological factors in the British Holocene fluvial record' *Quaternary Science Reviews* 24, 1873–89

Lewis, J. (2006) 'Normandykes Roman Camp, Peterculter, Aberdeen (Peterculter parish) excavation', *Discovery and Excavation in Scotland* New series, 7, 13

Lidén, O 1942 'De flinteggade Benspetsarnas nordiska Kulturfas. Studier i Anslutning till nya sydsvenska Fynd', *Skrifter utgivna av Kungliga Humanistiska Vetenskabssamfundet i Lund* XXXIII. Lund: C W K Gleerup

Little, A., Elliott, B., Conneller, C., Pomstra, D., Evans, A. A., Fitton, L. C., et al (2016) 'Technological analysis of the world's earliest shamanic costume: a multi-scalar, experimental study of a red deer headdress from the Early Holocene site of Star Carr, North Yorkshire, UK', *PLoS ONE* 11 (4): e0152136. https://doi.org/10.1371/journal.pone.0152136

Livens, R. G. (1956) 'Three tanged flint points from Scotland', *Proceedings of the Society of Antiquaries of Scotland* LXXXIX, 438–43.

Lochrie, J. (2010a) *Prehistoric Pottery Report, Westgate Residential Development, Blackhall Road, Inverurie* Unpublished client report for Murray Archaeological Services Ltd

Lochrie, J. (2010b) *Midmill, Kintore, Aberdeenshire, Prehistoric pottery report*. Unpublished specialist report for Murray Archaeological Services Ltd

Lochrie, J. (2010c) *Prehistoric Pottery Summary Report, Pitdrichie Quarry, Drumlithe, Aberdeenshire*, Unpublished Client Report for Murray Archaeological Services Ltd

Lochrie, J. (2013) '8.1 Prehistoric pottery' in Murray, J. C. and Murray HK *Site West of International Paper, Port Elphinstone, Inverurie, Aberdeenshire, Archaeological Investigation*, 28–40, Unpublished client report for Murray Archaeological Services Ltd

Lochrie, J. (2016) Land at Kirkton of Fetteresso, Stonehaven, Aberdeenshire. Finds Assessment, (Unpublished client report)

Long, D. J., Tipping, R., Carter, S., Davidson, D. A., Boag, B. and Tyler, A. (2000) 'The replication of pollen stratigraphies in soil pollen profiles: a test' in Harley, M. M., Morton, C. M. and Blackmore, S. (eds) *Pollen and Spores: Morphology and Biology*, 481–97, Kew

Lopez-Doriga, I. (2013) 'An experimental approach to the taphonomic study of charred hazelnut remains in archaeological deposits' *Archaeology, Anthropolology, Science* (Published online at DOI 10.1007/s12520–013–0154–3)

Lowe, J. J., Rasmussen, S. O., Björck, S., Hoek, W. Z., Steffensen, J. P., Walker, M. J., Yu, Z. C. and Intimate Group (2008) 'Synchronization of palaeoenvironmental events in the North Atlantic during the Last Termination: a revised protocol recommended by the INTIMATE Group' *Quaternary Science Reviews* 27, 6–17

Lynch, A. H., Hamilton, J. and Hedges, R. E. M. (2008) 'Where the wild things are: aurochs and cattle in England' *Antiquity* 82, 1025–239

Lynch, M. and Dingwall, C. (2002) 'Aberdeen and the sea', in Dennison, E. P., Ditchburn, D. and Lynch, M. (eds) *Aberdeen before 1800: a new history*, 154–94, East Linton

Macgregor, G., Donnelly, M., Miller, J., Ramsay, S. and Alldritt, D. (1994) 'A Mesolithic scatter from Littlehill Bridge, Girvan, Ayrshire' *Scottish archaeological Journal* 23, 1–14

Macinnes, L. (2004) 'Historic landscape characterization' in Bishop, K. and Phillips, A. (eds) *Countryside Planning: New Approaches to Management and Conservation*, 155–69, London

Macinnes, L. (2010) 'The protection and management of the historic landscape in Scotland in the context of the European Landscape Convention' in Bloemers, T., Hars, H. and van der Valk, A. (eds) *The Cultural Landscape and Heritage Paradox: Protection and Development of the Dutch Archaeological- Historical Landscape and its European Dimension*, 151–60, Amsterdam

Macklin, M. G. and Lewin, J. (2003) 'River sediments, great floods and centennial-scale Holocene climate change' *Journal of Quaternary Science* 18, 101–5

Macklin, M. G., Johnstone, E. and Lewin, J. (2005) 'Pervasive and long-term forcing of Holocene river instability and flooding in Great Britain by centennial-scale climate change' *The Holocene* 15, 937–43

MacSween, A. (2001) 'Pottery' in Barclay, G. J., Carter, S. P., Dalland, M., Hastie, M., Holden, T. G., MacSween, A. and Wickham-Jones CR 'A possible Neolithic settlement and Kinbeachie, Black Isle, Highland' *Proceedings of the Society of Antiquaries of Scotland* 131, 57–85

MacSween, A. (2002) 'Pottery' in Cameron K 'The excavation of Neolithic pits and Iron Age souterrains at Dubton Farm, Brechin, Angus' *Tayside and Fife Archaeological Journal* 8, 34–42

MacSween, A. (2007) 'The Meldon Bridge period: the pottery from south and east Scotland twenty years on', in Burgess, C., Topping, P. and Lynch, F. (eds) *Beyond Stonehenge: Essays on the Bronze Age in Honour of Colin Burgess,* 367–76. Oxbow Books, Oxford

MacSween, A. (2008) 'The prehistoric pottery' in Cook, M. and Dunbar L *Rituals, Roundhouses and Romans. Excavations at Kintore, Aberdeenshire 2000–2006. Volume 1 Forest Road* STAR Monograph 1, 173–89, Loanhead

Madsen, B 1992 'Hamburgkulturens flintteknologi i Jels' in Holm, J. and Rieck, F Istidsjægere ved Jelssøerne. Hamburgkulturen i Danmark. 93–131. Skrifter fra Museumsrådet for Sønderjyllands Amt 5. Haderslev: Haderslev Museum.

Maizels, J. and Aitken, J. (1991) 'Palaeohydrological change during deglaciation in upland Britain: a case study from northeast Scotland' in Starkel, L., Gregory, K. J. and Thornes, J. B. (eds) *Temperate Palaeohydrology: fluvial processes in the temperate zone during the last 15,000 years,* 105–45, Chichester,

Mann, L. (1903) 'Report on the excavation of prehistoric pile-structures in Wigtownshire' *Proceedings of the Society of Antiquaries of Scotland* 37, 370–415

Maroo, S. and Yaldon, D. W. (2000) 'The Mesolithic mammal fauna of Great Britain' *Mammal Review* 30 (3–4), 243–48

Marshall, P. (2009) 'The radiocarbon dating of the pit alignment and the timber hall' in Murray, H. K., Murray, J. C. and Fraser, S. (eds) *A Tale of the Unknown Unknowns: a Mesolithic pit alignment and a Neolithic timber hall at Warren Field, Crathes, Aberdeenshire,* 72–80, Oxford

Marshall, P. D. and Cook G 2014 'Radiocarbon dating', in H. K. Murray and J. C. Murray, 'Mesolithic and Early Neolithic activity along the Dee: excavations at Garthdee Road, Aberdeen', *Proceedings of the Society of Antiquaries of Scotland* 144, 10–16

Mason, D. (2003) *Roman Britain and the Roman Navy* Tempus

Mason, S. L. R. (forthcoming) *The Ethnography of Hazel Nut Exploitation* Report commissioned as part of the AWPR/B-T project and to be submitted for publication to Journal of Anthropological Archaeology.

McClatchie, M., Bogaard, A., Colledge, S., Whitehouse, N. J., Schulting, R. J., Barratt, P. and McLaughlin, T. R. (2014) 'Neolithic farming in north-western Europe: archaeobotanical evidence from Ireland' *Journal of Archaeological Science* 51, 206–15

McCullagh, R. and Tipping, R. (1998) *The Lairg Project 1988–1996: The Evolution of an Archaeological Landscape in Northern Scotland* Edinburgh

McDonnell, G. (1994) 'Slag report', in Ballin Smith, B. (ed) *Howe: Four Millennia of Orkney Prehistory. Excavations 1978–82* Monograph Series Number 9,228–34, Edinburgh

McDonnell, G. (2000) 'Ironworking and other residues', in Lane, A. and Campbell E *Dunadd: an Early Dalriadic Capital,* 218–20, Oxford

McDonnell, G. (2013) 'Metallurgical and vitrified material', in Armit, I. and McKenzie J *An Inherited Place: Broxmouth Hillfort and the south-east Scottish Iron Age,* 393–402, Edinburgh

McKinley JI 2000 'The analysis of cremated bone' in Cox, M. and Mays, S. (eds) *Human Osteology in Archaeology and Forensic Science* Greenwich Medical Media, 403–21, London,

McLaren, D. (2010) 'The vitrified material', in White, R. and Richardson P 'The excavation of Bronze Age roundhouses at Oldmeldrum, Aberdeenshire', *Scottish Archaeological Internet Reports (SAIR)* 43, 19

McLaren, D. (2012) *The vitrified material from Bellfield, North Kessock* (Unpublished client report) Headland Archaeology (UK) Ltd

McLaren, D. (2013) 'Slag and vitrified material' in Suddaby I 'Excavations of post-built roundhouses and a circular ditched enclosure at Kirtaraglen, Portree, Isle of Skye, 2006–7' *Scottish Archaeological Internet Reports* (SAIR) 54, 47–8, Edinburgh, Available: <http://archaeologydataservice.ac.uk/archives/view/sair/contents.cfm? vol=54> Accessed 29 May 2017.

McLaren, D (forthcoming) 'The Stone Artefacts' in Hatherley C & Murray R *Culduthel: An Iron Age Craft Centre in North-East Scotland*

McLaren, D. and Dungworth, D. (2012) *The manufacture of iron at Culduthel: ferrous metalworking debris and iron metallurgy* (Unpublished client report) Headland Archaeology (UK) Ltd

McLaren, D. and Dungworth, D. (2016) 'The ferrous metalworking' in Cook M 'Prehistoric settlement patterns in the north-east of Scotland. Excavations at Grantown Road, Forres, 2002–2013' *Scottish Archaeological Internet Reports (SAIR)* 61, 45–61, Edinburgh

McLaren, D. and Engl, R. (forthcoming) 'The excavations of Neolithic and Beaker pit groups and a late prehistoric settlement at East Beechwood Farm, Inverness' *Scottish Archaeological Internet Report (SAIR)* Edinburgh

McLaren, F. (2000) 'Revising the wheat crops of Neolithic Britain, in Fairbairn A 'Plants in Neolithic Britain and beyond' *Neolithic Studies Group Seminar Papers* 5, 91–100

McVean, D. N. (1964) 'Woodland and scrub' in Burnett, J. (ed) *The Vegetation of Scotland,* 144–67, Edinburgh

Mears, R. and Hillman, G. (2007) *Wild Food* London.

Meldrum, E. (1957) 'Mounth passes and Motehills' *The Deeside Field,* 2nd series, 2, 20

Mercer, J. (1968) 'Stone tools from a washing-limit deposit of the highest post-glacial transgression, Lealt Bay, Isle of Jura', *Proceedings of the Society of Antiquaries of Scotland* 100, 1–46

Mercer, R. (1981) *Grimes Graves, Norfolk Volume 1: Excavations 1971–2* London

Merritt, J. W., Auton, C. A., Connell, E. R., Hall, A. M. and Peacock, J. D. (2003) *Cainozoic Geology and Landscape Evolution of North-east Scotland* Edinburgh

Mesolithic Deeside website 2018 Mapping Mesolithic Deeside http://www.mesolithicdeeside.org/index.asp? pageid=679279, accessed 10 February 2018

Millican, K 2016 'Seeing the wood in the trees' in Brophy et al (eds) 2016 *The Neolithic of Mainland Scotland,* 139–68, Edinburgh

Mithen, S. and Finlay, N 2000 'Staosnaig, Colonsay: excavations 1989–1995' in Mithen S *Hunter-gatherer Landscape Archaeology: the Southern Hebrides Mesolithic Project 1988–98. Vol. 2: Archaeological fieldwork on Colonsay, computer modelling, experimental archaeology and final interpretation* McDonald Institute Monographs, 359–441, Cambridge

Mithen, S., Finlay, N., Carruthers, W., Mason, S., Hather, J. and Carter, S. (2000) 'Occupation and activity at Staosnaig' in Mithen, S. (ed) *Hunter-gatherer Landscape Archaeology: the Southern Hebrides Mesolithic Project 1988–98. Vol. 2: Archaeological fieldwork on Colonsay, computer modelling, experimental archaeology and final interpretation* McDonald Institute Monographs, 407–15, Cambridge

Mithen, S., Finlay, N., Carruthers, W., Carter, S. and Ashmore, P. (2001) 'Plant use in the Mesolithic: evidence from Staosnaig, Isle of Colonsay, Scotland' *Journal of Archaeological Science* 28, 223–34

Mithen, S., Wicks, K., Pirie, A., Riede, F., Lane, C., Banerjea, R., Cullen, V., Gittins, M. and Pankhurst, N. (2015) 'A Lateglacial archaeological site in the far north-west of Europe at Rubha Port an t-Seilich, Isle of Islay, western Scotland: Ahrensburgian-style artefacts, absolute dating and geoarchaeology', *Journal of Quaternary Science* 30 (5), 396–416

Moore, H. and Wilson, G. (1999) 'Burnt Mounds in Shetland' *Proceedings of the Society of Antiquities of Scotland* 129, 203–37

Moore, P. (2014) *Aberdeen Western Peripheral Route/Balmedie-Tipperty Lot 1 – Balmedie to Tipperty Invasive Archaeological Investigations* [unpublished client report] report No. 3090, CFA Archaeology Ltd

Munro, M. (1986) *Geology of the Country around Aberdeen* London

Murdoch, W. (1975) 'The geomorphology and glacial deposits of the area around Aberdeen' in Gemmell, A. M. D. (ed) *Quaternary Studies in North East Scotland,* 14–18, Aberdeen

Murray, J. C. and Murray, H. K. (2013) *Site West of International Paper, Port Elphinstone, Inverurie, Aberdeenshire, Archaeological Investigation* 28–40 (Unpublished client report) Murray Archaeological Services Ltd

Murray, H. K. (2005) 'David Lloyd Leisure Centre, Garthdee Road' *Discovery and Excavation in Scotland* New series 6, 8–9

Murray, H. K. and Murray, J. C. (2006) *Thainstone Business Park, Inverurie, Aberdeenshire* SAIR 21, Edinburgh

Murray, H. K. and Murray, J. C. (2008) *Midmill Industrial Estate, Kintore, Aberdeenshire* (Unpublished client report) Murray Archaeology

Murray, H. K. and Murray, J. C. (2014) 'Mesolithic and Early Neolithic activity along the Dee: excavations at Garthdee Road, Aberdeen' *Proceedings of the Society of Antiquaries of Scotland* 144, 1–64

Murray, H. K., Murray, J. C., Shepherd, A. N., and Shepherd, I. A. G. (1992) 'Evidence of agricultural activity of the later second millennium BC at Rattray, Aberdeenshire' *Proceedings of the Society of Antiquaries of Scotland* 122, 113–26

Murray, H. K., Murray, J. C. and Fraser, S. (2009) *A Tale of the Unknown Unknowns. A Mesolithic Pit Alignment and a Neolithic Timber Hall at Warren Field, Crathes, Aberdeenshire* Oxford.

Murray, R. (2007) *Culduthel Mains Farm Inverness, Phase 5. Excavation of a later prehistoric settlement; assessment report* (Unpublished client report) Headland Archaeology (UK) Ltd

Murray, R. (2008) *Data structure report of an archaeological excavation at Culduthel Mains Farm, Phase 7 & 8* (Unpublished client report) Headland Archaeology (UK) Ltd

Murray, R. (2011) *Bellfield Farm, North Kessock. Area 2 & 3 archaeological excavation* (Unpublished client report) Headland Archaeology (UK) Ltd

Murray, R. (2012a) *Access from the North Proposal (The Third Don Crossing) Topographic Survey: Cruives Enclosure Wall (Site A29)* (Unpublished client report) Headland Archaeology (UK) Ltd

Murray, R. (2012b) *Access from the North Proposal (The Third Don Crossing) Historic Building Recording and Photographic Survey: Grandholm Canalised Water Course (Site A25), Grandholm Mill Lades (Site A26), and Danestone Policy Wall (D1)* (Unpublished client report) Headland Archaeology (UK) Ltd

Murray, R. (2015) *Aberdeen Western Peripheral Route/ Balmedie-Tipperty Lot 3 – Southern Leg: Sites SL/003-SL/005 Aberdeenshire: Post-Excavation Assessment and Mitigation Excavation Assessment Report* (Unpublished client report) Headland Archaeology (UK) Ltd

Murray, R. and Wilson, D. (2017) *Results of Archaeological Monitoring & Mitigation during Post-Excavation Assessment and Assessment Report* (Unpublished client report) Headland Archaeology (UK) Ltd

Needham, S. (2005) 'Transforming Beaker Culture in North-West Europe: processes of fusion and fission' *Proceedings of the Prehistoric Society* 71, 171–218

Neighbour, T. and Johnson, M. (2005) 'A Bronze Age burnt mound in lowland Cumbria: excavations at Garlands Hospital, Carlisle, 1997' *Transactions Cumberland & Westmorland Antiquarian and Archaeological Society* 5, 11–23

Nicol, I., Johnston, A. and Campbell, L. (1996) *Landscape Character Assessment of Aberdeen.* Scottish Natural Heritage Review 80, Edinburgh

Noble, G 2006 *Neolithic Scotland. Timber, Stone, Earth and Fire* Edinburgh

Noble, G. and Brophy, K. (2011) 'Ritual and remembrance at a prehistoric ceremonial complex in central Scotland: excavations at Forteviot, Perth & Kinross' *Antquity* 85 (329) 787–804.

Noble, G. and Brophy, K. (2014) Construction process, environment: altering the landscape in Neolithic Lowland Scotland' in Furholt, M., Hinz, M., Mischka, D., Noble, G. and Olausson, D. (eds) *Landscapes, Histories and Societies in the Northern European Neolithic,* 65–77, Kiel: German Research Foundation

Noble, G. and Gondek, M 2016 Rhynie Environs Archaeological Project, Excavation, *Discovery and Excavation in Scotland* New series 16, 30

Noble, G., Greig, M., Millican, K., Anderson, S., Clarke, A., Johnson, M., McLaren, D. and Sheridan, A. (2012) 'Excavations at a multi-period site at Greenbogs, Aberdeenshire, Scotland and the four-post timber architecture tradition of Late Neolithic Britain and Ireland' *Proceedings of the Prehistoric Society* 78, 146–71

Noble, G., Gondek, M., Campbell, E. and Cook, M. (2013) 'Between prehistory and history: the archaeological detection of social change among the Picts' *Antiquity* 87 (338), 1136–50

Noble, G., Christie, C. and Philip, E. (2016a) 'Life is the Pits! Ritual, refuse and Mesolithic–Neolithic settlement traditions in North-east Scotland' in Brophy, K., MacGregor, G. and Ralston, I. (eds) *The Neolithic of Mainland Scotland,* 171–99, Edinburgh

Noble,, G., Turner,, J., Hamilton,, D., Hastie,, L., Knecht,, R., Stirling,, L., Sveinbjarnarson,, O., Upex, B. and Milek, K 2016b 'Early medieval shellfish gathering at the Sands of Forvie, Aberdeenshire: feast or famine?' *Proceedings of the Society of Antiquaries of Scotland 146, 121–52*

Noble,, G., Gondek,, M., MacIver,, C., MacLean, D. and Campbell, E 2017 'Rhynie Environs Archaeological Project, excavation' *Discovery and Excavation in Scotland* New series, 18, 25–26

Noe-Nygaard, N., Price, T. D. and Hede, S. U. (2005) 'Diet of aurochs and cattle in southern Scandinavia: evidence from ^{15}N and ^{13}C stable isotopes' *Journal of Archaeological Science* 32, 855–71

O'Dell, A. C. and Walton, K. (1962) *The Highlands and Islands of Scotland* Edinburgh

O'Kelly, M. J. (1954), 'Excavations and experiments in ancient Irish cooking-places' *Journal of the Royal Society of Antiquaries of Ireland* 84, 105–55

O'Néill, J. (2000) 'Just another fulacht fiadh story' *Archaeology Ireland* 14, 2–19

O'Néill, J. (2009) *Burnt mounds in Northern and Western Europe: A study of prehistoric technology and society* Saarbrücken

O'Sullivan, A. (1996) 'Neolithic, bronze age and iron age woodworking techniques' in Rafterty, B. and Ballie, G. L. (eds) *Trackway Excavations in the Mountdillon bogs, Co. Longford*, 291–342, Dublin

Olausson, D. and Larsson, L. (1982) 'Heat treatment of flint in the Scandinavian stone age?' *Papers of the Archaeological Institute University of Lund* (4), 5–25

Ordnance Survey (1962) *Sheet 77* Soil Survey of Scotland

Parker Pearson, M., Chamberlain, A. T., Collins, M. J., Craig, O. E., Marshall, P., Mulville, J., Smith, C., Chenery, G., Cook, G., Craig, J., Evans, J., Hiller, J., Montgomery, J., Schwenninger, I., Taylor, G. and Wess, T. (2005) 'Evidence for mummification in Bronze Age Britain' *Antiquity* 79, 529–46

Paterson, H. M. L. and Lacaille, A. D. (1936) 'Banchory microliths' *Proceedings of the Society of Antiquaries of Scotland* 70, 419–34

Paynter, S. (2006) 'Regional variations in bloomery smelting slag of the Iron Age and Romano-British periods' *Archaeometry* 48, 271–92

Peacock, J. D. and Merritt, J. W. (2000) 'Glacial deposits at the Boyne Limestone Quarry, Portsoy, and the late-Quaternary history of coastal Banffshire' *Journal of Quaternary Science* 15, 543–55

Penczak, T. (2009) 'Fish assemblage compositions after implementation of the IndVal method on the Narew River system' *Ecological Modelling* 220, 419–23

Peterken, G. F. (1996) *Natural Woodland: Ecology and Conservation in Northern Temperate Regions* Cambridge

Peterson, R. (1997) 'Fordhouse Barrow (Dun Parish)' *Discovery and Excavation in Scotland*, 13

Peterson, R. and Proudfoot, E. (1996) 'Fordhouse Barrow (Dun Parish)' *Discovery and Excavation in Scotland*, 12

Photos-Jones, E., Ballin Smith, B., Hall, A. J. and Jones, R. E. (2007) 'On the intent to make cramp: an interpretation of vitreous seaweed cremation "waste" from prehistoric burial sites in Orkney, Scotland' *Oxford Journal of Archaeology* 26 (1), 1–23

Pickett, S. T. A. and White, P. S. (1985) *The Ecology of Natural Disturbance and Patch Dynamics* New York

Pollard, T. and Morrison, A. (eds) 1996 *The Early Prehistory of Scotland* Edinburgh

Pope, R. (2003) *Prehistoric Dwelling, Circular Structures in North and Central Britain c 2500 BC–AD 500* Unpublished PhD thesis, University of Durham

Pope, R. (2007) 'Ritual and the roundhouse: a critique of recent ideas on the use of domestic space in later British prehistory' in Haselgrove, C. and Pope, R. (eds) *The Earlier Iron Age in Britain and the Near Continent,* 204–28, Oxford

Pope, R. (2015) 'Bronze Age architectural traditions: dates and landscapes' in Hunter, F. and Ralston I *Scotland in Later Prehistoric Europe,* 159–84, Edinburgh

Porter, A. (2009) *A Road to the Past: Excavations along the A1 at Loughbrickland* Ballycastle

Price, T. D. (1986) 'The reconstruction of Mesolithic diets' in Bonsall, C. (ed) *The Mesolithic in Europe,* 48–59, Edinburgh

Pyne, S. J. (2013) 'Consumed by either fire or fire: a review of the environmental consequences of anthropogenic fire' reproduced in McNeill, J. R. and Roe, A. (eds) *Global Environmental History. An introductory reader,* 88–109, London

Quinn, B. and Moore, D. (2007) 'Ale, brewing and Fulachta Fiadh' *Archaeology Ireland* 21 (3), 8–11

Rackham, O. (1980) *Ancient Woodland* Cambridge

Raisen, P. and Rees, T. (1996) 'Excavation of three crop-mark sites at Melville Nurseries, Dalkeith', *Glasgow Archaeological Journal* 19, 31–50

Ralston, I. (1997) 'Pictish homes' in Henry, D. (ed) *The Worm, the Germ and the Thorn: Pictish and related studies presented to Isabel Henderson,* 18–34, Brechin

Rasmussen, M. (ed) (2007) *Iron Age Houses in Flames. Testing house reconstructions at Lejre.* Studies in Technology and Culture 3 Lejre.

Rasmussen, S. O., Seierstad, I. K., Andersen, K. K., Bigler, M., Dahl-Jensen, D. and Johnsen, S. J. (2008) 'Synchronisation of the NGRIP, GRIP and GRIP2 ice cores across MIS2 and palaeoclimatic implications' *Quaternary Science Reviews* 27, 18–28

Rasmussen, S. O., Bigler, M., Blockley, S. P., Blunier, T., Buchardt, S. L., Clausen, H. B., Cvijanovic, I., Dahl-Jensen, D., Johnsen, S. J., Fischer, H., Gkinis, V., Guillevic, M., Hoek, W. Z., Lowe, J. J., Pedro, J. B., Popp, T., Seierstad, I. K., Steffensen, J. P., Svensson, A. M., Vallelonga, P., Vinther, B. M., Walker, M. J. C., Wheatley, J. J. and Winstrup, M. (2014) 'A stratigraphic framework for abrupt climatic changes during the Last Glacial period based on three synchronized Greenland ice-core records: refining and extending the INTIMATE event stratigraphy' *Quaternary Science Reviews* 106, 14–28

Rausing, G. (1984) *Prehistoric Boats and Ships of Northwestern Europe* Lund

RCAHMS (1990) *North East Perth. An Archaeological Landscape* Edinburgh

RCAHMS (2007) *In the Shadow of Bennachie. A Field Archaeology of Donside, Aberdeenshire* 2nd edition, Edinburgh

Rees, T. (1997) 'The excavation of Cairnwell ring-cairn, Portlethen, Aberdeenshire' *Proceedings of the Society of Antiquaries of Scotland 127,* 255–80

Reid, M. L. (1989) 'A room with a view: an examination of round-houses, with particular reference to northern Britain' *Oxford Journal of Archaeology* 8 (1), 1–39

Reimer, P. J., Bard, E., Bayliss, A. and Beck, J. W. (2013) 'IntCal13 and Marine13 radiocarbon age calibration curves 0–50,000 years cal BP', *Radiocarbon* 55, 1869–87

Reynolds, D. M. (1982) 'Aspects of later timber construction in south-east Scotland' in Harding, D. W. (ed) *Later Prehistoric Settlement in South-East Scotland*, 44–56, Edinburgh

Rideout, J. S. (1995) 'Carn Dubh, Moulin, Perthshire: survey and excavation of an archaeological landscape 1987–90' *Proceedings of the Society of Antiquaries of Scotland* 125, 139–96

Rippon, S., Smart P and Pears, B. (2012) *The Fields of Britannia: Continuity and Change in the Late Roman and Early Medieval Landscape* Oxford

Robertson, A. (2014) *Aberdeen Western Peripheral Route/ Balmedie-Tipperty Lot 2 – Northern Leg: Blackdog to Kingswells: Assessment Report on the Results of Trial Trenching and Sample Excavations* (Unpublished client report) Headland Archaeology (UK) Ltd

Robertson, A., Lochrie, J., Timpany, S., Bailey, L., Mynett, A., Shillto, L. M. and Smith, S. (2013) 'Built to last: Mesolithic and Neolithic settlement at two sites beside the Forth estuary, Scotland' *Proceedings of the Society of Antiquaries of Scotland* 143, 73–136

Robertson, J. (1813) *General View of the Agriculture of Kincardineshire* Edinburgh

Rodwell, J. S. (1991) *British Plant Communities. 1. Woodlands and Scrub* Cambridge

Roland, T. P., Daley, T. J., Caseldine, C. J., Charman, D. J., Turney, C. S. M., Amesbury, M. J., Thompson, G. J. and Woodley, E. J. (2015) 'The 5.2 ka climate event: Evidence from stable isotope and multi-proxy palaeoecological peatland records in Ireland' *Quaternary Science Reviews* 124, 209–23

Romans, J. C. C. and Robertson, L. (1983) 'The environment of north Britain: soils' in Chapman, J. C. and Mytum, H. C. (eds) *Settlement in North Britain 1000BC–AD1000* BAR British Series 118, 55–82, Oxford

Rose, J., Turner, C., Coope, G. R. and Bryan, M. D. (1980) 'Channel changes in a lowland river catchment over the last 13,000 years' in Cullingford, R. A., Davidson, D. A. and Lewin, J. (eds) *Timescales in Geomorphology*, 159–75, Chichester

Roth, J. P. (1999) *The Logistics of the Roman Army at War: 264BC–AD235* Brill

Ruggles, C. (1999) *Astronomy in Prehistoric Britain and Ireland* London

Russell-White, C. J. (1995) 'The excavation of a Neolithic and Iron Age settlement at Wardend of Durris, Aberdeenshire' *Proceedings of the Society of Antiquaries of Scotland* 125, 9–27

Russell-White, C. J. and Barber, J. (1990) 'Bute and Islay' in Buckley, V. (ed) *Burnt Offerings: International Contributions to Burnt Mound Archaeology*, 82, Dublin

Sadovnik, M., Robin, V., Nadeau, M. J., Bork, H. R. and Nelle, O. (2013) 'Neolithic human impact on landscapes related to megalithic structures: palaeoecological evidence from the Krähenberg, northern Germany' *Journal of Archaeological Science* 51, 164–73

Salisbury EJ and Jane, F. W. (1940) 'Charcoals from Maiden Castle and their significance in relation to the vegetation and climatic conditions in prehistoric times' *Journal of Ecology* 28, 310–25

Sanderson, D. C. W. and Murphy, S. (2010) 'Using simple portable OSL measurements and laboratory characterisation to help understand complex and heterogeneous sediment sequences for luminescence dating' *Quaternary Geochronology* 5, 299–305

Sansum, P. A. (2004) *Recent Woodland Management Practice in Western Scottish Oak Woods: a Palynological and Documentary History* Unpublished PhD thesis, University of Stirling

Saville, A. (2004) 'The material culture of Mesolithic Scotland' in Saville, A. (ed) *Mesolithic Scotland and its Neighbours. The Early Holocene Prehistory of Scotland, its British and Irish Context, and some Northern European Perspectives*, 185–220, Edinburgh

Saville, A. (2005) 'Prehistoric quarrying of a secondary flint source: evidence from north-east Scotland' in Topping, P. and Lynott, M. (eds) *The Cultural Landscape of Prehistoric Mines*, 1 13, Oxford

Saville, A. (2006) 'The Early Neolithic lithic assemblage in Britain: some chronological considerations', in Allard, P., Bostyn, F. and Zimmermann, A. (eds) *Contribution of Lithics to Early and Middle Neolithic Chronology in France and Neighbouring Regions*. BAR International Series 1494, 1–14

Saville, A. (2008) 'The beginning of the later Mesolithic in Scotland' in Sulgostowska, Z. and Tomaszewski, A. J. (eds) *Man – Millennia – Environment: Studies in Honour of Romuald Schild* Polish Academy of Sciences Institute of Archaeology and Ethnology, 207–13, Warsaw

Saville, A. and Ballin, T. B. (2009) 'Upper Palaeolithic evidence from Kilmelfort Cave, Argyll: a re-evaluation of the lithic assemblage', *Proceedings of the Society of Antiquaries of Scotland* 139, 9–45

Savory, G. (2015) *Aberdeen Western Peripheral Route/ Balmedie-Tipperty, Lot 4 – Fastlink, Invasive Archaeological Investigations, Mitigation Excavation, AWPR/B-T/FL/007* (Unpublished client report) CFA Archaeology Ltd, Report No. 3206

ScARF (2012a) Saville, A. and Wickham-Jones, C. (eds) *Palaeolithic and Mesolithic Panel Report Scottish Archaeological Research Framework: Society of Antiquaries of Scotland* Available online at http://www.scottishheritagehub.com/content/palaeolithic-mesolithic-panel-report

ScARF (2012b) 'Places to live and ways of living' in Brophy, K. and Sheridan, A. (eds) *Neolithic Panel Report Scottish Archaeological Research Framework: Society of Antiquaries of Scotland* Available online at http://www.scottishheritagehub.com/content/scarf-neolithic-panel-report

ScARF (2012c) Downes, J. (ed) *Bronze Age Panel Report. Scottish Archaeological Research Framework: Society of Antiquaries of Scotland* Available online at http://www.scottishheritagehub.com/content/scarf-bronze-age-panel-report

ScARF (2012d) Hunter F and Carruthers, M. (eds) *Iron Age Panel Report. Scottish Archaeological Research Framework: Society of Antiquaries of Scotland* Available online at https://www.scottishheritagehub.com/content/sites/scarf-ironage-panel-report

ScARF (2012e) *Modern Scotland: Archaeology, the modern past and the modern present Summary of the Modern Panel document* Accessed September 2012

SEPA http://apps. sepa.org.uk/FRMStrategies/pdf/pva/PVA_06_18_Full.pdf

Seppä, H., Birks, H. J. B., Giesecke, T., Hammarlund, D., Alenius, T., Antonsson, K., Bjune, A. E., Heikkilä, M., MacDonald, G. M., Ojala, A. E. K., Telford, R. J. and Veski, S. (2007) 'Spatial structure of the 8200 cal yr BP event in northern Europe' *Climates of the Past* 3, 225–36

Serjeantson, D. (1990) 'The introduction of mammals to the Outer Hebride and the role of boats in stock management' *Anthropozoologica* 13, 7–18

Sheehan, J. (1990) 'The excavation of a fulacht fiadh at Coarhamore, Vantia Island, Co. Kerry' in Buckley, V. (ed) *Burnt Offerings: International Contributions to Burnt Mound Archaeology,* 98–101, Dublin

Shennan, S., Downey, S. S., Timpson, A., Edinborough, K., Colledge, S., Kerig, T., Manning, K. and Thomas, M. G. (2013) 'Regional population collapse followed initial agriculture booms in mid-Holocene Europe' *Nature Communications* 4, 2486

Shepherd, C. (2009) 'Foggieton, Aberdeen City (Peterculter parish), historic landscape survey', *Discovery and Excavation in Scotland* New series, 10, 14

Shepherd, C. (2010) 'Kirkhill Forest, Aberdeen (Dyce parish), historic landscape survey' *Discovery and Excavation in Scotland* New series, 11, 12

Shepherd, I. (1983) 'Foveran Links, flint working site' *Discovery and Excavation in Scotland,* 11

Shepherd, I. A. G. (1984) 'Bairnie Hillock (Belhelvie p): round cairn/barrow', *Discovery and Excavation in Scotland,* 11

Shepherd, I. (1996) *Aberdeen and North-East Scotland, Exploring Scotland's Heritage series,* Edinburgh

Sheridan, A. (2002) 'The radiocarbon dating programmes of the National Museums of Scotland' *Antiquity* 76 (293), 794–96

Sheridan, A. (2007) 'Chapter 11. Scottish Beaker dates: the good, the bad and the ugly', in Larson, M. and Parker Pearson M *From Stonehenge to the Baltic: Living with Cultural Diversity in the Third Millennium BC.* BAR International Series, 91–123, Oxford: Archaeopress,

Sheridan, A. (2009) 'The prehistoric pottery' in Murray, H. K., Murray, J. C. and Fraser, S. M. A. *A Tale of the Unknown Unknowns. A Mesolithic Pit Alignment and a Neolithic Timber Hall at Warren Field, Crathes, Aberdeenshire* Oxford

Sheridan, A. (2010) 'The Neolithization of Britain and Ireland: the "big picture"' in Finlayson, B. and Warren, G. (eds) *Landscapes in Transition,* 89–105, Oxford

Sheridan, A. (2013) 'Early Neolithic habitation structures in Britain and Ireland: a matter of circumstance and context' in Hoffman, D. and Smyth, J. (eds) *Tracking the Neolithic House in Europe,* 283–300, New York

Sheridan, A. (forthcoming) 'The stone artefacts' in Hatherley, C. and Murray, R *Culduthel: An Iron Age Craft Centre.* Society of Antiquaries of Scotland, Edinburgh

Simmons, I. G. (1996) *The Environmental Impact of Later Mesolithic Cultures* Edinburgh

Sheridan, A. and Hammersmith, H. (2006) 'The Beaker', in Suddaby I and Sheridan A 'A pit containing an undecorated Beaker and associated artefacts from Beechwood Park, Raigmore, Inverness', *Proceedings of the Society of Antiquaries of Scotland* 136, 80–81

Simmons, I. G. (2003) *The Moorlands of England and Wales. An Environmental History 8000 BC–AD 2000* Edinburgh

Simmons, I. G. and Innes, J. B. (1996a) 'Disturbance phases in the mid-Holocene vegetation at North Gill, North York

Moors: form and process' *Journal of Archaeological Science* 23, 183–191

Simmons, I. G. and Innes, J. B. (1996b) 'An episode of prehistoric canopy manipulation at North Gill, North Yorkshire, England' *Journal of Archaeological Science* 23, 337–41

Simmons, I. G. and Innes, J. B. (1996c) 'Prehistoric charcoal in peat profiles at North Gill, Yorkshire Moors, England' *Journal of Archaeological Science* 23, 193–97

Simpson, D. D. A. and Cole, J. M. (1990) 'Excavations at Grantully, Perthshire' *Proceedings of the Society of Antiquaries of Scotland* 120, 33–44

Smedley, P. L., Ó Dochartaigh, B. É., MacDonald, A. M. and Darling, W. G. (2009) *Baseline Scotland: groundwater Chemistry of Aberdeenshire* British Geological Survey Open Report, OR/09/065, 90

Smith, D. E., Cullingford, R. A. and Brooks, C. L. (1983) 'Flandrian relative sea level changes in the Ythan valley, northeast Scotland' *Earth Surface Processes & Landforms* 8, 423–38

Smith, D. E., Firth, C. R., Brooks, C. L., Robinson, M. and Collins, P. E. F. (1999) 'Relative sea-level rise during the main postglacial transgression in NE Scotland, UK' *Transactions of the Royal Society of Edinburgh: Earth Sciences* 90, 1–27

Smith, I 1991 'Sprouston, Roxburghshire: an early Anglian centre of the eastern Tweed Basin' *Proceedings of the Society of Antiquaries of Scotland* 121, 261–94

Speak, S. and Burgess, C. (1999) 'Meldon Bridge: a centre of the third millennium BC in Peeblesshire' *Proceedings of the Society of Antiquaries of Scotland* 129, 1–118

Spearman, R. M. (1997) 'The smithy and metalworking debris from Mills Mount' in Driscoll, S. and Yeoman P *Excavations within Edinburgh Castle in 1988–91,* 164–8, Edinburgh

Speller, K., Banks, I., Duffy, P. and MacGregor, G. (1997) 'Ladywell Farm, Girvan (Girvan Parish), burnt mound: prehistoric and medieval features' *Discovery and Excavations Scotland,* 73–4

Squair, R. and Jones, A. (2002) 'Prehistoric pottery' in Atkinson JA 'Excavation of a Neolithic occupation site at Chapelfield, Cowie, Stirling' *Proceedings of the Society of Antiquaries of Scotland* 132, 139–92

Starley, D. (1995) *Hammerscale. Archaeology Datasheet no. 10.* Historical Metallurgy Society

Starley, D. (2000) 'Metalworking debris', in Buxton, K. and Howard-Davis, C. (eds) *Bremetenacum: Excavations at Roman Ribchester 1980, 1989–1990,* 337–47, Lancaster

Stevens, C. J. and Fuller, D. Q. (2012) 'Did Neolithic farming fail? The case for a Bronze Age agricultural revolution in the British Isles' *Antiquity* 86, 707–22

Stevenson, J. B. (1975) 'Survival and discovery' in Evans, J. G., Limbrey, S. and Cleere, H. (eds) *The Effect of Man on the Landscape: the highland zone,* 104–7, London

Stoops, G. (2003) *Guidelines for Analysis and Description of Soil and Regolith Thin Sections* 184, Wisconsin

Strachan, D., Sneddon, D., Paterson, D. and Tipping, R. (in press) 'Early medieval settlement on the Scottish mainland: a rare survivor from Perthshire' in Ralston, I. B. M. and Hunter, F. (eds) *Scotland in Early Medieval Europe* Edinburgh

Strachan, R. and Dunwell, A. (2003) 'Excavations of Neolithic and Bronze Age sites near Peterhead, Aberdeenshire, 1998' *Proceedings of the Society of Antiquaries of Scotland* 133, 137–71

Stratigos, M. and Noble, G. (2014) 'Crannogs, castles and lordly residences: new research and dating of crannogs in northeast Scotland' *Proceedings of the Society of Antiquaries of Scotland, 144*, 205–22

Sturt, F., Garrow, D. and Bradley, S. (2013) 'New models of Holocene palaeogeography and inundation' *Journal of Archaeological Science* 40 (11), 3963–76

St Joseph, J. K. (1970) 'The camps at Ardoch, Stracathro and Ythan Wells: recent excavations', *Britannia* I, 163–78

Suddaby, I. (2009) 'The excavation of an Early Bronze Age burnt mound at Arisaig, Lochaber, Highland' *Scottish Archaeological Internet Reports* 39 https://doi.org/10.5284/1017938

Suddaby, I. (2014a) *Aberdeen Western Peripheral Route/Balmedie-Tipperty, Lot 1 – Balmedie to Tipperty, Invasive Archaeological Investigations, Mitigation Excavation AWPR/B-T/BT/001* (Unpublished client report) CFA Archaeology report No. 3220

Suddaby, I. (2015a) *Aberdeen Western Peripheral Route/Balmedie-Tipperty, Lot 1 – Balmedie to Tipperty, Invasive Archaeological Investigations, Mitigation Excavation AWPR/B-T/BT/002* (Unpublished client report) CFA Archaeology report No. 3221

Suddaby, I. (2015b) *Aberdeen Western Peripheral Route/Balmedie-Tipperty, Lot 1 – Balmedie-Tipperty, Archaeological Mitigation, Excavation Trench BT/003.* (Unpublished client report) CFA Archaeology report No. 3222

Suddaby, I. and Ballin, T. B. (2010) 'Late Neolithic and Late Bronze Age lithic assemblages associated with a cairn and other prehistoric features at Stoneyhill Farm, Longhaven, Peterhead, Aberdeenshire, 2002–03', *Scottish Archaeological Internet Reports (SAIR)* 45 https://doi.org/10.5284/1017938

Tabor, J. (2016) 'Early Neolithic pits and artefact scatters at North Fen, Sutton Gault, Cambridgeshire' *Proceedings of the Society of Antiquaries* 82, 161–91

Tallantire, P. A. (2002) 'The early Holocene spread of hazel (*Corylus avellana* L.) in Europe north and west of the Alps: an ecological hypothesis' *The Holocene* 12, 81–96

Taylor, A. (2016) *A96 Park & Choose Scheme: Archaeological Watching Brief and Excavation* (Unpublished client report) Headland Archaeology (UK) Ltd

Terry, J. (1995) 'Excavations at Lintshie Gutter unenclosed platform settlement, Crawford, Lanarkshire, 1991' *Proceedings of the Society of Antiquaries of Scotland* 125, 369–427

Thomas, J. (1999) *Understanding the Neolithic* London

Thomas, J. (2004) 'The later Neolithic architectural repertoire: the case of the Dunragit complex' in Cleal, R. and Pollard, J. (eds) *Monuments and Material Culture. Papers in Honour of an Avebury Archaeologist: Isobel Smith*, 98–108, Salisbury

Thomas, J. (2007) *Place and Memory: Excavations at the Pict's Knowe, Holywood and Holm Farm, Dumfries and Galloway, 1994–8* Oxford

Thomas, J. (2011) 'Introduction: beyond the mundane?' in Anderson-Whymark, H. and Thomas J *Regional Perspectives on Neolithic Pit Deposition: Beyond the Mundane*, 1–12, Oxford

Thomas, J. (2013) *The Birth of Neolithic Britain. An interpretive account* Oxford

Thoms, A. V. (2009) 'Rock of ages: propagation of hot-rock cookery in western North America' *Journal of Archaeological Science* 36, 573–91

Thomson, S. (2015) *A96 Park and Ride, Aberdeen – Archaeological Excavation* (Unpublished client report) Headland Archaeology (UK) Ltd

Tilley, C. (1994) *A Phenomenology of Landscape: Places, Paths and Monuments* Oxford

Timpany, S. (2012a) *Aberdeen Western Peripheral Route Package (Fastlink). Red Moss Wetland (Site 67) and Blackburn Moss (Site 119). Palaeoenvironmental Assessment* (Unpublished client report) Headland Archaeology (UK) Ltd

Timpany, S. (2012b) *Aberdeen Western Peripheral Route Package (Northern Leg). Red Moss (Site 314). Palaeoenvironmental Assessment* (Unpublished client report) Headland Archaeology (UK) Ltd

Timpany, S. (2012c) *Aberdeen Western Peripheral Route Package (Southern Leg). Hare Moss Wetland (Site 153): Palaeoenvironmental Assessment* (Unpublished client report) Headland Archaeology (UK) Ltd

Timpany, S. (2014a) 'Environmental evidence', in Murray, H. K. and Murray JC 'Mesolithic and Early Neolithic activity along the Dee: excavations at Garthdee Road, Aberdeen', *Proceedings of the Society of Antiquaries of Scotland* 144, 16–20

Timpany, S. (2014b) *Aberdeen Western Peripheral Route. Balmedie–Tipperty. Lot 3 Southern Leg: Palaeoenvironmental Sampling and Analysis at Hare Moss Wetland (Site 153)* (Unpublished client report) Headland Archaeology (UK) Ltd

Timpany, S. and Masson, D. (2009) *WGI-07: Mid Mill, Kintore, Aberdeenshire: sample assessment report* (Unpublished client report) Headland Archaeology (UK) Ltd

Tipping, R. (1994) 'The form and fate of Scotland's woodlands' *Proceedings of the Society of Antiquaries of Scotland* 124, 1–55

Tipping, R. (1997) 'Pollen analysis, late Iron Age and Roman agriculture around Hadrian's Wall' in Gwilt, A. and Haselgrove, C. (eds) *Reconstructing Iron Age Societies*, 239–47, Oxford

Tipping, R. (1998) 'The chronology of Late Quaternary fluvial activity in part of the Milfield Basin, northeast England' *Earth Surface Processes & Landforms* 23, 845–56

Tipping, R. (2007) 'Landscape history of the Don Valley and north east Scotland' in Royal Commission on Ancient and Historical Monuments (Scotland) *In the Shadow of Bennachie: A Field Archaeology of the Valley of the Don*, 25–44, Edinburgh

Tipping, R. (2008) 'Blanket peat in the Scottish Highlands: timing, cause, spread and the myth of environmental determinism' *Biodiversity & Conservation* 17, 2097–2113

Tipping, R. (2010a) *Bowmont. An Environmental History of the Bowmont Valley and the Northern Cheviot Hills* Edinburgh

Tipping, R. (2010b) 'The case for climatic stress forcing choice in the adoption of agriculture in the British Isles' in Finlayson, B. and Warren, G. (eds) *Landscapes in Transition*, 66–77, Oxford

Tipping, R. (2015) 'I have not been able to find anything of interest in the peat: landscapes and environment in the Later Bronze and Iron Ages in Scotland' in Hunter, F. and Ralston, I. (eds) *Scotland in Later Prehistoric Europe*, 101–17, Edinburgh

Tipping, R. and Tisdall, E. (2006) 'The landscape context of the Antonine Wall: a review of the literature' *Proceedings of the Society of Antiquaries of Scotland* 135, 443–70

Tipping, R., Long, D., Carter, S., Davidson, D. A., Tyler, A. and Boag, B. (1999) 'Testing the potential of soil-stratigraphic palynology in podsols' in Pollard, A. M. (ed) *Geoarchaeology: exploration, environments, resources*, 79–90, London

Tipping, R., Davies, A. L. and Tisdall, E. (2006) 'Long term woodland stability and instability in West Glen Affric, northern Scotland' *Forestry* 79, 351–59

Tipping, R., Davies, A., McCulloch, R. and Tisdall, E. (2008) 'Response to late Bronze Age climate change of farming communities in north east Scotland' *Journal of Archaeological Science* 35, 2379–86

Tipping, R., Bunting, M. J., Davies, A. L., Murray, H., Fraser, S. and McCulloch, R. (2009) 'Modelling land use around an early Neolithic timber "hall" in north east Scotland from high spatial resolution pollen analyses' *Journal of Archaeological Science* 36, 140–49

Tipping, R., Bradley, R., McCulloch, R., Sanders, J. and Wilson, R. (2013) 'Moments of crisis: from coincidence to hypothesis testing in defining the impacts of abrupt climate change in Scottish prehistory' *Proceedings of the Society of Antiquaries of Scotland* 142, 1–17

Transport Scotland –https://web.archive.org/web/20160117123025/http://www.transportscotland.gov.uk/project/aberdeen-western-peripheral-route-balmedie-tipperty accessed 21 September 2017

Tylecote, R. F. (1986) *The Prehistory of Metallurgy in the British Isles* London

Tyson, R. E. (1985) 'The population history of Aberdeenshire, 1695–1755' *Northern Scotland* 6, 113–31

Usher, M. B. (1999) *Landscape Character: perspectives on management and change* Edinburgh

van Geel, B., van der Plicht, J., Kilian, M. R., Klaver, E. R., Kouwenberg, J. H. M., Renssen, H., Reynaud-Ferrara, I. and Waterbolk, H. T. (1998) 'The sharp rise of $\Delta^{14}C$ ca. 800 cal BC: possible causes, related climatic teleconnections and the impact on human environments' *Radiocarbon* 40, 535–50

van Wessel, J. (2012a) *Aberdeen Western Peripheral Route Package (Northern Leg). Topographic Surveys: Ashtown Boundary Stone (Site 120), Parkhill Pumping Station (Site 170), Cranfield Farm Consumption Dyke (Site 201), Goval Standing Stone (Site 218), Overton Stone Wall (Site 279)* (Unpublished client report) Headland Archaeology (UK) Ltd

van Wessel, J. (2012b) *Aberdeen Western Peripheral Route Package (Fastlink). Topographic Surveys: Howieshill Farmstead (Site 32), Burnhead Cairns (Site 121), Scottish North Eastern Railway (Site 257) and Crossley Clearance Cairn (Site 506)* (Unpublished client report) Headland Archaeology (UK) Ltd

van Wessel, J. (2012c) *Aberdeen Western Peripheral Route Package (Southern Leg). Topographic Surveys: Auchintoul Croft (Site 129), Hillhead, Charleston – Consumption Dyke (Site 205), Charlestown Consumption Dyke (Site 212), West Charleston Dyke (3) (Site 222), West Charleston Dyke (1) (Site 223), Lochview Croft Dyke (2) (Site 225), West Charleston Dyke (4) (Site 230), Hillside Dyke (Site 234), Lochview Croft Dyke (1) (Site 236), West Charlestown Dyke (5) (Site 242), Deeside Railway (Site 246), Nether Beanshill Sheepfold (1) (Site 285), Nether Beanshill Well (Site 286), Nether Beanshill Sheepfold (2) (Site 287), Beans Hill Pen (1) (Site 346), Beans Hill Rig (4) (Site 349), West Hatton Dyke (2) (Site 441), West Hatton Dyke (1) (Site 443), Denhead of Cloghill Dyke (3) (Site 450), Denhead Of Cloghill Dyke (4) (Site 451), Cloghill – Consumption Dyke (Site 462), Newpark Ruined Farmstead (Site 494), Sunnyside Field System (Site 496), Nether Beanshill*

Sheep Fold (Site 519) and Nether Beanshill Dyke (Site 520) (Unpublished client report) Headland Archaeology (UK) Ltd

van Wessel, J. (2012d) *Aberdeen Western Peripheral Route (Northern Leg). Building Recording Survey: Dyce Airfield – Radio Station (Site 154c)* (Unpublished client report) Headland Archaeology (UK) Ltd

van Wessel, J. (2012e) *Aberdeen Western Peripheral Route Package (Southern Leg). Building Recording Surveys: Kingcausie Bridge (Site 514) and Silverburn Bridge (Site 522)* (Unpublished client report) Headland Archaeology (UK) Ltd

van Wessel, J. (2012f) *Aberdeen Western Peripheral Route Package (A90 Balmedie to Tipperty). Topographic and Photographic Surveys: Snarleshow (Dambrae) Possible Lade (Site 42), Kirkhill Upright Stone (Site 51), Overhill Cattle Rubbing Stones (Site 57) and Mill of Foveran Lade (Site 72)* (Unpublished client report) Headland Archaeology (UK) Ltd

van Wessel, J. (2014) *Aberdeen Western Peripheral Route/ Balmedie-Tipperty, Lot 2-Northern Leg: Site AWPR/B-T/ NL-009. Topographic Survey* (Unpublished client report) Headland Archaeology (UK) Ltd

van Wessel, J. (2015) *Aberdeen Western Peripheral Route/ Balmedie-Tipperty Lot 2 – Northern Leg: Post-Excavation Assessment and Mitigation Excavation Assessment Report* (Unpublished client report) Headland Archaeology (UK) Ltd

van Wessel, J. and Bailey, L. (2012) *A96 (T) Dyce Drive Park and Choose and Associated Link Road (Dyce). Photographic Survey: Walton Farmhouse (Site 128)* (Unpublished client report) Headland Archaeology (UK) Ltd

Vasari, Y. N. (1977) 'Radiocarbon dating of the Late-Glacial and early Flandrian vegetational succession in the Scottish Highlands and the Isle of Skye' in Gray, J. M. and Lowe, J. J. (eds) *Studies in the Scottish Lateglacial Environment*, 143–62, Oxford

Vasari, Y. N. and Vasari, A. (1968) 'Late- and post-glacial macrophytic vegetation in the lochs of northern Scotland' *Acta Botanica Fennici* 80, 1–20

Vermeersch, PM 2015 *An Ahrensburgian site at Zonhoven-Molenheide (Belgium)*. BAR International Series 2471. Oxford

Waddington, C., Bailey, G., Boomer, I., Milner, N., Pederson, K., Shiel, R. and Stevenson, T. (2003) 'A Mesolithic settlement at Howick, Northumberland' *Antiquity* http://antiquity.ac.uk/projgall/waddington295/

Waddington, C. (ed) (2007) *Mesolithic Settlement in the North Sea Basin. A Case Study from Howick, North-East England* Oxford

Waddington, C. (2011) 'Towards synthesis: research and discovery in Neolithic North-East England' *Proceedings of the Prehistoric Society* 77, 279–319

Waddington, C. and Pedersen, K. L. R. (2007) 'Chipped stone tools' in Waddington, C. (ed) *Mesolithic Settlement in the North Sea Basin. A Case Study from Howick, North-East England*, 75–109, Oxford

Waddington, C. and Wicks, K. (2017) 'Resilience or wipe out? Evaluating the convergent impacts of the 8.2 ka event and Storegga tsunami on the Mesolithic of northeast Britain' *Journal of Archaeological Science: Reports* 14, 692–714

Walker, A. and Longford, C. (2017) *Milltimber (Sites SL/001 and SL/002) Wood Charcoal Analysis Report* (Unpublished assessment report) Headland Archaeology (UK) Ltd

Walker, B., McGregor, C. and Stark, G. (1996) *Thatchers and Thatching Techniques. A Guide to Conserving Scottish Thatching Traditions* Edinburgh

Walker, M. J. C., Bohncke, S. J. P., Coope, G. R., O'Connell, M., Usinger H and Verbruggen, C. (1994) 'The Devensian/ Weichselian Late-glacial in northwest Europe (Ireland, Britain, north Belgium, The Netherlands, northwest Germany)' *Journal of Quaternary Science* 9, 109–18

Walton, K. (1950) 'The distribution of population in Aberdeenshire, 1696' *Scottish Geographical Magazine* 66, 17–26

Walton, K. (1963) 'The site of Aberdeen' *Scottish Geographical Magazine* 79 (2), 69–73.

Ward, T. (2005) 'Daer Valley Project, South Lanarkshire (Crawford parish), excavation; survey' *Discovery and Excavation in Scotland* New series, 6, 134

Ward, T. (2010) Prehistory Howburn Farm Report Biggar Archaeology Group accessed at http://www.biggararchaeology. org.uk/pdf_reports/HOWBURN_REPORT2010.pdf 06/05/18

Warren, G. (2005) *Mesolithic Lives in Scotland* Gloucester

Warren, G., Davis, S., Mc Clatchie, M. and Sands, R. (2014) 'The potential role of humans in structuring the wooded landscapes of Mesolithic Ireland: a review of data and discussion of approaches' *Vegetation History and Archaeobotany* 23, 629–46

Warren, G., Fraser, S., Clarke, A., Driscoll, K., Mitchell, W., Noble, G., Paterson, D., Schulting, R., Tipping, R., Verbaas, A., Wilson, C. and Wickham-Jones C 2018 'Little house in the mountains? A small Mesolithic structure from the Cairngorm Mountains, Scotland' *Journal of Archaeological Science* 18, 936–45

Weber, MJ 2012 *From Technology to Tradition – re-evaluating the Hamburgian-Magdalenian relationship. Untersuchungen und Materialien zur Steinzeit in Schleswig-Holstein und im Ostseeraum* 5. Neumünster

Welfare, A. (2007) 'The antiquarian tradition' in RCAHMS *In the Shadow of Bennachie. A Field Archaeology of Donside, Aberdeenshire* 2nd edition, 7–16, Edinburgh

Welfare, A. (2011) *Great Crowns of Stone. The Recumbent Stone Circles of Scotland* Edinburgh

Welfare, H. and Swan, V. G. (1995) *Roman Camps in England: the field archaeology* London

Werritty, A. and Hoey, T. B. (2004) *Geomorphological Changes and Trends in Scotland: river channels and processes* Scottish Natural Heritage.

White, R. and Richardson, P. (2010) 'The excavation of Bronze Age Roundhouses at Oldmeldrum, Aberdeenshire' *Scottish Archaeological Internet Report* 43

Whitehouse, N. J. (2006) 'The Holocene British and Irish ancient woodland fossil beetle fauna: implications for woodland history, biodiversity and faunal colonisation' *Quaternary Science Reviews* 25 (15–16), 1755–89

Whitehouse, N. J., Schulting, R. J., McClatchie, M., Barratt, P., McLaughlin, T. R., Bogaard, A., Colledge, S., Marchant, R., Gaffrey, J. and Bunting, M. J. (2013) 'Neolithic agriculture on the European western frontier: the boom and bust of early farming in Ireland' *Journal of Archaeological Science* 40, 1–25

Whitehouse, N. J. and Smith, D. (2010) 'How fragmented was the British Holocene wildwood? Perspectives on the "Vera" grazing debate from the fossil beetle record' *Quaternary Science Reviews* 29, 539–53

Whittington, G. (1975) 'Placenames and the settlement pattern of dark-age Scotland' *Proceedings of the Society of Antiquaries of Scotland* 106, 99–110

Whittington G and Edwards, K. J. (1993) 'Ubi solitudinem faciunt pacem appellant: the Romans in Scotland, a palaeoenvironmental contribution' *Britannia* 24, 13–25

Whittle, A., Healy, F. and Bayliss, A. (2011) *Gathering Time. Dating the early Neolithic enclosures of southern Britain and Ireland* Oxford

Wickham-Jones, C. R. (1990) *Rhum: Mesolithic and Later Sites at Kinloch* Society of Antiquaries of Scotland Monograph 7

Wickham-Jones, C. R. (2004) 'Structural evidence in the Scottish Mesolithic' in Saville, A. (ed) *Mesolithic Scotland and its Neighbours. The Early Holocene Prehistory of Scotland, its British and Irish Context, and some Northern European Perspectives*, 229–42, Edinburgh

Wickham-Jones, C. and Dalland, M. (1998) 'A small mesolithic site at Fife Ness, Fife, Scotland' *Internet Archaeology* 5. Available: <http://dx.doi.org/10.11141/ia.5.1> Accessed 31 August 2017

Wickham-Jones, C. and Hardy, K. (2004) 'Camas Daraich: a Mesolithic site at the Point of Sleat, Skye', *Scottish Archaeological Internet Reports (SAIR)* 12

Wickham-Jones, C. and Holden, T. (1998) 'The opportunistic exploitation of flint at Easter Hatton, Aberdeenshire' *Lithics* 20, 23–29

Wicks, K. and Mithen, S. (2013) 'The impact of the abrupt 8.2 ka cold event on the Mesolithic population of western Scotland: a Bayesian chronological analysis using "activity events" as a population proxy' *Journal of Archaeological Science* 45, 240–69

Wickham-Jones, C. R., Kenworthy, J. B., Gould, A., MacGregor, G. and Noble, G. (2017) 'Archaeological Excavations at Nethermills Farm, Deeside, 1978–81' *Proceedings of the Society of Antiquaries of Scotland* 146, 7–55

Williams, A. N. (2012) 'The use of summed radiocarbon probability distributions in archaeology; a review of methods' *Journal of Archaeological Science* 39, 578–89

Williams, G. (1990) 'Burnt mounds in south-west Wales' in Buckley V *Burnt Offerings. International Contributions to Burnt Mound Archaeology*, 129–40, Dublin

Williamson, T. (2003) *Shaping Medieval Landscapes. Settlement, Society & Environment* Macclesfield

Williamson, T. (2015) *Environment, Society and Landscape in Early Medieval England: Time and Topography* Woodbridge

Wilson, C. A., Cloy, J. M., Graham, M. C. and Hamlet, L. (2013) 'A microanalytical study of iron, aluminium and organic matter relationships in soils with contrasting hydrological regimes' *Geoderma* 202–203, 71–81

Wilson, D. (2017) *Construction Phase Archaeological Monitoring Areas for the Aberdeen Western Peripheral Route (AWPR): Results of Archaeological Monitoring & Mitigation during Post-Excavation Assessment and Assessment Report* (Unpublished client report) Headland Archaeology (UK) Ltd

Withrington, D. J. (ed) (1972) *Deeside* Wakefield

Withrington, D. J. and Grant, I. R. (eds) (1982) *The Statistical Account of Scotland 1791–1799. Volume XIV. Kincardineshire and South-West Aberdeenshire* Wakefield

Woodbridge, J., Fyfe, R. M., Roberts, N., Downey, S., Edinborough, K. and Shennan, S. (2013) 'The impact of the Neolithic agricultural transition in Britain: a comparison of pollen-based land-cover and archaeological ^{14}C date-inferred population change' *Journal of Archaeological Science* 51, 216–24

Woodley, N. (forthcoming) An Iron Age & Early Historic Settlement and Metal Working Site at Walton Road, Dyce. Submitted to Tayside and Fife Archaeological Journal

Wright, A. D. (nd)'The lithic assemblage' in Innes, L., Wright, A. D. and Duncan J *Rescue excavation of an enclosure and lithic material at Climpy, Forth, South Lanarkshire* (Unpublished report) GUARD

Yalden, D. (1999) *The History of British Mammals* London

Yeoman,, P., A. (1988) 'Mottes in Northeast Scotland', *Scot Archaeological Review,* vol. 5, 130

Zvelebil, M. (1994) 'Plant use in the Mesolithic and its role in the transition to farming' *Proceedings of the Prehistoric Society* 60, 35–74

Maps

Gordon R 1636–52 Aberdeen, Banf [sic], Murrey [sic] & c. to Inverness: [and] Fra the north water to Ross/Robertus Gordonius a Strathloch describebat 1640. Adv. MS.70.2.10 (Gordon 25) https://maps.nls.uk/view/00000356

Gordon R 1636–52 Marre from Kincairne Pueill to the Springis of Dee; The Draught of Dee River fra Kincarne to Durris. The Draught of Dee River fra Kincarne to Durris. Adv. MS.70.2.10 (Gordon 28) https://maps.nls.uk/view/00000360

Gordon, R 1636–52 [A map of the district along the north side of the River Dee near Crathes and Durres, showing "Ye Lyne of Leys possession" and "Lyne of Leys clayme"] Adv. MS.70.2.10 (Gordon 31) https://maps.nls.uk/view/00000363

Robertson, J. (1822) *Topographical and military map of the counties of Aberdeen, Banff and Kincardine*

Roy 1747–55 Military Survey of Scotland 1747–55 https://maps.nls.uk/roy/index.html

Thomson, J. (1826) *Northern Part of Aberdeen & Banff Shires. Southern Part.*

Taylor and Skinners (1776) *Survey and maps of the roads of North Britain; the road from Aberdeen to Fraserburgh*

Digital appendices contents

The digital appendices are available at https://doi.org/10.5284/1050093

Appendix 1: Assessment Reports

Appendix 2: Technical Reports

Appendix 2.1 Environmental Reports

Appendix 2.2 Artefact Reports

Appendix 3: Radiocarbon Certificates

Appendix 4: Report Concordance

Site	Charcoal	Plant	Hazelnut	Wood	Bone	OSL dating	Bayesian modelling	Ethnographic study	Pottery	Lithics	Coarse stone	Industrial Waste	Use-wear	Site Name	Chapter in monograph
SL/001	x													Milltimber	2
SL/002A	x					x	x			x		x		Milltimber	2
SL/002B	x					x	x		x	x		x		Milltimber	2
SL/002C	x					x			x	x				Milltimber	2
SL/002D	x		x			x		x	x	x			x	Milltimber	2
AMA09	x	x							x	x	x			Milltimber	2
SL/003B	x				x				x	x		x		Nether Beanshill	3
SL/004A	x			x							x			Gairnhill	3
SL/004B	x									x	x			Gairnhill	3
SL/004C									x					Gairnhill	3
SL/004D	x			x	x				x	x	x	x		Gairnhill	3
NL/001C	x								x	x	x			Chapel of Stoneywood	3
NL/003B	x		x					x		x			x	Standingstones	4
NL/006A	x								x	x				Goval	5
NL/006B	x									x				Goval	5
NL/012	x								x	x				Blackdog	6
NL/013										x				Middlefield	6
AMA022	x	x							x	x	x			Wester Hatton	6

Index

Page numbers in *italics* are illustrations; with 't' are figures.